Class XI

# Statistics for Economics

**T.R. Jain**
Former Principal
S.A. Jain College
Ambala City

**Dr. V.K. Ohri**
Associate Professor(Retd.)
Shyam Lal College
(Delhi University), Delhi

Printing History: Edition: 2016-17

Syllabus Covered: Central Board of Secondary Education, Delhi

Medium: ENGLISH (Hindi medium is also available)

Price: Three Hundred Twenty Five Rupees (₹ 325/-)

ISBN: 978-93-80735-01-6



Published By: **VK Global Publications Pvt. Ltd.**

**Regd. Office:**
4323/3, Ansari Road, Darya Ganj, New Delhi-110002
Ph: 91-11-23250105, 23250106 Fax: 91-11-23250141

**Corporate Office:**
15/1, Main Mathura Road, Faridabad (NCR)
Haryana-121003
Phone: 0129-7117719 (30 lines) Fax: 0129-2250322

Email: mail@vkpublications.com
www.vkpublications.com

Printed At: Prince Print Process, Delhi

# Contents

## Statistics for Economics



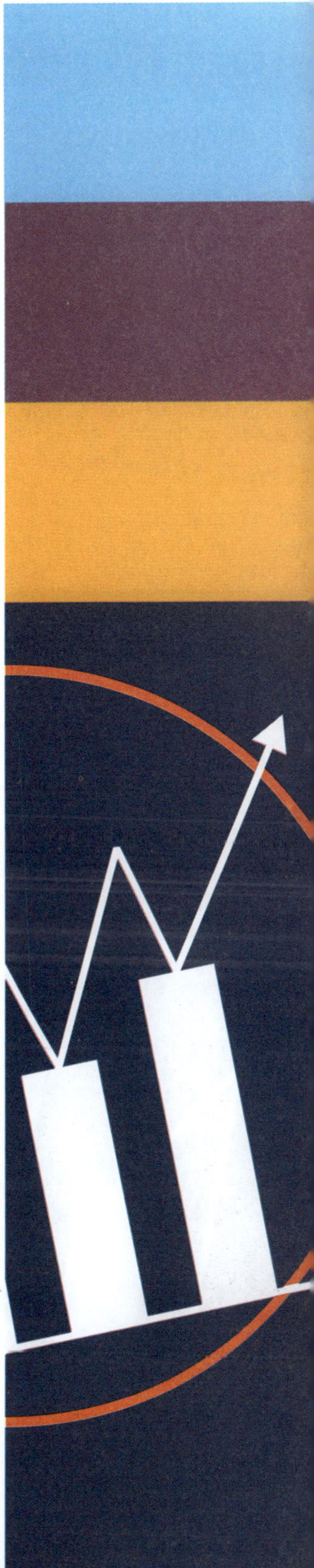

# Syllabus

## Central Board of Secondary Education, Delhi

Economics

Class–XI (2016-17)

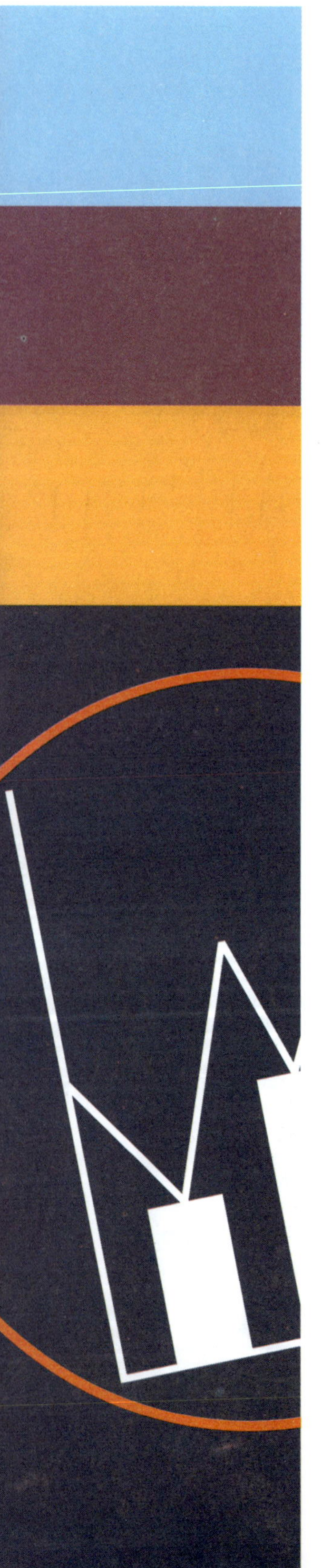

| 3 Hours | | Marks: 90 |
|---|---|---|
| Units | Periods | Marks |
| **Part–A: Statistics for Economics** | | |
| 1. Introduction | 07 | 13 |
| 2. Collection, Organisation and Presentation of Data | 27 | |
| 3. Statistical Tools and Interpretation | 66 | 27 |
| | **100** | **40** |
| **Part–B: Indian Economic Development** | | |
| 4. Development Experience (1947-90) and Economic Reforms since 1991 | 34 | 18 |
| 5. Current Challenges facing Indian Economy | 60 | 22 |
| 6. Development Experience of India– A Comparison with Neighbours (OTBA) | 14 | 10 |
| **Theory Paper (40+50= 90 marks)** | **108** | **50** |
| **Part–C: Project Work** | **12** | **10** |

**Note:** The question paper will include a Section on **Open Text Based Assessment** (OTBA) of 10 marks from Unit-6 of Part-B. From this unit, no other questions will be asked in the theory examination. The OTBA will be asked only during the annual examination to be held in the March 2017. The open text material on the identified unit will be supplied to students in advance. The OTBA is designed to test the analytical and higher order thinking skills of the students.

### PART–A: STATISTICS FOR ECONOMICS

In this course, the learners are expected to acquire skills in collection, organisation and presentation of quantitative and qualitative information pertaining to various simple economic aspects systematically. It also intends to provide some basic statistical tools to analyse, and interpret any economic information and draw appropriate inferences. In this process, the learners are also expected to understand the behaviour of various economic data.

**Unit–1: Introduction** **(07 Periods)**

What is Economics?

Meaning, scope and importance of statistics in Economics.

**Unit–2: Collection, Organisation and Presentation of Data** **(27 Periods)**

Collection of Data–sources of data–primary and secondary; how basic data is collected, with concepts of sampling; methods of collecting data; some important sources of secondary data: Census of India and National Sample Survey Organisation.

Organisation of Data: Meaning and types of variables; Frequency Distribution.

Presentation of Data: Tabular Presentation and Diagrammatic Presentation of Data: (i) Geometric forms (bar diagrams and pie diagrams), (ii) Frequency diagrams (histogram, polygon and ogive), and (iii) Arithmetic line graphs (time series graph).

**Unit–3: Statistical Tools and Interpretation** **(66 Periods)**

(For all the numerical problems and solutions, the appropriate economic interpretation may be attempted. This means, the students need to solve the problems and provide interpretation for the results derived.)

Measures of Central Tendency–mean (simple and weighted), median and mode.

Measures of Dispersion–absolute dispersion (range, quartile deviation, mean deviation and standard deviation); relative dispersion (co-efficient of range, co-efficient of quartile-deviation, co-efficient of mean deviation, co-efficient of variation); Lorenz Curve: Meaning, construction and its application.

Correlation–meaning, scatter diagram; Measures of correlation–Karl Pearson's method (two variables ungrouped data); Spearman's rank correlation.

Introduction to Index Numbers–meaning, types–wholesale price index, consumer price index and index of industrial production, uses of index numbers; Inflation and index numbers.

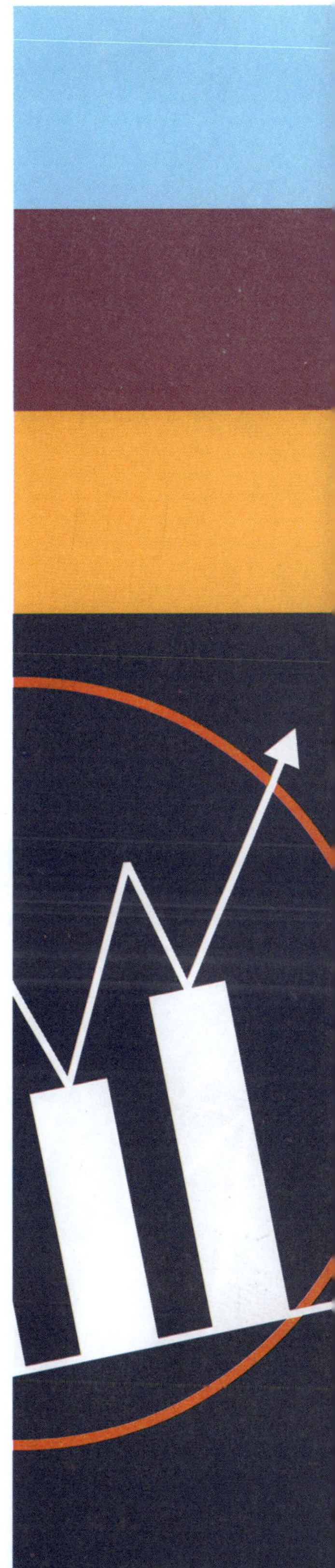

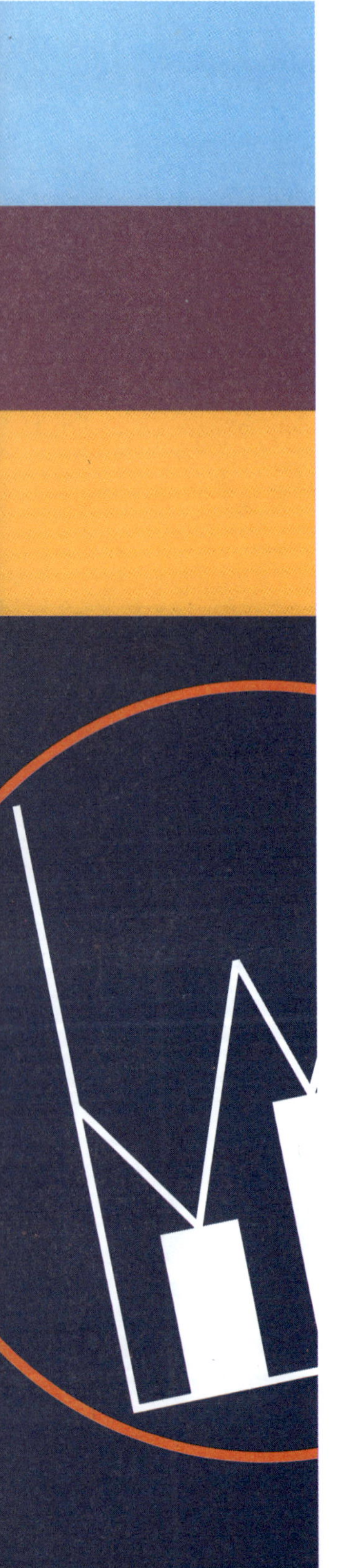

## PART–B: INDIAN ECONOMIC DEVELOPMENT

### Unit–4: Development Experience (1947-90) and Economic Reforms since 1991 (34 Periods)

A brief introduction of the state of Indian economy on the eve of independence.

Common goals of Five Year Plans.

Main features, problems and policies of agriculture (institutional aspects and new agricultural strategy, etc.), industry (industrial licensing, etc.) and foreign trade.

**Economic Reforms since 1991**

Need and main features–liberalisation, globalisation and privatisation.

An appraisal of LPG policies.

### Unit–5: Current Challenges facing Indian Economy (60 Periods)

Poverty–absolute and relative; Main programmes for poverty alleviation: A critical assessment.

Rural Development: Key issues–credit and marketing–role of cooperatives; agricultural diversification; alternative farming–organic farming.

Human Capital Formation: How people become resource; Role of human capital in economic development; Growth of Education Sector in India.

Employment: Formal and informal, growth and other issues: Problems and policies.

Inflation: Problems and Policies.

Infrastructure: Meaning and Types: Case Studies: Energy and Health: Problems and Policies–A critical assessment.

Sustainable Economic Development: Meaning, Effects of Economic Development on Resources and Environment, including global warming.

### Unit–6: Development Experience of India– A Comparison with Neighbours (OTBA) (14 Periods)

India and Pakistan

India and China

Issues: growth, population, sectoral development and other developmental indicators.

## PART–C: DEVELOPING PROJECTS IN ECONOMICS (12 Periods)

The students may be encouraged to develop projects, as per the suggested project guidelines. Case studies of a few organisations/ outlets may also be encouraged. Under this the students will do only one comprehensive project using concepts from both Part–A and Part–B.

Some of the examples of the projects are as follows (they are not mandatory but suggestive):

(i) A report on demographic structure of your neighborhood.

(ii) Changing consumer awareness amongst households.

(iii) Dissemination of price information for growers and its impact on consumers.

(iv) Study of a Cooperative Institution: milk cooperatives, marketing cooperatives, etc.

(v) Case studies on public private partnership, outsourcing and outward Foreign Direct Investment.

(vi) Global warming.

(vii) Designing eco-friendly projects applicable in school such as paper and water recycle.

The idea behind introducing this unit is to enable the students to develop the ways and means by which a project can be developed using the skills learned in the course. This includes all the steps involved in designing a project starting from choosing a title, exploring the information relating to the title, collection of primary and secondary data, analysing the data, presentation of the project and using various statistical tools and their interpretation and conclusion.

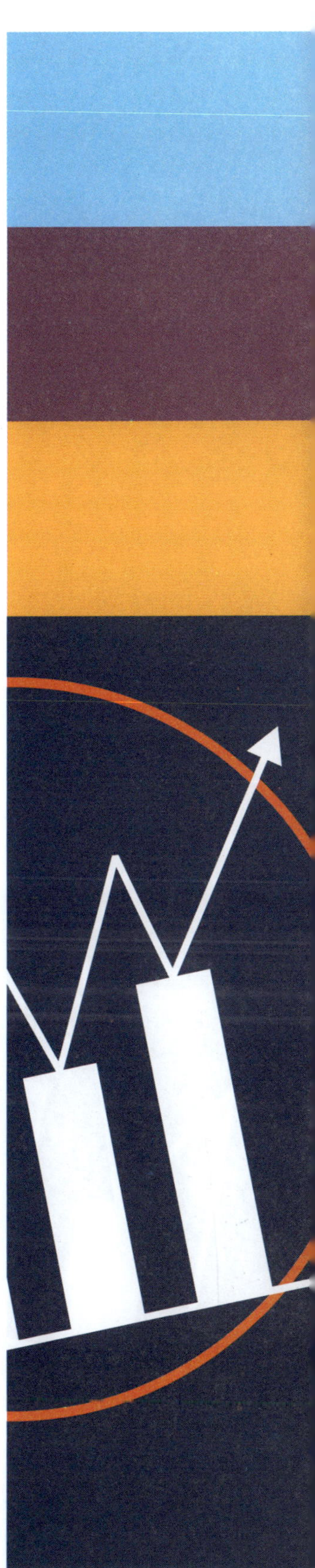

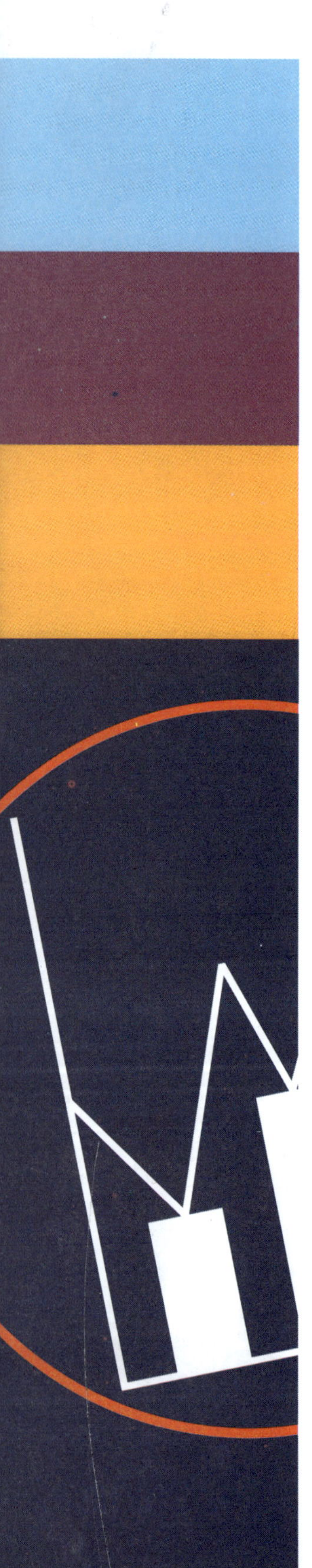

# Design of Question Paper

## Central Board of Secondary Education, Delhi

### Economics

Class XI

**Theory: 90 marks + project : 10 marks** **Duration: 3 Hours**

| S. No. | Typology of Questions | Very Short Answer/ MCQ 1 Mark | Short Answer I 3 Marks | Short Answer II 4 Marks | Long Answer 6 Marks | OTBA 5 Marks | Marks | Percentage |
|---|---|---|---|---|---|---|---|---|
| 1. | **Remembering:** (Knowledge based simple recall questions, to know meaning of specific facts, terms, concepts, principles, or theories; identify, information) | – | 2 | 1 | 2 | – | 22 | 25% |
| 2. | **Understanding:** (Comprehension–to be familiar with meaning and to understand conceptually, interpret, compare, contrast, explain, paraphrase, or interpret information) | 1 | 2 | 1 | 2 | – | 23 | 25% |
| 3. | **Application:** (Use abstract information in concrete situation, to apply knowledge to new situations; Use given content to interpret a situation, provide an example, or solve a problem) | 2 | 2 | 1 | 1 | – | 18 | 20% |
| 4. | **High Order Thinking Skills:** (Analysis & Synthesis–Classify, compare, contrast, or differentiate between different pieces of information, Organise and/or integrate unique pieces of information from a variety of sources) | 2 | 2 | – | 1 | 1 | 19 | 21% |
| 5. | **Evaluation:** (Appraise, judge, and/or justify the value or worth of a decision or outcome, or to predict outcomes based on values) | 0 | 1 | – | – | 1 | 8 | 9% |
| | **Total** | **5×1 = 5** | **9×3 = 27** | **3×4 = 12** | **6×6 = 36** | **2×5 = 10** | **Theory 90+10 projects =100 marks** | **100** |

**Note:** The question paper will include a Section on Open Text Based Assessment (OTBA) of 10 marks from Unit-6 of Part-B. From this unit, no other questions will be asked in the theory examination. The OTBA will be asked only during the annual examination to be held in the March 2017. The open text material on the identified unit will be supplied to students in advance. The OTBA is designed to test the analytical and higher order thinking skills of students.

There will be Internal choice in questions of 3 marks, 4 marks and 6 marks in both sections (A and B). (Total 3 internal choices in section A and total 3 internal choices in section B.)

# Statistics for Economics

This chapter [illegible]
matter of [illegible]
the issues [illegible]
The chapter [illegible]
Economics [illegible]
Statistics [illegible]
statistics in [illegible]

advise the [illegible]
of Economics [illegible]
(routine) bus[illegible]

Very unde[illegible]
economic act[illegible]
needs, and [illegible]
services for [illegible]

consum[illegible]

Consumption [illegible]
direct satisf[illegible]
goods and serv[illegible]

Production is [illegible]
engaged in [illegible]
generation of [illegible]

A producer is [illegible]
of income [illegible]

Production [illegible]
goods as they [illegible]

Saving and [illegible]
savers and [illegible]
or for invest[illegible]

# Concept of Economics and Significance of Statistics in Economics

1

This chapter orients the students of Economics (Class XI) to the subject matter of Statistics and its usefulness in understanding and analysing the issues and problems arising out of economic activities of man. The chapter begins with an introductory discussion of the concept of Economics, followed by a brief discussion of the meaning and scope of Statistics. It concludes with a comprehensive view of the importance of Statistics in Economics; it analyses why Statistics is studied in Economics.

## 1. What is Economics?

We advise the young readers of Class XI to comprehend the concept of Economics through the following discussion relating to ordinary (or routine) business (or activities) of our life.

Every individual, ranging from a child to an old man, is engaged in some economic activity or the other. Consumption is an important economic activity; and we all are consumers, consuming different goods and services for the satisfaction of our wants.

**Who is a Consumer?**

A consumer is one who consumes goods and services for the satisfaction of his wants.

**What is Consumption?**

Consumption is the process of using up utility value of goods and services for the direct satisfaction of our wants. Utility value of goods means inherent capacity of goods and services to satisfy human wants.

Production is another economic activity, and many of us are producers, engaged in the production of different goods and services for the generation of income.

**Who is a Producer?**

A producer is one who produces and/or sells goods and services for the generation of income.

**What is Production?**

Production is the process of converting raw material into useful things. Things become useful as they acquire utility value in the process of production.

Saving and investment are also economic activities, and many of us are savers and investors. We save a part of our income for future consumption or for investment in shares and bonds to generate income.

> **What is Saving?**
> It is that part of income which is not consumed. It is an act of abstinence from consumption.
>
> **What is Investment?**
> It is expenditure by the producers on the purchase of such assets which help to generate income.

Thus, we are consumers, producers, savers and investors. We are all engaged in diverse economic activities. Economic activities include consumption, production, saving, investment, and many more.

> **What is Economic Activity?**
> It is an activity which is related to the use of scarce means (also called scarce resources). Means are always scarce in relation to our wants. Imagine yourself as the richest person on the earth. Still you can't have everything you wish to have at a point of time. It implies the scarcity of your means/resources in relation to your wants.

Engaged in diverse economic activities, we are performing 'ordinary business of life', according to **Alfred Marshall**, a great propounder of Modern Economics. Thus, he defines Economics as "*the study of mankind in the ordinary business of life*."

> ***Learning by doing***
> *How would you distinguish between economic activity and non-economic activity? Draw a list of economic and non-economic activities of your family members. Give logical reasoning in support of your answer.*
>
> ***Hint:*** *Non-economic activities are not related to the use of scarce resources. Scarce resources must have some market value.*

## Scarcity is the Undercurrent of Economic Problem and therefore of Economics

Resources are always scarce in relation to our wants. Also, resources have alternative uses: A ten-rupee note in your pocket may be spent on a cup of coffee or a cold drink. Likewise, a worker may render his services in factory A, rather than B and C. Because, resources are scarce and have alternative uses, we cannot escape from the problem of allocation of limited means to alternative uses. This is what we call economic problem or the problem of choice.

> **What is Economic Problem?**
> It is the problem of choice (or the problem of allocating scarce resources to alternative uses) arising on account of the fact that resources are scarce and these have alternative uses.

Economics is essentially the study of economic problems that we must confront owing to the fact that our means are scarce in relation to our wants, and that the means have alternative uses. *If there is no scarcity, there is no economic problem, and there is no economics if there is no economic problem*. Thus, **Robbins** defines Economics as "*A science that studies human behaviour as a relationship between ends and scarce means which have alternative uses*."

## Three Distinct Components of Economics: Consumption, Production and Distribution

### Consumption

Here, we, as students of Economics, study behaviour of human beings as consumers or buyers of different goods and services for the satisfaction of their wants. As consumers, people have limited means, while their wants are unlimited. How do they allocate their given means (or income) on the purchase of different goods and services, (given their market prices) so that their satisfaction is maximised? This is the study of consumption or the study of consumer behaviour. When we formulate a set of standard relationships (like the inverse relationship between price of good and its purchase) explaining how consumers tend to behave, we call it consumption theory.

### Production

Producers also have limited means while they have a wide range of goods and services to choose from for their firms and factories. Given prices of different inputs, how do they choose such combination(s) which are least expensive, so that they are able to minimise their cost of production. Also, given prices of different goods, how do they choose to produce those, the production of which offers them maximum revenue, so that their profit (profit = revenue – costs) is maximised. This is the study of production, or the study of producers' behaviour. When we formulate a set of standard relationships (like greater the productivity of a factor, greater is its employment) explaining the behaviour of producers or their production decisions, we call it production theory.

### Distribution

As students of Economics we are also interested in knowing how income (generated in the process of production) is distributed among those who have worked as agents of production. Who are agents of production? These are owners of factors of production, viz. land, labour, capital and entrepreneurship. A part of income generated will go to the owners of land (used in production) in the form of rent; a part will go to labourers (for rendering their services) in the form of wage; a part will go to the owners of capital (used in production) in the form of interest; and a part will go to the entrepreneurs in the form of profits. Distribution of income refers to the distribution of GDP (gross domestic product) among the owners of the factors of production (land, labour, capital and entrepreneurship). What are the economic principles on the basis of which income is distributed among owners of the factors of production? Such a study is called distribution theory in Economics.

Besides these three major components of Economics, the economists also address such questions which are of social significance, like the question of poverty and unemployment, the question of growth with social justice and the question of environmental degradation as linked to various economic activities. Issues of social significance or collective significance are categorised as issues of macroeconomics. These are distinct from the issues of microeconomics which revolve around the problems of choice confronted by microeconomic units like a household, a firm or an industry.

**Microeconomics and Macroeconomics**

Microeconomics deals with economic issues or economic problems related to microeconomic units like a household, a firm or an industry. These issues and problems are studied and addressed largely with a view to maximising individual welfare. Macroeconomics deals with economic issues or economic problems at the level of economy as a whole. These issues or problems are studied and addressed keeping in mind the goals of social welfare or collective welfare.

## 2. What is Statistics?

Even to a layman this should not be a difficult question. If asked to define Statistics, we can expect a layman to say that Statistics is something like a store of quantitative information. **Yes, it is true.** Statistics means quantitative information or quantification of the facts and findings. But, how do we get quantitative information? There must be a system, method or technique to collect quantitative information. Also, statistical information may be a raw information. It needs to be classified, tabulated or it needs to be systematically presented. One must learn the system of presentation and classification of data. Also, there must be a set of methods and techniques to condense the data. May be, we find averages or percentages. And above all, there must be a set of methods or techniques on the analysis and interpretation of quantitative information. A student of Economics has to study all these methods and techniques to understand and master the subject matter of Statistics.

Thus, unlike a layman, a student of Economics cannot relax taking Statistics just as a pool of quantitative information. Instead he is also to look into the methods or techniques relating to its collection, classification, presentation, analysis as well as interpretation.

In view of such a vastness of the subject matter, Statistics is defined both in **singular sense** and **plural sense,** as under:

### Statistics–A Plural Noun

In its plural sense, Statistics refers to information in terms of numbers or numerical data, such as Population Statistics, Employment Statistics, Statistics concerning Public Expenditure, etc. However, any numerical information is not Statistics. **Example:** Ram gets ₹ 100 per month as pocket allowance is not Statistics (it is neither an aggregate nor an average) whereas average pocket allowance of the students of Class X is ₹ 100 per month, or there are 80 students in Class XI compared to just 8 in Class XII of your school are Statistics.

**Always bear in mind**

Only the averages or aggregates of data that relate to some 'enquiry' (like population growth in India) or some phenomenon (like the inverse relationship between price of a commodity and its demand) are to be taken as statistics.

Do not take statistics as some quantitative information relating to any individual like you have two brothers or three sisters.

The following table shows a set of data which is Statistics, and another set which is not Statistics. The figures used are hypothetical.

| Data which are not Statistics | Data which are Statistics |
|---|---|
| (i) A cow has 4 legs. | (i) Average height of the 26-plus male people in India is 6 feet compared to 5 feet in Nepal. |
| (ii) Ram has 200 rupees in his pocket. | (ii) Birth rate in India is 18 per thousand compared to 8 per thousand in USA. |
| (iii) A young lady was run over by a speeding truck at 100 km per hour. | (iii) Over the past 10 years, India has won 60 test matches in cricket and lost 50. |

> *Learning by doing*
> *List five examples each of 'data which are Statistics', and 'data which are not Statistics'. Information should be related to the performance of your school in sports and academics.*

Thus:

All Statistics are data, but all data are not Statistics.

### Definition

In its plural sense, this is how Statistics is defined by different authors:

> *"Statistics are numerical statements of facts in any department of enquiry placed in relation to each other."* **—Bowley**

> *"By Statistics we mean quantitative data affected to a marked extent by multiplicity of causes."* **—Yule and Kendall**

### Features or Characteristics of Statistics in the Plural Sense or as Numerical Data

Main characteristics of Statistics in terms of numerical data are as follows:

**(1) Aggregate of Facts:** A single number does not constitute Statistics. No conclusion can be drawn from it. It is only the aggregate number of facts that is called Statistics, as the same can be compared and conclusions can be drawn from them. For example, if it is stated that there are 1,000 students in our college, then it has no statistical significance. But if it is stated that there are 300 students in arts faculty, 400 in commerce faculty and 300 in science faculty in our college, it makes statistical sense as this data conveys statistical information. Similarly, if it is stated that population of India is 121 crore or that the value of total exports from India is ₹ 11,66,439 crore, then these aggregate of facts will be termed as Statistics. It can, therefore, be concluded 'All Statistics are expressed in numbers but all numbers are not Statistics'.

**(2) Numerically Expressed:** Statistics are expressed in terms of numbers. Qualitative aspects like 'small' or 'big'; 'rich' or 'poor'; etc. are not called Statistics. For instance, to say, Irfan Pathan is tall and Sachin is short, has no statistical sense. However, if it is stated that height of Irfan Pathan is 6 ft and 2-inches and that of Sachin is 5 ft and 4-inches, then these numericals will be called Statistics.

**(3) Affected by Multiplicity of Causes:** Statistics are not affected by any single factor; but are influenced by many factors. Had they been affected by one factor alone then by removing that factor they would lose all their significance. For instance, 30 per cent rise in prices may have been due to several causes, like reduction in supply, increase in demand, shortage of power, rise in wages, rise in taxes, etc.

**(4) Reasonable Accuracy:** A reasonable degree of accuracy must be kept in view while collecting statistical data. This accuracy depends on the purpose of investigation, its nature, size and available resources.

**(5) Placed in Relation to each other:** Such numericals alone will be called Statistics as are mutually related and so comparable. Unless they have the quality of comparison they cannot be called Statistics.

> **Distinction between Quantitative and Qualitative Data**
>
> This is related to the distinction between quantitative variables and qualitative attributes. There are quantitative variables like income, expenditure and investment which can be expressed in numerical terms, viz., per capita income in India was (say) ₹ 4,000 per month, per capita expenditure was (say) ₹ 3,000 per month, and net investment (or capital formation) was (say) ₹ 10,000 crore in the year 2003-04. All such data are called **quantitative data**. On the other hand, there are qualitative attributes like 'IQ' level of different individuals or beauty of the individuals which cannot be expressed in numerical terms. These attributes refer to qualitative characteristics of the objects. These can be ranked or rated as good, very good, or excellent. We may give them ranks as 1,2,3, etc. All such data are called **qualitative data**. Briefly, while quantitative data refers to quantitative variables, qualitative data refers to qualitative attributes of the different objects.

For example, if it is stated "Ram is 40 years old, Mohan is 5 ft tall, Sohan has 60 kg of weight", then these numbers will not be called Statistics, as they are not mutually related nor subject to comparison. However, if the age, height and weight of all the three are inter-related, then the same will be considered as Statistics.

(6) **Pre-determined Purpose:** Statistics are collected with some pre-determined objective. Any information collected without any definite purpose will only be a numerical value and not Statistics. If data pertaining to the farmers of a village is collected, there must be some pre-determined objective. Whether the Statistics are collected for the purpose of knowing their economic position, or distribution of land among them or their total population, or for any other purpose, all these objectives must be pre-determined.

(7) **Enumerated or Estimated:** Statistics may be collected by enumeration or the same be estimated. If the field of investigation is vast, the procedure of estimation may be helpful. For example, 1 lakh people attended the rally addressed by the Prime Minister in Delhi and 2 lakh in Mumbai. These Statistics are based on estimation. As against it, if the field of enquiry is limited, the enumeration method is appropriate. For example, it can be verified by enumeration whether 20 students are present in the class or 10 workers are working in the factory.

(8) **Collected in a Systematic Manner:** Statistics should be collected in a systematic manner. Before collecting them, a plan must be prepared. No conclusion can be drawn from Statistics collected in haphazard manner. For instance, data regarding the marks secured by the students of a college without any reference to the class, subject, examination or maximum marks, etc., will lead to no conclusion.

In short, it can safely be concluded that "*all numerical data cannot be called Statistics but all Statistics are called numerical data.*"

> ***Learning by doing***
> *Write five examples each of 'quantitative variables' and 'qualitative variables'. Quantitative variables should be the well known terms of Economics, like production of wheat in India over the last 10 years.*

## Statistics–A Singular Noun

In the singular sense, Statistics means science of Statistics or statistical methods. It refers to techniques or methods relating to collection, classification, presentation, analysis and interpretation of quantitative data.

**Focus of the Study**

Statistics as a singular noun is focus of the study for the students of Class XI. You are to learn and understand how to collect data, organise data, present data as well as analyse and interpret data.

### Definition

"*Statistics may be defined as the collection, presentation, analysis and interpretation of numerical data.*" **—Croxton and Cowden**

"*Statistics is the science which deals with the collection, classification and tabulation of numerical facts as a basis for the explanation, description and comparison of phenomena.*" **—Lovitt**

"*Statistics is the science which deals with the methods of collecting, classifying, presenting, comparing and interpreting numerical data collected to throw some light on any sphere of enquiry.*" **—Seligman**

## Stages of Statistical Study

Studying Statistics as a singular noun implies the knowledge of various stages of statistical study. These stages are:

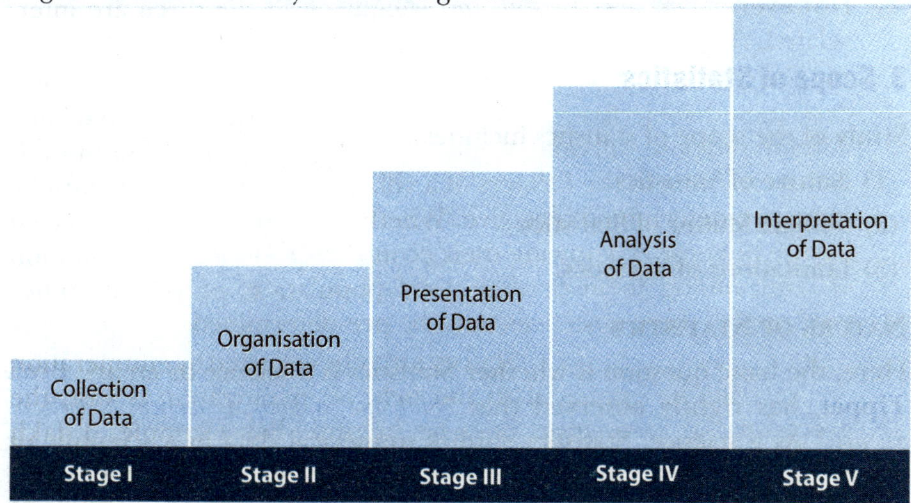


Obviously, at the first stage, we collect statistical data. Second, we organise the data in some systematic order. Third, we present the data in the form of graphs, diagrams or tables. Fourth, we analyse the data in terms of averages or percentages. Fifth, and finally, we interpret the data to find certain conclusions.

## Statistical Tools

Each stage of the statistical study involves the use of certain standard techniques or methods. These techniques or methods are called statistical tools. Thus, there are statistical tools used for the collection of data, like the 'Sample' and 'Census' techniques. Array of data and tally bars are the standard techniques used for organisation of data. Tables, graphs and diagrams are the well-known statistical tools for the presentation of data.

**What are Statistical Tools?**

These refer to the methods or techniques used for the collection, organisation and presentation of data, as well as for the analysis and interpretation of data.

Averages and percentages are the commonly used techniques for the analysis of data. Interpretation of data is often done in terms of the magnitude of averages, percentages or coefficients of correlation/regression. The following table gives an overall view of the various stages of statistical study and the related sets of statistical tools.

**Stages of Statistical Study and the Related Statistical Tools**

| Stages | Statistical Study | Statistical Tools |
|---|---|---|
| Stage I | Collection of Data | Census or Sample Techniques |
| Stage II | Organisation of Data | Array of Data and Tally Bars |
| Stage III | Presentation of Data | Tables, Graphs and Diagrams |
| Stage IV | Analysis of Data | Percentages, Averages, Correlation and Regression Coefficients |
| Stage V | Interpretation of Data | Magnitude of Percentages, Averages and the Degree of Relationship between different economic variables |

> **Note:** All the terms used to describe various statistical tools are comprehensively explained in the relevant chapters of the book. Students are not expected to mug up these terms at this stage of their study.

## 3. Scope of Statistics

Study of the scope of statistics includes:

(1) Nature of Statistics.

(2) Subject Matter of Statistics.

(3) Limitations of Statistics.

### Nature of Statistics

Here, the basic question is whether Statistics is a science or an art. **Prof. Tippet**, has rightly observed that "*Statistics is both a science as well as an art.*" As a science, Statistics studies numerical data in a scientific or systematic manner. As an art, Statistics relates to quantitative data to the real life problems. By using statistical data, we are able to analyse and understand real life problems much better than otherwise. Thus, the problem of unemployment in India is more meaningfully analysed when the size of unemployment is supported with quantitative data.

### Subject Matter of Statistics

Subject matter of statistics includes two components: Descriptive Statistics and Inferential Statistics.

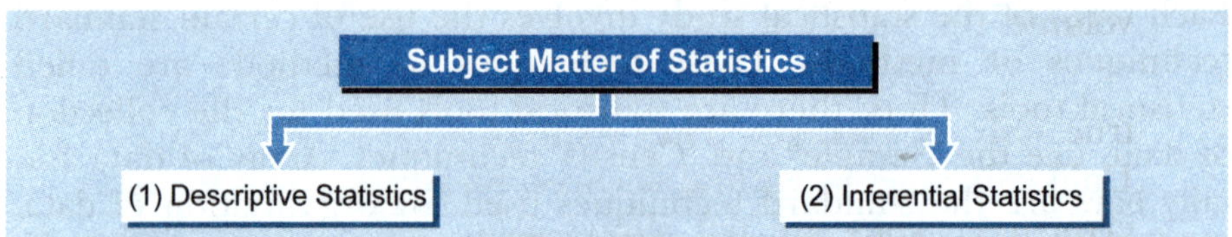


> **The Concept of Universe or Population**
>
> It should be interesting for the students of Class XI to note that the concept of universe or population has a specific meaning in Statistics. It refers to the aggregate of all items or units relating to your statistical study. **Example:** Universe or population size is 1,000 if you are studying 1,000 students for your statistical study.

(1) **Descriptive Statistics:** Descriptive Statistics refers to those methods which are used for the collection, presentation as well as analysis of data. These methods relate to such estimations as 'measurement of central tendencies' (average mean, median, mode), 'measurement of dispersion' (mean deviation, standard deviation, etc.), 'measurement of correlation', etc. Example: Descriptive statistics is used when you estimate average height of the secondary students in your school. Likewise, descriptive statistics is used when you find that marks in science and mathematics of the students in all classes are intimately related to each other.

(2) **Inferential Statistics:** Inferential Statistics refers to all such methods by which conclusions are drawn relating to the universe or population on the basis of a given sample. (In Statistics, the term universe or population refers to the aggregate of all items or units relating to any subject.) For example, if your class teacher estimates average weight of the entire class (called universe or population) on the basis of average weight of only a sample of students of the class, he is using inferential statistics.

## Limitations of Statistics

In modern times, Statistics has emerged to be of crucial significance in all walks of life. However, it has certain limitations. Thus, writes **Newshome** that, "*Statistics must be regarded as an instrument of research of great value but barring severe limitations which are not possible to overcome*." Following are some notable limitations of Statistics:

**(1) Study of Numerical Facts only:** Statistics studies only such facts as can be expressed in numerical terms. It does not study qualitative phenomena like honesty, friendship, wisdom, health, patriotism, justice, etc.

**(2) Study of Aggregates only:** Statistics studies only the aggregates of quantitative facts. It does not study statistical facts relating to any particular unit. Example: It may be a statistical fact that your class teacher earns ₹ 50,000 per month. But, as this fact relates to an individual, it is not to be deemed as a subject matter of Statistics. However, it becomes a subject matter of Statistics if we study income of school teachers across all parts of the country, for purpose of finding regional differences in income.

**(3) Homogeneity of Data, an essential Requirement:** To compare data, it is essential that statistics are uniform in quality. Data of diverse qualities and kinds cannot be compared. For example, production of food grains cannot be compared with the production of cloth. It is because cloth is measured in metres and food grains in tonnes. Nevertheless, it is possible to compare their value instead of the volume.

**(4) Results are True only on an Average:** Most statistical findings are true only as averages. They express only the broad tendencies. Unlike the laws of natural sciences, statistical observations are not error-free. They are not always valid under all conditions. For instance, if it is said that per capita income in India is ₹ 50,000 per annum, it does not mean that the income of each and every Indian is ₹ 50,000 per annum. Some may have more and some may have less.

**(5) Without Reference, Results may Prove to be Wrong:** In order to understand the conclusions precisely, it is necessary that the circumstances and conditions under which these conclusions have been drawn are also studied. Otherwise, they may prove to be wrong.

Example: In the business of cloth, profits earned during three years may be ₹ 1,000, ₹ 2,000 and ₹ 3,000 respectively. On the other hand, in the paper business profits earned during the same three years may be ₹ 3,000, ₹ 2,000 and ₹ 1,000 respectively. Thus, the average profit in both the businesses comes to ₹ 2,000 per annum. It may lead to the conclusion that both the businesses have similar economic status, but it may not be true. We may actually find that whereas cloth-business is making progress, paper-business is on the decline.

(6) **Can be used only by the Experts:** Statistics can be used only by those persons who have special knowledge of statistical methods. Those who are ignorant about these methods cannot make sensible use of statistics. It can, therefore, be said that data in the hands of an unqualified person is like a medicine in the hands of a quack who may abuse it, leading to disastrous consequences. In the words of **Yule** and **Kendall,** "*Statistical methods are most dangerous tools in the hands of an inexpert.*"

(7) **Prone to Misuse:** Misuse of Statistics is very common. Statistics may used to support a pre-drawn conclusion even when it is absolutely false. It is usually said, "*Statistics are like clay by which you can make a god or a devil, as you please.*" Misuse of statistics is indeed its greatest limitation.

## 4. Importance of Statistics in Economics

Following words of **Prof. Tippet** very aptly capture the importance of Statistics in Economics: "*A day might come when the department of Economics in the universities will go out of the control of economic theoreticians and come under the control of statistical workshops, in the same manner as the department of physics and chemistry have come under the control of experimental laboratories.*" Indeed, Statistics has emerged as the lifeline of Economics. It is because of the growing use of Statistics by the economists that the subjects like econometrics have been added to the horizons of Economics. Students of Class XI may note the following points to highlight the significance of Statistics in Economics.

(1) **Quantitative Expression of Economic Problems:** Consider any economic problem, be it the problem of unemployment, the problem of price rise or the problem of shrinking exports. The first task of the economists is to understand its magnitude through its quantitative expression.

For example, if it is the problem of unemployment, we make its quantitative expression stating that (say) 20 per cent of the India's working population is unemployed or that between the years 1995-2010 the percentage of unemployed working population has tended to increase from 18 per cent to 9.4 per cent.

(2) **Inter-sectoral and Inter-temporal Comparisons:** Economists do not stop merely at the quantitative expression of the problems. They would try to further comprehend it through inter-sectoral and inter-temporal comparisons. From inter-sectoral comparisons we mean, comparisons across different sectors of the economy. Thus, analysing the problem of unemployment, the economists would like to know the magnitude of unemployment across rural and urban sectors of the economy. They would like to know what percentage of rural population is unemployed compared to the urban population. Inter-temporal comparison means understanding of change in the magnitude of the problem over time. This would mean making a

comparison (say) over different plan periods of the rural and urban unemployment.

**(3) Working out Cause and Effect Relationship:** Economists try to find out cause and effect relationship between different sets of data. This enables them to attempt an effective diagnosis of the problem and accordingly to suggest some effective remedies. Thus, through their statistical studies, if the economists come to know that it is because of the decline in demand that investment in the economy has tended to shrink, they can suggest the government to adopt such measures as would increase the level of demand in the economy.

**(4) Construction of Economic Theories or Economic Models:** What is economic theory? It is an established statistical relationship between different sets of statistical data, offering conclusions of economic significance. The well-known inverse relationship between price of a commodity and its demand (*i.e.*, more is purchased when price falls) is an established statistical relationship, and therefore, is a part of economic theory. Is the construction of theoretical relationships or models possible without statistical experiments? Certainly not.

**(5) Economic Forecasting:** Economists do forecasting through statistical studies. By the term forecasting we do not mean some astrological predictions. We only mean to assess and ascertain the future course of certain events which are of economic significance. Thus, on studying the behaviour of price level over several years, the economists can make statistical forecasting about the likely trend or pattern of the price level in the near future. This helps us in future planning.

**(6) Formulation of Policies:** How does the finance minister decide to increase or decrease taxation as a source of government revenue? Obviously through statistical studies. It is through statistical investigations that the finance minister gets a feedback on the tax-paying capacity of the people, and revenue needs of the government. Accordingly, tax rates are fixed to get maximum possible revenue with minimum possible discomfort to the people.

**(7) Economic Equilibrium:** What is economic equilibrium? It is a state of balance for the producer or the consumer where the producer finds that his profits are maximum or where the consumer finds that his satisfaction is maximum. It is through the use of statistical methods that the economists have evolved some eco-fundamentals (which you will study in Class XII) telling us how profits of the producers are maximised or how consumers get maximum satisfaction.

Thus, so much is the significance of Statistics in Economics that **Marshall** (a great economist of the past century) had to concede that "*Statistics are the straw out of which I, like every other economist, have to make bricks*." Surely, Statistics is the hub of the wheel of economic studies, and the beginners of Class XI must focus on the hub to precisely understand the movement of the entire wheel.

**Two Important points on the Significance of Statistics in Economics**

(i) Statistics facilitates inter-sectoral and inter-temporal comparison.

(ii) Statistics helps to establish cause and effect relationship between different economic variables that have facilitated the construction of economic theories.

### Statistical Methods are No Substitute for Common Sense

This is a statement of caution to the students of Statistics. It urges the students not to use Statistics devoid of their common sense. You may find some spurious relationships, like larger the number of doctors in an area greater are the deaths in that area. It may be true statistically, but does not match with common sense. Hence, never propagate any statistical conclusion in case it offends your common sense. Likewise, average size of shoes for the 50 students in your class may be 'six'. But it would be foolish if the school authorities place an order of 50 shoes of the size-six for all of you. Surely this size may not fit many of you.

### Distrust of Statistics

Some people have misgivings about Statistics and make observations like the following:

(i) Statistics is a rainbow of lies.
(ii) Statistics are tissues of falsehood.
(iii) Statistics can prove anything.
(iv) Statistics cannot prove anything.
(v) Statistics are like clay of which you can make a god or a devil, as you please.

According to **Disraeli**, "There are three kinds of lies–lies, damned lies and Statistics."

Indeed, one can present statistical information in a manner that tends to distort the facts and thereby mislead the people. For instance, the government claimed that in 2011, per capita income in India increased by about 17 per cent. On the other hand, the opposition party claimed that in 2011, per capita income increased by 5 per cent only. But the difference lies in the fact that whereas government estimates are based on current prices, those of the opposition party are based on the 2004-05 prices. It is difficult for a layman to understand this difference. He will just be confused or perhaps befooled by the claims and counterclaims of the government and the opposition party.

#### What Causes Distrust?

Distrust of Statistics arises not because there is anything wrong with Statistics as a subject matter. It arises because the users of Statistics tend to manipulate it to suit or support their pre-drawn conclusions or observations.

Main causes for the distrust of Statistics are as under:

(i) Different kinds of Statistics are obtained in respect of a given problem.
(ii) Statistics can be altered to match the predetermined conclusions.
(iii) Authentic Statistics can also be presented in such a manner as to confuse the reader.
(iv) When Statistics are collected in a partial manner, the results are generally wrong. Consequently, people lose faith in them.

However, it may be noted that if Statistics are presented wrongly, then the fault does not lie with Statistics as a subject matter. The fault lies with those people who collect wrong Statistics or those who draw wrong conclusions. **Statistics, as such, do not prove anything. They are simply tools in the hands of the statisticians. If a statistician misuses the data, then the blame lies squarely on him and not on the subject matter. A competent doctor can cure a disease by making good use of the medicine but the same medicine in the hands of an incompetent doctor becomes a poison. The fault in this case is not of the medicine but of the unqualified doctor. In the same way, Statistics is never faulty but the fault lies with the users.**

In fact, Statistics should not be relied upon blindly nor distrusted outright. "Statistics should not be used as a blind man uses a lamp post for support rather than for illumination, whereas its real purpose is to serve as illumination and not as a support."

In making use of Statistics one should be cautious and vigilant. In the words of King, "The science of Statistics is the most useful servant, but only of great value to those who understand its proper use."

It is the duty of the students of Economics to make use of know-how of Statistics to discover the truth rather than to cover the truth.

**How to Remove Distrust?**

Following are some essential remedies of the distrust of Statistics:

(i) **Consideration of Statistical Limitations:** While making use of Statistics, limitations of Statistics must be taken care of.

(ii) **No Bias:** The user should be impartial. He should make use only of the relevant data and draw conclusions without any bias or prejudice.

(iii) **Application by Experts:** Statistics should be used only by the experts to minimise the possibility of misuse.

## EXERCISE

### 1. Very Short Answer Type Questions [1 mark]

#### A. Multiple Choice Questions: Choose the Correct Answer

1. Which of the following statements is not an example of Statistics?
   (a) Birth rate in India is 18 per thousand as compared to 8 per thousand in the US.
   (b) Ramesh has a ₹ 100 note in his pocket.
   (c) Over the last 10 years, India has won 60 text matches in cricket and lost 50.
   (d) Average pocket allowance of the students of Class XI is ₹ 500 per month.
2. Which of the following is correct regarding Statistics?
   (a) Aggregate of facts (b) Numerically expressed
   (c) Affected by multiplicity of causes (d) All of these
3. In singular sense Statistics means:
   (a) statistical science (b) statistical law
   (c) both (a) and (b) (d) none of these
4. The aggregate of data is called:
   (a) Statistics (b) editing of data
   (c) analysis of data (d) collection of data
5. Which of the following indicates a stage of statistical study?
   (a) Collection of data (b) Presentation of data
   (c) Analysis of data (d) All of these
6. In plural sense, which of the following is not a characteristic of Statistics?
   (a) Aggregate of data (b) Only expressed in words
   (c) Affected by multiplicity of causes (d) Collected in a systematic manner

7. With regards to distrust of Statistics which of the following statements is not correct?
   (a) Statistics is a rainbow of lies
   (b) Statistics are tissues of falsehood
   (c) Statistics express the facts in numbers
   (d) There are three kinds of lies–lies, damned lies and statistics
8. Which of the following is an economic activity?
   (a) Production (b) Consumption
   (c) Distribution (d) All of these
9. Which of the following statements is incorrect?
   (a) Resources have alternative uses
   (b) All numbers are Statistics
   (c) Macroeconomics studies large aggregates
   (d) Statistics studies only the aggregates of quantitative facts
10. The process of converting raw material into goods is called:
   (a) production (b) saving
   (c) investment (d) exchange

Ans. 1. (b), 2. (d), 3. (c), 4. (a), 5. (d), 6. (b), 7. (c), 8. (d), 8. (d), 9. (b), 10. (a).

### B. True or False

State whether the following statements are True or False:

1. The data collected without any objective is called numbers. (True/False)
2. Statistics studies both quantitative and qualitative variables. (True/False)
3. All numerical information is not Statistics. (True/False)
4. Tendulkar has a long bat. The statement is Statistics. (True/False)
5. Microeconomics studies economic activity of an individual unit. (True/False)
6. Inferential Statistics refers to those methods by which conclusions are drawn relating to the population on the basis of a given sample. (True/False)

Ans. 1. True, 2. False, 3. True, 4. False, 5. True, 6. True.

### C. Concepts/Definitions & Knowledge-based Questions

1. Define Economics.

Ans. Economics is the study of economic issues (or Economic problems) arising out of the fact that resources are scarce in relation to our needs/desires and the scarce resources have alternative uses.

2. Define economic activity.

Ans. Economic activity is an activity which is related to the use of scarce means (also called scarce resources).

3. Who is a consumer?

Ans. A consumer is one who consumes goods and services for the satisfaction of his wants.

4. What is consumption?

Ans. Consumption is the process of using up utility value of goods and services for the direct satisfaction of our wants. Utility value of goods means inherent capacity of goods and services to satisfy human wants.

5. Who is a producer?

Ans. A producer is one who produces and/or sells goods and services for the generation of income.

6. What is production?

Ans. Production is the process of converting raw material into useful things. Things become useful when they acquire utility value in the process of production.

7. What is saving?

Ans. Saving is that part of income which is not consumed. It is an act of abstinence from consumption.

8. Define investment.

Ans. Investment is expenditure by the producers on the purchase of such assets which help to generate income.

9. Define Statistics as a singular noun.

Ans. In the singular sense, Statistics means science of Statistics or statistical methods. It refers to techniques or methods relating to collection, classification, presentation, analysis and interpretation of quantitative data.

10. Define Statistics as a plural noun.

Ans. In the plural sense, Statistics refers to information in terms of numbers or numerical data, such as population statistics, employment statistics, statistics concerning public expenditure, etc.

11. What is meant by Descriptive Statistics?

Ans. Descriptive Statistics refers to those methods which are used for the collection, presentation as well as analysis of data. These methods relate to such estimations as 'measurement of central tendencies', 'measurement of dispersion', 'measurement of correlation', etc.

12. What is meant by Inferential Statistics?

Ans. Inferential Statistics refers to all such methods by which conclusions are drawn relating to the universe or population on the basis of a given sample.

## 2. Short Answer Type Questions [3-4 marks]

1. Scarcity causes economic problem. How?
2. Problem of choice is unavoidable in the ordinary business of life. How?
3. Explain how scarcity is the undercurrent of Economics.
4. Briefly explain the three distinct components of Economics.
5. Distinguish between microeconomics and macroeconomics.
6. Define Statistics as a singular noun and as a plural noun.
7. Name the stages of statistical study and statistical tools for the presentation of data.
8. Distinguish between 'quantitative' and 'qualitative' data, and give some examples of both.
9. Write three sentences highlighting the importance of Statistics in Economics.
10. What are the main features of Statistics as a numerical data? Describe any four.
11. State the main limitations of Statistics.
12. "Statistical methods are dangerous weapons in the hands of an unqualified person." Explain.

## 3. Long Answer Type Questions **[6 marks]**

1. Explain the scope of Statistics.
2. Absence of scarcity would mean absence of Economics. Explain with logical reasoning.
3. Define Statistics. What are its basic characteristics?
4. Explain the main limitations of Statistics?
5. Describe the main stages of Statistics and the related tools.
6. "Statistics is defined as aggregate of numerical facts." Give a few examples.
7. "Statistics is defined as the 'science' which deals with the analysis of statistical data." Give examples.
8. "There are three kinds of lies–lies, damned lies and Statistics." Explain the statement.

## 4. Essential Practicals

1. Complete the following observations:
   (i) Statistics means ____________.
   (ii) Statistics and economics are ____________.
   (iii) The term population refers to ____________.
   (iv) Descriptive Statistics means those methods ____________.
2. Prepare a list of statistical information that you will facilitate comparison of academic performance of your school with others in your neighbourhood.
3. Write two such pairs of statistical variables that show cause and effect relationship with each other.

## 5. NCERT Textbook Questions [With Hints to Answers]

1. Mark the following statements as true or false:
   (i) Statistics can only deal with quantitative data.
   (ii) Statistics solves economic problems.
   (iii) Statistics is of no use to Economics without data.

   [(i) True, (ii) False, (iii) True]
2. Make a list of activities that constitute the ordinary business of life. Why are these called economic activities?

   [Production, consumption, distribution are the some examples of economic activities. These are economic activities, as these are related to the use of scarce means for the satisfaction of human wants].
3. 'The government and policy makers use statistical data to formulate suitable policies of economic development'. Illustrate with two examples.

   [Page 13]
4. You have unlimited wants and limited resources to satisfy them. Explain by giving two examples.

   [Page 3, 4]
5. What are the reasons for studying Economics?

   [Page 12, 13]
6. Statistical methods are no substitute for common sense. Comment.

   [Page 14]

# Collection of Data

# 2

Now we know that, in the plural sense, **Statistics means data** or quantitative information capable of some meaningful conclusions. In other words, in data, we include that information which is capable of numerical expression. Let us recall some examples of data:

- that there are eight sugar mills in Haryana compared to 20 in Punjab.
- 20 per cent of the people in the working age group are unemployed in India compared to only 2 per cent in USA.
- of the total cattle population of the world, 50 per cent belongs to India.

The present chapter focuses on the collection of data, including: (i) sources of data, and (ii) methods of collecting data. But before that we must know why do we collect data. For a student of Economics, the purpose of data collection is to understand, analyse and explain a socio-economic problem, for example, the problem of unemployment or the problem of poverty. While analysing the problem we also try to understand the causes behind the problem as also the possible solutions. The entire exercise needs a comprehensive support of numerical facts, called data.

## 1. Primary and Secondary Sources of Data

There are two sources of data:

(i) Primary Source, and
(ii) Secondary Source.

**Primary Source:** You want to know about the quality of life of the people in your town. You may like to ascertain the quality of life in terms of per capita expenditure of different households in your town. You decide to collect the basic data yourself through statistical survey(s), of course with the help of investigators or field workers. While doing this exercise you are relying on primary source of the data. Thus, primary source of data implies collection of data from its source of origin. It offers you first-hand quantitative information relating to your statistical study. You or your team of investigators are contacting the respondents (people offering basic information) and obtaining the desired quantitative information on per capita expenditure of different households in your town.

Primary source of data implies collection of data from its source of origin. It offers you first-hand quantitative information relating to your statistical study.

**Secondary Source:** Secondary Source of collection of data implies obtaining the relevant statistical information from an agency, or an institution which is already in possession of that information. To continue with the previous example, data relating to the quality of life of the people of your town (or the data on per capita expenditure) may have already been collected by the State Government. You can simply approach the concerned Government department and request for the desired information. This will be a Secondary Source of data for you. Thus, secondary source implies that the desired statistical information already exists and you are simply to collect it from the concerned agency or the department. You are not to conduct statistical survey(s) yourself and you are not to contact the respondents (people offering basic information). Of course, you are not getting first hand information relating to your statistical study. You are simply relying on the information which is already existing.

Secondary source of data implies collection of data from some agency or institution which already happens to have collected the data through statistical survey(s). It does not offer you first-hand information relating to your statistical study. You are to rely on the information which is already existing.

## Primary and Secondary Data

Primary source of collecting data offers you, **'Primary data'** and secondary source offers you **'Secondary data'**. Let us clarify the difference.

**Primary Data:** Data collected by the investigator for his own purpose, for the first time, from beginning to end, are called primary data. These are collected from the source of origin. In the words of **Wessel** "*Data originally collected in the process of investigation are known as primary data*." Primary data are original. The concerned investigator is the first person who collects these information. The primary data are, therefore, a first-hand information. To illustrate, you may be interested in studying the socio-economic state of those students in your Class XI who secured first division in their matriculation examination. You collect information regarding their pocket allowance, their family income, educational status, their family members and the like. All this information would be termed as primary information or primary data, since you happen to be the first person to collect this information from the source of its origin.

**Secondary Data:** In the words of **M.M. Blair**, "*Secondary data are those which are already in existence, and which have been collected, for some other purpose than the answering of the question in hand*." According to **Wessel**, "*Data collected by other persons are called secondary data*." These data are, therefore, called second-hand data. Obviously, since these data have already been collected by somebody else, these are available in the form of published or unpublished reports. For example, data relating to Indian Railways which are annually published by the Railway Board, would be secondary data for any researcher.

### Principal Differences between Primary and Secondary Data

The following are some principal differences between primary and secondary data:

(1) **Difference in Originality:** Primary data are original because these are collected by the investigator from the source of their origin. Against this, secondary data are already in existence and therefore, are not original.

(2) **Difference in the Suitability of Objectives:** Primary data are always related to a specific objective of the investigator. These data, therefore, do not need any adjustment for the concerned study. On the other hand, secondary data have already been collected for some other purpose. Therefore, these data need to be adjusted to suit the objective of study in hand.

(3) **Difference in Cost of Collection:** Primary data are costlier in terms of time, money and efforts involved than the secondary data. This is because primary data are collected for the first time from their source of origin. Secondary data are simply collected from the published or unpublished reports. Accordingly, these are much less expensive.

Of course, it may be noted that there are no fundamental differences between primary data and secondary data. Data are data, whether primary or secondary. These are classified as primary or secondary just on the basis of their collection: first-hand or second-hand. Thus, a particular set of data when collected by the investigator for a specific purpose from the source of origin, would be primary data. And the same set of data, when used by some other investigator for his own purpose, would be known as secondary data. Thus, **Secrist** has rightly pointed out, "*The distinction between primary and secondary data is one of the degree. Data which are primary in the hands of one party may be secondary in the hands of other.*"

**Primary and Secondary Data– the Basic Difference**

- If we are collecting data from its source of origin, for the first time, it is primary data.
- If we are using data which have already been collected by somebody else, it is secondary data.

**Note:** If you are getting data from somebody else who collected it from its source of origin but did not use it for his own study, it will be deemed as primary data.

## 2. How Basic Data is Collected: Some Statistical Methods/Modes of Data Collection

When basic data is to be collected from its primary source, how do we do it? It involves the study of a set of statistical methods or statistical techniques. The following are some of the well-known methods of collecting primary data:

- Direct Personal Investigation
- Indirect Oral Investigation
- Information from Local Sources or Correspondents
- Information through Questionnaires and Schedules
  (i) Mailing Method, and (ii) Enumerator's Method.

### Direct Personal Investigation

The direct personal investigation is the method by which data are personally collected by the investigator from the informants. In other words, the investigator establishes direct relation with the persons from

whom the information is to be obtained. The success of this method, however, requires that the investigator should be very diligent, efficient, impartial and tolerant.

Direct contact with the workers of an industry to obtain information about their economic conditions is an example of this method.

### Suitability

This method of collecting primary data is suitable particularly when:

(1) the field of investigation is limited or not very large.

(2) a greater degree of originality of the data is required.

(3) information is to be kept secret.

(4) accuracy of data is of great significance, and

(5) when direct contact with the informants is required.

### Merits

Data, thus, collected have the following merits:

**(1) Originality:** Data have a high degree of originality.

**(2) Accuracy:** Data are fairly accurate when personally collected.

**(3) Reliability:** Because the information is collected by the investigator himself, reliability of the data is not doubted.

**(4) Related Information:** When in direct contact with the informants, the investigator may obtain other related information as well.

**(5) Uniformity:** There is a fair degree of uniformity in the data collected by the investigator himself from the informants. It facilitates comparison.

**(6) Elastic:** This method is fairly elastic because the investigator can always make necessary adjustments in his set of questions.

### Demerits

However, the method of direct personal investigation suffers from certain demerits, as under:

**(1) Difficult to Cover Wide Areas:** Direct personal investigation becomes very difficult when the area of the study is very wide.

**(2) Personal Bias:** This method is highly prone to personal bias of the investigator. As a result, the data may lose their credibility.

**(3) Costly:** This method is very expensive in terms of the time, money and efforts involved.

**(4) Limited Coverage:** In this method, area of investigation is generally small. The results are, therefore, less representative. This may lead to wrong conclusions.

> ***Learning by doing***
>
> *You are to conduct direct personal investigation on the quality of teaching in a school. Who are your informants? What difficulties do you expect to encounter in such an exercise?*

## Indirect Oral Investigation

*Indirect oral investigation is the method by which information is obtained not from the persons regarding whom the information is needed. It is collected orally from other persons who are expected to possess the necessary information. These other persons are known as witnesses.* For example, by this method, the data on the economic conditions of the workers may be collected from their employers rather than the workers themselves.

### Suitability

This method is suitable particularly when:

(1) the field of investigation is relatively large.

(2) it is not possible to have direct contact with the concerned informants.

(3) the concerned informants are not capable of giving information because of their ignorance or illiteracy.

(4) investigation is so complex in nature that only experts can give information.

This method is mostly used by government or non-government committees or commissions.

### Merits

Some of the notable merits of this method are as under:

(1) **Wide Coverage:** This method can be applied even when the field of investigation is very wide.

(2) **Less Expensive:** This is relatively a less expensive method as compared to Direct Personal Investigation.

(3) **Expert Opinion:** Using this method an investigator can seek opinion of the experts and thereby can make his information more reliable.

(4) **Free from Bias:** This method is relatively free from the personal bias of the investigator.

(5) **Simple:** This is relatively a simple approach of data collection.

### Demerits

However, there are some demerits, as under:

(1) **Less Accurate:** The data collected by this method are relatively less accurate. This is because the information is obtained from persons other than the concerned informants.

(2) **Biased:** There is possibility of personal bias of the witnesses giving information.

(3) **Doubtful Conclusions:** This method may lead to doubtful conclusions due to carelessness of the witnesses.

## Difference between Direct Personal Investigation and Indirect Oral Investigation

The difference between direct personal investigation and indirect oral investigation is as under:

(1) In the case of direct personal investigation, the investigator establishes direct contact with the informants. On the other hand, in the case of indirect oral investigation, information is obtained by contacting other than those about whom information is sought.

(2) Direct Personal Investigation is generally possible when the field of investigation is small. On the other hand, indirect oral investigation is generally preferred when the field of investigation is relatively large.

(3) In the Direct Personal Investigation, the investigator must be well versed in the language and cultural habits of the informants. There is no such requirement in the case of Indirect Oral Investigation.

(4) Direct investigation is relatively costlier than the indirect investigation.

> *Learning by doing*
>
> *You are keen on finding statistical information on available Health Care facilities in your locality comprising 200 families. How would you approach the issue, and which method of investigation would you prefer to adopt? Give reasons.*

## Information from Local Sources or Correspondents

Under this method, the investigator appoints local persons or correspondents at different places. They collect information in their own way and furnish the same to the investigator.

### Suitability

This method is suitable particularly when:

(1) regular and continuous information is needed.

(2) the area of investigation is large.

(3) the information is to be used by journals, magazines, radio, TV, etc. and

(4) a very high degree of accuracy of information is not required.

### Merits

Principal merits of this method are as under:

(1) **Economical:** This method is quite economical in terms of time, money or efforts involved.

(2) **Wide Coverage:** This method allows a fairly wide coverage of investigation.

(3) **Continuity:** The correspondents keep on supplying almost regular information.

(4) **Suitable for Special Purpose:** This method is particularly suitable for some special-purpose investigations, *e.g.*, price quotations from the different grain markets for the construction of Index Number of agricultural prices.

### Demerits

Following are some notable demerits of this method:

(1) **Loss of Originality:** Originality of data is sacrificed owing to the lack of personal contact with the respondents.

(2) **Lack of Uniformity:** There is lack of uniformity of data. This is because data is collected by a number of correspondents.

(3) **Personal Bias:** This method suffers from the personal bias of the correspondents.

(4) **Less Accurate:** The data collected by this method are not very accurate.

(5) **Delay in Collection:** Generally, there is a delay in the collection of information through this method.

## Information through Questionnaires and Schedules

Under this method, the investigator prepares a questionnaire keeping in view the objective of the enquiry. There are two ways of collecting information on the basis of questionnaire:

(1) Mailing Method, and

(2) Enumerator's Method.

## (1) Mailing Method

Under this method, questionnaires are mailed to the informants. A letter is attached with the questionnaire giving the purpose of enquiry. It is also assured that the information would be kept secret. The informant notes the answers against the questions and returns the completed questionnaire to the investigator.

### Suitability

This method is most suited when:

(1) the area of the study is very wide, and

(2) the informants are educated.

### Merits

The following are the main merits of this method:

(1) **Economical:** This method is economical in terms of time, money and efforts involved.

(2) **Original:** This method is original and therefore, fairly reliable. This is because the information is duly supplied by the concerned persons themselves.

(3) **Wide Coverage:** This method allows wide coverage of the area of study.

### Demerits

However, there are certain demerits of this method as under:

(1) **Lack of Interest:** Generally, the informants do not take interest in questionnaires and fail to return the questionnaires. Those who return, often send incomplete answers.

(2) **Lack of Flexibility:** This method lacks flexibility. When questions are not properly replied, these cannot be changed to obtain the required information.

(3) **Limited Use:** This method has limited use owing to the fact that the questionnaires can be answered only by the educated informants. Thus, this method cannot be used when the informants are uneducated.

(4) **Biased:** If the informants are biased, then the information will also be biased.

(5) **Less Accuracy:** The conclusions based on such investigation have only limited accuracy. This is because some questions may be difficult, and consequently accurate answers may not be offered.

### (2) Enumerator's Method

Under this method, a questionnaire is prepared according to the purpose of enquiry. The enumerator himself approaches the informant with the questionnaire. The questionnaires which are filled by the enumerators themselves by putting questions are called schedules. Thus, under this method, the enumerator himself fills the schedules after seeking information from the informants. Enumerators are those persons who help the investigators in collecting the data. The enumerators are given training to fill the schedules and put the questions intelligently to obtain accurate information.

#### Suitability

This method is mostly used when:

(1) field of investigation is large.

(2) the investigation needs specialised and skilled investigators, and

(3) the investigators are well versed in the local language and cultural norms of the informants.

**Define Investigator, Enumerator and Respondent**

- Investigator is a person who plans and conducts an empirical investigation independently or with the help of others.
- Enumerator is a person who actually collects the desired statistical information or statistical data. Often the enumerators are trained personnel hired by the investigator for field work.
- Respondent is a person who answers/ responds to the set of questions included in the questionnaire.

#### Merits

This method has the following merits:

(1) **Wide Coverage:** This method is capable of a wide coverage in terms of the area involved. Even illiterates can furnish the required information.

(2) **Accuracy:** There is a fair degree of accuracy in the results. This is because investigations are done by specialized enumerators.

(3) **Personal Contact:** Unlike in the case of mailing questionnaires, there is personal contact with the informants in this method. Accordingly, accurate and right answers are obtained.

(4) **Impartiality:** This method is impartial. This is because the enumerators themselves do not need the required information, so they are impartial to the nature of information that they obtain.

(5) **Completeness:** Schedules have the merit of completeness because these are filled in by the enumerators themselves.

#### Demerits

The following are the main demerits of this method:

(1) **Expensive:** This is a very expensive method of investigation because of the involvement of trained investigators.

(2) **Availability of Enumerators:** Competent enumerators may not be available. Accuracy of the information accordingly suffers.

(3) **Time Consuming:** Enumerators may need specialised training for particular investigation. The process of investigation thus becomes time consuming.

(4) **Not Suitable for Private Investigation:** Since this method is very expensive, it is generally not suitable for private investigation. This method is generally used by the Government institutions.

(5) **Partial:** If the enumerators are biased, then the data will not be accurate.

## Construction of Questionnaires and Schedules and their Qualities

In the context of collection of Primary data, construction of questionnaires and schedules has the special significance.

The set of questions in questionnaires and schedules are similar. The only difference that lies between the two is that, *in questionnaires, the entire information is recorded by the informants themselves. In the schedules, on the other hand, the information as supplied by the informants is recorded by the enumerators*.

**The Basic Difference between a Questionnaire and a Schedule**

Both show a set of questions. But in case of a questionnaire, the answers are to be recorded/written by the respondents themselves, while in the case of a schedule, answers are to be written/recorded by the enumerators specifically hired for the purpose.

### Qualities of a Good Questionnaire

Following are some of the desired qualities of a good questionnaire:

(1) **Limited Number of Questions:** The number of questions in a questionnaire should be as limited as possible. Questions should be only relating to the purpose of enquiry.

(2) **Simplicity:** Language of the questions should be simple, lucid and clear. Questions should be short, not long or complex. Mathematical questions must be avoided.

(3) **Proper Order of the Questions:** Questions must be placed in a proper order.

(4) **No Undesirable Questions:** Undesirable questions or personal questions must be avoided. The questions should not offend the informants.

(5) **Non-Controversial:** Questions should be such as can be answered impartially. No controversial questions should be asked.

(6) **Calculations:** Questions involving calculations by the respondents must be avoided. Investigator himself should do the calculation job.

(7) **Pre-Testing Pilot Survey:** Some questions be asked from the informants on trial basis. If their answers involve some difficulty these can be reframed accordingly. Such testing is technically called pilot survey.

(8) **Instructions:** A questionnaire must show clear instructions for filling in the form.

(9) **Cross Verification:** Such questions may be asked which help cross verifications.

(10) **Request for Return:** Request should be made to the respondents to return the questionnaire completed in all respects. The informant must be assured that the information conveyed by him will be treated as confidential.

### Types of Questions: Some Examples

There are four possible types of questions, as under:

(1) **Simple Alternative Questions:** These questions are answered in 'Yes' or 'No', 'Right or Wrong' and 'Good or Bad.'

**EXAMPLE**

Do you have a car? ......................Yes/No

Or

Government decides to introduce 10+2 system in the college. Do you agree? ......................Yes/No

(2) **Multiple Choice Questions:** When there are various possibilities of a particular event, multiple choice questions are generally asked. A number of possible answers are given for such questions. The informant is to tick-mark the one that he feels fit.

**EXAMPLE**

What is your mode of conveyance from home to college?

1. On foot ☐
2. Cycle ☐
3. Bus ☐
4. Scooter ☐

Correct answer be tick-marked (✓) in the box.

(3) **Specific Information Questions:** Only specific information is obtained through such questions.

**EXAMPLE**

In which class do you read?

Or

How much pocket allowance do you get?

(4) **Open Questions:** In such questions, the informant is requested to give his views on specific issues.

**EXAMPLE**

How can prices in India be controlled?

Or

How can power shortage in the country be overcome?

*Learning by doing*

You are studying in a school which is nearly 500 km away from your home town. As a student you are keen to collect statistical information relating to literacy rate in your town. Which mode of data collection will you prefer to adopt? Give reasons in support of your answer.

**Example of an Ideal Questionnaire**

Objective of this questionnaire is to know about the monthly income and expenditure of the 10+2 students living in the hostels. You are requested to fill in this questionnaire, and return at your earliest convenience. Information furnished in this questionnaire will be kept strictly confidential. The information will be used only for the present investigation.

1. Student's Name ..............................................................
2. Age ..............................................................
3. Faculty .............................................. Art/Commerce/Science
4. Name of the School/College ..............................................................
5. Father's name and address ..............................................................
6. Father's Occupation ........................................ Income ........................................
7. Income (if any) of other members in the family ..............................................................
8. Monthly income received by the student
   - (i) From the family ..............................................................
   - (ii) Personal earning ..............................................................
   - (iii) Scholarship ..............................................................
   - (iv) Others ..............................................................
9. Monthly Expenditure of the Student

| Items of Expenditure | Amount of Expenditure |
|---|---|
| (i) School/College fee | ........................................ |
| (ii) Stationery | ........................................ |
| (iii) Books | ........................................ |
| (iv) Conveyance | ........................................ |
| (v) Hostel expenses | ........................................ |
| (vi) Entertainment | ........................................ |
| (vii) Other items (specify) | ........................................ |

10. Is your monthly income enough for you? Yes .................. No ..................
11. If your monthly income is not enough, how do you propose to increase it?
12. Can you save anything from your monthly income? If yes, under which of the above-noted heads of expenditures can you save and how much?

**Principal Steps in the Planning of a Field Survey (or Field Investigation)**

While planning a field survey, you are required to focus on the following steps:

(i) Design questionnaire with utmost care and be sure that:
   - (a) the questionnaire has a reasonable length.
   - (b) the questionnaire includes only precise and short questions.
   - (c) the set of questions in the questionnaire can be cross-checked with each other.
   - (d) the questions do not involve serious/difficult calculations for the respondent.

(ii) Decide the mode of enquiry, viz. direct personal oral investigation (also called interview method) or mailing the questionnaire.

(iii) Arrange a proper training programme for the enumerators, explaining to them the purpose and mode of enquiry and also the nature of various questions in the questionnaire.

(iv) Conduct a pilot survey (a small preliminary investigation) when the field of investigation is very large.

**Pilot Survey**

What it is? It refers to a try-out survey covering a very small sample of the universe of your study. Why do it? This is a sort of pre-testing of your questionnaire. This helps you to assess quality of your questionnaire and the way respondents respond to the set of questions. Accordingly you are able to know in advance the shortcomings/drawbacks of your questionnaire. Required changes in the questionnaire may be introduced before you are set out for a final survey.

**Pilot Survey helps:**

(i) in assessing the quality and suitability of questions

(ii) in assessing performance of the enumerators

(iii) in designing a set of instructions for the enumerators

(iv) in assessing the cost and time involved in the final survey.

**Main Sources of Errors in Collection of Data**

These are the following:

(i) Errors related to the measurement of objects which may occur when: (a) the scale of measurement happens to be different for different enumerators, and (b) different enumerators may be allowing different degree of approximation in their measurement, even while using identical scales.

(ii) Errors occurring due to wrong responses simply because the respondents are not able to handle/ understand the questions precisely.

(iii) Errors occurring due to the lack of response. Some respondents may not respond to the questionnaire. Lack of information thus occurring infuses an element of error in the collection of data.

(iv) Errors occurring due to miscalculations, also called arithmetical errors.

(v) Errors occurring due to 'communication gap' or due to lack of recording of the information.

## 3. Collection of Secondary Data

There are two main sources of secondary data: **(1) Published Sources**, and **(2) Unpublished Sources.**

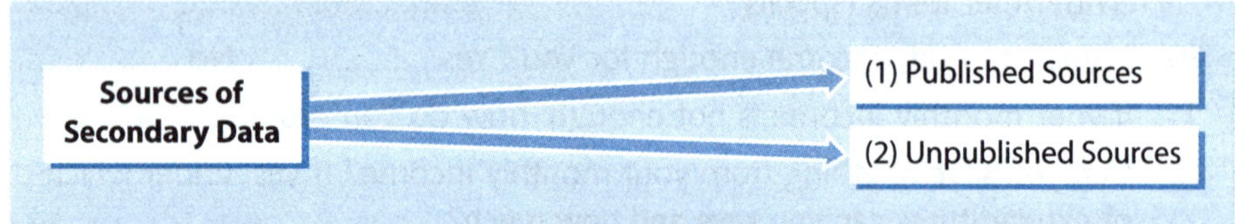


### (1) Published Sources

Some of the published sources of secondary data are:

**(1) Government Publications:** Ministries of the Central and State Governments in India publish a variety of Statistics as their routine activity. As these are published by the Government, data are fairly reliable. Some of the notable Government publications on Statistics are: Statistical Abstract of India, Annual Survey of Industries, Agricultural Statistics of India, Report on Currency and Banking, Labour Gazette, Reserve Bank of India Bulletin, etc.

**(2) Semi-Government Publications:** Semi-Government bodies (such as Municipalities and Metropolitan Councils) publish data relating to education, health, births and deaths. These data are also fairly reliable and useful.

(3) **Reports of Committees and Commissions:** Committees and Commissions appointed by the Government also furnish a lot of statistical information in their reports. Finance Commission, Monopolies Commission, Planning Commission are some of the notable commissions in India which supply detailed statistical information in their reports.

(4) **Publications of Trade Associations:** Some of the big trade associations, through their statistical and research divisions, collect and publish data on various aspects of trading activity. For example, Sugar Mills Association publishes information regarding sugar mills in India.

(5) **Publications of Research Institutions:** Various universities and research institutions publish information as findings of their research activities. In India, for example, Indian Statistical Institute, National Council of Applied Economic Research publish a variety of statistical data as a regular feature.

(6) **Journals and Papers:** Many newspapers such as **'The Economic Times'** as well as magazines such as **Commerce, Facts for You** also supply a large variety of statistical information.

(7) **Publications of Research Scholars:** Individual research scholars also sometimes publish their research work containing some useful statistical information.

(8) **International Publications:** International organisations such as UNO, IMF, World Bank, ILO, and foreign governments etc., also publish a lot of statistical information. These are used as secondary data.

### (2) Unpublished Sources

There are some unpublished secondary data as well. These data are collected by the government organisations and others, generally for their self use or office record. These data are not published. These unpublished numerical information may, however, be used as secondary data.

### Precautions in the Use of Secondary Data

We know that secondary data are collected by others to suit their specific requirements. Therefore, one needs to be very careful while using these data. **Connor** has rightly stated, "*Statistics especially other people's Statistics are full of pitfalls for the users.*" Some of the notable questions to be borne in mind while dealing with the secondary data are:

(a) Whether the data are reliable?

(b) Whether the data are suitable for the purpose of enquiry?

(c) Whether the data are adequate?

In order to assess the reliability, suitability and adequacy of the data, the following points must be kept in mind:

(1) **Ability of the Collecting Organisation:** One should check the ability of the organisation which initially collected the data. The data should be used only if it is collected by able, experienced and impartial investigators.

**A Note of Caution for the Users of Secondary Data**

Users of secondary data must check:

(i) reliability of data,

(ii) suitability of data, and

(iii) adequacy of data.

(2) **Objective and Scope:** One should note the objective of collecting data as well as the scope of investigation. Data should be used only if the objective and scope of the study as undertaken earlier match with the objective and scope of the present study.

(3) **Method of Collection:** The method of collection of data by the original investigator should also be noted. The method adopted must match the nature of investigation.

(4) **Time and Conditions of Collection:** One should also make sure of the period of investigation as well as the conditions of investigations. For example, data collected during war times may not be suitable to generalise certain facts during peace times.

(5) **Definition of the Unit:** One should also make sure that the units of measurement used in the initial collection of data are the same as adopted in the present study. If the unit of measurement differs, data must be modified before use.

(6) **Accuracy:** Accuracy of the data should also be checked. If the available data do not conform to the required degree of accuracy, these should be discarded.

In short, as stated by **Bowley,** "*It is never safe to take published Statistics at their face value without knowing their meaning and limitations*."

### Two Important Sources of Secondary Data: 'Census of India' and 'Reports and Publications of National Sample Survey Office'

(1) **Census of India:** Census of India is a decennial publication of the Government of India. It is published by Registrar General & Census Commissioner, India. It is a very comprehensive source of secondary data. It relates to population size and the various aspects of demographic changes in India. Broadly, it includes statistical information on the following parameters:

(i) Size, growth rate and distribution of population in India.

(ii) Population projections.

(iii) Density of population.

(iv) Sex composition of population.

(v) State of literacy.

Information on these parameters relates to country as a whole as well as different states and union territories of the country. As the name suggests, Census of India is a comprehensive enquiry on population size and the related parameters of change covering each and every household of the country.

> **Important**
>
> The statistical data collected by NSSO are released through its quarterly journal, called SARVEKSHANA and its reports, popularly known as NSSO Reports.

(2) **Reports and Publications of National Sample Survey Office (NSSO):** Reports and publications of NSSO is another important source of secondary data in India. NSSO is a government organisation under the Ministry of Statistics and Programme Implementation. This organisation conducts regular sample surveys to collect basic statistical information relating to a variety of economic activity in rural as well as urban parts of the country. For example, the 69th round of NSSO survey (July–December 2012) was on "Drinking Water, Sanitation,

Hygiene, Housing Conditions and Slum Conditions". Broadly, reports and publications of NSSO offers statistical information of the following parameters of economic change:

(i) Land and Livestock Holdings.

(ii) Housing Conditions and Migration with special emphasis on slum dwellers.

(iii) Employment and Unemployment status in India.

(iv) Consumer Expenditure in India, including level and pattern of consumer expenditure of diverse categories of the people.

(v) Sources of Household income in India.

Unlike Census of India, Reports and Publications of National Sample Survey Office are based on 'sample' study of the population/universe.

> Important Agencies at the national level which collect, process and tabulate the statistical data: NSSO (National Sample Survey Office), RGI (Registrar General of India), DGCIS (Directorate General of Commercial Intelligence and Statistics) and Labour Bureau.

## EXERCISE

### 1. Very Short Answer Type Questions [1 mark]

#### A. Multiple Choice Questions: Choose the Correct Answer

1. Data collected for the first time from the source of origin is called:

   (a) primary data (b) secondary data

   (c) internal data (d) none of these

2. What kind of data are contained in the census of population and national income estimates, for the government?

   (a) Primary data (b) Secondary data

   (c) Internal data (d) None of these

3. Which of the following is a method of secondary data collection?

   (a) Direct personal investigation

   (b) Direct oral investigation

   (c) Collection of information through questionnaire

   (d) None of these

4. Which of the following is a merit of a good questionnaire?

   (a) Difficulty (b) Less number of questions

   (c) Not in proper order (d) Invalid questions

5. Which of the following methods is used when an investigator collects the required information with the informant?

   (a) Direct Personal Investigation (b) Indirect Oral Investigation

   (c) Mailing Method (d) Enumerator's Method

6. In order to know the likings and dislikings of the listeners of the programmes broadcast by the Himachal Akashvani, the latter is keen to collect data. Which method of collecting data will be suitable for it?

   (a) Direct Personal Investigation (b) Indirect Oral Investigation

   (c) Mailing Method (d) Enumerator's Method

7. Questionnaires are filled by the:

   (a) investigator (b) enumerator

   (c) informant (d) none of these

8. Which of the following is a source of secondary data?

   (a) Government publication (b) Private publication

   (c) Report published by the State Bank of India (d) All of these

Ans. 1. (a), 2. (b), 3. (d), 4. (b), 5. (a), 6. (d), 7. (b), 8. (a).

## B. True or False

State whether the following statements are True or False:

1. If we use the data collected by some other person, it is known as secondary data. (True/False)
2. Indirect oral investigation is applied when the field of investigation is very limited. (True/False)
3. Primary data involve more time and more expenses. (True/False)
4. Investigator is a person who plans and conducts an empirical investigation independently. (True/False)
5. Approximation errors occur due to miscalculation. (True/False)

Ans. 1. True, 2. False, 3. True, 4. True, 5. False.

## C. Concepts/Definitions & Knowledge-based Questions

1. Define primary data.

Ans. Data collected by the investigator for his own purpose, for the first time, from beginning to end, are called primary data. These are collected from the source of origin.

2. Define secondary data.

Ans. According to Wessel, "Data collected by other persons are called secondary data." These data are, therefore, called second-hand data. Since these data have already been collected by somebody else, these are available in the form of published or unpublished reports.

3. What are the sources of data?

Ans. There are two sources of data: (i) Primary source of data, which implies collection of data from its source of origin. It offers you first-hand quantitative information relating to your statistical study.

(ii) Secondary source of data, which implies collection of data from some agency or institution which already happens to have collected the data through statistical survey.

4. Name two important sources of secondary data.

Ans. Government Publications: Ministries of the Central and State Governments in India publish a variety of Statistics as their routine activity.

Semi-Government Publications: Semi-Government bodies (such as Municipalities and Metropolitan Councils) publish data relating to education, health, births and deaths.

5. What will be the kind of data published by the railway department regarding the progress of railway for an investigator?

Ans. Data published by the railway department regarding the progress of railway for an investigator would be treated as secondary data for the investigator.

6. Write down a few parameters on which statistical information is published in Census of India.

Ans. (i) Size, growth rate and distribution of population in India.

(ii) Population projections.

(iii) Density of population.

(iv) Sex composition of population.

## 2. Short Answer Type Questions [3-4 marks]

1. Define data. What are the main sources of data?
2. Distinguish between primary and secondary source of data.
3. Define primary and secondary data. Give one example of each.
4. Differentiate between primary and secondary data.
5. What are the main methods of collecting primary data?
6. What is meant by direct personal investigation? Give its merits and demerits.
7. What is meant by indirect oral investigation? Give its merits and demerits.
8. What is meant by questionnaire? What is the difference between questionnaire and schedule?
9. What are the qualities of a good questionnaire?
10. What are the main sources of secondary data?
11. What precautions are necessary to use secondary data?
12. Define the terms (i) investigator, (ii) enumerator, and (iii) respondent.
13. What are (i) measurement errors, and (ii) recording mistakes?
14. What are the main sources of errors in the collection of data?
15. "Census of India provide statistical information on various aspects of demographic changes in India." Explain.
16. "Secondary data are those which are already in existence, and which have been collected, for some other purpose than the answering of the question in hand." Substantiate this statement focusing on the difference between primary and secondary data.
17. Statistical tables giving district-wise birth and death rates (number of births and deaths per 1,000 of population) are obtained from publications of the Census of India 2011. Would you call them primary or secondary data? Give two reasons in support of your answer.

## 3. Long Answer Type Questions [6 marks]

1. What are primary data? Enumerate the various methods of collecting primary data. Discuss the merits and demerits of any one of them.
2. What are secondary data? Discuss the various sources of collecting secondary data.
3. Distinguish between primary data and secondary data. Which of these two sets of data is more reliable and why?

4. Describe the questionnaire method of collecting primary data. What precautions must be taken while preparing a questionnaire? Is there any difference between a questionnaire and a schedule?
5. Distinguish between primary and secondary data. State the relevant situations when primary or secondary data are to be used.
6. What are the kinds of errors that you envisage in the process of collection of data?
7. What are the advantages and disadvantages of collecting primary data by (i) personal interview, and (ii) mailing questionnaires to respondents?
8. What are important types of data as published in 'Census of India' and 'Reports and publications of NSSO'?

## 4. Essential Practicals

1. Frame five 'two-way' questions and five 'multiple choice' questions relating to a questionnaire that you intend to design for collecting primary data on the Level and Composition of Expenditure of the People in your locality.

   **Example: Two-way question:** Does your monthly expenditure ever exceed your monthly income during an year?

   | Yes | No |
   |---|---|

   **Multiple choice question:** Which of the following is your major item of expenditure during the month?

   | School Fee | Tuition Fee | Food |
   |---|---|---|
   | Clothing | House Rent | Others |

2. Complete the following observations:
   (i) Secondary data is the data ______________.
   (ii) Sources of secondary data are ______________.
   (iii) Primary data are always collected directly from the individuals ______________.
   (iv) Pilot survey is conducted to assess ______________.

## 5. NCERT Textbook Questions [With Hints to Answers]

1. (i) There are many sources of data (true/false).
   (ii) Telephone survey is the most suitable method of collecting data, when the population is literate and spread over a large area (true/false).
   (iii) Data collected by investigator is called the secondary data (true/false).
   [(i) True, (ii) True, (iii) False]

# Census and Sample Methods of Collection of Data

3

There are 2,000 students in a college. An investigator wants to collect data regarding their family background. He has two possible choices. First, he collects information relating to all the 2,000 students. Second, he collects information relating to some of the students (sample of students) who would represent all the 2,000 students. In Statistics, the first approach for collecting data is called **Census Method** and the second approach is called **Sample Method.** The present chapter focuses on a comprehensive study of the census and sample methods of data collection. Beginning with the concepts of Census and Sample techniques the chapter offers a detailed discussion of the merits and demerits of the two techniques. Also, various techniques of 'sampling' are discussed with a comparative look at their merits and demerits.

## 1. Concepts of 'Census' and 'Sample'

Chapter 2 of the book introduces the concept of universe or population. It would be useful to recapitulate this concept for a comprehensive understanding of the concepts of 'Census' and 'Sample'.

*In Statistics, universe or population simply refers to an aggregate of items to be studied for an investigation*. Ordinarily, the term population is used to mean total number of people living in a country. Population of India was approximately 121.02 crore in 2010-11. But in Statistics, the term population is used differently. *In Statistics, the term population means the aggregate of all items about which we want to obtain information.* To illustrate, there are 2,000 students in a particular college. If an investigation relates to all the 2,000 students, then 2,000 would be taken as universe or population. Each unit of these 2,000 is called Item. To further illustrate, 1 sugar mill out of the 10 sugar mills we are studying, would be called an item. All the 10 sugar mills would constitute population or the universe.

If a statistical inquiry is based on all items of the universe, it is called a census inquiry. For example, if you want to know quality of life of the 25,000 households in your town and you decide to collect the relevant statistical data of all 25,000 households (that is, your statistical inquiry is covering all the items of the universe or is covering the entire universe) you are relying on census method of your statistical inquiry. Alternative is that you collect statistical data for every 5th or 10th household of your town, which you think should represent all the 25,000 households of the town. Now you are not covering each and every item of the universe; instead you are covering only a 'sample' of the universe. Characteristics of the 'sample' are supposed to represent characteristics of the entire universe. Or, quality of life of a sample of (say) 2,500 families is supposed to represent quality of life of all the 25,000 families of your town. This is called a sample method of a statistical inquiry.

The concepts of 'Sample' and 'Population' are projected in Fig. 1. Bigger part of this picture is comprising the entire 27 items showing population or universe and the corresponding part comprising of 3 items shows sample.

Now you must be sure that Sample is only a part of the population or the universe. But it must be that part which, in terms of its characteristics, represents the entire population.

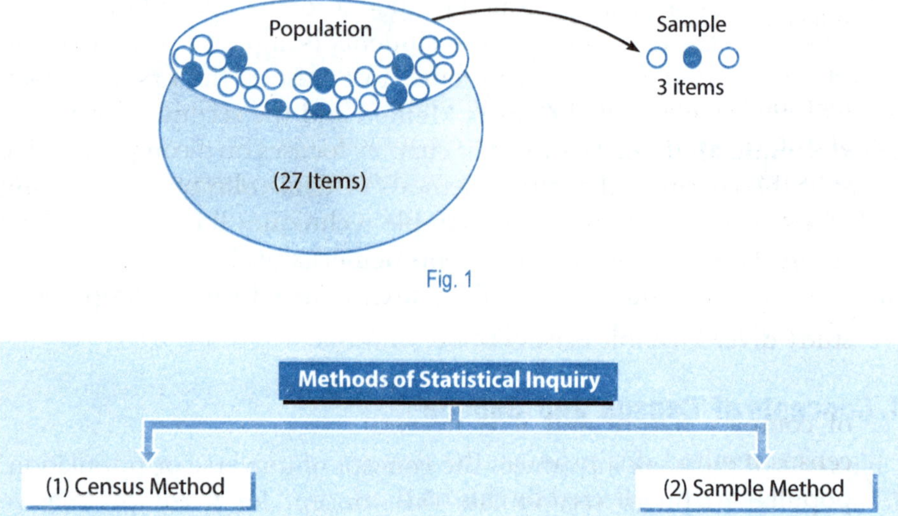


Fig. 1

Methods of Statistical Inquiry

(1) Census Method

(2) Sample Method

## 2. Census Method

*Census method is that method in which data are collected covering every item of the universe or population relating to the problem under investigation.*

To illustrate, you may be interested in the investigation of colour composition of the *Maruti* cars in India. According to the Census Method, you are required to collect data on the colour of each and every *Maruti* car sold in India.

Census method implies complete enumeration of the universe/ population. Census of population is the most suitable example of the census method of a statistical enquiry. For the estimation of the country's population, house to house enquiry is conducted and even people living at the roadside are contacted in India, census of population is conducted every ten years, and the last census was conducted in February 2011.

Census of India 2011 reveals that in terms of the size of population. India is the second largest country in the world next only to China.

## Suitability of the Census Method

Census method is suitable particularly for such statistical investigations which have (1) small size of population, (2) widely diverse items in the population, (3) requirement of intensive examination of different items, and (4) high degree of accuracy and reliability.

## Merits

Principal merits of census method are as under:

(1) **Reliable and Accurate:** Results based on census method are accurate and highly reliable. This is because each and every item of the population is studied.

(2) **Less Biased:** Results based on census method are less biased. It is because of the absence of investigator's discretion regarding the selection of sample items.

(3) **Extensive Information:** Information collected through the census method is quite exhaustive and therefore, more meaningful because all the items of a universe are examined. For example, population census in India gives exhaustive information relating to the number of people in different parts of the country, their age and sex composition, education, status, occupation, and the like.

(4) **Study of Diverse Characteristics:** By using census method, one can study diverse characteristics of the universe.

(5) **Study of Complex Investigation:** When items in a universe are of complex nature and it is necessary to study each item, only census method can produce the desired results. Data on country's population are collected by this method.

(6) **Indirect Investigation:** Census method can be successfully used in indirect investigations relating to unemployment, poverty, corruption, etc.

## Demerits

However, there are certain demerits of census method as under:

(1) **Costly:** Census method is very costly and is, therefore, generally not used for ordinary investigations. Only the Government or some big institutions can afford to use this method and that too for specific purposes only.

(2) **Large Manpower:** Census method requires lot of manpower. Training of a large number of enumerators becomes essential, which is a very difficult process.

(3) **Not Suitable for Large Investigations:** If the universe comprises a large number of items, then it may not be possible to cover each and every item. Census method becomes practically inoperative in such situations.

## 3. Sample Method

*Sample method is that method in which data is collected about the sample on a group of items taken from the population for examination and conclusions are drawn on their basis.*

Sample method is widely used in our day-to-day life. A lady in the kitchen, for example, tests only a grain or two of the rice to know whether the rice is boiled or not. By examining only a few drops of blood, a doctor determines the blood group of a person.

### Suitability of the Sample Method

Sample method is particularly suitable when: (1) the size of population is very large, (2) very high degree of accuracy is not needed, (3) intensive examination of diverse items is not required, and (4) when different units of the universe are broadly similar to each other.

### Merits of the Sample Method

Some of the principal merits of the sample method are as under:

(1) **Economical:** Sample method of investigation is economical because only some units of the population are studied.

(2) **Time Saving:** In this method, only limited number of the items are investigated. As such the process of investigation is time-saving, not time-consuming.

(3) **Identification of Error:** Because only a limited number of items are covered, errors can be easily identified. To that extent sampling method shows better accuracy.

(4) **Large Investigations:** Sample method is more feasible in situations of large investigations than the census method which generally involves unaffordable cost.

(5) **Administrative Convenience:** There is an administrative convenience in handling a limited number of items. More capable and efficient investigators can be appointed.

(6) **More Scientific:** According to R. Fisher, Sample Method is more scientific because the sample data can be conveniently investigated from various angles.

### Demerits of the Sample Method

Yet there are some demerits of the sample method as under:

(1) **Partial:** It is only a partial investigation of the universe. The investigator's bias in the selection of the sample is not ruled out. Accordingly, the results may be biased as well.

(2) **Wrong Conclusions:** If the selected sample does not represent the characteristics of the universe, the study may end up with wrong conclusions.

(3) **Difficulty in Selecting Representative Sample:** It is not very easy to select a sample which would represent the characteristics of the entire population.

(4) **Difficulty in Framing a Sample:** Sometimes the universe may be so diverse that it becomes difficult to frame a sample.

(5) **Specialised Knowledge:** Sampling involves a set of technical procedures. One must have the technical knowledge of choosing a representative sample from the universe. Persons who are well-versed with all the techniques of sampling are not easily available.

### Essentials of a Sample

In order to arrive at an unbiased and right conclusions, a sample must have the following qualities or essentials:

(1) **Representative:** A sample must represent all the characteristics of the universe. It is possible only when each unit of the universe stands equal chances of being selected in the sample.

(2) **Independent:** All units of a sample must be independent of each other. In other words, inclusion of one item in the sample should not be dependent upon the inclusion of some other items of the universe.

(3) **Homogeneity:** If more than one sample are selected from a universe, these samples should be homogeneous (and not contradictory) to each other.

(4) **Adequacy:** The number of items in the sample should be fairly adequate so that some reliable conclusions are drawn covering the characteristics of the universe as a whole.

**Two Basic Essentials of a Good Sample**

These are:

(i) that the sample must represent characteristics of the entire universe/ population.

(ii) that the sample must be adequate enough to offer reliable conclusions.

***Learning by doing***

- *Which method — census or sample — would you prefer if you are to study economic conditions of the people in your area?*
- *Would you opt for a census method if you are to assess performance of Economics teacher in your school? Give reasons.*
- *If your teacher is to assess IQ level of the students in your class, would a sample of 10 students out of 50 be enough to get good results?*

## Methods of Sampling

Following are the principal methods or techniques of sampling:

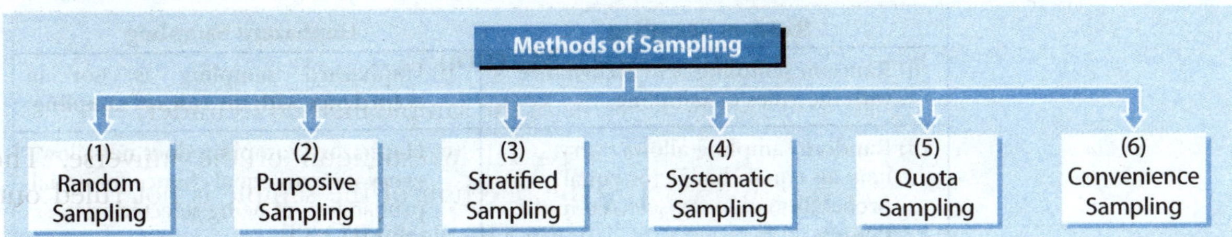


### (1) Random Sampling

*Random sampling is that method of sampling in which each and every item of the universe has equal chance of being selected in the sample.* In other words, there is an equal probability for every item of the universe being selected in the sample.

Which of the various items of the universe would get selected in the sample is beyond the control of the investigator. The selection is left entirely to the chance factors. This method is used particularly when various items of the universe are homogeneous or identical to each other. This method is impartial and economical. Random Sampling may be done in any of the following ways:

(i) **Lottery Method:** In this method, paper-slips are made for each item of the universe. These slips are shuffled in a box. Then, impartially, some of the slips are drawn to form a sample of the universe.

(ii) **Tables of Random Numbers:** Some statisticians have prepared a set of tables called Tables of Random Numbers. A sample is framed with reference to these tables. Of all these tables Tippet's Table is most widely used. Using 41,600 figures, Tippet has involved 10,400 numbers comprising of four units each. For the use of this method, all items of the universe are first arranged in an order. Then using Tippet's Table the required number of items are selected as are needed for a sample.

### Merits

**The Principal Merit of Random Sampling**

It is that each and every item of the universe has equal chance (or equal probability) of being selected.

Following points may be noted on the merits of random sampling:

(1) This method is free from personal bias of the investigator.

(2) Each and every item of the universe stands equal chances of being selected.

(3) The universe gets fairly represented by the sample.

(4) This is a very simple and straightforward method.

### Demerits

However, there are two notable demerits of this method. These are as under:

(1) This method does not guarantee proportionate representation of different items in the universe.

(2) Random sampling does not give weightage to certain important items in the universe.

**Random sampling is not Haphazard sampling. Note the difference:**

| Random Sampling | Haphazard Sampling |
|---|---|
| (i) Random sampling is in accordance with the rules of sampling. | (i) Haphazard sampling is not in accordance with the rules of sampling. |
| (ii) Random sampling allows every item an equal chance (or equal probability) of being selected in the sample. | (ii) Haphazard sampling does not allow every item an equal chance (or equal probability) of being selected in the sample. |

**Random Sampling and Exit Polls**

Exit polls is an interesting example of random sampling. What does it mean? It means a small percentage of the people exiting the poll booths are contacted and asked whom they voted to. From the sample of information thus collected, a prediction is made about the victory chances of different candidates contesting election.

### (2) Purposive or Deliberate Sampling

*Purposive sampling is that method in which the investigator himself makes the choice of the sample items which in his opinion are the best representative of the universe.* Thus, in this method of sampling, selection of the sample items is not left to the chance factors; it is simply made by choice.

This method of sampling is specifically suitable when some of the items in the universe are of special significance and ought to be included in the sample. For example, if an investigation is to be made relating to the iron and steel industry in India, then the inclusion of such industries as the Tata Iron and Steel Company is obviously a purposive selection.

However, there is a considerable possibility of personal bias in purposive sampling. As a result, it loses its credibility.

#### Merits

(1) This method is flexible to allow the inclusion of those items in the sample which are of special significance.

(2) Selection of items can be deliberately tuned to the purpose of study.

(3) It is a very simple technique of selection of the sample items.

#### Demerits

(1) There is a possibility of personal bias in the selection of items.

(2) Because of the possibilities of personal bias, reliability of the results becomes doubtful.

### (3) Stratified or Mixed Sampling

This method of sampling is generally adopted when population consists of different groups with different characteristics. *According to this method of sampling, population is divided into different strata having different characteristics and some of the items are selected from each strata, so that the entire population gets represented.* Each stratum should be represented in correct proportion in the sample. To illustrate, suppose there are 50 students in Class XI. Out of them, 30 have studied Mathematics and 20 have studied Home Science in their Class X. Thus, the population of the 50 students gets divided into two strata consisting of 30 and 20 students respectively. From each of these strata, items would be selected proportionately such that the sample represents the characteristics of the entire population. If, of the total 50 students, only a sample of five is to be selected, then we shall randomly select three out of the first stratum (comprising 30 students) and two out of the second stratum (comprising 20 students). However, items may also be selected unproportionately from different strata.

An investigator may prefer to select four students from amongst those who studied Mathematics and only one from amongst those who studied Home Science. The choice will be governed by the nature of the enquiry and wisdom of the investigator.

Stratified Sampling is also called Mixed technique of sampling because this method involves the mixture of both purposive sampling and random sampling. The division of population into different strata is purposely done while selection of the items is done at random.

**The Principal Merit of Stratified Sampling**

It allows selection of such items which represent diverse characteristics of the population.

### Merits

(1) This method covers diverse characteristics of the population.

(2) On the basis of diverse characteristics of the population, a comparative analysis of the data becomes possible.

(3) This method of sampling offers reliable as well as meaningful results.

### Demerits

(1) This method is suitable only when there is a complete knowledge about the diverse characteristics of the population. Therefore, this has a limited scope.

(2) There is a possibility of bias at the time of classification of the population into different strata.

(3) When the size of population is already small, it may be difficult to further divide it into smaller parts/strata.

## (4) Systematic Sampling

*According to this method, units of the population are numerically, geographically and alphabetically arranged. Every nth item of the numbered items is selected as a sample item.* To illustrate, if 10 out of 100 students are to be selected for a sample, then 100 students would be numbered and systematically arranged. One item of the first 10 would be selected at random. Subsequently, every 10th item from the selected number will be selected to frame a sample. If the first selected number is 5th item, then the subsequent numbers would be 15th, 25th, 35th, 45th, 55th, 65th, 75th, 85th and 95th. This method of sampling is, in fact, a short-cut method of Random Sampling.

### Merits

(1) This is a very simple method. Sample is easily determined.

(2) There is hardly any possibility of personal bias in this method.

**Principal Demerit of Systematic Sampling**

It does not allow every item of the universe equal chance (or equal probability) of being selected in the sample.

### Demerits

(1) Every item in the population does not get equal chance of being selected because only the first item is selected on the basis of random sampling.

(2) If all the items in the population are homogeneous, this method of sampling serves no specific purpose.

## (5) Quota Sampling

*In this method, the population is divided into different groups or classes according to different characteristics of the population.* Some percentage of different groups in total population is fixed. Further, some quota of the items to be selected as sample-items is fixed for each group. The investigator selects the fixed number of items from each group to frame a sample.

This method of sampling is not very expensive. But there is a high possibility of personal bias at the time of selection of the items by the investigator. Accordingly, the reliability of results becomes questionable.

### (6) Convenience Sampling

*In this method, sampling is done by the investigator in such a manner that suits his convenience.* To illustrate, an investigator may select a sample of teachers merely by referring to the college prospectus. This method is the simplest and least expensive, but unscientific and unreliable. It depends too much on the whims of enumerators.

## Reliability of Sampling Data

The reliability of the sampling data means that the characteristics of the universe are fully represented by the sample. It depends mainly on the following factors:

(1) **Size of the Sample:** Reliability of sampling depends on the size of the sample. If its size is very small, it will fail to represent the population. Accordingly, the conclusions would lack reliability.

(2) **Method of Sampling:** If the method of sampling is not simple and exhaustive, it will not adequately represent the population. Consequently, the results will not be dependable.

(3) **Bias of Correspondents and Enumerators:** Personal bias of the correspondents and enumerators should be as less as possible. Otherwise, reliability of the sampling data is bound to suffer.

(4) **Training of Enumerators:** Reliability of sample also depends upon the training of the investigators. If they are not trained to make them expert in their field of investigation, the sample will lack reliability.

## Census and Sampling Methods: A Comparative Look

Some of the principal differences between census and sampling methods are as under:

(1) **Coverage:** In the census technique, an investigator collects information relating to all the items in the population. In sampling method, on the other hand, only some of the items which represent the population are covered for an investigation.

(2) **Suitability:** Census method is suitable when the area of investigation is relatively small. On the other hand, when the area of investigation is large, it is the sampling method which is generally used.

(3) **Accuracy:** There is generally a greater degree of accuracy in the results based on the census method than the sampling method. This is because in the census method each and every item of the population is studied. As against it, there is less accuracy and reliability in the sampling method because it studies only a few items of population. However, errors can be easily detected and removed in the sampling method because of the small number of items. To that extent sampling method shows greater accuracy than the census method.

(4) **Cost:** Sampling method is certainly much less expensive than the census method. Smaller the sample size out of the given population, lesser the cost of investigation.

(5) **Time:** Sample method is less time consuming than the census method.

(6) **Nature of Items:** Census method is particularly suitable when the items in the population have diverse characteristics. On the other hand, sample method is suitable when items in the population are homogeneous.

(7) **Verification:** Verification of the statistical information obtained through census method is generally not possible. It would involve huge expenses and the repetition of the whole process. Sample information, on the other hand, can be easily verified. In case of doubt, enumeration can be done again and facts verified accordingly.

In short, sample method of statistical investigation is generally preferred to the census method because the former is less expensive in terms of the time, money and efforts involved. However, for the successful application of the sample method, it is very essential that the sample items represent the characteristics of population as a whole.

**Statistical Errors: Sampling and Non-Sampling Errors**

Statistical errors are broadly classified as (i) sampling errors, and (ii) non-sampling errors. Following are the details:

(i) **Sampling Errors:** These are related to the size or nature of the sample selected for the study. Due to a very small size of the sample selected for study or due to non-representative nature of the sample, the estimated value may differ from the actual value of a parameter. The error thus emerging is called sampling error. For example, if the estimated value of a parameter is found to be 10 while the actual/true value is 20 then, the sampling error
= estimated value of the parameter – true value of the parameter
= 10 – 20 = –10.

(ii) **Non-sampling Errors:** These are errors related to the collection of data. These are of the following types:

**Error of Measurement:** Error of measurement may occur due to: (i) difference in the scale of measurement, and (ii) difference in the rounding off procedure adopted by different investigators.

**Error of Non-response:** This arises when the respondents do not offer the required information.

**Error of Misinterpretation:** This arises when the respondent fails to interpret the questions in the questionnaire.

**Error of Calculation or Arithmetical Error:** It occurs in the course of addition, subtraction or multiplication of data.

**Error of Sampling Bias:** It occurs when, for some reason or the other, a part of target population, cannot be included in the choice of a sample.

**Larger the field of investigation or larger the population size, greater is the possibility of errors related to the collection of data, or data acquisition. It must be noted here that a non-sampling error is more serious than a sampling error. Because a sampling error can be minimised by opting for a larger sample size. No such possibility exists in case of non-sampling errors.**

# EXERCISE

## 1. Very Short Answer Type Questions [1 mark]

### A. Multiple Choice Questions: Choose the Correct Answer

1. Census method is suitable for that investigation in which:
   (a) the size of population is large
   (b) high degree of accuracy is not required
   (c) there are widely diverse items
   (d) intensive examination of diverse items is not required
2. Which of the following methods is used for the estimation of population in a country?
   (a) Census method (b) Sampling method
   (c) Both (a) and (b) (d) None of these
3. Reliability of sampling data depends on:
   (a) size of sample (b) method of sampling
   (c) training of enumerators (d) all of these
4. For drawing lottery ________________ sampling is used.
   (a) random (b) purposive
   (c) stratified (d) quota
5. Personal bias is possible under:
   (a) random sampling (b) purposive sampling
   (c) stratified sampling (d) quota sampling
6. If the investigator wants to select a sample on the basis of diverse characteristics of the population, which method should he use?
   (a) Convenience sampling method (b) Quota sampling method
   (c) Stratified sampling method (d) Both (b) and (c)
7. Which of the following factor(s) are considered when comparison between sampling and census method is made?
   (a) Area of survey (b) Accuracy of data
   (c) Cost of collection (d) All of these
8. Under random sampling, each item of the universe has ________ chance of being selected.
   (a) equal (b) unequal
   (c) zero (d) none of these

Ans. 1. (c), 2. (a), 3. (d), 4. (a), 5. (b), 6. (d), 7. (d), 8. (a).

### B. True or False

State whether the following statements are True or False:

1. Every item of population is included under the random sampling method. (True/False)
2. Sampling method is comparatively less expensive. (True/False)

3. Under purposive sampling, population is divided into different groups having different characteristics. (True/False)
4. Sampling errors are related to the size or nature of the sample selected. (True/False)
5. Census method needs less number of enumerators. (True/False)

Ans. 1. False, 2. True, 3. False, 4. True, 5. False.

### C. Concepts/Definitions & Knowledge-based Questions

1. What is meant by universe?

Ans. In Statistics, universe or population refers to an aggregate of items to be studied for an investigation.

2. What is meant by sample?

Ans. Sample is a group or collection of items from the universe wherein the characteristics of the former are supposed to represent characteristics of the latter.

3. What is meant by census method?

Ans. Census method is that method in which data are collected covering every item of the universe relating to the problem under investigation.

4. What is meant by sample method?

Ans. Sample method is that method in which data is collected about the sample on a group of items taken from the population for examination and conclusions are drawn on their basis.

5. What is meant by random sampling?

Ans. Random sampling is that method of sampling in which each and every item of the universe has equal chance of being selected in the sample.

6. What is meant by purposive or deliberate sampling?

Ans. Purposive sampling is that method in which the investigator himself makes the choice of the sample items which in his opinion are the best representative of the universe.

7. What is meant by stratified or mixed sampling?

Ans. According to stratified sampling, population is divided into different strata having different characteristics and some of the items are selected from each strata, so that the entire population gets represented.

8. Define systematic sampling.

Ans. According to systematic sampling, units of the population are numerically, geographically and alphabetically arranged. Every nth item of the numbered items is selected as a sample item.

9. Define quota sampling.

Ans. In quota sampling, the population is divided into different groups or classes according to different characteristics of the population.

10. Define convenience sampling.

Ans. In convenience sampling, sampling is done by the investigator in such a manner that suits his convenience.

## 2. Short Answer Type Questions [3-4 marks]

1. What is meant by census method? What are its uses?
2. What is meant by sample method? What are its uses?

3. What is the difference between census method and sampling method?
4. Mention four main merits of census method.
5. Mention four main demerits of census method.
6. Mention the four main merits of the sample method.
7. Mention the four demerits of the sample method.
8. What are the advantages of sampling method of collection of data over the census method?
9. Discuss how you would use the lottery method to select 3 students out of 10 in your class.
10. Does the lottery method always give you a random sample? Explain.
11. Explain the procedure of selecting a random sample of 3 students out of 10 in your class, by using random number tables.
12. What is meant by census method? In what conditions is this method used?
13. What is meant by sample method? Under what circumstances this method is more suitable?
14. What are the main elements of sampling?
15. What are the main methods of sampling?
16. What are the main merits of random sampling?
17. What are the main demerits of random sampling?
18. What is the difference between universe and sample?
19. Distinguish between (i) sampling, and (ii) non-sampling errors.
20. Define random sampling. How is it different from haphazard sampling?

## 3. Long Answer Type Questions [6 marks]

1. What is meant by census method? Give its merits and demerits.
2. Explain the meaning of sampling survey. What are its advantages and disadvantages?
3. Distinguish between random sampling and systematic sampling. Give suitable examples.
4. Distinguish between census and sample surveys. List four important types of sampling methods. Explain the reasons for preparing sample surveys in the collection of Statistics.
5. Compare the census and sample methods of collecting data with reference to reliability, time involved and cost.
6. Describe the various methods of sampling. How is random sampling better than systematic sampling?
7. What are the kinds of errors you would expect in a field survey by census method?
8. Distinguish between 'random sampling' and 'stratified sampling', clearly explaining the two in detail. Give examples of both.

## 4. Essential Practicals

1. There are 10 students in your school who excel in the game of cricket. All are equally brilliant, but you are to select only 3 out of 10 for representing your school in the inter-zonal cricket tournament. How would you do it? Give details with reason.
2. There are 40 students in your school who are cricket players. You are to form a team of 11 players. How would you do it? Would you resort to random sampling technique? Give reasons in support of your answer.

3. You want to conduct a survey on the popularity of Noodles among the students of different schools in your town. How would you design and choose your sample of study? Give reasons in support of your answer.
4. In a village comprising 300 small and big farmers, you are to select a sample of 10% farming households. The idea is to study cropping pattern in the village. How would you take your decisions on selecting the sample?
5. How would you use the random sampling method when you are to select a sample of 3 out of 10 students in your class?

## 5. NCERT Textbook Questions [With Hints to Answers]

1. (i) There is a certain bias involved in the non-random selection of samples (true/false).

   (ii) Non-sampling errors can be minimised by taking large samples (true/false).

   [(i) True, (ii) False]
2. In a village of 200 farms, a study was conducted to find the cropping pattern. Out of the 50 farms surveyed, 50% grew only wheat. Identify the population and the sample here.

   [Population = 200, Sample = 50.]
3. Give two examples each of sample and population.

   [Page 37, 38]
4. Which of the following is a preferred method of statistical studies, and why?

   (a) Census (b) Sample

   [Sample method of statistical investigation is generally preferred to the census method because the former is less expensive in terms of the time, money and efforts involved. However, for the successful application of the sample method, it is very essential that the sample items represent the characteristics of population as a whole.]
5. Which of the following errors is more serious and why?

   (a) Sampling error. (b) Non-sampling error.

   [Non-sampling error is more serious than a sampling error. Because a sampling error can be minimised by opting for a larger sample size. No such possibility exists in case of non-sampling errors.]
6. Suppose there are 10 students in your class. You want to select three out of them. How many samples are possible?

   [Selecting 3 students out of 10 is given by ${}^{10}C_3 = 120$.

   ∴ 120 samples are possible.]
7. Discuss how you would use the lottery method to select 3 students out of 10 in your class?

   [Page 42]
8. Explain the procedure of selecting a random sample of 3 students out of 10 in your class, by using random number tables.

   [Page 42]

# Organisation of Data

# 4

When an investigator collects data for an investigation, these are just raw data. Raw data are not capable of offering any meaningful conclusion. This is just like a lump of clay without any specific shape or identity. Data are to be organised before these are presented for final observations or conclusions. "*Organisation of the data refers to the arrangement of figures in such a form that comparison of the mass of similar data may be facilitated and further analysis may be possible*." An important method of organisation of data is to distribute these into different classes on the basis of their characteristics. This process is called **classification of data**. It involves conversion of raw data into statistical series in a manner such that some meaningful conclusions can be drawn out of them. The present chapter deals with classification of data, focusing on the conversion of raw data into various types of statistical series.

## 1. What is Classification?

There are 200 families in your locality. You have collected data regarding their income, expenditure, education, religion, size of family, etc. But this data will be of little use unless you know how many families are educated and how many are uneducated. How many families earn an income exceeding ₹ 5,000 per month and how many earn ₹ 500 or less per month.

In other words, in order to make the raw data meaningful, these must be classified on the basis of their different characteristics, such as educated families and uneducated families, rich families and poor families, etc.

Each such division of data is called **Class** and the process by which data is divided into different 'classes' on the basis of their similarity or diversity is called "Classification". Thus, classification is the grouping of related facts into different classes. In the words of **Conner**, "*Classification is the process of arranging things (either actually or notionally) in groups or classes according to their resemblances and affinities, and gives expression to the unity of attributes that may exist amongst a diversity of individuals.*" This definition suggests two important features of classification:

(i) Data are divided into different groups. For example, on the basis of education, persons may be classified as **educated** and **uneducated**.

(ii) Data are grouped or classified on the basis of their class similarities. All similar units are put in one class and as the similarity changes, class also changes.

**What is the Principal Objective of Classification of Data?**

It is to capture and distinctively present the diverse characteristics of data.

## Objectives of Classification

Main objectives of Classification are as under:

(1) **Simplification and Briefness:** Main objective of classification is to present data in a form that appears to be brief and simple.

(2) **Utility:** Classification enhances utility of the data as it brings out similarity within the diverse set of data.

(3) **Distinctiveness:** Classification renders obvious differences among the data more distinctly.

(4) **Comparability:** It makes data comparable and estimative.

(5) **Scientific Arrangement:** Classification facilitates arrangement of data in a scientific manner which increases their reliability.

(6) **Attractive and Effective:** Classification makes data more attractive and effective.

## Characteristics of a Good Classification

(1) **Comprehensiveness:** Classification of the raw data should be so comprehensive that each and every item of the data gets into some group or class. No item should be left out.

(2) **Clarity:** Classification of the raw data into classes should be absolutely clear and simple. That is, there should be no confusion about the placement of any item in a group.

(3) **Homogeneity:** All items in a group or class must be homogeneous or similar to each other.

(4) **Suitability:** The composition of the classes must suit the objective of enquiry. For example, in order to determine the income and expenditure of the students in a school, their classification on the basis of weight or marital status would make no sense. The data must be classified on the basis of different levels of income and expenditure.

(5) **Stability:** A particular kind of investigation should be based on the same set of classification. This base should not change with each investigation.

(6) **Elastic:** Classification should be elastic. There should be scope for change in the classification matching with the change in the purpose or objective of our study.

## Basis of Classification

There may be different basis of classifying a statistical information as shown in chart below.

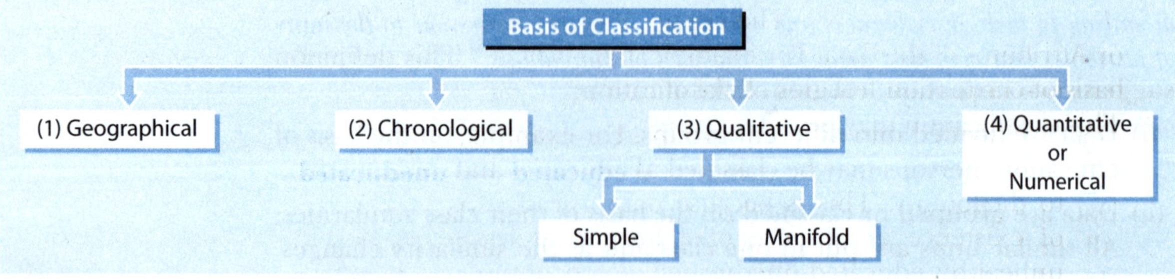

(1) **Geographical (or Spatial) Classification:** This classification of data is based on the geographical or locational differences of the data. To illustrate, data relating to the number of firms producing bicycles in India would be classified as under:

**Table 1. Number of Firms Producing Bicycles in 2013 Across Different Locations**

| Place | Number of Firms |
|---|---|
| Punjab | 30 |
| Haryana | 20 |
| U.P. | 25 |

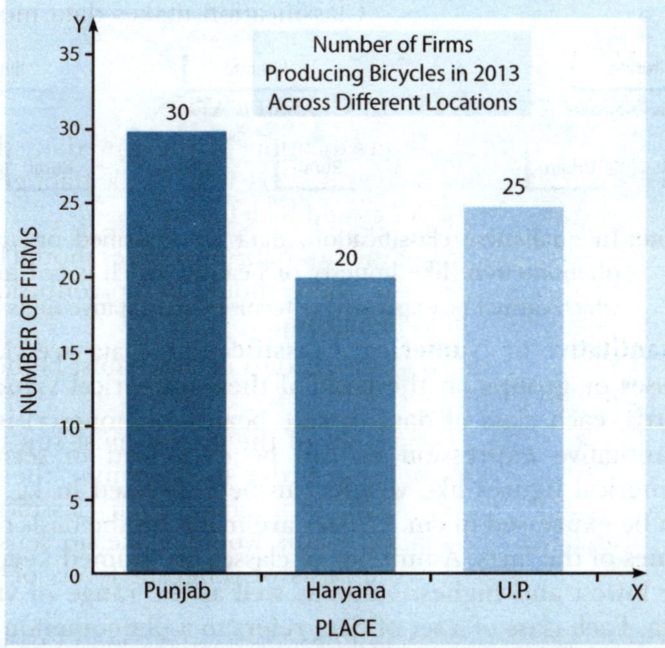


(2) **Chronological Classification:** When data are classified on the basis of time, it is known as chronological classification. This is illustrated in the following table:

**Table 2. Sales of a Firm (2011-2013)**

| Year | Sales (₹) |
|---|---|
| 2011 | 80 lakh |
| 2012 | 90 lakh |
| 2013 | 95 lakh |

**The Principal Difference between Geographical Classification and Chronological Classification**

While geographical classification presents data into different classes corresponding to different geographical locations, chronological classification presents data into different classes corresponding to different time intervals.

(3) **Qualitative Classification:** This classification is according to Qualities or Attributes of the data. For example, data may be classified on the basis of occupation, religion, level of intelligence of the population. This classification may be of two types:

(i) **Simple Classification:** It is called classification according to dichotomy. This is because data are divided on the basis of existence or absence of a quality. Male-female, healthy-unhealthy, educated-uneducated, are examples of dichotomy.

**(ii) Manifold Classification:** When classification according to quality of data involves more than one characteristic, it is called manifold classification or multiple classification. As a result of it, there may be more than two classes. To illustrate, factory workers may be classified as 'skilled' and 'unskilled'. These may be further classified as literate or illiterate and still further as rural or urban. This classification may take the following form:

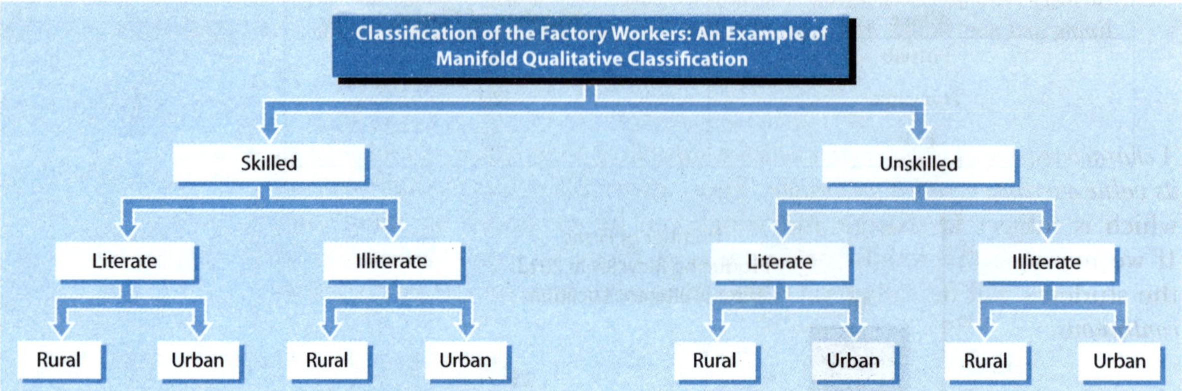


[**Note:** In qualitative classification, data are classified on the basis of a phenomenon (like honesty or beauty) which is not measurable or which cannot be expressed in terms of quantitative units like 2, 3 or 4.]

**(4) Quantitative or Numerical Classification:** Data are classified into classes or groups on the basis of their numerical values. In other words, each class of data (unlike beauty or honesty) is capable of quantitative expression or can be expressed in terms of some numerical figures like weight can be expressed in kg, and height can be expressed in cm. Classes are made on the basis of numerical values of the facts. A number of classes are framed keeping in view the lowest and highest value as well as the range of values in the data. Each class of a set of data refers to a phenomenon like 'wages' or 'profits' in the automobile industry which can be expressed in figures like Indian rupees. Table 3 below is an illustration of quantitative classification:

**Table 3. Annual Profit of small scale firms in the state of UP: Hypothetical data, just for an illustration of quantitative classification.**

| Annual Profit (₹) | Number of Firms |
|---|---|
| 0–1,00,000 | 5 |
| 1,00,000–2,00,000 | 150 |
| 2,00,000–3,00,000 | 1500 |
| 3,00,000–4,00,000 | 800 |
| 4,00,000–5,00,000 | 400 |
| Above 5,00,000 | 200 |

In the above classification, profit is the phenomenon under study. It is a quantifiable phenomenon. Hence, it is called quantitative classification of data.

It is important to note that the phenomenon under study (like profit in the above illustration) assumes different values over time or across different regions. When a phenomenon assumes different values it is called 'variable' in Statistics. Accordingly, **quantitative classification is also called 'classification by variables.'**

> ***Learning by doing***
> *Identify 10 important objects that impact your environment. Classify them, as living and non-living. Is it a quantitative classification? If not, give reasons.*

## 2. Concept of Variable

*A characteristic or a phenomenon which is capable of being measured and changes its value overtime is called a variable.* Thus, a variable refers to that quantity which is subject to change and which can be measured by some unit. If we measure the weight of students of Class XI, then the weight of the students will be called variable. A variable may be either *discrete or continuous*.

(a) **Discrete Variable: Discrete variables are those variables that increase in jumps or in complete numbers.** For example, the number of students in Class XI could be 1, 2, 3, 10, 11,15 or 20 etc. but cannot be $1\frac{1}{4}, 1\frac{1}{2}, 1\frac{3}{4}$, etc. In other words, discrete variables are expressed in terms of complete numbers, or one may simply say that values of these variables are in complete numbers as 1, 2, 3 and not continuous as between 1 to $1\frac{1}{4}$ or $1\frac{3}{4}$ and so on.

(b) **Continuous Variable: Variables that assume a range of values or increase not in jumps but continuously or in fractions are called continuous variables.** For example, height of the boys in a school is expressed as 5′1″, 5′2″, 5′3″, and so on.

In short, *while the values of discrete variables are in complete numbers (1, 2, 3, etc.), values of continuous variables are in fractions (5′4″, 5′2″, etc.) or are in any range such as 10–15, 15–20, etc.*

> **Principal difference between Discrete Variable and Continuous Variable**
>
> It is that while discrete variable assumes values in complete numbers like 2, 4, 6 and 8, continuous variables assume values in fractions like 2.4, 4.6 and 6.8 or values in some range like 2–4, 4–6 etc.

> **Difference between Variable and Attribute**
>
> Ordinarily, anything that varies/changes over time is taken as a variable. But not in Statistics. Colour of your hair may change over time. Is it a variable? No, not at all. Why? Because this change cannot be numerically expressed. In Statistics, only that change of an object is taken as a variable which can be **numerically** expressed. For example, average height of the students of Class X in the year 2005 is found to be (say) 5′6″ compared to 5′5″ in the previous year. **Qualitative** change, like a change in IQ level of the students of Class X is called 'attribute'. A change in the attributes is only qualitatively expressed as good, excellent and outstanding. Qualitative changes can at best be ranked as 1, 2, 3 where 1 stands for outstanding, 2 stands for excellent and 3 stands for good.

> ***Learning by doing***
> *Identify the following variables as discrete and continuous: volume, height, weight, temperature, snowfall, population, crop-production, no. of scooters on the ring road of Delhi, no. of houses demolished by the MCD.*

## 3. Raw Data

A mass of data in its crude form is called raw data. It is an unorganised mass of the various items. These are yet to be organised by the investigator. To illustrate, marks obtained by 30 students of class XI in Statistics, may be expressed as in Table 4.

**Univariate, Bivariate and Multivariate**

'Uni' means one, 'bi' means two, 'multi' means many. Accordingly, **univariate** refers to a series of statistical data with one variable only, like the data on income of the households of a particular region.

**Bivariate** refers to a series of statistical data with two variables like the data on income as well as expenditure of the households of a particular region.

**Multivariate** refers to a series of statistical data with many (and more than two) variables, like the data on age, sex, education, income and expenditure of the households of a particular region.

Table 4. **Marks obtained by the Students of Class XI in Statistics**

| | | | | | |
|---|---|---|---|---|---|
| 30 | 20 | 40 | 20 | 15 | 20 |
| 25 | 10 | 20 | 15 | 25 | 20 |
| 15 | 45 | 10 | 30 | 20 | 25 |
| 30 | 20 | 30 | 20 | 15 | 35 |
| 25 | 10 | 25 | 15 | 35 | 10 |

Data presented in this table are raw data. These are not homogeneous data or the data classified into different groups or classes with similarities. No meaningful conclusion is possible from this data. Only that data are useful to Statistics which are homogeneous. An item of the data, like the price of a commodity, income of a farmer, etc. is called observation, or value, or measure, or item, or magnitude, etc. To draw any conclusion from these data, an investigator has to first organise them. To do so, an investigator has to classify the same in the form of series.

**Series:** Raw data are classified in the form of series. Series refer to those data which are presented in some order and sequence. Arranging of data in different classes according to a given order is called **series.** Thus, if the marks obtained by the students of Class XI are arranged according to their roll numbers in the ascending or descending order, the data so arranged would be known as statistical series. According to **Horace Secrist,** "*A series as used statistically may be defined as things or attributes of things arranged according to some logical order.*"

## 4. Conversion of Raw Data into Statistical Series

Classification of data implies conversion of raw data into statistical series. As stated earlier, classes are formed keeping in mind the nature of variables involved in the study and the range of values that the variables tend to assume.

### Types of Statistical Series

Broadly, statistical series are of two types:

(1) *Individual Series or Series without Frequencies,* and

(2) *Frequency Series or Series with Frequencies*

Frequency series are further divided as:

(i) *Discrete Series or Frequency Array*, and

(ii) *Frequency Distribution or Series with Class-Intervals.*

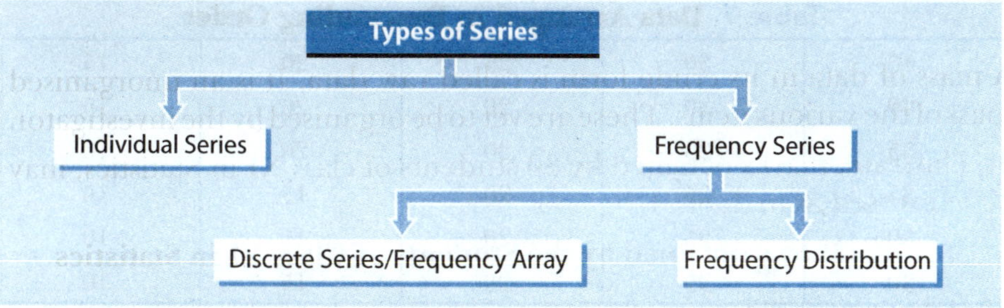


### (1) Individual Series

Individual series are those series in which the items are listed singly. For example, if the marks obtained by 30 students of Class XI are listed singly, the series would be called **Individual Series.** In these series there is no class of the items and also there is no frequency of the items. These series may be presented in two ways:

(i) **According to Serial Numbers:** One way of presenting an individual series is that all the items are arranged in a serial order. Thus, marks obtained by the students may be arranged in order of their roll numbers. Data on the monthly expenses of the hostel students may be arranged in order of their room numbers. Data given in Table 4 on the marks obtained by 30 students are presented in Table 5 in order of their roll numbers.

**Table 5. Marks Obtained by the Students in Statistics**

| Roll Number | Marks | Roll Number | Marks | Roll Number | Marks | Roll Number | Marks |
|---|---|---|---|---|---|---|---|
| 1 | 30 | 9 | 20 | 17 | 15 | 25 | 35 |
| 2 | 25 | 10 | 10 | 18 | 30 | 26 | 20 |
| 3 | 15 | 11 | 40 | 19 | 20 | 27 | 20 |
| 4 | 30 | 12 | 20 | 20 | 15 | 28 | 25 |
| 5 | 25 | 13 | 10 | 21 | 15 | 29 | 35 |
| 6 | 20 | 14 | 30 | 22 | 25 | 30 | 10 |
| 7 | 10 | 15 | 25 | 23 | 20 | | |
| 8 | 45 | 16 | 20 | 24 | 15 | | |

(ii) **Ascending or Descending Order of Data:** The other way of presenting an individual series is a simple ascending or descending order. In the ascending order, the smallest value is placed first, while in the descending order the highest value is placed first. Tables 6 and 7 show the arrangement of data in the ascending and descending orders respectively.

**Table 6. Data Arranged in Ascending Order**

| | | | | |
|---|---|---|---|---|
| 10 | 15 | 20 | 25 | 30 |
| 10 | 15 | 20 | 25 | 30 |
| 10 | 15 | 20 | 25 | 35 |
| 10 | 20 | 20 | 25 | 35 |
| 15 | 20 | 20 | 30 | 40 |
| 15 | 20 | 25 | 30 | 45 |

Table 7. **Data Arranged in Descending Order**

| | | | | |
|---|---|---|---|---|
| 45 | 30 | 25 | 20 | 15 |
| 40 | 30 | 20 | 20 | 15 |
| 35 | 25 | 20 | 20 | 10 |
| 35 | 25 | 20 | 15 | 10 |
| 30 | 25 | 20 | 15 | 10 |
| 30 | 25 | 20 | 15 | 10 |

Organisation of data in the form of individual series is a very simple form of presentation of data. But this method is not of much use when the number of items is very large.

***Learning by doing***

1. *Following data relate to the pocket expenses (rupees) of 10 students of Class XI. Arrange them in the ascending and descending orders:*
   *50, 20, 30, 15, 45, 35, 40, 25, 20, 43.*
2. *In a sample investigation, 20 persons are found to have the following money in their pockets as office expenses. Arrange the data in the ascending and descending orders:*
   *114, 108, 100, 98, 101, 109, 117, 119, 121, 136*
   *131, 136, 143, 156, 169, 182, 195, 207, 219, 255.*
3. *Collect data of weekly expenditure on food by your family. Arrange the data in an order. Also, convert the data into monthly expenditure. Find the total number of observations.*

### (2) Frequency Series

Frequency series or series with frequencies may be of two types: **(i) Discrete Series or Frequency Array**, and **(ii) Frequency Distribution.** Before we discuss these two types of series, let us understand the meaning of the following terms:

**(a) Frequency:** Frequency is the number of times an item occurs (or repeats itself) in the series. In other words, the number of times an item repeats itself in the population, is called the frequency of that item. For example, in Table 4, 10 has occurred 4 times. This means 4 students have secured 10 marks; or the frequency of 10 is 4.

**(b) Class Frequency:** The number of times an item repeats itself corresponding to a range of value (or class interval) is called class frequency. For example, if there are 4 students securing marks between 10–15, then 4 is the frequency corresponding to the class interval 10–15. Thus, 4 will be called class frequency.

**(c) Tally Bars:** Every time an item occurs, a tally bar, (|) is marked against that item. Corresponding to a particular class interval, each tally bar signifies 'one' occurrence of that item. Two tally bars would mean that the concerned item has occurred twice in the series. After every four tallies the fifth tally will crossout all the previous four tallies. Thus, making a group of five, *i.e.*, ~~||||~~. *This method of marking and counting is known as Four and Cross Method*. To illustrate, Table 5 shows that 4 students obtained 10 marks, 5 students obtained 15 marks, 8 students obtained 20 marks, 5 students obtained 25 marks, 4 students obtained 30 marks, 2 students obtained 35 marks, 1 student obtained 40 marks and 1 student obtained 45 marks. All these frequencies have been presented in Table 8, using Four and Cross Method.

**Table 8. Four and Cross Method of converting Raw Data into Frequency Series (data as in Table 5 or 6)**

| Marks | Tally Bars | Frequency |
|---|---|---|
| 10 | 𝍷𝍷𝍷𝍷 | 4 |
| 15 | 𝍸 | 5 |
| 20 | 𝍸𝍷𝍷𝍷 | 8 |
| 25 | 𝍸 | 5 |
| 30 | 𝍷𝍷𝍷𝍷 | 4 |
| 35 | 𝍷𝍷 | 2 |
| 40 | 𝍷 | 1 |
| 45 | 𝍷 | 1 |

In this table, to express 8 tally bars, first of all four tally bars (||||) are marked, fifth tally bar has been marked across the four 𝍸. The sign 𝍸 signifies that an item occurs five times in the series. Likewise, three tally bars are further marked ||| to make it equal to eight, *i.e.*, 𝍸 + ||| = 8. Thus, 1 = |; 2 = ||; 3 = |||; 4 = ||||; 5 = 𝍸; 6 = 𝍸 |; 7 = 𝍸 ||; and so on.

### (i) Discrete Series or Frequency Array

*A discrete series or frequency array is that series in which data are presented in a way that exact measurements of items are clearly shown.* In such series there are no class intervals, and a particular item in the series is numbered rather than measured with some range.

**ILLUSTRATION.**

Twenty students of Class XI have secured the following marks:

11, 12, 14, 11, 16, 11, 17, 16, 17, 14
17, 18, 20, 14, 20, 17, 20, 17, 14, 20.

Present the data as a frequency array.

**SOLUTION:**

Table 9 presents these data in the form of a frequency array. The table shows that 3 students secured 11 marks, 4 students secured 14 marks, again 4 students secured 20 marks, and the like. As it is clear from the table, in such series the items are arranged in the ascending (or descending) order. Frequencies are noted in front of each item to signify the number of times that the item occurs in the series. In this table, the marks secured are shown in ascending order. Against these marks are shown their frequencies, that is, the number of students who have secured these marks.

**Table 9. Discrete Series or Frequency Array**

| Marks | Tally Bars of the Frequency | Frequency (Total) |
|---|---|---|
| 11 | 𝍷𝍷𝍷 | 3 |
| 12 | 𝍷 | 1 |
| 14 | 𝍷𝍷𝍷𝍷 | 4 |
| 16 | 𝍷𝍷 | 2 |
| 17 | 𝍸 | 5 |
| 18 | 𝍷 | 1 |
| 20 | 𝍷𝍷𝍷𝍷 | 4 |
| | Total | 20 |

Thus, 3 is the frequency for 11; so 3 is written against it. This means 11 is occurring 3 times in the series, or 3 students have secured 11 marks. Likewise, 5 is written against 17; 5 is the frequency of 17 or 5 students have secured 17 marks.

Discrete series present the data in a very brief form. However, this type of presentation of the data becomes difficult when there is a large mass of data and a large number of small frequencies. In such situations, data are to be distributed in different classes.

### (ii) Frequency Distribution

It is that series in which items cannot be exactly measured. The items assume a range of values and are placed within the range or limits. In other words, data are classified into different classes with a range, the range is called class intervals. Each item in the series is written against a particular class interval by way of a tally bar. The number of times an item occurs is shown as frequency against the class intervals to which that item belongs.

#### Illustration.

Following table offers an illustration of a frequency distribution. The table shows different class intervals (each showing a range of marks in Statistics) and the corresponding frequencies (each showing the number of students).

**Table 10. Frequency Distribution**

| Marks | Tally Bars | Frequency |
|---|---|---|
| 10–15 | \|\|\|\| | 4 |
| 15–20 | ~~\|\|\|\|~~ | 5 |
| 20–25 | ~~\|\|\|\|~~ \|\|\| | 8 |
| 25–30 | ~~\|\|\|\|~~ | 5 |
| 30–35 | \|\|\|\| | 4 |
| 35–40 | \|\| | 2 |
| 40–45 | \| | 1 |
| 45–50 | \| | 1 |

It is clear from Table 10 that frequency of class interval 10–15 is 4. It means that there are 4 students who have secured marks between 10–15. Likewise, frequency of class interval 20–25 is 8 which means that there are 8 students who have secured marks between 20–25. But, it is not clear that how many students have secured 10 marks in the class interval 10–15 and how many have secured 11 and 14 marks in the same class interval.

**Concept of Relative Frequency**

If the frequency values are expressed as percentages of the total frequency, we get relative frequencies. Example: In Table 10 above, total frequency is 4 + 5 + 8 + 5 + 4 + 2 + 1 + 1 = 30. Relative frequencies would be:

$\frac{4}{30} \times 100$, $\frac{5}{30} \times 100$, $\frac{8}{30} \times 100$, .... and so on.

## Frequency Distribution and Frequency Array—The Difference

Both 'frequency array' and 'frequency distribution' show the arrangement of data, with frequencies as variables corresponding to different values of some X-variable. The difference lies in the fact that in case of frequency arrays, the X-variable must be a discrete variable. In case of a frequency distribution, X-variable is not a discrete variable; rather it is a distribution with different class intervals. Here is an example:

| Frequency Array | | Here, | Frequency Distribution | | Here, |
|---|---|---|---|---|---|
| X | Y | Values of the X-variable are discrete values, showing rating by the students of their principal. Values of Y-variable are the frequencies corresponding to different values of X-variable. | X | Y | X-variable does not show discrete values; rather it shows a range of values or different class intervals. Like (say) daily pocket money of the students of Class X between ₹ 5–10 or between ₹ 10–15, or between ₹ 15–20. Values of Y-variable shows the frequencies. |
| 1 | 50 | | 5–10 | 10 | |
| 2 | 70 | | 10–15 | 8 | |
| 3 | 90 | | 15–20 | 15 | |
| 4 | 120 | | 20–25 | 20 | |
| 5 | 200 | | | | |

Briefly, frequency array refers to discrete series showing frequencies corresponding to some discrete values while frequency distribution refers to series showing frequencies corresponding to different class intervals.

**[Note:** Frequency Distribution is also known as Continuous Series or Series with class intervals, or Series of Grouped Data; students are advised to keep this in mind while reading the subsequent chapters of the book.]

**Some Important Terms**

Let us understand some important terms before a detailed study of different types of frequency distribution in the next section.

**(i) Class:** A range of values which incorporate a set of items is called a class. For example, 5–10, 10–15 are the classes.

**(ii) Class Limits: The extreme values of a class are limits.** Every class interval has two limits, **lower limit** and **upper limit. Of the class interval 5–10 in the above example, the lower limit is 5 and the upper limit is 10.**

**(iii) Magnitude of a Class Interval: Magnitude of a class interval is the difference between the upper limit and the lower limit of a class.** For example, in a class interval 10–15, the magnitude of the class interval would be 15 - 10 = 5. Thus,

Magnitude of a Class Interval ($i$) = Upper limit ($l_2$) – Lower limit ($l_1$)

The following formula is used to find out Class Interval.

**Formula**

$$i = l_2 - l_1$$

Where, $i$ = magnitude of a class interval

$l_2$ = upper limit of the class interval

$l_1$ = lower limit of the class interval.

**Size of Class**

'Size of Class' refers to size of the class interval, or it refers to width of the class. If 'range' (the difference between highest value and lowest value of the series) is (say) 100 and the number of classes is 20, then size of the class will be 100/20=5. Thus:

Size of the Class (S) $= \frac{\text{Range (r)}}{\text{No. of Classes (n)}}$

Or, $s = \frac{r}{n}$

$= \frac{100}{20} = 5$

considering the above example.

**Note:** Size of the class must be such that all values belonging to the particular class-interval tend to converge on the mid-value of the class interval. Only then it becomes an ideal class-size. Otherwise, our result would have a high degree of statistical error.

**(iv) Mid-value:** Mid-value is the average value of the upper and lower limits. It is known by adding up the upper limit and lower limit values and dividing the total by 2. Thus,

$$\text{Mid-value} = \frac{\text{Upper Limit} + \text{Lower Limit}}{2}$$

$$m = \frac{l_2 + l_1}{2}$$

Where, $m$ = mid-value

$l_1$ = lower limit

$l_2$ = upper limit.

For example, mid-value of 10–20 class interval = $\frac{20 + 10}{2}$ = 15.

## 5. Types of Frequency Distribution

Frequency Distribution is of five types:

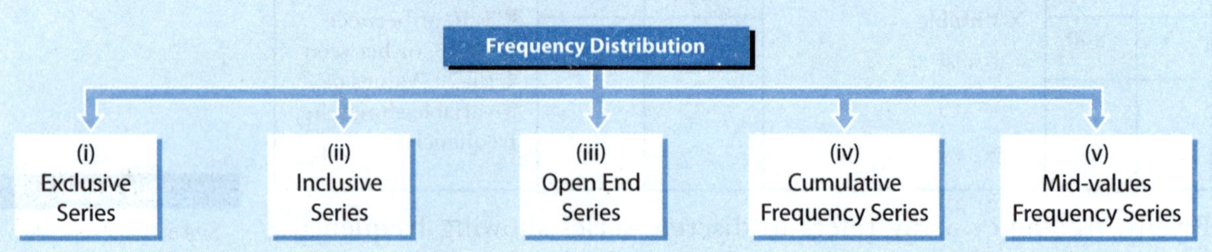


### (I) Exclusive Series

Exclusive series is that series in which every class interval excludes items corresponding to its upper limit. In this series the upper limit of one class interval is the lower limit of the next class interval. It is called exclusive series because frequencies of the upper limit of each class interval is not included in that class.

For example, in a class interval, 10–15, only such items would be included, the value of which is between 10 and 14. Any item of the value of 15 would be included in the next class interval, *viz.*, 15–20.

**Illustration.**

**Exclusive Series**

| Marks | Frequency |
|---|---|
| 10–15 | 4 |
| 15–20 | 5 |
| 20–25 | 8 |
| 25–30 | 5 |
| 30–35 | 4 |
| | Total = 26 |

It is clear from this table that the upper limit of a class interval repeats itself as the lower limit of the next class interval. Also, it may be noted that all values corresponding to, say 15, have been incorporated not in the class interval of 10–15, but in the class interval of 15–20. Likewise, value of 20 will be included in the class interval 20–25 and not in class interval 15–20.

### (II) Inclusive Series

An inclusive series is that series which includes all items upto its upper limit. In such series, the upper limit of class interval does not repeat itself as a lower limit of the next class interval. Thus, there is a gap between the upper limit of a class interval and the lower limit of the next class interval. The gap ranges between 0.1 to 1.0. For example, 10–14, 15–19, 20–24, etc. represents an inclusive series. Thus, all the items ranging between 10–14 are included in that class interval. Likewise, all the items ranging between 15–19 would be included in that class interval.

In short, while in the exclusive series there is an overlapping of the class limits (upper class limit of one class interval being the lower class limit of the next class interval), there is no such overlapping in the inclusive series.

**What is the Basic Difference between Exclusive Series and Inclusive Series?**

In case of exclusive series upper limit of one class interval repeats itself as lower limit of the next class interval. While in case of inclusive series, it does not.

**Illustration.**

**Inclusive Series**

| Marks | Frequency |
|---|---|
| 10–14 | 4 |
| 15–19 | 5 |
| 20–24 | 8 |
| 25–29 | 5 |
| 30–34 | 4 |
| | Total = 26 |

#### Conversion of Inclusive Series into Exclusive Series

Inclusive series are used when there is some definite difference between the values of various items in the population. In the above table if a student has obtained, 14.5 or 19.5 marks these can be expressed only if the inclusive series is converted into an exclusive series. Following steps are involved in the conversion of an inclusive series into an exclusive series:

(i) First, we find the difference between the upper limit of class interval and the lower limit of the next class interval.

(ii) Half of that difference is added to the upper limit of a class interval and half is subtracted from the lower limit of the class interval.

Using these two steps, inclusive series of the above table have been converted into an exclusive series as under.

**Conversion of the Above Inclusive Series into an Exclusive Series**

| Marks | Frequency |
|---|---|
| 9.5–14.5 | 4 |
| 14.5–19.5 | 5 |
| 19.5–24.5 | 8 |
| 24.5–29.5 | 5 |
| 29.5–34.5 | 4 |

### Difference between Exclusive and Inclusive Series

Main differences between exclusive and inclusive series are as under:

(1) In case of exclusive series, the upper limit of one class interval is the lower limit of the next class interval. However, in inclusive series there is generally a difference between the upper limit of one class interval and the lower limit of the other class interval.

(2) In case of exclusive series, value of the upper limit of a class interval is not included in that class; rather it is included in the lower limit of the next class interval. On the contrary, in the case of inclusive series, value of the upper limit of a class is included in that very class interval.

(3) Exclusive series is useful whether the value is in complete number or in decimals, but inclusive series is useful only when value is in complete number.

(4) Counting can be done in all cases under exclusive series. However, to facilitate counting it becomes necessary to convert inclusive series into exclusive series.

**What is an Open End Series?**

It is that series in which

(i) lower limit of the first class interval is missing, or

(ii) upper limit of the last class interval is missing.

### (III) Open End Series

In some series, the lower class limit of the first class interval and the upper limit of the last class interval are missing. Instead, '*less than*' or below is specified in place of the lower class limit of the first class interval and '*more than*' or above is specified in place of the upper class limit of the last class interval. Such series are called 'Open-end' series. Thus, an Open end series is that series in which lower limit of the first class interval and (or) the upper limit of last class interval is missing. Table below shows such a Series.

**Open End Series**

| Marks | Frequency |
|---|---|
| Below 5 | 1 |
| 5–10 | 3 |
| 10–15 | 4 |
| 15–20 | 6 |
| 20 and above | 1 |

In order to determine the limits of the open-end class intervals, the general practice is to give same magnitude to these class intervals as is of the other class intervals in the series. However, this practice is adopted when the known magnitudes of different class intervals in the series are equal to each other. For example, in the above table since the magnitude of the class interval is the same throughout the series, first class interval will be assumed as 0–5 and last as 20–25.

### (IV) Cumulative Frequency Series

Cumulative frequency series is that series in which the frequencies are continuously added corresponding to each class interval in the series.

Let us proceed with an illustration of converting Simple Frequency Series into a Cumulative Frequency Series. Here is a simple frequency series.

**ILLUSTRATION.**

**Simple Frequency Series**

| Marks | Frequency |
|---|---|
| 5–10 | 3 |
| 10–15 | 8 |
| 15–20 | 9 |
| 20–25 | 4 |
| 25–30 | 4 |

There are two ways of converting this series into cumulative frequency series. These are:

(i) **Cumulative frequencies may be expressed on the basis of upper limits of the class intervals,** *e.g.*, less than 10, less than 15, less than 20, when the class intervals are 5–10, 10–15 and 15–20.

(ii) **Cumulative frequencies may be expressed on the basis of lower class limits of the class intervals,** *e.g.*, more than 5, more than 10, more than 15, when the class intervals are 5–10, 10–15 and 15–20.

Thus, when a frequency distribution is to be converted into a cumulative frequency distribution, the cumulative frequencies would correspond to either the lower class limits or the upper class limits of the class intervals in a series. Accordingly, the class intervals would get converted into 'less than' or 'more than' values. Following is an example of how a frequency distribution is converted into a cumulative frequency distribution.

**Cumulative Frequency Series**

| Method I | | Method II | |
|---|---|---|---|
| **Marks** | **Number of Students** | **Marks** | **Number of Students** |
| Less than 10 | 0 + 3 = 3 | More than 5 | 28 |
| Less than 15 | 3 + 8 = 11 | More than 10 | 28 – 3 = 25 |
| Less than 20 | 11 + 9 = 20 | More than 15 | 25 – 8 = 17 |
| Less than 25 | 20 + 4 = 24 | More than 20 | 17 – 9 = 8 |
| Less than 30 | 24 + 4 = 28 | More than 25 | 8 – 4 = 4 |

### Conversion of Cumulative Frequency Series into Simple Frequency Series

Cumulative Frequency Series may be converted into Simple Frequency Series. Following illustration explains this process:

**ILLUSTRATION.**

Convert the following cumulative frequency series into a simple frequency series.

4 students obtained less than 10 marks

20 students obtained less than 20 marks

40 students obtained less than 30 marks

48 students obtained less than 40 marks

50 students obtained less than 50 marks

**SOLUTION:**

**Conversion of a Cumulative Frequency Series into a Simple Frequency Series**

| Cumulative Frequency Series | | Simple Frequency Series | |
|---|---|---|---|
| **Marks less than** | **Number of Students** | **Marks** | **Number of Students** |
| 10 | 4 | 0–10 | 4 |
| 20 | 20 | 10–20 | 20 – 4 = 16 |
| 30 | 40 | 20–30 | 40 – 20 = 20 |
| 40 | 48 | 30–40 | 48 – 40 = 8 |
| 50 | 50 | 40–50 | 50 – 48 = 2 |

### (v) MID-VALUES FREQUENCY SERIES

Mid-values frequency series are those series in which we have only mid-values of the class intervals and the corresponding frequencies.

**For example:**

| **Mid-value** | 5 | 15 | 25 | 35 | 45 |
|---|---|---|---|---|---|
| **Frequency** | 6 | 5 | 11 | 9 | 8 |

Such series may be converted into simple frequency series using the following method: (i) First, mutual difference between mid-values (*i*) is determined; and (ii) Second, the difference so obtained is reduced to half $\left(\frac{1}{2}i\right)$ which when deducted from the mid-value gives lower limit of the class interval and when added to the mid-value gives the corresponding upper limit.

Thus, Lower limit: $l_1 = m - \frac{1}{2}i$

Upper limit: $l_2 = m + \frac{1}{2}i$

(Where, $m$ = mid-value; $i$ = difference between mid-values; $l_1$= lower limit and $l_2$ = upper limit.)

In the above frequency series with mid-values, the mutual difference between mid-values ($i$) = 15 – 5 = 10. Half of it is 5. Deducting 5 from each mid-value we get lower limits and adding 5 to each mid-value we get the corresponding upper limits.

Following table shows the process of this conversion.

**Conversion of a Series with Mid-values into a Series with Class Intervals**

| Mid-value | Frequency | Classes | Technique |
|---|---|---|---|
| 5 | 6 | 0–10 | $l_1 = 5 - \frac{10}{2} = 0, l_2 = 5 + \frac{10}{2} = 10$ |
| 15 | 5 | 10–20 | $l_1 = 15 - \frac{10}{2} = 10, l_2 = 15 + \frac{10}{2} = 20$ |
| 25 | 11 | 20–30 | $l_1 = 25 - \frac{10}{2} = 20, l_2 = 25 + \frac{10}{2} = 30$ |
| 35 | 9 | 30–40 | $l_1 = 35 - \frac{10}{2} = 30, l_2 = 35 + \frac{10}{2} = 40$ |
| 45 | 8 | 40–50 | $l_1 = 45 - \frac{10}{2} = 40, l_2 = 45 + \frac{10}{2} = 50$ |

**ILLUSTRATION.**

Class mid-values of a frequency distribution of marks in Economics of a group of students in Class XI are given as 25, 32, 39, 46, 53 and 60.

Find the size of the class interval and class limits.

**SOLUTION:**

Size of class interval = Mutual difference between mid-values

$$= 32 - 25 = 39 - 32 = 46 - 39 = \ldots = 60 - 53$$
$$= 7$$

Thus, the size of the class is 7.

Given the size of the class as 7 and mid-values of classes as 25, 32, 39, 46, 53 and 60, we can now obtain the class limits by using the following formulae:

$$\text{Lower limit: } l_1 = m - \frac{1}{2}i$$

$$\text{Upper limit: } l_2 = m + \frac{1}{2}i$$

Where, $m$ = mid-values; $i$ = difference between mid-values or the size of class.

Accordingly, the class limits of the first class will be:

$$l_1 = 25 - \frac{1}{2} \times 7 = 25 - 3.5 = 21.5$$

$$l_2 = 25 + \frac{1}{2} \times 7 = 25 + 3.5 = 28.5$$

and so on.

Thus, the various classes with class limits are given as:

| Classes | Mid-value | Technique |
|---|---|---|
| 21.5–28.5 | 25 | $l_1 = 25 - \frac{7}{2} = 21.5, l_2 = 25 + \frac{7}{2} = 28.5$ |
| 28.5–35.5 | 32 | $l_1 = 32 - \frac{7}{2} = 28.5, l_2 = 32 + \frac{7}{2} = 35.5$ |
| 35.5–42.5 | 39 | $l_1 = 39 - \frac{7}{2} = 35.5, l_2 = 39 + \frac{7}{2} = 42.5$ |
| 42.5–49.5 | 46 | $l_1 = 46 - \frac{7}{2} = 42.5, l_2 = 46 + \frac{7}{2} = 49.5$ |
| 49.5–56.5 | 53 | $l_1 = 53 - \frac{7}{2} = 49.5, l_2 = 53 + \frac{7}{2} = 56.5$ |
| 56.5–63.5 | 60 | $l_1 = 60 - \frac{7}{2} = 56.5, l_2 = 60 + \frac{7}{2} = 63.5$ |

## MISCELLANEOUS ILLUSTRATIONS

**ILLUSTRATION 1.**

In a survey, it was found that 50 families bought milk in the following quantities in a particular month. Classify the following data in an individual, discrete, continuous and cumulative frequency series.

| | | | | |
|---|---|---|---|---|
| 19 | 25 | 12 | 21 | 20 |
| 11 | 7 | 9 | 11 | 14 |
| 20 | 15 | 22 | 15 | 17 |
| 10 | 23 | 18 | 11 | 19 |
| 25 | 22 | 5 | 18 | 17 |
| 11 | 6 | 21 | 24 | 26 |
| 8 | 5 | 9 | 20 | 23 |
| 16 | 22 | 22 | 23 | 13 |
| 16 | 11 | 16 | 22 | 17 |
| 23 | 22 | 10 | 7 | 21 |

**SOLUTION:**

### 1. Individual Series: In the Ascending Order of the items

| | | | | |
|---|---|---|---|---|
| 5 | 11 | 16 | 20 | 22 |
| 5 | 11 | 16 | 20 | 22 |
| 6 | 11 | 16 | 20 | 23 |
| 7 | 11 | 17 | 21 | 23 |
| 7 | 11 | 17 | 21 | 23 |
| 8 | 12 | 17 | 21 | 23 |
| 9 | 13 | 18 | 22 | 24 |
| 9 | 14 | 18 | 22 | 25 |
| 10 | 15 | 19 | 22 | 25 |
| 10 | 15 | 19 | 22 | 26 |

### 2. Discrete Series: In the Ascending Order of the items

| Quantity of Milk | Tally Bars | Frequency | Quantity of Milk | Tally Bars | Frequency |
|---|---|---|---|---|---|
| 5 | \|\| | 2 | 16 | \|\|\| | 3 |
| 6 | \| | 1 | 17 | \|\|\| | 3 |
| 7 | \|\| | 2 | 18 | \|\| | 2 |
| 8 | \| | 1 | 19 | \|\| | 2 |
| 9 | \|\| | 2 | 20 | \|\|\| | 3 |
| 10 | \|\| | 2 | 21 | \|\|\| | 3 |
| 11 | ~~\|\|\|\|~~ | 5 | 22 | ~~\|\|\|\|~~ \| | 6 |
| 12 | \| | 1 | 23 | \|\|\|\| | 4 |
| 13 | \| | 1 | 24 | \| | 1 |
| 14 | \| | 1 | 25 | \|\| | 2 |
| 15 | \|\| | 2 | 26 | \| | 1 |

### 3. Frequency Distribution

| Class Interval | Tally Bars | Frequency (f) |
|---|---|---|
| 5–10 | ~~\|\|\|\|~~ \|\|\| | 8 |
| 10–15 | ~~\|\|\|\|~~ ~~\|\|\|\|~~ | 10 |
| 15–20 | ~~\|\|\|\|~~ ~~\|\|\|\|~~ \|\| | 12 |
| 20–25 | ~~\|\|\|\|~~ ~~\|\|\|\|~~ ~~\|\|\|\|~~ \|\| | 17 |
| 25–30 | \|\|\| | 3 |
| | | $\Sigma f = 50$ |

## 4. Cumulative Frequency Distribution

| Quantity of Milk | Number of Buyers | Quantity of Milk | Number of Buyers |
|---|---|---|---|
| Less than 5 | 0 | More than 5 | 50 |
| " " 10 | 8 | " " 10 | 42 |
| " " 15 | 18 | " " 15 | 32 |
| " " 20 | 30 | " " 20 | 20 |
| " " 25 | 47 | " " 25 | 3 |
| " " 30 | 50 | " " 30 | 0 |

**ILLUSTRATION 2.**

Prepare a frequency series of the ages of 25 students of Class XI in your school.

15, 16, 16, 17, 18, 18, 17, 15, 15, 16, 16, 17, 15,

16, 16, 15, 16, 16, 15, 17, 17, 18, 19, 16, 15

**SOLUTION:**

In this question, minimum age is 15 years and the maximum age is 19 years. Therefore, the distribution of frequencies would correspond to the values between 15 and 19.

**Frequency Series**

| Age | Tally Bars | Frequency (f) |
|---|---|---|
| 15 | 𝍸 II | 7 |
| 16 | 𝍸 IIII | 9 |
| 17 | 𝍸 | 5 |
| 18 | III | 3 |
| 19 | I | 1 |
| | | $\Sigma f = 25$ |

**ILLUSTRATION 3.**

We have the following data on the monthly expenditure on food (in rupees) for 30 households in a locality.

| | | | | | |
|---|---|---|---|---|---|
| 115 | 159 | 196 | 205 | 212 | 223 |
| 256 | 271 | 310 | 129 | 335 | 169 |
| 184 | 234 | 245 | 241 | 265 | 298 |
| 144 | 135 | 172 | 173 | 229 | 243 |
| 220 | 238 | 278 | 243 | 220 | 238 |

(i) Obtain a frequency distribution using following class intervals 100–150, 150–200, 200–250, 250–300, 300–350

(ii) What percentage of households spends less than ₹ 250 per month and what percentage of households spends more than ₹ 200 per month?

**SOLUTION:**

(i) The data may be presented in the form of an exclusive series:

| Class Interval | Tally Bars | Frequency (f) |
|---|---|---|
| 100–150 | \|\|\|\| | 4 |
| 150–200 | ~~\|\|\|\|~~ \| | 6 |
| 200–250 | ~~\|\|\|\|~~ ~~\|\|\|\|~~ \|\|\| | 13 |
| 250–300 | ~~\|\|\|\|~~ | 5 |
| 300–350 | \|\| | 2 |
| | | $\Sigma f = 30$ |

(ii) Number of households spending less than ₹ 250 per month

$= 4 + 6 + 13 = 23$

Percentage of households spending less than ₹ 250 per month

$$= \frac{23}{10} \times 100 = 76.6\%$$

Number of households spending more than ₹ 200

$= 13 + 5 + 2 = 20$

Percentage of households spending more than ₹ 200 per month

$$= \frac{20}{30} \times 100 = 66.6\%$$

**ILLUSTRATION 4.**

Make a frequency distribution (inclusive) series of the following data. The class interval is to be taken as 6.

| | | | | | | | |
|---|---|---|---|---|---|---|---|
| 24 | 26 | 28 | 32 | 1 | 7 | 9 | 11 |
| 15 | 13 | 14 | 18 | 23 | 6 | 4 | 2 |
| 9 | 18 | 27 | 36 | 15 | 21 | 27 | 33 |
| 4 | 8 | 12 | 16 | 10 | 3 | 8 | 1 |
| 4 | 9 | 6 | 2 | 18 | 27 | 23 | 1 |
| 22 | 15 | 29 | 17 | | | | |

**SOLUTION:**

In this question, the lowest value is 1 and the highest value is 36. Accordingly, we take 0–6 as the initial class interval.

**Frequency Distribution (Inclusive Method)**

| Class Interval | Tally Bars | Frequency (f) |
|---|---|---|
| 0–6 | ~~\|\|\|\|~~ ~~\|\|\|\|~~ \| | 11 |
| 7–13 | ~~\|\|\|\|~~ ~~\|\|\|\|~~ | 10 |
| 14–20 | ~~\|\|\|\|~~ \|\|\|\| | 9 |
| 21–27 | ~~\|\|\|\|~~ \|\|\|\| | 9 |
| 28–34 | \|\|\|\| | 4 |
| 35–41 | \| | 1 |
| | | $\Sigma f = 44$ |

**ILLUSTRATION 5.**

Convert the following cumulative frequency distribution into a simple frequency distribution.

| Marks | Number of Students |
|---|---|
| More than 0 | 55 |
| More than 5 | 51 |
| More than 10 | 43 |
| More than 15 | 28 |
| More than 20 | 16 |
| More than 25 | 6 |
| More than 30 | 0 |

**SOLUTION:**

**Conversion of Cumulative Frequency Distribution into Simple Frequency Distribution**

| Marks | Number of Students (f) |
|---|---|
| 0–5 | 55 – 51 = 4 |
| 5–10 | 51 – 43 = 8 |
| 10–15 | 43 – 28 = 15 |
| 15–20 | 28 – 16 = 12 |
| 20–25 | 16 – 6 = 10 |
| 25–30 | 6 – 0 = 6 |
| 30–35 | 0 |

**ILLUSTRATION 6.**

The following are the marks obtained by 30 students of Class XI in Statistics.

| Marks out of 50 | | | | | |
|---|---|---|---|---|---|
| 15 | 10 | 8 | 7 | 6 | 11 |
| 20 | 12 | 14 | 16 | 18 | 13 |
| 0 | 5 | 4 | 7 | 9 | 17 |
| 8 | 16 | 18 | 19 | 20 | 0 |
| 24 | 28 | 26 | 25 | 29 | 4 |

Prepare a frequency distribution by taking a class interval of 5 on exclusive basis.

**SOLUTION:**

The lowest value is 0 and highest is 29. We have to take a class interval of 5. The various classes will be 0–5, 5–10, and so on up to 25–30.

**Frequency Distribution**

| Marks | Tally Bars | Frequency (f) |
|---|---|---|
| 0–5 | \|\|\|\| | 4 |
| 5–10 | ~~\|\|\|\|~~ \|\| | 7 |
| 10–15 | ~~\|\|\|\|~~ | 5 |
| 15–20 | ~~\|\|\|\|~~ \|\| | 7 |
| 20–25 | \|\|\| | 3 |
| 25–30 | \|\|\|\| | 4 |
| | | $\sum f = 30$ |

**Errors of Grouping or Loss of Information**

Error of grouping occurs when data are grouped into different class intervals. There is a hidden assumption in the process of grouping that all frequencies (or observations) corresponding to a particular class interval are equal to mid-value of the class interval. Obviously, there is an element of error in this assumption. Or, there is a loss of information regarding different values of observation in a class interval. It is this error which is called the **error of grouping**. To the extent that this error occurs, our results are not accurate.

# EXERCISE

## 1. Very Short Answer Type Questions [1 mark]

### A. Multiple Choice Questions: Choose the Correct Answer

1. Which of the following is the objective of classification?

   (a) Simplification (b) Briefness

   (c) Comparability (d) All of these

2. Classification of data on the basis of time period is called:

   (a) geographical classification (b) chronological classification

   (c) qualitative classification (d) quantitative classification

3. The characteristic of a fact that can be measured in the form of numbers is called:

   (a) frequency (b) variable

   (c) attribute (d) none of these

4. A series in which every class interval excludes items corresponding to its upper limit is called:

   (a) exclusive series (b) inclusive series

   (c) both (a) and (b) (d) none of these

5. An open end series is that series in which:

   (a) lower limit of the first class interval is missing

   (b) upper limit of the last class interval is missing

   (c) both (a) and (b)

   (d) none of these

6. Formula for finding mid-value is given by:

   (a) $l_2 - l_1$ (b) $\frac{l_2 - l_1}{2}$

   (c) $l_1 + l_2$ (d) $\frac{l_1 + l_2}{2}$

7. According to tally bar method, which of the following symbols indicate the frequency of five?

   (a) 𝍸 | (b) ||||

   (c) 𝍸 (d) None of these

8. In a series, the number of times an item occurs is known as:

(a) number (b) class frequency

(c) frequency (d) cumulative frequency

9. The difference between upper limit and lower limit of a class is known as:

(a) range (b) magnitude

(c) frequency (d) class limits

10. Which of the following equations is correct?

(a) $s = r + n$ (b) $s = r - n$

(c) $s = r \times n$ (d) $s = \frac{r}{n}$

[s = Size of the class; r = Range; n = Number of classes]

Ans. 1. (d), 2. (b), 3. (b), 4. (a), 5. (c), 6. (d), 7. (c), 8. (c), 9. (b), 10. (d).

### B. True or False

State whether the following statements are True or False

1. Raw data are collected by investigator during the investigation. (True/False)
2. In case of discrete variable data are expressed in fractions. (True/False)
3. In an inclusive series, the upper limit of one class interval is the lower limit of the next class. (True/False)
4. The number of variables or items that come under any class is called class frequency.(True/False)
5. Arranging the data in different classes according to a given order is called 'series'. (True/False)
6. Cumulative frequency is the frequency of a class. (True/False)

Ans. 1. True, 2. False, 3. False, 4. True, 5. True, 6. False.

### C. Concepts/Definitions & Knowledge-based Questions

1. What is meant by classification?

Ans. Classification is the grouping of related facts into different classes. In other words, the process by which data is divided into different classes on the basis of their similarity or diversity is called classification.

2. Define a variable.

Ans. A characteristic or a phenomenon which is capable of being measured and changes its value overtime is called a variable.

3. What is meant by individual series?

Ans. Individual series are those series in which the items are listed singly. In these series there is no class of the items and also there is no frequency of the items.

4. What is a discrete series?

Ans. A discrete series is that series in which data are presented in a way that exact measurements of items are clearly shown. In such series there are no class intervals and a particular item in the series is numbered rather than measured with some range.

5. What is meant by a continuous series or frequency distribution?

Ans. Continuous series or frequency distribution is that series in which items cannot be exactly measured. The items assume a range of values and are placed within the range or limits.

6. What is meant by frequency?

Ans. Frequency is the number of times an item occurs or repeats itself in the series.

7. What are the class limits?

Ans. The extreme values of a class are limits. Every class interval has two limits, lower limit and upper limit.

8. What is meant by magnitude of a class interval?

Ans. Magnitude of a class interval is the difference between the upper limit and the lower limit of a class.

9. What is meant by exclusive series?

Ans. Exclusive series is that series in which every class interval excludes items corresponding to its upper limit.

10. What is meant by inclusive series?

Ans. An inclusive series is that series which includes all items upto its upper limit.

11. What is an open end series?

Ans. An open end series is that series in which lower limit of the first class interval and (or) the upper limit of last class interval is missing.

12. What is meant by cumulative frequency series?

Ans. Cumulative frequency series is that series in which the frequencies are continuously added corresponding to each class interval in the series.

13. What is meant by mid-values frequency series?

Ans. Mid-value frequency series are those series in which we have only mid-values of the class intervals and the corresponding frequencies.

## 2. Short Answer Type Questions [3-4 marks]

1. What is meant by statistical series? Give the names of statistical series.
2. What is meant by classification of data? State its objectives.
3. Mention two series from the point of view of their construction. Give an example of each.
4. What are the four main merits of classification?
5. What is frequency distribution? What are the main points underlying the construction of a frequency distribution?
6. What are the different types of frequency distribution?
7. Describe the concept of individual series. Give one example.
8. Describe the concept of discrete series. Give one example.
9. Describe the concept of continuous series. Give one example.
10. Describe the concept of cumulative frequency. Give one example.

11. Distinguish between (i) variable, and (ii) attribute. Explain with examples.
12. Distinguish between (i) continuous, and (ii) discrete variables. Explain with examples.
13. What is meant by inclusive series? Illustrate with one example.
14. What is meant by exclusive series? Illustrate with one example.

## 3. Long Answer Type Questions [6 marks]

1. What do you mean by classification? Explain its various objectives.
2. Discuss the different methods of classification of data.
3. What is meant by statistical data? Explain and illustrate various types of statistical series.
4. Explain the concepts of:
   (i) Class interval,
   (ii) Individual series,
   (iii) Frequency array, and
   (iv) Frequency distribution.
5. What is statistical classification? What is the importance of such a classification?
6. Explain with examples two ways of presenting cumulative frequency series.
7. How many classes should we choose? How does one decide about the size of class intervals?

## 4. Essential Practicals

1. In an examination, 25 students secured the following marks:

| | | | | | | | | | | | | |
|---|---|---|---|---|---|---|---|---|---|---|---|---|
| 23 | 28 | 30 | 32 | 35 | 35 | 36 | 40 | 41 | 43 | 44 | 45 | 45 |
| 48 | 49 | 52 | 53 | 54 | 56 | 56 | 58 | 61 | 62 | 65 | 68 | |

   (i) Arrange these data in the form of a frequency distribution using the following class as intervals: 20–29, 30–39, 40–49, 50–59, and 60–69.
   (ii) Arrange the data with cumulative frequencies.

2. The following data is of the age of 25 students of Class XI.
   Arrange these data in the form of a frequency distribution.

| | | | | | | | | | | | | |
|---|---|---|---|---|---|---|---|---|---|---|---|---|
| 15 | 16 | 16 | 17 | 18 | 18 | 17 | 15 | 15 | 16 | 16 | 17 | 15 |
| 16 | 15 | 16 | 16 | 18 | 15 | 17 | 17 | 18 | 10 | 16 | 15 | |

3. Students of Class XI obtained following marks in Economics. Classify the data in the form of individual series, discrete series, continuous series and cumulative frequency series.

| | | | | | | | | | | | | | | |
|---|---|---|---|---|---|---|---|---|---|---|---|---|---|---|
| 15 | 15 | 18 | 16 | 20 | 21 | 25 | 25 | 15 | 16 | 18 | 22 | 24 | 25 | 20 |
| 18 | 22 | 24 | 24 | 25 | 25 | 23 | 20 | 15 | 16 | 17 | 19 | 18 | 22 | 22 |

4. Arrange the following data in the form of an exclusive frequency distribution, using 5–10 as the initial class interval:

| | | | | | | | | | | | | | |
|---|---|---|---|---|---|---|---|---|---|---|---|---|---|
| 12 | 36 | 40 | 30 | 28 | 20 | 19 | 10 | 10 | 19 | 27 | 15 | 26 | 10 |
| 19 | 7 | 45 | 33 | 26 | 37 | 5 | 20 | 11 | 17 | 37 | 30 | 20 | |

5. Weight of 20 students is given in kilograms. Using class interval of 5, make a frequency distribution.

| 30 | 45 | 26 | 25 | 42 | 33 | 15 | 35 | 45 | 45 |
|---|---|---|---|---|---|---|---|---|---|
| 45 | 39 | 42 | 40 | 18 | 35 | 41 | 20 | 36 | 48 |

6. Convert the following data in a simple frequency distribution:

| 5 students obtained less than 3 marks |
|---|
| 12 students obtained less than 6 marks |
| 25 students obtained less than 9 marks |
| 33 students obtained less than 12 marks |

7. In the following statement, take the number of letters in a word as items and number of times a word (of the same size) repeats itself as frequencies. Prepare a discrete series.

"Success in the examination confers no absolute right to appointment unless government is satisfied after such an enquiry as may be considered necessary that the candidate is suitable in all respects for appointment."

[Hint: Note the number of letters in each word e.g., Success = 7, in = 2, the = 3, examination = 11, confers = 7, no = 2, absolute = 8, right = 5, to = 2, appointment = 11, unless = 6, government = 10, is = 2, satisfied = 9, after = 5, such = 4, an = 2, enquiry = 7, as = 2, may = 3, be = 2, considered = 10, necessary = 9, that = 4, the = 3, candidate = 9, is = 2, suitable = 8, in = 2, all = 3, respects = 8, for = 3, appointment = 11. Write these values as:

7, 2, 3, 11, 7, 2, 8, 5, 2, 11, 6, 10, 2, 9, 5, 4, 2, 7, 2, 3, 2, 10, 9, 4, 3, 9, 2, 8, 2,3, 8, 3, 11.

In these data, 2 is the smallest value and 11 is the largest value. So, we shall write,

(Ans. Size of Items: 2, 3, 4, 5, 6, 7, 8, 9, 10, 11.

Frequency: 9, 5, 2, 2, 1, 3, 3, 3, 2, 3; $\Sigma f = 33$)]

8. An economic survey revealed that 30 families in a town incur following expenditure in a day (rupees).

| 11 | 12 | 14 | 16 | 16 | 17 | 18 | 18 | 20 | 20 | 20 | 21 | 21 | 22 | 22 |
|---|---|---|---|---|---|---|---|---|---|---|---|---|---|---|
| 23 | 23 | 24 | 25 | 25 | 26 | 27 | 28 | 28 | 31 | 32 | 32 | 33 | 36 | 38 |

(i) Convert these data in the form of a frequency distribution, using the following class intervals. 10–14, 15–19, 20–24, 25–29, 30–34 and 35–39.

(ii) How many families spend more than 29 rupees a day?

(Ans. 6 or 20%)

9. From the following data related to the weight of college students in kg, prepare a frequency distribution with a class interval of 10 on exclusive and inclusive basis:

| 40 | 70 | 63 | 53 | 85 |
|---|---|---|---|---|
| 92 | 72 | 65 | 53 | 79 |
| 49 | 42 | 43 | 47 | 50 |
| 52 | 50 | 48 | 65 | 42 |
| 69 | 60 | 54 | 82 | 55 |

10. Construct the simple frequency distribution from the following data:

| Mid-value | 5 | 15 | 25 | 35 | 45 | 55 |
|---|---|---|---|---|---|---|
| Frequency | 2 | 8 | 15 | 12 | 7 | 6 |

11. Classify the following data by taking class interval such that their mid-values are 17, 22, 27, 32 and so on:

| | | | | | | | | | | | |
|---|---|---|---|---|---|---|---|---|---|---|---|
| 30 | 42 | 30 | 54 | 40 | 48 | 14 | 17 | 51 | 42 | 25 | 41 |
| 30 | 27 | 42 | 36 | 28 | 28 | 37 | 54 | 44 | 31 | 36 | 40 |
| 36 | 22 | 30 | 31 | 19 | 48 | 16 | 42 | 32 | 21 | 22 | 40 |
| 33 | 41 | 21 | 16 | 17 | 36 | 37 | 41 | 46 | 47 | 52 | 53 |

## 5. NCERT Textbook Questions [With Hints to Answers]

1. Which of the following alternatives is true?

   (i) The class mid-point is equal to:

   (a) the average of the upper class limit and the lower class limit

   (b) the product of upper class limit and the lower class limit

   (c) the ratio of the upper class limit and the lower class limit

   (d) none of the above

   (ii) The frequency distribution of two variables is known as:

   (a) univariate distribution

   (b) bivariate distribution

   (c) multivariate distribution

   (d) none of the above

   (iii) Statistical calculations in classified data are based on:

   (a) the actual values of observations

   (b) the upper class limits

   (c) the lower class limits

   (d) the class mid-points

   (iv) Under exclusive method:

   (a) the upper class limit of a class is excluded in the class interval

   (b) the upper class limit of a class is included in the class interval

   (c) the lower class limit of a class is excluded in the class interval

   (d) the lower class limit of a class is included in the class interval

   (v) Range is the:

   (a) difference between the largest and the smallest observations

   (b) difference between the smallest and the largest observations

   (c) average of the largest and the smallest observations

   (d) ratio of the largest to the smallest observation

[(i) (a), (ii) (b), (iii) (d), (iv) (a & d), (v) (a)]

2. What is a variable? Distinguish between a discrete and a continuous variable.

[A variable refers to that quantity which is subject to change and which can be measured by some unit.

The principle difference between a discrete and a continuous variable is that while discrete variable assumes values in complete numbers like 2, 4, 6 and 8, continuous variable assumes values in fractions like 2.4, 4.6 and 6.8 or values in some range like 2–4, 4–6, etc.]

3. Explain the 'exclusive' and 'inclusive' methods used in classification of data.

[Page 62, 63]

4. Use the data in following table that relate to monthly household expenditure (in ₹) on food of 50 households, and

   (i) Obtain the range of monthly household expenditure on food.

   (ii) Divide the range into appropriate number of class intervals and obtain the frequency distribution of expenditure.

   (iii) Find the number of households whose monthly expenditure on food is

   (a) less than ₹ 2,000.

   (b) more than ₹ 3,000.

   (c) between ₹ 1,500 and ₹ 2,500.

Table. Monthly Household Expenditure (in ₹) on Food of 50 Households

| | | | | |
|---|---|---|---|---|
| 1,904 | 1,559 | 3,473 | 1,735 | 2,760 |
| 2,041 | 1,612 | 1,753 | 1,855 | 4,439 |
| 5,090 | 1,085 | 1,823 | 2,346 | 1,523 |
| 1,211 | 1,360 | 1,110 | 2,152 | 1,183 |
| 1,218 | 1,315 | 1,105 | 2,628 | 2,712 |
| 4,248 | 1,812 | 1,264 | 1,183 | 1,171 |
| 1,007 | 1,180 | 1,953 | 1,137 | 2,048 |
| 2,025 | 1,583 | 1,324 | 2,621 | 3,676 |
| 1,397 | 1,832 | 1,962 | 2,177 | 2,575 |
| 1,293 | 1,365 | 1,146 | 3,222 | 1,396 |

[ (i) Range = Highest value of the series – Lowest value of the series

= 5,090 – 1,007

= 4,083

(ii) **Frequency Distribution**

| Class Interval | Tally Bars of the Frequency | Frequency (f) |
|---|---|---|
| 1,000–1,500 | 𝍸 𝍸 𝍸 𝍸 | 20 |
| 1,500–2,000 | 𝍸 𝍸 ||| | 13 |
| 2,000–2,500 | 𝍸 | | 6 |
| 2,500–3,000 | 𝍸 | 5 |
| 3,000–3,500 | || | 2 |
| 3,500–4,000 | | | 1 |
| 4,000–4,500 | || | 2 |
| 4,500–5,000 | — | 0 |
| 5,000–5,500 | | | 1 |
| | | $\sum f = 50$ |

(iii) (a) Number of households whose monthly expenditure on food is less than ₹ 2,000 = 20 + 13 = 33.

(b) Number of households whose monthly expenditure on food is more than ₹ 3,000 = 2 + 1 + 2 + 1 = 6.

(c) Number of households whose monthly expenditure on food is between ₹ 1,500 and ₹ 2,500 = 13 + 6 = 19.]

5. In a city 45 families were surveyed for the number of domestic appliances they used. Prepare a frequency array based on their replies as recorded below.

| 1 | 3 | 2 | 2 | 2 | 2 | 1 | 2 | 1 | 2 | 2 | 3 | 3 | 3 | 3 |
|---|---|---|---|---|---|---|---|---|---|---|---|---|---|---|
| 3 | 3 | 2 | 3 | 2 | 2 | 6 | 1 | 6 | 2 | 1 | 5 | 1 | 5 | 3 |
| 2 | 4 | 2 | 7 | 4 | 2 | 4 | 3 | 4 | 2 | 0 | 3 | 1 | 4 | 3 |

[ **Frequency Array or Discrete Series**

| Number of Domestic Appliances | Tally Bars of the Frequency | Frequency (f) |
|---|---|---|
| 0 | | | 1 |
| 1 | 𝍸 || | 7 |
| 2 | 𝍸 𝍸 𝍸 | 15 |
| 3 | 𝍸 𝍸 || | 12 |
| 4 | 𝍸 | 5 |
| 5 | || | 2 |
| 6 | || | 2 |
| 7 | | | 1 |
| | | $\sum f = 45$ |

6. What is 'loss of information' in classified data?

[Page 72]

7. Do you agree that classified data is better than raw data?

[Yes. Classified data is better than raw data because classification of data involves conversion of raw data into statistical series in a manner such that some meaningful conclusions can be drawn out of them.]

8. Distinguish between univariate and bivariate frequency distribution.

[Univariate frequency distribution refers to a series of statistical data with one variable only, like the data on income of the households of a particular region.

Bivariate frequency distribution refers to a series of statistical data with two variables like the data on income as well as savings of the households.]

9. Prepare a frequency distribution by inclusive method taking class interval of 7 from the following data:

| 28 | 17 | 15 | 22 | 29 | 21 | 23 | 27 | 18 | 12 | 7 | 2 | 9 | 4 | 6 |
|---|---|---|---|---|---|---|---|---|---|---|---|---|---|---|
| 1 | 8 | 3 | 10 | 5 | 20 | 16 | 12 | 8 | 4 | 33 | 27 | 21 | 15 | 9 |
| 3 | 36 | 27 | 18 | 9 | 2 | 4 | 6 | 32 | 31 | 29 | 18 | 14 | 13 | 15 |
| 11 | 9 | 7 | 1 | 5 | 37 | 32 | 28 | 26 | 24 | 20 | 19 | 25 | 19 | 20 |

[The lowest value is 1 and highest value is 37. We have to take a class interval of 7. The various classes may be 0–7, 8–15, 16–23, 24–31 and 32–39.

**Frequency Array or Discrete Series**

| Class Interval | Tally Bars of the Frequency | Frequency (f) |
|---|---|---|
| 0–7 | ~~IIII~~ ~~IIII~~ ~~IIII~~ | 15 |
| 8–15 | ~~IIII~~ ~~IIII~~ ~~IIII~~ | 15 |
| 16–23 | ~~IIII~~ ~~IIII~~ IIII | 14 |
| 24–31 | ~~IIII~~ ~~IIII~~ I | 11 |
| 32–39 | ~~IIII~~ | 5 |
| | | $\Sigma f = 60$ |

# Presentation of Data—Textual and Tabular Presentation

5

The classification of data leads to the problem of presentation of data. *The presentation of data means exhibition of the data in such a clear and attractive manner that these are easily understood and analysed.* There are many forms of presentation of data of which the following three are well known: (i) Textual or Descriptive Presentation, (ii) Tabular Presentation, and (iii) Diagrammatic Presentation. The present chapter focuses on Textual and Tabular Presentation of data. Diagrammatic Presentation of data is discussed in the next chapter.

## 1. Textual Presentation

In textual presentation, data are a part of the text of study or a part of the description of the subject matter of study. Such a presentation is also called descriptive presentation of data. This is the most common form of data presentation when the quantity of data is not very large. Here are some examples:

### Example 1

In a strike call given by the trade unions of shoe making industry in the city of Delhi, 50% of the workers reported for the duty, and only 2 out of the 20 industries in the city were totally closed.

### Example 2

Surveys conducted by a Non-government Organisation reveal that, in the state of Punjab, area under pulses has tended to shrink by 40% while the area under rice and wheat has tended to expand by 20%, between the years 1991-2001.

### Suitability

Textual presentation of data is most suitable when the quantum of data is not very large. A small volume of data presented as a part of the subject matter of study becomes a useful supportive evidence to the text. Thus, rather than saying that price of gold is sky-rocketing, a statement like price of gold has risen by 50% during the financial year 2011-12 is much more meaningful and precise. One need not support the text with voluminous data in the form of tables or diagram when the textual matter itself is very small and includes only a few observations. Indeed, textual presentation of data is an integral component of a small quantitative description of a phenomenon. It gives an emphasis of statistical truth to the otherwise qualitative observations.

### Drawbacks

A serious drawback of the textual presentation of data is that one has to go through the entire text before quantitative facts about a phenomenon become evident. A picture or a set of bars showing increase in the price of gold during a specified period is certainly quite informative even on a casual glance of the reader. Textual presentation of data, on the other hand, does not offer anything to the reader at a mere glance of the text matter. The reader must read and comprehend the entire text. When the subject under study is vast and involves comparison across different areas/countries, textual presentation of data would only add to discomfort of the reader.

> ***Learning by doing***
>
> *Using some hypothetical data, and descriptive form of data presentation:*
>
> - *describe the impact of strike by the traders in your city.*
> - *describe the impact of increase in the price of petrol on the demand for cars and scooters.*

## 2. Tabular Presentation

In the words of **Neiswanger,** "*A statistical table is a systematic organisation of data in columns and rows.*" Vertical dissections of table (| |) are known as columns and horizontal dissections (═) are known as rows.

Tabulation is the process of presenting data in the form of a table. According to **Prof. L.R. Connor**, "*Tabulation involves the orderly and systematic presentation of numerical data in a form designed to elucidate the problem under consideration.*"

In the words of **Prof. M.M. Blair**, "*Tabulation in its broadest sense is an orderly arrangement of data in columns and rows.*"

> **Note the Difference between Table and Tabulation**
>
> While tabulation refers to the method or process of presenting data in the form of rows and columns, table refers to the actual presentation of data in the form of rows and columns. Table is the consequence of tabulation.

### Components of a Table

Following are the principal components of a table:

(1) **Table Number:** First of all, a table must be numbered. Different tables must have different numbers, *e.g.*, 1, 2, 3, ..., etc. These numbers must be in the same order as the tables. Numbers facilitate location of the tables.

(2) **Title:** A table must have a title. Title must be written in bold letters. It should attract the attention of the readers. The title must be simple, clear and short. A good title must reveal: (i) the problem under consideration, (ii) the time period of the study, (iii) the place of study, and (iv) the nature of classification of data. *A good title is short but complete in all respects.*

(3) **Head Note:** If the title of the table does not give complete information, it is supplemented with a head note. Head note completes the information in the title of the table. Thus, units of the data are generally expressed in the form of lakhs, tonnes, etc. and preferably in brackets as a head-note.

(4) **Stubs:** Stubs are titles of the rows of a table. These titles indicate information contained in the rows of the table.

(5) **Caption:** Caption is the title given to the columns of a table. A caption indicates information contained in the columns of the table.

A caption may have sub-heads when information contained in the columns is divided in more than one class. For example, a caption of 'Students' may have boys and girls as sub-heads.

(6) **Body or Field:** Body of a table means sum total of the items in the table. Thus, body is the most important part of a table. It indicates values of the various items in the table. Each item in the body is called 'cell'.

(7) **Footnotes:** Footnotes are given for clarification of the reader. These are generally given when information in the table need to be supplemented.

(8) **Source:** When tables are based on secondary data, source of the data is to be given. Source of the data is specified below the footnote. It should give: name of the publication and publisher, year of publication, reference, page number, etc.

Check the following **Format of a Table** showing its various components:

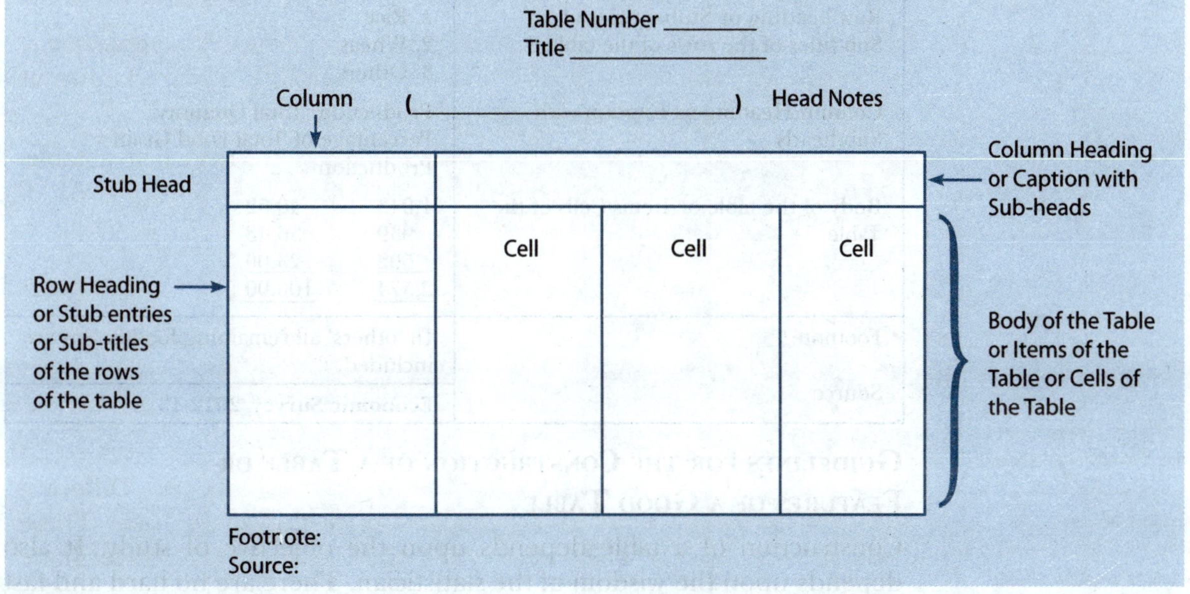


## Let us be Practical

Let us construct a table, showing its various components, given the following information:

In 2011-12, total production of food grains was 2,574 lakh tonnes of which production of rice, wheat and other crops was 1,043, 939 and 592 lakh tonnes, respectively. Percentage share of rice, wheat and other crops in the total production of food grains was 40.52, 36.48 and 23 respectively.

Table 1 is a tabular presentation of the given statistical information.

**Table 1. Production of Food Grains in India in 2011-12**

(Total in Lakh Tonnes, and Percentage)

| Food Grain | Production | |
|---|---|---|
| | Total Quantity | Percentage of Total Food Grain Production |
| 1. Rice | 1,043 | 40.52 |
| 2. Wheat | 939 | 36.48 |
| 3. Others | 592 | 23.00 |
| Total | 2,574 | 100.00 |

**Footnote:** In 'others', all remaining food grains are included.

**Source:** Economic Survey, 2012–13.

Compare this table with the format of Table 1 given on p. 102 Confirm the following components of a Table:

| Format of Table | Actual Table |
|---|---|
| Table No. ______________ | Table 1 |
| Title ______________ | Production of Food Grains in India in 2011-12 |
| Head Notes ______________ | Total in Lakh Tonnes, and Percentage |
| Stub Head ______________ | Food Grain |
| Row heading or Stub entries or Sub-titles of the rows of the table | 1. Rice<br>2. Wheat<br>3. Others |
| Column Heading or Caption with Sub-heads | Production, Total Quantity, Percentage of Total Food Grain Production |
| Body of the table or Items/Cells of the Table | 1,043 40.52<br>939 36.48<br>592 23.00<br>2,574 100.00 |
| Footnote | In 'others' all remaining food grains are included. |
| Source | Economic Survey, 2012-13. |

## Guidelines for the Construction of a Table or Features of a Good Table

Construction of a table depends upon the objective of study. It also depends upon the wisdom of the statistician. There are no hard and fast rules for the construction of a table. However, some important guidelines should be kept in mind. These guidelines are features of a good table. These are as under:

(1) **Title as compatible with the Objective of the Study:** Title of a table must be provided at the top center of the table and it must be compatible with the objective of the study.

(2) **Comparison:** It should be kept in mind that items (cells) which are to be compared with each other are placed in columns or rows close to each other. This facilitates comparison.

(3) **Special Emphasis:** Some items in the table may need special emphasis. Such items should be placed in the head rows (top above)

or head columns (extreme left). Moreover, such items should be presented in bold figures.

(4) **Ideal Size:** Table must be of an ideal size. To determine an ideal size of a table, a rough draft or sketch must be drawn. Rough draft will give an idea as to how many rows and columns should be drawn for presentation of the data.

**A Point You Must Note**

Before deciding on the size of the table (number of rows and columns) you must draw a rough format. Make sure that the size of the table does not become too large to be comprehended.

(5) **Stubs:** If rows are very long, stubs may be given at the right hand side of the table also.

(6) **Use of Zero:** Zero should be used only to indicate the quantity of a variable. It should not be used to indicate the non-availability of data. If the data are not available, it should be indicated by 'n.a.' or (–) hyphen sign.

(7) **Headings:** Headings should generally be written in the singular form. For example, in the columns indicating goods, the word 'good' should be used.

(8) **Abbreviations:** Use of abbreviations should be avoided in the headings or sub-headings of the table. Short forms of the words such as Govt., m.p. (monetary policy), etc. should not be used. Also such signs as "(ditto)" should not be used in the body of the table.

(9) **Footnote:** Footnote should be given only if needed. However, if footnote is to be given, it must bear some asterisk mark (*) corresponding to the concerned item.

(10) **Units:** Units used must be specified above the columns. If figures are very large, units may be noted in the short form as '000' hectare or '000' tonnes.

(11) **Total:** In the table, sub-totals of the items must be given at the end of each row. Grand total of the items must also be noted.

(12) **Percentage and Ratio:** Percentage figures should be provided in the table, if possible. This makes the data more informative.

(13) **Extent of Approximation:** If some approximate figures have been used in the table, the extent of approximation must be noted. This may be indicated at the top of the table as a part of head note or at the foot of the table as a footnote.

(14) **Source of Data:** Source of data must be noted at the foot of the table. It is generally noted next to the footnote.

(15) **Size of Columns:** Size of the columns must be uniform and symmetrical.

(16) **Ruling of Columns:** Columns may be divided into different sections according to similarities of the data.

(17) **Simple, Economical and Attractive:** A table must be simple, attractive and economical in space.

## Kinds of Tables

There are three basis of classifying tables, viz., (i) purpose of a table, (ii) originality of a table, and (iii) construction of a table. According to each of these basis, statisticians have classified tables in the Flow Chart, given on the next page:

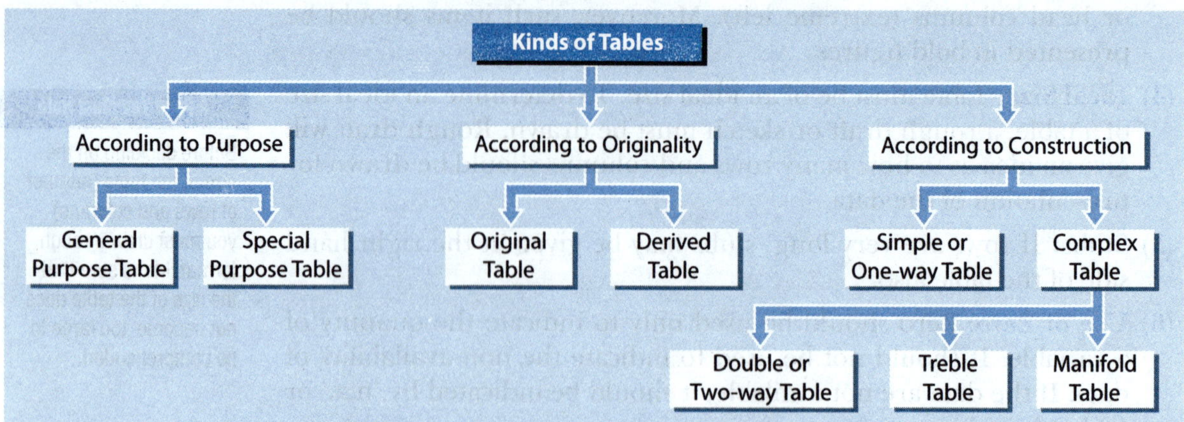


Let us attempt a brief description of the various kinds of tables:

### (1) Tables According to Purpose

According to purpose, there are two kinds of tables:

(i) **General Purpose Table:** General purpose table is that table which is of general use. It does not serve any specific purpose or specific problem under consideration. Such tables are just 'data bank' for the use of researchers for their various studies. These tables are generally attached to some official reports, like Census Reports of India. These are also called **Reference Tables.**

(ii) **Special Purpose Table:** Special purpose table is that table which is prepared with some specific purpose in mind. Generally these are small tables limited to the problem under consideration. In these tables data are presented in the form of result of the analysis. That is why these tables are also called **summary tables.**

### (2) Tables According to Originality

On the basis of originality, tables are of two kinds:

(i) **Original Table:** An original table is that in which data are presented in the same form and manner in which they are collected.

(ii) **Derived Table:** A derived table is that in which data are not presented in the form or manner in which these are collected. Instead the data are first converted into ratios or percentage and then presented.

### (3) Tables According to Construction

According to construction, tables are of two kinds:

(i) **Simple or One-way Table:** A simple table is that which shows only one characteristic of the data. Table 2 below is an example of a simple table. It shows number of students in a college:

**Table 2. Number of Students in a College**

| Class | Number of Students |
|---|---|
| XI | 200 |
| B.A. (I) | 100 |
| B.A. (II) | 80 |
| B.A. (III) | 60 |
| Total | 440 |

**(ii) Complex Table:** A complex table is one which shows more than one characteristic of the data. On the basis of the characteristics shown, these tables may be further classified as:

**(a) Double or Two-way Table:** A two-way table is that which shows two characteristics of the data. For example, Table 3, showing the number of students in different classes according to their sex, is a two-way table:

**Table 3. Number of Students in a College**
(According to Sex and Class)

| Class | Number of Students | | Total |
|---|---|---|---|
| | Boys | Girls | |
| XI | 160 | 40 | 200 |
| B.A. (I) | 40 | 60 | 100 |
| B.A. (II) | 60 | 20 | 80 |
| B.A. (III) | 50 | 10 | 60 |
| Total | 310 | 130 | 440 |

**(b) Treble Table:** A treble table is that which shows three characteristics of the data. For example, Table 4 shows number of students in a college according to class, sex and habitation.

**Table 4. Number of Students in a College**
**(According to Class, Sex and Habitation)**

| Class | Boys | | | Girls | | | Total | | |
|---|---|---|---|---|---|---|---|---|---|
| | Rural | Urban | Total | Rural | Urban | Total | Rural | Urban | Total |
| XI | 50 | 110 | 160 | 10 | 30 | 40 | 60 | 140 | 200 |
| B.A. (I) | 10 | 30 | 40 | 15 | 45 | 60 | 25 | 75 | 100 |
| B.A. (II) | 15 | 45 | 60 | 5 | 15 | 20 | 20 | 60 | 80 |
| B.A. (III) | 10 | 40 | 50 | 5 | 5 | 10 | 15 | 45 | 60 |
| Total | 85 | 225 | 310 | 35 | 95 | 130 | 120 | 320 | 440 |

**(c) Manifold Table:** A manifold table is the one which shows more than three characteristics of the data. Table 5, for example, shows number of students in a college according to their sex, class, habitation and marital status:

**Table 5. Number of Students in a College**
**(According to their Sex, Class, Habitation and Marital Status)**

| Class | Boys | | | | Girls | | | | Total |
|---|---|---|---|---|---|---|---|---|---|
| | Rural | | Urban | | Rural | | Urban | | |
| | Married | Unmarried | Married | Unmarried | Married | Unmarried | Married | Unmarried | |
| XI | 5 | 55 | 10 | 90 | 2 | 8 | 5 | 25 | 200 |
| B.A. (I) | 5 | 15 | 15 | 35 | 4 | 4 | 4 | 18 | 100 |
| B.A. (II) | 5 | 10 | 15 | 30 | 2 | 3 | 5 | 10 | 80 |
| B.A. (III) | 5 | 5 | 20 | 20 | 3 | 2 | 2 | 3 | 60 |
| Total | 20 | 85 | 60 | 175 | 11 | 17 | 16 | 56 | 440 |

## Classification of Data and Tabular Presentation

Tabular presentation is based on four fold classification of data, viz., qualitative, quantitative, temporal, and spatial. Following are the details with suitable illustrations.

**(i) Qualitative Classification of Data and Tabular Presentation:** Qualitative classification occurs when data are classified on the basis of qualitative attributes or qualitative characteristics of a phenomenon. Example: Data of unemployment may relate to rural-urban areas, skilled and unskilled workers, or male and female job seekers. Table 6 below is an example of tabular presentation of data when data are classified on the basis of qualitative attributes or qualitative characteristics.

**Table 6. Unemployment in Punjab by Sex and Location (per cent)**

| Sex | Location | |
|---|---|---|
| | Rural | Urban |
| Male | 20 | 10 |
| Female | 30 | 20 |
| Total | 25 | 15 |

(This is an imaginary table. In this table, male and female are such characteristics/attributes which are qualitative and cannot be quantified.)

**(ii) Quantitative Classification of Data and Tabular Presentation:** Quantitative classification occurs when data are classified on the basis of quantitative characteristics of a phenomenon. **Example:** Data on marks in Mathematics by the students of Class XII in CBSE examination. Table 7 shows tabular presentation of data when data are classified on the basis of quantitative characteristics.

**Table 7. Marks Obtained by Students of Class XII of XYZ School**

| Marks | Number of Students |
|---|---|
| 20–30 | 3 |
| 30–40 | 7 |
| 40–50 | 12 |
| 50–60 | 22 |
| 60–70 | 32 |
| 70–80 | 36 |
| 80–90 | 09 |
| 90–100 | 01 |

**Source:** Result Sheets

Here, marks are a quantifiable variable and data are classified in terms of different class intervals of marks.

*Learning by doing*

- *Construct a table presenting data collected by you on preferential liking of your class-mates of different teachers in your school.*
- *Construct a table on marks in English secured by the students of Class X in your school in the house examination.*
- *Construct a table on the runs scored by different players in the inter-school cricket tournament hosted by your school.*

**(iii) Temporal Classification of Data and Tabular Presentation:** In temporal classification, data are classified according to time, and time becomes the classifying variable. **Example:** Sale of Cell phones in different years during the period 2010-2014 in the city of Delhi. Table 8 shows tabular presentation of data on the basis of temporal classification.

**Table 8. Annual Sale of Cell Phones in the City of Delhi (2010-2014)**

| Year | Sale (Units) |
|---|---|
| 2010 | 50,000 |
| 2011 | 70,000 |
| 2012 | 90,000 |
| 2013 | 1,00,000 |
| 2014 | 2,00,000 |

*Learning by doing*

- *Check with your Principal. Request him to provide you information on the number of students in the school over the last 10 years. Present the data in a table based on temporal classification.*
- *Go to the office of Registrar, Births and deaths, of your town. Make a request for data on the number of births and deaths registered during different years over the last 10 years. Present the data in the form of table, showing temporal classification of data.*

**(iv) Spatial Classification:** In spatial classification, place/location becomes the classifying variable. It may be a village, a town, a district, a state or a country as a whole. **Example:** Number of Indian students studying in different countries of the world during a particular year. Table 9 is an example of tabular presentation based on spatial classification of data.

**Table 9. Indian Students in different Countries of the World (2014)**

| Country | Number of Students |
|---|---|
| USA | 50,000 |
| UK | 15,000 |
| Japan | 5,000 |
| Russia | 2,000 |
| Australia | 7,000 |

*Learning by doing*

- *Get information on the native state of the students in your school. Present the data in the form of a table, showing spatial classification of data.*
- *Get information on the location of Head-office of different banks in your locality. Present the data in the form of a table, showing spatial classification of data.*

### Merits of Tabular Presentation

Following are the principal merits of tabular presentation of data:

(1) **Simple and Brief Presentation:** Tabular presentation is perhaps the most simplest form of data presentation. Data, therefore, are easily understood. Also, a large volume of statistical data is presented in a very brief form.

(2) **Facilitates Comparison:** The tabulation facilitates comparison of data by presenting the data in different classes.

(3) **Easy Analysis:** It is very easy to analyse the data from tables. It is by organising the data in the form of table that one finds out their central tendency, dispersion and correlation.

(4) **Highlights Characteristics of Data:** Tabulation highlights characteristics of data. Accordingly, it becomes easy to remember the statistical facts.

(5) **Economical:** Tabular presentation is a very economical mode of data presentation. It saves time as well as space.

## MISCELLANEOUS ILLUSTRATIONS

### Illustration 1.

Prepare a blank table to show the percentage of rural and urban population in India in 1981, 1991, 2001 and 2011.

**Solution:**

**Table 10. Percentage Distribution of Urban and Rural Population in India**

| Census Year | Percentage of Population | | Total |
|---|---|---|---|
| | Rural | Urban | |
| 1981 | | | |
| 1991 | | | |
| 2001 | | | |
| 2011 | | | |

### Illustration 2.

Point out the mistakes in the following table and rearrange it in the form of a good table.

| Literate | Less than 20 | 20–30 | 30–40 | 40 and above |
|---|---|---|---|---|
| Male | | | | |
| Female | | | | |

**Solution:**

The following mistakes may be noted in the above table:

1. There is no table number and no title of the table.
2. The table is without any head note.
3. Caption and sub-entries have not been properly noted. Literacy and age be divided according to caption and sub-entries respectively.
4. Total of the rows and columns has not been indicated.

**Table 11. Distribution of Population**
(According to Age, Sex and Literacy) (in lakh)

| Age (Years) | Literate | | | Illiterate | | |
|---|---|---|---|---|---|---|
| | Male | Female | Total | Male | Female | Total |
| Less than 20 years | | | | | | |
| 20–30 years | | | | | | |
| 30–40 years | | | | | | |
| 40 and above | | | | | | |
| Total | | | | | | |

**ILLUSTRATION 3.**

In a sample study about the coffee habits in two towns, following data were observed:

Town X: 52% persons were males,
25% were coffee drinkers, and
16% were male coffee drinkers

Town Y: 55% persons were males
28% were coffee drinkers, and
18% were male coffee drinkers.

Represent the above data in a tabular form.

**SOLUTION:**

**Table 12. Percentage of Coffee Drinkers in Town X and Town Y**

| Attribute | Town X | | | Town Y | | |
|---|---|---|---|---|---|---|
| | Males | Females | Total | Males | Females | Total |
| Coffee Drinkers | 16 | 9 | 25 | 18 | 10 | 28 |
| Non-coffee Drinkers | 36 | 39 | 75 | 37 | 35 | 72 |
| Total | 52 | 48 | 100 | 55 | 45 | 100 |

**ILLUSTRATION 4.**

There were 80 persons in a trip organised by a school. Out of which 60 were students, 14 were teachers and 6 (all males) were peons. Out of total persons, 16 were females including one lady teacher. Present the above information in a table.

**SOLUTION:**

Total number of females = 16

Number of females amongst teachers = 1 ...(given)

Number of females amongst peons = 0 ...(given)

Hence, number of females amongst students

= Total number of females – Female teachers

= 16 – 1 = 15

Number of males amongst students

= Total number of students – Female students

= 60 – 15 = 45

Number of males amongst teachers

= Total number of teachers – Female teachers

= 14 – 1 = 13

| Trip Goers | Sex | | |
|---|---|---|---|
| | **Male** | **Female** | **Total** |
| Students | 45 | 15 | 60 |
| Teachers | 13 | 1 | 14 |
| Peons | 6 | Nil | 6 |
| Total | 64 | 16 | 80 |

## EXERCISE

### 1. Very Short Answer Type Questions [1 mark]

#### A. Multiple Choice Questions: Choose the Correct Answer

1. The process of presenting data in the form of a table is called:
   (a) organisation (b) classification
   (c) presentation (d) tabulation
2. The principal component of a table is:
   (a) table number (b) title
   (c) head note (d) all of these
3. Which of the following is a basis of classification of a table?
   (a) Purpose (b) Construction
   (c) Originality (d) All of these
4. Which of the following are titles of the rows of a table?
   (a) Title (b) Stub
   (c) Caption (d) None of these
5. Complex table may be classified as:
   (a) general purpose and special purpose table (b) original and derived
   (c) double, treble and manifold table (d) none of these
6. In temporal classification, data are classified on the basis of:
   (a) location (b) time
   (c) originality (d) purpose
7. Table is the consequence of:
   (a) classification (b) organisation
   (c) presentation (d) tabulation

Ans. 1. (d), 2. (d), 3. (d), 4. (b), 5. (c), 6. (b), 7. (d).

#### B. True or False

State whether the following statements are True or False:

1. The collection and classification of data leads to the problem of analysis of data. (True/False)
2. Tabulation is an orderly arrangement of data in columns and rows. (True/False)
3. The title of a table must be provided at the bottom centre of the table. (True/False)
4. In tabulation, the table number should be followed by title. (True/False)

5. In derived table, data are presented in the raw form. (True/False)
6. A simple table is that table which shows only one characteristic of the data. (True/False)

Ans. 1. False, 2. True, 3. False, 4. True, 5. False, 6. True.

### C. Concepts/Definitions & Knowledge-based Questions

1. What is meant by presentation of data?

Ans. The presentation of data means exhibition of the data in such a clear and attractive manner that these are easily understood and analysed.

2. What is meant by tabulation?

Ans. Tabulation refers to the method or process of presenting data in the form of a table.

3. What is a table?

Ans. Table refers to the systematic presentation of data in the form of rows and columns.

4. What is a simple table?

Ans. A simple table is that which shows only one characteristic of the data.

5. What is a complex table?

Ans. A complex table is one which shows more than one characteristic of the data. They are further classified as: (a) Double or Two-way Table, (b) Treble Table, and (c) Manifold table.

6. Define derived table.

Ans. A derived table is that in which data are not presented in the form in which these are collected. Instead the data are first converted into ratios or percentage and then presented.

7. What are the two principal parts of a table?

Ans. (1) Table Number: A table must be numbered. Different tables must have different numbers, e.g., 1, 2, 3, ..., etc. These numbers must be in the same order as the tables.

(2) Title: A table must have a title. Title must be written in bold letters. It should attract the attention of the readers. The title must be simple, clear and short.

8. What are the kinds of tables?

Ans. Tables can be classified according to:

(1) Purpose: (i) General purpose table, (ii) Special purpose table;

(2) Originality: (i) Original table, (ii) Derived table; and

(3) Construction: (i) Simple or one-way table,
(ii) Complex table: (a) Double or Two-way table, (b) Treble table, and (c) Manifold table.

## 2. Short Answer Type Questions [3-4 marks]

1. What is the difference between table and tabulation?
2. What is meant by tabulation? What are the main objectives of tabulation?
3. Discuss the main forms of a table.
4. What is meant by a two-way table? Give an illustration.
5. Make a format of table presenting all its parts.
6. Explain the main parts of a table.
7. Describe the four general guidelines for the construction of a table.

## 3. Long Answer Type Questions [6 marks]

1. What is statistical table? Explain briefly the main characteristics of a good statistical table.
2. Describe the major parts of statistical table. Draw a format of a table showing all these parts.
3. Define tabulation. Explain its merits.
4. What is tabulation? Describe functional parts of a statistical table. Draw the specimen of a table.
5. Draw a flow chart showing different kinds of tables. Also, explain the various kinds of tables.

## 4. Essential Practicals

1. In 2009–10, the contribution of primary, secondary and tertiary sectors to India's GDP was 17.6%, 28.2% and 54.2% respectively. In 2010–11, these shares were 17.7%, 27.0% and 55.3% respectively. This information is based on the India 2013 (EPW Research Foundation). Present this information in the form of a table.
2. Prepare a sketch of such a table that exhibits the following types of information on the number of students of your college:
   (i) Faculty-wise: Arts, Commerce and Science.
   (ii) Class-wise: XI ; B.A. (I); B.A. (II); and B.A. (III).
   (iii) Sex-wise: Boys and Girls.
3. Following information relates to the exports from India to USSR and UK in the years 2011, 2012, 2013 and 2014. Present it in the form of a table.

| Year | 2011 | 2012 | 2013 | 2014 |
|---|---|---|---|---|
| Exports to USSR (₹ crore) | 209 | 416 | 1,305 | 1,655 |
| Exports to UK (₹ crore) | 170 | 421 | 550 | 670 |

4. Point out the mistakes in the following table. Rearrange it correctly.

| Number of Students | Subjects | | | |
|---|---|---|---|---|
| | Economics | English | Hindi | History |
| Boys | | | | |
| Girls | | | | |

5. Following information relates to the marks secured by 50 students in Economics. Present the information in the form of a table.

| Marks | 0–10 | 10–20 | 20–30 | 30–40 |
|---|---|---|---|---|
| Students | 15 | 12 | 18 | 5 |

6. Following information relates to the marks secured by 50 boys and girls in their paper in Economics. Present the information in the form of a two-way table.

| Marks | 0–10 | 10–20 | 20–30 | 30–40 |
|---|---|---|---|---|
| Boys | 10 | 7 | 6 | 1 |
| Girls | 5 | 5 | 12 | 4 |

7. Draw a blank table to show the distribution of population according to sex, literacy, and income.
8. Present the following information in a suitable tabular form:
   (i) In 2007, out of total 2,000 workers in a factory, 1,550 were members of a trade union. The number of women workers employees was 250, out of which 200 did not belong to any trade union.
   (ii) In 2013, the number of union workers was 1,725 of which 1,600 were men. The number of non-union workers was 380, among which 155 were women.

# Diagrammatic Presentation of Data: Bar Diagrams and Pie Diagrams

6

Data may be presented in a simple and attractive manner in the form of diagrams. Diagrammatic presentation is broadly classified as of three types, viz.,

(i) Geometric form including bar diagrams and pie diagrams,

(ii) Frequency diagrams including histograms, polygon and ogive, and

(iii) Arithmetic Line-Graphs or Time Series Graphs.

Following chart shows different types of diagrammatic presentation as specified in the syllabus for the CBSE students of Class XI.

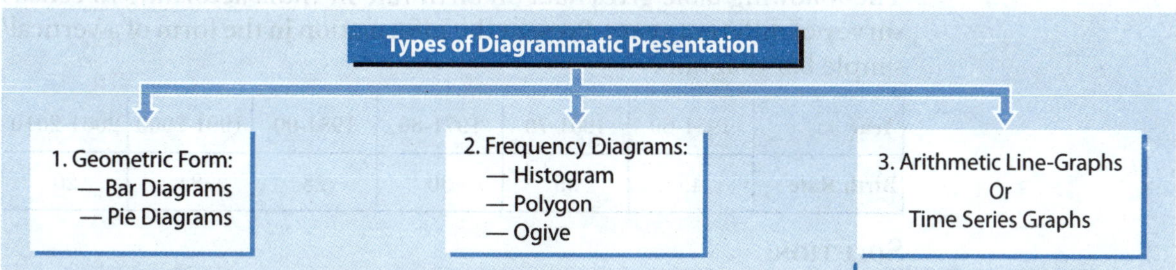


The present chapter focuses on Geometric form of diagrammatic presentation, including (i) Bar diagrams, and (ii) Pie diagrams.

## 1. Bar Diagrams

*Bar diagrams are those diagrams in which data are presented in the form of bars or rectangles. Bars are also called columns.*

### Bar and its Features

Bar usually means a rectangle or some rectangular form. It shows some value of the variable. It has the following features:

(1) The length or height of the bars differs according to different values of the variable, that is, length may be more or less but **breadth remains the same.**

(2) Bars may be either vertical or horizontal. However, usually these are used in their vertical form.

(3) Bars are **equidistant** from each other.

(4) All bars are based on some **common base line.**

(5) Unless data assume some specific ordering, these should be presented to form bars of the **ascending or descending order.**

(6) To make the bars attractive, these may be shaded with different colours.

### Types of Bar Diagrams

(i) **Simple Bar Diagrams:** *Simple bar diagrams are those diagrams which are based on a single set of numerical data*. The different items or values are represented by different bars.

Data relating to birth rate, death rate, production level of a commodity, are generally presented in the form of simple bar diagrams. These bar diagrams present only a single set of numerical data. These diagrams are more useful to present time series data, such as, individual value like weight of students; time series like birth-rate according to 2001-2011 census surveys; geographical conditions like per capita income in different states of India, namely, Haryana, Punjab, Himachal Pradesh, etc. The main limitation of simple bar diagrams is that these diagrams can show only a single set of numerical data. Illustration 1 and 2 explain the construction of simple bar diagram.

### Illustration.

The following table gives data on birth rate in India according to census survey of different years. Present the information in the form of a vertical/simple bar diagram.

| **Year** | 1951-60 | 1961-70 | 1971-80 | 1981-90 | 1991-2000 | 2001-2010 |
|---|---|---|---|---|---|---|
| **Birth Rate** | 45 | 35 | 30 | 28 | 24 | 20 |

### Solution:

**Birth Rate in India**

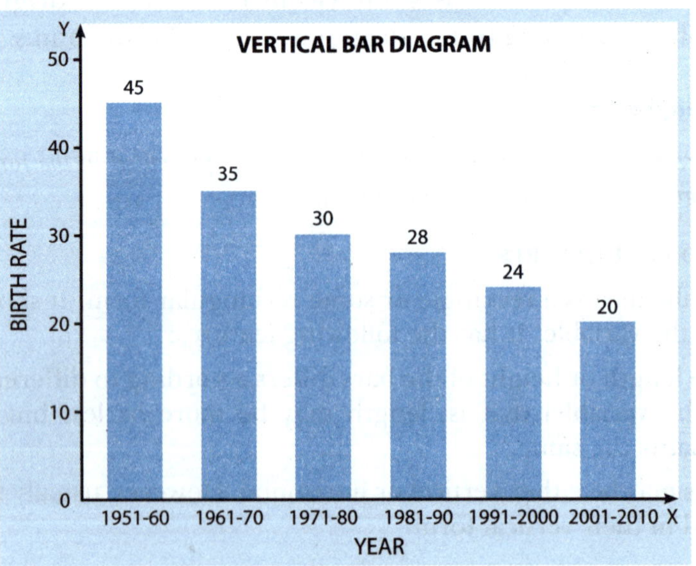

**ILLUSTRATION.**

Present the following data in the form of horizontal bar diagram:

| Students | A | B | C | D | E | F |
|---|---|---|---|---|---|---|
| Marks | 300 | 250 | 200 | 150 | 100 | 50 |

**SOLUTION:**

Marks obtained by different categories of students:

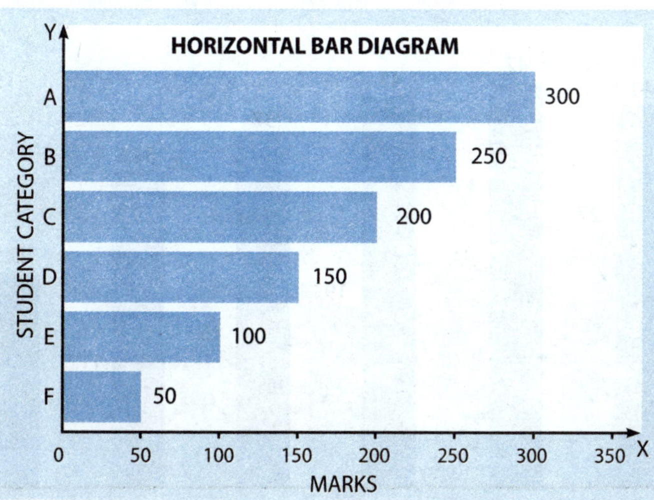


In the above diagram data are presented in the form of horizontal bars. *All the bars are of equal breadth. These are also equidistant from each other.*

> **Learning by doing**
>
> 1. *Get information from your school office about the CBSE result (2013) for the students of Class XII in your school. Draw a bar diagram (showing their aggregate marks classified as 1st division, 2nd division and 3rd division).*
> 2. *Collect data on the literacy rate in major states of India. Refer to Census 2011. Present the data in terms of a bar diagram. Write your observations how different states have performed in improving literacy among the masses.*

**(ii) Multiple Bar Diagrams:** Multiple Bar Diagrams are those diagrams which show two or more sets of data simultaneously. Generally, these diagrams are used to make comparison between two sets of series, such as birth-rate and death-rate series. Separate bars are drawn to present separate sets of values. Generally, bars are differentiated by colours to simultaneously indicate, the behaviour of two sets of series.

**ILLUSTRATION.**

The following table shows birth and death rate in India according to the Census Reports between 1931-40 to 2013-14 (hypothetical figures). Present the data in the form of a multiple bar diagram.

| Year | 1931-40 | 1941-50 | 1951-60 | 1961-70 | 1971-80 | 1981-90 | 1991-2000 | 2013-14 |
|---|---|---|---|---|---|---|---|---|
| Birth Rate | 46 | 45 | 40 | 42 | 41 | 37 | 32.5 | 22.5 |
| Death Rate | 36 | 31 | 27 | 23 | 19 | 15 | 11.5 | 7.3 |

**SOLUTION:**

**Birth Rate and Death Rate in India**
(Per Thousand) (1931-40 to 2013-14)

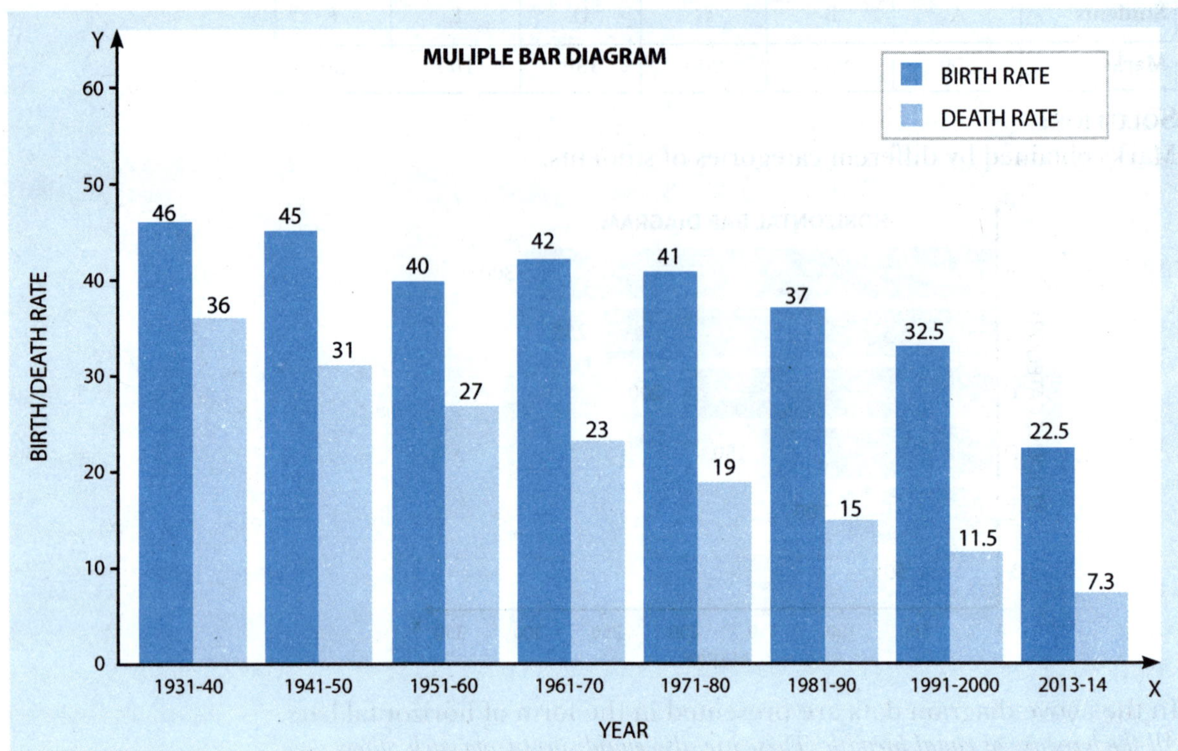


**(iii) Sub-divided Bar Diagrams or Differential Bar Diagrams:** Sub-divided bar diagrams are those diagrams which simultaneously present, total values as well as part values of a set of data. Different parts of the bars are shaded with colours. However, different parts of a bar must be shown in the same order for all bars of a diagram.

**ILLUSTRATION.**

The following table shows Production of Electricity from different Sources in India during 2010-11 to 2013-14 (hypothetical data). Present the data in a sub-divided bar diagram.

**(000' Million KWTs)**

| Year | Hydro Electricity | Thermal Electricity | Total Production |
|---|---|---|---|
| 2010-11 | 46 | 64 | 110 |
| 2011-12 | 49 | 72 | 121 |
| 2012-13 | 48 | 82 | 130 |
| 2013-14 | 51 | 89 | 140 |

**SOLUTION:**

**Hydro/Thermal Electricity Production in India**
2010-11 to 2013-14 (000' Million KWTs)

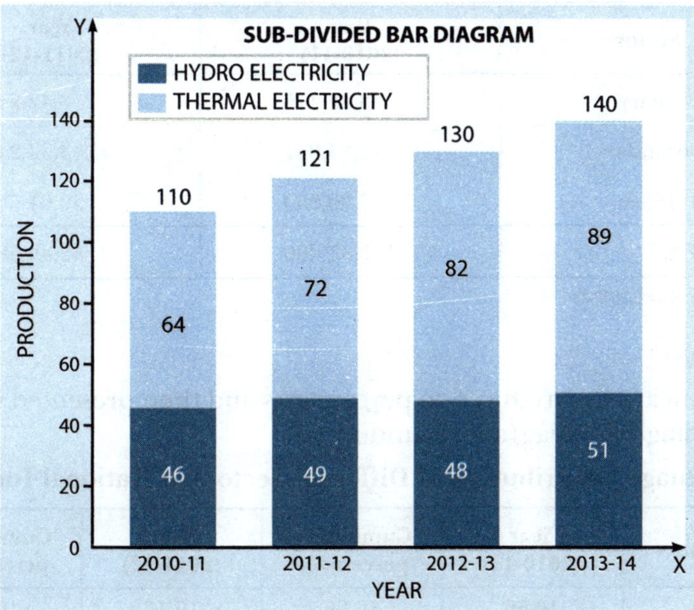


> *Learning by doing*
>
> *Check your school records on admissions. See how many students were admitted every year during the last 10 years. Classify the data as male and female students. Present the data in the form of a multiple bar diagram.*

**(iv) Percentage Bar Diagrams:** *Percentage bar diagrams are those diagrams which show simultaneously, different parts of the values of a set of data in terms of percentages.* Total value, indicated by total length of a bar is assumed to be 100. Each part thereof is shown as a part of 100. These parts may be shaded with different colours in order to highlight the difference. In fact, these diagrams are a different form of sub-divided bar diagrams. *The percentage bar diagrams are used generally when the values are of high magnitude.* In such cases, the use of sub-divided bar diagrams may not be appropriate. Because, when the values are of high magnitude, some parts of the bar may look very small compared to the others. Wide differences in parts of the bars makes comparison difficult. Percentage distribution of the bars in such cases should certainly be a better mode of presenting the data. Example given below illustrates percentage bar diagram.

**ILLUSTRATION.**

Gross Domestic Product by Industry of origin (at 2004-05 prices) is given for the years 2010-11 and 2011-12. Present this data in terms of percentage bar diagram.

**Gross Domestic Product by Industry of Origin (at 2004-05 prices) in 2010-11 and 2011-12**

(₹ crore)

| Sector | Year (2010-11) | Year (2011-12) |
|---|---|---|
| Primary | 8,22,415 | 8,47,744 |
| Secondary | 12,84,941 | 13,34,249 |
| Tertiary | 28,29,650 | 30,61,589 |
| Total | 49,37,006 | 52,43,582 |

**Source:** Economic Survey 2012-13

**SOLUTION:**

These data are first reduced to percentages and then presented in terms of percentage bar diagram, as under:

**Percentage Contribution of Different Sectors to National Income**

| Sector | Year (2010-11) | Cumulative percentage | Year (2011-12) | Cumulative percentage |
|---|---|---|---|---|
| Primary | 16.66 | 16.66 | 16.17 | 16.17 |
| Secondary | 26.03 | 42.69 | 25.45 | 41.62 |
| Tertiary | 57.31 | 100 | 58.38 | 100 |
| Total | 100 | | 100 | |

**Gross Domestic Product by Industry of Origin in 2010-11 and 2011-12 (₹ crore)**

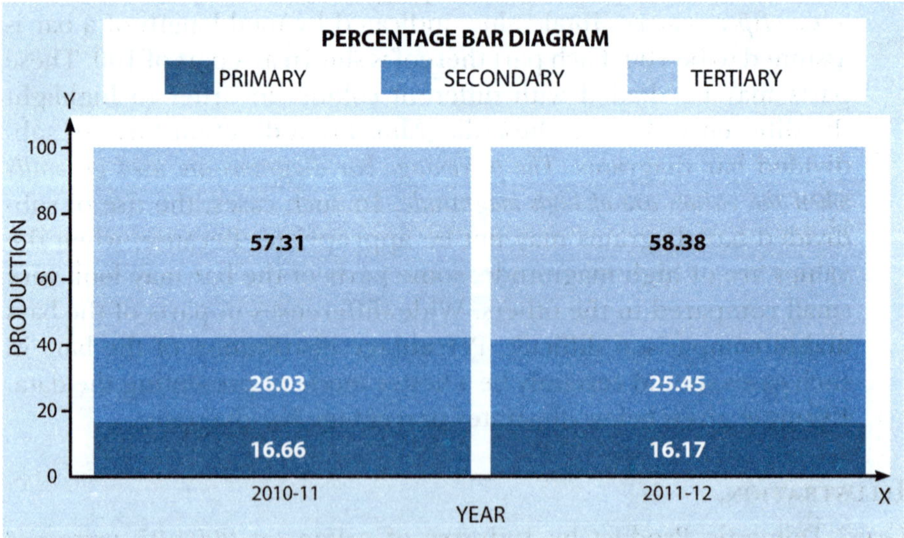


(v) **Deviation Bar Diagrams:** The deviation bar diagrams are used to compare the net deviation of related variables with respect to time and location. Bars representing positive and negative deviations are drawn above and below the base line. Such type of diagrams represent the deviations in magnitude as well as in direction.

**ILLUSTRATION.**

Represent the following data by a deviation bar diagram:

| Year | 2009 | 2010 | 2011 | 2012 | 2013 | 2014 |
|---|---|---|---|---|---|---|
| Saving/Deficit (in '000 ₹) | 30 | –20 | 10 | 15 | –25 | 20 |

**SOLUTION:**

**Saving/Deficit 2009 to 2014 (in '000 ₹)**

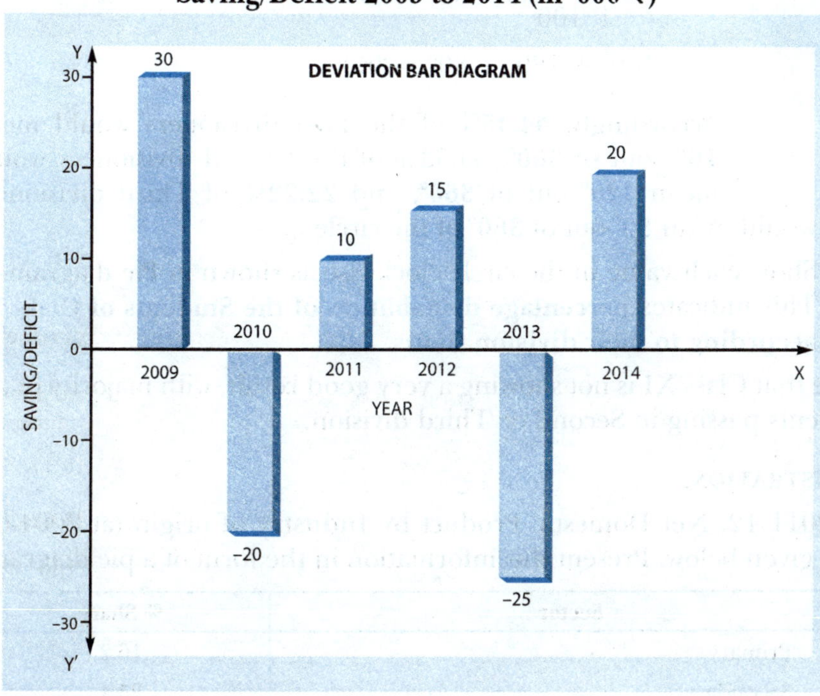


## 2. Pie or Circular Diagrams

Pie diagram is a circle divided into various segments showing the per cent values of a series. This diagram does not show absolute values. Construction of a pie diagram involves the following steps:

(1) As a first step, absolute values of the series are converted into per cent values. To illustrate, if in a class of 45 students, 20 are first divisioners, 15 are second divisioners and 10 are third divisioners, then in terms of per cent values it would mean $\frac{20}{45} \times 100$ or **44.45%** are first divisioners, $\frac{15}{45} \times 100$ or **33.33%** are second divisioners, and $\frac{10}{45} \times 100$ or **22.22%** are third divisioners.

(2) Second, draw a circle and note the fact that within a circle we can draw 4 angles of 90° each (See the adjacent figure), so that a circle comprises 90° × 4 = 360°.

$\angle abc + \angle abd + \angle ebc + \angle ebd = 360°$

However, the circle called PIE, is to be finally divided on the basis of the given/actual data. Thus, given the percentage share of first divisioners, second divisioners and third divisioners as 44.45, 33.33 and 22.22 respectively

**You must note it**

That pie diagrams are drawn only when percentage distribution of the value is to be diagrammatically presented.

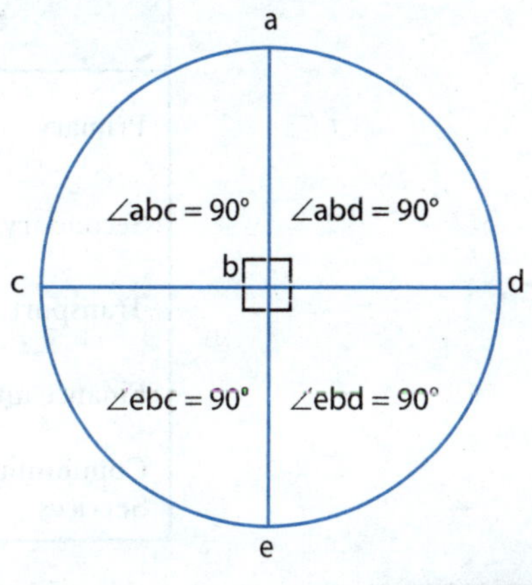

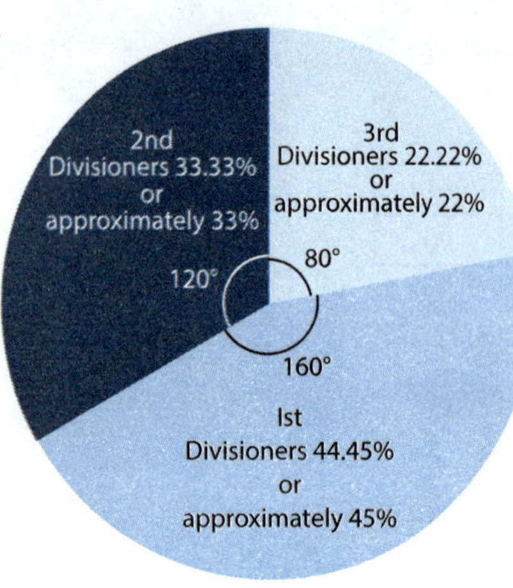


Pie Diagram–1

(adding upto 100) we divide the circle in terms of different angles as under:

$$\frac{44.45}{100} \times 360° = 160°$$

$$\frac{33.33}{100} \times 360° = 120°$$

$$\frac{22.22}{100} \times 360° = 80°$$

$$\therefore \quad 160° + 120° + 80° = 360°$$

Accordingly, **44.45%** of the First divisioners would mean **160°** out of **360°**, **33.33%** of the Second divisioners would mean **120°** out of **360°**, and **22.22%** of Third divisioners would mean **80°** out of **360°** of the circle.

(3) Show each value in the circle clockwise as shown in Pie diagram–1. This indicates **percentage distribution of the Students of Class XI according to their division status.**

**Note** that Class XI is not showing a very good result, with majority of the students passing in Second or Third division.

### Illustration.

In 2011-12, Net Domestic Product by Industry of origin (at 2004-05) is as given below. Present this information in the form of a pie diagram.

| Sector | % Share |
|---|---|
| Primary | 16.2 |
| Secondary | 25.4 |
| Transport | 27.5 |
| Finance and Insurance | 18.1 |
| Community and Social Services | 12.8 |
| Total | 100 |

**Source:** Economic Survey 2012-13

### Solution:

Percentage value are converted into component parts of 360° of a circle, and then shown as different components of the circle.

| Sector | % Share | Share in terms of Components of 360° |
|---|---|---|
| Primary | 16.2 | $\frac{16.2}{100} \times 360° = 58.32°$ |
| Secondary | 25.4 | $\frac{25.4}{100} \times 360° = 91.44°$ |
| Transport | 27.5 | $\frac{27.5}{100} \times 360° = 99°$ |
| Finance and Insurance | 18.1 | $\frac{18.1}{100} \times 360° = 65.16°$ |
| Community and Social Services | 12.8 | $\frac{12.8}{100} \times 360° = 46.08°$ |

**Gross Domestic Product according to the Industry of Origin**

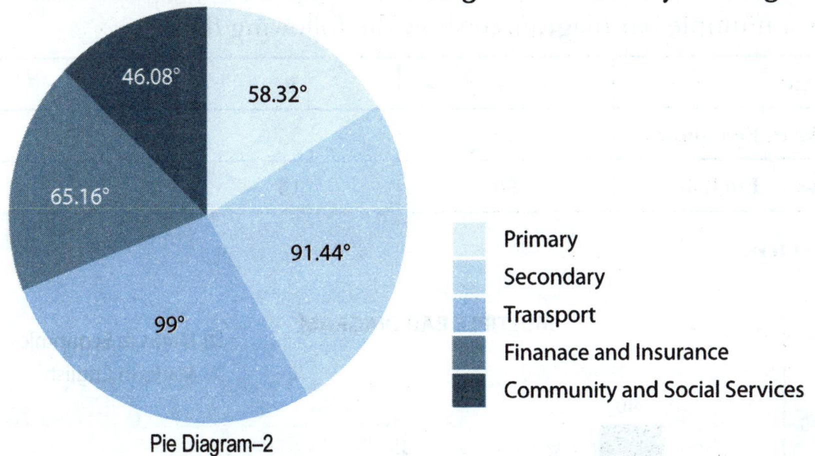


Pie Diagram–2

> *Learning by doing*
>
> *Here is an exercise for the students of Class XI. Draw a programme to conduct direct personal oral investigation of all the students of your school. Find out which mode of transport they use to come to the school. Present your information in terms of a pie diagram.*

## MISCELLANEOUS ILLUSTRATIONS

### ILLUSTRATION 1.

The strength of a school from 2010 to 2014 are given below:

| Year | 2010 | 2011 | 2012 | 2013 | 2014 |
|---|---|---|---|---|---|
| Strength of School | 500 | 600 | 500 | 700 | 750 |

Represent the data by a simple bar diagram.

**SOLUTION:**

The simple bar diagram of the above data is given below:

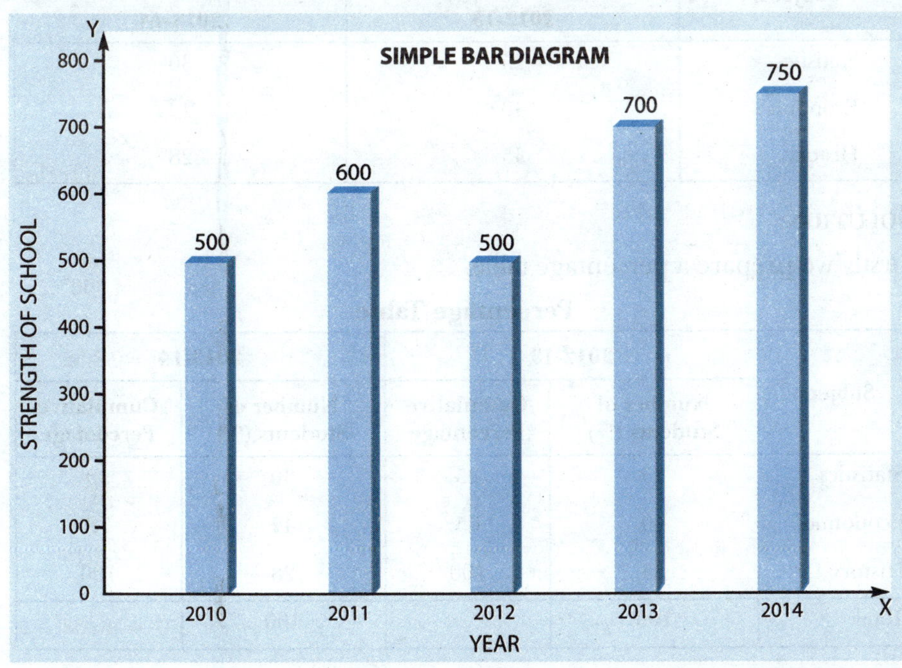

**ILLUSTRATION 2.**

Draw a multiple bar diagram to show the following data:

| Student | A | B | C |
|---|---|---|---|
| Marks in Economics | 40 | 35 | 30 |
| Marks in English | 30 | 15 | 25 |

**SOLUTION:**

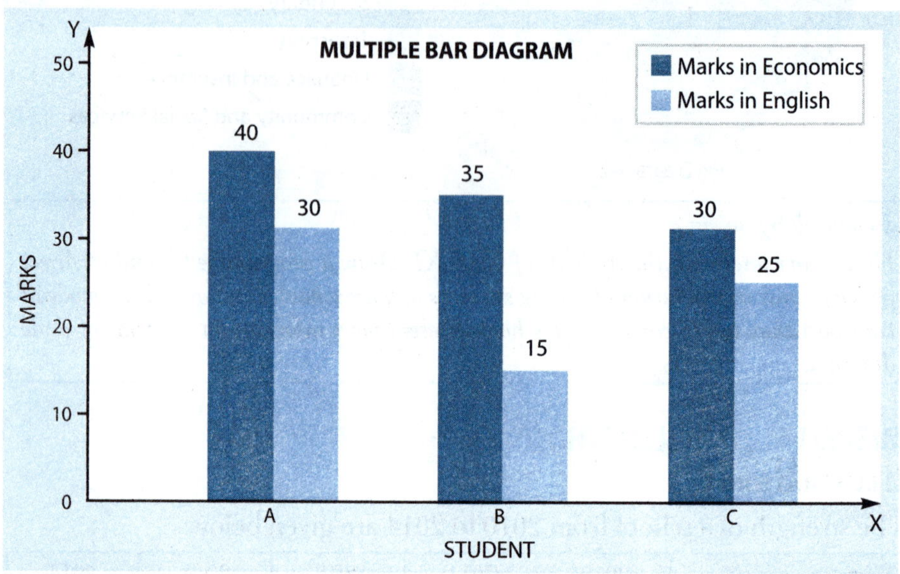


**ILLUSTRATION 3.**

Represent the following data by a percentage bar diagram:

(in '000)

| Subjects | Number of Students | |
|---|---|---|
| | 2012-13 | 2013-14 |
| Statistics | 25 | 30 |
| Economics | 40 | 42 |
| History | 35 | 28 |

**SOLUTION:**

Firstly we prepare a percentage table.

**Percentage Table**

| Subject | 2012-13 | | 2013-14 | |
|---|---|---|---|---|
| | Number of Students (%) | Cumulative Percentage | Number of Students (%) | Cumulative Percentage |
| Statistics | 25 | 25 | 30 | 30 |
| Economics | 40 | 65 | 42 | 72 |
| History | 35 | 100 | 28 | 100 |
| Total | 100 | | 100 | |

Now, we draw bars of equal length (100%) corresponding to each year. Then each bar is divided according to percentage of different constituents and should be different.

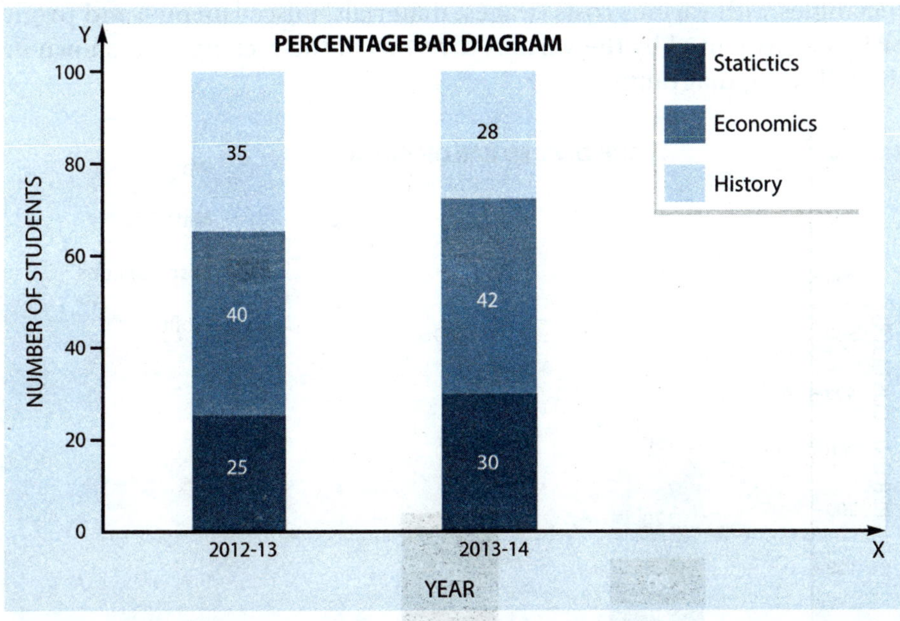


**ILLUSTRATION 4.**

Draw a suitable diagram to represent the following information:

| Factory | Selling Price per unit (in ₹) | Quantity Sold | Cost Components (in ₹) | | | |
|---|---|---|---|---|---|---|
| | | | Wages | Materials | Miscellaneous | Total |
| X | 400 | 20 | 3,200 | 2,400 | 1,600 | 7,200 |
| Y | 600 | 30 | 6,000 | 6,000 | 9,000 | 21,000 |

Also show the profit or loss as the case may be.

**SOLUTION:**

First of all we shall calculate the cost (wages, materials, miscellaneous) and profit per unit as given in the following table:

| | Factory X (20 units) | | Factory Y (30 units) | |
|---|---|---|---|---|
| | Total Cost (₹) | Per Unit Cost (₹) | Total Cost (₹) | Per Unit Cost (₹) |
| Wages | 3,200 | 160 | 6,000 | 200 |
| Materials | 2,400 | 120 | 6,000 | 200 |
| Miscellaneous | 1,600 | 80 | 9,000 | 300 |
| Profit/Loss | 800 (8,000 – 7,200) | 40 | –3,000 (18,000 – 21,000) | –100 |

[**Note:** Negative profit is regarded as loss.]

An appropriate diagram for representing this data would be the rectangles whose widths are in the ratio of the quantities sold, *i.e.*, 20 : 30, *i.e.*, 2 : 3. Selling prices would be represented by the corresponding heights of the rectangles with various costs (wages, materials, miscellaneous) and profit or loss represented by the various divisions of the rectangles as shown in the following diagram:

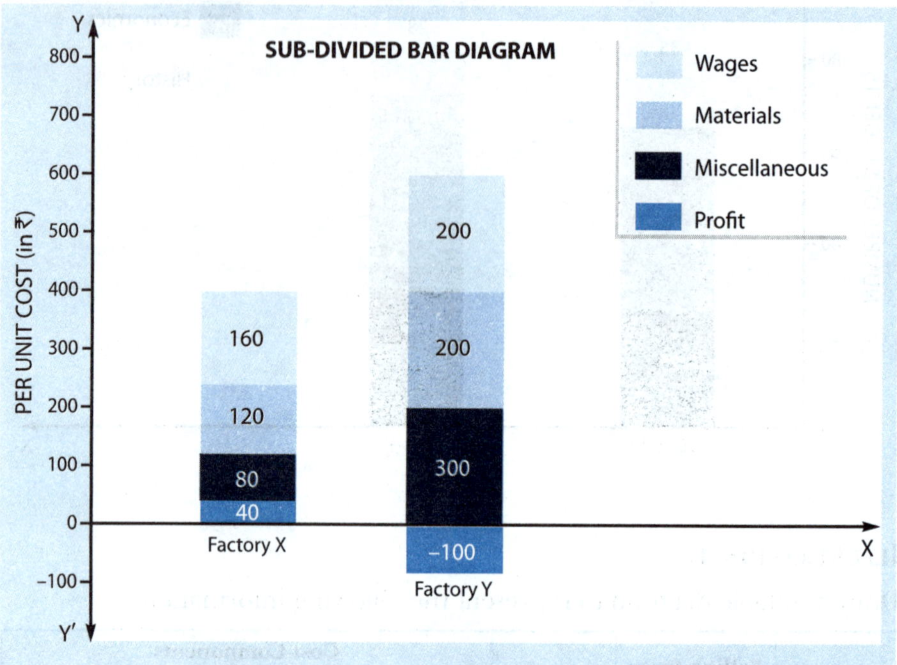


[**Note:** In case of profit, *i.e.*, when SP > CP, the entire rectangle will lie above the X-axis. But in case of loss, *i.e.*, when SP < CP, we will have rectangle with a portion lying below the X-axis which will reflect the loss incurred, *i.e.*, it cannot be recovered through sales.]

**ILLUSTRATION 5.**

Following are the data about the market share of 4 brands of TV sets sold in Panipat and Ambala. Present the data by a pie diagram.

| Brands of Sets | Units Sold in Panipat | Units Sold in Ambala |
|---|---|---|
| Samsung | 480 | 625 |
| Akai | 360 | 500 |
| Onida | 240 | 438 |
| Sony | 120 | 312 |

**SOLUTION:**

Total sets sold in Panipat and Ambala are 1,200 and 1,875 respectively. Data are to be represented by two circles whose radii are in the ratio of square roots of total TV sets sold in each city in the ratio of $\sqrt{1,200} : \sqrt{1,875}$ or 1 : 1.18. The calculations regarding construction of pie diagram are as follows:

| Brands of Sets | Panipat | | | Ambala | | |
|---|---|---|---|---|---|---|
| | Sets Sold | Sales (%) | Sales in terms of Components of 360° | Sets Sold | Sales (%) | Sales in terms of Components of 360° |
| Samsung | 480 | 40 | $\frac{40}{100} \times 360° = 144°$ | 625 | 33.3 | $\frac{33.3}{100} \times 360° = 119.88°$ |
| Akai | 360 | 30 | $\frac{30}{100} \times 360° = 108°$ | 500 | 26.7 | $\frac{26.7}{100} \times 360° = 96.12°$ |
| Onida | 240 | 20 | $\frac{20}{100} \times 360° = 72°$ | 438 | 23.4 | $\frac{23.4}{100} \times 360° = 84.24°$ |
| Sony | 120 | 10 | $\frac{10}{100} \times 360° = 36°$ | 312 | 16.6 | $\frac{16.6}{100} \times 360° = 59.76°$ |
| Total | 1,200 | | 360° | 1,875 | | 360° |

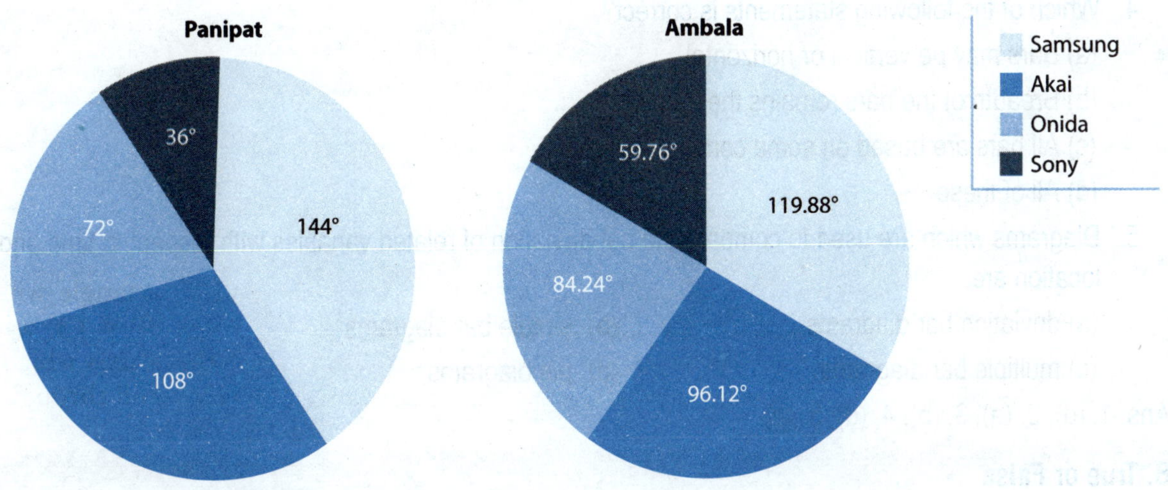


Pie Diagram-3

## EXERCISE

### 1. Very Short Answer Type Questions [1 mark]

#### A. Multiple Choice Questions: Choose the Correct Answer

1. Which of the following refer to geometric form of data presentation?
   (a) Bar diagrams (b) Histogram
   (c) Pie diagrams (d) Both (a) and (c)
2. The other name of pie diagram is:
   (a) circular diagram (b) bar diagram
   (c) histogram (d) polygon
3. Diagrams which show total values of a set of data simultaneously are known as:
   (a) percentage bar diagrams (b) differential bar diagrams
   (c) deviation bar diagrams (d) multiple bar diagrams
4. Which of the following statements is correct?
   (a) Bars may be vertical or horizontal
   (b) Breadth of the bars remains the same
   (c) All bars are based on some common base line
   (d) All of these
5. Diagrams which are used to compare the net deviation of related variables with respect to time and location are:
   (a) deviation bar diagrams (b) simple bar diagrams
   (c) multiple bar diagrams (d) pie diagrams

Ans. 1. (d), 2. (a), 3. (b), 4. (d), 5. (a).

#### B. True or False

State whether the following statements are True or False:

1. Bar diagrams are those diagrams in which data are presented in the form of bars or rectangles. (True/False)
2. In pie diagrams, absolute values of the series are converted into cumulative values. (True/False)
3. Bars in bar diagrams are equidistant from each other. (True/False)
4. Multiple bar diagrams are those diagrams which show two or more sets of data simultaneously. (True/False)
5. Percentage bar diagrams present only part values of a set of data. (True/False)

Ans. 1. True, 2. False, 3. True, 4. True, 5. False.

#### C. Concepts/Definitions & Knowledge-based Questions

1. What is meant by bar diagram?

Ans. Bar diagrams are those diagrams in which data are presented in the form of bars or rectangles. Bars are also called columns.

2. What is a multiple bar diagram?

Ans. Multiple bar diagrams are those diagrams which show two or more sets of data simultaneously. Generally, these diagrams are used to make comparison between two sets of series, such as birth-rate and death-rate series.

3. What does sub-divided bar diagram show?

Ans. Sub-divided bar diagrams are those diagrams which simultaneously present, total values as well as part values of a set of data.

4. Define percentage bar diagram.

Ans. Percentage bar diagrams are those diagrams which show simultaneously, different parts of the values of a set of data in terms of percentages.

5. Define deviation bar diagram.

Ans. The deviation bar diagrams are used to compare the net deviation of related variables with respect to time and location. Bars representing positive and negative deviations are drawn above and below the base line.

6. What is a circular or pie diagram?

Ans. Pie diagram is a circle divided into various segments showing the per cent values of a series.

## 2. Short Answer Type Questions [3-4 marks]

1. What is meant by bar? What are its features?
2. What is meant by simple bar diagram? What are their types?
3. What is meant by diagrammatic presentation of data? What are its main methods?
4. Which diagrams are known as bar diagrams? Explain the methods of its construction.
5. What is meant by pie diagram? Explain the method of its construction.

## 3. Long Answer Type Questions [6 marks]

1. What is meant by bar diagram? Explain its types.
2. What are the various types of statistical diagrams? Explain the geometric form of diagrammatic presentation.
3. Write brief notes on the following (use imaginary data for appropriate representation):
   (i) Bar diagram, and (ii) Pie diagram.

## 4. Essential Practicals

1. Make a suitable diagram of the following data on population in India:

| Year | 1951 | 1961 | 1971 | 1981 | 1991 | 2001 | 2011 |
|---|---|---|---|---|---|---|---|
| Population (crore) | 36.1 | 43.9 | 54.8 | 68.3 | 84.6 | 102.8 | 121.0 |

2. Give a diagrammatic presentation of the following data on India's Exports and Imports:

| Year | Export (₹ crore) | Import (₹ crore) |
|---|---|---|
| 2010-11 | 8,45,534 | 13,63,736 |
| 2011-12 | 11,42,922 | 16,83,467 |
| 2012-13 | 14,65,959 | 23,45,463 |

3. Make a bar diagram of the following data on India's population:

| Year | 1971 | 1981 | 1991 | 2001 | 2011 |
|---|---|---|---|---|---|
| Population (crore) | 54.8 | 68.3 | 84.6 | 102.8 | 121.0 |

4. Make a multiple bar diagram of the following data:

| Faculty | Number of Students | | |
|---|---|---|---|
| | 2011-12 | 2012-13 | 2013-14 |
| Arts | 600 | 550 | 500 |
| Science | 400 | 500 | 600 |
| Commerce | 200 | 250 | 300 |

5. Following table shows estimates of cost of production of certain commodities. Present the data in the form of a sub-divided bar diagram:

| Estimate of Cost | Goods | | | |
|---|---|---|---|---|
| | A | B | C | D |
| Raw material | 50 | 40 | 45 | 50 |
| Wages | 40 | 40 | 40 | 40 |
| Fixed costs | 10 | 12 | 15 | 15 |
| Office expenses | 10 | 8 | 10 | 5 |
| Total Cost | 110 | 100 | 110 | 110 |

6. Present the following data in the form of a multiple bar diagram:

| Year | Export (₹ crore) | Import (₹ crore) |
|---|---|---|
| 2010-11 | 8,40,755 | 13,74,436 |
| 2011-12 | 8,45,534 | 13,63,736 |
| 2012-13 | 11,42,922 | 16,83,467 |
| 2013-14 | 14,65,959 | 23,45,463 |

7. What do you mean by a circular diagram? Present the data on the expenditure of a labour-family in the form of a circular diagram:

| Items of Expenditure | Food | Clothing | Housing | Fuel and Light | Others |
|---|---|---|---|---|---|
| Percentage of Income Spent | 65 | 15 | 12 | 5 | 3 |

8. Following data relate to the construction of a house in Delhi. Present the information in the form of a pie diagram:

| Items | Labour | Bricks | Cement | Steel | Timber | Supervision |
|---|---|---|---|---|---|---|
| Percentage Expenditure | 25 | 15 | 20 | 15 | 10 | 15 |

9. For the years 2012-13 and 2013-14, value of gross domestic product at factor cost by the industry of origin is given in the following table. Present the information in the form of Pie Diagram showing differences in the percentage contribution of different sectors between the said years.

| Sector | Year | |
|---|---|---|
| | 2012-13 | 2013-14 |
| Primary | 17 | 16.7 |
| Secondary | 57 | 26 |
| Tertiary | 26 | 57.3 |
| Total | 100 | 100 |

[Hint: Make separate pie diagrams for the years 2012-13 and 2013-14.]

10. Present the following data on the production of food grains in the form of a sub-divided bar diagram:

| Year | Wheat | Rice | Gram | Total |
|---|---|---|---|---|
| 2012 | 30 | 20 | 10 | 60 |
| 2013 | 45 | 30 | 15 | 90 |

11. Present the following data by a deviation bar diagram, showing the difference between sale proceeds and costs of a firm.

| Year | Sale Proceeds (₹ in lakh) | Costs (₹ in lakh) |
|---|---|---|
| 2008-09 | 115 | 100 |
| 2009-10 | 140 | 115 |
| 2010-11 | 145 | 155 |
| 2011-12 | 150 | 140 |
| 2012-13 | 160 | 145 |
| 2013-14 | 170 | 165 |

## 5. NCERT Textbook Questions [With Hints to Answers]

1. Bar diagram is a
   (i) one-dimensional diagram
   (ii) two-dimensional diagram
   (iii) diagram with no dimension
   (iv) none of the above
   [(i)]
2. Width of bars in a bar diagram need not be equal (true/false).
   [True]
3. What kind of diagrams are more effective in representing the following?
   (i) Monthly rainfall in a year
   (ii) Composition of the population of Delhi by religion
   (iii) Components of cost in a factory
   [(i) Time series graphs, (ii) Pie diagram, (iii) Sub-divided bar diagram.]

4. The Indian Sugar Mills Association reported that, 'Sugar production during the first fortnight of December 2001 was about 3,87,000 tonnes, as against 3,78,000 tonnes during the same fortnight last year (2000). The off-take of sugar from factories during the first fortnight of December 2001 was 2,83,000 tonnes for internal consumption and 41,000 tonnes for exports as against 1,54,000 tonnes for internal consumption and nil for exports during the same fortnight last season.'

(i) Present the data in tabular form.

(ii) Suppose you were to present these data in diagrammatic form which of the diagrams would you use and why?

(iii) Present these data diagrammatically.

[ (i) **Production and Off-take of Sugar in India (in tonnes)**

| Time Period | Total Production of Sugar | Off-take of Sugar | |
|---|---|---|---|
| | | Internal Consumption | Exports |
| First Fortnight of December 2000 | 3,78,000 | 1,54,000 | — |
| First Fortnight of December 2001 | 3,87,000 | 2,83,000 | 41,000 |

(ii) Multiple bar diagram is used, because we are given more than two sets of data simultaneously.

(iii)

**Multiple Bar Diagram**

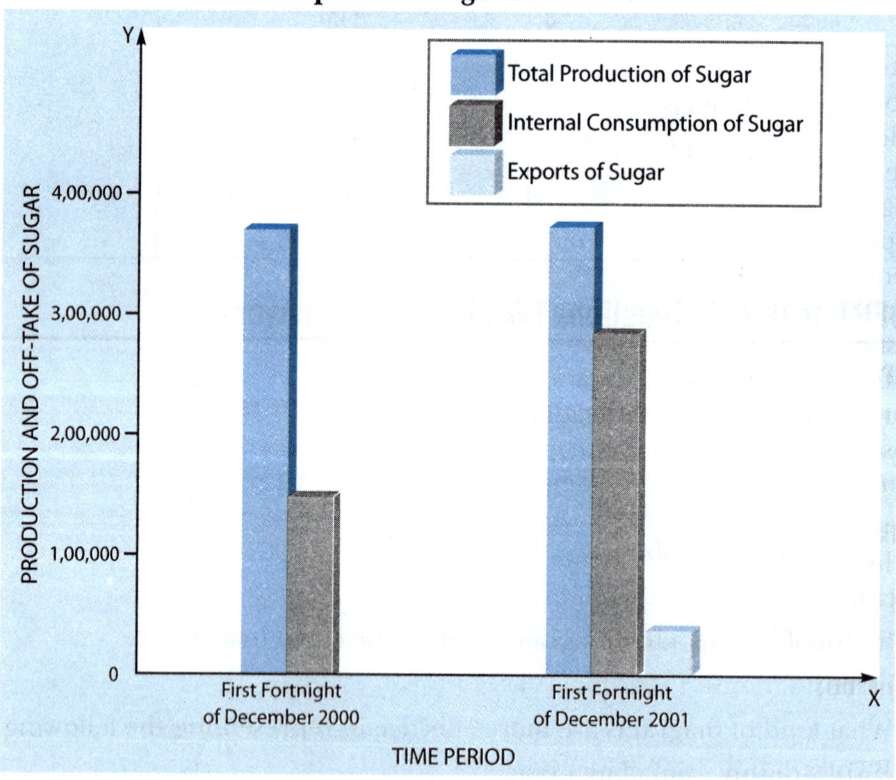

# Frequency Diagrams: Histogram, Polygon and Ogive

7

Frequency Diagrams relate to diagrammatic presentation of 'frequency distributions'. In such series, values of a variable repeat themselves number of times. That is, different values of a variable happen to occur different number of times. Like, for example, corresponding to the range of marks between 40–50, there are 50 students, corresponding to the range of marks between 50–60 there are 40 students; corresponding to the range of marks between 60–70 there are 20 students, and so on. There are three important forms of frequency diagrams, *viz*., (i) Histogram, (ii) Polygon, and (iii) Ogive. The present chapter focuses on these frequency diagrams.

## 1. Histogram

A Histogram is a graphical presentation of a frequency distribution of a continuous series. While constructing a Histogram, values of the variable are shown on the X-axis, and their frequencies on the Y-axis. Frequencies (corresponding to different class intervals) are shown by rectangles. The width of the rectangles are according to the width of the corresponding class intervals. Height of the rectangles is in proportion to the frequencies of the class intervals. Different rectangles meet each other from left to right. If the data are in the form of an inclusive series, these are first converted into exclusive series. It may be noted that Histograms are different from Bar diagrams because these are two-dimensional diagrams. Both length and breadth of the rectangles are considered for purpose of a comparison. Bar diagrams are only one-dimensional where only length of the bars is considered for purpose of a comparison.

**Note**

Histograms are drawn only when data are in the form of grouped frequency distribution or when the data are in the form of frequency distribution of continuous series. Histograms are never drawn for a discrete variable or for a data set making a discrete series.

If frequencies are expressed in terms of percentage in the distribution, then the same are shown as percentage on the graph instead of the number of items. Histograms of Frequency Distribution are of two types:

(i) Histograms of Equal Class Intervals, and

(ii) Histograms of Unequal Class Intervals.

**(i) Histograms of Equal Class Intervals:** Histograms of equal class intervals are those which are based on the data with equal class intervals. A series with equal class intervals would make a histogram including rectangles of equal width. Length of the rectangles would be different in proportion to the frequencies of the class intervals.

**ILLUSTRATION.**

The table below shows number of students of a college corresponding to different range of marks in Statistics.

Present the information in the form of a histogram:

| Marks | 0–10 | 10–20 | 20–30 | 30–40 | 40–50 | 50–60 | 60–70 |
|---|---|---|---|---|---|---|---|
| Number of Students | 5 | 10 | 15 | 20 | 12 | 8 | 4 |

**SOLUTION:**

**Number of Students Corresponding to Different Range of Marks in Statistics**

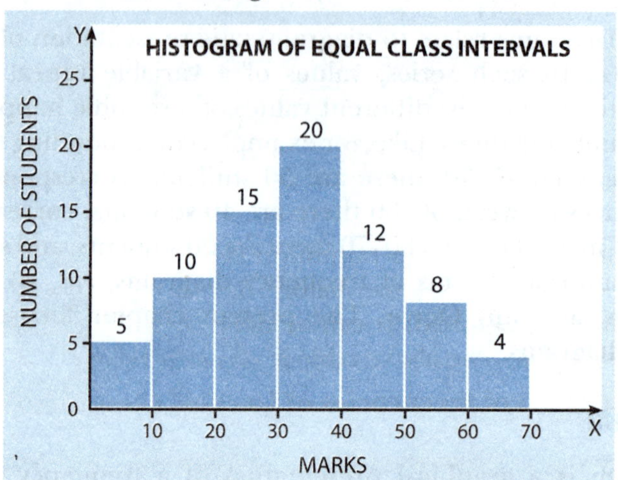


**(ii) Histograms of Unequal Class Intervals:** A histogram of unequal class interval is the one which is based on the data with unequal class intervals. When the data of class intervals are unequal, width of the rectangles would be different. The width of the rectangles would increase or decrease depending upon the increase or decrease in the size of the class intervals. *Before presenting the data in the form of graphs, frequencies of unequal class-intervals are adjusted.* First, we note a class of the smallest intervals. Other classes are noted in the increasing order of their class-intervals. If the size of one class interval is twice the smallest size in the series, frequency of that class is divided by '2'. Likewise, if the size of a class interval is three times the size of the smallest class interval in the series, frequency of that class is divided by '3' and so on.

**Adjustment Factor for any Class**

$$= \frac{\text{Class Interval of the Concerned Class}}{\text{Lowest Class Interval}}$$

To illustrate, suppose the class with the smallest intervals is 5–10, and the class with the largest interval is 10–20 the frequency of which is 12. Here the class interval of the bigger class is 10 which is twice as much as the size of the class interval of the smallest class, *i.e.*, 5. The bigger class interval is divided in two parts 10–15 and 15–20 and accordingly, the frequency of the bigger class, 12 would be divided by 2, that is 12 ÷ 2 = 6. The divider 2 in this case is called Adjustment Factor.

**Illustration.**

Present the following data in the form of a histogram:

| Weekly Wages (₹) | Number of Workers |
|---|---|
| 10–15 | 7 |
| 15–20 | 10 |
| 20–25 | 27 |
| 25–30 | 15 |
| 30–40 | 12 |
| 40–60 | 12 |
| 60–80 | 8 |

**Solution:**

In this frequency distribution minimum class interval is 5. Other class intervals are 10 and 20. Hence, before drawing the graph, frequency density should be calculated. It can be done by dividing frequencies by an adjustment factor. The above table is adjusted below:

**Adjustment of Frequencies of Unequal Class Intervals**

| Weekly Wages (₹) | Number of Workers | Adjustment Factor | Frequency Density |
|---|---|---|---|
| 10–15 | 7 | $\frac{5}{5} = 1$ | 7 ÷ 1 = 7 |
| 15–20 | 10 | $\frac{5}{5} = 1$ | 10 ÷ 1 = 10 |
| 20–25 | 27 | $\frac{5}{5} = 1$ | 27 ÷ 1 = 27 |
| 25–30 | 15 | $\frac{5}{5} = 1$ | 15 ÷ 1 = 15 |
| 30–40 | 12 | $\frac{10}{5} = 2$ | 12 ÷ 2 = 6 |
| 40–60 | 12 | $\frac{20}{5} = 4$ | 12 ÷ 4 = 3 |
| 60–80 | 8 | $\frac{20}{5} = 4$ | 8 ÷ 4 = 2 |

In the above table, the class interval for the first four classes is 5. Fifth class, however, is of the interval of 10 (40 – 30 = 10) which is twice as much as the class interval of the first four classes. Accordingly, frequency of the fifth class is divided by 2. Further, class interval of the 6th class is 20 (60 – 40 = 20) which is 4 times the minimum class interval of 5. Accordingly, frequency of this class is divided by 4. Likewise, the frequencies of other classes have been adjusted. It is based on this table that the histogram is drawn, on the next page:

## Number of Workers Corresponding to Different Range of Weekly Wages

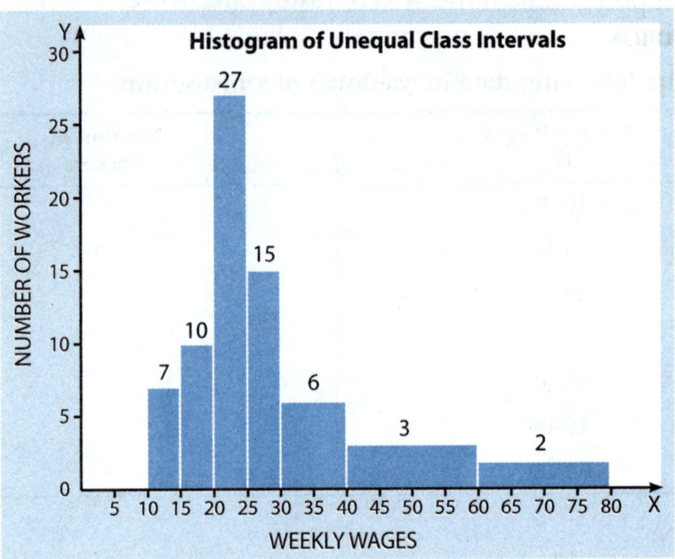


**What is the Difference between a Histogram and a Frequency Polygon?**

A histogram becomes a frequency polygon if we draw a line joining mid-points of the tops of all rectangles in a Histogram. It is important that the mid-points are joined using a foot-rule to make a straight line.

***Learning by doing***

*Visit different schools in your locality. Collect information on the daily wage earners. Your information should include (i) daily earnings, and (ii) number of wage earners. Convert the raw data into a continuous frequency distribution, and present your information in the form of a histogram.*

## 2. Polygon

Polygon is another form of diagrammatic presentation of data. It is formed by joining mid-points of the tops of all rectangles in a histogram. However, a polygon can be drawn even without constructing a histogram. For this, mid-values of the classes of a frequency distribution are marked on X-axis of the graph; the corresponding frequencies are marked on the Y-axis. Using a foot rule, all points indicating frequencies of the different classes are joined to make a graph, called frequency polygon. Both the sides of the frequency polygon are extended to meet the X-axis, at the mid-points of the immediately lower or higher imagined class intervals of zero frequency. This is done to ensure that the area of a frequency polygon is the same as that of the corresponding histogram.

**An Important Note**

It may be noted that while more than one polygon may be drawn on one graph paper, it is not possible to draw more than one histogram. Thus, when comparison of two frequency distribution is involved it is appropriate to present the data in the form of frequency polygons rather than histograms. When comparison is involved, frequency polygons are constructed using percentage value of the frequencies rather than their absolute values.

**ILLUSTRATION.**

Following table shows number of students of a college corresponding to different range of marks in Statistics. Make a frequency polygon.

| Marks | 0–10 | 10–20 | 20-30 | 30–40 | 40–50 | 50–60 | 60–70 |
|---|---|---|---|---|---|---|---|
| Number of Students | 5 | 10 | 15 | 20 | 12 | 8 | 5 |

**SOLUTION:**

A frequency polygon of the above data is presented in the following graph. In this graph, data have been first presented in the form of a histogram. Mid-points of the tops of rectangles in the Histogram have been marked and then joined using a scale or foot rule. The end-points of the polygon be joined to the immediate lower or higher mid-points (as the case may be) at zero frequency with the base-line. It is done to equate the area of polygon with the area of histogram. Here is an illustration of constructing a frequency polygon by making a histogram.

**Number of Students Corresponding to Different Range of Marks in Statistics**

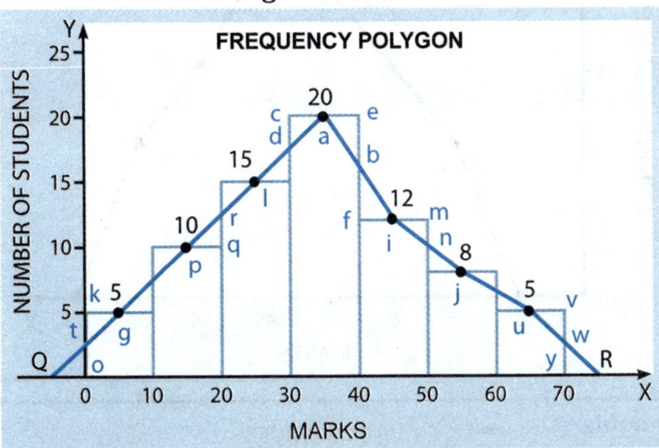


Frequency polygon can also be constructed without the help of histogram. Under this method, mid-points of various class intervals are taken and the corresponding frequencies to each mid-points are plotted. We can present the following data in the form of a frequency polygon without constructing a histogram.

**ILLUSTRATION.**

Present the following data in the form of frequency polygon:

| Marks | 10–20 | 20–30 | 30–40 | 40–50 | 50–60 | 60–70 |
|---|---|---|---|---|---|---|
| Number of Students | 10 | 15 | 20 | 22 | 15 | 10 |

**SOLUTION:**

To construct a frequency polygon without first constructing a histogram, one should first mark mid-points of the class intervals on the X-axis. Frequencies are then marked corresponding to those mid-points. Different points of frequencies are joined to make a frequency polygon.

| Marks | Mid-value | Number of Students |
|---|---|---|
| 10–20 | $\frac{10+20}{2} = 15$ | 10 |
| 20–30 | $\frac{20+30}{2} = 25$ | 15 |
| 30–40 | $\frac{30+40}{2} = 35$ | 20 |
| 40–50 | $\frac{40+50}{2} = 45$ | 22 |
| 50–60 | $\frac{50+60}{2} = 55$ | 15 |
| 60–70 | $\frac{60+70}{2} = 65$ | 10 |

Based on these data, frequency polygon has been drawn without constructing a histogram as given below.

**A Necessary Caution on the area Under a Histogram and Frequency Polygon**

Total area under a histogram should be equal to total area under a polygon. While joining mid-points on the top of the rectangles (in a histogram) some area like that of Δaeb or Δacd gets excluded. But some area as of Δpqr or Δifb gets included. Sum of the excluded area should be equal to sum of the included area so that total area under a histogram is equal to the total area under a polygon. Accordingly, to compensate for the loss of the area Δgkt we extend the Ist class interval (0–10) to the left by the same equal width and mark half of its size (10/2 = 5) as the starting point (Q in the figure) of the polygon. Likewise, to compensate for the loss of the area Δuvw, we extend the last class interval (60–70) to the right by the same equal width and mark half of its size (10/2 = 5) as the end point (R) in the picture of the polygon. Thus, the extended area of ΔotQ compensates for the area of Δgkt in the beginning and the extended area of ΔyRw compensates for the area of Δuvw at the end.

### Number of Students Corresponding to Different Range of Marks

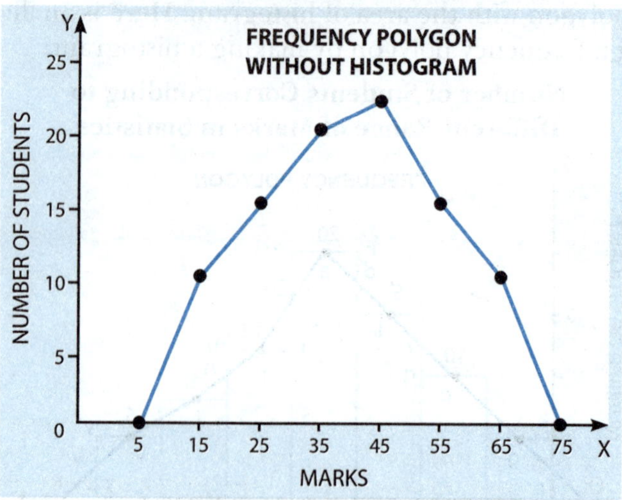


> *Learning by doing*
>
> *Collect data on the CBSE result (2014) for Class X in your school. Discuss with your teacher how can you present the information in terms of a frequency polygon. Write your observations on the performance of your school students.*

## 3. Frequency Curve

It is just a variant of polygon. A Frequency Curve is a curve which is plotted by joining the mid-points of all tops of a histogram by **freehand smoothed curves** and not by straight lines. Area of a frequency curve is equal to the area of a histogram or frequency polygon of a given data set. While drawing a frequency curve, we should eliminate angularity of the polygon. Accordingly, points of a frequency polygon are joined through a freehand smoothed curve rather than straight lines.

> **The basic difference between a Frequency Polygon and a Frequency Curve**
>
> Both frequency polygon and frequency curve are drawn by joining the mid-points of all tops of a histogram. But in case of frequency polygon the points are joined using a foot-rule (to make a straight line), whereas in case of frequency curve the points are joined using a freehand.

**ILLUSTRATION.**

Make a frequency curve of the following data:

| Age (Years) | 0–10 | 10–20 | 20–30 | 30–40 | 40–50 | 50–60 | 60–70 | 70–80 |
|---|---|---|---|---|---|---|---|---|
| Number of Residents | 150 | 300 | 500 | 800 | 1,000 | 900 | 400 | 100 |

**SOLUTION:**

The given data set is first converted into a histogram. Mid-points of the top of the rectangles of the histogram are marked. These points are joined through a freehand smoothed curve, on the next page:

**Number of Residents Corresponding to Different Age Groups**

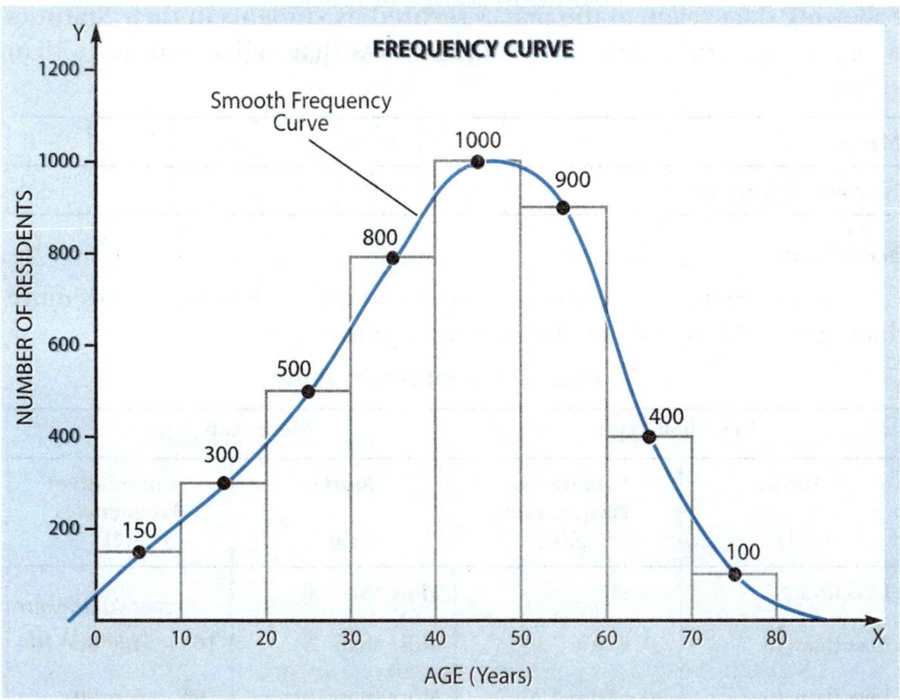


## 4. Ogive or Cumulative Frequency Curve

*Ogive or Cumulative Frequency Curve is the curve which is constructed by plotting cumulative frequency data on the graph paper, in the form of a smooth curve.*

A cumulative frequency curve or ogive may be constructed in two ways:

**(i) Less than Method:** In this method, beginning from upper limit of the 1st class interval we go on adding the frequencies corresponding to every next upper limit of the series. Thus in a series showing 0–5, 5–10 and 10–15 as different class intervals, we will find the frequency for less than 5, for less than 10 and for less than 15. The frequencies are added up to make '*Less than Ogive*'.

**(ii) More than Method:** In this method, we take cumulative total of the frequencies beginning with lower limit of the 1st class interval. Thus, in a series showing 0–5, 5–10 and 10–15 as different class intervals, we find the frequency for more than 0, for more than 5 and for more than 10. The frequencies thus presented make a '*More than Ogive*'.

**The Basic Difference between 'Less than' and 'More than' Ogives**

In less than ogives, frequencies are added starting from the upper limit of the 1st class interval of the frequency distribution. On the other hand, in case of 'more than' ogives, frequencies are added starting from the lower limit of the 1st class interval of the frequency distribution. Accordingly, while in case of 'less than' ogive the cumulative total tends to increase, in case of 'more than' ogive, the cumulative total tends to decrease.

**ILLUSTRATION.**

Following data relate to the marks secured by students in their Statistics paper. Graph these data in the form of less than ogive and more than ogive.

| Marks | 0–5 | 5–10 | 10–15 | 15–20 | 20–25 | 25–30 | 30–35 | 35–40 |
|---|---|---|---|---|---|---|---|---|
| Number of Students | 4 | 6 | 10 | 10 | 25 | 22 | 18 | 5 |

**SOLUTION:**

First we construct a cumulative frequency table of 'less than' and 'more than' type, and then draw the graphs, as under:

**Cumulative Frequency Table**

| Less than Type | | More than Type | |
|---|---|---|---|
| Marks (1) | Cumulative Frequencies (2) | Marks (3) | Cumulative Frequencies (4) |
| Less than 5 | 4 | More than 0 | 100 |
| Less than 10 | 4 + 6 = 10 | More than 5 | 100 – 4 = 96 |
| Less than 15 | 10 +10 = 20 | More than 10 | 96 – 6 = 90 |
| Less than 20 | 20 +10 = 30 | More than 15 | 90 – 10 = 80 |
| Less than 25 | 30 +25 = 55 | More than 20 | 80 – 10 = 70 |
| Less than 30 | 55 +22 = 77 | More than 25 | 70 – 25 = 45 |
| Less than 35 | 77 +18 = 95 | More than 30 | 45 – 22 = 23 |
| Less than 40 | 95 + 5 = 100 | More than 35 | 23 – 18 = 5 |
| | | More than 40 | 5 – 5 = 0 |

Graph A shows 'less than' cumulative frequencies, Graph B shows 'more than' cumulative frequencies, and Graph C shows both the 'less than' as well as 'more than' frequencies simultaneously.

**Students obtaining Marks in Statistics**

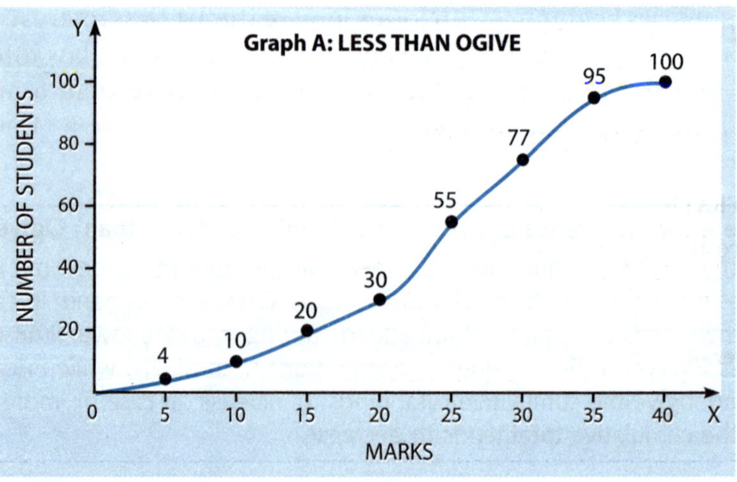

**Students obtaining Marks in Statistics**

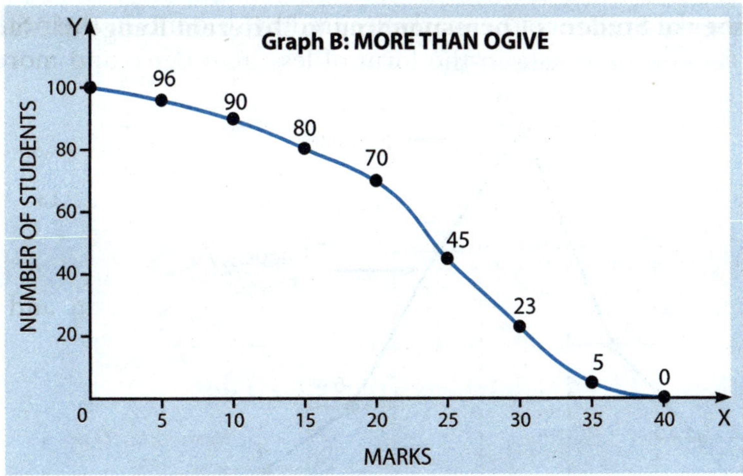


**Students obtaining Marks in Statistics**

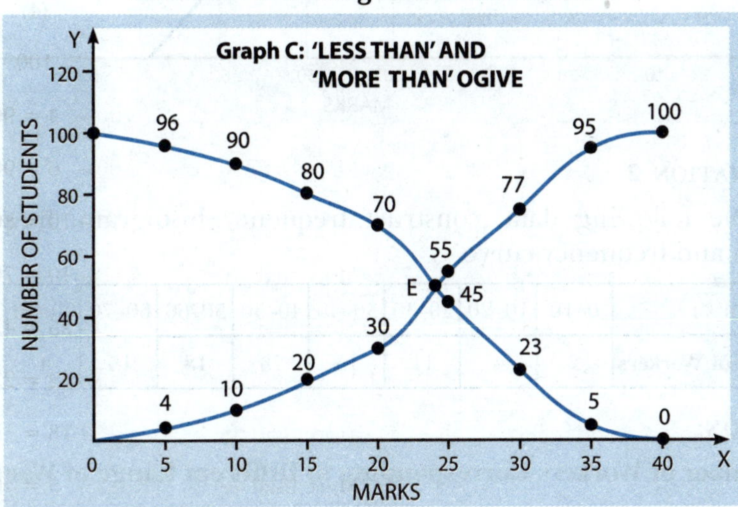


> ***Learning by doing***
>
> *Get information from your class mates on the monthly pocket allowance they get from their parents. Present the raw data in terms of a continuous frequency distribution. Show cumulative frequencies of your statistical series. Present your information in the form of (i) Less than ogive, and (ii) More than ogive.*

## MISCELLANEOUS ILLUSTRATIONS

### ILLUSTRATION 1.

Prepare histogram and frequency polygon from the following data:

| Marks | 0–10 | 10–20 | 20–30 | 30–40 | 40–50 | 50–60 |
|---|---|---|---|---|---|---|
| Number of Students | 5 | 8 | 15 | 11 | 6 | 4 |

**SOLUTION:**

**Number of Students Corresponding to Different Range of Marks**

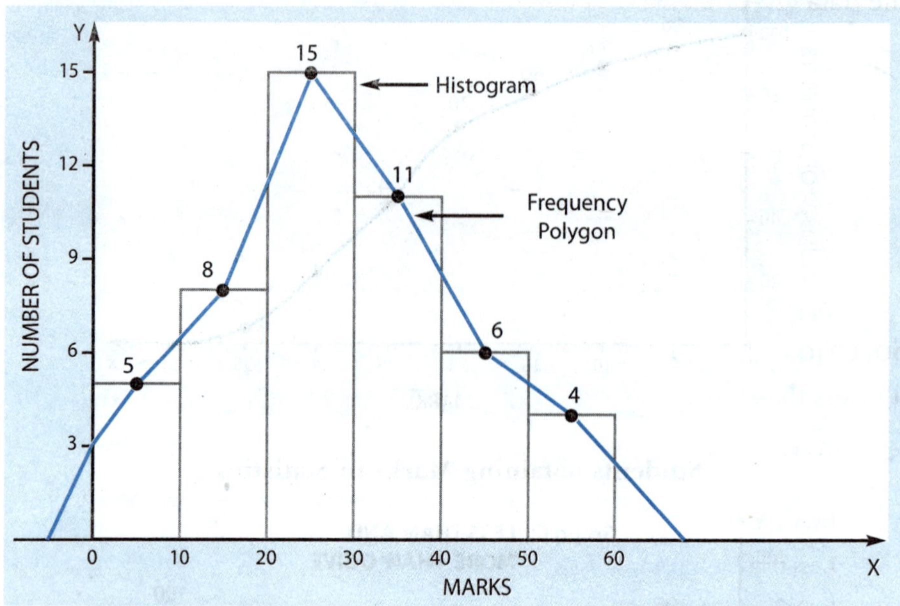


**ILLUSTRATION 2.**

From the following data, construct frequency histogram, frequency polygon and frequency curve.

| Wages (in ₹) | 0–10 | 10–20 | 20–30 | 30–40 | 40–50 | 50–60 | 60–70 | 70–80 | 80–90 |
|---|---|---|---|---|---|---|---|---|---|
| Number of Workers | 2 | 4 | 11 | 15 | 25 | 18 | 15 | 4 | 1 |

**SOLUTION:**

**Number of Workers Corresponding to Different Range of Wages**

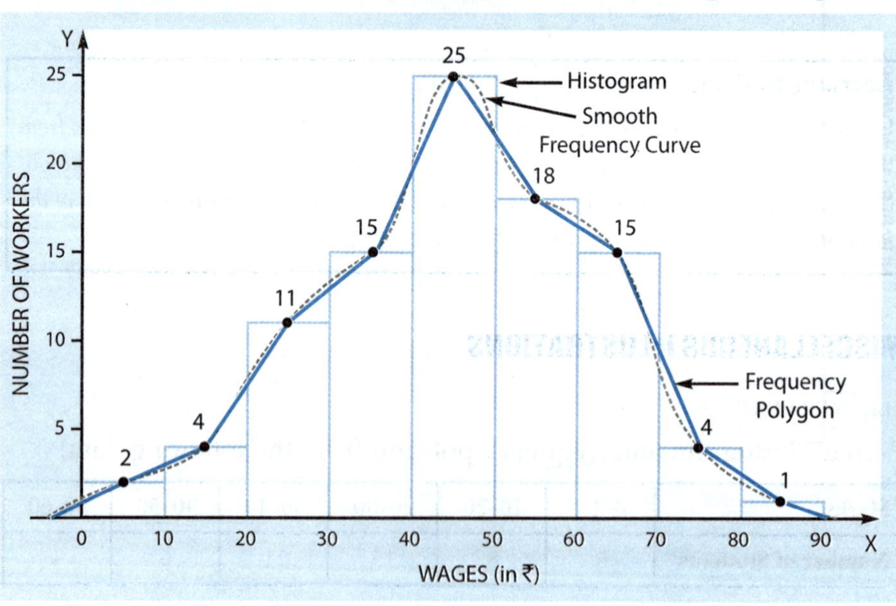

**ILLUSTRATION 3.**

Draw the 'less than' and 'more than' ogive on the same graph paper from the data given below:

| Weekly Wages (₹) | Number of Workers |
|---|---|
| 0–20 | 10 |
| 20–40 | 20 |
| 40–60 | 40 |
| 60–80 | 20 |
| 80–100 | 10 |

**SOLUTION:**

(i) 'Less than' method

| Weekly Wages (₹) | c.f. |
|---|---|
| Less than 20 | 10 |
| Less than 40 | 30 |
| Less than 60 | 70 |
| Less than 80 | 90 |
| Less than 100 | 100 |

(ii) 'More than' method

| Weekly Wages (₹) | c.f. |
|---|---|
| More than 0 | 100 |
| More than 20 | 90 |
| More than 40 | 70 |
| More than 60 | 30 |
| More than 80 | 10 |

Both 'less than' and 'more than' ogives based on the above data are presented in the following graph:

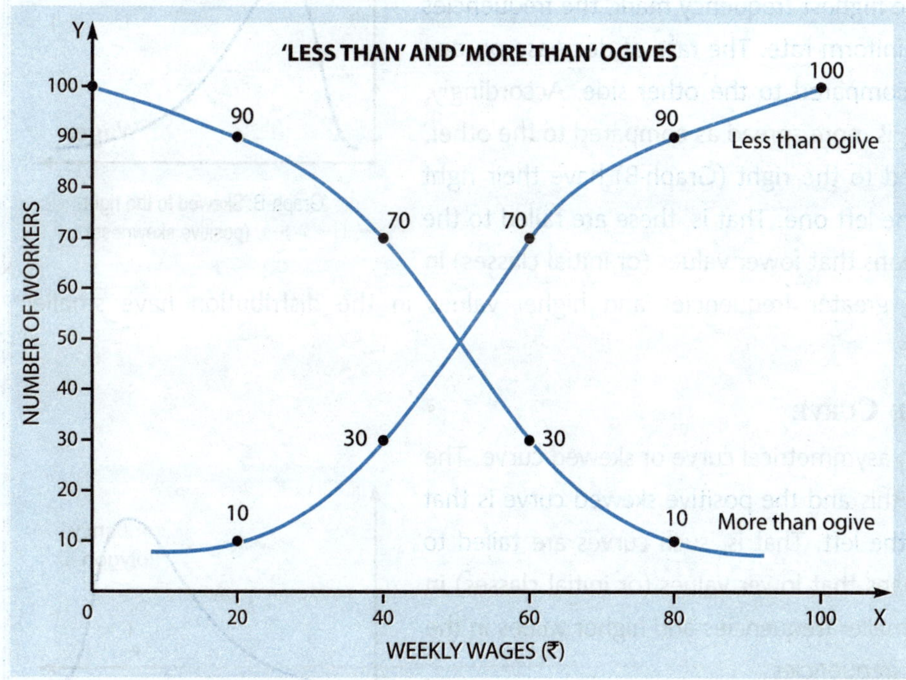

# APPENDIX

## Different Shapes of Frequency Curves

Frequency Curves are of different shapes. These shapes indicate the nature of frequency distributions of different data-sets. Some of the important shapes of frequency curves are as under:

### (1) Normal Curve or Symmetrical Curve

Graph-A shows a normal curve or symmetrical curve. In such curves, frequencies tend to increase gradually, followed by the tendency to stabilise and finally the tendency to decline. The highest frequency in such curves lies at the top center of the curve. The highest frequency, decreases on its either side at the uniform rate.

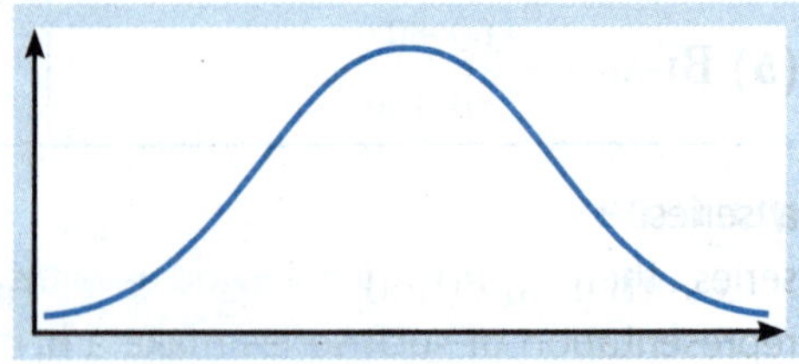

Graph-A: Symmetrical of Bell Shaped

This type of curve is symmetrical about a line which divides the curve in two equal parts. Such curves are also called Bell shaped. In practical life normal curves are very rare. However, these are of immense significance in the context of statistical analysis. Normal curves are extremely useful in understanding problems relating to sampling of data.

### (2) Positive Skewed Curve

This is one of the asymmetrical curves or skewed curves. Asymmetry or Skewness is that feature of a statistical distribution which indicates that, on both sides of the highest frequency mark, the frequencies do not decrease at the uniform rate. The rate of decrease on one side is less or more as compared to the other side. Accordingly, the one side of the curve is more spread as compared to the other. Curves which are skewed to the right (Graph-B) have their right side more spread than the left one. That is, these are tailed to the right. Obviously, this means that lower values (or initial classes) in such distributions have greater frequencies and higher values in the distribution have smaller frequencies.

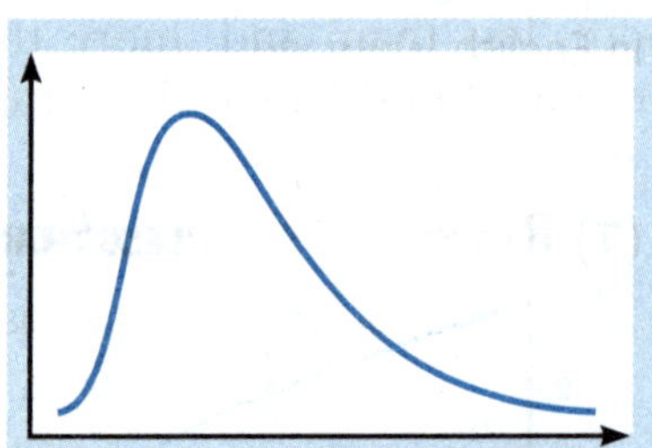

Graph-B: Skewed to the right (positive skewness)

### (3) Negative Skewed Curve

This is another kind of an asymmetrical curve or skewed curve. The only difference between this and the positive skewed curve is that this curve is skewed to the left. That is, such curves are tailed to the left (Graph-C). It means that lower values (or initial classes) in such distributions have smaller frequencies and higher values in the distribution have greater frequencies.

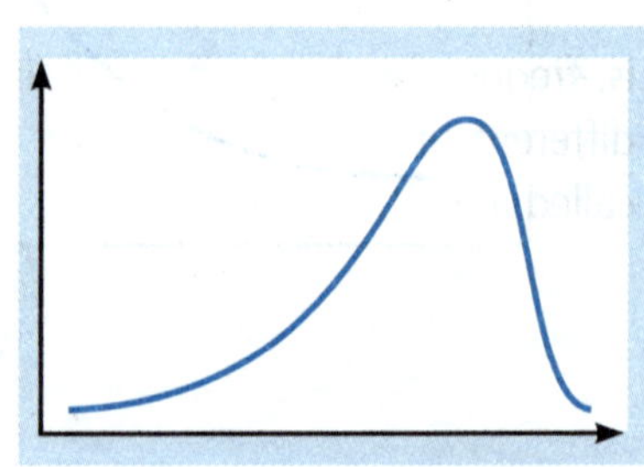

Graph-C: Skewed to the left (negative skewness)

## (4) U-Shaped Curve

U-shaped curves are formed if there are two high points in a series both having equal or nearly equal frequency, at the lowest and highest values (Graph-D). Most of the frequencies of a distribution are thus concentrated around the lowest and highest class intervals. There are only few frequencies marks corresponding to middle class intervals.

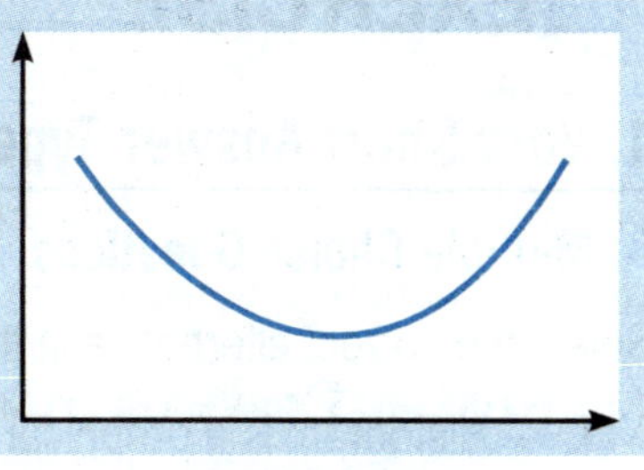

Graph-D: U-Shaped

## (5) Bi-modal Curve

Graph-E shows a Bi-modal curve. This curve is drawn when, in a series, there are two classes with highest frequencies. In such series, there is no unique modal value. That is why the graphic representation of such series make a Bi-modal curve.

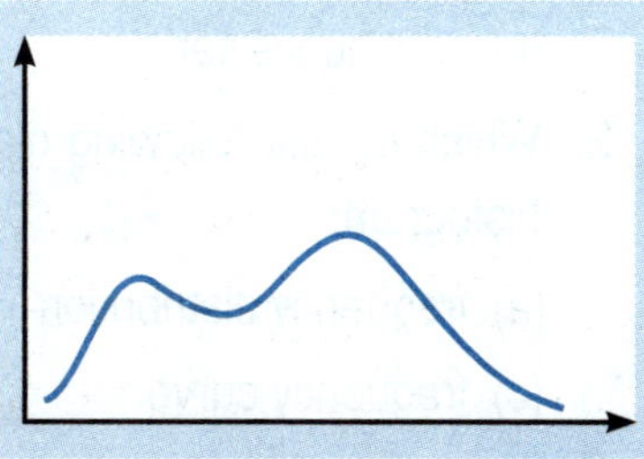

Graph-E: Bi-modal

## (6) J-Shaped Curve

Graph-F shows a J-shaped curve. This is drawn when, in a distribution, frequencies tend to increase with each class interval. In other words the curve moves from the low frequencies to the high frequencies. Thus, highest frequencies are found around the upper end of the curve. Such curves are shaped like the letter 'J' in English language.

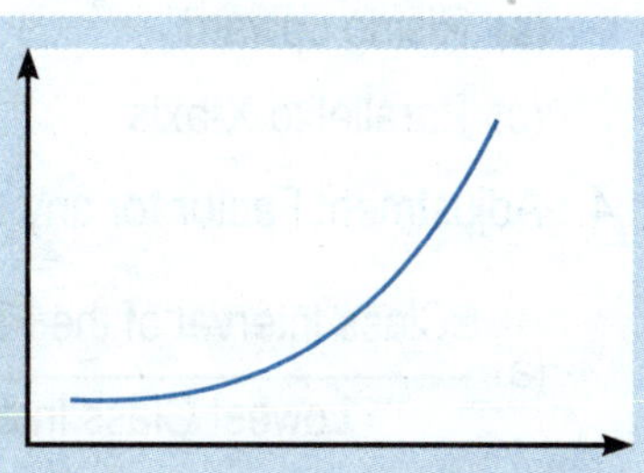

Graph-F: J-Shaped

## (7) Reverse J-Shaped Curve

Graph-G shows a reverse J-shaped curve. This type of curve is drawn when there are highest frequencies corresponding to lowest values in the distribution. Conversely, there are lowest frequencies corresponding to highest values in the distribution.

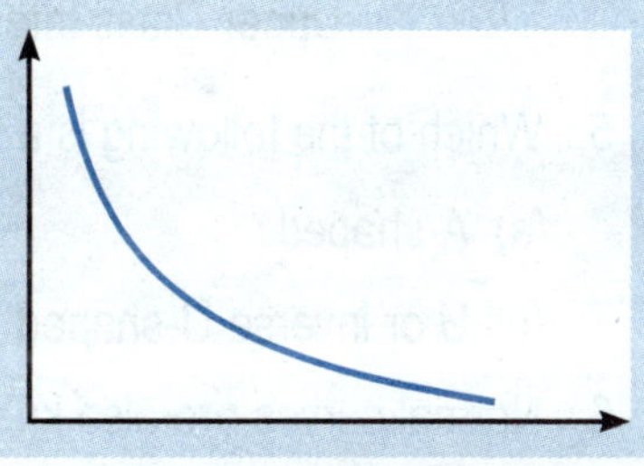

Graph-G: Reverse J-Shaped

## (8) Mixed Curve or Multi-modal Curve

These curves are formed when there is no specific pattern of the frequencies corresponding to different values (or classes) in the given distribution of data. That is, frequencies keep on increasing and decreasing corresponding to different classes in the data set. Graph H shows a mixed curve, also called a multi-modal curve.

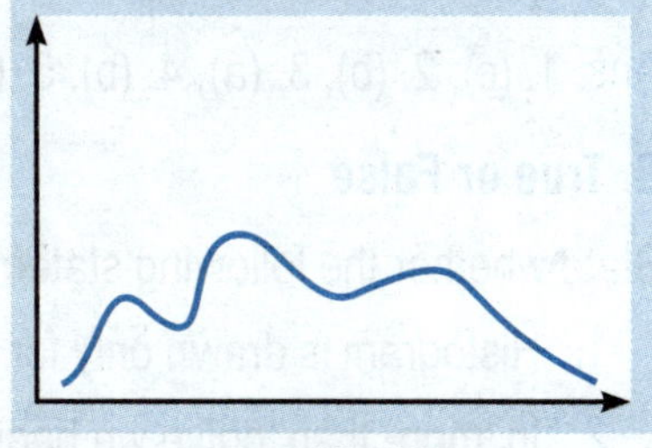

Graph-H: Mixed Curve

# EXERCISE

## 1. Very Short Answer Type Questions [1 mark]

### A. Multiple Choice Questions: Choose the Correct Answer

Select the correct alternative in the following questions:

1. A Histogram is a graphical presentation of a frequency distribution of a:
   (a) individual series (b) discrete series
   (c) continuous series (d) none of these
2. Which of the following diagrams is drawn by joining mid-points of the tops of all rectangles in a histogram:
   (a) frequency distribution (b) frequency polygon
   (c) frequency curve (d) none of these
3. What is the shape of 'less than ogive'?
   (a) Rising upward (b) Falling downward
   (c) Parallel to X-axis (d) Parallel to Y-axis
4. Adjustment Factor for any Class is equal to:
   (a) $\frac{\text{Class Interval of the First Class}}{\text{Lowest Class Interval}}$ (b) $\frac{\text{Class Interval of the Concerned Class}}{\text{Lowest Class Interval}}$
   (c) $\frac{\text{Class Interval of the First Class}}{\text{Upper Class Interval}}$ (d) $\frac{\text{Class Interval of the Concerned Class}}{\text{Upper Class Interval}}$
5. Which of the following is a shape of frequency distribution curve?
   (a) A-shaped (b) B-shaped
   (c) U or inverse U-shaped (d) All of these
6. Normal curves are also known as:
   (a) J-shaped curves (b) L-shaped curves
   (c) U-shaped curves (d) bell-shaped curves

Ans. 1. (c), 2. (b), 3. (a), 4. (b), 5. (c), 6. (d).

### B. True or False

State whether the following statements are True or False:

1. Histogram is drawn only for equal class intervals. (True/False)
2. In 'more than' ogive we begin from lower limit of the first class interval. (True/False)
3. A frequency curve is drawn by joining the mid-points of all tops of a histogram by straight lines. (True/False)

4. When a curve is drawn based on a series where there are two classes with highest frequencies is called bi-modal curve. (True/False)
5. Positively skewed curves have their tail more spread towards right. (True/False)

Ans. 1. False, 2. True, 3. False, 4. True, 5. True.

### C. Concepts/Definitions & Knowledge-based Questions

1. What are the frequency diagrams?

Ans. Frequency Diagrams relate to diagrammatic presentation of 'frequency distributions'.

2. What is meant by a histogram?

Ans. A Histogram is a graphical presentation of a frequency distribution of a continuous series.

3. Define frequency polygon.

Ans. All mid-points indicating frequencies of the different classes joined to make a graph are called frequency polygon.

4. What is a frequency curve?

Ans. A Frequency Curve is a curve which is plotted by joining the mid-points of all tops of a histogram by freehand smoothed curves and not by straight lines.

5. What is meant by an ogive?

Ans. Ogive is the curve which is constructed by plotting cumulative frequency data on the graph paper, in the form of a smooth curve.

## 2. Short Answer Type Questions [3-4 marks]

1. What is a histogram? Describe its types.
2. Explain frequency polygon.
3. Explain frequency curve.
4. What is the difference between histogram and frequency polygon?
5. Describe cumulative frequency curve.
6. Differentiate between histogram and bar diagrams.
7. Describe the procedure of drawing a histogram, when class intervals are (i) equal, and (ii) unequal.
8. Describe the procedure of drawing a (i) frequency polygon, and (ii) frequency curve.

## 3. Long Answer Type Questions [6 marks]

1. How is a frequency polygon different from a frequency curve? Draw the two diagrams taking an imaginary set of data.
2. (i) What does the total area under a frequency curve represent?
   (ii) What does the area, under a frequency curve, to the left of the ordinate at X = $\alpha$, represent; where $\alpha$ is some value of X within the total range?

## 4. Essential Practicals

1. Represent the following frequency distribution graphically:

| Number of Children | Number of Families |
|---|---|
| 0 | 5 |
| 1 | 10 |
| 2 | 20 |
| 3 | 25 |
| 4 | 30 |
| 5 | 10 |
| | Total = 100 |

2. Construct histogram, frequency polygon and frequency curve from the following data:

| Marks Obtained | 0–10 | 10–20 | 20–30 | 30–40 | 40–50 | 50–60 | 60–70 | 70–80 |
|---|---|---|---|---|---|---|---|---|
| Number of Students | 10 | 16 | 20 | 20 | 22 | 15 | 8 | 5 |

3. Make a frequency polygon and histogram using the given data:

| Marks Obtained | 10-20 | 20-30 | 30-40 | 40-50 | 50-60 | 60-70 |
|---|---|---|---|---|---|---|
| Number of Students | 5 | 12 | 15 | 22 | 14 | 4 |

4. Draw 'less than' and 'more than' ogive curves from the following data:

| Marks | 0–5 | 5–10 | 10–15 | 15–20 | 20–25 | 25–30 | 30–35 | 35–40 |
|---|---|---|---|---|---|---|---|---|
| Number of Students | 7 | 10 | 20 | 13 | 12 | 19 | 14 | 9 |

5. What is meant by ogive or cumulative frequency curve? From the following distribution construct the 'less than' ogive:

| Capital (in lakh) | 0–10 | 10–20 | 20–30 | 30–40 | 40–50 | 50–60 | 60–70 |
|---|---|---|---|---|---|---|---|
| Number of Companies | 2 | 3 | 7 | 11 | 15 | 7 | 23 |

6. Present the data given in the table below in a histogram:

| Marks | 0–10 | 10–20 | 20–30 | 30–40 | 40–50 | 50–60 | 60–70 | 70–80 |
|---|---|---|---|---|---|---|---|---|
| Frequency | 4 | 10 | 16 | 22 | 26 | 18 | 8 | 2 |

7. Draw a histogram from the following data relating to the monthly pocket allowance of the students of Class XI of a school:

| Size | 0–5 | 5–10 | 10–15 | 15–20 | 20–25 | 25–30 | 30–35 | 35–40 |
|---|---|---|---|---|---|---|---|---|
| Number of Students | 5 | 10 | 15 | 20 | 25 | 15 | 10 | 5 |

8. We are given the following marks secured by 25 students in an examination.

23, 28, 30, 32, 35, 36, 36, 40, 41, 43, 44, 44, 45, 48, 49, 52, 53, 54, 56, 56, 58, 61, 62, 65, 68.

(i) Arrange this data in the form of a frequency distribution taking the following class intervals. 20–29, 30–39, 40–49, 50–59 and 60–69.

(ii) Draw the frequency polygon and ogive for the above data.

9. Present the following data in the form of a histogram:

| **Mid-point** | 115 | 125 | 135 | 145 | 155 | 165 | 175 | 185 | 195 |
|---|---|---|---|---|---|---|---|---|---|
| **Size** | 6 | 55 | 48 | 72 | 116 | 60 | 38 | 22 | 3 |

[Hint: First, convert the data into a continuous frequency table; *e.g.*, 115 will be 110–120.]

10. The frequency distribution of marks obtained by students in a class test is given below. Draw frequency polygon and ogive.

| **Marks** | 0–10 | 10–20 | 20–30 | 30–40 | 40–50 |
|---|---|---|---|---|---|
| **Number of Students** | 3 | 10 | 14 | 10 | 3 |

11. (i) Construct a histogram and frequency polygon of the following distribution:

| **Marks** | 0–10 | 10–20 | 20–30 | 30–40 | 40–50 |
|---|---|---|---|---|---|
| **Number of Students** | 8 | 18 | 35 | 25 | 14 |

(ii) Show that the area under frequency polygon is equal to the area under histogram.

[**Hints:** (a) Make class intervals of 10 taking first class interval as 0–10.

(b) Area of histogram and polygon are equal, because the area which is left out of the histogram is included in the polygon.]

12. Draw a frequency polygon from the following data by using (i) histogram, and (ii) without using histogram:

| **Daily Wages (in ₹)** | 10–15 | 15–20 | 20–25 | 25–30 | 30–35 |
|---|---|---|---|---|---|
| **Number of Workers** | 40 | 70 | 60 | 80 | 60 |

13. Draw 'less than' as well as 'more than' ogives for the following data:

| **Weight (in kg)** | 30–34 | 35–39 | 40–44 | 45–49 | 50–54 | 55–59 | 60–64 |
|---|---|---|---|---|---|---|---|
| **Frequency** | 3 | 5 | 12 | 18 | 14 | 6 | 2 |

[Hint: Convert into Exclusive Series]

## 5. NCERT Textbook Questions [With Hints to Answers]

1. Data represented through a histogram can help in finding graphically the:

(i) mean (ii) mode

(iii) median (iv) all of the above

[(ii)]

2. Ogives can be helpful in locating graphically the:

   (i) mode (ii) mean

   (iii) median (iv) none of the above

   [(iii)]

3. Width of rectangles in a histogram should essentially be equal (true/false).

   [True]

4. Histogram can only be formed with continuous classification of data (true/false).

   [True]

5. Histogram and column diagram are the same method of presentation of data (true/false).

   [False]

6. Mode of a frequency distribution can be known graphically with the help of histogram (true/false).

   [True]

7. Median of a frequency distribution cannot be known from the ogives (true/false).

   [False]

8. How does the procedure of drawing a histogram differ when class intervals are unequal in comparison to equal class intervals in a frequency table?

   [Page 113-116]

# Arithmetic Line-Graphs or Time Series Graphs

# 8

When a set of statistical data are presented on a graph paper, it is called a graph. Presenting the data on a graph paper, we get different points, each point corresponding to a value of a statistical series. By joining the points we get a line which shows how a variable tends to change. Each point on the line corresponds to an arithmetic value of the variable under study, like, for example the value of exports or imports. Therefore, a graph showing arithmetic values of a variable (on a graph paper) is called 'arithmetic line-graph'. Often such graphs are constructed to present time series data, that is, the data (like the value of exports or imports) corresponding to different weeks, months or the years. Therefore, arithmetic line-graphs are often called **'time series graphs'.**

## 1. Construction of a Graph

Keeping in mind the size and nature of data, a suitable intersecting point on the graph paper is assumed as a *Point of Origin* as point 'O' in the adjacent picture. Horizontal and vertical lines intersecting through this point are shown as bold lines. These bold lines are called *Axis*. Horizontal line from left to right is called *Horizontal Axis*, *Abscissa* or *X-axis*. The line going upward or downward is called *Vertical Axis, Ordinate or Y-axis*. The X-axis and Y-axis are mutually perpendicular to each other. These axes divide the plain of the paper in four parts. Each part is called 'quadrant' as in the adjoining graph.

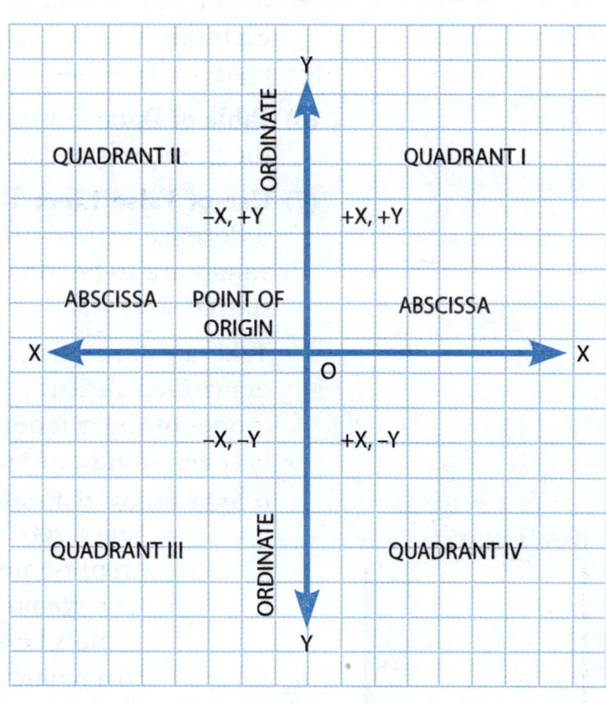


Point of origin in the graph is indicated by the English letter 'O'. Positive values of X are taken towards right side on the horizontal axis and of Y towards upper side on the vertical line. Negative values of X are taken towards the left side on horizontal line and of Y towards the lower side on vertical line. Thus, in the first quadrant, both X and Y are positive, in the second, X is –ve while Y is +ve; in the third quadrant both X and Y are –ve; and in the fourth X is +ve while

Y is –ve. In most cases, the data are positive figures. These are therefore presented only in the first quadrant.

## Rules for Constructing a Graph

The following points must be kept in mind while constructing a graph:

(1) **Heading:** Every graph must have a suitable and precise heading. Heading must be self-explanatory about the nature of information in the graph.

(2) **Choice of Scale:** One should fix an appropriate scale on which data should be presented. An appropriate scale is the one by which the entire data are easily represented by the graph. The graph should be on the middle of the graph paper to make it attractive.

> **You Must Note it**
>
> Graphs are always drawn with reference to some scale. The choice of scale depends on the values and volume of data.

(3) **Proportion of Axis:** As far as possible, length of X-axis on the graph paper should be one and a half (1½) times the length of Y-axis.

(4) **Method of Plotting the Points:** Economics and business Statistics are generally positive. These are to be presented in the first quadrant. Accordingly, the point of origin is fixed to the left and lower portion of the graph paper. On the X-axis, the points are plotted from left to right and on the Y-axis, the points are plotted upward from bottom to top.

(5) **Lines of Different Types:** If more than one line or curve are to be drawn in the same graph, these lines should be differentiated from each other in the form of broken lines (- - - - -), dotted lines (.....), bold lines (———), etc.

(6) **Table of Data:** It would be useful to give the table of data along with the graph of the data. This helps verification of the graph.

(7) **Use of False Line:** If the values in a series are very large and the difference between the smallest value and zero is high and if these values are to be indicated on Y-axis of the graph, then the Y-axis is started somewhere above the point 'O'.

Take an illustration. Suppose, in 2011, 35,000 tonnes of sugar is demanded, in 2012, 35,200 tonnes of sugar is demanded, and 35,800 tonnes of sugar is demanded in 2013. In such a case, the difference between minimum quantity of sugar (*i.e.*, 35,000 tonnes) and zero is very large. It would not be proper to write 35,000 immediately after zero on the Y-axis. If done, the entire data will be represented on a very small portion of the graph paper. A large portion of the graph paper will go waste. It would simply be a clumsy presentation of the statistical data. We overcome this difficulty by showing a cut or kink on the Y-axis, as in the adjoining picture. On the other hand, if these values are to be indicated on X-axis, then a cut or kink is marked on the X-axis.

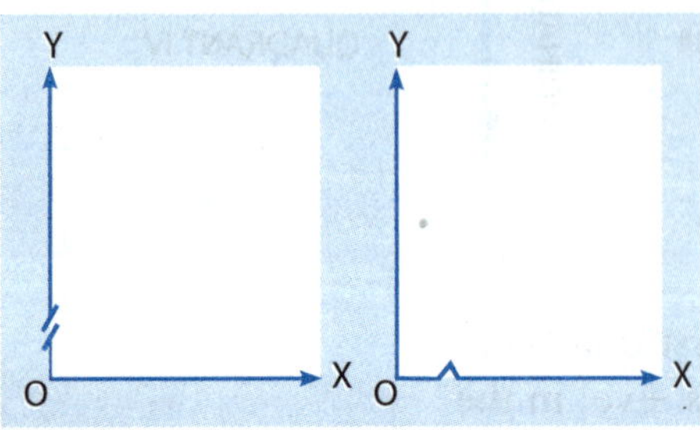

(8) **To Draw a Line or Curve:** We mark different points on the graph paper corresponding to different values of a series. These points are joined to make a line or a curve. The joining line must be uniform throughout its length. It should not be of different thickness at its different points.

## One Variable Graphs

One variable graphs are those graphs in which values of only one variable are shown with respect to some time period. Graphic presentation of the production of a factory between the months of January and June of a year, would be one variable graph.

**ILLUSTRATION.**

Following table shows production of a factory between January and June. Present the information in the form of a one variable time series graph.

| Month | January | February | March | April | May | June |
|---|---|---|---|---|---|---|
| Production (Quintals) | 5 | 7.5 | 5 | 10 | 12.5 | 15 |

**SOLUTION:**

Take the following steps:

(i) Indicate time period (in terms of months) on the X-axis, and production on the Y-axis.

(ii) Mark different points on the graph indicating values of production corresponding to different months.

(iii) Join the points to get a graph showing the behaviour of production over time.

**Monthly Production of a Factory (Quintals)**

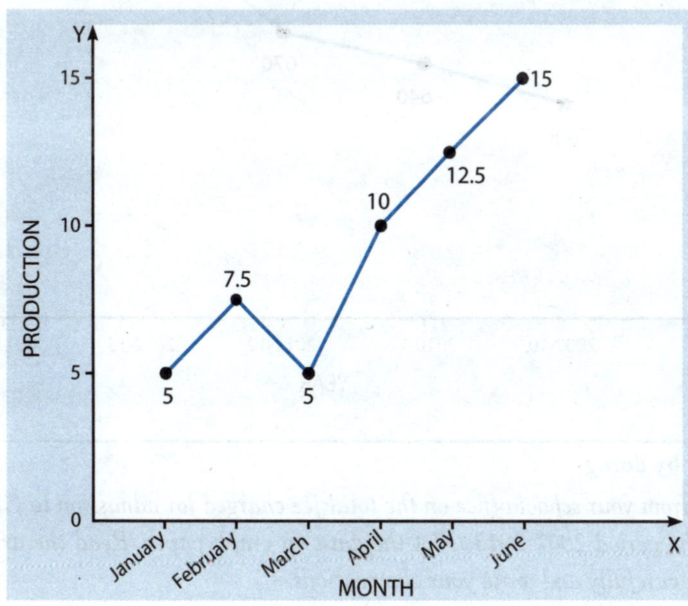

**Use of False Line:** The use of false line is very common with respect to time series data. Following illustration explains how exactly it is done.

**Illustration.**

Following table gives hypothetical figures of exports from India during the years 2009-10 to 2013-14. Present the information in the form of a suitable graph.

| Year | 2009-10 | 2010-11 | 2011-12 | 2012-13 | 2013-14 |
|---|---|---|---|---|---|
| **Exports (₹ crore)** | 600 | 640 | 670 | 780 | 900 |

**Solution:**

Presentation of these data involves the construction of a false line. Because: (i) difference between the minimum export value and zero is very large, and (ii) various values of exports show large difference. Data are presented in a graph with a false base line as under:

**Exports from India (2009-10 to 2013-14)**
**(₹ crore)**

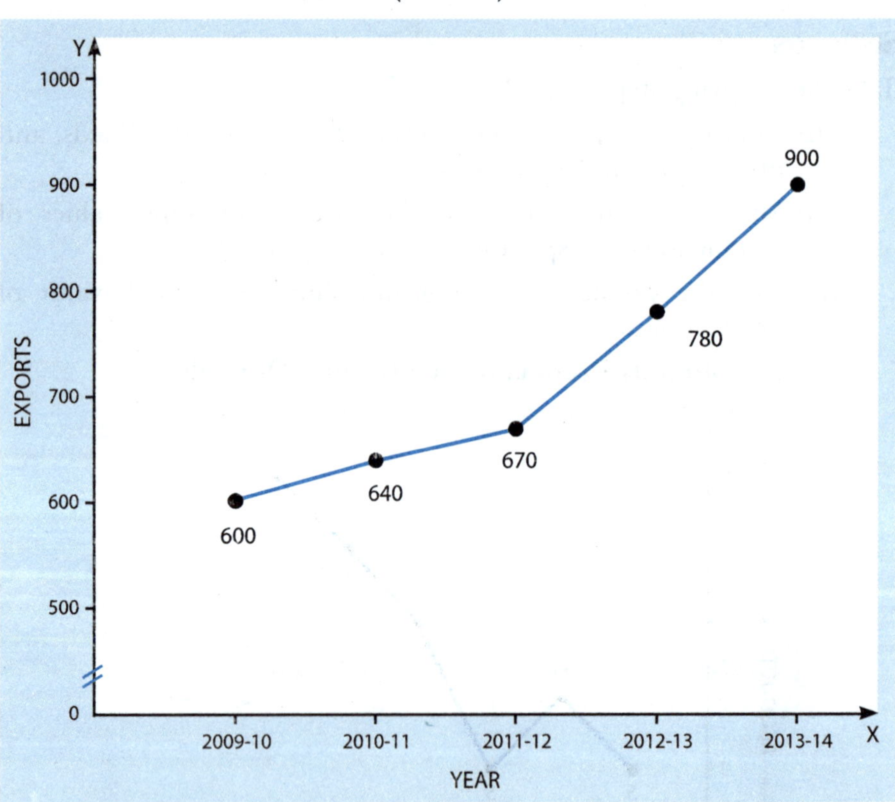


> ***Learning by doing***
>
> *Get data from your school office on the total fee charged for admission to Class XI, between the period 2007-2013. Plot the data on graph paper. Read the arithmetic line graph carefully and write your observations.*

## Two or More than Two Variable Graphs

*These are the graphs in which values of two (or more than two) variables are simultaneously shown with respect to some period of time*. Data on the production and sale of a factory in different months would make a two variable graph. Following illustration should make this point clear.

**ILLUSTRATION.**

The following table gives data on the production and sales of a factory (in thousand rupees) between January and June. Present the information in the form of a two variable arithmetic-line graph.

| Month | January | February | March | April | May | June |
|---|---|---|---|---|---|---|
| **Production** | 5 | 7.5 | 5 | 10 | 12.5 | 15 |
| **Sales** | 7.5 | 10 | 7.5 | 12.5 | 15 | 17.5 |

**SOLUTION:**

These data will also be presented in the form of graph in the same manner as shown in the above graph. In graph, following data pertaining to both production and sales are shown on Y-axis. These are represented by two different graph lines in the same graph.

**Monthly Production and Sales of a Factory (000' ₹)**

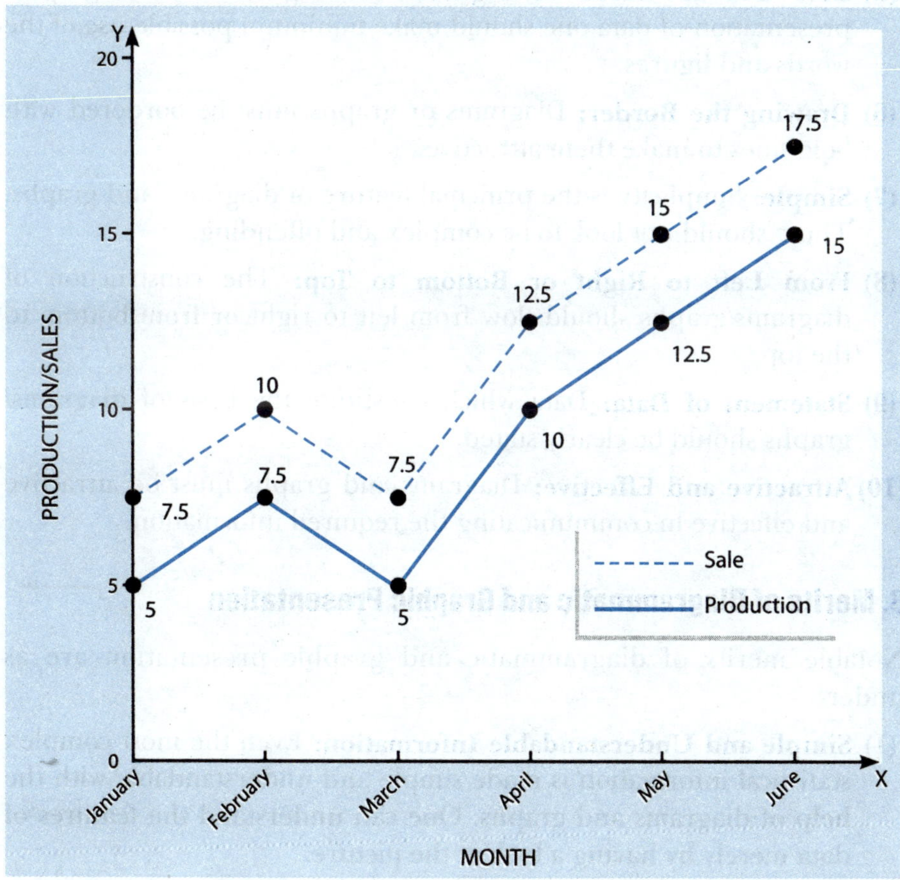

**Learning by doing**

Find out the data from your father about monthly family expenditure during the year 2013. Get similar information from your trustworthy close friend. Make an arithmetic line graph. Write your observations on the quality of life of the two families.

## 2. General Rules for Constructing Diagrams and Graphs

Some of the general rules for constructing diagrams and graphs are as follows:

**Restrict yourself**

To make the diagrams look attractive and simple, you must restrict yourself on the use of words and figures.

(1) **Proper Size:** Diagrams or graphs must suit the size of the paper. It should be neither too big nor too small.

(2) **Proper Heading:** Diagrams or graphs must bear proper heading. A heading must be simple, short and informative.

(3) **Proper Scale:** Before making a diagram/graph its scale should be properly determined and indicated.

(4) **Use of Signs and Colours only:** Diagrams or graphs must carry some signs on the nature and classification of information. Colours may be used to indicate different aspects of a diagram. These signs and colours must be clarified.

(5) **Less Use of Words or Figures:** In diagrammatic or graphic presentation of data one should make minimum possible use of the words and figures.

(6) **Drawing the Border:** Diagrams or graphs must be bordered with bold lines to make them attractive.

(7) **Simple:** Simplicity is the principal feature of diagrams and graphs. These should not look to be complex and offending.

(8) **From Left to Right or Bottom to Top:** The construction of diagrams/graphs should flow from left to right or from bottom to the top.

(9) **Statement of Data:** Data which constitute the basis of diagrams/graphs should be clearly stated.

(10) **Attractive and Effective:** Diagrams and graphs must be attractive and effective in communicating the required information.

## 3. Merits of Diagrammatic and Graphic Presentation

Notable merits of diagrammatic and graphic presentation are as under:

(1) **Simple and Understandable Information:** Even the most complex statistical information is made simple and understandable with the help of diagrams and graphs. One can understand the features of data merely by having a look at the picture.

(2) **Lasting Impact:** Diagrammatic or graphic presentation leaves a lasting impact on the reader's mind. Information is not easily forgotten.

(3) **No Need of Training or Specialised Knowledge:** One needs no training or specialised knowledge in reading the diagrams and graphs. These are easily understood even by a layman.

(4) **Attractive and Effective Means of Presentation:** Diagrams and graphs are very attractive and effective means of presenting data. It is rightly said that *a picture is worth of a thousand words*.

(5) **A Quick Comparative Glance:** Diagrams/graphs facilitate a comparative glance at the data. Thus, data on investment in Private and Public sectors, when presented in the form of (say) bar diagrams, can be easily compared. One can easily note the broad differences between the two.

(6) **Informative and Entertaining:** Besides being informative, diagrammatic or graphic presentation is an entertaining means of data presentation. The beginners are just fascinated to draw pictures in the form of diagrams and graphs.

(7) **Location of Averages:** Using graphic technique, we can easily locate the values of certain averages, such as mode and median.

(8) **Study of Correlation:** Graphic presentation of data corresponding to different variables helps identify correlation between the variables. For example, if time series data on income and expenditure are plotted on the same graph, one is very likely to observe a very high degree of positive correlation between the two variables. Higher level of income is very likely to be associated with higher level of consumption, and vice versa.

## 4. Limitations of Diagrammatic and Graphic Presentation

Some of the limitations of diagrammatic and graphic presentation of statistical data are as follows:

(1) **Limited Use:** Only a limited set of data can be presented in the form of a diagram. In fact, diagrams and graphs are generally used only when comparisons are involved or when time-series data are to be presented.

(2) **Misuse:** Diagrams may be misused for false projection of the statistical facts, especially in case of advertisements.

(3) **Only Preliminary Conclusions:** It may not be always easy to arrive at final conclusions after seeing the diagrams. Multiple information in the form of diagrams and graphs may offer only preliminary conclusions.

## MISCELLANEOUS ILLUSTRATIONS

### Illustration 1.

Represent the following data graphically:

| Year | 2008 | 2009 | 2010 | 2011 | 2012 | 2013 | 2014 |
|---|---|---|---|---|---|---|---|
| **Production of Wheat (in million tonnes)** | 5 | 8 | 13 | 16 | 20 | 17 | 22 |

**Solution:**

**Production of Wheat (2008 to 2014) (million tonnes)**

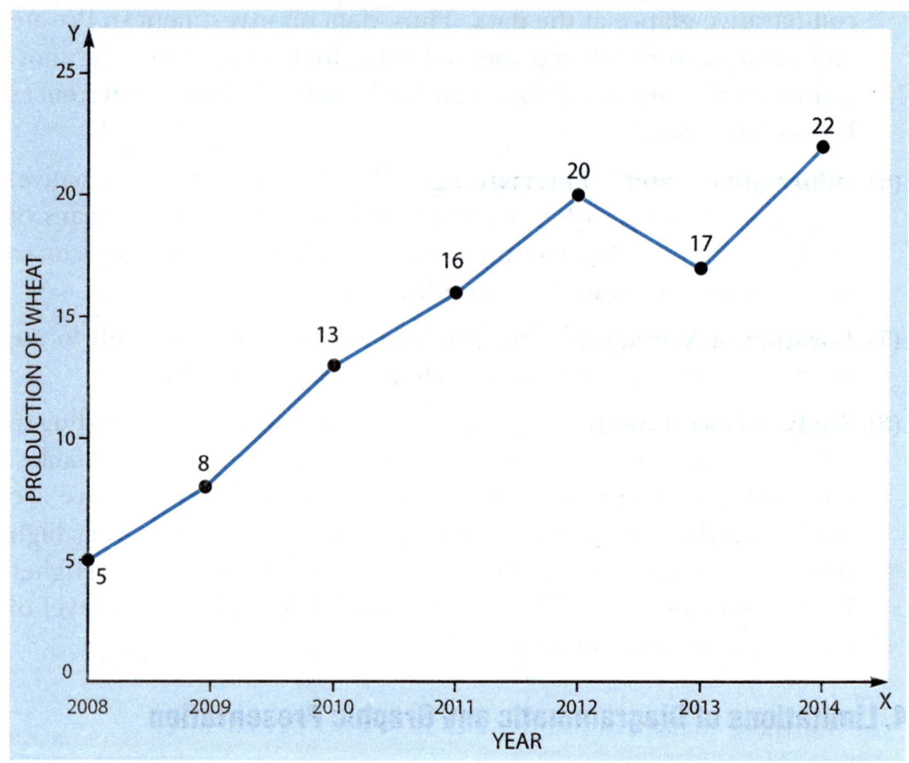


### Illustration 2.

Represent the following data related to exports and imports of India (hypothetical figures) graphically:

| Year | 2008 | 2009 | 2010 | 2011 | 2012 | 2013 | 2014 |
|---|---|---|---|---|---|---|---|
| **Exports (in ₹ crore)** | 300 | 350 | 400 | 380 | 450 | 280 | 250 |
| **Imports (in ₹ crore)** | 420 | 460 | 600 | 480 | 550 | 450 | 400 |

**SOLUTION:**

**Exports and Imports of India (2008 to 2014) (₹ crore)**

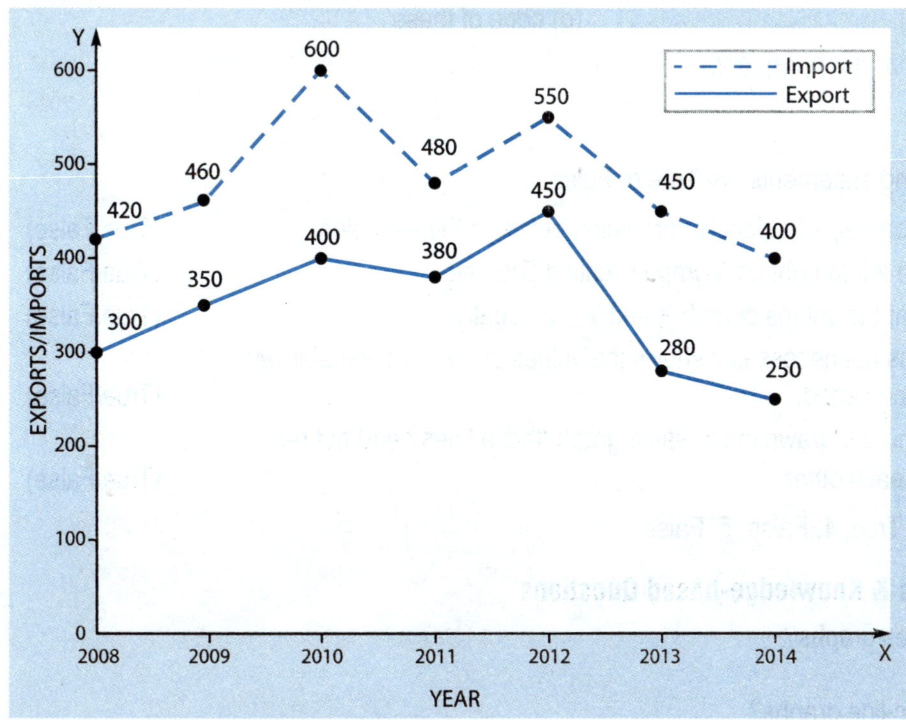


## EXERCISE

### 1. Very Short Answer Type Questions [1 mark]

**A. Multiple Choice Questions: Choose the Correct Answer**

1. Arithmetic line-graphs are also known as:
   (a) linear graphs (b) non-linear graphs
   (c) time series graphs (d) none of these
2. Axis divides the plain of a paper into:
   (a) two quadrants (b) three quadrants
   (c) four quadrants (d) none of these
3. In the first quadrant, the values of X and Y are:
   (a) +ve (b) –ve
   (c) X is +ve and Y is –ve (d) none of these
4. If the values in a series are very large and the difference between the smallest value and zero is high, then we use ________ base line.
   (a) original (b) false
   (c) true (d) none of these
5. In which quadrant, the value of X will be positive but that of Y will be negative?
   (a) 1st (b) 2nd
   (c) 3rd (d) 4th

6. Graphs are always drawn with reference to:

(a) scale (b) origin

(c) both (a) and (b) (d) none of these

Ans. 1. (c), 2. (c), 3. (a), 4. (b), 5. (d), 6. (a).

### B. True or False

State whether the following statements are True or False:

1. Graphic presentation helps to identify correlation between the variables. (True/False)
2. Horizontal line from left to right on a graph is called Ordinate. (True/False)
3. In the third quadrant the values of both X and Y are negative. (True/False)
4. One variable graphs not necessarily shows the values of only one variable with respect to some time period. (True/False)
5. If more than one line are drawn in the same graph, these lines need not be differentiated from each other. (True/False)

Ans. 1. True, 2. False, 3. True, 4. False, 5. False.

### C. Concepts/Definitions & Knowledge-based Questions

1. What are time series graphs?

Or

What are arithmetic-line graphs?

Ans. A graph showing arithmetic values of a variable (on a graph paper) is called 'arithmetic line-graph'. Often such graphs are constructed to present time series data, that is, the data (like the value of exports or imports) corresponding to different weeks, months or years. Therefore, arithmetic line-graphs are often called 'time series graphs'.

2. What is false base line?

Ans. If the values in a series are very large and the difference between the smallest value and zero is high and if these values are to be indicated on X/Y-axis of the graph, we overcome this difficulty by showing a cut or kink on the X/Y-axis, as in the adjoining picture.

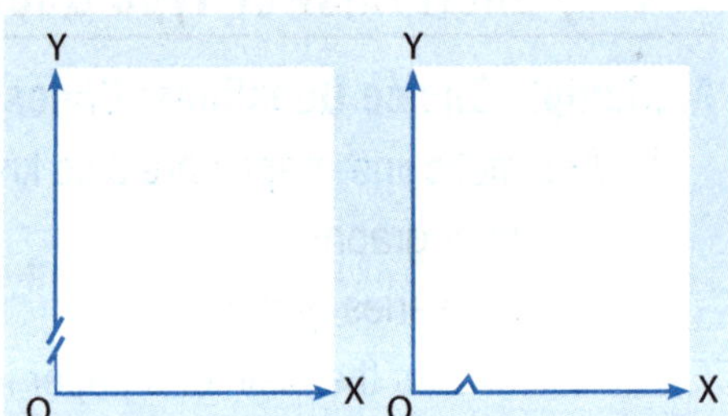


3. How many types are there of time series graphs?

Ans. There are two types of time series graphs:

(1) One variable graph, and (2) Two or more than two variable graphs.

4. State one merit of graphic presentation of time series data.

Ans. Graphic presentation leaves a **lasting impact** on the reader's mind. The information is not easily forgotten.

5. State one limitation of graphic presentation of time series data.

Ans. Graphic presentation may be **misused** for false projection of the statistical facts, especially in case of advertisements.

## 2. Short Answer Type Questions [3-4 marks]

1. Define a graph. Describe its types.
2. What is graphic presentation? Explain the rules for the construction of a graph.

3. Describe the general rules of constructing a diagram.
4. Describe the advantages of graphic presentation.
5. Describe the limitations of graphic presentation.

## 3. Long Answer Type Questions [6 marks]

1. What is meant by graphic presentation of a data? Discuss the procedure you would adopt in constructing graphs.
2. What are the uses or advantages of graphic presentation of the statistical data? Discuss its limitations.
3. Explain how a time series graph is prepared. Also distinguish between one variable and two variable time series graphs.

## 4. Essential Practicals

1. Plot the annual profits of a firm on a time series graph:

| **Year** | 2009 | 2010 | 2011 | 2012 | 2013 | 2014 |
|---|---|---|---|---|---|---|
| **Profit ('000 ₹)** | 60 | 72 | 75 | 65 | 80 | 95 |

2. Plot the following hypothetical figures on a time series graph:

| **Year** | **Imports (₹ thousand crore)** | **Exports (₹ thousand crore)** |
|---|---|---|
| 2009-10 | 123 | 106 |
| 2010-11 | 178 | 140 |
| 2011-12 | 215 | 159 |
| 2012-13 | 231 | 203 |
| 2013-14 | 245 | 209 |

3. The following are the figures of sales of two firms A and B for the years 2007-2014. Present the data graphically.

| **Year** | **Sales of Firm A (in thousand units)** | **Sales of Firm B (in thousand units)** |
|---|---|---|
| 2007 | 15 | 4 |
| 2008 | 17 | 9 |
| 2009 | 20 | 11 |
| 2010 | 19 | 12 |
| 2011 | 25 | 8 |
| 2012 | 28 | 10 |
| 2013 | 29 | 13 |
| 2014 | 27 | 12 |

4. The following are the sales figures of TVs of Firm A, during 2009-2014:

| **Year** | 2009 | 2010 | 2011 | 2012 | 2013 | 2014 |
|---|---|---|---|---|---|---|
| **Sale (in thousand units)** | 2,155 | 2,201 | 2,250 | 2,190 | 2,095 | 2,170 |

Plot the above data on time series graph.

## 5. NCERT Textbook Questions [With Hints to Answers]

1. Data represented through arithmetic line graph help in understanding:
   (i) long term trend (ii) cyclicity in data
   (iii) seasonality in data (iv) all of the above

   [(i)]

2. The following table shows the estimated sectoral real growth rates (percentage change over the previous year) in GDP at factor cost.

| Year<br>(1) | Agriculture and Allied Sectors<br>(2) | Industry<br>(3) | Services<br>(4) |
|---|---|---|---|
| 1994–95 | 5.0 | 9.2 | 7.0 |
| 1995–96 | –0.9 | 11.8 | 10.3 |
| 1996–97 | 9.6 | 6.0 | 7.1 |
| 1997–98 | –1.9 | 5.9 | 9.0 |
| 1998–99 | 7.2 | 4.0 | 8.3 |
| 1999–2000 | 0.8 | 6.9 | 8.2 |

Represent the data as multiple time series graph.

[ **Sectoral Real Growth Rates in GDP at Factor Cost**

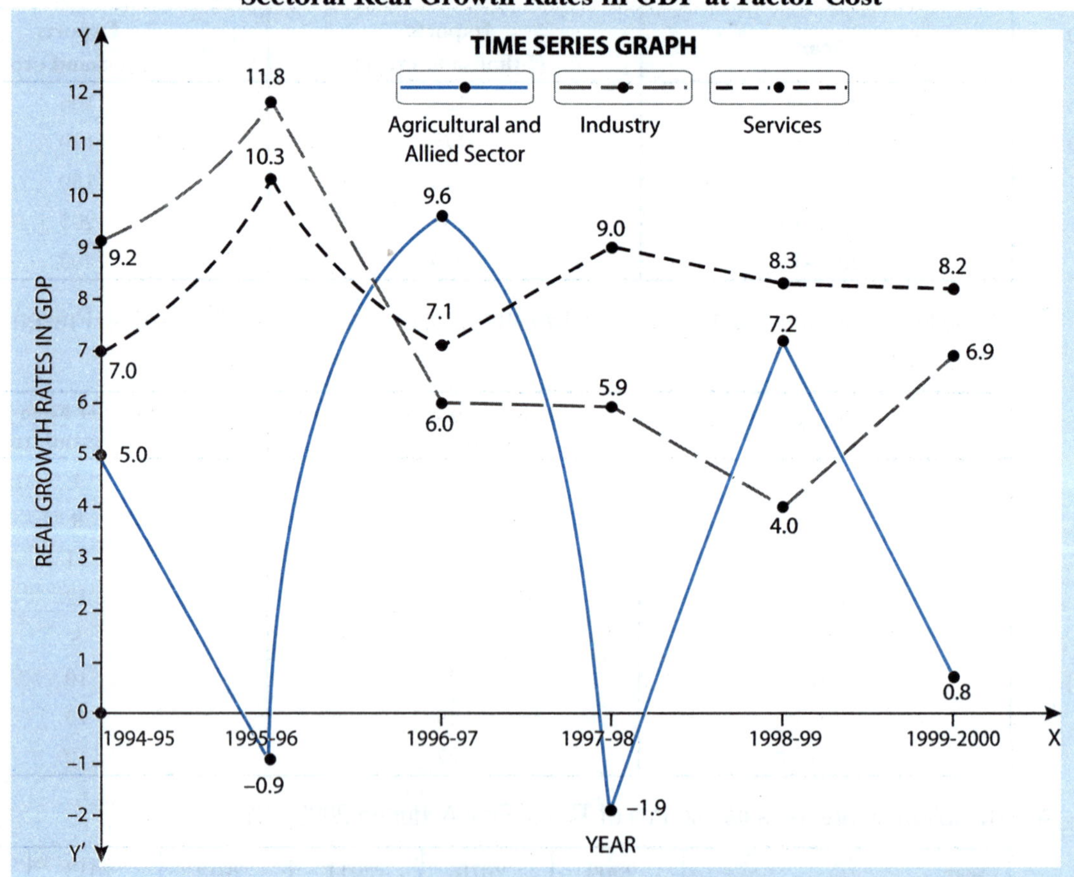

# Measures of Central Tendency— Arithmetic Mean

9

## 1. What is a Central Tendency?

A Central Tendency refers to a central value or a representative value of a statistical series.

It is difficult for anyone to understand or remember a large group of raw data. One would like to know the critical value which represents all the items in a series. Such a value is called 'central tendency' or 'average value'. For instance it is very difficult to remember and understand the data concerning the income of millions of Indians. However, if it is said that in 2011-12, provisional estimates for average income of the people in India was ₹ 38,037 per annum, it will be easy for us to guess the economic condition of most of the Indians. It is this average value which is called central tendency of the series. It is also called measure of location. Thus, measures of central tendency refer to all those methods of statistical analysis by which averages of the statistical series are worked out.

### Definition

According to **Croxton and Cowden,** *"An average is a single value within the range of the data that is used to represent all of the values in the series. Since an average is somewhere within the range of data, it is sometimes called measure of central value."*

According to **Clark,** *"An average is a figure that represents the whole group."*

## 2. Purpose and Functions of Averages

Study of averages is of central significance in statistical methods. That is why **Bowley** defines statistics as, *"A Science of Averages"*.

According to **Moroney,** *"The purpose of an average is brief and simple representation of a group of individual values so that the brain may quickly grasp the general basis of the units of the group."* Some of the main purposes and functions of averages are as under:

**What is the Basic Purpose of Finding an Average Value of a Series?**

It is to identify such a value that represents characteristics of all the items in the series.

**(1) Brief Description:** The main purpose of an average is to present a simple and systematic description of the principal features of the raw data. As a result of it, data can be easily understood.

(2) **Comparison:** Averages help in making comparison of different sets of data. For example, a comparison of the per capita income of India and USA shows that per capita income of India is much less than the per capita income of USA. Accordingly, it is concluded that India is a poor country.

(3) **Formulation of Policies:** Averages help in formulation of policies. For example, in India the per capita income is ₹ 31,801 per annum which is much less than many countries in the world. Accordingly, it becomes clear for the government to focus on such economic policies as are likely to increase per capita income.

(4) **Statistical Analysis:** Averages constitute the basis of statistical analysis. For example, if one knows the average marks secured by the students of a class in their different subjects, one can easily analyse the subjects in which the students are weak.

(5) **One Value for All:** Averages represent the universe or the mass of statistical data. One value represents all values of the series. Accordingly, conclusion can be drawn in respect of the universe as a whole.

## 3. Essentials of a Good Average

A good and satisfactory average should have the following features:

(1) **Clear and Stable Definition:** A good and a satisfactory average should be clear and stable in definition.

(2) **Representative:** An average value should be representative of the entire mass of data. It should be based on all the observations of the series.

(3) **Simplicity:** Simplicity is another essential feature of a good average. It must be so simple that it is easily worked out.

(4) **Certainty:** A good average must be certain in character. Only then an average value can be used as the basis of statistical analysis.

(5) **Absolute Number:** A good average should be an absolute number. A percentage or a relative value does not serve as a good average.

(6) **Least Effect of a Change in the Sample:** An average of a series should be least affected by a change in the sample on which the average is based.

(7) **Algebraic Treatment:** A good average should be capable of further mathematical or algebraic treatment.

## 4. Types of Statistical Averages

Averages are broadly classified into two categories:

(1) *Mathematical Averages*, and

(2) *Positional Averages*.

Following chart reveals their further categorisation:

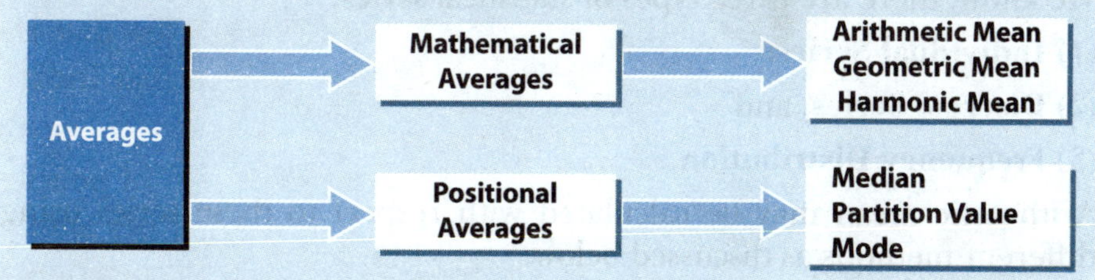


In the present chapter we discuss arithmetic mean.

## 5. Arithmetic Mean

Arithmetic Mean is a simple average of all items in a series. It is the simplest measure of central tendencies. The arithmetic mean of a series is simply called 'Mean'. If, for example, Ram plays 5 matches, Shyam 6, Mohan 7, Kishan 8 and Ravi 9 matches a week, the average number of matches played by Ram, Shyam, Mohan, Kishan and Ravi would be determined as under:

Number of Matches = 5 + 6 + 7 + 8 + 9 = 35

Number of Boys = 5

$$\text{Mean} = \frac{\text{Total Value of the Items}}{\text{Number of Items}} = \frac{35}{5} = 7$$

### Definition

*Arithmetic Mean or Mean is the number which is obtained by adding the values of all the items of a series and dividing the total by the number of items.*

In the words of **H. Secrist,** "*The Arithmetic Mean is the amount secured by dividing the sum of value of the items in a series by their numbers.*"

### FORMULA

Arithmetic mean is generally written as $\overline{X}$. It may be expressed in the form of following formula:

$$\overline{X} = \frac{X_1 + X_2 + X_3 + \ldots\ldots + X_n}{N} = \frac{\Sigma X}{N}$$

Here, $X_1, X_2, X_3, \ldots\ldots, X_n$ are the values of different items in the series. Thus, $X_1$ = matches played by Ram, 5; $X_2$= matches played by Shyam, 6 and $X_3$= matches played by Mohan, 7, etc.

N = Total number of items (in the above example, it is 5 comprising of five boys, Ram, Shyam, Mohan, Kishan and Ravi.)

Σ is a sign called Sigma. It refers to the sum total of the values of different items in the series.

### Types of Arithmetic Mean

Arithmetic mean is of two types:

**(1) Simple Arithmetic Mean:** In it, all items of a series are given equal importance.

**(2) Weighted Arithmetic Mean:** In it, different items of a series are accorded different weights in accordance with their relative importance.

**What is the Basic Difference between Simple Arithmetic Mean and Weighted Arithmetic Mean?**

In simple arithmetic mean, all items of the series are taken as of equal importance. In the weighted average, on the other hand, different items are taken as of different importance; accordingly weights are accorded to different items depending on their relative importance.

## Methods of Calculating Simple Arithmetic Mean

We know, there are three types of statistical series:

**(1) Individual Series,**

**(2) Discrete Series,** and

**(3) Frequency Distribution.**

Arithmetic mean may be calculated with respect to these series using different methods as discussed below:

## Calculation of Simple Arithmetic Mean in Case of Individual Series

In the case of individual series, arithmetic mean may be calculated by two methods:

**(1) Direct Method,** or

**(2) Short-cut Method.**

### (1) Direct Method

Following steps are involved in this method:

(i) Add up values of all the items of a series ($\Sigma X$);

(ii) Find out total number of items in the series (N); and

(iii) Divide the total of value of all the items ($\Sigma X$) with the number of items (N). Thus,

$$\overline{X} = \frac{\Sigma X}{N} \text{ or } \overline{X} = \frac{\text{Total Value of the Items}}{\text{Number of Items}}$$

**Illustration.**

Pocket allowance of 10 students is ₹ 15, 20, 30, 22, 25, 18, 40, 50, 55 and 65. Find out the average pocket allowance.

**Solution:**

| Pocket Allowance (₹) (X) |
|---|
| 15 |
| 20 |
| 30 |
| 22 |
| 25 |
| 18 |
| 40 |
| 50 |
| 55 |
| 65 |
| $\Sigma X = 340$ |

$$\overline{X} = \frac{\Sigma X}{N} = \frac{X_1 + X_2 + ... + X_{10}}{10} = \frac{340}{10} = 34$$

Average pocket allowance of the 10 students = ₹ 34.

### (2) Short-cut Method

This method is used when the size of items is very large.

The use of short-cut method involves the following steps:

(i) Before finding an actual average, some value in the series is taken as 'assumed average'. Assumed average should preferably be the middle item of the series. It facilitates the calculation of deviation from the assumed average.

(ii) Assumed average is generally taken by dividing by 2, the total of maximum and minimum values of the items. It is always a complete number. In statistics, assumed average is often denoted as 'A'.

(iii) Deviations of different values from the assumed average are found and each deviation is written against the concerned value in the series. Thus,

$$d \text{ (deviation)} = X - A$$

Where, X is the actual value in the series and A is the assumed average. If value of the item (X) is less than the assumed average (A), then 'd' or X – A would be negative. Thus, in the earlier illustration, if A is 40, 'd' corresponding to 1st value in the series (15) would be, 15 – 40 = (–) 25. Likewise corresponding to 8th value in the series (50) it would be, 50 – 40 = (+) 10.

While noting down the deviation against a particular item, sign of the deviation (+) or (–) must also be specified. Thus, 'd' of the first value would be written as, – 25 and of the 8th value as, +10.

(iv) Find the sum/total of all deviations. Add up positive deviations and negative deviations separately; and then find out the difference. If the sum of negative deviations is more than that of positive deviations then net sum of all the deviations will be negative and vice versa.

(v) Divide the net sum of the deviations by the number of items in the series. If the dividend is positive (+) then it gets added to A, the assumed average. And, if the dividend is negative (–), then it gets subtracted from A, the assumed average. The value, thus, obtained would be the actual average of the series.

**FORMULA**

$$\overline{X} = A + \frac{\Sigma d}{N}$$

(Here, $\overline{X}$ = Arithmetic mean; A = Assumed average; Σd = Net sum of the deviations of the different values from the assumed average; and N = Number of items in the series.)

**ILLUSTRATION.**

Following is the pocket allowance of 10 students. Find out arithmetic mean using Short-cut Method.

| Pocket Allowance (₹) | 15 | 20 | 30 | 22 | 25 | 18 | 40 | 50 | 55 | 65 |
|---|---|---|---|---|---|---|---|---|---|---|

**SOLUTION:**

(Assumed Average, A = 40)

| Number of Students | Pocket Allowance (₹) (X) | Deviation from the Assumed Average (d = X – A), (A = 40) | |
|---|---|---|---|
| 1 | 15 | 15 – 40 = – 25 | |
| 2 | 20 | 20 – 40 = – 20 | |
| 3 | 30 | 30 – 40 = – 10 | |
| 4 | 22 | 22 – 40 = – 18 | –110 |
| 5 | 25 | 25 – 40 = – 15 | |
| 6 | 18 | 18 – 40 = – 22 | |
| 7 | 40 (A) | 40 – 40 = 0 | |
| 8 | 50 | 50 – 40 = +10 | |
| 9 | 55 | 55 – 40 = +15 | +50 |
| 10 | 65 | 65 – 40 = +25 | |
| N = 10 | | Σd = – 110 + 50 = – 60 | |

The sum of '+' deviations = + 50

The sum of '–' deviations = – 110

The net sum of deviations, Σd= – 110 + 50 = – 60

Dividing the aggregate of deviations (Σd) by the number of items (N),

$$\frac{\Sigma d}{N} = \frac{-60}{10} = -6$$

Substituting this value of $\frac{\Sigma d}{N}$ in the following formula:

$$\overline{X} = A + \frac{\Sigma d}{N}$$

We have,

$$\overline{X} = 40 + (-)\ 6$$
$$= 40 - 6$$
$$= 34$$

Arithmetic Mean = ₹ 34.

***Learning by doing***

1. *Following is the monthly income of eight families in a locality.*
   *Monthly Income (₹) : 70, 10, 500, 75, 13, 250, 8, 42*
   *Find out arithmetic mean using Direct Method and Short-cut Method.*
   *(Ans. $\overline{X}$ = ₹ 121)*
2. *Students of Class XI secured following marks in their Statistics paper. Calculate arithmetic mean using Direct Method and Short-cut Method.*
   *20, 44, 65, 28, 45, 67, 30, 50, 68, 39, 53, 70, 40, 60, 75*
   *(Ans. $\overline{X}$ = 50.27)*
3. *Find out mean height of girl-students in your school. Compare it with the mean height of boy-students.*

## CALCULATION OF SIMPLE ARITHMETIC MEAN IN DISCRETE SERIES OR FREQUENCY ARRAY

In discrete series, there are frequencies corresponding to different items in the series. There are three methods of calculating mean of the discrete series.

That discrete series (also called frequency array) do not have class intervals. An item in the series does not assume any range of values but each item has corresponding frequency.

**Recall again**

– that individual series do not have frequencies of the items. These series show only values of different items.

(1) **Direct Method,**

(2) **Short-cut Method,** and

(3) **Step-deviation Method.**

### (1) Direct Method

Direct method of calculating mean of the discrete series involves the following steps:

(i) Values of the various items in the series are indicated by X, and their frequencies by 'f'.

(ii) Each item is multiplied by its frequency to get 'fX'. These multiples are added to get $\Sigma fX$. That is,

$\Sigma fX = f_1X_1 + f_2X_2 + ... + f_nX_n$

(iii) Frequencies are added up to get $\Sigma f$. That is,

$\Sigma f = f_1 + f_2 + f_3 + ..... + f_n$

(iv) $\Sigma fX$ is divided by $\Sigma f$ to obtain the mean, $\overline{X}$.

**FORMULA**

$$\overline{X} = \frac{\Sigma fX}{\Sigma f}$$

**ILLUSTRATION.**

Following is the weekly wage earnings of 19 workers:

| Wages (₹) | 10 | 20 | 30 | 40 | 50 |
|---|---|---|---|---|---|
| Number of Workers | 4 | 5 | 3 | 2 | 5 |

Calculate arithmetic mean using Direct Method.

**SOLUTION:**

| Wages (₹) (X) | Number of Workers or Frequency (f) | Multiple of the Value of X and Frequency (fX) |
|---|---|---|
| 10 | 4 | 4 × 10 = 40 |
| 20 | 5 | 5 × 20 = 100 |
| 30 | 3 | 3 × 30 = 90 |
| 40 | 2 | 2 × 40 = 80 |
| 50 | 5 | 5 × 50 = 250 |
| | Σf = 19 | ΣfX = 560 |

$$\overline{X} = \frac{\Sigma fX}{\Sigma f} = \frac{560}{19} = 29.47$$

Mean wage earnings of 19 workers = ₹ 29.47.

### (2) Short-cut Method

Short-cut method of estimating mean of the discrete frequency series uses the following formula:

**FORMULA**

$$\overline{X} = A + \frac{\Sigma fd}{\Sigma f}$$

**Steps**

(i) Before calculating the actual average of the series, some value which lies in the middle of the series is taken as assumed average. This may be indicated by 'A'. In the earlier example, assumed average may be taken as 50.

(ii) Deviation of each value of different items in the series is calculated from the assumed average. The deviation is noted against the concerned item of the series. The deviation may be positive (+) or negative (–). Accordingly, the (+) or (–) sign is to be noted against each deviation. If the deviation is zero, no sign needs to be specified.

(iii) Find the multiple of 'd' and its corresponding 'f', that is, 'fd'. Add up, separately, the positive (+) and negative (–) values of all 'fd'. Find out the difference between the two to get '$\Sigma$fd'.

(iv) Add up all frequencies, to get $\Sigma f$.

(v) Divide $\Sigma$fd by $\Sigma$f that is, $\frac{\Sigma fd}{\Sigma f}$.

If the value of $\frac{\Sigma fd}{\Sigma f}$ is positive, it gets added to the assumed average. If this value is negative, it gets subtracted from the assumed average. The result would be the actual average of the series.

**Illustration.**

Following are the wages of 19 workers:

| Wages (₹) | 10 | 20 | 30 | 40 | 50 |
|---|---|---|---|---|---|
| Number of Workers | 4 | 5 | 3 | 2 | 5 |

Calculate arithmetic mean, using Short-cut Method.

**Solution:**

**(Assumed Average, A = 30)**

| Wages (₹) (X) | Number of Workers or Frequency (f) | Deviation (d = X – A) (A = 30) | Multiple of Deviation and Frequency (fd) | |
|---|---|---|---|---|
| 10 | 4 | 10 – 30 = – 20 | 4 × (– 20)= – 80 | – 130 |
| 20 | 5 | 20 – 30 = – 10 | 5 × (–10) = – 50 | |
| 30 | 3 | 30 – 30 = 0 | 3 × 0 = 0 | |
| 40 | 2 | 40 – 30 = 10 | 2 × 10 = 20 | + 120 |
| 50 | 5 | 50 – 30 = 20 | 5 × 20 = 100 | |
| | $\Sigma$f = 19 | | $\Sigma$fd = –130 + 120 = –10 | |

$$\overline{X} = A + \frac{\Sigma fd}{\Sigma f} = 30 + \frac{-10}{19} = 30 - \frac{10}{19}$$

$$= 30 - 0.53 = 29.47$$

Arithmetic Mean = ₹ 29.47.

### (3) Step-deviation Method

This method is a variant of short-cut method. It is adopted when deviations from the assumed mean have some *common factor*. In the above example, all the deviations (d) can be divided by 10 which is a common factor in this case. The common factor may be indicated by 'C'. The deviation (d) when divided by the common factor C is called step-deviation. This may be indicated by d′.

**Steps**

(i) Step deviation d′ is obtained by dividing the deviation (of the actual value from the assumed average) by the common factor.

$$d' = \frac{X - A}{C} = \frac{d}{C}$$

(Here, d′ = Step deviation; C = Common factor; d = Deviation; X = Value of the item; and A = Assumed average.)

(ii) Each step deviation is multiplied with its frequency to get fd′. Sum total of the fd′ is obtained to get Σfd′.

(iii) Σfd′ is divided by Σf, and then multiplied by the common factor 'C'. The resultant value is added to A to get the actual average of the series. Thus,

**FORMULA**

$$\overline{X} = A + \frac{\Sigma fd'}{\Sigma f} \times C$$

**ILLUSTRATION.**

Wage rate of 19 workers is given below:

| Wages (₹) | 10 | 20 | 30 | 40 | 50 |
|---|---|---|---|---|---|
| Number of Workers | 4 | 5 | 3 | 2 | 5 |

Calculate arithmetic mean using 'Step-deviation Method.'

**SOLUTION:**

(Assumed Average, A = 30)

| Wages (₹) (X) | Number of Workers or Frequency (f) | Deviation (d = X – A) (A = 30) | Step-deviation $\left(d' = \frac{X-A}{C}\right)$ (C = 10) | Multiple of Step-deviation and Frequency (fd′) |
|---|---|---|---|---|
| 10 | 4 | 10 – 30 = 20 | $\frac{-20}{10} = 2$ | 4 × (–2) = – 8 |
| 20 | 5 | 20 – 30 = – 10 | $\frac{-10}{10} = 2$ | 5 × (–1) = – 5 |
| 30 | 3 | 30 – 30 = 0 | $\frac{0}{10} = 0$ | 3 × 0 = 0 |
| 40 | 2 | 40 – 30 = 10 | $\frac{10}{10} = 1$ | 2 × 1 = 2 |
| 50 | 5 | 50 – 30 = 20 | $\frac{20}{10} = 2$ | 5 × 2 = 10 |
| | Σf = 19 | | | Σfd′ = –1 |

$$\bar{X} = A + \frac{\Sigma fd'}{\Sigma f} \times C$$

$A = 30$, $C = 10$ and $\frac{\Sigma fd'}{\Sigma f} = \frac{-1}{19} = -0.053$

Putting these values in the formula:

$$\bar{X} = 30 + \frac{-1}{19} \times 10 = 30 - 0.053 \times 10$$

$$= 30 - 0.53 = 29.47$$

Arithmetic Mean = ₹ 29.47.

*Learning by doing*

1. *Calculate arithmetic mean of the following series.*

   *Take 15 as assumed average and use Short-cut Method.*

| **Size** | 20 | 19 | 18 | 17 | 16 | 15 | 14 | 13 | 12 | 11 |
|---|---|---|---|---|---|---|---|---|---|---|
| **Frequency** | 1 | 2 | 4 | 8 | 11 | 10 | 7 | 4 | 2 | 1 |

*(Ans. $\bar{X}$ = 15.54)*

2. *Students of your class obtained following marks in Statistics in the weekly test:*

| **Marks** | 4 | 5 | 6 | 7 | 8 |
|---|---|---|---|---|---|
| **Number of Students** | 12 | 10 | 18 | 20 | 24 |

*Calculate arithmetic mean using Direct and Short-cut Methods.*

*(Ans. $\bar{X}$ = 6.40 marks)*

3. *The following table gives height of certain persons:*

| **Height (inches)** | 57 | 59 | 61 | 63 | 65 | 67 | 69 | 71 | 73 |
|---|---|---|---|---|---|---|---|---|---|
| **Number of Persons** | 1 | 3 | 7 | 10 | 11 | 15 | 10 | 7 | 2 |

*Calculate arithmetic mean.* *(Ans. $\bar{X}$ = 65.82" approx.)*

4. *Following is the number of heads of 8 coins when tossed 205 times:*

| **Number of Heads** | 0 | 1 | 2 | 3 | 4 | 5 | 6 | 7 | 8 |
|---|---|---|---|---|---|---|---|---|---|
| **Frequency** | 2 | 19 | 46 | 62 | 47 | 20 | 5 | 2 | 2 |

*Calculate arithmetic mean (mean number of heads per toss), using Direct Method and Short-cut Method.* *(Ans. $\bar{X}$ = 3.15)*

## Calculation of Simple Arithmetic Mean in Case of Frequency Distribution

In case of a frequency distribution, items are classified into different class intervals like 5–10, 10–15, etc. Each class interval has its frequency. There are three methods of calculating mean in frequency distribution: **(1) Direct Method, (2) Short-cut Method,** and **(3) Step-deviation Method.**

**You Must be Remembering**

– that in a frequency distribution each item has a range of values or class intervals. Each class interval has its respective frequency.

### (1) Direct Method

This method involves the following steps:

(i) The mid-values of the class intervals are calculated. These may be indicated by 'm'. To find the mid-value of class intervals, the lower and upper limits of that class are added and then divided by '2'. Thus, mid-value of the class 10–20 would be determined as:

$$m = \frac{l_1 + l_2}{2} = \frac{10 + 20}{2} = \frac{30}{2} = 15$$

(Here, m = Mid-value; $l_1$ = Lower limit of the class; $l_2$ = Upper limit of the class.)

(ii) Mid-values are multiplied by their corresponding frequencies. The multiples 'fm' are added up to get Σfm.

(iii) Σfm is divided by Σf. The resultant value would be the mean value.

**FORMULA**

$$\bar{X} = \frac{\sum fm}{\sum f}$$

**ILLUSTRATION.**

The following table shows marks in English secured by students of Class X in your school in their examination. Calculate mean marks using Direct Method.

| **Marks** | 0–10 | 10–20 | 20–30 | 30–40 | 40–50 |
|---|---|---|---|---|---|
| **Number of Students** | 20 | 24 | 40 | 36 | 20 |

**SOLUTION:**

| **Marks** | **Mid-value** $\left(m = \frac{l_1 + l_2}{2}\right)$ | **Number of Students or Frequency (f)** | **Multiple of Mid-value and Frequency (fm)** |
|---|---|---|---|
| 0–10 | $\frac{0 + 10}{2} = 5$ | 20 | 20 × 5 = 100 |
| 10–20 | $\frac{10 + 20}{2} = 15$ | 24 | 24 × 15 = 360 |
| 20–30 | $\frac{20 + 30}{2} = 25$ | 40 | 40 × 25 = 1,000 |
| 30–40 | $\frac{30 + 40}{2} = 35$ | 36 | 36 × 35 = 1,260 |
| 40–50 | $\frac{40 + 50}{2} = 45$ | 20 | 20 × 45 = 900 |
| | | Σf = 140 | Σfm = 3,620 |

$$\bar{X} = \frac{\Sigma fm}{\Sigma f} = \frac{3,620}{140} = 25.86$$

Mean Marks = 25.86.

**(2) Short-cut Method**

This method involves the following steps:

(i) Mid-values of the classes are determined, and indicated by 'm'.

(ii) Deviations of the mid-values from the assumed average (A) are determined and indicated by 'd'. If negative, these deviations are written as –d, and if positive, these are written as +d.

(iii) Deviations (d) are multiplied by the frequencies (f) to get 'fd'. These are then added up to get Σfd.

(iv) Σfd is divided by Σf. The dividend is added to the assumed average. The resultant value would be the mean value.

**FORMULA**

$$\overline{X} = A + \frac{\Sigma fd}{\Sigma f}$$

**ILLUSTRATION.**

The following table shows marks secured by the students of a class in an examination in English:

| Marks | 0–10 | 10–20 | 20–30 | 30–40 | 40–50 |
|---|---|---|---|---|---|
| Number of Students | 20 | 24 | 40 | 36 | 20 |

Calculate mean marks using Short-cut Method.

**SOLUTION:**

**(Assumed Average, A = 25)**

| Marks (X) | Mid-value $\left(m = \frac{l_1 + l_2}{2}\right)$ | Number of Students or Frequency (f) | Deviation (d = m – A) (A = 25) | Multiple of Deviation and Frequency (fd) |
|---|---|---|---|---|
| 0–10 | $\frac{0+10}{2} = 5$ | 20 | 5 – 25 = –20 | 20 × – 20 = – 400 |
| 10–20 | $\frac{10+20}{2} = 15$ | 24 | 15 – 25 = –10 | 24 × –10 = – 240 |
| 20–30 | $\frac{20+30}{2} = 25$ | 40 | 25 – 25 = 0 | 40 × 0 = 0 |
| 30–40 | $\frac{30+40}{2} = 35$ | 36 | 35 – 25 = +10 | 36 × +10 = + 360 |
| 40–50 | $\frac{40+50}{2} = 45$ | 20 | 45 – 25 = +20 | 20 × + 20 = + 400 |
| | | Σf = 140 | | Σfd = 120 |

$$\frac{\Sigma fd}{\Sigma f} = \frac{120}{140} = 0.86$$

$$\overline{X} = A + \frac{\Sigma fd}{\Sigma f}$$

$$= 25 + 0.86 = 25.86$$

Mean Marks = 25.86.

### (3) Step-deviation Method

Step-deviation method is a very useful method of calculating mean value in the case of frequency distribution. It involves the following steps:

(i) Find out mid-values of the class intervals, indicated by 'm'.

(ii) Find out deviations of the mid-values from some assumed average. That is,

$$d = m - A$$

(iii) Find out step-deviations by dividing the deviations with some Common Factor (C) that is, $d' = \frac{d}{C}$.

(iv) Multiply step-deviations (d′) with the corresponding frequencies (f). Add up all the multiples to get Σfd′.

(v) Divide Σfd′ by Σf and then multiply it by C. The resultant value is added to A to get the mean value. Thus,

**FORMULA**

$$\overline{X} = A + \frac{\Sigma fd'}{\Sigma f} \times C$$

**ILLUSTRATION.**

The following table shows marks obtained by the students of a class in their test in English:

| **Marks** | 0–10 | 10–20 | 20–30 | 30–40 | 40–50 |
|---|---|---|---|---|---|
| **Number of Students** | 20 | 24 | 40 | 36 | 20 |

Calculate arithmetic mean using Step-deviation Method.

**SOLUTION:**

(Assumed Average, A = 25)

| **Marks** | **Mid-value** $\left(m = \frac{l_1 + l_2}{2}\right)$ | **Number of Students or Frequency (f)** | **Deviation (d = m – A) (A = 25)** | **Step-deviation (d′)** $\left(d' = \frac{m - A}{C}\right)$ **(C = 10)** | **Multiple of Step-deviation and Frequency (fd′)** |
|---|---|---|---|---|---|
| 0–10 | 5 | 20 | –20 | –2 | – 40 } – 64 |
| 10–20 | 15 | 24 | –10 | –1 | – 24 |
| 20–30 | 25 | 40 | 0 | 0 | 0 |
| 30–40 | 35 | 36 | +10 | +1 | + 36 } 76 |
| 40–50 | 45 | 20 | +20 | +2 | + 40 |
| | | Σf = 140 | | | Σfd′ = 12 |

$$\frac{\Sigma fd'}{\Sigma f} = \frac{12}{140} = 0.086$$

$$\text{Mean, } \overline{X} = A + \frac{\Sigma fd'}{\Sigma f} \times C$$

$$= 25 + 0.086 \times 10$$

$$= 25 + 0.86$$

$$= 25.86$$

Arithmetic Mean = 25.86 marks.

***Learning by doing***

1. *Find out the mean of the following distribution:*

| **Items** | 0–5 | 5–10 | 10–15 | 15–20 | 20–25 | 25–30 | 30–35 | 35–40 |
|---|---|---|---|---|---|---|---|---|
| **Frequency** | 2 | 5 | 7 | 13 | 21 | 16 | 8 | 3 |

(*Ans.* $\overline{X}$ = *21.9*)

2. *Find arithmetic mean from the following distribution:*

| **Marks** | 0–4 | 4–8 | 8–12 | 12–16 |
|---|---|---|---|---|
| **Number of Students** | 4 | 8 | 2 | 1 |

(*Ans.* $\overline{X}$ = *6 marks*)

## Calculation of Arithmetic Mean in Case of Cumulative Frequency Distribution

Here are two illustrations to facilitate your understanding.

### Illustration 1.

Marks in Statistics of the students of Class XI are given below. Find out arithmetic mean.

| Marks | Number of Students |
|---|---|
| Less than 10 | 5 |
| Less than 20 | 17 |
| Less than 30 | 31 |
| Less than 40 | 41 |
| Less than 50 | 49 |

### Solution:

A Cumulative Frequency Distribution should first be converted into a Simple Frequency Distribution, as under:

**Conversion of a Cumulative Frequency Distribution into a Simple Frequency Distribution**

| Marks | Number of Students |
|---|---|
| 0–10 | 5 |
| 10–20 | 17 – 5 = 12 |
| 20–30 | 31 – 17 = 14 |
| 30–40 | 41 – 31 = 10 |
| 40–50 | 49 – 41 = 8 |

Now, mean value of the data is obtained using Direct Method as under:

**Calculation of Mean**

| Marks (X) | Mid-value $\left(m = \frac{l_1 + l_2}{2}\right)$ | Number of Students or Frequency (f) | Multiple of Mid-value and Frequency (fm) |
|---|---|---|---|
| 0–10 | 5 | 5 | 25 |
| 10–20 | 15 | 12 | 180 |
| 20–30 | 25 | 14 | 350 |
| 30–40 | 35 | 10 | 350 |
| 40–50 | 45 | 8 | 360 |
| | | $\Sigma f = 49$ | $\Sigma fm = 1{,}265$ |

$$\overline{X} = \frac{\Sigma fm}{\Sigma f} = \frac{1{,}265}{49} = 25.82$$

Arithmetic Mean = 25.82 marks.

**ILLUSTRATION. 2**

The following table shows marks in Economics of the students of a class. Calculate arithmetic mean.

| Marks | Number of Students |
|---|---|
| More than 0 | 30 |
| More than 2 | 28 |
| More than 4 | 24 |
| More than 6 | 18 |
| More than 8 | 10 |

**SOLUTION:**

Converting Cumulative Frequency Distribution into a Simple Frequency Distribution, we get the following:

| Marks | Number of Students |
|---|---|
| 0–2 | 30 – 28 = 2 |
| 2–4 | 28 – 24 = 4 |
| 4–6 | 24 – 18 = 6 |
| 6–8 | 18 – 10 = 8 |
| 8–10 | 10 – 0 = 10 |

Arithmetic mean of this continuous series is estimated below, using Direct Method.

**Calculation of Arithmetic Mean using Direct Method**

| Marks | Mid-value $\left(m = \frac{l_1 + l_2}{2}\right)$ | Number of Students or Frequency (f) | Multiple of Mid-value and Frequency (fm) |
|---|---|---|---|
| 0–2 | 1 | 2 | 2 |
| 2–4 | 3 | 4 | 12 |
| 4–6 | 5 | 6 | 30 |
| 6–8 | 7 | 8 | 56 |
| 8–10 | 9 | 10 | 90 |
| | | $\Sigma f = 30$ | $\Sigma fm = 190$ |

$$\overline{X} = \frac{\Sigma fm}{\Sigma f} = \frac{190}{30} = 6.33$$

Arithmetic Mean = 6.33 marks.

**CALCULATION OF ARITHMETIC MEAN IN A MID-VALUE SERIES**

Here is an illustration.

**ILLUSTRATION.**

Following table gives marks in Statistics of the students of a class. Find out mean marks.

| Mid-value | 5 | 10 | 15 | 20 | 25 | 30 | 35 | 40 |
|---|---|---|---|---|---|---|---|---|
| Number of Students | 5 | 7 | 9 | 10 | 8 | 6 | 3 | 2 |

**SOLUTION:**

In this series, mid-values are already given. The calculation of arithmetic mean involves the same procedure as in the case of exclusive series.

**Calculation of Arithmetic Mean**

| Mid-value (m) | Number of Students or Frequency (f) | Multiple of Mid-value and Frequency (fm) |
|---|---|---|
| 5 | 5 | 25 |
| 10 | 7 | 70 |
| 15 | 9 | 135 |
| 20 | 10 | 200 |
| 25 | 8 | 200 |
| 30 | 6 | 180 |
| 35 | 3 | 105 |
| 40 | 2 | 80 |
| | $\Sigma f = 50$ | $\Sigma fm = 995$ |

$$\bar{X} = \frac{\Sigma fm}{\Sigma f} = \frac{995}{50} = 19.9$$

Mean Marks = 19.

## CALCULATION OF ARITHMETIC MEAN IN CASE OF INCLUSIVE SERIES

**ILLUSTRATION.**

The following table shows monthly pocket expenses of the students of a class. Find out the average pocket expenses.

| Pocket Expenses (₹) | 20–29 | 30–39 | 40–49 | 50–59 | 60–69 |
|---|---|---|---|---|---|
| Number of Students | 10 | 8 | 6 | 4 | 2 |

**SOLUTION:**

Calculation of arithmetic mean of inclusive series is the same as of exclusive series.

| Pocket Expenses (₹) | Mid-value $\left(m = \frac{l_1 + l_2}{2}\right)$ | Number of Students or Frequency (f) | Deviation (d = m – A) (A = 44.5) | Step-deviation $\left(d' = \frac{d}{C}\right)$ (C = 10) | Multiple of Step-deviation and Frequency (fd′) |
|---|---|---|---|---|---|
| 20–29 | 24.5 | 10 | – 20 | – 2 | – 20 |
| 30–39 | 34.5 | 8 | – 10 | – 1 | – 8 |
| 40–49 | 44.5 | 6 | 0 | 0 | 0 |
| 50–59 | 54.5 | 4 | +10 | +1 | + 4 |
| 60–69 | 64.5 | 2 | +20 | +2 | + 4 |
| | | $\Sigma f = 30$ | | | $\Sigma fd' = -20$ |

$$\bar{X} = A + \frac{\Sigma fd'}{\Sigma f} \times C$$

$$= 44.5 + \frac{-20}{30} \times 10$$

$$= 44.5 - \frac{20}{3}$$

$$= 44.5 - 6.67 = 37.83$$

Average Pocket Expenses = ₹ 37.83.

**CALCULATION OF 'CORRECTED' ARITHMETIC MEAN**

Sometimes, in the calculation of Arithmetic Mean, some items or values are wrongly written. Accordingly, the mean value goes wrong. But such mean value can be corrected, as illustrated below:

$$\overline{X} = \frac{\Sigma X(\text{Wrong}) + (\text{Correct value}) - (\text{Incorrect value})}{N}$$

**ILLUSTRATION.**

Mean marks obtained by 100 students are estimated to be 40. Later on it is found that one value was read as 83 instead of 53.

Find out the "corrected" mean.

**SOLUTION:**

$$\overline{X} = \frac{\Sigma X}{N}$$

Or, $\Sigma X = \overline{X}N$

Given: $\overline{X} = 40$; $N = 100$

$$40 = \frac{\Sigma X}{100}$$

$$\therefore \Sigma X(\text{wrong}) = 40 \times 100 = 4{,}000$$

Correct value = 53

Incorrect value = 83

Correct

$$\overline{X} = \frac{\Sigma X(\text{Wrong}) + (\text{Correct value}) - (\text{Incorrect value})}{N}$$

$$= \frac{4{,}000 + 53 - 83}{100}$$

$$= \frac{3{,}970}{100} = 39.70$$

Thus, Corrected Mean = 39.70.

### Finding the Missing Value

If mean of the series is known, but one value is missing, the missing value may be found using the following formula:

$$\overline{X} = \frac{X_1 + X_2 + X_3 + \ldots + X_n}{N}$$

**ILLUSTRATION.**

Suppose mean of a series of 5 items is 30. Four values are, 10, 15, 30 and 35 respectively. Find the missing (5th) value of the series.

**SOLUTION.**

Assume 5th value as $X_5$.

$$\overline{X} = \frac{X_1 + X_2 + X_3 + X_4 + X_5}{N}$$

Given: $X_1 = 10, X_2 = 15, X_3 = 30, X_4 = 35, X_5 = ?$

$$\overline{X} = 30, N = 5$$

$$30 = \frac{10 + 15 + 30 + 35 + X_5}{5} = \frac{90 + X_5}{5}$$

$\therefore \quad 30 \times 5 = 90 + X_5$

Or, $\quad 150 = 90 + X_5$

$\therefore \quad X_5 = 150 - 90$

$= 60$

Thus, Value of the 5th item = 60.

*Learning by doing*

1. *A polling agency interviewed 200 persons. The age distribution of those persons was recorded as under:*

| Age (Years) | 80–89 | 70–79 | 60–69 | 50–59 | 40–49 | 30–39 | 20–29 | 10–19 |
|---|---|---|---|---|---|---|---|---|
| Frequency | 2 | 2 | 6 | 20 | 56 | 40 | 42 | 32 |

*Calculate mean age of the persons by Direct Method.* *(Ans. $\overline{X}$ = 35.8 years)*

2. *Calculate mean of the following series by Direct Method:*

| Mid-value | 10 | 12 | 14 | 16 | 18 | 20 |
|---|---|---|---|---|---|---|
| Frequency | 5 | 8 | 12 | 20 | 10 | 5 |

*(Ans. $\overline{X}$ = 15.23)*

3. *In an examination in Hindi, the students of a class secured following marks. Calculate mean marks by Direct Method.*

| Marks | Number of Students |
|---|---|
| More than 0 | 50 |
| More than 10 | 46 |
| More than 20 | 40 |
| More than 30 | 20 |
| More than 40 | 10 |
| More than 50 | 3 |

*(Ans. $\overline{X}$ = 28.8 marks)*

## Weighted Arithmetic Mean

**What is Weighted Arithmetic Mean?**

It is the mean of weighted items of the series. Different items are accorded different weights depending on their relative importance. The weighted sum of the items is divided by the sum of the weights.

We have so far discussed *Simple Arithmetic Mean*. In simple arithmetic mean, all items of a series are taken as of equal significance. But sometimes we may give greater significance to some items and less to others. As household may, for example, give more significance to food, less to clothes and still less to entertainment. When different items of a series are weighed according to their relative importance, the average of such series is called *Weighted Arithmetic Average. A Weighted Arithmetic Average is, thus, the mean of weighted items.*

### Calculation of Weighted Mean

Calculation of weighted mean involves the following steps:

(1) Different items are weighed according to their significance. Weights are indicated by 'W'.

(2) Items (X) are multiplied by their corresponding weights (W) and added up to get ΣWX.

(3) ΣWX is divided by the sum total of weights, *i.e.*, ΣW, to get the mean value, that is,

## FORMULA

$$\overline{X}_w = \frac{\Sigma WX}{\Sigma W}$$

Here, $\overline{X}_w$ indicates weighted average.

**Illustration.**

Calculate weighted mean of the following data:

| **Marks (X)** | 81 | 76 | 74 | 58 | 70 | 73 |
|---|---|---|---|---|---|---|
| **Weight (W)** | 2 | 3 | 6 | 7 | 3 | 7 |

**Solution:**

**Calculation of Weighted Mean**

| Marks (X) | Weight (W) | WX |
|---|---|---|
| 81 | 2 | 162 |
| 76 | 3 | 228 |
| 74 | 6 | 444 |
| 58 | 7 | 406 |
| 70 | 3 | 210 |
| 73 | 7 | 511 |
| | ΣW = 28 | ΣWX = 1,961 |

Weighted Mean,

$$\overline{X}_w = \frac{\Sigma WX}{\Sigma W} = \frac{1,961}{28} = 70.04$$

Weighted Mean = 70.04 marks.

***Learning by doing***

1. *The following table shows prices per 100g of tea of different brands. Using quantities as weight, find out weighted arithmetic mean of the prices.*

| **Price per 100g in ₹** | 2.50 | 3 | 3.50 | 4 | 4.25 | 5 |
|---|---|---|---|---|---|---|
| **Quantity** | 10 | 8 | 8 | 4 | 4 | 2 |

*(Ans. $\overline{X}$ = 3.33)*

2. *Calculate weighted mean of the following data:*

| **Items (X)** | 5 | 10 | 25 | 20 | 25 | 30 |
|---|---|---|---|---|---|---|
| **Weight (W)** | 8 | 4 | 5 | 10 | 7 | 6 |

*(Ans. $\overline{X}$ = 19)*

## Combined Arithmetic Mean

Given the mean values of two or more parts of a series and the number of items in each part, one can get Combined Arithmetic Mean, or mean of the series as a whole. The following formula is used for the estimation of combined arithmetic mean:

**FORMULA**

$$\overline{X}_{1,2} = \frac{\overline{X}_1 N_1 + \overline{X}_2 N_2}{N_1 + N_2}$$

Here,

$\overline{X}_{1,2}$ = Combined arithmetic mean of parts 1 and 2 of a series;

$\overline{X}_1$ = Arithmetic mean of part 1 of the series;

$\overline{X}_2$ = Arithmetic mean of part 2 of the series;

$N_1$ = Number of items in part 1 of the series; and

$N_2$ = Number of items in part 2 of the series.

Likewise, when there are more than 2 parts of a series, the following formula is used to work out Combined Arithmetic Mean.

**Formula**

$$\overline{X}_{1,2,3,...,n} = \frac{\overline{X}_1 N_1 + \overline{X}_2 N_2 + ... + \overline{X}_n N_n}{N_1 + N_2 + ... + N_2}$$

**ILLUSTRATION.**

60 students of Section A of Class XI, obtained 40 mean marks in Statistics, 40 students of Section B obtained 35 mean marks in Statistics. Find out mean marks in Statistics for Class XI as a whole.

**SOLUTION:**

Given:

$$N_1 = 60, \overline{X}_1 = 40, N_2 = 40, \overline{X}_2 = 35$$

We know, $\overline{X}_{12} = \frac{\overline{X}_1 N_1 + \overline{X}_2 N_2}{N_1 + N_2}$

$\therefore$ $\overline{X}_{12} = \frac{40 \times 60 + 35 \times 40}{60 + 40}$

$\therefore$ $\overline{X}_{12} = \frac{2,400 + 1,400}{100} = \frac{3,800}{100} = 38$

Thus, Combined Arithmetic Mean = 38.

**ADDITION, SUBTRACTION, MULTIPLICATION AND DIVISION OF VALUES**

If some specific value is added to or subtracted from different items in a series, the mean value of the items would increase or decrease by the same specific value respectively. Likewise, if different items of a series are multiplied or divided by any specific value, the mean value of the items would be the multiple or divided by the same specific value. The following example illustrates this point:

| X | (X + 2) | (X – 2) | (X × 2) | (X ÷ 2) |
|---|---|---|---|---|
| 10 | 12 | 8 | 20 | 5 |
| 20 | 22 | 18 | 40 | 10 |
| 30 | 32 | 28 | 60 | 15 |
| 40 | 42 | 38 | 80 | 20 |
| 50 | 52 | 48 | 100 | 25 |
| $\Sigma X = 150$ <br> $N = 5$ <br> $\overline{X} = 30$ | $\Sigma X = 160$ <br> $N = 5$ <br> $\overline{X} = 32$ | $\Sigma X = 140$ <br> $N = 5$ <br> $\overline{X} = 28$ | $\Sigma X = 300$ <br> $N = 5$ <br> $\overline{X} = 60$ | $\Sigma X = 75$ <br> $N = 5$ <br> $\overline{X} = 15$ |

The example shows that: (i) if 2 is added to different items, the resultant average of the series also increases by 2 (30 + 2 = 32); (ii) if 2 is subtracted from the different items, the resultant average also decreases by 2 (30 – 2 = 28); (iii) if the items are multiplied by 2, the resultant average also increases by the multiple of 2 (30 × 2 = 60); and (iv) if different items are divided by 2 the resultant average will also be divided by 2 (30 ÷ 2 = 15).

### Location of Missing Item or Frequency

A missing item (referring to any value of a variable X) or a missing frequency (f) of a series can be located using the following equations:

$$\overline{X} = \frac{\Sigma X}{N} \qquad \overline{X} = \frac{\Sigma fX}{\Sigma f} \quad (N = \Sigma f)$$

$$\Sigma X = \overline{X}N \qquad \Sigma fX = \overline{X}\Sigma f$$

$$N = \frac{\Sigma X}{\overline{X}} \qquad \Sigma f = \frac{\Sigma fX}{\overline{X}}$$

### Illustration 1.

In the following frequency distribution, the frequency of the class interval (40–50) is not known. Find it, if the arithmetic mean of the distribution is 52.

| **Wages (₹)** | 10–20 | 20–30 | 30–40 | 40–50 | 50–60 | 60–70 | 70–80 |
|---|---|---|---|---|---|---|---|
| **Number of Workers** | 5 | 3 | 4 | ? | 2 | 6 | 13 |

### Solution:

| Wages (₹) | Mid-value (m) | Number of Workers or Frequency (f) | Multiple of Mid-value and Frequency (fm) |
|---|---|---|---|
| 10–20 | 15 | 5 | 75 |
| 20–30 | 25 | 3 | 75 |
| 30–40 | 35 | 4 | 140 |
| 40–50 | 45 | f | 45f |
| 50–60 | 55 | 2 | 110 |
| 60–70 | 65 | 6 | 390 |
| 70–80 | 75 | 13 | 975 |
| | | Σf = 33 + f | Σfm = 1,765 + 45f |

$$\overline{X} = \frac{\Sigma fm}{\Sigma f}$$

$$52 = \frac{1{,}765 + 45f}{33 + f}$$

Or, $52\,(33 + f) = 1{,}765 + 45f$

$$1{,}716 + 52f = 1{,}765 + 45f$$

$$52f - 45f = 1{,}765 - 1{,}716 \Rightarrow 7f = 49 \Rightarrow f = 7$$

Missing Frequency = 7.

**ILLUSTRATION 2.**

If the arithmetic mean of the following series is 115.86; find the missing value.

| Wages (₹) | 110 | 112 | 113 | 117 | ? | 125 | 128 | 130 |
|---|---|---|---|---|---|---|---|---|
| Number of Workers | 25 | 17 | 13 | 15 | 14 | 8 | 6 | 2 |

**SOLUTION:**

Let the missing value be X.

| Wages (₹) (X) | Number of Workers or Frequency (f) | Multiple of the Value of X and Frequency (fX) |
|---|---|---|
| 110 | 25 | 2,750 |
| 112 | 17 | 1,904 |
| 113 | 13 | 1,469 |
| 117 | 15 | 1,755 |
| X | 14 | 14X |
| 125 | 8 | 1,000 |
| 128 | 6 | 768 |
| 130 | 2 | 260 |
| | $\Sigma f = 100$ | $\Sigma fX = 9{,}906 + 14X$ |

$$\overline{X} = \frac{\Sigma fX}{\Sigma f}$$

$$115.86 = \frac{9{,}906 + 14X}{100}$$

$$115.86 \times 100 = 9{,}906 + 14X$$

$$14X = 11{,}586 - 9{,}906$$

$$14X = 1{,}680$$

$$X = \frac{1{,}680}{14} = 120$$

Missing Value = 120.

***Learning by doing***

1. *The arithmetic mean of the following series is 18, find out the missing frequency.*

| Class Interval | 11–13 | 13–15 | 15–17 | 17–19 | 19–21 | 21–23 | 23–25 |
|---|---|---|---|---|---|---|---|
| Frequency | 3 | 6 | 9 | 13 | ? | 5 | 4 |

(*Ans.* $f = 8$)

2. *The following series gives the weekly wages. The mean wages are ₹ 50.75. Find out the missing value.*

| Weekly Wages | 40–43 | 43–46 | 46–49 | 49–52 | 52–55 |
|---|---|---|---|---|---|
| Frequency | 3 | 6 | 9 | 13 | ? |

(*Ans.* $f = 36$)

3. *Mark the missing value of the following data. Mean marks are 11.66.*

| Weekly Wages | 5 | 6 | 7 | 8 | 12 | ? | 15 | 17 | 18 |
|---|---|---|---|---|---|---|---|---|---|
| Frequency | 3 | 10 | 5 | 10 | 12 | 15 | 11 | 13 | 1 |

(*Ans.* $X = 13$)

## A Notable Property of Arithmetic Mean

A notable property of arithmetic mean is that the sum of deviations of different items of a series, when deviations are taken from arithmetic mean, is always zero.

This important notable property of arithmetic mean can be proved by the following example. The sum of the deviations from its arithmetic mean would be zero. This is worked out as under:

**ILLUSTRATION.**

Show that in the series of marks 10, 20, 30, 40, 50 obtained by five students the sum of deviations from arithmetic mean is zero.

**SOLUTION:**

| Marks (X) | $\overline{X} = 30$ Deviations from Arithmetic Mean $(X - \overline{X})$ |
|---|---|
| 10 | 10 – 30 = – 20 |
| 20 | 20 – 30 = – 10 |
| 30 | 30 – 30 = 0 |
| 40 | 40 – 30 = + 10 |
| 50 | 50 – 30 = + 20 |
| $\Sigma X = 150$<br>$N = 5$<br>$\overline{X} = 30$ | $\Sigma(X-\overline{X}) = 0$ |

Thus, the sum of the deviations from arithmetic mean

$\Sigma(X-\overline{X})$ = zero.

**Properties of Arithmetic Mean (AM)**

(i) The sum of deviations of the items from AM is always zero.
(ii) The sum of squared deviations of the items from AM is minimum.
(iii) If each item of a series is increased, decreased, multiplied or divided by some constant then AM also increases, decreases, multiplies or is divided by the same constant.
(iv) The product of the AM and the number of items on which mean is based is equal to the sum of all given items.
(v) If each item of the original series is replaced by the actual mean, then the sum of these substitutions will be equal to the sum of the individual items.

## MERITS AND DEMERITS OF ARITHMETIC MEAN

### Merits

The following are some of the main merits of arithmetic mean:

**(1) Simplicity:** From the viewpoint of calculation and usage, arithmetic mean is the simplest of all the measures of central tendency.

**(2) Certainty:** Arithmetic mean is a certain value; it has no scope for estimated values.

**(3) Based on All Items:** Arithmetic mean is based on all the items in a series. It is, therefore, a representative value of the different items.

**(4) Algebraic Treatment:** Arithmetic mean is capable of further algebraic treatment. It is, therefore, extensively used in statistical analysis.

**(5) Stability:** Arithmetic mean is a stable measure of central tendency. This is because changes in the sample of a series have minimum effect on the arithmetic average.

**(6) Basis of Comparison:** Being stable and certain, arithmetic mean can be easily used for comparison.

**(7) Accuracy Test:** Arithmetic mean can be tested for its accuracy as a representative value of the series.

**The Principal Merit of Arithmetic Mean**

That it is based on all items of the series and is capable of further algebraic treatment.

**The Principal Demerit of Arithmetic Mean**

That arithmetic mean gets distorted by extreme values in the series, and that the value of arithmetic mean may not figure in the series at all.

### Demerits

Arithmetic mean suffers from following demerits:

(1) **Effect of Extreme Value:** The main defect of arithmetic mean is that it gets distorted by extreme values of the series. Therefore, it is not always an accurate measure. To illustrate, pocket expenditure of a rich student of Class XI may be ₹ 2,000, while his four friends incur pocket expenditure of ₹ 100, ₹ 80, ₹ 70 and ₹ 50 respectively. The average pocket expenditure of all the five students would be:

$$\overline{X} = \frac{2,000 + 100 + 80 + 70 + 50}{5} = \frac{2,300}{5} = ₹460$$

Certainly this is not such an accurate mean of the pocket expenditure of five students as 4 out of 5 students incur pocket expenditure just ranging between ₹ 50 to ₹ 100. The mean value of ₹ 460 is largely owing to the fact that there is an extreme value of ₹ 2,000 in the series. Such a mean is certainly not a representative value of all the items in the series.

(2) **Mean Value may not figure in the series at all:** The mean value may sometimes be that value which does not figure in the series at all. The average of 2, 3 and 7 is $\frac{2 + 3 + 7}{3} = 4$ which is not there in the series. It further erodes its representative character.

(3) **Laughable Conclusions:** Arithmetic mean sometimes offers laughable conclusions. If there are 50 students in Class XI and 51 students in Class XII, the average strength of these two classes would come to $\frac{50 + 51}{2} = 50.5$ students, which is indeed very funny because there cannot be half student.

(4) **Unsuitability:** Arithmetic mean is not a suitable measure in case of percentage or proportionate values.

(5) **Misleading Conclusions:** Arithmetic mean sometimes offers misleading conclusions. Following example illustrates this point:

**Income of Two Individuals A and B for the years 2012-2014**

| Year | Income (₹) | |
|---|---|---|
| | A | B |
| 2012 | 1,000 | 3,000 |
| 2013 | 2,000 | 2,000 |
| 2014 | 3,000 | 1,000 |
| | $\overline{X} = \frac{6,000}{3} = 2,000$ | $\overline{X} = \frac{6,000}{3} = 2,000$ |

In the given Table, average income of both A and B is same suggesting that A and B have been equally rich during the years 2012 to 2014. But a close examination of the series should reveal that while the income of A is increasing over years, that of B is decreasing. Thus, arithmetic mean offers misleading conclusions.

However, despite certain demerits of arithmetic mean as noted above, this is an ideal measure of the central tendency. This is the most widely used measure in practical life. Arithmetic mean is particularly significant in such series of which different items are equally important and therefore, equally weighed. Average output, average cost, average revenue, are some of the well known concepts in Economics based on arithmetic mean.

**Calculation of Arithmetic Mean for Different Series: A Glance**

| Series | Methods of Calculation of Arithmetic Mean |
|---|---|
| 1. Individual Series | (a) Direct Method: Formula: $\overline{X} = \frac{\Sigma X}{N}$ |
| | (b) Short-cut Method: Formula: $\overline{X} = A + \frac{\Sigma d}{N}$ |
| 2. Discrete Series/Frequency Array | (a) Direct Method: Formula: $\overline{X} = \frac{\Sigma fX}{\Sigma f}$ |
| | (b) Short-cut Method: Formula: $\overline{X} = A + \frac{\Sigma fd}{\Sigma f}$ |
| | (c) Step-deviation Method: Formula: $\overline{X} = A + \frac{\Sigma fd'}{\Sigma f} \times C$ |
| 3. Frequency Distribution Series | (a) Direct Method: Formula: $\overline{X} = \frac{\Sigma fm}{\Sigma f}$ |
| | (b) Short-cut Method: Formula: $\overline{X} = A + \frac{\Sigma fd}{\Sigma f}$ |
| | (c) Step-deviation Method: Formula: $\overline{X} = A + \frac{\Sigma fd'}{\Sigma f} \times C$ |

**Just Don't Miss it**

If a constant amount is added, subtracted, multiplied or divided, the arithmetic mean will be affected accordingly. Check the following illustration:

| X | X + 2 | X – 2 | X × 2 | $\frac{X}{2}$ |
|---|---|---|---|---|
| 10 | 12 | 8 | 20 | 5 |
| 12 | 14 | 10 | 24 | 6 |
| 14 | 16 | 12 | 28 | 7 |
| 16 | 18 | 14 | 32 | 8 |
| 52 | 60 | 44 | 104 | 26 |
| $\overline{X}$ = 13 | $\overline{X}$ = 15 | $\overline{X}$ = 11 | $\overline{X}$ = 26 | $\overline{X}$ = 6.5 |

## MISCELLANEOUS ILLUSTRATIONS

**ILLUSTRATION 1.**

Following are the marks obtained by 8 students in Statistics. Calculate the arithmetic mean.

| Marks | 15 | 18 | 16 | 45 | 32 | 40 | 30 | 28 |
|---|---|---|---|---|---|---|---|---|

**SOLUTION:**

| Marks (X) |
|---|
| 15 |
| 18 |
| 16 |
| 45 |
| 32 |
| 40 |
| 30 |
| 28 |
| $\Sigma X = 224$ |

$$\overline{X} = \frac{\Sigma X}{N} = \frac{X_1 + X_2 + ... + X_8}{N} = \frac{224}{8} = 28$$

Average marks of the 8 students = 28.

**ILLUSTRATION 2.**

Following are the marks obtained by 25 students in Economics. Find out the mean marks by using Direct and Short-cut Method.

| Marks | 10 | 20 | 30 | 40 | 50 | 60 |
|---|---|---|---|---|---|---|
| Number of Students | 5 | 2 | 3 | 8 | 4 | 3 |

**SOLUTION:**

**Direct Method:**

| Marks (X) | Number of Students or Frequency (f) | Multiple of the Value of X and Frequency (fX) |
|---|---|---|
| 10 | 5 | $10 \times 5 = 50$ |
| 20 | 2 | $20 \times 2 = 40$ |
| 30 | 3 | $30 \times 3 = 90$ |
| 40 | 8 | $40 \times 8 = 320$ |
| 50 | 4 | $50 \times 4 = 200$ |
| 60 | 3 | $60 \times 3 = 180$ |
| | $\Sigma f = 25$ | $\Sigma fX = 880$ |

$$\overline{X} = \frac{\Sigma fX}{\Sigma f} = \frac{880}{25} = 35.2$$

Mean Marks of 25 Students in Economics = 35.2.

**Short-cut Method:**

**(Assumed Average, A = 40)**

| Marks (X) | Number of Students or Frequency (f) | Deviation (d = X – A) (A = 40) | Multiple of Deviation and Frequency (fd) |
|---|---|---|---|
| 10 | 5 | 10 – 40 = – 30 | – 150 |
| 20 | 2 | 20 – 40 = – 20 | – 40 |
| 30 | 3 | 30 – 40 = – 10 | – 30 |
| 40 | 8 | 40 – 40 = 0 | 0 |
| 50 | 4 | 50 – 40 = 10 | 40 |
| 60 | 3 | 60 – 40 = 20 | 60 |
| | Σf =25 | | Σfd = – 120 |

$$\overline{X} = A + \frac{\Sigma fd}{\Sigma f}$$

$$= 40 + \frac{-120}{25} = 40 - \frac{120}{25}$$

$$= 40 - 4.8 = 35.2$$

Thus, Mean Marks = 35.2.

**ILLUSTRATION 3.**

Calculate mean salary by Step-deviation Method of the following data:

| Salary Group | Number of Employees |
|---|---|
| 60–75 | 3 |
| 75–90 | 4 |
| 90–105 | 5 |
| 105–120 | 5 |
| 120–135 | 7 |
| 135–150 | 6 |

**SOLUTION:**

**(Assumed Average, A = 112.5)**

| Salary Group (X) | Mid-value $\left(m = \frac{l_1 + l_2}{2}\right)$ | Number of Employees or Frequency (f) | Deviation (d = m – A) (A = 112.5) | Step-deviation (d′ = d/C) (C = 15) | Multiple of Step-deviation and Frequency (fd′) |
|---|---|---|---|---|---|
| 60–75 | 67.5 | 3 | – 45 | – 3 | – 9 |
| 75–90 | 82.5 | 4 | – 30 | – 2 | – 8 |
| 90–105 | 97.5 | 5 | – 15 | – 1 | – 5 |
| 105–120 | 112.5 | 5 | 0 | 0 | 0 |
| 120–135 | 127.5 | 7 | 15 | 1 | 7 |
| 135–150 | 142.5 | 6 | 30 | 2 | 12 |
| | | Σf = 30 | | | Σfd′ = –3 |

$$\overline{X} = A + \frac{\Sigma fd'}{\Sigma f} \times C$$

$$= 112.5 + \frac{-3}{30} \times 15 = 112.5 - \frac{3}{30} \times 15$$

$$= 112.5 - 1.5 = 111$$

Thus, Mean Salary = ₹ 111.

**ILLUSTRATION 4.**

Calculate mean from the following data:

| Marks | 10–20 | 10–30 | 10–40 | 10–50 | 10–60 | 10–70 | 10–80 | 10–90 |
|---|---|---|---|---|---|---|---|---|
| Number of Students | 4 | 16 | 56 | 97 | 124 | 137 | 146 | 150 |

**SOLUTION:**

The given data is in cumulative frequency form. It should first be converted into simple frequency.

**(Assumed Average, A = 45)**

| Marks | Number of Students or Frequency (f) | Mid-value $\left(m = \frac{l_1 + l_2}{2}\right)$ | Deviation (d = m – A) (A = 45) | Step-deviation (d′ = d/C) (C = 10) | Multiple of Step-deviation and Frequency (fd′) |
|---|---|---|---|---|---|
| 10–20 | 4 | 15 | – 30 | – 3 | – 12 |
| 20–30 | 16 – 4 = 12 | 25 | – 20 | – 2 | – 24 |
| 30–40 | 56 – 16 = 40 | 35 | – 10 | – 1 | – 40 |
| 40–50 | 97 – 56 = 41 | 45 | 0 | 0 | 0 |
| 50–60 | 124 – 97 = 27 | 55 | + 10 | + 1 | + 27 |
| 60–70 | 137 – 124 = 13 | 65 | + 20 | + 2 | + 26 |
| 70–80 | 146 – 137 = 9 | 75 | + 30 | + 3 | + 27 |
| 80–90 | 150 – 146 = 4 | 85 | + 40 | + 4 | + 16 |
| | Σf = 150 | | | | Σfd′ = 20 |

$$\text{Mean, } \overline{X} = A + \frac{\Sigma fd'}{\Sigma f} \times C$$

$$= 45 + \frac{20}{150} \times 10$$

$$= 45 + 1.33 = 46.33$$

Thus, Mean Marks = 46.33.

**ILLUSTRATION 5.**

A train runs 25 miles at a speed of 30 mph, another 50 miles at a speed of 40 mph, then due to repairs of the track travels for 6 minutes at a speed of 10 mph and finally covers the remaining distance of 24 miles at a speed of 24 mph. What is the average speed in miles per hour?

**SOLUTION:**

Time taken in covering 25 miles at a speed of 30 mph

$$= 50 \text{ minutes} \qquad \left(\because \text{ Time} = \frac{\text{Distance}}{\text{Speed}}\right)$$

Time taken in covering 50 miles at a speed of 40 mph

$$= 75 \text{ minutes}$$

Distance covered in 6 minutes at a speed of 10 mph = 1 mile

Time taken in covering 24 miles at speed of 24 mph = 60 minutes.

Therefore, taking the time taken as weights we have the weighted mean as

| Speed in mph (X) | Time Taken (W) | WX |
|---|---|---|
| 30 | 50 | 1,500 |
| 40 | 75 | 3,000 |
| 10 | 6 | 60 |
| 24 | 60 | 1,440 |
| | ΣW = 191 | ΣWX = 6,000 |

$$\text{Weighted Mean, } \overline{X}_W = \frac{\Sigma WX}{\Sigma W} = \frac{6,000}{191} = 31.41$$

Average Speed = 31.41 mph.

**ILLUSTRATION 6.**

If the average salary of a firm is 400 and the number of workers is 60, find the total salary bill of the firm.

**SOLUTION:**

Given: $\overline{X} = 400, N = 60$

$$\overline{X} = \frac{\Sigma X}{N}$$

$$\Rightarrow \qquad = N \times \overline{X}$$

$$= 60 \times 400 = 24,000$$

Total Salary Bill = ₹ 24,000.

**ILLUSTRATION 7.**

The mean of 5 observations is 7. Later on, it was found that two observations 4 and 8 were wrongly taken instead of 5 and 9. Find the corrected mean.

**SOLUTION:**

Given: $N = 5, \overline{X} = 7$

$$\overline{X} = \frac{\Sigma X}{N}$$

Or, $$\Sigma X = \overline{X}N$$

$$\therefore \qquad \Sigma X(\text{Wrong}) = 5 \times 7 = 35$$

$$\text{Correct } \Sigma X = 35 + \text{Correct items} - \text{Incorrect items}$$
$$= 35 + 5 + 9 - 4 - 8 = 37$$
$$\text{Correct } \overline{X} = \frac{\text{Correct } \Sigma X}{N} = \frac{37}{5}$$
$$= 7.4$$

Thus, Corrected Mean = 7.4.

**ILLUSTRATION 8.**

The mean monthly salary paid to all employees in a certain company was ₹ 600. The mean monthly salaries paid to male and female employees were ₹ 620 and ₹ 520 respectively. Find the percentage of male to female employees in the company.

**SOLUTION:**

Given: $\overline{X}_{12} = 600$, $\overline{X}_1 = 620$, $\overline{X}_2 = 520$

Let $N_1$ = Male Employees and $N_2$ = Female Employees

Using the formula of combined arithmetic mean, we have

$$\overline{X}_{12} = \frac{\overline{X}_1 N_1 + \overline{X}_2 N_2}{N_1 + N_2}$$

$$600 = \frac{(620)N_1 + (520)N_2}{N_1 + N_2}$$

Or, $600(N_1 + N_2) = 620N_1 + 520N_2$

Or, $600N_1 + 600N_2 = 620N_1 + 520N_2$

Or, $600N_2 - 520\,N_2 = 620N_1 - 600N_1$

$80N_2 = 20N_1$

Or, $\frac{N_1}{N_2} = \frac{80}{20} = \frac{4}{1}$

Or, $N_1 : N_2 = 4 : 1$

Hence, the percentage of male employees $= \frac{4}{4+1} \times 100 = 80\%$

and the percentage of female employees $= \frac{1}{4+1} \times 100 = 20\%$.

**Aliter:**

The problem can also be solved by using the following method:

Let $x$ be the percentage of male employees in the combined group. Therefore, the percentage of women employees $= 100 - x$.

We are given that $\overline{X}_1$ (male) = ₹ 620 and $\overline{X}_2$ (female) = ₹ 520

Also, $\overline{X}_{12}$ (combined mean) = 600

$$600 = \frac{620x + 520\,(100 - x)}{x + (100 - x)}$$

$$600 = \frac{620x + 52{,}000 - 520x}{x + (100 - x)}$$

$$600 = \frac{100x + 52{,}000}{100}$$

$\Rightarrow \quad 60,000 - 52,000 = 100x$

$\Rightarrow \quad x = \frac{8,000}{100}$

$\Rightarrow \quad x = 80\%$

Thus, there are 80% male employees and 20% female employees in the company.

**ILLUSTRATION 9.**

Find the missing information in the following table:

| | A | B | C | Combined |
|---|---|---|---|---|
| **Number (N)** | 10 | 8 | — | 24 |
| **Mean ($\overline{X}$)** | 20 | — | 6 | 15 |

**SOLUTION:**

Missing number for C = 24 – (10 + 8) = 6

Let mean for B = $x$

We know that,

$$X_{1,2,3} = \frac{\overline{X}_1 N_1 + \overline{X}_2 N_2 + \overline{X}_3 N_3}{N_1 + N_2 + N_3}$$

$$\therefore \quad 15 = \frac{(20 \times 10) + (8 \times x) + (6 \times 6)}{24}$$

$200 + 8x + 36 = 15 \times 24$

$\Rightarrow \quad 200 + 8x + 36 = 360$

$\Rightarrow \quad 8x = 360 - 236$

$\Rightarrow \quad 8x = 124$

$\Rightarrow \quad x = \frac{124}{8}$

$\Rightarrow \quad x = 15.5$

Thus, Missing Number for C = 6.

Mean of B = 15.5.

**ILLUSTRATION 10.**

In a class of 50 students 10 have failed and their average of marks is 2.5. The total marks secured by the entire class were 281. Find the average marks those who have passed.

**SOLUTION:**

Given: N = 50, Failed Students = 10

Mean marks of those who failed = 2.5

Total marks of 10 students who have failed = 2.5 × 10 = 25

Total marks secured by the entire class = 281

Total marks obtained by those who have passed = 281 – 25 = 256

Average marks obtained by those who have passed = $\frac{256}{40} = 6.4$

Average marks obtained by those who have passed = 6.4.

## EXERCISE

### 1. Very Short Answer Type Questions [1 mark]

**A. Multiple Choice Questions: Choose the Correct Answer**

1. Which of the following is a type of mathematical average?
   (a) Median (b) Partition value
   (c) Mode (d) None of these
2. Formula for finding arithmetic mean is:
   (a) $\overline{X} = \Sigma X$ (b) $\overline{X} = \frac{\Sigma X}{N}$
   (c) $\overline{X} = \Sigma X - N$ (d) $\overline{X} = \frac{N}{\Sigma X}$
3. Arithmetic mean of these items 5, 7, 9, 15, 20 is:
   (a) 10 (b) 10.2
   (c) 11.2 (d) 12
4. Arithmetic mean of these items: 10, 15, X, 20, 30 is 20. Find out the missing item.
   (a) 10 (b) 15
   (c) 5 (d) 25
5. By which formula is combined arithmetic mean estimated?
   (a) $\overline{X}_{12} = \frac{X_1 + X_2 + ... + X_n}{N_1 + N_2}$ (b) $\overline{X}_{12} = \frac{\overline{X}_1 N_1 + \overline{X}_2 N_2}{N_1 + N_2}$
   (c) $\overline{X}_{12} = \frac{\overline{X}_1 + \overline{X}_2}{N_1 + N_2}$ (d) None of these
6. Arithmetic mean of a series is 15 and if 5 is added in all the items of this series, the new arithmetic mean will be:
   (a) 5 (b) 20
   (c) 18 (d) 10
7. What is the formula to find out arithmetic mean through short-cut method in individual series?
   (a) $\overline{X} = \frac{\Sigma X}{N}$ (b) $\overline{X} = A + \frac{\Sigma d}{N}$
   (c) $\overline{X} = \frac{\Sigma X}{N} + A$ (d) $\overline{X} = \frac{\Sigma fX}{\Sigma f}$
8. Which of the following is not a measure of central tendency?
   (a) Mean (b) Mode
   (c) Standard deviation (d) Median
9. Which is not a method to find arithmetic mean?
   (a) Direct method (b) Short-cut method
   (c) Step-deviation method (d) Karl Pearson's method
10. Assumed mean is taken in which method?
    (a) Direct method (b) Step-deviation method
    (c) Karl Pearson's method (d) Spearman's method

11. Sum of deviations of different values from arithmetic mean is always equal to:

(a) zero (b) one

(c) less than one (d) more than one

Ans. 1. (d), 2. (b), 3. (c), 4. (d), 5. (b), 6. (b), 7. (b), 8. (c), 9. (d), 10. (b), 11. (a).

### B. True or False

State whether the following statements are True or False:

1. Central tendency refers to a central value of a statistical series. (True/False)
2. Averages help in the formulation of economic policies. (True/False)
3. The mean of weighted items is called weighted average. (True/False)
4. If a given number is subtracted from all the items in a series, then the arithmetic mean of that series will increase by the same specific value. (True/False)
5. There is least effect of marginal values on arithmetic mean. (True/False)
6. Arithmetic mean is shown by the following formula: (True/False)

   $\overline{X} = X_1 + X_2 + ... + X_n - N = \Sigma X - N$

Ans. 1. True, 2. True, 3. True, 4. False, 5. False, 6. False.

### C. Concepts/Definitions & Knowledge-based Questions

1. What do you mean by average value?

Ans. An average value refers to a central value or representative value of a statistical series.

2. Define arithmetic mean.

Ans. Arithmetic mean is the number which is obtained by adding the values of all the items of a series and dividing the total by the number of items.

3. Define weighted arithmetic mean.

Ans. Weighted arithmetic mean is the mean of weighted items of the series. Different items are accorded different weights depending on their relative importance. The weighted sum of the items is divided by the sum of the weights.

4. What are the types of arithmetic mean?

Ans. The two types of arithmetic mean are:

(i) Simple arithmetic mean, and (ii) Weighted arithmetic mean

5. Name any two mathematical averages.

Ans. The two mathematical averages are:

(i) Arithmetic mean, and (ii) Geometric mean

6. Give formula of calculating arithmetic mean of a continuous series using direct method.

Ans. $\overline{X} = \frac{\Sigma fm}{\Sigma f}$, Here, $\overline{X}$ = Arithmetic mean,

f = Frequency,

$m = \text{Mid-value} = \frac{\text{lower limit + upper limit}}{2} = \frac{l_1 + l_2}{2}$

7. Give formula of weighted average.

Ans. $\overline{X}_W = \frac{\Sigma WX}{\Sigma W}$, Here, $\overline{X}_W$ indicates weighted average, and W = Weights

8. State one notable property of arithmetic mean.

Ans. A notable property of arithmetic mean is that the sum of deviations of different items of a series, when deviations are taken from arithmetic mean, is always zero.

## 2. Short Answer Type Questions [3-4 marks]

1. What do you mean by statistical average or central tendency of a series? State its functions.
2. Explain the kinds of statistical averages.
3. Define and explain arithmetic mean.
4. Define and explain weighted arithmetic mean.
5. Discuss the various properties of arithmetic mean.
6. The arithmetic mean is described as the centre of gravity of the distribution of values of the variable. Explain.
7. Show that the sum of deviations of the values of the variable from their arithmetic mean is equal to zero.
8. Give the four objectives of statistical average.
9. State four merits of an ideal measure of central tendency.
10. State four merits of arithmetic mean.
11. State four demerits of arithmetic mean.

## 3. Long Answer Type Questions [6 marks]

1. What is statistical average? What desirable properties should an average possess?
2. Discuss the various methods of measuring arithmetic mean and point out its merits and demerits.
3. Why is the arithmetic mean the most commonly used measure of central tendency?
4. Explain the step-deviation method of calculating arithmetic mean, taking an imaginary set of data.

## 4. Essential Practicals

1. Eight workers earn the following income:

   30, 36, 34, 40, 42, 46, 54, 62

   Find out arithmetic mean. (Ans. Arithmetic Mean = ₹ 43)

2. Pocket allowance of 5 students respectively are:

   125, 75, 150, 175, 200

   Find out arithmetic mean. (Ans. Arithmetic Mean = ₹ 145)

3. Following is the height of 10 students:

| **Students** | A | B | C | D | E | F | G | H | I | J |
|---|---|---|---|---|---|---|---|---|---|---|
| **Height (cm)** | 155 | 153 | 168 | 160 | 162 | 166 | 164 | 180 | 157 | 165 |

   Calculate arithmetic mean using Direct and Short-cut Methods. (Ans. Arithmetic Mean = 163 cm)

4. Weight of 15 persons is as follows:

| **Weight (kg)** | 20 | 28 | 34 | 39 | 42 | 50 | 53 | 54 | 59 | 64 | 72 | 74 | 74 | 78 | 79 |
|---|---|---|---|---|---|---|---|---|---|---|---|---|---|---|---|

   Find out mean weight, using Direct Method as well as Short-cut Method.

   (Ans. Weighted Mean = 54.67 kg)

5. Calculate average of the following discrete series. Use Short-cut Method by taking 25 as assumed average.

| Size | 30 | 29 | 28 | 27 | 26 | 25 | 24 | 23 | 22 | 21 |
|---|---|---|---|---|---|---|---|---|---|---|
| Frequency (f) | 2 | 4 | 5 | 3 | 2 | 7 | 1 | 4 | 5 | 7 |

(Ans. Average = 24.925)

6. Marks secured by 42 students in Economics are:

| Marks | 15 | 20 | 22 | 23 | 27 | 35 | 18 |
|---|---|---|---|---|---|---|---|
| Number of Students | 8 | 4 | 7 | 3 | 8 | 7 | 5 |

Find average marks. (Ans. Average Marks = 23.2)

7. Average age of the people of a country is shown in the following table:

| Age (Years) | 10–20 | 20–30 | 30–40 | 40–50 | 50–60 |
|---|---|---|---|---|---|
| People ('000) | 30 | 32 | 15 | 12 | 9 |

Find out mean age by Direct Method. (Ans. Mean Age = 28.7 years)

8. Calculate the arithmetic mean of the following frequency distribution by Direct Method:

| Class Interval | 10–20 | 20–40 | 40–70 | 70–120 | 120–200 |
|---|---|---|---|---|---|
| Frequency | 4 | 10 | 26 | 8 | 2 |

(Ans. Arithmetic Mean = 57.4)

9. Calculate arithmetic mean from the following data by Short-cut Method:

| Class Interval | 20–25 | 25–30 | 30–35 | 35–40 | 40–45 | 45–50 | 50–55 |
|---|---|---|---|---|---|---|---|
| Frequency | 10 | 12 | 8 | 20 | 11 | 4 | 5 |

(Ans. Arithmetic Mean = 35.5)

10. Find out arithmetic mean from the following distribution by Short-cut Method:

| Items | 10–8 | 8–6 | 6–4 | 4–2 | 2–0 |
|---|---|---|---|---|---|
| Frequency | 10 | 8 | 6 | 4 | 2 |

(Ans. Arithmetic Mean = 6.33)

11. Sachin made the following runs in different matches:

| Runs | 5–15 | 15–25 | 25–35 | 35–45 | 45–55 |
|---|---|---|---|---|---|
| Frequency | 10 | 12 | 17 | 19 | 22 |

Calculate the average mean of the runs by Step-deviation Method.

(Ans. Average Mean = 33.875 runs)

12. Calculate arithmetic mean of the following frequency distribution:

| Class | less than 10 | 10–20 | 20–30 | 30–40 | 40–50 | 50–60 | more than 60 |
|---|---|---|---|---|---|---|---|
| Frequency | 5 | 12 | 18 | 22 | 6 | 4 | 3 |

(Ans. Arithmetic Mean = 30.14)

13. Mean marks obtained by a student in his five subjects are 15. In English he secures 8 marks, in Economics 12, in Mathematics 18, and in Commerce 9. Find out the marks he secured in Statistics.

(Ans. Marks secured in Statistics = 28 marks)

14. Mean value of the weekly income of 40 families is 265. But in the calculation, income of one family was read as 150 instead of 115. Find the "Corrected" mean. (Ans. Corrected Mean = ₹ 264.125)

15. Average pocket allowance of 6 students is ₹ 45. Of these, pocket allowance of 5 students is 20, 30, 22, 24 and 32 respectively. What is the pocket allowance of the sixth student?

(Ans. Pocket Allowance of the Sixth Student = ₹ 142)

16. The following table shows wages of the workers. Calculate the average wage of the workers.

| Wages (₹) | 10–19 | 20–29 | 30–39 | 40–49 | 50–59 |
|---|---|---|---|---|---|
| Number of Workers | 8 | 9 | 12 | 11 | 6 |

(Ans. Average Wage of the Workers = ₹ 34.07)

17. Ten players of the Australian team made an average of 63 runs and ten players of the Indian team made an average of 77 runs. Calculate the average run made by both the teams.

(Ans. Collective Average Run = 70)

18. Average income of 50 families is ₹ 3,000. Of these average income of 12 families is ₹ 1,800. Find out the average income of the remaining families.

(Ans. Average income of the remaining families = ₹ 3,378.95)

19. In the following frequency distribution, if the arithmetic mean is 45.6, find out missing frequency.

| Wages (₹) | 10–20 | 20–30 | 30–40 | 40–50 | 50–60 | 60–70 | 70–80 |
|---|---|---|---|---|---|---|---|
| Number of Workers | 5 | 6 | 7 | X | 4 | 3 | 9 |

(Ans. Missing Frequency = 16)

20. Calculate the weighted mean of the following data:

| Items | 96 | 102 | 104 | 124 | 148 | 164 |
|---|---|---|---|---|---|---|
| Weight | 5 | 6 | 3 | 7 | 12 | 9 |

(Ans. Weighted Mean = 131.52)

21. A student obtained 60 marks in English, 75 in Hindi, 63 in Mathematics, 59 in Economics and 55 in Statistics. Calculate weighted mean of the marks if weights are respectively 2, 1, 5, 5 and 3.

(Ans. Weighted Mean = 60.625 marks)

22. A housewife uses 10 kg of Wheat, 20 kg of Fuel, 5 kg of Sugar, and 2 kg of oil. Prices (per kg) of these items are ₹ 1.50 , 50 paise, ₹ 2.80 and ₹ 10 respectively. Taking quantities used as weights find out the weighted arithmetic average of the prices.

(Ans. Weighted Arithmetic Average = ₹ 1.59 per kg)

23. Calculate weighted mean of the following data by using Direct and Short-cut Methods:

| Items | 81 | 76 | 74 | 58 | 70 | 73 |
|---|---|---|---|---|---|---|
| Weight | 2 | 3 | 6 | 7 | 3 | 7 |

(Ans. Weighted Mean = 70.04)

## 5. NCERT Textbook Questions [With Hints to Answers]

1. Which average would be suitable in the following cases?
   (i) Average size of readymade garments.
   (ii) Average intelligence of students in a class.
   (iii) Average production in a factory per shift.
   (iv) Average wages in an industrial concern.
   (v) When the sum of absolute deviations from average is least.

(vi) When quantities of the variable are in ratios.

(vii) In case of open-ended frequency distribution.

[ (i) Mode (indicating a typical value of the series).

(ii) Mode (identifying modal value by ranking intelligence on the scale of 1–10).

(iii) Arithmetic mean.

(iv) Median (indicating 'less than or equal to wage' for 50% of the workers, and 'more than or equal to wage' for the other 50%).

(v) Arithmetic mean.

(vi) Weighted arithmetic mean.

(vii) Median (as it is not sensitive to all the values in a series).]

2. Indicate the most appropriate alternative from the multiple choices provided against each question.

(i) The most suitable average for qualitative measurement is:

(a) arithmetic mean (b) median

(c) mode

(ii) Which average is affected most by the presence of extreme items?

(a) median (b) mode

(c) arithmetic mean (d) geometric mean

(e) harmonic mean

(iii) The algebraic sum of deviation of a set of n values from A.M. is

(a) n (b) 0

(c) 1 (d) none of these

[(i) (c), (ii) (c), (iii) (b)]

3. The following table gives the daily income of ten workers in a factory. Find the arithmetic mean.

| Workers | A | B | C | D | E | F | G | H | I | J |
|---|---|---|---|---|---|---|---|---|---|---|
| Daily Income (in ₹) | 120 | 150 | 180 | 200 | 250 | 300 | 220 | 350 | 370 | 260 |

[

| Workers | Daily Income (in ₹) (X) |
|---|---|
| A | 120 |
| B | 150 |
| C | 180 |
| D | 200 |
| E | 250 |
| F | 300 |
| G | 220 |
| H | 350 |
| I | 370 |
| J | 260 |
| | $\Sigma X = 2,400$ |

$$\overline{X} = \frac{X_1 + X_2 + ... + X_{10}}{N}$$

$$= \frac{2,400}{10} = 240$$

∴ Arithmetic mean = ₹240.]

4. Following information pertains to the daily income of 150 families. Calculate the arithmetic mean.

| Income (in ₹) | Number of Families |
|---|---|
| More than 75 | 150 |
| More than 85 | 140 |
| More than 95 | 115 |
| More than 105 | 95 |
| More than 115 | 70 |
| More than 125 | 60 |
| More than 135 | 40 |
| More than 145 | 25 |

**[Conversion of a Cumulative Frequency Distribution into a Simple Frequency Distribution**

(Assumed Average, A = 110)

| Income (in ₹) | Mid-value $\left(m = \frac{l_1 + l_2}{2}\right)$ | Number of Families or Frequency (f) | Deviation (d = m – A) A = 110 | Step-deviation $\left(d' = \frac{m - A}{C}\right)$ C = 10 | Multiple of Step-deviation and Frequency (fd′) |
|---|---|---|---|---|---|
| 75–85 | 80 | 150 – 140 = 10 | – 30 | – 3 | – 30 |
| 85–95 | 90 | 140 – 115 = 25 | – 20 | – 2 | – 50 |
| 95–105 | 100 | 115 – 95 = 20 | – 10 | – 1 | – 20 |
| 105–115 | 110 | 95 – 70 = 25 | 0 | 0 | 0 |
| 115–125 | 120 | 70 – 60 = 10 | 10 | 1 | 10 |
| 125–135 | 130 | 60 – 40 = 20 | 20 | 2 | 40 |
| 135–145 | 140 | 40 – 25 = 15 | 30 | 3 | 45 |
| 145–155 | 150 | 25 | 40 | 4 | 100 |
| | | Σf = 150 | | | Σfd′ = 95 |

$$\overline{X} = A + \frac{\Sigma fd'}{\Sigma f} \times C$$

$$= 110 + \frac{95}{150} \times 10$$

$$= 110 + 6.3$$

$$= 116.3$$

∴ Arithmetic mean = ₹116.3.]

# Measures of Central Tendency—Median and Mode

10

In a statistical series, there may be a value which is centrally located or which occurs most frequently in the series. This is known as central value of the series. For example, if five friends watch, 5, 10, 15, 20 and 30 movies respectively, in a month, then 15 is the central value of the series. Take another example, suppose 80 out of 100 customers visiting a shoe shop buy shoes of size 8, then 8 occurs most frequently in a series of 100 observations. Accordingly, 8 will be taken as the central value of the series, though it includes other values as well like, 7, 9, 10, etc. In the first example, '15' is the central value and it is positioned somewhere in the middle of the series. Hence, it is called median value. In the second example, 8 happens to occur most frequently in the series (80 times out of 100). Hence, it is called modal value. Median and mode are the most important positional averages. These are called positional averages because their value is worked out on the basis of their position in the statistical series. There are other positional averages as well (besides median and mode) as indicated in the following flow chart.

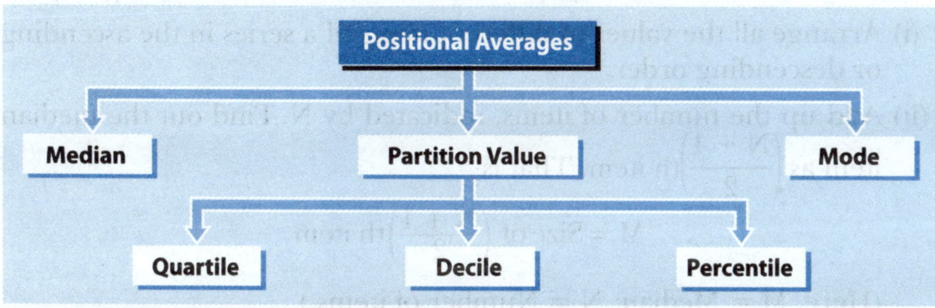


The present chapter focuses only on median and mode, in accordance with the CBSE guidelines. Only a passing reference is made to the estimation of one partition value, *viz*, 'Quartile' as its knowledge would help understand the estimation of 'Quartile Deviation' which is one of the various measures of dispersions, discussed in the next chapter.

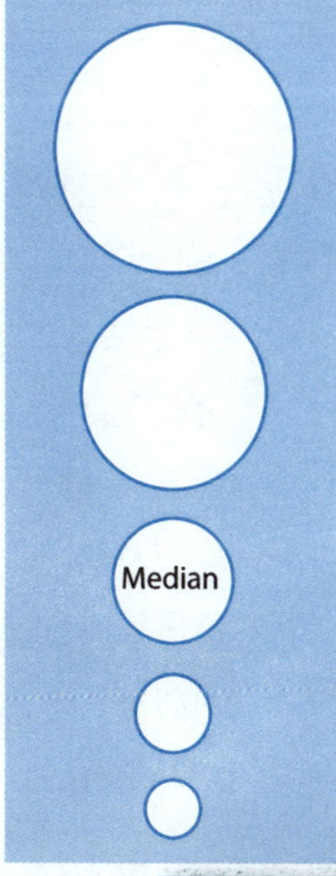


## 1. Median

Median is a centrally located value of a series such that half of the values (or items) of the series are above it and the other half below it. To illustrate if median height of the students of a class is to be determined, all the students may be asked to stand in the increasing or decreasing order of their heights. The student figuring in the middle would be taken as the central item of the series. Height of this student would be taken as median

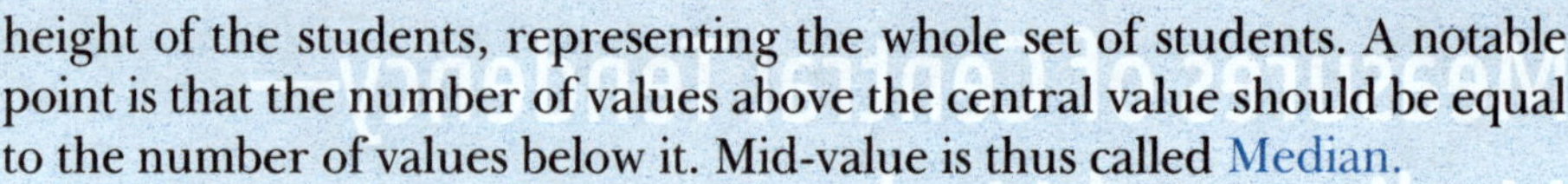

height of the students, representing the whole set of students. A notable point is that the number of values above the central value should be equal to the number of values below it. Mid-value is thus called Median.

### Definition

According to **Connor**, "*The Median is that value of the variable which divides the group into two equal parts, one part comprising all values greater than the median value and the other part comprising all the values smaller than the median value.*"

## How to Find the Median Value?

In Statistics, median is indicated by M. In order to locate the median value, all items of a series are arranged in either the ascending order or descending order. In ascending order, higher values follow the lower values. In the descending order, lower values follow the higher values. The median value is located, using the following formula:

### FORMULA

$$M = \text{Size of } \left(\frac{N+1}{2}\right)\text{th item}$$

(Here, M = Median; N = Number of items.)

Let us learn the application of this formula, taking different types of statistical series.

## Calculation of Median for Different Types of Statistical Series

### (1) Individual Series and the Median

Calculation of median in individual series involves the following steps:

(i) Arrange all the values of different items of a series in the ascending or descending order.

(ii) Add up the number of items, indicated by N. Find out the median item as $\left(\frac{N+1}{2}\right)$th item. That is,

$$M = \text{Size of } \left(\frac{N+1}{2}\right)\text{th item}$$

(Here, M = Median; N = Number of items.)

(iii) If N of series happens to be an odd number, that is, not divisible by 2, it is easier to find out median with the help of the above formula. For example, if the series is 4, 5, 6, 7, 8, then Median will be $\frac{5+1}{2}$ =3rd item.

4 5 6 7 8

↑

Median

↓

1 2 3 4 5

$$\text{Median} = \text{Size of } \left(\frac{N+1}{2}\right)\text{th} = \text{3rd item} = 6$$

(iv) If N of series happens to be an even number, $\frac{N+1}{2}$ will come in fractions. Thus, if the series is 4,10,12, and 18, then the $\frac{N+1}{2}$ would not be a complete number, but it would be like 2.5th value. In such cases, median value would be the arithmetic mean of the two middle values of the series. Thus, median value or the size of 2.5th item would be located as under:

$$\text{Median} = \frac{\text{Size of 2nd item} + \text{Size of 3rd item}}{2}$$

$$= \text{Size of 2.5th item}$$

$$= \frac{10+12}{2} = \frac{22}{2} = 11$$

When N of the series is an even number, median is estimated using the following formula:

$$M = \frac{\text{Size of}\left(\frac{N}{2}\right)\text{th item} + \text{Size of}\left(\frac{N}{2}+1\right)\text{th item}}{2}$$

**ILLUSTRATION.**

The following series show marks in Economics of 11 students of Class XI. Find the median marks.

| Marks | 17 | 32 | 35 | 33 | 15 | 21 | 41 | 32 | 11 | 10 | 20 |
|---|---|---|---|---|---|---|---|---|---|---|---|

| Ascending Order | | Descending Order | |
|---|---|---|---|
| S. No. | Marks | S. No. | Marks |
| 1 | 10 | 1 | 41 |
| 2 | 11 | 2 | 35 |
| 3 | 15 | 3 | 33 |
| 4 | 17 | 4 | 32 |
| 5 | 20 | 5 | 32 |
| 6 (M) | 21 | 6 (M) | 21 |
| 7 | 32 | 7 | 20 |
| 8 | 32 | 8 | 17 |
| 9 | 33 | 9 | 15 |
| 10 | 35 | 10 | 11 |
| 11 | 41 | 11 | 10 |
| N = 11 | | N = 11 | |

$$M = \text{Size of}\left(\frac{N+1}{2}\right)\text{th item}$$

$$= \text{Size of}\left(\frac{11+1}{2}\right)\text{th item}$$

$$= \text{Size of 6th item} = 21$$

Median = 21.

Important: Cumulative frequency as used in the formula for estimating the median value refers to the cumulative frequency of the class immediately preceding the median class.

**Learning by doing**

1. *Marks of 15 students in their Economics paper are:*
   *6, 9, 10, 12, 18, 19, 23, 23, 24, 28, 37, 48, 49, 53, 60*
   *Find the median marks.* *(Ans. M = 23 marks)*
2. *Height of seven students is measured in cm as,*
   *140, 142, 144, 145, 147, 149, 151*
   *Find the median height.* *(Ans. M = 145 cm)*
3. *Weight of eight students in kg is noted as,*
   *71, 72, 64, 68, 70, 76, 73, 75*
   *Find the median weight.* *(Ans. M = 71.5 kg)*

### (2) Discrete Series or Frequency Array and the Median

Calculation of median in case of discrete series or frequency array involves the following steps:

**Important**

Cumulative frequency as used in the formula for estimating the median value refers to the cumulative frequency of the class immediately preceding the median class.

(i) Arrange the data into ascending (or descending) order.

(ii) Convert the simple frequencies of a series into cumulative frequencies,

(iii) Determine the $\left(\frac{N+1}{2}\right)$th item of the series, N being equal to $\Sigma f$.

(iv) Find the median value corresponding to the $\left(\frac{N+1}{2}\right)$th item.

**ILLUSTRATION.**

Find the median of the following series:

| **Size** | 2 | 3 | 4 | 5 | 6 | 7 | 8 | 9 | 10 |
|---|---|---|---|---|---|---|---|---|---|
| **Frequency** | 2 | 3 | 8 | 10 | 12 | 16 | 10 | 8 | 6 |

**SOLUTION:**

**Estimation of the Median**

| Size | Frequency | Cumulative Frequency |
|---|---|---|
| 2 | 2 | 2 |
| 3 | 3 | 2 + 3 = 5 |
| 4 | 8 | 5 + 8 = 13 |
| 5 | 10 | 13 + 10 = 23 |
| 6 | 12 | 23 + 12 = 35 |
| 7 | 16 | 35 + 16 = 51 (M) |
| 8 | 10 | 51 + 10 = 61 |
| 9 | 8 | 61 + 8 = 69 |
| 10 | 6 | 69 + 6 = 75 |
| | N=75 | |

$$\text{Median or M} = \text{Size of}\left(\frac{N+1}{2}\right)\text{th item}$$

$$= \text{Size of}\left(\frac{75+1}{2}\right)\text{th item}$$

$$= \text{Size of 38th item}$$

It shows that median value corresponds to the 38th item in the series. This item appears first of all in 51st cumulative frequency of the series. Therefore, median shall be the value corresponding to the 51st cumulative frequency, which is 7.

Median = 7.

*Learning by doing*

1. *Find out median of the following series:*

| **Size** | 20 | 25 | 30 | 35 | 40 | 45 | 50 | 55 |
|---|---|---|---|---|---|---|---|---|
| **Frequency** | 14 | 18 | 33 | 30 | 20 | 15 | 13 | 7 |

*(Ans. M = 35)*

2. *Find out median of the following series:*

| **Selling Price (paise)** | 45 | 46 | 47 | 48 | 49 | 50 | 51 | 52 |
|---|---|---|---|---|---|---|---|---|
| **Frequency** | 23 | 20 | 42 | 50 | 41 | 12 | 8 | 4 |

*(Ans. M = 48 paise)*

### (3) Frequency Distribution Series and the Median

Calculation of median in a continuous series involves the following steps:

(i) The data are arranged in ascending or descending orders of their class interval.

(ii) The frequencies are then converted into cumulative frequencies.

(iii) Median class of the series is identified. It corresponds to that cumulative frequency which includes the $\left(\frac{N}{2}\right)$th item.

(iv) The following formula is applied to determine the actual median value.

**FORMULA**

$$M = l_1 + \frac{\frac{N}{2} - c.f.}{f} \times i$$

(Here, $l_1$ = Lower limit of the median class; c.f. = Cumulative frequency of the class preceding the median class; f = Frequency of the median class; $i$ = Size of the median class interval.)

**ILLUSTRATION.**

Find out median value of the following distribution:

| **Wage Rate (₹)** | 0–10 | 10–20 | 20–30 | 30–40 | 40–50 |
|---|---|---|---|---|---|
| **Number of Workers** | 22 | 38 | 46 | 35 | 20 |

**SOLUTION:**

| Wage Rate (₹) | Frequency (f) | Cumulative Frequency |
|---|---|---|
| 0–10 | 22 | 22 |
| 10–20 | 38 | **60 (c.f.)** |
| ($l_1$) **20–30** | **46 (f)** | 106 |
| 30–40 | 35 | 141 |
| 40–50 | 20 | 161 |
| | $\Sigma f = N = 161$ | |

$$\therefore \quad M = \text{Size of} \left(\frac{N}{2}\right)\text{th item; } N = \sum f = 161$$

$$\therefore \quad M = \text{Size of} \left(\frac{161}{2}\right)\text{th item} = \text{Size of 80.5th item}$$

80.5th item lies in 106th cumulative frequency. The class interval corresponding to this cumulative frequency is 20–30, which, therefore, is the median class interval. That is, the value of the median must lie within the range of 20–30. The following formula is applied to identify the exact value of the median.

$$M = l_1 + \frac{\frac{N}{2} - c.f.}{f} \times i$$

$$= 20 + \frac{\frac{161}{2} - 60}{46} \times 10 = 20 + \frac{80.5 - 60}{46} \times 10$$

$$= 20 + \frac{20.5}{46} \times 10 = 20 + 4.46 = 24.46$$

Median = ₹ 24.46.

**ILLUSTRATION.**

The following table gives distribution of marks secured by some students:

| Marks | 10–20 | 20–30 | 30–40 | 40–50 | 50–60 | 60–70 | 70–80 |
|---|---|---|---|---|---|---|---|
| Number of Students | 42 | 38 | 120 | 84 | 48 | 36 | 31 |

Calculate the median marks secured by the students.

**SOLUTION:**

**Calculation of Median**

| Marks | Frequency (f) | Cumulative Frequency |
|---|---|---|
| 10–20 | 42 | 42 |
| 20–30 | 38 | **80 (c.f.)** |
| ($l_1$) **30–40** | **120 (f)** | 200 |
| 40–50 | 84 | 284 |
| 50–60 | 48 | 332 |
| 60–70 | 36 | 368 |
| 70–80 | 31 | 399 |
| | N = 399 | |

$$M = \text{Size of} \left(\frac{N}{2}\right)\text{th item}$$

$$= \text{Size of} \left(\frac{399}{2}\right)\text{th item} = \text{Size of } 199.5\text{th item}$$

Hence, median lies in the class 30–40.

$$M = l_1 + \frac{\frac{N}{2} - \text{c.f.}}{f} \times i$$

$$= 30 + \frac{\frac{399}{2} - 80}{120} \times 10$$

$$= 30 + \frac{199.5 - 80}{120} \times 10 = 30 + \frac{119.5}{120} \times 10$$

$$= 30 + 9.96 = 39.96$$

Median Marks = 39.96.

*Learning by doing*

1. *Find out median of the following series:*

| **Items** | 20–30 | 30–40 | 40–50 | 50–60 | 60–70 | 70–80 | 80–90 |
|---|---|---|---|---|---|---|---|
| **Frequency** | 5 | 10 | 16 | 18 | 12 | 10 | 8 |

*(Ans. M = 54.7)*

2. *Find out median marks of the following marks distribution for 100 students.*

| **Marks** | 0–10 | 10–20 | 20–30 | 30–40 | 40–50 |
|---|---|---|---|---|---|
| **Number of Students** | 8 | 30 | 40 | 12 | 10 |

*(Ans. M = 23 marks)*

### (4) Cumulative Frequency Series and the Median

**Illustration.**

Calculate median of the following series:

| **Wage Rate (₹) (less than)** | 10 | 20 | 30 | 40 | 50 | 60 | 70 | 80 |
|---|---|---|---|---|---|---|---|---|
| **Number of Workers** | 15 | 35 | 60 | 84 | 96 | 127 | 198 | 250 |

**Solution:**

As a first step the cumulative frequency of 'less than' type is converted into a simple frequency distribution as under:

**Calculation of Median**

| **Wage Rate (₹)** | **Cumulative Frequency** | **Frequency (f)** |
|---|---|---|
| 0–10 | 15 | 15 |
| 10–20 | 35 | 35 – 15 = 20 |
| 20–30 | 60 | 60 – 35 = 25 |
| 30–40 | 84 | 84 – 60 = 24 |
| 40–50 | **96 (c.f.)** | 96 – 84 = 12 |
| ($l_1$) **50–60** | 127 | **127 – 96 = 31(f)** |
| 60–70 | 198 | 198 – 127 = 71 |
| 70–80 | 250 | 250 – 198 = 52 |
| | | $\Sigma f = N = 250$ |

M = Size of N/2th item or 250/2 = 125th item which lies in 127th cumulative frequency of the series. The corresponding class interval, 50–60 is, therefore, the median class interval. The actual value of the median is determined using the standard formula, *viz.*

$$M = l_1 + \frac{\frac{N}{2} - c.f.}{f} \times i$$

Imputing the values,

$l_1 = 50$, c.f. = 96, f = 31, $i = 10$

$$M = 50 + \frac{\frac{250}{2} - 96}{31} \times 10$$

$$= 50 + \frac{125 - 96}{31} \times 10$$

$$= 50 + \frac{29}{31} \times 10$$

$$= 50 + 9.35 = 59.35$$

Median Wage Rate = ₹ 59.35.

### (5) Inclusive Series and the Median

**ILLUSTRATION.**

Calculate median of the following data:

| Marks | 46–50 | 41–45 | 36–40 | 31–35 | 26–30 | 21–25 | 16–20 | 11–15 |
|---|---|---|---|---|---|---|---|---|
| Number of Students | 5 | 11 | 22 | 35 | 26 | 13 | 10 | 7 |

**SOLUTION:**

**Important**

Always convert inclusive series into exclusive series, before you start estimating median value of the series.

This is an inclusive series given in the descending order. It should first be converted into an exclusive series and placed in the ascending order, as in the following table:

| Conversion into Exclusive Series | Frequency (f) | Cumulative Frequency |
|---|---|---|
| 10.5–15.5 | 7 | 7 |
| 15.5–20.5 | 10 | 17 |
| 20.5–25.5 | 13 | 30 |
| 25.5–30.5 | 26 | **56 (c.f.)** |
| **($l_1$) 30.5–35.5** | **35 (f)** | 91 |
| 35.5–40.5 | 22 | 113 |
| 40.5–45.5 | 11 | 124 |
| 45.5–50.5 | 5 | 129 |
| | N = 129 | |

Median, M = Size of $\left(\frac{N}{2}\right)$th item; N = $\Sigma f$ = 129

= Size of $\left(\frac{129}{2}\right)$th item = Size of 64.5th item

64.5th item lies in 91st cumulative frequency of the series. The corresponding class interval, 30.5–35.5, would therefore, be the Median class interval.

Using the formula,

$$M = l_1 + \frac{\frac{N}{2} - c.f.}{f} \times i$$

$$= 30.5 + \frac{\frac{129}{2} - 56}{35} \times 5$$

$$= 30.5 + \frac{64.5 - 56}{35} \times 5 = 30.5 + \frac{8.5}{35} \times 5$$

$$= 30.5 + 1.2 = 31.7$$

Median = 31.7 marks.

### (6) Median of the Series with Unequal Class Intervals

**ILLUSTRATION.**

Calculate median of the following distribution of data:

| Class Interval | 0–5 | 5–10 | 10–20 | 20–30 | 30–50 | 50–70 | 70–100 |
|---|---|---|---|---|---|---|---|
| Number of Students | 12 | 15 | 25 | 40 | 42 | 14 | 8 |

**SOLUTION:**

In such distributions, no specific treatment of the data is needed. Median can be calculated straight away as in the case of other frequency distributions.

**Estimation of the Median**

| Class Interval | Frequency (f) | Cumulative Frequency |
|---|---|---|
| 0–5 | 12 | 12 |
| 5–10 | 15 | 27 |
| 10–20 | 25 | **52 (c.f.)** |
| ($l_1$) **20–30** | **40 (f)** | 92 |
| 30–50 | 42 | 134 |
| 50–70 | 14 | 148 |
| 70–100 | 8 | 156 |
| | N = 156 | |

$$M = \text{Size of } \left(\frac{N}{2}\right)\text{th item; } N = 156$$

$$= \text{Size of } \left(\frac{156}{2}\right)\text{th item} = \text{Size of 78th item}$$

This lies in 92th cumulative frequency and the corresponding Median class is 20–30.

$\therefore\ l_1 = 20$, c.f. = 52, f = 40 and $i = 10$.

Substituting the values in the formula, we have

$$M = l_1 + \frac{\frac{N}{2} - c.f.}{f} \times i$$

$$= 20 + \frac{\frac{156}{2} - 52}{40} \times 10$$

$$= 20 + \frac{78 - 52}{40} \times 10 = 20 + \frac{26}{40} \times 10$$

$$= 20 + 6.5 = 26.5$$

Median = 26.5.

### To Locate Missing Frequency

**ILLUSTRATION.**

Find the missing frequency in the following distribution if N=100 and M = 30.

| Marks | 0–10 | 10–20 | 20–30 | 30–40 | 40–50 | 50–60 |
|---|---|---|---|---|---|---|
| Number of Students | 10 | ? | 25 | 30 | ? | 10 |

**SOLUTION:**

Two frequencies are missing and let the missing frequencies be denoted by $f_1$ and $f_2$. We need two equations, we will get one from summation of frequencies and one from median formula.

| Marks | Frequency (f) | Cumulative Frequency |
|---|---|---|
| 0–10 | 10 | 10 |
| 10–20 | $f_1$ | $10 + f_1$ |
| 20–30 | 25 | $35 + f_1$ |
| **30–40** | **30** | $65 + f_1$ |
| 40–50 | $f_2$ | $65 + f_1 + f_2$ |
| 50–60 | 10 | $75 + f_1 + f_2$ |
| | N = 100 | |

1st Equation: From summation of frequencies,

$$75 + f_1 + f_2 = 100 \Rightarrow f_1 + f_2 = 25 \qquad \text{...(i)}$$

2nd Equation: From information regarding median,

M=30, Median class is 30–40.

Now,

$$M = l_1 + \frac{\frac{N}{2} - c.f.}{f} \times i$$

$$30 = 30 + \frac{50 - (35 + f_1)}{30} \times 10$$

$$0 = \frac{15 - f_1}{3} \quad \text{or} \quad f_1 = 15 \qquad \text{...(ii)}$$

Substituting $f_1 = 15$ from equation (ii), in equation (i)

As $\quad f_1 + f_2 = 25$

Put $f_1 = 15$

$\therefore \quad 15 + f_2 = 25$

$\therefore \quad f_2 = 25 - 15 = 10$

Thus, $f_1 = 15$, $f_2 = 10$.

**ILLUSTRATION.**

Find the missing frequency in the following distribution if N is 60 and median is 40.

| Marks | 0–10 | 10–30 | 30–60 | 60–80 | 80–90 |
|---|---|---|---|---|---|
| Frequency | 5 | $f_1$ | $f_2$ | 8 | 2 |

**Solution:**

| Marks | Frequency (f) | Cumulative Frequency |
|---|---|---|
| 0–10 | 5 | 5 |
| 10–30 | $f_1$ | $5 + f_1$ |
| 30–60 | $f_2$ | $5 + f_1 + f_2$ |
| 60–80 | 8 | $13 + f_1 + f_2$ |
| 80–90 | 2 | $15 + f_1 + f_2$ |
| | N = 60 | |

$\therefore$ N = 60

$\therefore 15 + f_1 + f_2 = 60 \qquad$ or $\qquad f_1 + f_2 = 45$

Median Size $= \frac{N}{2} = \frac{60}{2} = 30\text{th term}$

($\because$ Median is 40, so Median class is 30–60)

$$M = l_1 + \frac{\frac{N}{2} - c.f.}{f} \times i$$

$$\Rightarrow \qquad 40 = 30 + \frac{30 - (5 + f_1)}{f_2} \times 30$$

$$\Rightarrow \qquad 10 = \frac{(25 - f_1)}{f_2} \times 30$$

$$\Rightarrow \qquad 10f_2 = 750 - 30f_1$$

$$30f_1 + 10f_2 = 750$$

Thus, we get

$$f_1 + f_2 = 45 \qquad \text{...(i)}$$

$$30f_1 + 10f_2 = 750 \qquad \text{...(ii)}$$

Dividing equation (ii) by 10, we get

$$3f_1 + f_2 = 75 \qquad \text{...(iii)}$$

Now subtracting (i) from (iii), we get

$$3f_1 + f_2 = 75$$
$$f_1 + f_2 = 45$$
$$2f_1 = 30$$

$$\Rightarrow \qquad f_1 = 15$$

Now substituting $f_1 = 15$ in (i), we get

$$f_2 = 45 - 15 = 30$$

Hence, $f_1 = 15$, $f_2 = 30$.

*Learning by doing*

1. *Calculate median of the following data:*

| Marks (less than) | 15 | 30 | 45 | 60 | 75 | 90 |
|---|---|---|---|---|---|---|
| Number of Students | 18 | 35 | 62 | 81 | 95 | 100 |

(*Ans.* $M = 38.33$ *marks*)

2. *Find out median in the following series:*

| Size (less than) | 5 | 10 | 15 | 20 | 25 | 30 | 35 |
|---|---|---|---|---|---|---|---|
| Frequency | 1 | 3 | 13 | 17 | 27 | 36 | 38 |

(*Ans.* $M = 21$)

3. *Find out median of the following data-set:*

| Class Interval | 60–69 | 50–59 | 40–49 | 30–39 | 20–29 | 10–19 |
|---|---|---|---|---|---|---|
| Frequency | 13 | 15 | 21 | 20 | 19 | 12 |

(*Ans.* $M = 39$)

4. *Calculate median from the following series:*

| Class Interval | 10–20 | 20–40 | 40–70 | 70–120 | 120–140 |
|---|---|---|---|---|---|
| Frequency | 4 | 10 | 26 | 8 | 2 |

(*Ans.* $M = 52.69$)

5. *Calculate median from the following data-set:*

| Marks | Number of Students | Marks | Number of Students |
|---|---|---|---|
| 1–5 | 7 | 26–30 | 18 |
| 6–10 | 10 | 31–35 | 10 |
| 11–15 | 16 | 36–40 | 5 |
| 16–20 | 32 | 41–45 | 1 |
| 21–25 | 24 | | |

(*Ans.* $M = 19.95$ *marks*)

## Graphic Determination of Median

Median value of a series may also be determined through the graphic presentation of the data in the form of ogives. This may be done in two ways.

(1) Presenting the data graphically in the form of 'less than' or 'more than' ogives.

(2) Presenting the data graphically and simultaneously in the form of 'less than' and 'more than' ogives. That is, the two ogives are superimposed upon each other to determine the median value.

### (i) 'Less than' or 'More than' Ogive Approach

According to this approach, a frequency distribution series is first converted into a 'less than' or 'more than' cumulative series as in the case of ogives. Data are presented graphically to make a 'less than' or 'more than' ogive. $\left(\frac{N}{2}\right)$th item of the series is determined and from this point (on the Y-axis of the graph) a perpendicular is drawn to the right to cut the cumulative frequency curve. The median value of the series is the one where the cumulative frequency curve is cut by the perpendicular corresponding to the X-axis. The following illustration explains the method.

**ILLUSTRATION.**

Determine median value of the following series using graphic method:

| Marks | 0–5 | 5–10 | 10–15 | 15–20 | 20–25 | 25–30 | 30–35 | 35–40 |
|---|---|---|---|---|---|---|---|---|
| Number of Students | 4 | 6 | 10 | 10 | 25 | 22 | 18 | 5 |

**SOLUTION:**

Using 'Less than' ogive approach, the calculation of the median value involves the following steps:

(1) Convert the series into a '*less than*' cumulative frequency distribution and graph the data as under:

**Estimation of the Median: 'Less than' Ogive Approach**

| Marks | Cumulative Frequency |
|---|---|
| Less than 5 | 4 |
| Less than 10 | 10 |
| Less than 15 | 20 |
| Less than 20 | 30 |
| Less than 25 | 55 |
| Less than 30 | 77 |
| Less than 35 | 95 |
| Less than 40 | 100 |

(**Ans.** Median = 24)

(2) Find out $\left(\frac{N}{2}\right)$th item and mark it on the Y-axis. In the above illustration $\left(\frac{N}{2}\right)$th item is $\frac{100}{2} = 50$.

(3) Draw a perpendicular from 50 to the right to cut the cumulative frequency curve (ogive) at point E.

(4) From the point E where cumulative frequency curve (ogive) is cut, draw a perpendicular on X-axis. The point at which it touches X-axis will be the median value of the series, as shown in Graph A:

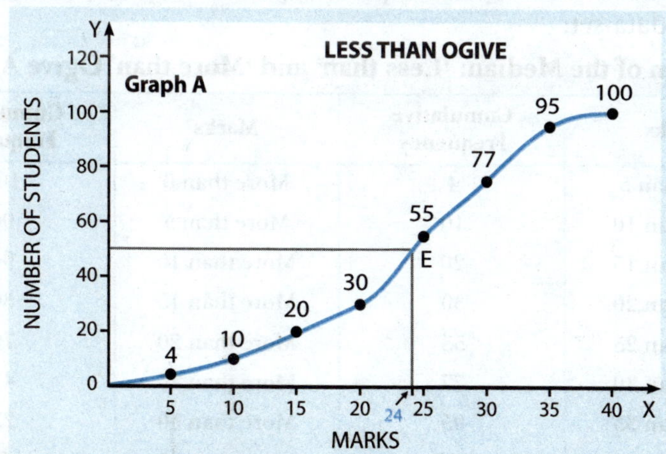


Using 'more than' ogive approach, the calculation of the median involves the similar procedure, as should be evident from the following table and Graph B:

**Estimation of the Median: 'More than' Ogive Approach**

| Marks | Cumulative Frequency |
|---|---|
| More than 0 | 100 |
| More than 5 | 96 |
| More than 10 | 90 |
| More than 15 | 80 |
| More than 20 | 70 |
| More than 25 | 45 |
| More than 30 | 23 |
| More than 35 | 5 |
| More than 40 | 0 |

(**Ans.** Median = 24)

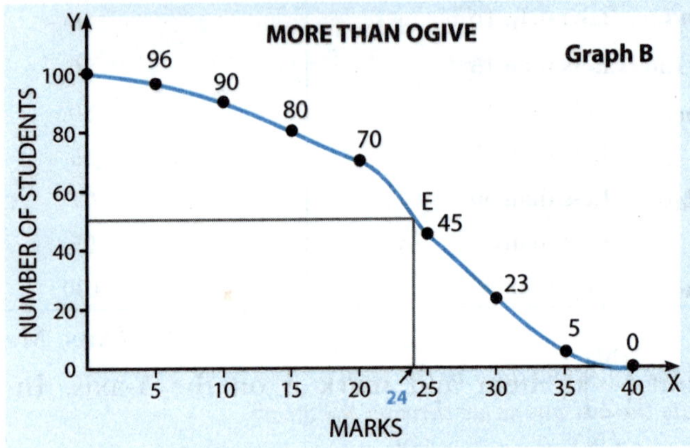


### (ii) 'Less than' and 'More than' Ogive Approach

Another way of the graphic determination of the median is *simultaneous graphic presentation of both the 'less than' and 'more than' ogives*. Mark the point E where the ogive curves cut each other; draw a perpendicular from that point on the X-axis; the corresponding value on the X-axis would be the median value. Graph C explains this process, based on the following data-set:

**Estimation of the Median: 'Less than' and 'More than' Ogive Approach**

| Marks | Cumulative Frequency | Marks | Cumulative Frequency |
|---|---|---|---|
| Less than 5 | 4 | More than 0 | 100 |
| Less than 10 | 10 | More than 5 | 96 |
| Less than 15 | 20 | More than 10 | 90 |
| Less than 20 | 30 | More than 15 | 80 |
| Less than 25 | 55 | More than 20 | 70 |
| Less than 30 | 77 | More than 25 | 45 |
| Less than 35 | 95 | More than 30 | 23 |
| Less than 40 | 100 | More than 35 | 5 |
| | | More than 40 | 0 |

(**Ans.** Median = 24)

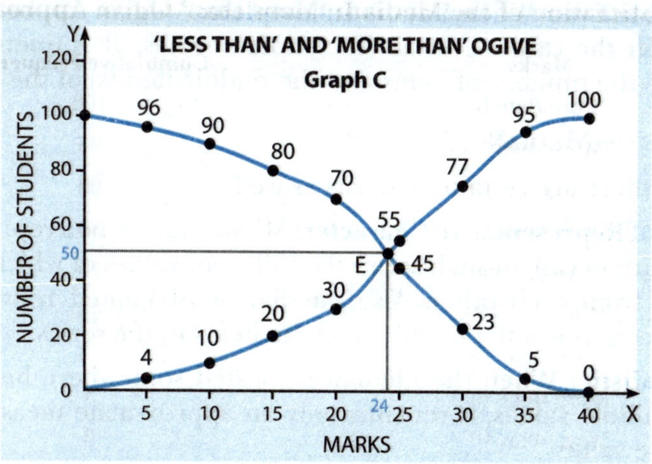


*Learning by doing*

1. *Find out median of the following series, using graphic technique:*

| Class Interval | 40–45 | 45–50 | 50–55 | 55–60 | 60–65 | 65–70 | 70–75 | 75–80 | 80–85 |
|---|---|---|---|---|---|---|---|---|---|
| Frequency | 4 | 6 | 8 | 10 | 7 | 6 | 5 | 3 | 1 |

(*Ans.* *M* = 58.5)

2. *Calculate median value of the following data-set using graphic technique:*

| Size | 0–10 | 10–20 | 20–30 | 30–40 | 40–50 | 50–60 |
|---|---|---|---|---|---|---|
| Frequency | 3 | 10 | 20 | 7 | 6 | 4 |

(*Ans.* *M* = 26)

3. *Graph the following data in the form of 'less than' and 'more than' ogives, and calculate the median value through the graph:*

| Marks | 0–5 | 5–10 | 10–15 | 15–20 | 20–25 | 25–30 | 30–35 | 35–40 |
|---|---|---|---|---|---|---|---|---|
| Number of Students | 7 | 10 | 20 | 13 | 17 | 10 | 14 | 9 |

(*Ans.* *M* = 20 marks)

## Merits of Median

Median is a widely used measure of the central tendency, particularly in the field of socio-economic studies. Some of its main merits are as under:

(1) **Simplicity:** It is a very simple measure of the central tendency of the series. In the case of simple statistical series, just a glance at the data is enough to locate the median value.

(2) **Free from the Effect of Extreme Values:** Unlike arithmetic mean, median value is not distorted by the extreme values of the series.

(3) **Certainty:** Certainty is another merit of the median. Median value is always a certain specific value in the series.

(4) **Real Value:** Median value is a real value and is a better representative value of the series compared to arithmetic average, the value of which may not exist in the series at all.

(5) **Graphic Presentation:** Besides algebraic approach, the median value can be estimated also through the graphic presentation of data.

**Two Principal Merits of Median as the Measure of Central Tendency of the Series are**

(i) Unlike arithmetic mean, median is free from the effect of extreme values of the series.

(ii) Median value can be estimated even in case of an incomplete statistical series.

(6) **Possible Even When Data is Incomplete:** Median can be estimated even in the case of certain incomplete series. It is enough if one knows the number of items and the middle item(s) of the series.

### DEMERITS OF MEDIAN

However, there are certain demerits as well:

**What is the Principal Demerit of Median as the measure of Central Tendency?**

That unlike arithmetic mean, the median value is not capable of further algebraic treatment, and that its estimation is not based on all items of the series.

(1) **Lack of Representative Character:** Median fails to be a representative measure in case of such series the different values of which are wide apart from each other. Also, median is of limited representative character as it is not based on all the items in the series.

(2) **Unrealistic:** When the median is located somewhere between the two middle values, it remains only an approximate measure, not a precise value.

(3) **Lack of Algebraic Treatment:** Arithmetic mean is capable of further algebraic treatment, but median is not. For example, multiplying the median with the number of items in the series will not give us the sum total of the values of the series.

However, median is quite a simple method of finding an average of a series. It is quite a commonly used measure in the case of such series which are related to qualitative observations as IQ, and health of the students.

**Methods of Calculating Median: A Glance**

| Type of Series | Method of Calculation |
|---|---|
| 1. Individual Series | (a) M = Size of $\left(\frac{N+1}{2}\right)$th item<br>(Here, N = Total of items.)<br>(b) If $\left(\frac{N+1}{2}\right)$comes to be in fractions, the median would be average of the two middle values of the series. |
| 2. Discrete Series/ Frequency Array | M = Size of $\left(\frac{N+1}{2}\right)$th item<br>(Here, N = Sum of the frequencies $\Sigma f$.) |
| 3. Frequency Distribution Series | M = Size of $\left(\frac{N}{2}\right)$th item<br>Median class corresponds to that cumulative frequency which includes the above value. Following formula is applied to determine actual median value:<br>$M = l_1 + \frac{\frac{N}{2} - c.f.}{f} \times i$ |

## 2. Partition Value : Quartile

The value that divides the series into more than two parts is called Partition Value. If a statistical series is divided into four equal parts, the end value of each part is called a quartile. It is written as Q. The First Quartile or $Q_1$ is also known as lower quartile. The Second Quartile, or $Q_2$ is the same as Median of the series. The Third Quartile, or $Q_3$ is also called upper quartile.

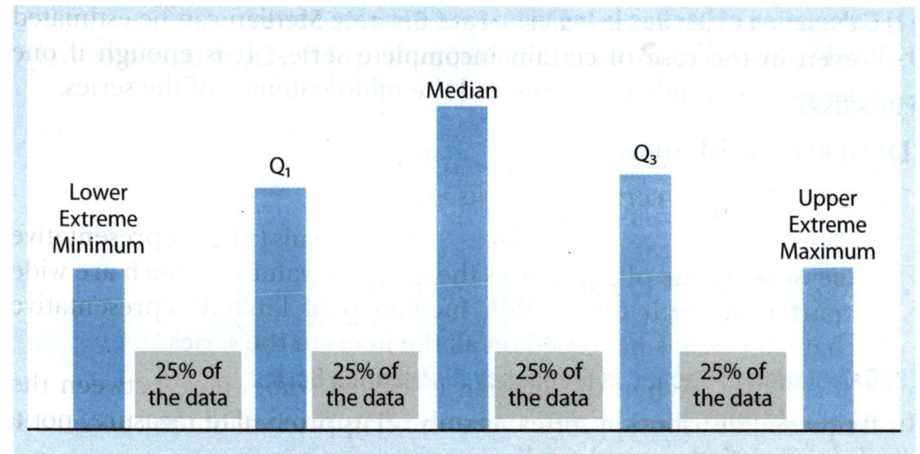


**Did you know?**

The first quartile ($Q_1$) or lower quartile has 25% of the items of the distribution below it and 75% of the items above it.

The second quartile ($Q_2$) or median has 50% of items below it and 50% of the items above it.

The third quartile ($Q_3$) or upper quartile has 75% of the items below it and 25% of items above it.

## Estimation of $Q_1$ and $Q_3$

Quartile values ($Q_1$ and $Q_3$) are estimated differently for different sets of series, as under:

### (i) Individual and Discrete Series

For the individual and discrete series, $Q_1$ and $Q_3$ are determined using the following formulae:

**FORMULAE**

$$Q_1 = \text{Size of} \left(\frac{N+1}{4}\right)\text{th item of the series}$$

$$Q_3 = \text{Size of } 3\left(\frac{N+1}{4}\right)\text{th item of the series}$$

In individual series, N = Number of items,
while in discrete series, N = Sum of frequencies, $\sum f$.

### (ii) Frequency Distribution Series

In frequency distribution series, the class interval of $Q_1$ and $Q_3$ are first identified as under:

$$\text{Class interval of } Q_1 = \text{Size of} \left(\frac{N}{4}\right)\text{th item}$$

$$\text{Class interval of } Q_3 = \text{Size of } 3\left(\frac{N}{4}\right)\text{th item}$$

**FORMULAE**

$$Q_1 = l_1 + \frac{\left[\frac{N}{4} - \text{c.f.}\right]}{f} \times i$$

$$Q_3 = l_1 + \frac{\left[3\left(\frac{N}{4}\right) - \text{c.f.}\right]}{f} \times i$$

## Deciles

Deciles distribute the series into ten equal parts, and is generally expressed as D. Accordingly, we have nine deciles, $D_1, D_2, D_3, \ldots, D_9$, of a series. These are estimated for different types of series as under:

#### (1) Calculation of Deciles in Individual and Discrete Series

Following formulae are used in the estimation of $D_1$, $D_4$ or $D_9$ respectively:

**FORMULAE**

$$D_1 = \text{Size of } \left(\frac{N+1}{10}\right)\text{th item}$$

$$D_4 = \text{Size of } 4\left(\frac{N+1}{10}\right)\text{th item}$$

$$D_9 = \text{Size of } 9\left(\frac{N+1}{10}\right)\text{th item}$$

#### (2) Calculation of Deciles in Frequency Distribution Series

In frequency distribution series, first the class interval of the concerned decile is identified using the following formulae:

$$\text{Class interval of } D_1 = \text{Size of } \left(\frac{N}{10}\right)\text{th item}$$

$$\text{Class interval of } D_4 = \text{Size of } 4\left(\frac{N}{10}\right)\text{th item}$$

$$\text{Class interval of } D_9 = \text{Size of } 9\left(\frac{N}{10}\right)\text{th item}$$

Actual value of the concerned decile is calculated using the following formulae:

**FORMULAE**

$$D_1 = l_1 + \left[\frac{\frac{N}{10} - \text{c.f.}}{\text{f}}\right] \times i$$

$$D_4 = l_1 + \left[\frac{4\left(\frac{N}{10}\right) - \text{c.f.}}{\text{f}}\right] \times i$$

$$D_9 = l_1 + \left[\frac{9\left(\frac{N}{10}\right) - \text{c.f.}}{\text{f}}\right] \times i$$

### PERCENTILES

Percentiles divide the series into 100 equal parts, and is generally expressed as P. There are 99 percentiles in a series ranging from $P_1, P_2, P_3, \ldots\ldots, P_{99}$. Obviously $P_{50}$ would be the median of the series as it is the centrally located value in the series. Likewise $P_{25}$ is the same as $Q_1$ and $P_{75}$ is the same as $Q_3$ of the series. If a student has secured 89 percentile in an MBA entrance examination, it means that his position is below 11 per cent of total candidates appeared in the examination. Percentiles are estimated for different types of series as under:

#### (1) Estimation of Percentiles in Individual and Discrete Series

In the individual and discrete series, $P_1, P_2, P_3, \ldots$ are estimated using the following formulae:

**FORMULAE**

$$P_1 = \text{Size of}\left(\frac{N+1}{100}\right)\text{th item}$$

$$P_4 = \text{Size of } 4\left(\frac{N+1}{100}\right)\text{th item}$$

$$P_{99} = \text{Size of } 99\left(\frac{N+1}{100}\right)\text{th item}$$

### (2) Estimation of Percentile in Frequency Distribution Series

In frequency distribution series, the class interval of $P_1, P_2, P_3, \ldots P_{99}$ are first identified using the following formulae:

$$\text{Class interval of } P_1 = \text{Size of}\left(\frac{N}{100}\right)\text{th item}$$

$$\text{Class interval of } P_4 = \text{Size of } 4\left(\frac{N}{100}\right)\text{th item}$$

$$\text{Class interval of } P_{99} = \text{Size of } 99\left(\frac{N}{100}\right)\text{th item}$$

(That is, class interval of $P_{99}$ corresponds to size of $99\left(\frac{N}{100}\right)$th item in the cumulative frequency of the series.)

Actual value of the concerned percentile is calculated using the following formulae:

**FORMULAE**

$$P_1 = l_1 + \left[\frac{\frac{N}{100} - \text{c.f.}}{\text{f}}\right] \times i$$

$$P_4 = l_1 + \left[\frac{4\left(\frac{N}{100}\right) - \text{c.f.}}{\text{f}}\right] \times i$$

$$P_{99} = l_1 + \left[\frac{99\left(\frac{N}{100}\right) - \text{c.f.}}{\text{f}}\right] \times i$$

The following table presents different partition values.

**Table of Partition Values**

| Partition Values | Divisions of a Series | Number of Partition Values in Series |
|---|---|---|
| Quartile | 4 | 3 |
| Decile | 10 | 9 |
| Percentile | 100 | 99 |

**ILLUSTRATION 1.**

From the following data, calculate $Q_1$, $Q_3$, $D_5$ and $P_{25}$.

| S. No. | 21 | 15 | 40 | 30 | 26 | 45 | 50 | 54 | 60 | 65 | 70 |
|---|---|---|---|---|---|---|---|---|---|---|---|

**SOLUTION:**

The data is first arranged in ascending order:

| S. No. | X |
|---|---|
| 1 | 15 |
| 2 | 21 |
| 3 | 26 |
| 4 | 30 |
| 5 | 40 |
| 6 | 45 |
| 7 | 50 |
| 8 | 54 |
| 9 | 60 |
| 10 | 65 |
| 11 | 70 |
| N = 11 | |

$$Q_1 = \text{Size of}\left(\frac{N+1}{4}\right)\text{th item}$$
$$= \text{Size of}\left(\frac{11+1}{4}\right)\text{th item}$$
$$= \text{Size of 3rd item} = 26$$

$$Q_3 = \text{Size of } 3\left(\frac{N+1}{4}\right)\text{th item}$$
$$= \text{Size of } 3\left(\frac{11+1}{4}\right)\text{th item}$$
$$= \text{Size of 9th item} = 60$$

$$D_5 = \text{Size of } 5\left(\frac{N+1}{10}\right)\text{th item}$$
$$= \text{Size of } 5\left(\frac{11+1}{10}\right)\text{th item}$$
$$= \text{Size of 6th item} = 45$$

$$P_{25} = \text{Size of } 25\left(\frac{N+1}{100}\right)\text{th item}$$
$$= \text{Size of } 25\left(\frac{11+1}{100}\right)\text{th item}$$
$$= \text{Size of 3rd item} = 26$$

Thus, $Q_1 = 26, Q_3 = 60, D_5 = 45, P_{25} = 26.$

**ILLUSTRATION 2.**

Calculate $Q_1$, $Q_3$, $D_6$ and $P_{85}$ from the following data:

| Size | 10 | 11 | 12 | 13 | 14 | 15 | 16 | 17 | 18 |
|---|---|---|---|---|---|---|---|---|---|
| Frequency | 3 | 4 | 5 | 12 | 10 | 7 | 5 | 2 | 1 |

**SOLUTION:**

| Size | Frequency (f) | Cumulative Frequency |
|---|---|---|
| 10 | 3 | 3 |
| 11 | 4 | 7 |
| 12 | 5 | 12 |
| 13 | 12 | 24 |
| 14 | 10 | 34 |
| 15 | 7 | 41 |
| 16 | 5 | 46 |
| 17 | 2 | 48 |
| 18 | 1 | 49 |
| | N = 49 | |

$$Q_1 = \text{Size of } \left(\frac{N+1}{4}\right)\text{th item} = \text{Size of } \left(\frac{49+1}{4}\right)\text{th item}$$

$$= \text{Size of 12.5th item} = 13$$

$$Q_3 = \text{Size of } 3\left(\frac{N+1}{4}\right)\text{th item} = \text{Size of } 3\left(\frac{49+1}{4}\right)\text{th item}$$

$$= \text{Size of 37.5th item} = 15$$

$$D_6 = \text{Size of } 6\left(\frac{N+1}{10}\right)\text{th item} = \text{Size of } 6\left(\frac{49+1}{10}\right)\text{th item}$$

$$= \text{Size of 30th item} = 14$$

$$P_{85} = \text{Size of } 85\left(\frac{N+1}{100}\right)\text{th item} = \text{Size of } 85\left(\frac{49+1}{100}\right)\text{th item}$$

$$= \text{Size of 42.5th item} = 16$$

Thus, $Q_1 = 13, Q_3 = 15, D_6 = 14, P_{85} = 16.$

**ILLUSTRATION 3.**

Calculate the values of $Q_1$, $Q_3$, $D_8$ and $P_{56}$ from the following data:

| Wages (₹) | 0–10 | 10–20 | 20–30 | 30–40 | 40–50 |
|---|---|---|---|---|---|
| Number of Workers | 22 | 38 | 46 | 35 | 19 |

**SOLUTION:**

**Calculation of $Q_1$, $Q_3$, $D_8$ and $P_{56}$**

| Wages (₹) | Frequency (f) | Cumulative Frequency |
|---|---|---|
| 0–10 | 22 | 22 |
| 10–20 | 38 | 60 |
| 20–30 | 46 | 106 |
| 30–40 | 35 | 141 |
| 40–50 | 19 | 160 |
| | N = 160 | |

$$Q_1 = \text{Size of } \left(\frac{N}{4}\right)\text{th item} = \text{Size of } \left(\frac{160}{4}\right)\text{th item}$$

$$= \text{Size of 40th item.}$$

$Q_1$ lies in 60th cumulative frequency. The class interval corresponding to this cumulative frequency is 10–20.

$$\text{Thus, } Q_1 = l_1 + \frac{\frac{N}{4} - \text{c.f.}}{f} \times i$$

$$= 10 + \frac{\frac{160}{4} - 22}{38} \times 10$$

$$= 10 + \frac{40 - 22}{38} \times 10 = 10 + \frac{18}{38} \times 10$$

$$= 10 + 4.74 = 14.74$$

$$Q_3 = \text{Size of } 3\left(\frac{N}{4}\right)\text{th item} = \text{Size of } 3\left(\frac{160}{4}\right)\text{th item}$$

$$= \text{Size of 120th item}$$

$Q_3$ lies in 141th cumulative frequency. The class interval corresponding to this cumulative frequency is 30–40.

$$\text{Thus, } Q_3 = l_1 + \frac{3\left(\frac{N}{4}\right) - \text{c.f.}}{f} \times i$$

$$= 30 + \frac{3\left(\frac{160}{4}\right) - 106}{35} \times 10$$

$$= 30 + \frac{120 - 106}{35} \times 10 = 30 + \frac{14}{35} \times 10$$

$$= 30 + 4 = 34$$

$$D_8 = \text{Size of } 8\left(\frac{N}{10}\right)\text{th item}$$

$$= \text{Size of } 8\left(\frac{160}{10}\right)\text{th item}$$

$$= \text{Size of 128th item}$$

$D_8$ lies in 141th cumulative frequency. The class interval corresponding to this cumulative frequency is 30–40.

$$\text{Thus, } D_8 = l_1 + \frac{8\left(\frac{N}{10}\right) - \text{c.f.}}{f} \times i$$

$$= 30 + \frac{8\left(\frac{160}{10}\right) - 106}{35} \times 10 = 30 + \frac{128 - 106}{35} \times 10$$

$$= 30 + \frac{22}{35} \times 10$$

$$= 30 + 6.29$$

$$= 36.29$$

$$P_{56} = \text{Size of } 56\left(\frac{N}{100}\right)\text{th item}$$

$$= \text{Size of } 56\left(\frac{160}{100}\right)\text{th item}$$

$$= \text{Size of } 89.6\text{th item}$$

$P_{56}$ lies in 106th cumulative frequency. The class interval corresponding to this cumulative frequency is 20–30.

$$\text{Thus, } P_{56} = l_1 + \frac{56\left(\frac{N}{100}\right) - \text{c.f.}}{f} \times i$$

$$= 20 + \frac{56\left(\frac{160}{100}\right) - 60}{46} \times 10 = 20 + \frac{89.6 - 60}{46} \times 10$$

$$= 20 + \frac{29.6}{46} \times 10$$

$$= 20 + 6.43$$

$$= 26.43$$

Thus, $Q_1 = 14.74$, $Q_3 = 34$, $D_8 = 36.29$, $P_{56} = 26.43$.

## 3. Mode

Mode is another important measure of central tendency of statistical series. It is the value which occurs most frequently in the series; that is, modal value has the highest frequency in the series. For example, if out of 100 students in a class, 70 students record their age as 15 years, the modal age of the students would be 15 years. The word *'Mode'* is derived from the French word *la Mode* which means a thing in vogue or fashion. In statistics, it is generally represented by the letter Z.

### Definition

According to **Kenny**, *"The value of the variable which occurs most frequently in a distribution is called the mode."*

**Croxton** and **Cowden** state, *"The mode may be regarded as the most typical of a series of value."*

### Calculation of Mode

Mode is calculated differently for different types of series.

#### (1) Calculation of Mode in Individual Series

There are two ways of calculating mode in individual series:

(i) By Inspection.

(ii) By Converting Individual Series into Discrete Frequency Series.

**(i) Mode by Inspection:** This method involves just an inspection of the series. One is to simply identify the value that occurs most frequently in the series. Such a value is called mode.

**ILLUSTRATION.**

Age of 15 students of a class is reported below. Find the modal age.

| Age (Years) | 22 | 24 | 17 | 18 | 17 | 19 | 18 | 21 | 20 | 21 | 20 | 23 | 22 | 22 | 22 |
|---|---|---|---|---|---|---|---|---|---|---|---|---|---|---|---|

**SOLUTION:**

Arrange the series in an ascending order as:

| Age (Years) | 17 | 17 | 18 | 18 | 19 | 20 | 20 | 21 | 21 | 22 | 22 | 22 | 22 | 23 | 24 |
|---|---|---|---|---|---|---|---|---|---|---|---|---|---|---|---|

An inspection of the series shows that 22 occurs most frequently in the series.

Hence, Mode (Z) = 22.

**(ii) By Converting Individual Series into Discrete Frequency Series:** When the number of items in a series is very large, Inspection Method of finding out the mode becomes very difficult, if not impossible. In such cases, individual series are first converted into discrete frequency series or frequency array. The mode is then identified as the value corresponding to which there is highest frequency.

**ILLUSTRATION.**

The table below presents death rate of population across different countries. Find the mode.

| Death Rate (Per Thousand) | 11.1 | 10.9 | 10.7 | 11.1 | 10.6 | 11.3 | 10.6 |
|---|---|---|---|---|---|---|---|
| | 10.7 | 10.6 | 10.9 | 10.6 | 10.5 | 10.4 | 10.6 |

**SOLUTION:**

First, we convert the series into a discrete frequency distribution in ascending order as under.

| Death Rate | 10.4 | 10.5 | 10.6 | 10.7 | 10.9 | 11.1 | 11.3 |
|---|---|---|---|---|---|---|---|
| Frequency | 1 | 1 | 5 | 2 | 2 | 2 | 1 |

10.6 is the value with highest frequency of 5. Hence,

Mode (Z) = 10.6.

**When to use Inspection Method to identify Modal Value of the Series?**

Inspection method is to be used only in case of such series where different items show different frequencies.

### (2) Calculation of Mode in Discrete Series or Frequency Array

There are two methods for calculation of mode in discrete frequency series: (i) Inspection Method; and (ii) Grouping Method.

#### (i) Inspection Method

As in the case of individual series, *Inspection Method* is sometimes used for the calculation of mode in discrete frequency series as well. An inspection of the series would show the mode or the value that has the highest frequency in the series, provided the series are regular and homogeneous.

**ILLUSTRATION.**

Find out mode of the following series:

| Income (₹) | 110 | 120 | 130 | 140 | 150 | 160 |
|---|---|---|---|---|---|---|
| Number of Persons | 2 | 4 | 8 | 10 | 5 | 4 |

**SOLUTION:**

A glance at the series reveals that 140 commands the highest frequency of 10 in the series.

Hence, 140 is the Mode (Z) of the series.

### (ii) Grouping Method

In the case of discrete frequency distribution, inspection method is possible only when there is regularity and homogeneity in the series. However, the series may sometimes not be regular or homogeneous.

More than one value may command the highest frequency in the series. In such cases, Grouping Method of the calculation of mode is used. The method involves the construction of: (a) Grouping Table, and (b) Analysis Table. The illustration below explains the calculation of mode using the grouping technique.

**ILLUSTRATION.**

Given the following data, calculate mode using the grouping technique.

| Size | 2 | 3 | 4 | 5 | 6 | 7 | 8 | 9 | 10 | 11 | 12 | 13 |
|---|---|---|---|---|---|---|---|---|---|---|---|---|
| Frequency | 3 | 8 | 10 | 12 | 16 | 14 | 10 | 8 | 17 | 5 | 4 | 1 |

**SOLUTION:**

**Table 1. Grouping Table for the Estimation of Mode**

| Size | (I) Frequency | (II) (1+2) | (III) (2+3) | (IV) (1+2+3) | (V) (2+3+4) | (VI) (3+4+5) |
|---|---|---|---|---|---|---|
| 2 | 3 | 3 + 8 = 11 | | 3 + 8 + 10 = 21 | | |
| 3 | 8 | | 8 + 10 = 18 | | 8 + 10 + 12 = 30 | |
| 4 | 10 | 10 + 12 = 22 | | | | 10 + 12 + 16 = (38) |
| 5 | 12 | | 12 + 16 = (28) | 12 + 16 + 14 = (42) | | |
| 6 | 16 | 16 + 14 = (30) | | | 16 + 14 + 10 = (40) | |
| 7 | 14 | | 14 + 10 = 24 | | | 14 + 10 + 8 = 32 |
| 8 | 10 | 10 + 8 = 18 | | 10 + 8 + 17 = 35 | | |
| 9 | 8 | | 8 + 17 = 25 | | 8 + 17 + 5 = 30 | |
| 10 | (17) | 17 + 5 = 22 | | | | 17 + 5 + 4 = 26 |
| 11 | 5 | | 5 + 4 = 9 | 5 + 4 + 1 = 10 | | |
| 12 | 4 | 4 + 1 = 5 | | | | |
| 13 | 1 | | | | | |

Check the following Tables 1 and 2 and the subsequent details.

There are 6 columns in the table on the frequency and its groupings, as in Table 1.

In **Column I,** the frequencies as given in the question are noted against the respective items.

In **Column II,** the frequencies are grouped in twos beginning with the 1st item.

In **Column III,** the frequencies are grouped in twos beginning with 2nd item.

In **Column IV,** the frequencies are grouped into threes beginning with 1st item.

In **Column V,** the frequencies are grouped into threes beginning with 2nd item.

In **Column VI,** the frequencies are grouped into threes beginning with 3rd item.

Highest value in all the columns are shown in bold letters or are underlined, or encircled.

**Table 2. Analysis Table**

| Column | Size of items containing maximum frequency | | | | | | | | | | | |
|---|---|---|---|---|---|---|---|---|---|---|---|---|
| | **2** | **3** | **4** | **5** | **6** | **7** | **8** | **9** | **10** | **11** | **12** | **13** |
| I | | | | | | | | | ✓ | | | |
| II | | | | | ✓ | ✓ | | | | | | |
| III | | | | ✓ | ✓ | | | | | | | |
| IV | | | | ✓ | ✓ | ✓ | | | | | | |
| V | | | | | ✓ | ✓ | ✓ | | | | | |
| VI | | | ✓ | ✓ | ✓ | | | | | | | |
| Total | — | — | 1 | 3 | 5 | 3 | 1 | — | 1 | — | — | — |

Analysis Table shows those items corresponding to which there are highest frequencies in different columns. Thus, in column I the highest total is 17 and this corresponds to the item 10. For column I a tick mark (√) is accordingly noted against 10 in the Analysis Table. Likewise, in column II the highest total is 30 and this corresponds to the items 6 and 7 (bracketed). A tick mark (✓) is accordingly noted against 6 as well as 7 in the Analysis Table. Similarly, in column III the highest total is 28 and it corresponds to the items 5 and 6. Thus, a tick mark is noted against 5 and 6. In column IV, the highest total is 42 and it corresponds to the items 5, 6 and 7. Thus, a tick mark is noted against 5, 6, and 7 in column IV. Likewise, tick marks are noted in other columns. The Analysis Table shows that item 6 has the largest number of tick marks. Thus, the Mode (Z) = 6.

*Learning by doing*

1. *Find out mode of the following series:*

   *7, 4, 10, 9, 15, 12, 7, 9, 7* *(Ans. Z = 7)*

2. *Weight of 50 students is given below. Calculate mode.*

| **Weight (in kg)** | 48 | 49 | 50 | 51 | 52 | 53 |
|---|---|---|---|---|---|---|
| **Number of Students** | 4 | 10 | 20 | 11 | 3 | 2 |

*(Ans. Z = 50 kg)*

### (3) Calculation of Mode in Frequency Distribution Series

As in the case of discrete frequency series, calculation of mode in continuous series has two methods: (i) Inspection Method, and (ii) Grouping Method.

However, in the case of continuous series, we first find out the modal class, using either of these two methods, and afterwards, calculate the exact value of mode with the aid of the following formula:

**FORMULA**

$$Z = l_1 + \frac{f_1 - f_0}{2f_1 - f_0 - f_2} \times i$$

(Here, Z = Value of the mode; $l_1$ = lower limit of the modal class; $f_1$ = The frequency of the modal class; $f_0$= The frequency of pre-modal class; $f_2$ = Frequency of the next higher class or post-modal class; $i$ = Size of the modal group.)

Below we discuss with illustrations the application of two methods for the calculation of mode in continuous series.

**You Must Understand it**

That in case of frequency distribution series, inspection method only helps in identification of the modal class interval, not the exact modal value.

#### (i) Inspection Method

When frequencies of a continuous series increase and decrease in some systematic order, the modal class may be found merely by an inspection of the series. The following illustration is an example of such series where modal class is found by inspection. Having found the modal class, the actual value of the mode is calculated using the formula given above.

**ILLUSTRATION.**

Calculate mode from the following data:

| Class Interval | 0–10 | 10–20 | 20–30 | 30–40 | 40–50 |
|---|---|---|---|---|---|
| Frequency | 2 | 5 | 7 | 5 | 2 |

**SOLUTION:**

**Calculation of Mode**

| Class Interval | Frequency |
|---|---|
| 0–10 | 2 |
| 10–20 | 5 ($f_0$) |
| **($l_1$) 20–30** | **7 ($f_1$)** |
| 30–40 | 5 ($f_2$) |
| 40–50 | 2 |

A glance at the series reveals that 20–30 is the modal class because it has the maximum frequency, *i.e.*, 7. Following formula is used to calculate modal value:

$$Z = l_1 + \frac{f_1 - f_0}{2f_1 - f_0 - f_2} \times i$$

$$= 20 + \frac{7-5}{2(7)-5-5} \times 10$$

$$= 20 + \frac{2}{14-10} \times 10$$

$$= 20 + \frac{2}{4} \times 10$$

$$= 20 + 5 = 25$$

Mode (Z) = 25.

**(ii) Grouping Method**

Inspection method of finding out modal class fails in case the frequencies of the series are not increasing or decreasing in some systematic pattern. It fails also, when there are more than one class intervals with higher frequencies in the distribution. In such cases, modal class is determined using the grouping method. We have already discussed the grouping method in the case of discrete frequency series; it is the same in the case of continuous series as well. After the modal class has been identified, the actual value of mode is calculated using the same formula, *viz.*

$$Z = l_1 + \frac{f_1 - f_0}{2f_1 - f_0 - f_2} \times i$$

**ILLUSTRATION.**

Calculate mode of the following series:

| Class Interval | 0–5 | 5–10 | 10–15 | 15–20 | 20–25 | 25–30 | 30--35 |
|---|---|---|---|---|---|---|---|
| Frequency | 1 | 2 | 10 | 4 | 10 | 9 | 2 |

**SOLUTION:**

Grouping of the frequencies is essential in this series, because there are two class intervals, *i.e.*, 10–15 and 20–25 with highest frequency, 10.

Hence, the grouping table and the subsequent Analysis Table are as follows:

**Grouping Table**

| Class Interval | (I) | (II) (1+2) | (III) (2+3) | (IV) (1+2+3) | (V) (2+3+4) | (VI) (3+4+5) |
|---|---|---|---|---|---|---|
| 0–5 | 1 | 1 + 2 = 3 | | 1 + 2 + 10 = 13 | | |
| 5–10 | 2 | | 2 + 10 = 12 | | 2 + 10 + 4 = 16 | |
| 10–15 | 10 | 10 + 4 = 14 | | | | 10 + 4 + 10 = 24 |
| 15–20 | 4 | | 4 + 10 = 14 | 4 + 10 + 9 = 23 | | |
| 20–25 | 10 | 10 + 9 = 19 | | | 10 + 9 + 2 = 21 | |
| 25–30 | 9 | | 9 + 2 = 11 | | | |
| 30–35 | 2 | | | | | |

**Analysis Table**

| Column | Class intervals corresponding to highest frequencies in the Grouping Table | | | | | | |
|---|---|---|---|---|---|---|---|
| | 0–5 | 5–10 | 10–15 | 15–20 | 20–25 | 25–30 | 30–35 |
| I | | | ✓ | | ✓ | | |
| II | | | | | ✓ | ✓ | |
| III | | | | ✓ | ✓ | | |
| IV | | | | ✓ | ✓ | ✓ | |
| V | | | | | ✓ | ✓ | ✓ |
| VI | | | ✓ | ✓ | ✓ | | |
| Total | — | — | 2 | 3 | 6 | 3 | 1 |

Analysis Table shows that of all the class intervals, 20–25 has the highest frequency (6). It has got the maximum (✓) marks. Accordingly, 20–25 is the modal class interval of the series. The actual value of mode is,

$$Z = l_1 + \frac{f_1 - f_0}{2f_1 - f_0 - f_2} \times i$$

$l_1$ = lower limit of modal group = 20

$f_1$ = frequency of modal class = 10

$f_0$ = frequency of class preceding the modal class (15–20) = 4

$f_2$ = frequency of class following the modal class (25–30) = 9

i = class interval = 25 – 20 = 5

$$\text{Hence, } Z = 20 + \frac{10-4}{20-4-9} \times 5 = 20 + \frac{6}{7} \times 5 = 20 + 4.29 = 24.29$$

Mode (Z) = 24.29

***Learning by doing***

1. *Calculate mode of the following series:*

| **Class Interval** | 0–5 | 5–10 | 10–15 | 15–20 | 20–25 | 25–30 |
|---|---|---|---|---|---|---|
| **Frequency** | 20 | 24 | 32 | 28 | 20 | 26 |

(*Ans.* *Z* = 13.33)

2. *Calculate mode, given the following distribution of data:*

| **Class Interval** | 4–8 | 8–12 | 12–16 | 16–20 | 20–24 | 24–28 | 28–32 | 32–36 | 36–40 |
|---|---|---|---|---|---|---|---|---|---|
| **Frequency** | 10 | 12 | 16 | 14 | 10 | 8 | 17 | 5 | 4 |

(*Ans.* *Z* = 14.67)

### (4) Calculation of Mode when Class Intervals are Unequal

In case of unequal class intervals, mode will be determined by a different method. To calculate mode, unequal class intervals are made equal, as in the following illustration.

**ILLUSTRATION.**

| **Class Interval** | 0–4 | 4–8 | 8–12 | 12–14 | 14–16 | 16–20 | 20–24 | 24–26 | 26–32 | 32–34 | 34–40 | 40–44 | 44–48 |
|---|---|---|---|---|---|---|---|---|---|---|---|---|---|
| **Frequency** | 2 | 4 | 7 | 5 | 8 | 3 | 2 | 1 | 13 | 5 | 3 | 3 | 9 |

**Solution:**

Change unequal class intervals into equal class-intervals and work out an analysis table, as under:

| Class Interval | (I) Frequency | (II) (1+2) | (III) (2+3) | (IV) (1+2+3) | (V) (2+3+4) | (VI) (3+4+5) |
|---|---|---|---|---|---|---|
| 0–8 | 2+4=6 $f_0$ | 6 + 20 = 26 | | 6 + 20 + 5 = 31 | | |
| 8–16 | 7+5+8=20 $f_1$ | | 20 + 5 = 25 | | 20 + 5 + 14 = 39 | |
| 16–24 | 3+2=5 $f_2$ | 5 + 14 = 19 | | | | 5 + 14 + 8 = 27 |
| 24–32 | 1+13=14 | | 14 + 8 = 22 | 14 + 8 + 12 = 34 | | |
| 32–40 | 5+3=8 | 8 + 12 = 20 | | | | |
| 40–48 | 3+9=12 | | | | | |

**Analysis Table**

| Column | 0–8 | 8–16 | 16–24 | 24–32 | 32–40 | 40–48 |
|---|---|---|---|---|---|---|
| I | | ✓ | | | | |
| II | ✓ | ✓ | | | | |
| III | | ✓ | ✓ | | | |
| IV | | | | ✓ | ✓ | ✓ |
| V | | ✓ | ✓ | ✓ | | |
| VI | | | ✓ | ✓ | ✓ | |
| Total | 1 | 4 | 3 | 3 | 2 | 1 |

Mode is in 8–16 class interval.

By using the formula,

$$Z = l_1 + \frac{f_1 - f_0}{2f_1 - f_0 - f_2} \times i$$

$l_1 = 8, f_1 = 20; f_0 = 6; f_2 = 5; i = 8$

$$Z = 8 + \frac{20 - 6}{2(20) - 6 - 5} \times 8 = 8 + \frac{14}{40 - 11} \times 8 = 8 + \frac{14}{29} \times 8$$

$$Z = 8 + 3.86$$
$$= 11.86$$

Mode (Z) = 11.86.

**Illustration.**

Calculate mode of the following data:

| **Marks** | 0–5 | 5–10 | 10–20 | 20–40 | 40–60 | 60–80 | 80–90 | 90–100 |
|---|---|---|---|---|---|---|---|---|
| **Number of Students** | 5 | 7 | 9 | 25 | 30 | 24 | 8 | 6 |

**Solution:**

This is a series with unequal class intervals. Calculation of mode requires that this series be converted into one with equal class interval of 20, as shown on the next page.

| Marks | Number of Students |
|---|---|
| 0–20 | 5 + 7+ 9 = 21 |
| 20–40 | 25 = 25 ($f_0$) |
| **($l_1$) 40–60** | **30 = 30 ($f_1$)** |
| 60–80 | 24 = 24 ($f_2$) |
| 80–100 | 8 + 6 = 14 |

A glance at the table reveals that 40–60 is the modal class. The actual value of mode is,

$$Z = l_1 + \frac{f_1 - f_0}{2f_1 - f_0 - f_2} \times i$$

$$= 40 + \frac{30 - 25}{2(30) - 25 - 24} \times 20 = 40 + \frac{5}{60 - 49} \times 20$$

$$= 40 + \frac{5}{11} \times 20 = 40 + 9.09 = 49.09$$

Mode (Z) = 49.09.

### (5) Calculation of Mode in Case of Inclusive Series

**ILLUSTRATION.**

Calculate mode of the following series:

| Class Interval | 10–19 | 20–29 | 30–39 | 40–49 | 50–59 | 60–69 | 70–79 |
|---|---|---|---|---|---|---|---|
| **Frequency** | 10 | 12 | 18 | 30 | 16 | 6 | 8 |

**Note**

That for the calculation of mode in case of inclusive series, the series must be converted into exclusive as a first step.

**SOLUTION:**

For the calculation of mode, inclusive series are first to be converted into exclusive series, as under:

| Class Interval | Exclusive Class Intervals | Frequency |
|---|---|---|
| 10–19 | 9.5–19.5 | 10 |
| 20–29 | 19.5–29.5 | 12 |
| 30–39 | 29.5–39.5 | 18 ($f_0$) |
| 40–49 | **($l_1$) 39.5–49.5** | **30 ($f_1$)** |
| 50–59 | 49.5–59.5 | 16 ($f_2$) |
| 60–69 | 59.5–69.5 | 6 |
| 70–79 | 69.5–79.5 | 8 |

A glance at the above table reveals that 39.5–49.5 is the modal class interval. The actual value of mode is,

$$Z = l_1 + \frac{f_1 - f_0}{2f_1 - f_0 - f_2} \times i$$

$$= 39.5 + \frac{30 - 18}{2(30) - 18 - 16} \times 10$$

$$= 39.5 + \frac{12}{60 - 34} \times 10$$

$$= 39.5 + \frac{12}{26} \times 10$$

$$= 39.5 + 4.62 = 44.12$$

Mode (Z) = 44.12.

### (6) Calculation of Mode when Only Mid-values of the Class Intervals are Known

**ILLUSTRATION.**

Calculate mode, given the following data-set:

| Mid-value | 15 | 25 | 35 | 45 | 55 | 65 | 75 | 85 |
|---|---|---|---|---|---|---|---|---|
| Frequency | 5 | 8 | 12 | 16 | 28 | 15 | 3 | 2 |

**SOLUTION:**

A series with 'mid-value' is first to be expanded as a series with class intervals, as under:

**Expansion of Mid-values as Class Intervals for the Estimation of Mode**

| Mid-value | Class Interval | Frequency |
|---|---|---|
| 15 | 10–20 | 5 |
| 25 | 20–30 | 8 |
| 35 | 30–40 | 12 |
| 45 | 40–50 | 16 ($f_0$) |
| 55 | **($l_1$) 50–60** | **28 ($f_1$)** |
| 65 | 60–70 | 15 |
| 75 | 70–80 | 3 |
| 85 | 80–90 | 2 |

Class interval 50–60 is the one with highest frequency. This is the modal class interval, as the frequencies are increasing or decreasing in a systematic pattern. The actual value of mode is,

$$Z = l_1 + \frac{f_1 - f_0}{2f_1 - f_0 - f_2} \times i$$

$$= 50 + \frac{28 - 16}{2(28) - 16 - 15} \times 10$$

$$= 50 + \frac{12}{56 - 31} \times 10$$

$$= 50 + \frac{12}{25} \times 10$$

$$= 50 + 4.8 = 54.8$$

Mode (Z) = 54.8.

**CALCULATION OF MODE IN 'LESS THAN' CUMULATIVE FREQUENCY DISTRIBUTION**

**ILLUSTRATION.**

Find out mode of the following series:

| Wages (₹) less than | 200 | 300 | 400 | 500 | 600 | 700 | 800 | 900 |
|---|---|---|---|---|---|---|---|---|
| Number of Workers | 5 | 18 | 38 | 70 | 90 | 95 | 98 | 100 |

**Solution:**

For the calculation of Mode, 'Less-than' cumulative frequency distribution is first to be converted into a normal continuous frequency distribution, as under:

| Wages (₹) | Number of Workers (f) |
|---|---|
| 100–200 | 5 |
| 200–300 | 18 – 5 = 13 |
| 300–400 | 38 – 18 = 20 ($f_0$) |
| **($l_1$) 400–500** | **70 – 38 = 32 ($f_1$)** |
| 500–600 | 90 – 70 = 20 ($f_2$) |
| 600–700 | 95 – 90 = 5 |
| 700–800 | 98 – 95 = 3 |
| 800–900 | 100 – 98 = 2 |

An inspection of the series reveals that 400–500 is the modal class. The value of mode is,

$$Z = l_1 + \frac{f_1 - f_0}{2f_1 - f_0 - f_2} \times i$$

$$= 400 + \frac{32 - 20}{2(32) - 20 - 20} \times 100$$

$$= 400 + \frac{12}{64 - 40} \times 100$$

$$= 400 + \frac{12}{24} \times 100$$

$$= 400 + 50 = 450$$

Mode (Z) = 450.

*Learning by doing*

1. *Calculate mode of the following series:*

| Class Interval | 30–59 | 60–89 | 90–119 | 120–149 | 150–179 | 180–209 | 210–239 |
|---|---|---|---|---|---|---|---|
| Frequency | 4 | 7 | 12 | 15 | 18 | 6 | 5 |

(*Ans.* $Z = 155.5$)

2. *The following data-set gives mid-values and frequencies. Calculate its mode.*

| Mid-value | 5 | 10 | 15 | 20 | 25 | 30 | 35 | 40 | 45 |
|---|---|---|---|---|---|---|---|---|---|
| Frequency | 7 | 13 | 19 | 24 | 32 | 28 | 17 | 8 | 6 |

(*Ans.* $Z = 25.83$)

## Calculation of Mode through Arithmetic Mean and Median

One can calculate mode of a series through mean and median of that series. The formula is:

**FORMULA**

$$Z = 3M - 2\overline{X}$$

(Here, Z = Mode; M = Median; and $\overline{X}$ = Mean.)

Here, it may be noted that in the case of normal distributions, or symmetrical distributions, mean, median and mode coincide with

**Note**

That in case of normal distributions, mean, median and mode of the series tend to coincide.

each other. Thus, this formula is most useful in this case. However, in asymmetrical distribution the formula may also be used for the calculation of mode.

### Illustration.

Calculate mode of a series, the mean and median values of which are 16 cm and 20 cm respectively.

### Solution:

Mode = 3 Median – 2 Mean

Or, $Z = 3M - 2\overline{X}$

Here, M = 20 cm, $\overline{X}$= 16 cm

$\therefore \quad Z = 3 \times 20 - 2 \times 16$

$= 60 - 32$

$= 28$

Thus, Mode (Z)= 28 cm.

*Learning by doing*

1. *Median and mean values of the marks obtained by the students of a class are 46.67 and 45.5 respectively. Find out mode of the marks.* (**Ans.** $Z = 49.01$)
2. *Median and mean weight of the students of a class are 35.83 and 37.06 respectively. Calculate the mode.* (**Ans.** $Z = 33.37$)
3. *If median and mean of a distribution are 18.8 and 20.2 respectively, what would be its mode?* (**Ans.** $Z = 16$)

### Graphic Method of Locating Mode

Mode of a series may be located through a graphic presentation of the data. It involves the following steps:

(i) Present the given information in the form of a histogram. Identify the highest rectangle. This corresponds to modal class of the series.

(ii) Join the top corners of the modal rectangle with the immediate next corners of the adjacent rectangles. The joining lines must cut each other.

(iii) The point where the joining lines cut each other points to the modal value. This value is determined by drawing a perpendicular from that point on to the X-axis. Illustration below should explain this process.

### Illustration.

Calculate mode of the following series, using the Graphic Technique:

| Expenditure | Number of Families |
|---|---|
| 0–10 | 14 |
| 10–20 | 23 |
| 20–30 | 27 |
| 30–40 | 21 |
| 40–50 | 15 |

**SOLUTION:**

The adjoining graph shows expenditure on the X-axis and number of families on the Y-axis. As is evident, class interval 20–30 corresponds to the highest rectangle in the graph, and is therefore, the modal class interval.

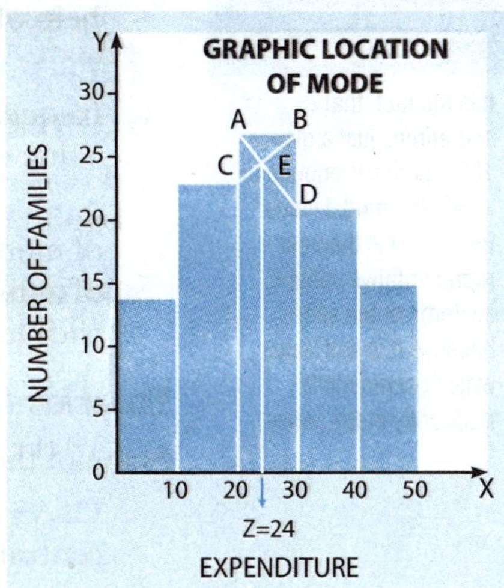


For the calculation of modal value, AD and BC lines are drawn to join the top ends of the modal rectangle with the immediate next ends of the adjoining rectangles. These lines are crossing each other at point E. A perpendicular is drawn from point E on the X-axis to locate the exact value of mode which is 24. A counter check of this modal value may be made by calculating mode with the following formula:

$$Z = l_1 + \frac{f_1 - f_0}{2f_1 - f_0 - f_2} \times i$$

$$= 20 + \frac{27 - 23}{2(27) - 23 - 21} \times 10$$

$$= 20 + \frac{4}{54 - 44} \times 10 = 20 + \frac{4}{10} \times 10$$

$$= 20 + 4 = 24$$

Thus, Mode (Z) = 24.

*Learning by doing*

1. *Present the following information in the form of a histogram and locate the modal value. Give a cross-check to your answer, calculating mode through its standard formula.*

| Class Interval | 0–10 | 10–20 | 20–30 | 30–40 | 40–50 | 50–60 | 60–70 |
|---|---|---|---|---|---|---|---|
| Frequency | 4 | 8 | 14 | 20 | 30 | 15 | 6 |

*(Ans. Z = 44)*

2. *Find out mode of the following distribution, using histogram.*

| Age | 20–25 | 25–30 | 30–35 | 35–40 | 40–45 | 45–50 |
|---|---|---|---|---|---|---|
| Frequency | 50 | 70 | 100 | 180 | 150 | 120 |

*(Ans. Z = 38.6)*

3. *Find out mode of the following data with the help of histogram.*

| Marks | 0–10 | 10–20 | 20–30 | 30–40 | 40–50 | 50–60 |
|---|---|---|---|---|---|---|
| Frequency | 6 | 8 | 16 | 25 | 12 | 8 |

*(Ans. Z = 34.1 marks)*

## MERITS OF MODE

Mode, as a measure of central tendency has the following main merits:

(1) **Simple and Popular:** Mode is a very simple measure of the central tendency. Sometimes, just a glance at the series is enough to locate the modal value. Because of its simplicity, it is a very popular measure of central tendency.

(2) **Less Effect of Marginal Values:** Compared to mean, mode is less affected by marginal values in the series. Mode is determined only by the value with the highest frequencies.

**What is the Principal Merit of mode as a Measure of Central Tendency?**

It is the fact that sometimes just a glance at the series is enough to locate the modal value. Besides, it is the best representative value of all items of the series, because it is that value which occurs most frequently in the series.

(3) **Graphic Determination:** Mode can be located graphically, with the help of histogram.

(4) **Best Representation:** Mode is that value which occurs most frequently in the series. Accordingly, mode is the best representative value of the series.

(5) **No Need of knowing all the items or Frequencies:** The calculation of mode does not require knowledge of all the items and frequencies of a distribution. In simple series, it is enough if one knows the item with highest frequency in the distribution.

## Demerits of Mode

Some of the demerits of mode are as under:

(1) **Uncertain and Vague:** Mode is an uncertain and vague measure of central tendency.

(2) **Not Capable of Algebraic Treatment:** Unlike mean, mode is not capable of further algebraic treatment.

(3) **Difficult:** When frequencies of all items are identical, it is difficult to identify the modal value.

(4) **Complex Procedure of Grouping:** Calculation of mode involves cumbersome procedure of grouping the data. If the extent of grouping changes, there will be a change in the modal value.

(5) **Ignores Extreme Marginal Frequencies:** It ignores extreme marginal frequencies. To that extent, modal value is not a representative value of all the items in a series.

Besides, one can question the representative character of the modal value as its calculation does not involve all items of the series.

**The Principal Demerit of Mode as a Measure of Central Tendency**

That it is difficult to identify modal value in case series are not regular or when different class intervals in a series show the same frequency.

## Uses of Mode

Owing to simplicity of its calculation and understanding, mode is becoming an increasingly popular measure of the central tendency. In the trading sector, this measure is frequently used. Average expenditure, average income of the customers or popularity of goods in the market invariably refers to modal value. Likewise, in Meteorological Department, average rainfall or temperature of a place invariably refers to the modal value. In other spheres of life as well, the use and application of mode is gaining popularity.

**Calculation of Mode: A Glance**

| Types of Series | Method of Calculation |
|---|---|
| 1. Individual Series | (a) The value that occurs the most in the series is identified as mode of the series by inspection method.<br>(b) If the frequency of all values is equal the same are changed into discrete frequency distribution and then mode is calculated. |

| 2. Discrete Series/Frequency Array | (a) The value that occurs the most in the series is identified by inspection method.<br>(b) If items with highest frequency are more than one, then grouping method is used. |
|---|---|
| 3. Frequency Distribution Series | (a) **Exclusive:** Series with highest frequency is called modal class. The actual value of mode is determined using the following formula:<br>$Z = l_1 + \frac{f_1 - f_0}{2f_1 - f_0 - f_2} \times i$<br>(b) **Inclusive:** Inclusive series is converted into exclusive series. |
| 4. Moderately Asymmetrical Distributions | $Z = 3M - 2\overline{X}$ |

## 4. Relationship among Mean, Mode and Median

Before knowing the relationship among mean, median and mode, it is necessary to know whether the distribution is symmetrical or asymmetrical.

(i) In case of symmetrical distribution, mean, median and mode will be identical and frequency curve will be bell-shaped.

(ii) In case of asymmetrical distribution, value of mean, median and mode will be different. As such, frequency curve will not be bell-shaped. It may be skewed either to the right or to the left.

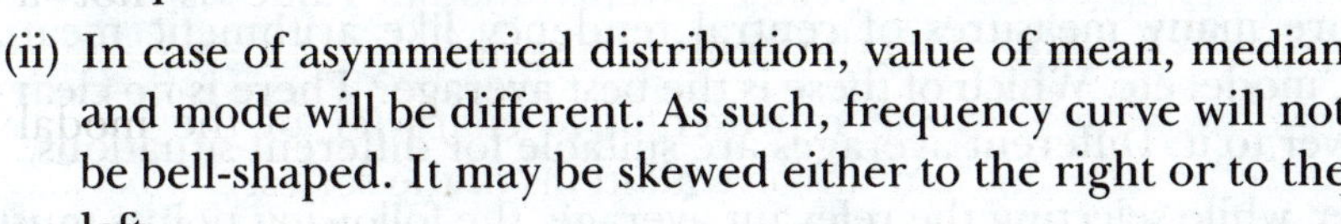

Bell-Shaped Curve

$\overline{X} = M = Z$

If the distribution is skewed more to the right, *i.e.*, positive, then mean ($\overline{X}$) and median (M) will be greater than mode (Z), *i.e.*, ($\overline{X}$, M > Z). In other words, mode is the minimum. If the distribution is skewed more to the left, *i.e.*, negative, then mean and median will be less than mode, *i.e.*, ($\overline{X}$, M < Z). In other words, mode (Z) will be maximum.

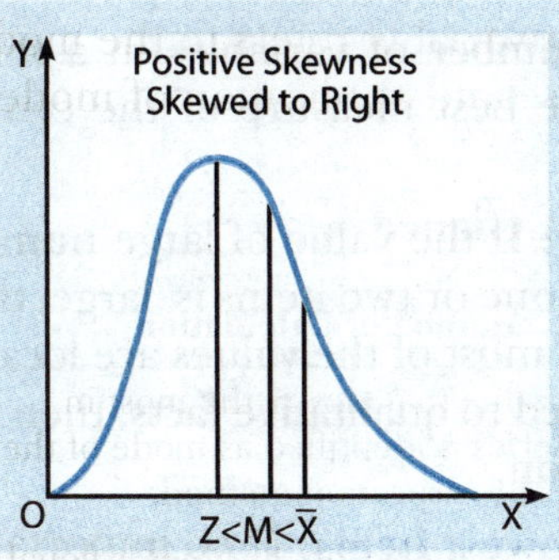


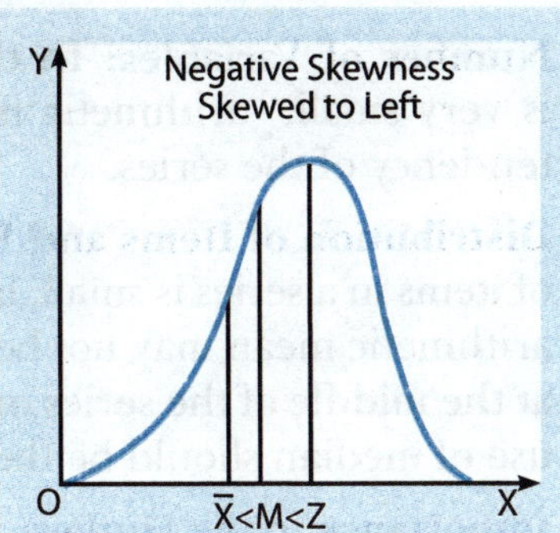


The following formula generalises the relationship between mode, median and mean of a series:

$$\text{Mode} = 3 \text{ Median} - 2 \text{ Mean}$$

$$Z = 3M - 2\overline{X}$$

Following example illustrates this relationship:

**ILLUSTRATION.**

If in an asymmetrical distribution, median is 280 and mean is 310, what will be the mode?

**SOLUTION:**

Mode = 3 Median – 2 Mean

Mode = 3 × 280 – 2 × 310

= 840 – 620

= 220

When Mode is 220 and Median is 280, Mean would be:

220 = 280 × 3 – 2 Mean

220 = 840 – 2 Mean

2 Mean = 840 – 220

2 Mean = 620

$\text{Mean} = \frac{620}{2} = 310$

When Mode is 220 and Mean is 310, Median would be:

220 = 3 Median – 2×310

220 = 3 Median – 620

3 Median = 220 + 620

3 Median = 840

$\text{Median} = \frac{840}{3} = 280$

## 5. Which is the Best Average?

**You Must Note**

That median and mode are not based on all items of the series. Only arithmetic mean is based on all items of the series. Also, only arithmetic mean is capable of furthrer algebraic treatment; mode and median are not.

There are many measures of central tendency like arithmetic mean, median, mode, etc. Which of these is the best average? There is no clear-cut answer to it. Different averages are suitable for different situations.

However, while selecting the relevant average, the following points must be kept in mind:

(1) **Objective:** Selection of average must conform to the objective of study. For instance, if all values are to be given equal importance, arithmetic mean will be most appropriate. However, if the value occurring most frequently in a series is to be identified, mode will be most relevant.

(2) **Number of Variables:** In case the number of variables in a series is very small, arithmetic mean is the best measure of the central tendency of the series.

(3) **Distribution of Items and Frequency:** If the value of large number of items in a series is small, but that of one or two items is large, then arithmetic mean may not be useful. If most of the values are located at the middle of the series or are related to qualitative facts, then the use of median should be the best option.

(4) **Importance to the Highest and the Lowest Items:** If no importance is to be attached to the highest and the lowest items of a series, then the use of median or mode should be most suitable.

(5) **Types of Series:** If in a series large number of items are similar to each other then the use of mode is not suitable.

## 6. Comparative Features

Following comparative features must be kept in view while making use of different measures of central tendency:

(1) Mean and median can always be estimated with certainty but not the mode.

(2) Median and mode are located in the middle of the frequency distribution, the mean may not be.

(3) It is difficult to calculate mode as compared to mean and median.

(4) Median and mode are not based on all the items of the distribution but mean is based on all the items of the distribution.

(5) Arithmetic examination of mean is possible. But it is not possible in case of median and mode.

(6) Selection of a sample influences mean but not the median and mode.

(7) Mean is influenced by the highest and the lowest items of the series. However, median and mode are not influenced by them.

(8) Median and mode can be graphically located, but not the mean unless it is a situation of normal distribution.

## MISCELLANEOUS ILLUSTRATIONS

### ILLUSTRATION 1.

The following series show marks in Statistics of 9 students in Class XI. Find the median marks.

| Marks | 22 | 16 | 18 | 13 | 15 | 19 | 17 | 20 | 23 |
|---|---|---|---|---|---|---|---|---|---|

**SOLUTION:**

The data is first arranged in ascending order:

| S. No. | Marks |
|---|---|
| 1 | 13 |
| 2 | 15 |
| 3 | 16 |
| 4 | 17 |
| 5 | 18 |
| 6 | 19 |
| 7 | 20 |
| 8 | 22 |
| 9 | 23 |
| N = 9 | |

$$M = \text{Size of}\left(\frac{N+1}{2}\right)\text{th item}$$

$$= \text{Size of}\left(\frac{9+1}{2}\right)\text{th item}$$

$$= \text{Size of 5th item} = 18$$

Hence, Median = 18.

**ILLUSTRATION 2.**

Calculate median from the following data:

| 200 | 217 | 316 | 264 | 296 | 282 | 317 | 299 |
|---|---|---|---|---|---|---|---|

**SOLUTION:**

The data is first arranged in ascending order:

| S. No. | X |
|---|---|
| 1 | 200 |
| 2 | 217 |
| 3 | 264 |
| 4 | 282 |
| 5 | 296 |
| 6 | 299 |
| 7 | 316 |
| 8 | 317 |
| N = 8 | |

$$M = \text{Size of}\left(\frac{N+1}{2}\right)\text{th item}$$

$$= \text{Size of}\left(\frac{8+1}{2}\right)\text{th item}$$

$$= \text{Size of 4.5th item}$$

$$= \frac{\text{Size of 4th item + Size of 5th item}}{2}$$

$$\therefore \quad M = \frac{282 + 296}{2} = \frac{578}{2} = 289$$

Median = 289.

**ILLUSTRATION 3.**

Following are the marks obtained by a batch of 10 students in a certain class test in Statistics (X) and Accountancy (Y):

| Roll Number | 1 | 2 | 3 | 4 | 5 | 6 | 7 | 8 | 9 | 10 |
|---|---|---|---|---|---|---|---|---|---|---|
| Statistics(X) | 63 | 64 | 62 | 32 | 30 | 60 | 47 | 46 | 35 | 28 |
| Accountancy(Y) | 68 | 66 | 35 | 42 | 26 | 85 | 44 | 80 | 33 | 72 |

In which subject is the level of knowledge of students higher?

**SOLUTION:**

**Calculation of Median**

| Roll Number | Statistics (X) | Accountancy (Y) |
|---|---|---|
| 1 | 28 | 26 |
| 2 | 30 | 33 |
| 3 | 32 | 35 |
| 4 | 35 | 42 |
| 5 | 46 | 44 |
| 6 | 47 | 66 |
| 7 | 60 | 68 |
| 8 | 62 | 72 |
| 9 | 63 | 80 |
| 10 | 64 | 85 |
| N = 10 | | |

$$\text{Median} = \text{Size of}\left(\frac{N+1}{2}\right)\text{th item} = \text{Size of}\left(\frac{10+1}{2}\right)\text{th item}$$

$$= \text{Size of}\left(\frac{11}{2}\right)\text{th item} = \text{Size of 5.5th item}$$

$$\text{Median (X)} = \frac{\text{Size of 5th item} + \text{Size of 6th item}}{2}$$

$$= \frac{46+47}{2} = \frac{93}{2} = 46.5 \text{ marks}$$

$$\text{Median (Y)} = \frac{\text{Size of 5th item} + \text{Size of 6th item}}{2}$$

$$= \frac{44+66}{2} = \frac{110}{2} = 55 \text{ marks}$$

Median marks of Accountancy (Y) are more than that of Statistics (X). Therefore, level of knowledge of students is higher in Accountancy.

**ILLUSTRATION 4.**

Calculate the median from the following data:

| Size | 10 | 12 | 14 | 16 | 18 | 20 | 22 |
|---|---|---|---|---|---|---|---|
| Frequency | 2 | 5 | 12 | 20 | 10 | 7 | 3 |

**SOLUTION:**

**Calculation of Median**

| Size | Frequency (f) | Cumulative Frequency |
|---|---|---|
| 10 | 2 | 2 |
| 12 | 5 | 7 |
| 14 | 12 | 19 |
| 16 | 20 | 39 (M) |
| 18 | 10 | 49 |
| 20 | 7 | 56 |
| 22 | 3 | 59 |
| | N = 59 | |

$$M = \text{Size of}\left(\frac{N+1}{2}\right)\text{th item}$$

$$= \text{Size of}\left(\frac{59+1}{2}\right)\text{th item} = \text{Size of 30th item}$$

The value of 30th item lies against 39 whose value is 16. Therefore, Median = 16.

**ILLUSTRATION 5.**

The following table gives the marks obtained by some students. Calculate the median marks obtained by the students.

| Marks | 0–5 | 5–10 | 10–15 | 15–20 | 20–25 | 25–30 | 30–35 | 35–40 | 40–45 |
|---|---|---|---|---|---|---|---|---|---|
| Number of Students | 6 | 12 | 17 | 30 | 10 | 10 | 8 | 5 | 2 |

**SOLUTION:**

| Marks | Frequency (f) | Cumulative Frequency |
|---|---|---|
| 0–5 | 6 | 6 |
| 5–10 | 12 | 18 |
| 10–15 | 17 | **35 (c.f.)** |
| **($l_1$) 15–20** | **30 (f)** | 65 |
| 20–25 | 10 | 75 |
| 25–30 | 10 | 85 |
| 30–35 | 8 | 93 |
| 35–40 | 5 | 98 |
| 40–45 | 2 | 100 |
| | $\Sigma f = N = 100$ | |

$$M = \text{Size of}\left(\frac{N}{2}\right)\text{th item}$$

$$= \text{Size of}\left(\frac{100}{2}\right)\text{th item} = \text{Size of 50th item}$$

50th item lies in 65th cumulative frequency and the corresponding median class is 15–20.

$$M = l_1 + \frac{\frac{N}{2} - \text{c.f.}}{f} \times i = 15 + \frac{\frac{100}{2} - 35}{30} \times 5$$

$$= 15 + \frac{50-35}{30} \times 5 = 15 + \frac{15}{30} \times 5$$

$$= 15 + 2.5 = 17.5$$

Median = 17.5 marks.

**ILLUSTRATION 6.**

Calculate median from the following data:

| Marks | Number of Students |
|---|---|
| Less than 10 | 4 |
| Less than 20 | 16 |
| Less than 30 | 40 |
| Less than 40 | 76 |
| Less than 50 | 96 |
| Less than 60 | 112 |
| Less than 70 | 120 |
| Less than 80 | 125 |

**SOLUTION:**

Since, we are given cumulative frequencies, firstly we find simple frequencies.

**Calculation of Median**

| Marks | Cumulative Frequency | Frequency (f) |
|---|---|---|
| 0–10 | 4 | 4 |
| 10–20 | 16 | 16 – 4 = 12 |
| 20–30 | **40 (c.f.)** | 40 – 16 = 24 |
| **($l_1$) 30–40** | 76 | **76 – 40 = 36 (f)** |
| 40–50 | 96 | 96 – 76 = 20 |
| 50–60 | 112 | 112 – 96 = 16 |
| 60–70 | 120 | 120 – 112 = 8 |
| 70–80 | 125 | 125 – 120 = 5 |
| | | Σf = N = 125 |

$$M = \text{Size of} \left(\frac{N}{2}\right)\text{th item}$$

$$= \text{Size of} \left(\frac{125}{2}\right)\text{th item} = \text{Size of 62.5th item}$$

Hence, median lies in the class 30–40.

$$M = l_1 + \frac{\frac{N}{2} - \text{c.f.}}{f} \times i$$

$$= 30 + \frac{\frac{125}{2} - 40}{36} \times 10 = 30 + \frac{62.5 - 40}{36} \times 10$$

$$= 30 + \frac{22.5}{36} \times 10 = 30 + 6.25 = 36.25$$

Median = 36.25 marks.

**ILLUSTRATION 7.**

Calculate median of the following distribution of data:

| Class Interval | 1–10 | 11–20 | 21–30 | 31–40 | 41–50 |
|---|---|---|---|---|---|
| Frequency | 4 | 12 | 20 | 9 | 5 |

**SOLUTION:**

Since we are given inclusive series, firstly we convert it into exclusive one by deducting 0.5 from the lower limits and adding 0.5 to the upper limits.

**Calculation of Median**

| Class Interval | Frequency (f) | Cumulative Frequency |
|---|---|---|
| 0.5–10.5 | 4 | 4 |
| 10.5–20.5 | 12 | **16 (c.f.)** |
| **($l_1$) 20.5–30.5** | **20 (f)** | 36 |
| 30.5–40.5 | 9 | 45 |
| 40.5–50.5 | 5 | 50 |
| | N = 50 | |

$$M = \text{Size of}\left(\frac{N}{2}\right)\text{th item}$$

$$= \text{Size of}\left(\frac{50}{2}\right)\text{th item} = \text{Size of 25th item}$$

∴ Median lies in the class 20.5–30.5.

$$M = l_1 + \frac{\frac{N}{2} - \text{c.f.}}{f} \times i$$

$$= 20.5 + \frac{\frac{50}{2} - 16}{20} \times 10$$

$$= 20.5 + \frac{25 - 16}{20} \times 10 = 20.5 + \frac{9}{20} \times 10$$

$$= 20.5 + 4.5 = 25$$

Median = 25.

**Illustration 8.**

Calculate the median from the following data-set:

| Size | 10–15 | 15–17.5 | 17.5–20 | 20–30 | 30–35 | 35–40 | 40–50 |
|---|---|---|---|---|---|---|---|
| Frequency | 10 | 15 | 17 | 25 | 28 | 30 | 40 |

**Solution:**

Even though the class intervals are unequal, no specific treatment of the data is needed. Median can be calculated straight away as in the case of other frequency distributions.

**Calculation of Median**

| Size | Frequency (f) | Cumulative Frequency |
|---|---|---|
| 10–15 | 10 | 10 |
| 15–17.5 | 15 | 25 |
| 17.5–20 | 17 | 42 |
| 20–30 | 25 | **67 (c.f.)** |
| **($l_1$) 30–35** | **28 (f)** | 95 |
| 35–40 | 30 | 125 |
| 40–50 | 40 | 165 |
| | N = 165 | |

$$M = \text{Size of}\left(\frac{N}{2}\right)\text{th item}$$

$$= \text{Size of}\left(\frac{165}{2}\right)\text{th item}$$

$$= \text{Size of 82.5th item}$$

Hence, median lies in the class 30–35.

$$M = l_1 + \frac{\frac{N}{2} - c.f.}{f} \times i$$

$$= 30 + \frac{\frac{165}{2} - 67}{28} \times 5$$

$$= 30 + \frac{82.5 - 67}{28} \times 5 = 30 + \frac{15.5}{28} \times 5$$

$$= 30 + 2.77 = 32.77$$

Median = 32.77.

**ILLUSTRATION 9.**

Compute median from the following data:

| **Mid-value** | 5 | 15 | 25 | 35 | 45 | 55 | 65 | 75 |
|---|---|---|---|---|---|---|---|---|
| **Frequency** | 15 | 7 | 11 | 10 | 13 | 8 | 20 | 16 |

**SOLUTION:**

Since, we are given the mid-values, we should first find out the upper and lower limits of the various classes. As the mid-values are 5, 15, 25, 35, 45, 55, 65, 75, so, class size is 10 (= 15 – 5). For determining limits of different classes, applying the formula:

Lower limit: $l_1 = m - \frac{1}{2} \times i$ and

Upper limit: $l_2 = m + \frac{1}{2} \times i$

where, $i$ = difference between two mid-values.

In this case, the upper and the lower limits of the first mid-value are:

$$l_1 = 5 - \frac{1}{2} \times 10 = 0 \text{ and } l_2 = 5 + \frac{1}{2} \times 10 = 10$$

*i.e.,* 0–10 class interval.

Similarly, class intervals for other mid-values are obtained as:

| Classes | Frequency (f) | Cumulative Frequency |
|---|---|---|
| 0–10 | 15 | 15 |
| 10–20 | 7 | 22 |
| 20–30 | 11 | 33 |
| 30–40 | 10 | **43 (c.f.)** |
| **($l_1$) 40–50** | **13 (f)** | 56 |
| 50–60 | 8 | 64 |
| 60–70 | 20 | 84 |
| 70–80 | 16 | 100 |
| | N = 100 | |

$$M = \text{Size of} \left(\frac{N}{2}\right)\text{th item}$$

$$= \text{Size of} \left(\frac{100}{2}\right)\text{th item} = \text{Size of 50th item}$$

Hence, median lies in the class 40–50.

$$M = l_1 + \frac{\frac{N}{2} - c.f.}{f} \times i$$

$$= 40 + \frac{\frac{100}{2} - 43}{13} \times 10 = 40 + \frac{50 - 43}{13} \times 10$$

$$= 40 + \frac{7}{13} \times 10 = 40 + 5.38 = 45.38$$

Median = 45.38.

**ILLUSTRATION 10.**

Find the missing frequency of the group 20–30 when the median is 28.

| **Class Interval** | 0–10 | 10–20 | 20–30 | 30–40 | 40–50 |
|---|---|---|---|---|---|
| **Frequency** | 5 | 8 | ? | 16 | 6 |

**SOLUTION:**

Let the missing frequency be denoted by $f_1$.

**Calculation of Missing Frequency**

| Class Interval | Frequency (f) | Cumulative Frequency |
|---|---|---|
| 0–10 | 5 | 5 |
| 10–20 | 8 | **13 (c.f.)** |
| **($l_1$) 20–30** | **$f_1$** | $13 + f_1$ |
| 30–40 | 16 | $29 + f_1$ |
| 40–50 | 6 | $35 + f_1$ |
| | $N = 35 + f_1$ | |

Since, Median = 28, it lies in the class 20–30.

$$M = l_1 + \frac{\frac{N}{2} - c.f.}{f} \times i$$

$$28 = 20 + \frac{\frac{35 + f_1}{2} - 13}{f_1} \times 10$$

$$8 = \frac{\frac{35 + f_1}{2} - 13}{f_1} \times 10$$

$$\Rightarrow \quad 8f_1 = \left(\frac{35 + f_1}{2} - 13\right) \times 10$$

$$\Rightarrow \quad 8f_1 = \left(\frac{35 + f_1 - 26}{2}\right) \times 10$$

$$16f_1 = 350 + 10f_1 - 260 \Rightarrow 6f_1 = 90$$

$$\therefore \quad f_1 = \frac{90}{6} = 15$$

Thus, Missing Frequency ($f_1$) = 15.

**Illustration 11.**

Calculate $Q_1$, $Q_3$, $D_9$ and $P_{70}$ from the following data:

| 120 | 187 | 170 | 180 | 192 | 150 | 190 | 181 | 200 | 210 |
|---|---|---|---|---|---|---|---|---|---|

**Solution:**

The date is first arranged in ascending order:

| S. No. | X |
|---|---|
| 1 | 120 |
| 2 | 150 |
| 3 | 170 |
| 4 | 180 |
| 5 | 181 |
| 6 | 187 |
| 7 | 190 |
| 8 | 192 |
| 9 | 200 |
| 10 | 210 |
| N = 10 | |

$$Q_1 = \text{Size of } \left(\frac{N+1}{4}\right)\text{th item} = \text{Size of } \left(\frac{10+1}{4}\right)\text{th item}$$

$= \text{Size of } 2.75\text{th item}$

$= \text{Size of 2nd item} + 0.75 \text{ (Size of 3rd item – Size of 2nd item)}$

$= 150 + \frac{3}{4}(170 - 150) = 150 + 15 = 165$

$$Q_3 = \text{Size of } 3\left(\frac{N+1}{4}\right)\text{th item} = \text{Size of } 3\left(\frac{10+1}{4}\right)\text{th item}$$

$= \text{Size of } 8.25\text{th item}$

$= \text{Size of 8th item} + 0.25 \text{ (Size of 9th item – Size of 8th item)}$

$= 192 + \frac{1}{4}(200 - 192) = 192 + 2 = 194$

$$D_9 = \text{Size of } 9\left(\frac{N+1}{10}\right)\text{th item} = \text{Size of } 9\left(\frac{10+1}{10}\right)\text{th item}$$

$= \text{Size of } 9.9\text{th item}$

$= \text{Size of 9th item} + 0.9 \text{ (Size of 10th item – Size of 9th item)}$

$= 200 + \frac{9}{10}(210 - 200) = 200 + 9 = 209$

$$P_{70} = \text{Size of } 70\left(\frac{N+1}{100}\right)\text{th item} = \text{Size of } 70\left(\frac{10+1}{100}\right)\text{th item}$$

$= \text{Size of } 7.7\text{th item}$

$= \text{Size of 7th item} + 0.7 \text{ (Size of 8th item – Size of 7th item)}$

$= 190 + \frac{7}{10}(192 - 190) = 190 + 1.4 = 191.4$

Thus, $Q_1 = 165$, $Q_3 = 194$, $D_9 = 209$, $P_{70} = 191.4$.

**ILLUSTRATION 12.**

Calculate median, quartiles, 6th decile and 70th percentile from the following data:

| Marks less than | 80 | 70 | 60 | 50 | 40 | 30 | 20 | 10 |
|---|---|---|---|---|---|---|---|---|
| Number of Students | 100 | 90 | 80 | 60 | 32 | 20 | 13 | 5 |

**SOLUTION:**

The data is given in the form of a cumulative frequency distribution. First we convert it into simple frequency distribution and write it in ascending order:

| Marks | Cumulative Frequency | Frequency (f) |
|---|---|---|
| 0–10 | 5 | 5 |
| 10–20 | 13 | 8 (= 13 – 5) |
| 20–30 | 20 | 7 (= 20 – 13) |
| 30–40 | 32 | 12 (= 32 – 20) |
| 40–50 | 60 | 28 (= 60 – 32) |
| 50–60 | 80 | 20 (= 80 – 60) |
| 60–70 | 90 | 10 (= 90 – 80) |
| 70–80 | 100 | 10 (= 100 – 90) |
| | | $\Sigma f = N = 100$ |

$$M = \text{Size of}\left(\frac{N}{2}\right)\text{th item} = \text{Size of}\left(\frac{100}{2}\right)\text{th item}$$

$$= \text{Size of 50th item}$$

Median lies in the class 40–50.

$$M = l_1 + \frac{\frac{N}{2} - \text{c.f.}}{f} \times i = 40 + \frac{\frac{100}{2} - 32}{28} \times 10$$

$$= 40 + \frac{50 - 32}{28} \times 10 = 40 + \frac{18}{28} \times 10$$

$$= 40 + 6.43 = 46.43$$

$$Q_1 = \text{Size of}\left(\frac{N}{4}\right)\text{th item}$$

$$= \text{Size of}\left(\frac{100}{4}\right)\text{th item} = \text{Size of 25th item}$$

$Q_1$ lies in the class 30–40.

$$Q_1 = l_1 + \frac{\frac{N}{4} - \text{c.f.}}{f} \times i = 30 + \frac{\frac{100}{4} - 20}{12} \times 10$$

$$= 30 + \frac{25 - 20}{12} \times 10 = 30 + \frac{5}{12} \times 10$$

$$= 30 + 4.17 = 34.17$$

$$Q_3 = \text{Size of } 3\left(\frac{N}{4}\right)\text{th item}$$

$$= \text{Size of } 3\left(\frac{100}{4}\right)\text{th item}$$

$$= \text{Size of 75th item}$$

$Q_3$ lies in the class 50–60.

$$Q_3 = l_1 + \frac{3\left(\frac{N}{4}\right) - \text{c.f.}}{f} \times i = 50 + \frac{3\left(\frac{100}{4}\right) - 60}{20} \times 10$$

$$= 50 + \frac{75 - 60}{20} \times 10$$

$$= 50 + \frac{15}{20} \times 10$$

$$= 50 + 7.5 = 57.5$$

$$D_6 = \text{Size of } 6\left(\frac{N}{10}\right)\text{th item}$$

$$= \text{Size of } 6\left(\frac{100}{10}\right)\text{th item}$$

$$= \text{Size of 60th item}$$

$D_6$ lies in the class 40–50.

$$D_6 = l_1 + \frac{6\left(\frac{N}{10}\right) - \text{c.f.}}{f} \times i = 40 + \frac{6\left(\frac{100}{10}\right) - 32}{28} \times 10$$

$$= 40 + \frac{60 - 32}{28} \times 10 = 40 + \frac{28}{28} \times 10$$

$$= 40 + 10 = 50$$

$$P_{70} = \text{Size of } 70\left(\frac{N}{100}\right)\text{th item}$$

$$= \text{Size of } 70\left(\frac{100}{100}\right)\text{th item}$$

$$= \text{Size of 70th item}$$

$P_{70}$ lies in the class 50–60.

$$P_{70} = l_1 + \frac{70\left(\frac{N}{100}\right) - \text{c.f.}}{f} \times i = 50 + \frac{70\left(\frac{100}{100}\right) - 60}{20} \times 10$$

$$= 50 + \frac{70 - 60}{20} \times 10$$

$$= 50 + \frac{10}{20} \times 10$$

$$= 50 + 5 = 55$$

$\therefore$ Median = 46.43, $Q_1$ = 34.17, $Q_3$ = 57.5, $D_6$ = 50, $P_{70}$ = 55.

**ILLUSTRATION 13.**

Following is the distribution of marks in Economics obtained by 50 students:

| Marks (more than) | 0 | 10 | 20 | 30 | 40 | 50 |
|---|---|---|---|---|---|---|
| Number of Students | 50 | 46 | 40 | 20 | 10 | 3 |

Calculate the median marks. If 60% of the students pass this test, find the minimum marks obtained by a pass candidate.

**SOLUTION:**

Let us first of all convert cumulative frequencies into simple frequencies.

| Marks | Frequency (f) | Cumulative Frequency |
|---|---|---|
| 0–10 | 50 – 46 = 4 | 4 |
| 10–20 | 46 – 40 = 6 | 10 |
| 20–30 | 40 – 20 = 20 | 30 |
| 30–40 | 20 – 10 = 10 | 40 |
| 40–50 | 10 – 3 = 7 | 47 |
| 50–60 | 3 | 50 |
| | Σf = N = 50 | |

(i) $M = \text{Size of} \left(\frac{N}{2}\right)\text{th item}$

$= \text{Size of} \left(\frac{50}{2}\right)\text{th item} = \text{Size of 25th item}$

Median lies in the class 20–30.

$$M = l_1 + \frac{\frac{N}{2} - c.f.}{f} \times i$$

$$= 20 + \frac{\frac{50}{2} - 10}{20} \times 10 = 20 + \frac{25 - 10}{20} \times 10$$

$$= 20 + \frac{15}{20} \times 10 = 20 + 7.5 = 27.5$$

(ii) Since, 60% candidates are passed and 40% have failed, the minimum pass marks are given by $P_{40}$. In other words, we have to find the value of $P_{40}$.

$$P_{40} = \text{Size of } 40\left(\frac{N}{100}\right)\text{th item}$$

$$= \text{Size of } 40\left(\frac{50}{100}\right)\text{th item}$$

$= \text{Size of 20th item}$

$P_{40}$ lies in the class 20–30.

$$P_{40} = l_1 + \frac{40\left(\frac{N}{100}\right) - c.f.}{f} \times i = 20 + \frac{40\left(\frac{50}{100}\right) - 10}{20} \times 10$$

$$= 20 + \frac{20 - 10}{20} \times 10 = 20 + \frac{10}{20} \times 10$$

$= 20 + 5 = 25$

Median = 27.5.

Minimum marks obtained by a pass candidate = 25.

**ILLUSTRATION 14.**

Find the mode from the following data:

8, 10, 5, 8, 12, 7, 8, 9, 11, 7

**SOLUTION:**

Arrange the series in an ascending order as:

5, 7, 7, 8, 8, 8, 9, 10, 11, 12

An inspection of the series shows that the value 8 occurs most frequently in the series.

Hence, Mode (Z) = 8.

**ILLUSTRATION 15.**

From the following data, determine the mode by grouping method:

| **Size** | 7 | 8 | 9 | 10 | 11 | 12 | 13 | 14 | 15 | 16 | 17 |
|---|---|---|---|---|---|---|---|---|---|---|---|
| **Frequency** | 2 | 3 | 6 | 12 | 20 | 24 | 25 | 7 | 5 | 3 | 1 |

**SOLUTION**

**Grouping Table for the Estimation of Mode**

| Size | I Frequency | II (1 + 2) | III (2 + 3) | IV (1+2+3) | V (2+3+4) | VI (3+4+5) |
|---|---|---|---|---|---|---|
| 7 | 2 | 2 + 3 = 5 | | 2 + 3 + 6 = 11 | | |
| 8 | 3 | | 3 + 6 = 9 | | 3 + 6 + 12 = 21 | |
| 9 | 6 | 6 + 12 = 18 | | | | 6 + 12 + 20 = 38 |
| 10 | 12 | | 12 + 20 = 32 | 12 + 20 + 24 = 56 | | |
| 11 | 20 | 20 + 24 = 44 | | | 20 + 24 + 25 = 69 | |
| 12 | 24 | | 24 + 25 = 49 | | | 24 + 25 + 7 = 56 |
| 13 | 25 | 25 + 7 = 32 | | 25 + 7 + 5 = 37 | | |
| 14 | 7 | | 7 + 5 = 12 | | 7 + 5 + 3 = 15 | |
| 15 | 5 | 5 + 3 = 8 | | | | 5 + 3 + 1 = 9 |
| 16 | 3 | | 3 + 1 = 4 | | | |
| 17 | 1 | | | | | |

**Analysis Table**

| Column | Size of items containing maximum frequency | | | | | | | | | | |
|---|---|---|---|---|---|---|---|---|---|---|---|
| | 7 | 8 | 9 | 10 | 11 | 12 | 13 | 14 | 15 | 16 | 17 |
| I | | | | | | | ✓ | | | | |
| II | | | | | ✓ | ✓ | | | | | |
| III | | | | | | ✓ | ✓ | | | | |
| IV | | | | ✓ | ✓ | ✓ | | | | | |
| V | | | | | ✓ | ✓ | ✓ | | | | |
| VI | | | | | | ✓ | ✓ | ✓ | | | |
| Total | — | — | — | 1 | 3 | 5 | 4 | 1 | — | — | — |

It is clear from the Analysis Table that the size 12 occurs the maximum number of times, *i.e.*, 5 times.

Thus, the Mode (Z) = 12.

**ILLUSTRATION 16.**

Calculate the mode from the following data:

| Wages (₹) | 0–5 | 5–10 | 10–15 | 15–20 | 20–25 | 25–30 | 30–35 |
|---|---|---|---|---|---|---|---|
| Number of Workers | 3 | 7 | 15 | 30 | 20 | 10 | 5 |

**SOLUTION:**

| Wages (₹) | Frequency (f) |
|---|---|
| 0–5 | 3 |
| 5–10 | 7 |
| 10–15 | 15 ($f_0$) |
| **($l_1$) 15–20** | **30 ($f_1$)** |
| 20–25 | 20 ($f_2$) |
| 25–30 | 10 |
| 30–35 | 5 |

Since, the series is regular, we may not do grouping for the location of model group. By inspection, modal class is 15–20.

$$Z = l_1 + \frac{f_1 - f_0}{2f_1 - f_0 - f_2} \times i$$

Here, $l_1 = 15, f_1 = 30, f_0 = 15, f_2 = 20, i = 5$

Substituting the values, we get

$$Z = 15 + \frac{30 - 15}{2(30) - 15 - 20} \times 5$$

$$= 15 + \frac{15}{60 - 35} \times 5$$

$$= 15 + \frac{15}{25} \times 5$$

$$= 15 + 3 = 18$$

Thus, Mode = 18.

**ILLUSTRATION 17.**

Calculate the mode from the following data:

| Class Interval | 20–24 | 25–29 | 30–34 | 35–39 | 40–44 | 45–49 | 50–54 | 55–59 |
|---|---|---|---|---|---|---|---|---|
| Frequency | 3 | 5 | 10 | 20 | 12 | 6 | 3 | 1 |

**SOLUTION:**

Since we are given inclusive class intervals, we first convert it into exclusive series as under:

| Class Interval | Frequency (f) |
|---|---|
| 19.5–24.5 | 3 |
| 24.5–29.5 | 5 |
| 29.5–34.5 | 10 $f_0$ |
| **34.5–39.5** | **20 $f_1$** |
| 39.5–44.5 | 12 $f_2$ |
| 44.5–49.5 | 6 |
| 49.5–54.5 | 3 |
| 54.5–59.5 | 1 |

A glance at the above table reveals that modal class is 34.5–39.5. The actual value of mode is,

$$Z = l_1 + \frac{f_1 - f_0}{2f_1 - f_0 - f_2} \times i$$

$$= 34.5 + \frac{20 - 10}{2\,(20) - 10 - 12} \times 5$$

$$= 34.5 + \frac{10}{40 - 22} \times 5$$

$$= 34.5 + \frac{10}{18} \times 5$$

$$= 34.5 + 2.78$$

$$= 37.28$$

Mode = 37.28.

**ILLUSTRATION 18.**

The mode and mean are 26.6 and 28.1 respectively in an asymmetrical distribution. Find out the value of median.

**SOLUTION:**

Given: Mode (Z) = 26.6, Mean ($\overline{X}$) = 28.1

$$Z = 3M - 2\overline{X}$$

Substituting the values, we get

$$26.6 = 3M - 2 \times 28.1$$

$$\Rightarrow \quad 26.6 = 3M - 56.2$$

$$\Rightarrow \quad 3M = 26.6 + 56.2 = 82.8$$

$$\Rightarrow \quad M = \frac{82.8}{3} = 27.6$$

Median Value = 27.6.

# EXERCISE

## 1. Very Short Answer Type Questions [1 mark]

### A. Multiple Choice Questions: Choose the Correct Answer

1. Median divides a series into how many parts?
   (a) Two (b) Three
   (c) Four (d) All of these
2. Which of the following is a kind of partition value?
   (a) Arithmetic mean (b) Median
   (c) Quartile (d) Both (b) and (c)
3. Which of the following formulae is used to find out median?
   (a) $M = l_1 + \frac{\frac{N}{4} - c.f.}{f} \times i$ (b) $M = l_2 + \frac{\frac{N}{4} - c.f.}{f} \times i$
   (c) $M = l_1 + \frac{N - c.f.}{f} \times i$ (d) None of these
4. Dividing a series into ten equal parts is called:
   (a) decile (b) quartile
   (c) percentile (d) none of these
5. For calculating median, all items of the series are arranged in:
   (a) descending order (b) ascending order
   (c) ascending or descending order (d) none of these
6. Quartile is a type of:
   (a) mathematical average (b) statistical average
   (c) partition value (d) none of these
7. Mode refers to that value of a series that occurs ____________ times in the series.
   (a) zero (b) infinite
   (c) maximum (d) minimum
8. What is the relationship between mode, mean and median?
   (a) $Z = 3M + 2\overline{X}$ (b) $Z = 3M - 2\overline{X}$
   (c) $\overline{X} = \frac{3M - Z}{2}$ (d) Both (b) and (c)
9. Out of the following, by which method mode can be calculated?
   (a) Inspection method (b) Grouping method
   (c) Both (a) and (b) (d) None of these

10. Which of the following formulae is used to find out $P_{77}$ in frequency distribution?

(a) $l_1 - \dfrac{77\left(\frac{N}{10}\right) - \text{c.f.}}{f} \times i$

(b) $l_1 + \dfrac{77\left(\frac{N}{10}\right) - \text{c.f.}}{f} \times i$

(c) $l_1 - \dfrac{77\left(\frac{N}{100}\right) - \text{c.f.}}{f} \times i$

(d) $l_1 + \dfrac{77\left(\frac{N}{100}\right) - \text{c.f.}}{f} \times i$

11. Median of these numbers: 3, 5, 7, 9, 12 is:

(a) 3
(b) 6
(c) 7
(d) 12

12. Formula of $D_7$ in individual series is:

(a) size of $\left(\frac{N+1}{100}\right)$th item
(b) size of $7\left(\frac{N+1}{10}\right)$th item
(c) size of $7\left(\frac{N}{100}\right)$th item
(d) none of these

Ans. 1. (a), 2. (c), 3. (d), 4. (a), 5. (c), 6. (c), 7. (c), 8. (d), 9. (c), 10. (d), 11. (c), 12. (b).

### B. True or False

State whether the following statements are True or False:

1. Quartile divides a series into three equal parts. (True/False)
2. Cumulative frequency indicates 'less than' or 'more than' value of the series. (True/False)
3. Mode of 3, 4, 3, 5, 5, 3, 2 numbers is 5. (True/False)
4. $Q_1$ is known as upper quartile of the series. (True/False)
5. In percentiles, series is divided in hundred equal parts. (True/False)
6. The point where 'less than ogive' and 'more than ogive' intersect each other determines median. (True/False)
7. Median is free from the effect of extreme values. (True/False)

Ans. 1. False, 2. True, 3. False, 4. False, 5. True, 6. True, 7. True.

### C. Concepts/Definitions & Knowledge-based Questions

1. Define median.

Ans. Median is a centrally located value of a series such that half of the values (or items) of the series are above it and the other half below it.

2. Define mode.

Ans. Mode is the value which occurs most frequently in the series; that is, modal value has the highest frequency in the series.

3. Define partition value.

Ans. The value that divides the series into more than two parts is called Partition Value.

4. Define quartile.

Ans. If a statistical series is divided into four equal parts, the end value of each part is called a quartile. It is written as Q.

5. What is positional average?

Ans. Positional average are those averages whose value is worked out on the basis of their position in the statistical series.

6. Give the formula for finding out median of a continuous series.

Ans. Median class is identified. It corresponds to that cumulative frequency which includes the $\left(\frac{N}{2}\right)$th item. The following formula is then applied to determine the actual median value.

$$M = l_1 + \frac{\frac{N}{2} - c.f.}{f} \times i$$

(Here, $l_1$ = Lower limit of the median class; c.f. = Cumulative frequency of the class preceding the median class; f = Frequency of the median class; $i$ = Size of the median class interval.)

7. Give the formula for estimating mode in case of continuous series.

Ans. The following formula is used to calculate the exact value of the mode in case of continuous series after finding the modal class.

$$Z = l_1 + \frac{f_1 - f_0}{2f_1 - f_0 - f_2} \times i$$

(Here, Z = Value of the mode; $l_1$ = lower limit of the modal class; $f_1$ = The frequency of the modal class; $f_0$ = The frequency of pre-modal class; $f_2$ = Frequency of the next higher class or post-modal class; $i$ = Size of the modal group.)

## 2. Short Answer Type Questions [3-4 marks]

1. What are the main differences between mode and median?
2. What are the uses of mode? How are quartiles calculated?
3. 'Arithmetic mean is affected by very large and very small values, but median and mode are not affected by them.' Explain.
4. State four merits of median.
5. State four demerits of median.
6. State four merits of mode.
7. State four demerits of mode.
8. Describe the relationship between mean, median and mode.

## 3. Long Answer Type Questions [6 marks]

1. Define median. What are its merits and demerits?
2. What is mode? Discuss the merits, demerits and uses of the mode.
3. Define an average and describe its chief properties.
4. How is median class interval located in case of continuous series? Explain taking an imaginary set of data.
5. Compare the arithmetic mean, median and mode as measures of central tendency. Describe situations where one is more suitable than the others.

## 4. Essential Practicals

1. Given below is the data of the age of 9 children of a street. Find the median.
   5, 8, 7, 3, 4, 6, 2, 9, 1 (Ans. Median = 5)
2. Find the median of the following values:
   30, 20, 15, 10, 25, 35, 18, 21, 28, 40, 36 (Ans. Median = 25)
3. Find out median of the series of the following table:

| Items | 3 | 4 | 5 | 6 | 7 | 8 |
|---|---|---|---|---|---|---|
| Frequency | 6 | 9 | 11 | 14 | 23 | 10 |

(Ans. Median = 6)

4. Data relating to wages of some workers are given below. Find out median wage.

| Wages (₹) | 20–30 | 30–40 | 40–50 | 50–60 | 60–70 |
|---|---|---|---|---|---|
| Number of Workers | 25 | 12 | 15 | 13 | 5 |

(Ans. Median Wage = ₹ 38.33)

5. The following table expresses the age of eight students. Find the median age.

| S. No. | 1 | 2 | 3 | 4 | 5 | 6 | 7 | 8 |
|---|---|---|---|---|---|---|---|---|
| Age (Years) | 18 | 16 | 14 | 11 | 13 | 10 | 9 | 2 |

(Ans. Median Age = 12 years)

6. Number of persons living in a house is reported to be as under for 500 houses in a village. Find the median number of persons in a house in the village.

| Number of Persons in a House | 1 | 2 | 3 | 4 | 5 | 6 | 7 | 8 | 9 | 10 |
|---|---|---|---|---|---|---|---|---|---|---|
| Number of Houses | 26 | 113 | 120 | 95 | 60 | 42 | 21 | 14 | 5 | 4 |

(Ans. Median = 3)

7. Find out median of the following series:

| Size | 15 | 20 | 25 | 30 | 35 | 40 |
|---|---|---|---|---|---|---|
| Frequency | 10 | 15 | 25 | 5 | 5 | 20 |

(Ans. Median = 25)

8. Distribution of marks obtained by 100 student of a class is given below. Find out the median marks.

| Marks | 0 | 5 | 10 | 15 | 20 | 25 | 30 | 35 | 40 | 45 |
|---|---|---|---|---|---|---|---|---|---|---|
| Number of Students | 4 | 6 | 15 | 5 | 8 | 12 | 28 | 14 | 3 | 5 |

(Ans. Median = 30 marks)

9. Find out median wage rate from the following data-set:

| Wage Rate (₹) | 5-15 | 15–25 | 25–35 | 35–45 | 45–55 | 55–65 |
|---|---|---|---|---|---|---|
| Number of Workers | 4 | 6 | 10 | 5 | 3 | 2 |

(Ans. Median Wage Rate = ₹ 30)

10. Find out median of the following series:

| Wage Rate (₹) | 25–30 | 20–25 | 15–20 | 10–15 | 5–10 | 0–5 |
|---|---|---|---|---|---|---|
| Number of Workers | 5 | 10 | 20 | 5 | 8 | 2 |

(Ans. Median = ₹ 17.5)

11. Calculate the median from the following series:

| Age (Years) | 55–60 | 50–55 | 45–50 | 40–45 | 35–40 | 30–35 | 25–30 | 20–25 |
|---|---|---|---|---|---|---|---|---|
| Number of Students | 7 | 13 | 10 | 15 | 30 | 33 | 28 | 14 |

(Ans. Median = 35 years)

12. 50 students of economics, secured the following marks in an examination:

| Marks | 20–25 | 25–30 | 30–35 | 35–40 | 40–45 | 45–50 | 50–55 | 55–60 | 60–65 | 65–70 |
|---|---|---|---|---|---|---|---|---|---|---|
| Students | 6 | 3 | 7 | 4 | 6 | 4 | 2 | 8 | 3 | 7 |

Calculate median. (Ans. Median = 44.16 marks)

13. Given the following data, find out median:

| Age | 20–25 | 25–30 | 30–35 | 35–40 | 40–45 | 45–50 | 50–55 | 55–60 |
|---|---|---|---|---|---|---|---|---|
| Number of Students | 50 | 70 | 100 | 180 | 150 | 120 | 70 | 60 |

(Ans. Median = 40)

14. Find out median, with the help of the following data:

| Price Level | 10–20 | 20–30 | 30–40 | 40–50 | 50–60 | 60–70 |
|---|---|---|---|---|---|---|
| Number of Commodity | 2 | 5 | 8 | 4 | 6 | 3 |

(Ans. Median = 38.75)

15. Calculate median, given the following data:

| Mid-value | 20 | 30 | 40 | 50 | 60 | 70 |
|---|---|---|---|---|---|---|
| Male (c.f.) | 12 | 25 | 42 | 46 | 48 | 50 |

c.f. = Cumulative Frequency

(**Note:** Before solving the question, the student should first convert cumulative frequency into class frequency.) (Ans. Median = 35)

16. Calculate mode of the following series using the graphic technique. Counter check the modal value with the formula.

| Wage | 0–10 | 10–20 | 20–30 | 30–40 | 40–50 |
|---|---|---|---|---|---|
| Number of Workers | 28 | 46 | 54 | 42 | 30 |

(Ans. Model Value = 24)

17. Calculate mode from the following data:

| Wages | 25 | 50 | 75 | 80 | 85 | 90 |
|---|---|---|---|---|---|---|
| Number of Workers | 4 | 6 | 9 | 3 | 2 | 1 |

(Ans. Mode = 75)

18. Find out mode from the following data:

| Class Interval | 5–10 | 10–15 | 15–20 | 20–25 | 25–30 | 30–35 | 35–40 |
|---|---|---|---|---|---|---|---|
| Number of Children | 4 | 5 | 3 | 2 | 6 | 7 | 3 |

(Ans. Mode = 31)

19. Calculate mode of the following series, using grouping method:

| Size | 40 | 44 | 48 | 52 | 56 | 60 | 64 | 68 | 72 | 76 |
|---|---|---|---|---|---|---|---|---|---|---|
| Frequency | 10 | 12 | 14 | 20 | 15 | 20 | 18 | 10 | 8 | 4 |

(Ans. Mode = 60)

20. Calculate mode of the following distribution:

| Marks | 10–19 | 20–29 | 30–39 | 40–49 | 50–59 | 60–69 | 70–79 | 80–89 | 90–99 |
|---|---|---|---|---|---|---|---|---|---|
| Number of Students | 29 | 87 | 181 | 247 | 263 | 133 | 40 | 9 | 2 |

(Ans. Mode = 50.59)

21. Find out mode, given the following information:

| Size | 6–10 | 11–15 | 16–20 | 21–25 | 26–30 |
|---|---|---|---|---|---|
| Frequency | 20 | 30 | 50 | 40 | 10 |

(Ans. Mode = 18.83)

22. Calculate mode from the following data:

| Wages (₹) | Number of Workers |
|---|---|
| Less than 10 | 15 |
| Less than 20 | 35 |
| Less than 30 | 60 |
| Less than 40 | 84 |
| Less than 50 | 96 |
| Less than 60 | 127 |
| Less than 70 | 198 |
| Less than 80 | 250 |

(Ans. Mode = 66.78)

23. Calculate mode from the following series:

| Size | 1 | 2 | 3 | 4 | 5 | 6 | 7 | 8 | 9 | 10 |
|---|---|---|---|---|---|---|---|---|---|---|
| Frequency | 8 | 6 | 10 | 12 | 20 | 12 | 5 | 3 | 2 | 4 |

(Ans. Mode = 5)

24. Calculate the mean, median and mode of the number of persons per house in a village with the help of the following information:

| Number of Persons per House | 1 | 2 | 3 | 4 | 5 | 6 | 7 | 8 | 9 | 10 |
|---|---|---|---|---|---|---|---|---|---|---|
| Number of Houses | 26 | 113 | 120 | 95 | 60 | 42 | 21 | 14 | 5 | 4 |

[Ans. $\overline{X}$ = 3.78, M = 3, Z = 1.44 (Mode = 3 Median – 2 Mean)]

25. Calculate the median and mode from the following data:

| Marks | 0–10 | 10–20 | 20–30 | 30–40 | 40–50 | 50–60 | 60–70 | 70–80 |
|---|---|---|---|---|---|---|---|---|
| Number of Students | 2 | 18 | 30 | 45 | 35 | 20 | 6 | 3 |

(Ans. Median = 36.55, Mode = 36)

26. Calculate the median value, given the following statistical information:

| Age | 20–25 | 25–30 | 30–35 | 35–40 | 40–45 | 45–50 | 50–55 | 55–60 |
|---|---|---|---|---|---|---|---|---|
| Number of Students | 50 | 70 | 100 | 180 | 150 | 120 | 70 | 60 |

(Ans. Median Value = 40)

27. Obtain the mean, median and mode of the following data:

| Marks | 0–10 | 10–20 | 20–30 | 30–40 | 40–50 | 50–60 | 60–70 | 70–80 |
|---|---|---|---|---|---|---|---|---|
| Number of Students | 5 | 7 | 15 | 25 | 20 | 15 | 8 | 5 |

[Ans. $\overline{X}$ = 40, M = 39.2, Z = 37.60 (Mode = 3 Median – 2 Mean)]

28. Calculate median in an asymmetrical distribution if mode is 83 and arithmetic mean is 92.

(Ans. Median = 89)

29. Calculate mode when arithmetic mean is 146 and median is 130. (Ans. Mode = 98)

30. If mode is 63 and median is 77, calculate arithmetic mean. (Ans. Arithmetic Mean = 84)

31. Calculate arithmetic mean, median and mode of the following series:

| Marks | Number of Students |
|---|---|
| Less than 10 | 12 |
| Less than 20 | 26 |
| Less than 30 | 40 |
| Less than 40 | 58 |
| Less than 50 | 80 |
| Less than 60 | 110 |
| Less than 70 | 138 |
| Less than 80 | 150 |

[Ans. $\overline{X}$ = 44.07, M = 47.73, Z = 55.05 (Mode = 3 Median – 2 Mean)]

## 5. NCERT Textbook Questions [With Hints to Answers]

1. Comment whether the following statements are true or false:
   (i) The sum of deviation of items from median is zero.
   (ii) An average alone is not enough to compare series.
   (iii) Arithmetic mean is a positional value.
   (iv) Upper quartile is the lowest value of top 25% of items.
   (v) Median is unduly affected by extreme observations.

   [(i) False, (ii) True, (iii) False, (iv) True, (v) False]

2. If the arithmetic mean of the data given below is 28, find (a) the missing frequency, and (b) the median of the series:

| Profit per Retail Shop (in ₹) | 0–10 | 10–20 | 20–30 | 30–40 | 40–50 | 50–60 |
|---|---|---|---|---|---|---|
| Number of Retail Shops | 12 | 18 | 27 | f | 17 | 6 |

[

| Profit per Retail Shop (in ₹) | Mid-value $\left(m = \frac{l_1 + l_2}{2}\right)$ | Number of Retail Shops or Frequency (f) | Multiple of Mid-value and Frequency (fm) |
|---|---|---|---|
| 0–10 | 5 | 12 | 60 |
| 10–20 | 15 | 18 | 270 |
| 20–30 | 25 | 27 | 675 |
| 30–40 | 35 | f | 35f |
| 40–50 | 45 | 17 | 765 |
| 50–60 | 55 | 6 | 330 |
| | | Σf = 80 + f | Σfm = 2,100 + 35f |

$$\overline{X} = \frac{\Sigma fm}{\Sigma f}$$

$$28 = \frac{2{,}100 + 35f}{80 + f}$$

$$28\,(80 + f) = 2{,}100 + 35f$$

$$2{,}240 + 28f = 2{,}100 + 35f$$

$$7f = 140$$
$$f = 20$$

| Profit per Retail Shop (in ₹) | Number of Retail Shops or Frequency (f) | Cumulative Frequency |
|---|---|---|
| 0–10 | 12 | 12 |
| 10–20 | 18 | **30** |
| **20–30** | **27** | 57 |
| 30–40 | 20 | 77 |
| 40–50 | 17 | 94 |
| 50–60 | 6 | 100 |
| | N = Σf = 100 | |

$$M = \text{Size of}\left(\frac{N}{2}\right)\text{th item} = \text{Size of}\left(\frac{100}{2}\right)\text{th item} = \text{Size of 50th item}$$

Hence, median lies in the class 20–30.

$$M = l_1 + \frac{\frac{N}{2} - \text{c.f.}}{f} \times i$$

$$= 20 + \frac{\frac{100}{2} - 30}{27} \times 10 = 20 + \frac{50 - 30}{27} \times 10$$

$$= 20 + \frac{20}{27} \times 10 = 20 + 7.41 = 27.41$$

∴ Value of missing frequency = 20 and value of the median = ₹ 27.41.]

3. The size of land holdings of 380 families in a village is given below. Find the median size of land holdings.

| Size of Land Holdings (in acres) | Less than 100 | 100–200 | 200–300 | 300–400 | 400 and above |
|---|---|---|---|---|---|
| Number of Families | 40 | 89 | 148 | 64 | 39 |

[

| Size of Land Holdings (in acres) | Number of Families or Frequency (f) | Cumulative Frequency |
|---|---|---|
| 0–100 | 40 | 40 |
| 100–200 | 89 | **129** |
| **200–300** | **148** | 277 |
| 300–400 | 64 | 341 |
| 400–500 | 39 | 380 |
| | N = Σf = 380 | |

$$M = \text{Size of}\left(\frac{N}{2}\right)\text{th item} = \text{Size of}\left(\frac{380}{2}\right)\text{th item} = \text{Size of 190th item}$$

190th item lies in the 277th cumulative frequency and the corresponding class interval is 200–300.

$$M = l_1 + \frac{\frac{N}{2} - \text{c.f.}}{f} \times i$$

$$= 200 + \frac{\frac{380}{2} - 129}{148} \times 100 = 200 + \frac{190 - 129}{148} \times 100$$

$$= 200 + \frac{61}{148} \times 100 = 200 + 41.22$$

$$= 241.22$$

Therefore, Median = 241.22.]

**4.** The following series relates to the daily income of workers employed in a firm. Compute (a) highest income of lowest 50% workers, (b) minimum income earned by the top 25% workers, and (c) maximum income earned by lowest 25% workers.

| **Daily Income (in ₹)** | 10–14 | 15–19 | 20–24 | 25–29 | 30–34 | 35–39 |
|---|---|---|---|---|---|---|
| **Number of Workers** | 5 | 10 | 15 | 20 | 10 | 5 |

[This is an inclusive series to be converted into an exclusive series, as in the following table:

| **Conversion into Exclusive Series** | **Frequency (f)** | **Cumulative Frequency** |
|---|---|---|
| 9.5–14.5 | 5 | 5 |
| 14.5–19.5 | 10 | **15** |
| **19.5–24.5** | **15** | **30** |
| **24.5–29.5** | **20** | 50 |
| 29.5–34.5 | 10 | 60 |
| 34.5–39.5 | 5 | 65 |
| | N = Σf = 65 | |

(a) $$M = \text{Size of } \left(\frac{N}{2}\right)\text{th item}$$

$$= \text{Size of } \left(\frac{65}{2}\right)\text{th item} = \text{Size of 32.5th item}$$

32.5th item lies in 50th cumulative frequency and the corresponding median class is 24.5–29.5.

Using the formula,

$$M = l_1 + \frac{\frac{N}{2} - \text{c.f.}}{f} \times i$$

$$= 24.5 + \frac{\frac{65}{2} - 30}{20} \times 5 = 24.5 + \frac{32.5 - 30}{20} \times 5$$

$$= 24.5 + \frac{2.5}{20} \times 5 = 24.5 + 0.625 = 25.125$$

(b) $$Q_1 = \text{Size of } \left(\frac{N}{4}\right)\text{th item}$$

$$= \text{Size of} \left(\frac{65}{4}\right)\text{th item} = \text{Size of 16.25th item}$$

16.25th item lies in 30th cumulative frequency and the corresponding median class is 19.5–24.5.

Using the formula,

$$Q_1 = l_1 + \frac{\frac{N}{4} - \text{c.f.}}{f} \times i$$

$$= 19.5 + \frac{\frac{65}{4} - 15}{15} \times 5 = 19.5 + \frac{16.25 - 15}{15} \times 5$$

$$= 19.5 + \frac{1.25}{15} \times 5 = 19.5 + 0.42$$

$$= 19.92$$

(c) $Q_1 = \text{Size of } 3\left(\frac{N}{4}\right)\text{th item}$

$$= \text{Size of } 3\left(\frac{65}{4}\right)\text{th item} = \text{Size of 48.75th item}$$

48.75th item lies in 50th cumulative frequency and the corresponding median class is 24.5–29.5.

$$Q_3 = l_1 + \frac{3\left(\frac{N}{4}\right) - \text{c.f.}}{f} \times i$$

$$= 24.5 + \frac{3\left(\frac{65}{4}\right) - 30}{20} \times 5 = 24.5 + \frac{48.75 - 30}{20} \times 5$$

$$= 24.5 + \frac{18.75}{20} \times 5 = 24.5 + 4.69$$

$$= 29.19$$

∴ (a) Highest income of lowest 50% workers = ₹25.125.

(b) Minimum income earned by the top 25% workers = ₹19.92.

(c) Maximum income earned by lowest 25% workers = ₹29.19.]

**5.** The following table gives production yield in kg per hectare of wheat of 150 farms in a village. Calculate the mean, median and mode of the production yield.

| **Production Yield (kg per hectare)** | 50–53 | 53–56 | 56–59 | 59–62 | 62–65 | 65–68 | 68–71 | 71–74 | 74–77 |
|---|---|---|---|---|---|---|---|---|---|
| **Number of Farms** | 3 | 8 | 14 | 30 | 36 | 28 | 16 | 10 | 5 |

[

| **Production Yield** | **Mid-value** $\left(m = \frac{l_1 + l_2}{2}\right)$ | **Number of Farms or Frequency (f)** | **Cumulative Frequency** | **Deviation (d = X – A) A = 63.5** | **Step-deviation** $\left(d' = \frac{m - A}{C}\right)$ **C = 3** | **Multiple of Step-deviation and Frequency (fd′)** |
|---|---|---|---|---|---|---|
| 50–53 | 51.5 | 3 | 3 | –12 | – 4 | – 12 |
| 53–56 | 54.5 | 8 | 11 | –9 | – 3 | – 24 |
| 56–59 | 57.5 | 14 | 25 | –6 | – 2 | – 28 |
| 59–62 | 60.5 | 30 | 55 | –3 | – 1 | – 30 |
| 62–65 | 63.5 | 36 | 91 | 0 | 0 | 0 |
| 65–68 | 66.5 | 28 | 119 | 3 | 1 | 28 |
| 68–71 | 69.5 | 16 | 135 | 6 | 2 | 32 |
| 71–74 | 72.5 | 10 | 145 | 9 | 3 | 30 |
| 74–77 | 75.5 | 5 | 150 | 12 | 4 | 20 |
| | | Σf = 150 | | | | Σfd′ = –94 + 110 = 16 |

$$\overline{X} = A + \frac{\Sigma fd'}{\Sigma f} \times C$$

$$= 63.5 + \frac{16}{150} \times 3$$

$$= 63.5 + 0.32 = 63.82$$

$$M = \text{Size of} \left(\frac{N}{2}\right)\text{th item}$$

$$= \text{Size of} \left(\frac{150}{2}\right)\text{th item}$$

$$= \text{Size of 75th item}$$

This lies in the 91th cumulative frequency and the corresponding class is 62–65.

$$M = l_1 + \frac{\frac{N}{2} - \text{c.f.}}{f} \times i$$

$$= 62 + \frac{\frac{150}{2} - 55}{36} \times 3$$

$$= 62 + \frac{75 - 55}{36} \times 3$$

$$= 62 + \frac{20}{36} \times 3$$

$$= 62 + 1.67$$

$$= 63.67$$

A glance at the series reveals that 62–65 is the modal class because it has the maximum frequency, *i.e.*, 36. Following formula is used to calculate modal value.

$$Z = l_1 + \frac{f_1 - f_0}{2f_1 - f_0 - f_2} \times i$$

$$= 62 + \frac{36 - 30}{2(36) - 30 - 28} \times 3$$

$$= 62 + \frac{6}{72 - 58} \times 3$$

$$= 62 + \frac{6}{14} \times 3$$

$$= 62 + 1.29$$

$$= 63.29$$

∴ Mean = 63.82 kg per hectare.

Median = 63.67 kg per hectare.

Mode = 63.29 kg per hectare.]

# Measures of Dispersion

11

## 1. What is Dispersion?

In the last two chapters, we studied Averages or Measures of Central Tendency. Average indicates representative value of the series around which other values of the series tend to converge. So that average represents the series as a whole. One may now be keen to know how far the various values of the series tend to disperse from each other, or from their average. This brings us to yet another important branch of statistical methods, *viz.*, Measures of Dispersion. Only when we study dispersion along with average of a series that we can have a comprehensive information about the nature and composition of a statistical series. Let us take an illustration to understand the point better. The following data relates to wages paid to 5 workers in three factories, A, B and C.

| Factory A | Factory B | Factory C |
|---|---|---|
| 400 | 350 | 50 |
| 400 | 380 | 75 |
| 400 | 400 | 400 |
| 400 | 420 | 725 |
| 400 | 450 | 750 |

In all the three factories the arithmetic mean and median is same, *i.e.*, 400. But in factory A, there is no variation between the average wage and the wages paid to the different labourers. In factory 'B', there is a small variation between average wage and wages paid to the different workers. But in factory C, there is large variation in the average wage and the wages paid to different workers. The minimum wage is ₹ 50 and maximum wage is ₹ 750. It shows that mean and median do not provide complete information about the composition and character of a series. In order to get a comprehensive picture of the series, we should study measures of dispersion as well.

**How is Dispersion of the Series Different from Average of the Series?**

Average of the series refers to central tendency of the series. It represents behaviour of all items in the series. But different items tend to differ from each other and from their average. Dispersion measures the extent of this difference. Or, dispersion measures the extent to which different items tend to disperse away from the central tendency.

### Definition

According to **Dr. Bowley**, *"Dispersion is the measure of the variation of the items."*

In the words of **Spiegel**, *"The degree to which numerical data tend to spread about an average value is called the variation or dispersion of the data."*

## 2. Objectives Related to the Measurement of Dispersion

**What is the Basic Objective Related to the Measurement of Dispersion?**

It is to know about the composition of the statistical series by estimating the extent to which different items of the series tend to move away from their average value or the central tendency.

Following are some specific objectives related to the measurement of dispersion:

(1) To know the variation of different values of the items from the average value of a series.

(2) To know about the composition of a series or the dispersal of values on either sides of the central tendency.

(3) To know the range of values (i.e., difference between the highest and the lowest value).

(4) To compare the disparity between two or more series in order to find out the degree of variation.

(5) To know whether the central tendency truly represents the series or not.

### Absolute and Relative Measures of Dispersion

There are two measures of dispersion, as discussed under:

#### (i) Absolute Measure

*When dispersion of the series is expressed in terms of the original unit of the series, it is called absolute measure of dispersion.* Thus, dispersion of price series would be expressed in terms of rupees; dispersion of weight series would be expressed in terms of kilograms; and so on. For example, if one states that the average wage of a group of the workers is ₹ 100 and dispersion of the wage is ₹ 10, one is referring to absolute dispersion. Absolute measure of dispersion is used when only one set of statistical distribution is under consideration. It cannot be used when comparison is involved across two or more sets of statistical series with different units of measurement (like 'rupee' in one case and 'kilogram' in the other).

#### (ii) Relative Measure

*The relative measure of dispersion expresses the variability of data in terms of some relative value or percentage.* Thus, if one states that 26 per cent of the people in India are below poverty line, one is referring to the relative variability of data. In such cases, absolute variability is divided by the mean value of the series or percentage of the absolute variability is determined. This measure of dispersion is used when one studies two or more series simultaneously. *Relative measure of dispersion is known as Coefficient of Dispersion.*

## 3. Methods of Measuring Dispersion

Following are the methods of absolute and relative measures of dispersion:

| Absolute Measure | Relative Measure |
|---|---|
| (1) Range | Coefficient of Range |
| (2) Quartile Deviation; Inter Quartile Range | Coefficient of Quartile Deviation |
| (3) Mean Deviation | Coefficient of Mean Deviation |
| (4) Standard Deviation | Coefficient of Standard Deviation, Coefficient of Variation |
| (5) Lorenz Curve | |

## Range

It is the simplest method of measuring dispersion of data. Range *is the difference between the highest value and the lowest value in a series.*

Thus:

**FORMULA**

$$R = H - L$$

Here, R = Range; H = Highest value in the series;

L = Lowest value in the series.

To illustrate, pocket expenses of 5 students are reported to be ₹ 20, ₹ 30, ₹ 40, ₹ 50 and ₹ 100 per month. The highest value (H) in this series is ₹ 100 and the lowest value (L) is ₹ 20. Accordingly,

$R = H - L$

$R = ₹\,100 - ₹\,20 = ₹\,80$

Thus, $R = ₹\,80$.

### Coefficient of Range

Range is an absolute measure of dispersion. As such it cannot be used for comparisons. To make it comparable we find its coefficient. It is the ratio between (i) the difference between the highest and lowest values of the series and (ii) the sum of the lowest and highest values of the series. It is calculated as under:

**FORMULA**

$$\text{Coefficient of Range, CR} = \frac{H - L}{H + L}$$

(Here, CR = Coefficient of range; H = Highest value in the series; L = Lowest value in the series.)

Thus of the given illustration,

$$\text{Coefficient of Range, (CR)} = \frac{100 - 20}{100 + 20} = \frac{80}{120} = 0.67$$

### Calculation of Range and Coefficient of Range for Different Types of Statistical Series

Let us understand through different illustrations how range and its coefficient are calculated for different types of statistical series.

#### (1) Individual Series and Range

In the individual series, range is calculated as the difference between the highest and lowest value of the series.

**Illustration.**

Monthly wages of workers of a factory are stated below. Find out the range and the coefficient of range.

| Wages (₹) | 50 | 60 | 80 | 90 | 200 | 225 | 250 | 300 | 340 | 360 | 400 | 415 | 425 | 450 | 500 |
|---|---|---|---|---|---|---|---|---|---|---|---|---|---|---|---|

**Solution:**

**Why should we measure Dispersion about some particular value?**

All measures of dispersion do not measure variation about some particular value of the series. Range, for example, is simply the difference between the highest and the lowest values of a statistical series. Likewise, quartile deviation is defined as half of the difference between $Q_3$ (third quartile) and $Q_1$ (first quartile). But measures of dispersion like mean deviation and standard deviation are worked out as deviations from some central tendency of the statistical series. Deviations from some central tendency (or central value like mean or median) of the series offers a better picture of dispersion. Why? Because: (i) then we can assess how precise is the central tendency as the representative value of all the observations in the series. Greater value of dispersion implies lesser representativeness of the central tendency and vice versa, and (ii) we can precisely assess how scattered are the actual observations from their representative value. Actual observations may show both a positive variation as well as negative variation from the observed central tendency of the series. A summary measure of variation (which is what a measure of dispersion focuses on) is possible only when all the variations are duly considered.

Range (R) = H – L

Here, H = 500; L = 50

Thus, R = 500 – 50 = 450

Coefficient of Range (CR) = $\frac{H-L}{H+L} = \frac{500-50}{500+50} = \frac{450}{550} = 0.82$

Range = 450

Coefficient of Range = 0.82.

*Learning by doing*

1. *5 students obtained following marks in statistics:*
   *20, 35, 25, 30, 15*
   *Find out range and coefficient of range.* *(Ans. R = 20, CR = 0.4)*
2. *Prices of shares of a company were noted as under from Monday through Saturday. Find out range and the coefficient of range.*

| **Day** | Mon. | Tues. | Wed. | Thu. | Fri. | Sat. |
|---|---|---|---|---|---|---|
| **Price (₹)** | 200 | 210 | 208 | 160 | 220 | 250 |

*(Ans. R = 90, CR = 0.22)*

3. *You know share market is going bullish during the last several months. Collect weekly data on the share price of any two important industries during the past six months. Calculate the range of share prices. Comment on how volatile are the share prices.*

### (2) Discrete Frequency Series or Frequency Array and Range

As in the case of individual series, range of the discrete series is determined as the difference between the highest value and the lowest value of the series. Frequency of the series is not taken into account.

**Illustration.**

Calculate range and coefficient of range of the following series.

| **Size** | 10 | 11 | 12 | 13 | 14 | 15 | 16 | 18 |
|---|---|---|---|---|---|---|---|---|
| **Frequency** | 1 | 13 | 24 | 14 | 15 | 13 | 16 | 20 |

**Note**

That in the estimation of range or coefficient of range, frequency of the items is not taken into consideration.

**Solution:**

Here, H = 18; L = 10

Range (R) = H – L = 18 – 10 = 8

Coefficient of Range (CR) = $\frac{H-L}{H+L} = \frac{18-10}{18+10} = \frac{8}{28} = 0.29$

Range = 8

Coefficient of Range = 0.29.

*Learning by doing*

1. *Calculate range and the coefficient of range of the following series:*

| **Marks** | 10 | 20 | 30 | 40 | 50 | 60 | 70 |
|---|---|---|---|---|---|---|---|
| **Number of Students** | 15 | 18 | 25 | 30 | 16 | 10 | 9 |

*(Ans. R = 60, CR = 0.75)*

2. *Find out the range and the coefficient of range from the following data:*

| **Daily Wage (₹)** | 6 | 7 | 8 | 9 | 10 | 11 | 12 | 15 |
|---|---|---|---|---|---|---|---|---|
| **Number of Workers** | 10 | 15 | 12 | 18 | 25 | 20 | 10 | 4 |

*(Ans. R = 9, CR = 0.429)*

### (3) Frequency Distribution Series and Range

The following two methods are used to find out the range of the frequency distribution series.

**Method I:**

Mid-values of the class intervals are found. Difference between the highest and the lowest mid-values would be the range of the series. Frequencies of the distribution are not taken into account.

**ILLUSTRATION.**

Find out range and the coefficient of range of the following series.

| Size | 5–10 | 10–15 | 15–20 | 20–25 | 25–30 |
|---|---|---|---|---|---|
| Frequency | 4 | 9 | 15 | 30 | 40 |

**SOLUTION:**

| Size | Mid-value | Frequency |
|---|---|---|
| 5–10 | 7.5 | 4 |
| 10–15 | 12.5 | 9 |
| 15–20 | 17.5 | 15 |
| 20–25 | 22.5 | 30 |
| 25–30 | 27.5 | 40 |

Range (R) = H – L = 27.5 – 7.5 = 20

Coefficient of Range (CR) = $\frac{H - L}{H + L} = \frac{27.5 - 7.5}{27.5 + 7.5} = \frac{20}{35} = 0.57$

Range = 20

Coefficient of Range = 0.57.

**Method II:**

According to this method, we find the difference between lower limit of the first class interval.and upper limit of the last class interval in the series. Difference between these values would be the range of the series. That is,

**FORMULA**

R = Upper Limit of the Last Class Interval
– Lower Limit of the First Class Interval

**ILLUSTRATION.**

Find out the range and the coefficient of range of the following series:

| Marks | 20-29 | 30-39 | 40-49 | 50-59 | 60-69 |
|---|---|---|---|---|---|
| Number of Students | 8 | 12 | 20 | 7 | 3 |

**SOLUTION:**

This is an inclusive series. For the estimation of range, this must be converted into exclusive series, as below:

| Marks | Number of Students |
|---|---|
| 19.5–29.5 | 8 |
| 29.5–39.5 | 12 |
| 39.5–49.5 | 20 |
| 49.5–59.5 | 7 |
| 59.5–69.5 | 3 |

$L = 19.5;\ H = 69.5$

Range (R) $= 69.5 - 19.5 = 50$

Coefficient of Range (CR) $= \dfrac{69.5 - 19.5}{69.5 + 19.5} = \dfrac{50}{89} = 0.562$

Range = 50

Coefficient of Range = 0.562.

*Learning by doing*

1. *Marks obtained by 100 students of a class are given below. Find out range and coefficient of range of the marks.*

| Marks | 10–20 | 20–30 | 30–40 | 40–50 | 50–60 | 60–70 | 70–80 | 80–90 | 90–100 |
|---|---|---|---|---|---|---|---|---|---|
| Number of Students | 4 | 10 | 16 | 22 | 20 | 18 | 8 | 2 | 5 |

(*Ans.* $R = 90$, $CR = 0.8$)

2. *In an examination, 25 students obtained the following marks. Find out coefficient of range of the marks.*

| Marks | 5–9 | 10–14 | 15–19 | 20–24 | 25–29 | 30–34 | 35–39 |
|---|---|---|---|---|---|---|---|
| Number of Students | 1 | 3 | 8 | 5 | 4 | 2 | 2 |

(*Ans.* $CR = 0.79$)

## Merits and Demerits of Range

### Merits

(1) **Simple:** It is a very simple measure of the dispersion of the series. It is simple to calculate as well as understand.

(2) **Wide Application:** Range is widely used in statistical series relating to quality control in production. Control charts are prepared on the basis of range. If the quality of goods produced is within the range prescribed in the charts then the production process is said to be under control, otherwise not. Likewise range is a commonly used measure of dispersion in case of changes in interest rates, exchange rates and share prices.

### Demerits

(1) **Unstable:** It is an unstable measure of dispersion. It depends upon the extreme values of the series. Any change in the extreme values or a change in the sample immediately affects the range of the series.

(2) **Not Based on all Values:** The calculation of range is not based on all the values of a series. It does not give importance to other values other than the extreme ones.

(3) **No Knowledge of the Formation of the Series:** Range gives no precise knowledge about the formation of series.

(4) **Irrelevant for Open-ended Frequency Distribution:** Range cannot be calculated in case of open-ended frequency distributions. It just becomes irrelevant.

## Inter Quartile Range and Quartile Deviation (QD) and Their Coefficient

### Inter Quartile Range

Difference between third Quartile ($Q_3$) and first Quartile ($Q_1$) of a series, is called **Inter Quartile Range.**

**FORMULA**

$$\text{Inter Quartile Range} = Q_3 - Q_1$$

### Quartile Deviation

Quartile Deviation is Half of Inter Quartile Range.

**FORMULA**

$$\text{Quartile Deviation} = \frac{Q_3 - Q_1}{2}$$

It is also called Semi-inter Quartile Range.

### Coefficient of Quartile Deviation

Coefficient of quartile deviation is calculated using the following formula:

**FORMULA**

$$\text{Coefficient of QD} = \frac{Q_3 - Q_1}{2} \div \frac{Q_3 + Q_1}{2} = \frac{Q_3 - Q_1}{Q_3 + Q_1}$$

$$\text{Coefficient of Quartile Deviation} = \frac{Q_3 - Q_1}{Q_3 + Q_1}$$

## Calculation of Quartile Deviation and Coefficient of Quartile Deviation for Different Types of Statistical Series

Through different illustrations, let us understand how quartile deviation and coefficient of quartile deviation are calculated for different statistical series.

### (1) Individual Series and Quartile Deviation

In order to calculate quartile deviation in case of individual series, we first find out the values of third quartile and first quartile using the following equations:

$$Q_1 = \text{Size of} \left(\frac{N+1}{4}\right) \text{th item}$$

$$Q_3 = \text{Size of } 3\left(\frac{N+1}{4}\right) \text{th item}$$

Quartile Deviation (QD) and the coefficient of QD are then calculated using the following formulae:

**FORMULAE**

$$QD = \frac{Q_3 - Q_1}{2}$$

$$\text{Coefficient of QD} = \frac{Q_3 - Q_1}{Q_3 + Q_1}$$

**ILLUSTRATION.**

Find out the quartile deviation and coefficient of quartile deviation of the following series:

| S. No. | 1 | 2 | 3 | 4 | 5 | 6 | 7 | 8 | 9 | 10 | 11 |
|---|---|---|---|---|---|---|---|---|---|---|---|
| Marks | 10 | 15 | 20 | 25 | 30 | 35 | 40 | 45 | 50 | 55 | 60 |

**SOLUTION:**

$$Q_1 = \text{Size of} \left(\frac{N+1}{4}\right)\text{th item} = \text{Size of} \left(\frac{11+1}{4}\right)\text{th item}$$

$$= \text{Size of 3rd item} = 20 \text{ marks}$$

$$Q_3 = \text{Size of } 3\left(\frac{N+1}{4}\right)\text{th item} = \text{Size of } 3\left(\frac{11+1}{4}\right)$$

$$= \text{Size of 9th item} = 50 \text{ marks}$$

**Note**

$(Q_3-Q_1)/2$ or quartile deviation is average of the difference between two quartiles ($Q_3$ and $Q_1$).

$$\text{Quartile Deviation (QD)} = \frac{Q_3 - Q_1}{2} = \frac{50-20}{2} = 15$$

$$\text{Coefficient of Quartile Deviation} = \frac{Q_3 - Q_1}{Q_3 + Q_1} = \frac{50-20}{50+20} = \frac{30}{70}$$

$$= 0.43$$

QD = 15, Coefficient of QD = 0.43

**ILLUSTRATION.**

The following table shows monthly wages of 10 workers:

| Monthly Wages (₹) | 120 | 150 | 170 | 180 | 181 | 187 | 190 | 192 | 200 | 210 |
|---|---|---|---|---|---|---|---|---|---|---|

Calculate first, third quartiles and quartile deviation.

**SOLUTION:**

**Calculation of the Partition Values**

| S. No. | 1 | 2 | 3 | 4 | 5 | 6 | 7 | 8 | 9 | 10 |
|---|---|---|---|---|---|---|---|---|---|---|
| Monthly Wages (₹) | 120 | 150 | 170 | 180 | 181 | 187 | 190 | 192 | 200 | 210 |

$$Q_1 = \text{Size of} \left(\frac{N+1}{4}\right)\text{th item}$$

$$= \text{Size of} \left(\frac{10+1}{4}\right)\text{th item}$$

$$= \text{Size of 2.75th item}$$

$$= \text{Size of 2nd item} + \frac{3}{4}(\text{Size of 3rd item} - \text{Size of 2nd item})$$

$$= ₹\ 150 + \frac{3}{4}(170 - 150)$$

$$Q_1 = ₹\ 165$$

$$Q_3 = \text{Size of } 3\left(\frac{N+1}{4}\right)\text{th item} = \text{Size of 8.25th item}$$

$$= \text{Size of 8th item} + \frac{1}{4}\text{ (Size of 9th item – Size of 8th item)}$$

$$Q_3 = ₹\,192 + \frac{1}{4}(200 - 192) = ₹\,194$$

$$QD = \frac{Q_3 - Q_1}{2} = \frac{194 - 165}{2} = \frac{29}{2} = 14.5$$

***Learning by doing***

1. *Estimate quartile deviation and the coefficient of quartile deviation of the following data:*

   *8, 9, 11, 12, 13, 17, 20, 21, 23, 25, 27*

   *Show that QD is the average of the difference between two quartiles.*

   *(**Ans.** QD = 6, Coefficient of QD = 0.353)*

2. *Find out quartile deviation and coefficient of quartile deviation of the following series:*

   *28, 18, 20, 24, 30, 15, 47, 27*

   *(**Ans.** QD = 5.5, Coefficient of QD = 0.23)*

### (2) Discrete Series or Frequency Array and Quartile Deviation

In a discrete series, quartile deviation is calculated by converting simple frequencies of series into cumulative frequencies. It is illustrated as below.

**Illustration.**

The following data shows daily wages of 199 workers of a factory. Find out quartile deviation and the coefficient of quartile deviation.

| **Wages (₹)** | 10 | 20 | 30 | 40 | 50 | 60 | 70 | 80 | 90 | 100 |
|---|---|---|---|---|---|---|---|---|---|---|
| **Number of Workers** | 2 | 8 | 20 | 35 | 42 | 20 | 28 | 26 | 16 | 2 |

**Solution:**

The above series is first converted into a cumulative frequency distribution series.

| Wages (₹) | Frequency (f) | Cumulative Frequency |
|---|---|---|
| 10 | 2 | 2 |
| 20 | 8 | 10 |
| 30 | 20 | 30 |
| **($Q_1$) 40** | **35** | **65** |
| 50 | 42 | 107 |
| 60 | 20 | 127 |
| **($Q_3$) 70** | **28** | **155** |
| 80 | 26 | 181 |
| 90 | 16 | 197 |
| 100 | 2 | 199 |
| | N = 199 | |

$$Q_1 = \text{Size of }\left(\frac{N+1}{4}\right)\text{th item}$$

$$= \text{Size of }\left(\frac{199+1}{4}\right)\text{th item} = \text{Size of 50th item}$$

50th item lies in 65th cumulative frequency of the series. Wage corresponding to 65th cumulative frequency is ₹ 40 which therefore is first quartile of the wage distribution. Likewise,

$$Q_3 = \text{Size of } 3\left(\frac{N+1}{4}\right)\text{th item}$$

$$= \text{Size of } 3\left(\frac{199+1}{4}\right)\text{th item} = \text{Size of 150th item}$$

150th item falls in 155th cumulative frequency of the series. Wage corresponding to 155th cumulative frequency is ₹ 70 which therefore is the third quartile of the series.

$$\text{Quartile Deviation (QD)} = \frac{Q_3 - Q_1}{2}$$

$$= \frac{70 - 40}{2} = \frac{30}{2} = 15$$

$$\text{Coefficient of QD} = \frac{Q_3 - Q_1}{Q_3 + Q_1}$$

$$= \frac{70 - 40}{70 + 40} = \frac{30}{110} = 0.27$$

***Learning by doing***

1. *Find out quartile deviation and the coefficient of quartile deviation of the following data:*

| Age | 20 | 30 | 40 | 50 | 60 | 70 | 80 |
|---|---|---|---|---|---|---|---|
| Members | 3 | 61 | 132 | 153 | 140 | 51 | 3 |

*(Ans. QD = 10, Coefficient of QD = 0.2)*

2. *Estimate quartile deviation and the coefficient of quartile deviation of the following series:*

| Height (inches) | 58 | 59 | 60 | 61 | 62 | 63 | 64 | 65 | 66 |
|---|---|---|---|---|---|---|---|---|---|
| Number of Students | 15 | 20 | 32 | 35 | 33 | 22 | 20 | 10 | 8 |

*(Ans. QD = 1.5, Coefficient of QD = 0.024)*

### (3) Frequency Distribution Series and Quartile Deviation

Following illustration should explain the calculation of quartile deviation in frequency distribution series:

**Illustration.**

Find out quartile deviation of the following series:

| Age (Years) | 0–20 | 20–40 | 40–60 | 60–80 | 80–100 |
|---|---|---|---|---|---|
| Number of Persons | 4 | 10 | 15 | 20 | 11 |

**Solution:**

| Age (Years) | Number of Persons (f) | Cumulative Frequency |
|---|---|---|
| 0–20 | 4 | 4 |
| 20–40 | 10 | 14 |
| 40–60 | 15 | 29 |
| 60–80 | 20 | 49 |
| 80–100 | 11 | 60 |

$$Q_1 = \text{Size of}\left(\frac{N}{4}\right)\text{th item} = \text{Size of}\left(\frac{60}{4}\right)\text{th item}$$

$$= \text{Size of 15th item}$$

15th item lies in group 40–60 and falls within 29th cumulative frequency of the series.

$$Q_1 = l_1 + \frac{\frac{N}{4} - \text{c.f.}}{f} \times i$$

(Here, $l_1$ = Lower limit of the class interval; N = Sum total of the frequencies; c.f. = Cumulative frequency of the class preceding the first quartile class; f = Frequency of the quartile class; $i$ = Class interval.)

Thus, $$Q_1 = 40 + \frac{\frac{60}{4} - 14}{15} \times 20 = 40 + \frac{15 - 14}{15} \times 20$$

$$= 40 + \frac{1}{15} \times 20$$

$$= 40 + 1.33 = 41.33$$

Likewise,

$$Q_3 = \text{Size of } 3\left(\frac{N}{4}\right)\text{th item}$$

$$= \text{Size of } 3\left(\frac{60}{4}\right)\text{th item}$$

$$= \text{Size of 45th item}$$

45th item falls within 49th cumulative frequency of the series.

Thus,

$$Q_3 = l_1 + \frac{3\left(\frac{N}{4}\right) - \text{c.f.}}{f} \times i$$

$$= 60 + \frac{3\left(\frac{60}{4}\right) - 29}{20} \times 20 = 60 + \frac{45 - 29}{20} \times 20$$

$$= 60 + \frac{16}{20} \times 20$$

$$= 60 + 16 = 76$$

Having known the values of $Q_1$ and $Q_3$, quartile deviation (QD) is found as,

$$QD = \frac{Q_3 - Q_1}{2}$$

$$= \frac{76 - 41.33}{2} = \frac{34.67}{2} = 17.34$$

And,

$$\text{Coefficient of QD} = \frac{Q_3 - Q_1}{Q_3 + Q_1}$$

$$= \frac{76 - 41.33}{76 + 41.33} = \frac{34.67}{117.33}$$

$$= 0.30$$

Thus,

QD = 17.34, and Coefficient of QD = 0.30.

*Learning by doing*

1. *Given the following data, find out quartile deviation and the coefficient of quartile deviation:*

| Wages (₹) | 0–5 | 5–10 | 10–15 | 15–20 | 20–25 | 25–30 |
|---|---|---|---|---|---|---|
| Number of Workers | 4 | 6 | 3 | 8 | 12 | 7 |

*(**Ans.** QD = 6.87, Coefficient of QD = 0.4)*

2. *Find out quartile deviation and coefficient of quartile deviation from the following data:*

| Class Interval | 0–10 | 10–20 | 20–30 | 30–40 | 40–50 | 50–60 |
|---|---|---|---|---|---|---|
| Frequency | 4 | 8 | 5 | 4 | 9 | 10 |

*(**Ans.** QD = 16.25, Coefficient of QD = 0.48)*

## Merits and Demerits of Quartile Deviation

### Merits

(1) **Simple:** It is very simple to calculate and understand.

(2) **Less Effect of Extreme Values:** Quartile deviation is less affected by extreme values of the series.

### Demerits

(1) **Not Based on all Values:** The calculation of quartile deviation is not based on all values of the series. It is, therefore, less representative.

(2) **Formation of Series not known:** This method does not show complete formation of the series.

(3) **Instability:** The calculation of quartile deviation is significantly influenced by change in sample of the population. Accordingly, it suffers from instability.

## Mean Deviation

Mean Deviation is the arithmetic average of the deviations of all the values taken from some average value (mean, median, mode) of the series, ignoring signs (+ or –) of the deviations.

In the words of **Clark** and **Schakde,** "*Mean Deviation is the Arithmetic Average of deviations of all the values taken from a statistical average (mean, median, or mode) of series. In taking deviation of values, algebraic signs + and – are not taken into consideration, that is negative deviations are also treated as positive deviations.*"

Calculation of mean deviation involves the following steps:

(1) We first of all find out mean, median or mode of a series.

(2) As a second step, we find out the deviations of different items from the (central value mean, median or mode of the series.) These deviations are added up. While adding up these deviations positive (+) and negative (–) signs are ignored. All deviations are treated as positive.

(3) On both sides of the deviation, from the mean, are drawn two straight lines signifying that while calculating deviation negative signs have been ignored and all deviations have been treated as positive.

(4) Mean deviation is known by dividing the sum total of the deviation by the number of items.

**Note:** Deviations are often found from median value of the series. Many a time mean is also used, but the use of Modal value is seldom made. Formula of mean deviation is as follows:

### FORMULA

If deviations are taken from median, the following formula is used:

$$MD_m = \frac{\Sigma|X - M|}{N} \text{ or } \frac{\Sigma|dm|}{N}$$

And, if deviations are taken from arithmetic average of the series, then

$$MD_{\overline{X}} = \frac{\Sigma|X - \overline{X}|}{N} \text{ or } \frac{\Sigma|d\overline{x}|}{N}$$

(Here, MD = Mean deviation; X – M = Deviation from the median; $X - \overline{X}$ = Deviation from the arithmetic average; N = Number of items.)

## Coefficient of Mean Deviation

In order to find out coefficient of mean deviation, mean deviation of the series is divided by the central tendency of the series. If the deviations are taken from arithmetic mean, the mean deviation is divided by the arithmetic mean. And, if the deviations are taken from median, the mean deviation is divided by the median. Likewise, if the deviations are taken from mode of the series, the mean deviation is divided by the mode value.

Thus,

(1) Coefficient of MD from Mean $= \frac{MD_{\overline{x}}}{\overline{X}} = \frac{\text{Mean Deviation}}{\text{Arithmetic Mean}}$

(2) Coefficient of MD from Median$= \frac{MD_m}{M} = \frac{\text{Mean Deviation}}{\text{Median}}$

(3) Coefficient of MD from Mode $= \frac{MD_z}{Z} = \frac{\text{Mean Deviation}}{\text{Mode}}$

## Calculation of Mean Deviation

### (1) Individual Series and Mean Deviation

Following illustration should explain the calculation of mean deviation in case of individual series:

**Illustration.**

The data below gives wages of workers in a factory. Find out mean deviation and its coefficient.

| **S. No.** | 1 | 2 | 3 | 4 | 5 | 6 | 7 | 8 | 9 |
|---|---|---|---|---|---|---|---|---|---|
| **Wages (₹)** | 40 | 42 | 45 | 47 | 50 | 51 | 54 | 55 | 57 |

**SOLUTION:**

| Steps: Estimating MD through Median | Steps: Estimating MD through Mean |
|---|---|
| (i) Arrange the data in ascending order. | (i) Calculate arithmetic mean by adding up the data. |
| (ii) Calculate the median $M = \text{Size of}\left(\frac{N+1}{2}\right)\text{th item}$ | (ii) Find out the deviation of the items from mean. Ignore (+) and (–) signs. Express it by $\lvert d\bar{x} \rvert$. |
| (iii) Find out the deviation of the items from median. Ignore (–) and (+) signs. Express it by $\lvert dm \rvert$ sign. | (iii) Sum up the deviations. |
| (iv) Sum up the deviations, and express the same by using the relevant formula to find the required answer. $MD_m = \frac{\Sigma\lvert dm \rvert}{N}$ | (iv) Use the relevant formula to find the required answer. $MD_{\bar{X}} = \frac{\Sigma\lvert d\bar{x} \rvert}{N}$ |
| (v) After that solve the question with the help of the formula. | |

| Calculation of Mean Deviation and Coefficient of Mean Deviation using Median | | | Calculation of Mean Deviation and Coefficient of Mean Deviation using Arithmetic Mean | | |
|---|---|---|---|---|---|
| S. No. | Wages (₹) | Deviation from Median $\lvert dm \rvert = \lvert X - M \rvert$ M = 50 | S. No. | Wages (₹) | Deviation from Arithmetic Mean $\lvert d\bar{x} \rvert = \lvert X - \bar{X} \rvert$ $\bar{X} = 49$ |
| 1 | 40 | 10 | 1 | 40 | 9 |
| 2 | 42 | 8 | 2 | 42 | 7 |
| 3 | 45 | 5 | 3 | 45 | 4 |
| 4 | 47 | 3 | 4 | 47 | 2 |
| 5 | 50 (M) | 0 | 5 | 50 | 1 |
| 6 | 51 | 1 | 6 | 51 | 2 |
| 7 | 54 | 4 | 7 | 54 | 5 |
| 8 | 55 | 5 | 8 | 55 | 6 |
| 9 | 57 | 7 | 9 | 57 | 8 |
| N=9 | | $\Sigma\lvert dm \rvert = 43$ | N= 9 | $\Sigma X = 441$ | $\Sigma\lvert d\bar{x} \rvert = 44$ |

| From Median | From Mean |
|---|---|
| (a) $M = \text{Size of}\left(\frac{N+1}{2}\right)\text{th item}$<br>$M = \text{Size of}\left(\frac{9+1}{2}\right)\text{th item}$<br>M = 5th item = ₹ 50 | (a) $\bar{X} = \frac{\Sigma X}{N}$<br>$= \frac{441}{9}$<br>= ₹ 49 |
| (b) $MD_m = \frac{\Sigma\lvert dm \rvert}{N} = \frac{43}{9}$ = ₹ 4.78 | (b) $MD_{\bar{X}} = \frac{\Sigma\lvert d\bar{x} \rvert}{N} = \frac{44}{9}$ = ₹ 4.89 |
| (c) Coefficient of $MD_m$<br>$= \frac{MD_m}{M} = \frac{4.78}{50} = 0.096$ | (c) Coefficient of $MD_{\bar{X}} = \frac{MD_{\bar{X}}}{\bar{X}} = \frac{4.89}{49}$<br>$= 0.10$ |

> ***Learning by doing***
>
> 1. *Find out mean deviation of the monthly income of the five families given below, using arithmetic mean of the data:*
>
>    *852, 635, 792, 836, 750* (**Ans.** $\overline{X} = 773$, $MD_{\overline{X}} = 64.4$)
>
> 2. *Weight of nine students of a class is given below. Calculate mean deviation, using median and arithmetic mean of the series. Also calculate coefficient of mean deviation:*
>
>    ***Weight (kg):*** *47, 50, 58, 45, 53, 59, 47, 60, 49*
>
>    (**Ans.** $MD_m = 4.67$, $CMD_m = 0.0934$, $MD_{\overline{X}} = 4.89$, $CMD_{\overline{X}} = 0.094$)

### (2) Discrete Series or Frequency Array and Mean Deviation

Following steps may be noted in the calculation of mean deviation for the discrete series:

(1) Find out central tendency of the series (mean or median) from which deviations are to be taken.

(2) Deviations of different items in the series are taken from central tendency, and signs (+) or (–) of the deviations are ignored. It is expressed as ($|d\bar{x}|$) or ($|dm|$).

(3) Each deviation value is multiplied by the frequency facing it, and the sum of these multiples is obtained. This is expressed as $\Sigma f|d|$.

(4) $\Sigma f|d|$ is divided by the sum total of frequencies, that is $\Sigma f$ or N. The resultant value would be mean deviation.

Thus,

$$MD_m = \frac{\Sigma f|dm|}{N}$$

(Here, 'dm' indicates that deviations are taken from median (M) of the series.)

**ILLUSTRATION.**

Using median and arithmetic mean respectively, calculate mean deviation and its coefficient from the following data:

| **Size of Items** | 5 | 6 | 7 | 8 | 9 | 10 | 11 | 12 | 13 |
|---|---|---|---|---|---|---|---|---|---|
| **Frequency** | 4 | 5 | 6 | 7 | 8 | 9 | 10 | 11 | 12 |

**SOLUTION:**

**(i) Calculation of Mean Deviation from Median**

| **Size of Items (X)** | **Frequency (f)** | **Cumulative Frequency** | **Deviation from Median $\lvert dm\rvert = \lvert X - M\rvert$ M=10** | **Multiple of Deviation and the Corresponding Frequency $f\lvert dm\rvert$** |
|---|---|---|---|---|
| 5 | 4 | 4 | 5 | 20 |
| 6 | 5 | 9 | 4 | 20 |
| 7 | 6 | 15 | 3 | 18 |
| 8 | 7 | 22 | 2 | 14 |
| 9 | 8 | 30 | 1 | 8 |
| **10** | **9** | **39** | 0 | 0 |
| 11 | 10 | 49 | 1 | 10 |
| 12 | 11 | 60 | 2 | 22 |
| 13 | 12 | 72 | 3 | 36 |
| | N = 72 | | | $\Sigma f\lvert dm\rvert = 148$ |

(a) Median or M = Size of $\left(\frac{N+1}{2}\right)$th item

$= \text{Size of } \left(\frac{72+1}{2}\right)\text{th item}$

= Size of 36.5th item = 10

(b) Mean Deviation from Median

Or, $MD_m = \frac{\Sigma f|dm|}{N} = \frac{148}{72} = 2.05$

(c) Coefficient of Mean Deviation from Median

$= \frac{MD_m}{M} = \frac{2.05}{10} = 0.205$

**(ii) Calculation of Mean Deviation from Arithmetic Mean**

| Size of Items (X) | Frequency (f) | fX | Deviation from Mean (9.83) (–), (+) ignored $|d\bar{x}|$ | Product of Deviation and the Corresponding Frequency ($f|d\bar{x}|$) |
|---|---|---|---|---|
| 5 | 4 | 20 | 4.83 | 19.32 |
| 6 | 5 | 30 | 3.83 | 19.15 |
| 7 | 6 | 42 | 2.83 | 16.98 |
| 8 | 7 | 56 | 1.83 | 12.81 |
| 9 | 8 | 72 | 0.83 | 6.64 |
| 10 | 9 | 90 | 0.17 | 1.53 |
| 11 | 10 | 110 | 1.17 | 11.70 |
| 12 | 11 | 132 | 2.17 | 23.87 |
| 13 | 12 | 156 | 3.17 | 38.04 |
| | $\Sigma f = 72$ | $\Sigma fX = 708$ | | $\Sigma f|d\bar{x}| = 150.04$ |

(a) $\bar{X} = \frac{\Sigma fX}{\Sigma f} = \frac{708}{72} = 9.83$

(b) Mean Deviation from Arithmetic Mean

Or, $MD_{\bar{x}} = \frac{\Sigma f|d\bar{x}|}{\Sigma f} = \frac{150.04}{72} = 2.08$

(c) Coefficient of Mean Deviation from Mean

$= \frac{MD_{\bar{x}}}{\bar{X}} = \frac{2.08}{9.83} = 0.21$

***Learning by doing***

1. *Find out mean deviation and its coefficient of the following data:*

| **Items** | 5 | 10 | 15 | 20 | 25 | 30 | 35 | 40 |
|---|---|---|---|---|---|---|---|---|
| **Frequency** | 8 | 16 | 18 | 22 | 14 | 9 | 6 | 7 |

*(**Ans.** $MD_{\bar{X}} = 7.656$, Coefficient of $MD_{\bar{X}} = 0.38$)*

2. *Calculate mean deviation from the following data, using mean and median, respectively.*

| **Size** | 4 | 6 | 8 | 10 | 12 | 14 | 16 |
|---|---|---|---|---|---|---|---|
| **Frequency** | 2 | 4 | 5 | 3 | 2 | 1 | 4 |

*(**Ans.** $MD_{\bar{X}} = 3.32$, $MD_m = 3.24$)*

### (3) Frequency Distribution Series and Mean Deviation

Continuous series are first converted into discrete series by finding mid-values of the class intervals. Afterwards, same procedure is followed for the calculation of mean deviation and its coefficient as in the case of discrete series.

**You Must Not Miss it**

That for the estimation of mean deviation, frequency distribution series are often converted in discrete series by finding mid-values of the class intervals.

**ILLUSTRATION.**

Find out mean deviation and coefficient of mean deviation, using arithmetic mean from the following data:

| **Profit (₹)** | 0–10 | 10–20 | 20–30 | 30–40 | 40–50 |
|---|---|---|---|---|---|
| **Shops (Number)** | 5 | 10 | 15 | 20 | 25 |

**SOLUTION:**

| Profit (₹) | Mid-value (m) | Frequency (f) | Multiple of Mid-value and Frequency (fm) | Deviation from Mean $\lvert d\bar{x}\rvert = \lvert m - \bar{X}\rvert$ $\bar{X} = 31.66$ | Multiple of Deviation and the Corresponding to Frequency ($f\lvert d\bar{x}\rvert$) |
|---|---|---|---|---|---|
| 0–10 | 5 | 5 | 25 | 26.66 | 133.30 |
| 10–20 | 15 | 10 | 150 | 16.66 | 166.60 |
| 20–30 | 25 | 15 | 375 | 6.66 | 99.90 |
| 30–40 | 35 | 20 | 700 | 3.34 | 66.80 |
| 40–50 | 45 | 25 | 1,125 | 13.34 | 333.50 |
| | | $\Sigma f = 75$ | $\Sigma fm = 2,375$ | $\Sigma\lvert d\bar{x}\rvert = 66.66$ | $\Sigma f\lvert d\bar{x}\rvert = 800.10$ |

$$\bar{X} = \frac{\Sigma fm}{\Sigma f} = \frac{2,375}{75} = 31.66$$

Mean Deviation from Arithmetic Mean

$$MD_{\bar{X}} = \frac{\Sigma f\lvert d\bar{x}\rvert}{\Sigma f} = \frac{800.10}{75} = 10.67$$

Coefficient of Mean Deviation

$$= \frac{MD_{\bar{X}}}{\bar{X}} = \frac{10.67}{31.67} = 0.34$$

Mean Deviation = 10.67, Coefficient of Mean Deviation = 0.34.

**ILLUSTRATION.**

Calculate mean deviation and its coefficient from the median of the following data:

| **Size** | 100–120 | 120–140 | 140–160 | 160–180 | 180–200 |
|---|---|---|---|---|---|
| **Frequency** | 4 | 6 | 10 | 8 | 5 |

**SOLUTION:**

| Size (X) | Mid-value (m) | Frequency (f) | Cumulative Frequency | Deviation from Median $\lvert dm\rvert = \lvert m - M\rvert$ M = 153 | Multiple of Deviation and the Corresponding Frequency ($f\lvert dm\rvert$) |
|---|---|---|---|---|---|
| 100–120 | 110 | 4 | 4 | 110 – 153 = 43 | 172 |
| 120–140 | 130 | 6 | 10 (c.f.) | 130 – 153 = 23 | 138 |
| 140–160 | 150 | 10 (f) | 20 | 150 – 153 = 3 | 30 |
| 160–180 | 170 | 8 | 28 | 170 – 153 = 17 | 136 |
| 180–200 | 190 | 5 | 33 | 190 – 153 = 37 | 185 |
| | | $\Sigma f = N = 33$ | | | $\Sigma f\lvert dm\rvert = 661$ |

$$M = \text{Size of}\left(\frac{N}{2}\right)\text{th item}$$

$$= \text{Size of}\left(\frac{33}{2}\right)\text{th item} = \text{Size of 16.5th item}$$

140–160 is the Median Class Interval.

The Median is calculated as

$$M = l_1 + \frac{\left(\frac{N}{2}\right) - c.f.}{f} \times i$$

$$M = 140 + \frac{16.5 - 10}{10} \times 20 = 140 + 13 = 153$$

Mean Deviation from Median

$$MD_m = \frac{\Sigma f|dm|}{\Sigma f} = \frac{661}{33} = 20.03$$

Coefficient of Mean Deviation

$$= \frac{MD_m}{M} = \frac{20.03}{153} = 0.1309$$

$MD_m = 20.03$, Coefficient of $MD_m = 0.1309$.

***Learning by doing***

1. *The following table gives distribution of marks for 50 students of a class. Calculate mean deviation from the mean and median respectively from the data:*

| Marks Obtained | 140–150 | 150–160 | 160–170 | 170–180 | 180–190 | 190–200 |
|---|---|---|---|---|---|---|
| Frequency | 4 | 6 | 10 | 18 | 9 | 3 |

*(**Ans.** $MD_{\bar{X}} = 10.56$, $MD_m = 10.24$)*

2. *Estimate the coefficient of mean deviation from the median from the following data:*

| Age Group | 20–30 | 30–40 | 40–50 | 50–60 | 60–70 |
|---|---|---|---|---|---|
| Number of Workers | 8 | 12 | 20 | 16 | 4 |

*(**Ans.** Coefficient of $MD_m = 0.19$)*

## Merits and Demerits of Mean Deviation

### Merits

**(1) Simple:** It is a very simple and easy measure of dispersion.

**(2) Based on all Values:** Mean deviation is based on all the items of the series. It is therefore more representative than the range or quartile deviation.

**(3) Less Effect of Extreme Values:** Mean deviation is less affected by extreme values than the range.

**What is the Principal Drawback of Mean Deviation as a Measure of Dispersion?**

It is that all deviations from the average value of the series are taken as positive, even when some of these are actually negative.

### Demerits

**(1) Inaccuracy:** Calculation of mean deviation suffers from inaccuracy, because the '+' or '–' signs are ignored.

**(2) Not Capable of Algebraic Treatment:** Mean deviation is not capable of any further algebraic treatment.

**(3) Unreliable:** In case deviations are taken from mode and mode being uncertain, mean deviation also becomes uncertain and therefore, unreliable.

## Standard Deviation

Standard deviation is a most satisfactory scientific method of dispersion. Accordingly, it is a widely used method in statistical analysis.

This was first used by **Karl Pearson**. *This is sometimes called as* ***'Root Mean Square Deviation'****. This is generally denoted by (sigma) of the Greek language. Standard Deviation is the square root of the arithmetic mean of the squares of deviations of the items from their mean value.* Standard deviation has two main features: (i) The value of its deviation is taken from arithmetic mean. (ii) Plus and minus signs of the deviations taken from the mean are not ignored. In fact, signs of the deviations become redundant once the deviations are squared. Finally, square root of the arithmetic mean of the squares of the deviation is calculated. It is this square root which is called Standard Deviation. This is always in positive value.

In the words of **Spiegel**, *"The Standard deviation is the square root of the arithmetic mean of the squares of all deviations. Deviations being measured from arithmetic mean of the items."*

### Coefficient of Standard Deviation

This is a relative measure of the dispersion of series. It is generally used whenever variation in different series is compared. Coefficient of standard deviation is estimated by dividing the value of standard deviation by the mean of the series. Thus,

$$\text{Coefficient of Standard Deviation} = \frac{\sigma}{\overline{X}}$$

### Calculation of Standard Deviation

#### (1) Individual Series and Standard Deviation

There are three methods of calculating standard deviation in case of individual series:

(i) **Direct Method,**

(ii) **Short-cut Method,** and

(iii) **Step-deviation Method.**

#### (i) Direct Method

Direct method of calculating standard deviation is most useful when mean value is in whole number. This method involves the following steps:

(1) First of all, mean value of the concerned series is determined. That is, we find out $\overline{X}$ as, $\overline{X} = \frac{\Sigma X}{N}$.

(2) Deviation of each item from $\overline{X}$ is determined. That is, we find the values of x as, $x = X - \overline{X}$

(3) Each value of the deviation is squared. The sum total of the square of the deviations is obtained. That is, we find out $\Sigma x^2$.

(4) $\Sigma x^2$ is divided by the number of items (N) in the series. Square root of $\frac{\Sigma x^2}{N}$ will be the standard deviation. That is, we calculate the value

**How Standard Deviation differs from Mean Deviation?**

Standard deviation is a most satisfactory scientific method of dispersion. Accordingly, it is a widely used method in statistical analysis.

Two main differences between standard deviation and mean deviation are:

(i) In the calculation of standard deviation, deviations are taken only from the mean value of the series. On the other hand, in the calculation of mean deviation, deviations may be taken from mean, median or mode.

(ii) In the calculation of mean deviation, signs of deviations (+) or (−) are ignored. But in the calculation of standard deviation, signs are not ignored.

of $\sqrt{\frac{\Sigma x^2}{N}}$. Thus, following is the formula for the calculation of standard deviation:

**FORMULA**

$$\text{SD or } \sigma = \sqrt{\frac{\Sigma x^2}{N}} \text{ or } \sqrt{\frac{\Sigma(X-\overline{X})^2}{N}}$$

(Here, $\sigma$ = Standard deviation; $\Sigma x^2$ = Sum total of the squares of deviations; $\overline{X}$ = Mean value; $X - \overline{X}$ = Deviation from mean value; N = Number of items.)

**ILLUSTRATION.**

Following are the marks obtained by 10 students of a class. Calculate standard deviation and coefficient of standard deviation.

| Marks | 12 | 8 | 17 | 13 | 15 | 9 | 18 | 11 | 6 | 1 |
|---|---|---|---|---|---|---|---|---|---|---|

**SOLUTION:**

**Calculation of Standard Deviation Using Direct Method**

| S. No. | Marks (X) | Deviation ($x = X - \overline{X}$) $\overline{X}$ =11 | Square of Deviation $x^2$ (= $X - \overline{X})^2$ |
|---|---|---|---|
| 1 | 12 | 12 – 11 = 1 | 1 |
| 2 | 8 | 8 – 11 = – 3 | 9 |
| 3 | 17 | 17 – 11 = 6 | 36 |
| 4 | 13 | 13 – 11 = 2 | 4 |
| 5 | 15 | 15 – 11 = 4 | 16 |
| 6 | 9 | 9 – 11 = – 2 | 4 |
| 7 | 18 | 18 – 11 = 7 | 49 |
| 8 | 11 | 11 – 11 = 0 | 0 |
| 9 | 6 | 6 – 11 = – 5 | 25 |
| 10 | 1 | 1 – 11 = – 10 | 100 |
| N = 10 | $\Sigma X$=110 | $\Sigma x = 0$ | $\Sigma x^2 = 244$ |

$$\overline{X} = \frac{\Sigma X}{N} = \frac{110}{10} = 11$$

$$\sigma = \sqrt{\frac{\Sigma x^2}{N}} = \sqrt{\frac{244}{10}} = \sqrt{24.4} = 4.94$$

$$\text{Coefficient of SD} = \frac{\sigma}{\overline{X}} = \frac{4.94}{11} = 0.45$$

SD = 4.94 marks, Coefficient of SD = 0.45.

**(ii) Short-cut Method**

Short-cut method of calculating standard deviation involves the following steps:

(1) We take any value of the series as assumed average, generally written as A.

(2) Deviations of all the items are obtained from the assumed average. Sum total of these deviations is obtained as $\Sigma(X - A)$ or $\Sigma dx$.

Also, we square up the deviations and obtain their sum total as $(X - A)^2$ or $\Sigma dx^2$.

(3) The following formula is applied to calculate the value of standard deviation:

**FORMULA**

$$\sigma = \sqrt{\frac{\sum dx^2}{N} - \left(\frac{\sum dx}{N}\right)^2}$$

**ILLUSTRATION.**

Find out standard deviation, given the following data:

8, 10, 12, 14, 16, 18, 20, 22, 24, 26

**SOLUTION:**

| S. No. | Size (X) | Deviation from Assumed Average (dx = X – A) A = 20 | Square of Deviation ($dx^2$) |
|---|---|---|---|
| 1 | 8 | 8 – 20 = – 12 | 144 |
| 2 | 10 | 10 – 20 = – 10 | 100 |
| 3 | 12 | 12 – 20 = – 8 | 64 |
| 4 | 14 | 14 – 20 = – 6 | 36 |
| 5 | 16 | 16 – 20 = – 4 | 16 |
| 6 | 18 | 18 – 20 = – 2 | 4 |
| 7 | 20 (A) | 20 – 20 = 0 | 0 |
| 8 | 22 | 22 – 20 = + 2 | 4 |
| 9 | 24 | 24 – 20 = + 4 | 16 |
| 10 | 26 | 26 – 20 = + 6 | 36 |
| N = 10 | | $\Sigma dx = -30$ | $\Sigma dx^2 = 420$ |

$$\sigma = \sqrt{\frac{\Sigma dx^2}{N} - \left(\frac{\Sigma dx}{N}\right)^2} = \sqrt{\frac{420}{10} - \left(\frac{-30}{10}\right)^2}$$

$$= \sqrt{42 - (-3)^2} = \sqrt{33} = 5.74$$

Standard Deviation = 5.74.

### (iii) Step-deviation Method

This method involves the following steps:

(i) We take any value of the series as assumed average.

(ii) Deviations are taken from the assumed average as $dx = (X - A)$.

(iii) The deviations are divided by some common factor, as $dx' = \frac{dx}{C}$ where C is the common factor and $dx'$ are step-deviations.

(iv) Sum of the step-deviations is obtained. Also, step-deviations are squared and then sum total is obtained as $\Sigma dx'^2$.

(v) The following formula is applied to calculate the value of standard deviation.

**FORMULA**

$$\sigma = \sqrt{\frac{\sum dx'^2}{N} - \left(\frac{\sum dx'}{N}\right)^2} \times C$$

**ILLUSTRATION.**

Find out standard deviation of the monthly income of 5 persons, as stated below:

| S. No. of Persons | Monthly Income (in ₹) |
|---|---|
| 1 | 500 |
| 2 | 700 |
| 3 | 1,000 |
| 4 | 1,500 |
| 5 | 1,300 |

**SOLUTION:**

| S. No. | Monthly Income | Deviation from Assumed Average (dx = X – A) A = 1,000 | $dx' = \frac{dx}{C}$ C = 100 | $dx'^2$ |
|---|---|---|---|---|
| 1 | 500 | – 500 | – 5 | 25 |
| 2 | 700 | – 300 | – 3 | 9 |
| 3 | 1,000 (A) | 0 | 0 | 0 |
| 4 | 1,500 | + 500 | + 5 | 25 |
| 5 | 1,300 | + 300 | + 3 | 9 |
| N = 5 | | | $\Sigma dx'=0$ | $\Sigma dx'^2=68$ |

$$\sigma = \sqrt{\frac{\Sigma dx'^2}{N} - \left(\frac{\Sigma dx'}{N}\right)^2} \times C$$

$$= \sqrt{\frac{68}{5} - \left(\frac{0}{5}\right)^2} \times 100$$

$$= \sqrt{13.6} \times 100 = 368.78$$

Standard Deviation (σ) = 368.78.

*Learning by doing*

1. *The following Table gives marks obtained by 7 students of a class. Find out standard deviation of the marks.*

   *40, 42, 38, 44, 46, 48, 50* *(Ans. σ = 4)*

2. *Weight of some students is given below in kilograms. Find out standard deviation.*

   *41, 44, 45, 49, 50, 53, 55, 55, 58, 60* *(Ans. σ = 5.97)*

3. *Using step-deviation method, calculate standard deviation of the following series:*

| Marks | 0–10 | 10–20 | 20–30 | 30–40 | 40–50 | 50–60 | 60–70 | 70–80 |
|---|---|---|---|---|---|---|---|---|
| Number of Students | 5 | 10 | 20 | 40 | 30 | 20 | 10 | 4 |

*(Ans. σ = 15.7)*

**(iv) Yet another Method**

Standard deviation in case of individual series can be calculated using the following formula:

$$\sigma = \sqrt{\frac{\sum X^2}{N} - \left(\frac{\sum X}{N}\right)^2}$$

**ILLUSTRATION.**

Using electronic calculator, find out standard deviation of the following data:

| Marks | 10 | 20 | 30 | 40 | 50 |
|---|---|---|---|---|---|

**SOLUTION:**

**Calculation of Standard Deviation**

| S. No. | Marks (X) | $X^2$ |
|---|---|---|
| 1 | 10 | 100 |
| 2 | 20 | 400 |
| 3 | 30 | 900 |
| 4 | 40 | 1,600 |
| 5 | 50 | 2,500 |
| N = 5 | $\Sigma X = 150$ | $\Sigma X^2 = 5{,}500$ |

$$\sigma = \sqrt{\frac{\sum X^2}{N} - \left(\frac{\sum X}{N}\right)^2}$$

$$= \sqrt{\frac{5,500}{5} - \left(\frac{150}{5}\right)^2} = \sqrt{1,100 - (30)^2}$$

$$= \sqrt{1,100 - 900} = \sqrt{200} = 14.14$$

Standard Deviation ($\sigma$) = 14.14.

### (2) Discrete Series or Frequency Array and Standard Deviation

There are two methods of calculating standard deviation in discrete series:

**(i) Direct Method**, and **(ii) Short-cut Method**.

#### (i) Direct Method

This method involves the following steps:

(1) We first determine mean value of the series as

$$\overline{X} = \frac{\Sigma fX}{N}$$

(2) Deviations of various items are obtained from the mean value as

$$x = X - \overline{X}$$

(3) Squares of deviations are obtained as $x^2$.

(4) Squared deviations are multiplied by their corresponding frequencies, and their sum total is obtained as $\Sigma fx^2$.

(5) The following formula is applied to calculate the value of standard deviation.

**FORMULA**

$$\sigma = \sqrt{\frac{\sum fx^2}{N}} \quad \text{or} \quad \sigma = \sqrt{\frac{\sum f(X - \overline{X})^2}{N}}$$

**ILLUSTRATION.**

Find out standard deviation of the following data, using direct method:

| Size | 4 | 6 | 8 | 10 | 12 | 14 | 16 |
|---|---|---|---|---|---|---|---|
| Frequency | 1 | 2 | 3 | 5 | 3 | 2 | 1 |

**SOLUTION:**

| Size (X) | Frequency (f) | Multiple of Size and Frequency (fX) | Deviation from Mean ($x = X - \bar{X}$) $\bar{X} = 10$ | Square of Deviation ($x^2$) | $fx^2$ |
|---|---|---|---|---|---|
| 4 | 1 | 4 | –6 | 36 | 36 |
| 6 | 2 | 12 | –4 | 16 | 32 |
| 8 | 3 | 24 | –2 | 4 | 12 |
| 10 | 5 | 50 | 0 | 0 | 0 |
| 12 | 3 | 36 | +2 | 4 | 12 |
| 14 | 2 | 28 | +4 | 16 | 32 |
| 16 | 1 | 16 | +6 | 36 | 36 |
| | N = 17 | $\Sigma fX = 170$ | | | $\Sigma fx^2 = 160$ |

$$\bar{X} = \frac{\Sigma fX}{N} = \frac{170}{17} = 10$$

$$\sigma = \sqrt{\frac{\Sigma fx^2}{N}} = \sqrt{\frac{\Sigma f(X-\bar{X})^2}{N}} = \sqrt{\frac{160}{17}} = \sqrt{9.41} = 3.07$$

Standard Deviation ($\sigma$) = 3.07.

**(ii) Short-cut Method**

This method involves the following steps:

(1) We take any value of the series as assumed average, written as A. Generally, the value of the item with the highest frequency is taken as assumed average.

(2) Deviations of different items from assumed average are obtained as $d = (X - A)$.

(3) Deviations are multiplied by their corresponding frequencies and then sum total is obtained as $\Sigma fd$. Also, deviations are squared and multiplied by the corresponding frequencies to obtain $\Sigma fd^2$.

(4) The following formula is applied to calculate the value of standard deviation:

**FORMULA**

$$\sigma = \sqrt{\frac{\sum fd^2}{N} - \left(\frac{\sum fd}{N}\right)^2}$$

**ILLUSTRATION.**

Find out standard deviation of the following data:

| Size | 1 | 2 | 3 | 4 | 5 | 6 | 7 | 8 |
|---|---|---|---|---|---|---|---|---|
| Frequency | 5 | 10 | 15 | 20 | 15 | 10 | 10 | 15 |

**SOLUTION:**

**Calculation of Standard Deviation (σ) in Discrete Series (Short-cut method)**

| Size (X) | Frequency (f) | Deviation from Assumed Average (dx = X – A) A = 5 | Square of Deviation ($dx^2$) | Multiple of Deviation and the Corresponding Frequency (fdx) | $fdx^2$ |
|---|---|---|---|---|---|
| 1 | 5 | – 4 | 16 | –20 | 80 |
| 2 | 10 | – 3 | 9 | –30 | 90 |
| 3 | 15 | – 2 | 4 | –30 | 60 |
| 4 | 20 | – 1 | 1 | –20 | 20 |
| 5 | 15 | 0 | 0 | 0 | 0 |
| 6 | 10 | +1 | 1 | +10 | 10 |
| 7 | 10 | +2 | 4 | +20 | 40 |
| 8 | 15 | +3 | 9 | +45 | 135 |
| | Σf =100 | | | Σfdx = –25 | $\Sigma fdx^2$=435 |

$$\sigma = \sqrt{\frac{\Sigma fdx^2}{N} - \left(\frac{\Sigma fdx}{N}\right)^2} = \sqrt{\frac{435}{100} - \left(\frac{-25}{100}\right)^2}$$

$$\sigma = \sqrt{\frac{435}{100} - \left(\frac{-1}{4}\right)^2} = \sqrt{\frac{435}{100} - \frac{1}{16}} = \sqrt{4.29} = 2.07$$

Standard Deviation (σ) = 2.07.

***Learning by doing***

1. *Find out standard deviation of the savings of the following 10 persons:*

| Persons | 1 | 2 | 3 | 4 | 5 | 6 | 7 | 8 | 9 | 10 |
|---|---|---|---|---|---|---|---|---|---|---|
| Savings (₹) | 114 | 108 | 100 | 98 | 101 | 109 | 117 | 119 | 121 | 126 |

*(**Ans.** σ = 9.14)*

2. *Find out standard deviation and its coefficient of the following series:*

| Size | 10 | 20 | 30 | 40 | 50 | 60 | 70 |
|---|---|---|---|---|---|---|---|
| Frequency | 6 | 8 | 16 | 15 | 33 | 11 | 12 |

*(**Ans.** SD = 16.36, Coefficient of SD = 0.37)*

## (3) Frequency Distribution Series and Standard Deviation

Three methods are available for the calculation of standard deviation in case of frequency distribution series:

**(i) Direct Method,**

**(ii) Short-cut Method,** and

**(iii) Step-deviation Method.**

### (i) Direct Method

This method involves the following steps:

(1) First, mean of the series ($\overline{X}$) is determined.

(2) Deviations of various mid-values are taken from the mean value, $x = m - \bar{X}$ (Here, mid-value is m).

(3) Deviations are squared ($x^2$) and then multiplied by their corresponding frequencies to get $\Sigma fx^2$.

(4) Following formula is used to calculate the value of standard deviation:

**FORMULA**

$$\sigma = \sqrt{\frac{\Sigma fx^2}{N}} \text{ or } \sigma = \sqrt{\frac{\Sigma f(X - \bar{X})^2}{N}}$$

**ILLUSTRATION.**

Given the following series, calculate standard deviation by direct method:

| Size | 0–2 | 2–4 | 4–6 | 6–8 | 8–10 | 10–12 |
|---|---|---|---|---|---|---|
| Frequency | 2 | 4 | 6 | 4 | 2 | 6 |

**SOLUTION:**

| Size (X) | Mid-value (m) | Frequency (f) | Multiple of Mid-value and Frequency (fm) | Deviation from Mean Value ($x = m - \bar{X}$) $\bar{X} = 6.5$ | Square of Deviation ($x^2$) | $fx^2$ |
|---|---|---|---|---|---|---|
| 0–2 | 1 | 2 | 2 | – 5.5 | 30.25 | 60.50 |
| 2–4 | 3 | 4 | 12 | – 3.5 | 12.25 | 49.00 |
| 4–6 | 5 | 6 | 30 | – 1.5 | 2.25 | 13.50 |
| 6–8 | 7 | 4 | 28 | + 0.5 | 0.25 | 1.00 |
| 8–10 | 9 | 2 | 18 | + 2.5 | 6.25 | 12.50 |
| 10–12 | 11 | 6 | 66 | + 4.5 | 20.25 | 121.50 |
| | | N = 24 | $\Sigma fm = 156$ | | | $\Sigma fx^2 = 258$ |

$$\bar{X} = \frac{\Sigma fm}{N} = \frac{156}{24} = 6.5$$

$$\sigma = \sqrt{\frac{\Sigma fx^2}{N}} = \sqrt{\frac{258}{24}} = \sqrt{10.75} = 3.28$$

Standard Deviation ($\sigma$) = 3.28.

### (ii) Short-cut Method

This method is the same as used in case of discrete series. The only difference is that whereas in discrete series, deviations are obtained of the actual values of the series, in case of frequency distribution series deviations are obtained of the mid-values of the class intervals. In both the cases, deviations are taken from the mean value of the series. Thus,

**FORMULA**

$$\text{SD or } \sigma = \sqrt{\frac{\Sigma fdx^2}{N} - \left(\frac{\Sigma fdx}{N}\right)^2}$$

**ILLUSTRATION.**

Using short-cut method, calculate standard deviation of the following series:

| Size | 0–2 | 2–4 | 4–6 | 6–8 | 8–10 | 10–12 |
|---|---|---|---|---|---|---|
| Frequency | 2 | 4 | 6 | 4 | 2 | 6 |

**SOLUTION:**

| Size (X) | Mid-value (m) | Frequency (f) | Deviation from Assumed Average (dx=m – A) A=5 | Square of Deviation ($dx^2$) | Multiple of Deviation and the Corresponding Frequency (fdx) | $fdx^2$ |
|---|---|---|---|---|---|---|
| 0–2 | 1 | 2 | – 4 | 16 | – 8 | 32 |
| 2–4 | 3 | 4 | – 2 | 4 | – 8 | 16 |
| 4–6 | 5 | 6 | 0 | 0 | 0 | 0 |
| 6–8 | 7 | 4 | + 2 | 4 | + 8 | 16 |
| 8–10 | 9 | 2 | + 4 | 16 | + 8 | 32 |
| 10–12 | 11 | 6 | + 6 | 36 | + 36 | 216 |
| | | N = 24 | | | $\Sigma fdx=36$ | $\Sigma fdx^2=312$ |

$$\sigma = \sqrt{\frac{\Sigma fdx^2}{N} - \left(\frac{\Sigma fdx}{N}\right)^2} = \sqrt{\frac{312}{24} - \left(\frac{36}{24}\right)^2}$$

$$= \sqrt{13 - 2.25} = \sqrt{10.75} = 3.28$$

Standard Deviation ($\sigma$) = 3.28.

### (iii) Step-deviation Method

This is the most popular method of calculating standard deviation in case of frequency distribution series. It involves the following steps:

(1) Take any value as assumed average, A.

(2) Find out mid-values of the class intervals. Take deviations of the mid-values from A, expressed as 'dx'.

(3) Divide the deviations by their common factor to get $\left(\frac{dx}{C}\right)$, expressed as dx′.

(4) Multiply dx′ with the corresponding frequencies and find their sum total as $\Sigma fdx'$. Also take squares of ($dx'^2$), and multiply them by the corresponding frequencies to get $\Sigma fdx'^2$.

(5) Calculate the value of standard deviation, using the following formula:

**FORMULA**

$$\sigma = \sqrt{\frac{\Sigma fdx'^2}{N} - \left(\frac{\Sigma fdx'}{N}\right)^2} \times C$$

**ILLUSTRATION.**

Using step-deviation method, calculate standard deviation of the following series:

| Marks | 0–10 | 10 20 | 20–30 | 30–40 | 40–50 | 50–60 | 60–70 | 70–80 |
|---|---|---|---|---|---|---|---|---|
| Number of Students | 5 | 10 | 20 | 40 | 30 | 20 | 10 | 4 |

**SOLUTION:**

**Frequency Distribution Series and Standard Deviation (Step-deviation Method)**

| Marks (X) | Mid-value (m) | Frequency (f) | Deviation from Assumed Average (dx = m – A) A = 35 | $dx' = \frac{dx}{C}$ C = 10 | fdx' | $fdx'^2$ |
|---|---|---|---|---|---|---|
| 0–10 | 5 | 5 | – 30 | – 3 | – 15 | 45 |
| 10–20 | 15 | 10 | – 20 | – 2 | – 20 | 40 |
| 20–30 | 25 | 20 | – 10 | – 1 | – 20 | 20 |
| 30–40 | 35(A) | 40 | 0 | 0 | 0 | 0 |
| 40–50 | 45 | 30 | + 10 | +1 | +30 | 30 |
| 50–60 | 55 | 20 | + 20 | +2 | +40 | 80 |
| 60–70 | 65 | 10 | + 30 | +3 | +30 | 90 |
| 70–80 | 75 | 4 | + 40 | +4 | +16 | 64 |
| | | N = 139 | | | $\Sigma fdx'=61$ | $\Sigma fdx'^2=369$ |

$$\sigma = \sqrt{\frac{\Sigma fdx'^2}{N} - \left(\frac{\Sigma fdx'}{N}\right)^2} \times C$$

$$\sigma = \sqrt{\frac{369}{139} - \left(\frac{61}{139}\right)^2} \times 10$$

$$= \sqrt{2.655 - 0.193} = \sqrt{2.462} \times 10 = 15.69$$

Standard Deviation (σ) = 15.69.

**ILLUSTRATION.**

Find out standard deviation of the following data-set, using step-deviation method:

| **Marks** | 20–40 | 40–60 | 60–80 | 80–100 | 100–120 | 120–140 |
|---|---|---|---|---|---|---|
| **Number of Students** | 6 | 9 | 8 | 10 | 11 | 6 |

**SOLUTION:**

| Marks (X) | Mid-value (m) | Frequency (f) | Deviation from Assumed Average (dx = m – A) A = 90 | $dx' = \frac{dx}{C}$ C = 20 | fdx' | $fdx'^2$ |
|---|---|---|---|---|---|---|
| 20–40 | 30 | 6 | – 60 | – 3 | – 18 | 54 |
| 40–60 | 50 | 9 | – 40 | – 2 | – 18 | 36 |
| 60–80 | 70 | 8 | – 20 | – 1 | – 8 | 8 |
| 80–100 | 90 | 10 | 0 | 0 | 0 | 0 |
| 100–120 | 110 | 11 | +20 | +1 | 11 | 11 |
| 120–140 | 130 | 6 | +40 | +2 | 12 | 24 |
| | | N = 50 | | | $\Sigma fdx' = -21$ | $\Sigma fdx'^2 = 133$ |

$$\sigma = \sqrt{\frac{\Sigma fdx'^2}{N} - \left(\frac{\Sigma fdx'}{N}\right)^2} \times C$$

$$\sigma = \sqrt{\frac{133}{50} - \left(\frac{-21}{50}\right)^2} \times 20 \qquad \text{[Here, C = 20]}$$

$$\sigma = \sqrt{2.66 - 0.1764} \times 20 = \sqrt{2.4836} \times 20 = 31.52$$

Standard Deviation (σ) = 31.52.

***Learning by doing***

1. *Calculate standard deviation of the following series:*

| **Size** | 0–5 | 5–10 | 10–15 | 15–20 | 20–25 | 25–30 | 30–35 | 35–40 |
|---|---|---|---|---|---|---|---|---|
| **Frequency** | 2 | 5 | 7 | 13 | 21 | 16 | 8 | 3 |

*(**Ans.** SD or $\sigma$ = 7.80)*

2. *Calculate standard deviation of the following data, using step-deviation method.*

| **Age** | 20–30 | 30–40 | 40–50 | 50–60 | 60–70 | 70–80 | 80–90 |
|---|---|---|---|---|---|---|---|
| **Frequency** | 3 | 61 | 132 | 153 | 140 | 51 | 2 |

*(**Ans.** SD or $\sigma$ = 11.9)*

3. *Find out standard deviation of the distribution of population in 104 villages of a Tehsil, as given below by step-deviation method.*

***Distribution of Population***

| **Population** | **No. of Villages** |
|---|---|
| 0–200 | 10 |
| 200–400 | 28 |
| 400–1,000 | 42 |
| 1,000–2,000 | 18 |
| 2,000–5,000 | 6 |

*(**Ans.** $\sigma$ = 789.11)*

4. *Calculate mean and standard deviation of the following data by short-cut method:*

| **Class Interval** | 10–20 | 20–30 | 30–40 | 40–50 | 50–60 | 60–70 | 70–80 |
|---|---|---|---|---|---|---|---|
| **Frequency** | 5 | 10 | 15 | 20 | 25 | 18 | 7 |

*(**Ans.** $\overline{X}$ = 48.2, SD or $\sigma$ = 15.80)*

## Combined Standard Deviation

Just as it is possible to calculate combined mean of two or more groups, similarly the combined standard deviation of two or more groups can be calculated. The combined standard deviation of two groups is denoted by $\sigma_{12}$ and is computed as follows:

**FORMULA**

$$\sigma_{12} = \sqrt{\frac{N_1\sigma_1^2 + N_2\sigma_2^2 + N_1d_1^2 + N_2d_2^2}{N_1 + N_2}}$$

Where, $\sigma_{12}$ = Combined standard deviation;

$\sigma_1$ = Standard deviation of the first group;

$\sigma_2$ = Standard deviation of the second group;

$d_1 = \overline{X}_1 - \overline{X}_{12}$, $d_2 = \overline{X}_2 - \overline{X}_{12}$.

The above formula can be extended to calculate the standard deviation of three or more groups. For example, combined standard deviation of three groups is given by:

**FORMULA**

$$\sigma_{123} = \sqrt{\frac{N_1\sigma_1^2 + N_2\sigma_2^2 + N_3\sigma_3^2 + N_1d_1^2 + N_2d_2^2 + N_3d_3^2}{N_1 + N_2 + N_3}}$$

Where, $d_1 = \overline{X}_1 - \overline{X}_{123}$; $d_2 = \overline{X}_2 - \overline{X}_{123}$; $d_3 = \overline{X}_3 - \overline{X}_{123}$

**ILLUSTRATION.**

Two samples of size 100 and 150 respectively have means 50 and 60 and standard deviations 5 and 6. Find the mean and standard deviation of the combined sample of size 250.

**SOLUTION:**

Given: $N_1 = 100, \quad \overline{X}_1 = 50, \quad \sigma_1 = 5$

$N_2 = 150, \quad \overline{X}_2 = 60, \quad \sigma_2 = 6$

Now,
$$\overline{X}_{12} = \frac{N_1\overline{X}_1 + N_2\overline{X}_2}{N_1 + N_2}$$

$$= \frac{100 \times 50 + 150 \times 60}{100 + 150} = \frac{5,000 + 9,000}{250}$$

$$= \frac{14,000}{250} = 56$$

$$d_1 = \overline{X}_1 - \overline{X}_{12} = 50 - 56 = -6$$

$$d_2 = \overline{X}_2 - \overline{X}_{12} = 60 - 56 = +4$$

$$\sigma_{12} = \sqrt{\frac{N_1\sigma_1^2 + N_2\sigma_2^2 + N_1d_1^2 + N_2d_2^2}{N_1 + N_2}}$$

$$= \sqrt{\frac{100 \times (5)^2 + 150 \times (6)^2 + 100 \times (-6)^2 + 150 \times (4)^2}{100 + 150}}$$

$$= \sqrt{\frac{100 \times 25 + 150 \times 36 + 100 \times 36 + 150 \times 16}{250}}$$

$$= \sqrt{\frac{2,500 + 5,400 + 3,600 + 2,400}{250}} = \sqrt{\frac{13,900}{250}}$$

$$= \sqrt{55.6} = 7.46$$

Hence, the Combined Mean = 56 and the Combined Standard Deviation = 7.46.

**VARIANCE**

Variance is another measure of dispersion. The term variance was first used by **R.A. Fisher** in 1918. Variance is the square of the standard deviation. Symbolically,

**FORMULA**

$$\text{Variance} = (SD)^2 = \sigma^2$$

Calculation of Variance

(i) $\text{Variance} = \dfrac{\sum f(X - \overline{X})^2}{N}$ (Actual Mean Method)

(ii) $\text{Variance} = \dfrac{\sum fd^2}{N} - \left(\dfrac{\sum fd}{N}\right)^2$ (Assumed Mean Method)

(iii) $\text{Variance} = \left[\dfrac{\sum fd'^2}{N} - \left(\dfrac{\sum fd'}{N}\right)^2\right] \times C^2$ (Step-deviation Method)

**ILLUSTRATION.**

Calculate the mean and variance from the data given below:

| Daily Wages | 0–10 | 10–20 | 20–30 | 30–40 | 40–50 |
|---|---|---|---|---|---|
| Number of Workers | 2 | 7 | 10 | 5 | 3 |

**SOLUTION:**

**Calculation of Mean and Variance**

| Daily Wages | Frequency (f) | Mid-value (m) | Deviation from Assumed Average (d = m – 25) A = 25 | $d' = \frac{d}{C}$ C = 10 | fd′ | $fd'^2$ |
|---|---|---|---|---|---|---|
| 0–10 | 2 | 5 | – 20 | – 2 | – 4 | 8 |
| 10–20 | 7 | 15 | – 10 | – 1 | – 7 | 7 |
| 20–30 | 10 | 25 (A) | 0 | 0 | 0 | 0 |
| 30–40 | 5 | 35 | + 10 | + 1 | +5 | 5 |
| 40–50 | 3 | 45 | + 20 | + 2 | +6 | 12 |
| | Σf = N= 27 | | | | Σfd′=0 | $\Sigma fd'^2=32$ |

$$\overline{X} = A + \frac{\Sigma fd'}{\Sigma f} \times C$$

$$= 25 + \frac{0}{27} \times 10 = 25$$

$$\text{Variance } (\sigma^2) = \left[\frac{\sum fd'^2}{N} - \left(\frac{\sum fd'}{N}\right)^2\right] \times C^2$$

$$= \left[\frac{32}{27} - \left(\frac{0}{27}\right)^2\right] \times 10^2$$

$$\Rightarrow \quad \sigma^2 = 1.185 \times 100 = 118.51$$

Mean = 25, Variance ($\sigma^2$) = 118.51.

**COEFFICIENT OF VARIATION**

Coefficient of variation is 100 times the coefficient of dispersion based on standard deviation of a statistical series. It was first used by the famous statistician **Karl Pearson**. That is the reason why it is called **Karl Pearson's Coefficient of Variation**. In the words of **Karl Pearson**, *"Coefficient of variation is the percentage variation in the mean, the standard deviation being considered as the total variation in the mean."*

In order to calculate coefficient of variation, standard deviation of the series is divided by mean of the series and multiplied by 100. It is estimated using the following formula:

**Important**

Coefficient of variation and variance are the different concepts.

Coefficient of variation is estimated as $\frac{\sigma}{\overline{X}} \times 100$; variance is simply the square of standard deviation.

(Variance = $\sigma^2$)

**FORMULA**

Coefficient of Variation or CV

$$= \frac{\sigma}{\overline{X}} \times 100$$

= Coefficient of Standard Deviation × 100

Coefficient of Variation (CV) is 100 times the coefficient of dispersion based on standard deviation of a statistical series.

Coefficient of variation is used to compare the variability, homogeneity, stability and uniformity of two different statistical series. Higher value of coefficient of variation suggests greater degree of variability and lesser degree of stability. On the other hand, a lower value of coefficient of variation suggests lower degree of variability and higher degree of stability, uniformity, homogeneity and consistency.

## Calculation of Coefficient of Variation

### (1) Individual Series and Coefficient of Variation

**Illustration.**

Calculate coefficient of variation of the following series:

| **S. No.** | 1 | 2 | 3 | 4 | 5 | 6 | 7 | 8 | 9 | 10 |
|---|---|---|---|---|---|---|---|---|---|---|
| **Marks** | 53 | 58 | 25 | 30 | 54 | 42 | 32 | 48 | 46 | 52 |

**Solution:**

**Calculation of CV—Individual Series**

| S. No. | Marks (X) | Deviation from Mean ($x = X - \overline{X}$) $\overline{X} = 44$ | Square of Deviation $(X - \overline{X})^2$ or $x^2$ |
|---|---|---|---|
| 1 | 53 | 9 | 81 |
| 2 | 58 | 14 | 196 |
| 3 | 25 | – 19 | 361 |
| 4 | 30 | – 14 | 196 |
| 5 | 54 | 10 | 100 |
| 6 | 42 | – 2 | 4 |
| 7 | 32 | – 12 | 144 |
| 8 | 48 | 4 | 16 |
| 9 | 46 | 2 | 4 |
| 10 | 52 | 8 | 64 |
| N = 10 | $\Sigma X = 440$ | | $\Sigma x^2 = \Sigma(X - \overline{X})^2 = 1,166$ |

$$\overline{X} = \frac{\Sigma X}{N} = \frac{440}{10} = 44$$

$$\sigma = \sqrt{\frac{\Sigma x^2}{N}} = \sqrt{\frac{\Sigma (X - \overline{X})^2}{N}}$$

$$= \sqrt{\frac{1,166}{10}} = \sqrt{116.6} = 10.8$$

$$CV = \frac{\sigma}{\overline{X}} \times 100 = \frac{10.8}{44} \times 100$$

$$= 24.55$$

Coefficient of Variation = 24.55.

### (2) Discrete Series or Frequency Array and Coefficient of Variation

Following illustration explains the calculation of CV for discrete frequency series.

**ILLUSTRATION.**

Calculate coefficient of variation of the following data:

| **Items** | 10 | 12 | 14 | 16 | 18 | 20 | 22 |
|---|---|---|---|---|---|---|---|
| **Frequency** | 4 | 6 | 10 | 15 | 9 | 4 | 2 |

**SOLUTION:**

**Calculation of CV**

| Items | Frequency (f) | Deviation from Assumed Average (dx = X – A) A=16 | fdx | $fdx^2$ |
|---|---|---|---|---|
| 10 | 4 | – 6 | – 24 | 144 |
| 12 | 6 | – 4 | – 24 | 96 |
| 14 | 10 | – 2 | – 20 | 40 |
| 16 | 15 | 0 | 0 | 0 |
| 18 | 9 | 2 | +18 | 36 |
| 20 | 4 | 4 | +16 | 64 |
| 22 | 2 | 6 | +12 | 72 |
| | N = 50 | | Σfdx=–22 | $\Sigma fdx^2$=452 |

$$\bar{X} = A + \frac{\Sigma fdx}{N} = 16 + \frac{-22}{50} = 15.56$$

$$\sigma = \sqrt{\frac{\Sigma fdx^2}{N} - \left(\frac{\Sigma fdx}{N}\right)^2}$$

$$\sigma = \sqrt{\frac{452}{50} - \left(\frac{-22}{50}\right)^2} = \sqrt{9.04 - (-0.44)^2}$$

$$\sigma = \sqrt{9.04 - 0.1936} = \sqrt{8.8464} = 2.97$$

$$CV = \frac{\sigma}{\bar{X}} \times 100 = \frac{2.97}{15.56} \times 100 = 19.09$$

Coefficient of Variation = 19.09.

### (3) Frequency Distribution Series and Coefficient of Variation

**ILLUSTRATION.**

Calculate coefficient of variation, given the following data-set:

| **Marks** | 0–10 | 10–20 | 20–30 | 30–40 | 40–50 | 50–60 | 60–70 |
|---|---|---|---|---|---|---|---|
| **Number of Students** | 2 | 4 | 5 | 9 | 10 | 5 | 15 |

**SOLUTION:**

**Calculation of CV**

| Marks | Mid-value (m) | Frequency (f) | Deviation from Assumed Average (dx = m – A) A = 35 | $dx' = \frac{dx}{C}$ C = 10 | $dx'^2$ | fdx' | $fdx'^2$ |
|---|---|---|---|---|---|---|---|
| 0–10 | 5 | 2 | – 30 | – 3 | 9 | – 6 | 18 |
| 10–20 | 15 | 4 | – 20 | – 2 | 4 | – 8 | 16 |
| 20–30 | 25 | 5 | – 10 | – 1 | 1 | – 5 | 5 |
| 30–40 | 35 (A) | 9 | 0 | 0 | 0 | 0 | 0 |
| 40–50 | 45 | 10 | +10 | +1 | 1 | +10 | 10 |
| 50–60 | 55 | 5 | +20 | +2 | 4 | +10 | 20 |
| 60–70 | 65 | 15 | +30 | +3 | 9 | +45 | 135 |
| | | N = 50 | | | | Σfdx' = 46 | Σfdx'²= 204 |

$$\overline{X} = A + \frac{\Sigma fdx'}{N} \times C$$

$$= 35 + \frac{46}{50} \times 10 = 44.2$$

$$\sigma = \sqrt{\frac{\Sigma fdx'^2}{N} - \left(\frac{\Sigma fdx'}{N}\right)^2} \times C$$

$$= \sqrt{\frac{204}{50} - \left(\frac{46}{50}\right)^2} \times 10 = \sqrt{4.08 - (0.92)^2} \times 10$$

$$= \sqrt{4.08 - 0.8464} \times 10 = \sqrt{3.2336} \times 10$$

$$= 1.798 \times 10$$

$$= 17.98$$

$$CV = \frac{\sigma}{\overline{X}} \times 100$$

$$= \frac{17.98}{44.2} \times 100 = 40.68$$

Coefficient of Variation = 40.68.

**ILLUSTRATION.**

Batsmen X and Y score following runs in different innings they played in a test series. Which of the two is a better scorer? Who is more consistent?

| X | 12 | 115 | 6 | 73 | 7 | 19 | 119 | 36 | 84 | 29 |
|---|---|---|---|---|---|---|---|---|---|---|
| Y | 47 | 12 | 76 | 42 | 4 | 51 | 37 | 48 | 13 | 0 |

**SOLUTION:**

In order to determine which of the two is a better scorer, we should compare average runs scored by two batsmen in different innings. And, in order to determine consistency of batting we should compare CV of the runs scored by the batsmen in different series.

**Estimation of Mean and CV**

| Batsman-X | | | Batsman-Y | | |
|---|---|---|---|---|---|
| X | (x=X – $\bar{X}$) $\bar{X}$ = 50 | $x^2$ | Y | (y=Y – $\bar{Y}$) $\bar{Y}$ = 33 | $y^2$ |
| 12 | – 38 | 1,444 | 47 | + 14 | 196 |
| 115 | + 65 | 4,225 | 12 | – 21 | 441 |
| 6 | – 44 | 1,936 | 76 | + 43 | 1,849 |
| 73 | + 23 | 529 | 42 | + 9 | 81 |
| 7 | – 43 | 1,849 | 4 | – 29 | 841 |
| 19 | – 31 | 961 | 51 | + 18 | 324 |
| 119 | + 69 | 4,761 | 37 | + 4 | 16 |
| 36 | – 14 | 196 | 48 | + 15 | 225 |
| 84 | + 34 | 1,156 | 13 | – 20 | 400 |
| 29 | – 21 | 441 | 0 | – 33 | 1,089 |
| ΣX=500 | | $\Sigma x^2$= 17,498 | ΣY=330 | | $\Sigma y^2$ = 5,462 |

**Batsman X:** $\bar{X} = \frac{\Sigma X}{N} = \frac{500}{10} = 50$

$$\sigma_X = \sqrt{\frac{\Sigma x^2}{N}} = \sqrt{\frac{17,498}{10}} = \sqrt{1,749.8} = 41.83$$

and $CV_x = \frac{\sigma}{\bar{X}} \times 100 = \frac{41.83}{50} \times 100 = 83.66$

**Batsman Y:** $\bar{Y} = \frac{\Sigma Y}{N} = \frac{330}{10} = 33$

$$\sigma_Y = \sqrt{\frac{\Sigma y^2}{N}} = \sqrt{\frac{5,462}{10}} = \sqrt{546.2} = 23.37$$

and $CV_Y = \frac{\sigma}{\bar{Y}} \times 100 = \frac{23.37}{33} \times 100 = 70.82$

Since average score of X is more than that of Y, we conclude that X is a better batsman. But batting of X shows greater CV than Y. Hence, Y is relatively more consistent in batting than X.

**ILLUSTRATION.**

Two factories A and B are located in some Industrial estate. Average wage and its standard deviation are given below separately for A and B. Find out coefficient of variation.

| Factory | Average Weekly Wage | S.D. | Number of Workers |
|---|---|---|---|
| A | 35 | 5 | 476 |
| B | 30 | 10 | 524 |

**SOLUTION:**

| Coefficient of Variation of Factory A | Coefficient of Variation of Factory B |
|---|---|
| $CV_A = \frac{\sigma}{\bar{X}} \times 100$ <br> $= \frac{5}{35} \times 100 = 14.29$ | $CV_B = \frac{\sigma}{\bar{X}} \times 100$ <br> $= \frac{10}{30} \times 100 = 33.33$ |

***Learning by doing***

1. *Following are the marks obtained by 20 students in statistics. Find out coefficient of variation of the marks.*

| 62 | 85 | 73 | 81 | 74 | 58 | 66 | 72 | 54 | 84 |
|---|---|---|---|---|---|---|---|---|---|
| 65 | 50 | 83 | 62 | 85 | 52 | 80 | 86 | 71 | 75 |

(*Ans.* $\overline{X} = 70.9$, $\sigma = 11.44$, $CV = 16.14$)

2. *Calculate coefficient of variation of the following data:*

| S. No. | 1 | 2 | 3 | 4 | 5 | 6 | 7 | 8 |
|---|---|---|---|---|---|---|---|---|
| Value | 25 | 42 | 33 | 48 | 45 | 29 | 43 | 39 |

(*Ans.* $\overline{X} = 38$, $\sigma = 7.63$, $CV = 20.08$)

3. *Given the following data, calculate coefficient of variation:*

| Age | 20–30 | 30–40 | 40–50 | 50–60 | 60–70 | 70–80 | 80–90 |
|---|---|---|---|---|---|---|---|
| Number of Students | 3 | 61 | 132 | 153 | 140 | 51 | 2 |

(*Ans.* $\overline{X} = 54.72$, $\sigma = 11.87$, $CV = 21.69$)

### A Mathematical Property of Standard Deviation

The sum of the squares of the deviations of items from the arithmetic mean is minimum.

| Deviations taken from Mean | | | Deviations from Assumed Mean | | |
|---|---|---|---|---|---|
| X | $x = X - \overline{X}$ $\overline{X} = 6$ | $x^2$ | X | $d = X - A$ | $d^2$ |
| 2 | – 4 | 16 | 2 | – 2 | 4 |
| 4 | – 2 | 4 | 4 (A) | 0 | 0 |
| 6 | 0 | 0 | 6 | + 2 | 4 |
| 8 | + 2 | 4 | 8 | + 4 | 16 |
| 10 | + 4 | 16 | 10 | + 6 | 36 |
| $\Sigma X = 30$ | | $\Sigma x^2 = 40$ | | | $\Sigma d^2 = 60$ |

## Merits and Demerits of Standard Deviation

### Merits

(1) **Based on all Values:** The calculation of standard deviation is based on all the values of a series. It does not ignore any value. Accordingly, it is a comprehensive measure of dispersion.

(2) **Certain Measure:** Standard deviation is a clear and certain measure of dispersion. Therefore, it can be used in all situations.

(3) **Little Effect of a change in Sample:** Change in sample causes little effect on standard deviation. This is because deviation is based on all the values of a sample.

(4) **Algebraic Treatment:** Standard deviation is capable of further algebraic treatment.

### Demerits

(1) **Difficult:** It is difficult to calculate and make use of standard deviation as a measure of dispersion.

(2) **More Importance to Extreme Value:** In the calculation of standard deviation, extreme values tend to get greater importance.

## Lorenz Curve

Lorenz curve is another important measure of variability of the statistical series. This curve was first used by Max Lorenz. Hence, it is called Lorenz Curve. These curves are generally used to measure variability in the distribution of income and wealth.

**What is Lorenz Curve?**

It is a curve that shows deviation of actual distribution (of income or wealth) from the line showing equal distribution.

*Lorenz curve is a measure of deviation of actual distribution from the line of equal distribution*. This is a cumulative percentage curve. The extent of deviation of the actual distribution from the equal distribution is called Lorenz coefficient. Greater the distance of *Lorenz curve from the line of equal distribution more is the inequality or variability in its series. On the other hand, closer is the Lorenz curve to the line of equal distribution, lower will be the variability or degree of inequality*.

### Construction of Lorenz Curve

Following steps are involved in the construction of a Lorenz Curve:

(1) First of all, the series is converted into a cumulative frequency series. The cumulative sum of the items (or mid-values of class intervals) is assumed to be 100 and the different items are converted into percentages of the cumulative sum. Likewise, cumulative sum of the frequencies is assumed to be 100 and different frequencies are converted into percentages of the sum of the frequencies.

(2) Cumulative frequencies are plotted on X-axis of a graph, while cumulative items are plotted on the Y-axis.

(3) On both axes, we start from 0 to 100 and both X and Y axes take the values from 0 to 100.

(4) Draw a diagonal line joining the origin (0, 0) with the cumulative frequencies (100, 100). This shows equal distribution. It is, therefore, called 'Equality Line' or Line of Equal Distribution.

(5) Actual data are plotted on the graph and a curve is obtained by joining different points. This curve shows actual distribution.

(6) The actual distribution curve is called Lorenz curve. Closeness of Lorenz curve to the Equal Distribution Line shows lesser variation in the distribution. Larger the gap between the actual distribution curve and the Lorenz Line, greater is the variation. If two Lorenz curves are drawn on the same graph paper, the one which is further away from the equal distribution line shows greater variation.

### Illustration.

Draw a Lorenz curve of the data given below:

| Income (₹) | 100 | 200 | 400 | 500 | 800 |
|---|---|---|---|---|---|
| Number of Persons | 80 | 70 | 50 | 30 | 20 |

**SOLUTION:**

| Income (X) | Cumulative Sum | Cumulative Percentage | Number of Persons (Frequency) | Cumulative Frequency | Cumulative Percentage of Frequency |
|---|---|---|---|---|---|
| 100 | 100 | 5 | 80 | 80 | 32 |
| 200 | 300 | 15 | 70 | 150 | 60 |
| 400 | 700 | 35 | 50 | 200 | 80 |
| 500 | 1,200 | 60 | 30 | 230 | 92 |
| 800 | 2,000 | 100 | 20 | 250 | 100 |
| ΣX = 2,000 | | | Σf = 250 | | |

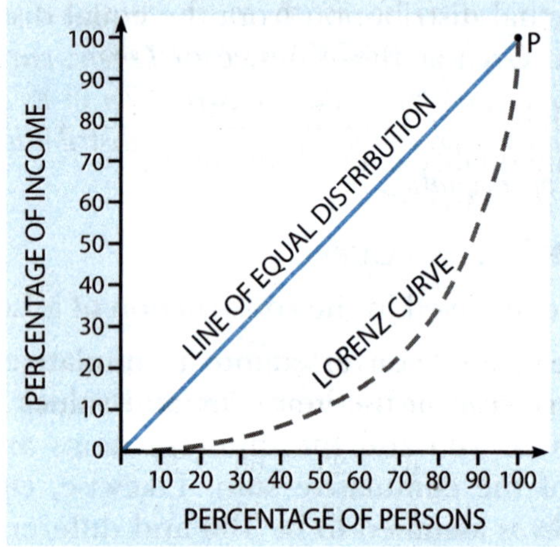


**ILLUSTRATION.**

Show inequality in wages in two different firms using Lorenz Curve approach, given the following data:

| Wages (₹) | 50–70 | 70–90 | 90–110 | 110–130 | 130–150 |
|---|---|---|---|---|---|
| Number of Workers A | 20 | 15 | 20 | 25 | 20 |
| Number of Workers B | 150 | 100 | 90 | 110 | 50 |

**SOLUTION:**

**Estimation of Cumulative Sum and Percentage**

| Wages (₹) | Mid-value (X) | Cumulative Sum | Cumulative % | Firm A | | | Firm B | | |
|---|---|---|---|---|---|---|---|---|---|
| | | | | Number of Workers or Frequency | Cumulative Frequency | Cumulative % | Number of Workers or Frequency | Cumulative Frequency | Cumulative % |
| 50–70 | 60 | 60 | 12 | 20 | 20 | 20 | 150 | 150 | 30 |
| 70–90 | 80 | 140 | 28 | 15 | 35 | 35 | 100 | 250 | 50 |
| 90–110 | 100 | 240 | 48 | 20 | 55 | 55 | 90 | 340 | 68 |
| 110–130 | 120 | 360 | 72 | 25 | 80 | 80 | 110 | 450 | 90 |
| 130–150 | 140 | 500 | 100 | 20 | 100 | 100 | 50 | 500 | 100 |
| | ΣX=500 | | | | | | | | |

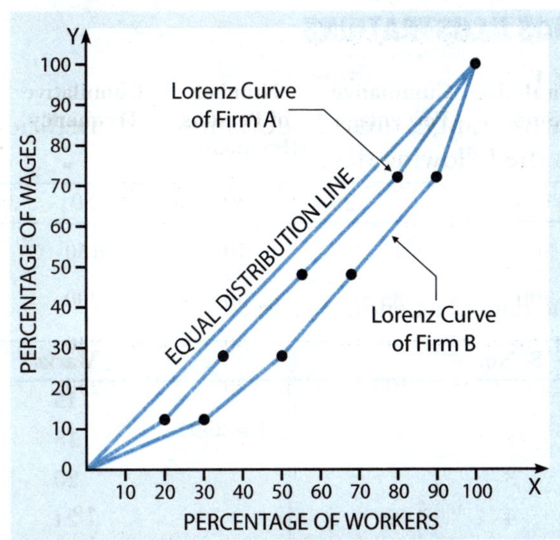


**Observation:** Both in firm A and firm B distribution of wages is far from equal. However, inequality is more pronounced in case of firm B than firm A as the Lorenz curve for firm B is farther away from the line of equal distribution.

***Learning by doing***

1. *The following table shows number of firms in two different areas 'A' and 'B' according to their annual profits. Present the data by way of Lorenz curve.*

| Profit ('000' ₹) | 6 | 25 | 60 | 84 | 105 | 150 | 170 | 400 |
|---|---|---|---|---|---|---|---|---|
| **Firms in Area A** | 6 | 11 | 13 | 14 | 15 | 17 | 10 | 14 |
| **Firms in Area B** | 2 | 38 | 52 | 28 | 38 | 26 | 12 | 4 |

2. *Make a Lorenz curve of the following data:*

| Income | 500 | 1,000 | 2,000 | 3,000 | 3,500 |
|---|---|---|---|---|---|
| **Number in Class 'A' (000)** | 4 | 6 | 8 | 12 | 10 |
| **Number in Class 'B' (000)** | 8 | 7 | 5 | 3 | 2 |

## Application of Lorenz Curve

Lorenz Curve is a graphic measure of dispersion in a statistical series. It is a very simple measure and provides an immediate glimpse of the degree of variation in a statistical distribution from its mean value. It was first used by **Prof. Lorenz** for the measurement of economic inequality relating to the distribution of income and wealth across different nations or across different periods of time for the same nation. With the passage of time the application of Lorenz curve has widely spread to measure disparity of distribution relating to various parameters like distribution of profits and wages. Briefly, Lorenz curve as a measure of dispersion is presently applied to the following parameters, *viz.*,

(i) distribution of income,
(ii) distribution of wealth,
(iii) distribution of wages,
(iv) distribution of profits,
(v) distribution of production, and
(vi) distribution of population.

## MISCELLANEOUS ILLUSTRATIONS

### ILLUSTRATION 1.

Find inter quartile range, quartile deviation and coefficient of quartile deviation from the following data:

| Marks | 28 | 18 | 20 | 24 | 27 | 30 | 15 |
|---|---|---|---|---|---|---|---|

**SOLUTION:**

First arrange the data in ascending order:

| S. No. | Marks |
|---|---|
| 1 | 15 |
| 2 | 18 |
| 3 | 20 |
| 4 | 24 |
| 5 | 27 |
| 6 | 28 |
| 7 | 30 |
| N = 7 | |

$$Q_1 = \text{Size of } \left(\frac{N+1}{4}\right)\text{th item} = \text{Size of } \left(\frac{7+1}{4}\right)\text{th item}$$

$$= \text{Size of 2nd item} = 18 \text{ marks}$$

$$Q_3 = \text{Size of } 3\left(\frac{N+1}{4}\right)\text{th item} = \text{Size of } 3\left(\frac{7+1}{4}\right)\text{th item}$$

$$= \text{Size of 6th item} = 28 \text{ marks}$$

$$\text{Inter Quartile Range} = Q_3 - Q_1 = 28 - 18 = 10$$

$$\text{Quartile Deviation} = \frac{Q_3 - Q_1}{2} = \frac{28 - 18}{2} = 5$$

$$\text{Coefficient of Quartile Deviation} = \frac{Q_3 - Q_1}{Q_3 + Q_1} = \frac{28-18}{28+18} = \frac{10}{46} = 0.217$$

### ILLUSTRATION 2.

Calculate inter quartile range, quartile deviation and the coefficient of quartile deviation from the following data:

| Wages (₹) | 31 | 33 | 35 | 37 | 39 | 41 | 43 |
|---|---|---|---|---|---|---|---|
| Number of Workers | 12 | 18 | 16 | 14 | 12 | 8 | 7 |

**SOLUTION:**

| Wages (₹) | Frequency (f) | Cumulative Frequency |
|---|---|---|
| 31 | 12 | 12 |
| 33 | 18 | 30 |
| 35 | 16 | 46 |
| 37 | 14 | 60 |
| 39 | 12 | 72 |
| 41 | 8 | 80 |
| 43 | 7 | 87 |
| | N = 87 | |

$$Q_1 = \text{Size of}\left(\frac{N+1}{4}\right)\text{th item} = \text{Size of}\left(\frac{87+1}{4}\right)\text{th item}$$

$$= \text{Size of 22nd item} = 33$$

$$Q_3 = \text{Size of } 3\left(\frac{N+1}{4}\right)\text{th item} = \text{Size of } 3\left(\frac{87+1}{4}\right)\text{ th item}$$

$$= \text{Size of 66th item} = 39$$

Inter Quartile Range = $Q_3 - Q_1 = 39 - 33 = 6$

Quartile Deviation = $\frac{Q_3 - Q_1}{2} = \frac{39-33}{2} = \frac{6}{2} = 3$

Coefficient of Quartile Deviation = $\frac{Q_3 - Q_1}{Q_3 + Q_1} = \frac{39-33}{39+33} = \frac{6}{72} = 0.083$

**ILLUSTRATION 3.**

Find the range which contains the middle 50% of the items and coefficient of quartile deviation from the following data:

| Class Interval | 11–20 | 21–30 | 31–40 | 41–50 | 51–60 |
|---|---|---|---|---|---|
| Frequency | 4 | 8 | 20 | 12 | 6 |

**SOLUTION:**

Since, we are given inclusive series, we first convert it into exclusive one:

**Calculation of Coefficient of Quartile Deviation**

| Class Interval | Frequency (f) | Cumulative Frequency |
|---|---|---|
| 10.5–20.5 | 4 | 4 |
| 20.5–30.5 | 8 | **12** |
| **30.5–40.5** | **20** | **32** |
| **40.5–50.5** | **12** | 44 |
| 50.5–60.5 | 6 | 50 |
| | $\Sigma f = N = 50$ | |

$$Q_1 = \text{Size of}\left(\frac{N}{4}\right)\text{th item}$$

$$= \text{Size of}\left(\frac{50}{4}\right)\text{th item} = \text{Size of 12.5th item}$$

$\therefore$ $Q_1$ lies in the class 30.5–40.5.

$$Q_1 = l_1 + \frac{\left(\frac{N}{4}\right) - \text{c.f.}}{f} \times i$$

$$= 30.5 + \frac{\frac{50}{4} - 12}{20} \times 10 = 30.5 + \frac{12.5 - 12}{20} \times 10$$

$$= 30.5 + \frac{0.5}{20} \times 10$$

$$= 30.5 + 0.25 = 30.75$$

$$Q_3 = \text{Size of } 3\left(\frac{N}{4}\right)\text{th item}$$

$$= \text{Size of } 3\left(\frac{50}{4}\right)\text{th item}$$

$$= \text{Size of 37.5th item}$$

$\therefore$ $Q_3$ lies in the class 40.5–50.5.

$$Q_3 = l_1 + \frac{3\left(\frac{N}{4}\right) - \text{c.f.}}{f} \times i$$

$$= 40.5 + \frac{3\left(\frac{50}{4}\right) - 32}{12} \times 10 = 40.5 + \frac{37.5 - 32}{12} \times 10$$

$$= 40.5 + \frac{5.5}{12} \times 10$$

$$= 40.5 + 4.58 = 45.08$$

**To find the middle 50% of the items**, compute $Q_3 - Q_1$, *i.e.*, inter quartile range.

Inter Quartile Range = $Q_3 - Q_1$ = 45.08 – 30.75 = 14.33

$$\text{Coefficient of Quartile Deviation} = \frac{Q_3 - Q_1}{Q_3 + Q_1}$$

$$= \frac{45.08 - 30.75}{45.08 + 30.75} = \frac{14.33}{75.83}$$

$$= 0.19$$

**ILLUSTRATION 4.**

Calculate the mean deviation from mean as well as from median and coefficient of mean deviation from the following data:

| Marks | 20 | 22 | 25 | 38 | 40 | 50 | 65 | 70 | 75 |
|---|---|---|---|---|---|---|---|---|---|

**SOLUTION:**

**Calculation of Mean Deviation**

| Marks (X) | Deviation from Mean $\lvert d\bar{x}\rvert = \lvert X - \bar{X}\rvert$ $\bar{X} = 45$ | Deviation from Median $\lvert dm\rvert = \lvert X - M\rvert$ M = 40 |
|---|---|---|
| 20 | 25 | 20 |
| 22 | 23 | 18 |
| 25 | 20 | 15 |
| 38 | 7 | 2 |
| 40 | 5 | 0 |
| 50 | 5 | 10 |
| 65 | 20 | 25 |
| 70 | 25 | 30 |
| 75 | 30 | 35 |
| N = 9, $\Sigma X = 405$ | $\Sigma\lvert d\bar{x}\rvert = 160$ | $\Sigma\lvert dm\rvert = 155$ |

$$\overline{X} = \frac{\Sigma X}{N} = \frac{405}{9} = 45$$

Mean Deviation from Mean

$$MD_{\overline{X}} = \frac{\Sigma|d\overline{x}|}{N} = \frac{160}{9} = 17.78$$

Coefficient of Mean Deviation

$$= \frac{MD_{\overline{X}}}{\overline{X}} = \frac{17.78}{45} = 0.40$$

$$\text{Median} = \text{Size of} \left(\frac{N+1}{2}\right)\text{th item}$$

$$= \text{Size of} \left(\frac{9+1}{2}\right)\text{th item}$$

$$= \text{Size of 5th item} = 40$$

Mean Deviation from Median

$$MD_m = \frac{\Sigma|dm|}{N} = \frac{155}{9} = 17.22$$

Coefficient of Mean Deviation

$$= \frac{MD_m}{M} = \frac{17.22}{40} = 0.43$$

**ILLUSTRATION 5.**

Calculate mean deviation and its coefficient from mean from the following data:

| Marks | 0–10 | 10–20 | 20–30 | 30–40 | 40–50 |
|---|---|---|---|---|---|
| Number of Students | 6 | 28 | 51 | 11 | 4 |

**SOLUTION:**

**Calculation of Mean Deviation from Mean**

| Marks (X) | Mid-value (m) | Frequency (f) | Multiple of Mid-value and Frequency (fm) | Deviation from Mean $\|d\overline{x}\| = \|m - \overline{X}\|$ $\overline{X} = 22.9$ | Multiple of Deviation and the Corresponding Frequency $(f\|d\overline{x}\|)$ |
|---|---|---|---|---|---|
| 0–10 | 5 | 6 | 30 | 17.9 | 107.4 |
| 10–20 | 15 | 28 | 420 | 7.9 | 221.2 |
| 20–30 | 25 | 51 | 1,275 | 2.1 | 107.1 |
| 30–40 | 35 | 11 | 385 | 12.1 | 133.1 |
| 40–50 | 45 | 4 | 180 | 22.1 | 88.4 |
| | | $\Sigma f = 100$ | $\Sigma fm = 2{,}290$ | | $\Sigma f\|d\overline{x}\| = 657.2$ |

$$\overline{X} = \frac{\Sigma fm}{\Sigma f} = \frac{2{,}290}{100} = 22.9$$

Mean Deviation from Mean

$$MD_{\overline{X}} = \frac{\Sigma f|d\overline{x}|}{\Sigma f} = \frac{657.2}{100} = 6.572$$

Coefficient of Mean Deviation

$$= \frac{MD_{\overline{X}}}{\overline{X}} = \frac{6.572}{22.9} = 0.287$$

$MD_{\overline{X}} = 6.572$, CMD = 0.287

**ILLUSTRATION 6.**

Calculate mean deviation and its coefficient from median from the following data:

| **Marks** | 0–10 | 10–20 | 20–30 | 30–40 | 40–50 |
|---|---|---|---|---|---|
| **Number of Students** | 5 | 8 | 15 | 16 | 6 |

**SOLUTION:**

**Calculation of Mean Deviation from Median**

| Marks (X) | Mid-value (m) | Frequency (f) | Cumulative Frequency | Deviation from Median $\|dm\| = \|m - M\|$ M = 28 | Multiple of Deviation and the Corresponding Frequency (f\|dm\|) |
|---|---|---|---|---|---|
| 0–10 | 5 | 5 | 5 | 23 | 115 |
| 10–20 | 15 | 8 | **13(c.f.)** | 13 | 104 |
| **($l_1$)20–30** | 25 | **15 (f)** | 28 | 3 | 45 |
| 30–40 | 35 | 16 | 44 | 7 | 112 |
| 40–50 | 45 | 6 | 50 | 17 | 102 |
| | | Σf=N=50 | | | Σf\|dm\|=478 |

$$M = \text{Size of } \left(\frac{N}{2}\right)\text{th item}$$

$$= \text{Size of } \left(\frac{50}{2}\right)\text{th item}$$

$$= \text{Size of 25th item}$$

20–30 is the median class interval.

$$M = l_1 + \frac{\frac{N}{2} - c.f.}{f} \times i$$

$$= 20 + \frac{\frac{50}{2} - 13}{15} \times 10 = 20 + \frac{25 - 13}{15} \times 10$$

$$= 20 + \frac{12}{15} \times 10 = 20 + 8 = 28$$

Mean Deviation from Median

$$MD_m = \frac{\Sigma f|dm|}{\Sigma f} = \frac{478}{50} = 9.56$$

Coefficient of Mean Deviation

$$= \frac{MD_m}{M} = \frac{9.56}{28} = 0.34$$

$MD_m = 9.56$, $CMD_m = 0.34$.

**ILLUSTRATION 7.**

Calculate the standard deviation from the following data:

| Size | 16 | 20 | 18 | 19 | 20 | 20 | 28 | 17 | 22 | 20 |
|---|---|---|---|---|---|---|---|---|---|---|

**SOLUTION:**

**Calculation of Standard Deviation**

| Size (X) | Deviation ($x = X - \overline{X}$) $\overline{X} = 20$ | Square of Deviation ($x^2$) |
|---|---|---|
| 16 | – 4 | 16 |
| 20 | 0 | 0 |
| 18 | – 2 | 4 |
| 19 | – 1 | 1 |
| 20 | 0 | 0 |
| 20 | 0 | 0 |
| 28 | 8 | 64 |
| 17 | – 3 | 9 |
| 22 | 2 | 4 |
| 20 | 0 | 0 |
| N = 10, $\Sigma X = 200$ | $\Sigma x = 0$ | $\Sigma x^2 = 98$ |

$$\overline{X} = \frac{\Sigma X}{N} = \frac{200}{10} = 20$$

$$\sigma = \sqrt{\frac{\Sigma x^2}{N}} = \sqrt{\frac{98}{10}} = \sqrt{9.8} = 3.13$$

Standard Deviation = 3.13.

**ILLUSTRATION 8.**

Using Short-cut Method, calculate the standard deviation from the data given below:

| Size | 3 | 4 | 5 | 6 | 7 | 8 | 9 |
|---|---|---|---|---|---|---|---|
| Frequency | 7 | 8 | 10 | 12 | 4 | 3 | 2 |

**SOLUTION:**

**Calculation of Standard Deviation—Short-cut Method**

| Size (X) | Frequency (f) | Deviation from Assumed Average (dx = X – A) A = 6 | Square of Deviation $(dx)^2$ | fdx | $fdx^2$ |
|---|---|---|---|---|---|
| 3 | 7 | – 3 | 9 | – 21 | 63 |
| 4 | 8 | – 2 | 4 | – 16 | 32 |
| 5 | 10 | – 1 | 1 | – 10 | 10 |
| 6 | 12 | 0 | 0 | 0 | 0 |
| 7 | 4 | + 1 | 1 | + 4 | 4 |
| 8 | 3 | + 2 | 4 | + 6 | 12 |
| 9 | 2 | + 3 | 9 | + 6 | 18 |
| | N = 46 | | | $\Sigma fdx = -31$ | $\Sigma fdx^2 = 139$ |

$$\sigma = \sqrt{\frac{\Sigma fdx^2}{N} - \left(\frac{\Sigma fdx}{N}\right)^2} = \sqrt{\frac{139}{46} - \left(\frac{-31}{46}\right)^2}$$

$$= \sqrt{3.0217 - 0.4542}$$

$$= \sqrt{2.5675} = 1.6$$

Standard Deviation = 1.6.

**ILLUSTRATION 9.**

Using Step-deviation Method, find out standard deviation from the following data-set:

| Age (under) | 10 | 20 | 30 | 40 | 50 | 60 |
|---|---|---|---|---|---|---|
| **Number of Persons** | 15 | 32 | 51 | 78 | 97 | 109 |

**SOLUTION:**

Since the cumulative frequencies are given, firstly we find the simple frequencies:

**Calculation of Standard Deviation—Step-deviation Method**

| Age | Mid-value (m) | Frequency (f) | Deviation from Assumed Average (dx=m – A) A=35 | $dx' = \frac{dx}{C}$ C = 10 | $dx'^2$ | $fdx'$ | $fdx'^2$ |
|---|---|---|---|---|---|---|---|
| 0–10 | 5 | 15 | – 30 | – 3 | 9 | – 45 | 135 |
| 10–20 | 15 | 17 | – 20 | – 2 | 4 | – 34 | 68 |
| 20–30 | 25 | 19 | – 10 | – 1 | 1 | – 19 | 19 |
| 30–40 | 35 (A) | 27 | 0 | 0 | 0 | 0 | 0 |
| 40–50 | 45 | 19 | +10 | +1 | 1 | 19 | 19 |
| 50–60 | 55 | 12 | +20 | +2 | 4 | 24 | 48 |
| | | N = 109 | | | | $\Sigma fdx'=-55$ | $\Sigma fdx'^2=289$ |

$$\sigma = \sqrt{\frac{\Sigma fdx'^2}{N} - \left(\frac{\Sigma fdx'}{N}\right)^2} \times C$$

$$= \sqrt{\frac{289}{109} - \left(\frac{-55}{109}\right)^2} \times 10$$

$$= \sqrt{2.6514 - 0.2546} \times 10 = \sqrt{2.3968} \times 10$$

$$= 1.548 \times 10$$

$$= 15.48$$

Standard Deviation = 15.48.

**ILLUSTRATION 10.**

If sum of squares of items = 2,430, arithmetic mean = 7, and number of items = 12, find the coefficient of variation.

**SOLUTION:**

Given: $\Sigma X^2 = 2{,}430,\ \overline{X} = 7,\ N = 12$

$$\sigma = \sqrt{\frac{\Sigma X^2}{N} - (\overline{X})^2}$$

$$= \sqrt{\frac{2{,}430}{12} - (7)^2} = \sqrt{202.5 - 49}$$

$$= \sqrt{153.5} = 12.39$$

$$CV = \frac{\sigma}{\overline{X}} \times 100$$

$$= \frac{12.39}{7} \times 100 = 177$$

Coefficient of Variation = 177.

**ILLUSTRATION 11.**

The coefficient of variation of a series is 58. The standard deviation is 21.2. What is the arithmetic mean?

**SOLUTION:**

Given: CV = 58, $\sigma$ = 21.2

$$CV = \frac{\sigma}{\overline{X}} \times 100$$

$$\Rightarrow \qquad \overline{X} = \frac{\sigma}{CV} \times 100$$

Substituting the values, we get

$$\overline{X} = \frac{21.2}{58} \times 100 = 36.6$$

Arithmetic Mean = 36.6.

**ILLUSTRATION 12.**

If the mean and standard deviation of 75 observations is 40 and 8 respectively, find the new mean and standard deviation if

(i) each observation is multiplied by 5.

(ii) 7 is added to each observation.

**SOLUTION:**

Given: $\overline{X} = 40, \sigma = 8, N = 75$

(i) A "change of scale" affects the value of both $\overline{X}$ and $\sigma$. A change of scale occurs when each observation is multiplied by a constant. As a result to that, $\overline{X}$ and $\sigma$ also get multiplied by that constant.

In our question, that constant is 5.

Hence,

$$\text{New } \overline{X} = \text{Old } \overline{X} \times 5$$
$$= 40 \times 5$$
$$= 200$$

and,

$$\text{New } \sigma = \text{Old } \sigma \times 5$$
$$= 8 \times 5$$
$$= 40$$

(ii) A "change of origin" affects the value of $\overline{X}$ but not that of $\sigma$. A change of origin occurs when each observation is increased by a constant. As a result to that, $\overline{X}$ also increases by the same constant, while $\sigma$ remains unchanged.

In our question, that constant is 7.

Hence,

$$\text{New } \overline{X} = \text{Old } \overline{X} + 7$$
$$= 40 + 7$$
$$= 47$$

while,

$$\text{New } \sigma = \text{Old } \sigma$$
$$= 8$$

## EXERCISE

### 1. Very Short Answer Type Questions [1 mark]

#### A. Multiple Choice Questions: Choose the Correct Answer

1. Which is the relative measure of dispersion?
   (a) Range (b) Mean deviation
   (c) Coefficient of standard deviation (d) None of these

2. Coefficient of range is:
   (a) $\left(\frac{H+L}{H-L}\right) \times 2$ (b) $\frac{H+L}{2}$
   (c) $\frac{H+L}{H-L}$ (d) $\frac{H-L}{H+L}$

3. Which of the following formulae is used to find out inter quartile range?
   (a) $\frac{Q_1 - Q_3}{2}$ (b) $\frac{Q_1 + Q_3}{2}$
   (c) $Q_3 - Q_1$ (d) $Q_3 + Q_1$

4. Quartile deviation is equal to:
   (a) $\frac{Q_1 - Q_3}{2}$ (b) $\frac{Q_1 + Q_3}{2}$
   (c) $\frac{Q_3 - Q_1}{2}$ (d) $\frac{Q_3 + Q_1}{2}$

5. Mean deviation can be calculated by using:
   (a) mean (b) mode
   (c) median (d) all of these

6. Coefficient of mean deviation from mean is:
   (a) $\frac{MD_{\overline{X}}}{\overline{X}}$ (b) $\frac{MD_m}{M}$
   (c) $\frac{MD_Z}{Z}$ (d) all of these

7. Formula of standard deviation is:
   (a) $\sigma = \frac{\Sigma(X-\overline{X})}{N}$ (b) $\sigma = \sqrt{\frac{\Sigma(X-\overline{X})^2}{N}}$
   (c) $\sigma = \sqrt{\frac{\Sigma(X-\overline{X})}{N}}$ (d) $\sigma = \sqrt{\frac{\Sigma X}{N}}$

8. Coefficient of variation is a percentage expression of:

(a) mean deviation (b) quartile deviation

(c) standard deviation (d) none of these

9. Which of these is the merit of standard deviation?

(a) Standard deviation is based on all values of the series

(b) Standard deviation shows little effect of changes in the sample

(c) In the estimation of standard deviation, more importance is given to difficult and extreme value

(d) Both (a) and (b)

10. $\sqrt{\dfrac{N_1\sigma_1^{\ 2} + N_2\sigma_2^{\ 2} + N_1 d_1^{\ 2} + N_2 d_2^{\ 2}}{N_1 + N_2}}$ is the formula of:

(a) combined mean deviation (b) combined quartile deviation

(c) combined standard deviation (d) coefficient of variation

11. In the calculation of standard deviation, deviations are taken only from the _____ value of the series.

(a) mean (b) mode

(c) median (d) quartile

12. Which of the following equations is correct?

(a) Variance = $\sigma$ (b) Variance = $\sigma^2$

(c) Variance = $\sigma^4$ (d) Variance = $\sqrt{\sigma} \times 2$

Ans. 1. (c), 2. (d), 3. (c), 4. (c), 5. (d), 6. (a), 7. (b), 8. (c), 9. (d), 10. (c), 11. (a), 12. (b).

### B. True or False

State whether the following statements are True or False:

1. Absolute measure of variation is that in which variability of data is expressed in terms of percentage. (True/False)
2. Aggregate of the highest value (H) in the series and the lowest value (L) in the series is called their range. (True/False)
3. In mean deviation, negative deviations are also treated as positive deviations. (True/False)
4. Coefficient of Standard Deviation is: $\dfrac{\sigma}{\overline{X}}$. (True/False)
5. Standard deviation is a better measure of dispersion compared to mean deviation as it is based on the squares of deviations from the mean. (True/False)
6. Lorenz curve does not measure variability of the statistical series. (True/False)

Ans. 1. False, 2. False, 3. True, 4. True, 5. True, 6. False.

### C. Concepts/Definitions & Knowledge-based Questions

1. Define dispersion.

Ans. Dispersion is the measure of the extent to which different items tend to disperse away from the central tendency.

2. What do you mean by coefficient of dispersion?

Ans. The coefficient of dispersion expresses the variability of data in terms of some relative value or percentage. Coefficient of dispersion is known as relative measure of dispersion.

3. Define range.

Ans. Range is the difference between the highest value and the lowest value in a series. Thus,

Range = Highest value in the series – Lowest value in the series

4. Define inter quartile range.

Ans. Difference between third Quartile ($Q_3$) and first Quartile ($Q_1$) of a series is called Inter quartile range. Thus,

$$\text{Inter Quartile Range} = Q_3 - Q_1$$

5. Define quartile deviation.

Ans. Quartile deviation is half of inter quartile range. It is also called semi-inter quartile range. Thus,

$$\text{Quartile Deviation} = \frac{Q_3 - Q_1}{2}$$

6. Give the formula for coefficient of quartile deviation?

Ans. Coefficient of quartile deviation is calculated using the following formula:

Formula:

$$\text{Coefficient of Quartile Deviation} = \frac{Q_3 - Q_1}{2} \div \frac{Q_3 + Q_1}{2} = \frac{Q_3 - Q_1}{Q_3 + Q_1}$$

7. Define mean deviation.

Ans. Mean Deviation is the arithmetic average of the deviations of all the values taken from some average value (mean, median, mode) of the series, ignoring signs (+ or –) of the deviations.

8. How is coefficient of mean deviation calculated?

Ans. In order to find out coefficient of mean deviation, mean deviation of the series is divided by the central tendency of the series. Accordingly,

(1) $\text{Coefficient of MD from Mean} = \frac{MD_{\bar{X}}}{\bar{X}} = \frac{\text{Mean Deviation}}{\text{Arithmetic Mean}}$

(2) $\text{Coefficient of MD from Median} = \frac{MD_m}{M} = \frac{\text{Mean Deviation}}{\text{Median}}$

(3) $\text{Coefficient of MD from Mode} = \frac{MD_Z}{Z} = \frac{\text{Mean Deviation}}{\text{Mode}}$

9. Define standard deviation.

Ans. Standard deviation is the square root of the arithmetic mean of the squares of deviations of the items from their mean value.

10. Define coefficient of variation.

Ans. Coefficient of variation is 100 times the coefficient of dispersion based on standard deviation of a statistical series. It is calculated as

$$\text{Coefficient of variation} = \frac{\sigma}{\bar{X}} \times 100$$

11. What is a lorenz curve?

Ans. Lorenz curve is curve that shows deviation of actual distribution (of income or wealth) from the line showing equal distribution.

12. Define variance.

Ans. Variance is another measure of dispersion. Variance is the square of the standard deviation. Symbolically,

$$\text{Variance} = (SD)^2 = \sigma^2$$

## 2. Short Answer Type Questions [3-4 marks]

1. Illustrate the meaning of the term dispersion with examples.
2. Discuss the main measures of dispersion.
3. How many are the absolute measures of dispersion?
4. How many are the relative measures of dispersion?
5. State the main merits and demerits of range.
6. Explain coefficient of range with the help of a formula.
7. Explain quartile deviation with the help of a formula.
8. What is meant by mean deviation? What are its main characteristics?
9. What is meant by standard deviation? What are its main merits or characteristics?
10. What are the main demerits of standard deviation?
11. What are the differences between standard deviation and mean deviation?
12. What are the main merits of Lorenz curve?
13. Why should we measure dispersion about some particular value? Do the range and quartile deviation measure dispersion about some value?
14. What are the properties of a good measure of dispersion?

## 3. Long Answer Type Questions [6 marks]

1. What is meant by mean deviation? What are the methods to calculate it? Give its merits and demerits.
2. What is standard deviation? How does it differ from mean deviation? What are its advantages and disadvantages?
3. What is meant by coefficient of variation? How will you calculate it in case of a discrete series?
4. Explain the construction of Lorenz curve taking an imaginary set of data.
5. What are the four alternative measures of absolute dispersion? Discuss their properties.
6. 'The coefficient of variation is a relative measure of dispersion.'

   We may calculate coefficient of variation using any of the measures of dispersion, such as, range, quartile deviation, mean deviation and standard deviation. Illustrate the use of coefficient of variation in these cases.

## 4. Essential Practicals

1. Calculate range and coefficient of range from the following data:

   4, 7, 8, 46, 53, 77, 8, 1, 5, 13 (Ans. R = 76, CR = 0.97)
2. Given the following data-set, calculate range and the coefficient of range:

| **Size** | 4.5 | 5.5 | 6.5 | 7.5 | 8.5 | 9.5 | 10.5 | 11.5 |
|---|---|---|---|---|---|---|---|---|
| **Frequency** | 4 | 5 | 6 | 3 | 2 | 1 | 3 | 5 |

(Ans. R = 7, CR = 0.44)

3. Find out the range and the coefficient of range, given the following data-set:

| Class Interval | 1-5 | 6-10 | 11-15 | 16-20 | 21-25 | 26-30 | 31-35 |
|---|---|---|---|---|---|---|---|
| Frequency | 2 | 8 | 15 | 35 | 20 | 10 | 14 |

(Ans. R = 30, CR = 0.833)

4. Find out quartile deviation and the coefficient of quartile deviation of the following series.

Wages of 9 Workers in Rupees:

170, 82, 110, 100, 150, 150, 200, 116, 250 (Ans. QD = 40, Coefficient of QD = 0.276)

5. Given the following data, estimate the coefficient of QD:

15, 20, 23, 23, 25, 25, 27, 40. (Ans. Coefficient of QD = 0.12)

6. Find out mean deviation of the following series from mean and median:

| Size | 4 | 6 | 8 | 10 | 12 | 14 | 16 |
|---|---|---|---|---|---|---|---|
| Frequency | 2 | 4 | 5 | 31 | 2 | 1 | 4 |

(Ans. $MD_{\bar{X}} = 1.49$, $MD_m = 1.43$)

7. Calculate mean deviation and coefficient of mean deviation with the help of median:

| Class Interval | 0–10 | 10–20 | 20–30 | 30–40 | 40–50 | 50–60 |
|---|---|---|---|---|---|---|
| Frequency | 15 | 19 | 14 | 20 | 18 | 14 |

(Ans. MD = 14.46, Coefficient of MD = 0.466)

8. Calculate mean deviation from mean of the following series:

| Size of Items | 3–4 | 4–5 | 5–6 | 6–7 | 7–8 | 8–9 | 9–10 |
|---|---|---|---|---|---|---|---|
| Frequency | 3 | 7 | 22 | 60 | 85 | 32 | 9 |

(Ans. MD = 0.92)

9. Given below are the marks obtained by the students of a class. Calculate mean deviation, and its coefficient, using median of data.

| Marks | 17 | 35 | 38 | 16 | 42 | 27 | 19 | 11 | 40 | 25 |
|---|---|---|---|---|---|---|---|---|---|---|

(Ans. $MD_m = 9.4$, $CMD_m = 0.36$)

10. Nine students of a class obtained following marks. Calculate mean deviation from median.

| S. No. | 1 | 2 | 3 | 4 | 5 | 6 | 7 | 8 | 9 |
|---|---|---|---|---|---|---|---|---|---|
| Marks | 68 | 49 | 32 | 21 | 54 | 38 | 59 | 66 | 41 |

(Ans. $MD_m = 12.77$)

11. Following data relate to the age-difference of husbands and wives of a particular community. Find out mean deviation from mean.

| Age-difference | 0–5 | 5–10 | 10–15 | 15–20 | 20–25 | 25–30 | 30–35 | 35–40 |
|---|---|---|---|---|---|---|---|---|
| Frequency | 449 | 705 | 507 | 281 | 109 | 52 | 16 | 4 |

(Ans. $MD_{\bar{X}} = 5.34$)

12. Find out the mean deviation and its coefficient using median of the following data:

| Number of Accidents | 1 | 2 | 3 | 4 | 5 | 6 | 7 | 8 | 9 | 10 | 11 | 12 |
|---|---|---|---|---|---|---|---|---|---|---|---|---|
| Number of Victims of Accidents | 16 | 21 | 10 | 17 | 8 | 4 | 2 | 1 | 2 | 2 | 2 | 2 |

(Ans. $MD_m$ = 5.41, Coeff. of $MD_m$ = 1.81)

13. Calculate standard deviation, given the following data:
10, 12, 14, 16, 18, 22, 24, 26, 28 (Ans. $\sigma$ = 6.05)

14. Calculate standard deviation and the coefficient of standard deviation, given the following data:

| Income (₹) | 5 | 10 | 15 | 20 | 25 | 30 | 35 | 40 |
|---|---|---|---|---|---|---|---|---|
| Number of Workers | 26 | 29 | 40 | 35 | 26 | 18 | 14 | 12 |

(Ans. SD = 10.02, Coefficient of SD = 0.516)

15. Of the two sets of income distribution of five and seven persons respectively, as given below calculate standard deviation:

| (i) Income (₹) | 4,000 | 4,200 | 4,400 | 4,600 | 4,800 | | |
|---|---|---|---|---|---|---|---|
| (ii) Income (₹) | 3,000 | 4,000 | 4,200 | 4,400 | 4,600 | 4,800 | 5,800 |

(Ans. (i) $\sigma$ = ₹ 282.84; (ii) $\sigma$ = ₹ 785.58)

16. Find out the standard deviation of the marks secured by 10 students:

| S. No. | 1 | 2 | 3 | 4 | 5 | 6 | 7 | 8 | 9 | 10 |
|---|---|---|---|---|---|---|---|---|---|---|
| Marks | 43 | 48 | 65 | 57 | 31 | 60 | 37 | 48 | 78 | 59 |

(Ans. $\sigma$ = 13.26)

17. Data of daily sale proceeds of a shop are as below. Calculate mean deviation and standard deviation.

| Daily Sales | 102 | 100 | 110 | 114 | 118 | 122 | 126 |
|---|---|---|---|---|---|---|---|
| Days | 3 | 9 | 25 | 35 | 17 | 10 | 1 |

(Ans. MD = 4.49, $\sigma$ = 5.96)

18. Calculate range, standard deviation and coefficient of variation of marks secured by students.

| 50 | 55 | 57 | 49 | 54 | 61 | 64 | 59 | 58 | 56 |
|---|---|---|---|---|---|---|---|---|---|

(Ans. R = 15, $\sigma$ = 4.38, CV = 7.78)

19. Following data show the number of runs made by Sachin and Sourabh in different innings. Find out who is a good scorer and who is a consistent player?

| Sachin | 92 | 17 | 83 | 56 | 72 | 76 | 64 | 45 | 40 | 32 |
|---|---|---|---|---|---|---|---|---|---|---|
| Sourabh | 28 | 70 | 31 | 00 | 59 | 108 | 82 | 14 | 3 | 95 |

(Ans. Sachin is a good scorer and Sachin is a consistent player.)

20. Calculate standard deviation of marks secured by 100 examinees in the examination:

| Marks | 10–20 | 20–30 | 30–40 | 40–50 | 50–60 | 60–70 | 70–80 | 80–90 |
|---|---|---|---|---|---|---|---|---|
| Number of Examinees | 19 | 3 | 2 | 49 | 24 | 2 | 0 | 1 |

(Ans. $\sigma$ = 14.9)

21. Calculate coefficient of variation from the following data:

| Variables | 10 | 20 | 30 | 40 | 50 | 60 | 70 |
|---|---|---|---|---|---|---|---|
| Frequencies | 6 | 8 | 16 | 15 | 32 | 11 | 12 |

(Ans. CV = 37.34)

22. Estimate coefficient of variation of the following data:

| Weight (kg) | 0–20 | 20–40 | 40–60 | 60–80 | 80–100 |
|---|---|---|---|---|---|
| Number of Persons | 81 | 40 | 66 | 49 | 14 |

(Ans. CV = 63.75)

## 5. NCERT Textbook Questions [With Hints to Answers]

1. A measure of dispersion is a good supplement to the central value in understanding a frequency distribution. Comment.
   [Page 245, 246]
2. Which measure of dispersion is the best and how?
   [Section 3, Page 246]
3. Some measures of dispersion depend upon the spread of values whereas some calculate the variation of values from a central value. Do you agree?
   [Section 3, Page 246]
4. In a town, 25% of the persons earned more than ₹ 45,000 whereas 75% earned more than 18,000. Calculate the absolute and relative values of dispersion.
   [Given: $Q_3$ = 45,000; $Q_1$ = 18, 000

$$\text{Quartile Deviation} = \frac{Q_3 - Q_1}{2} = \frac{45{,}000 - 18{,}000}{2} = \frac{27{,}000}{2} = 13{,}500$$

$$\text{Coefficient of Quartile Deviation} = \frac{Q_3 - Q_1}{Q_3 + Q_1} = \frac{45{,}000 - 18{,}000}{45{,}000 + 18{,}000} = \frac{27{,}000}{63{,}000} = 0.43$$

Therefore, Absolute value of dispersion = 13,500

Relative value of dispersion = 0.43.]

**5.** The yield of wheat and rice per acre for 10 districts of a state is as under:

| District | 1 | 2 | 3 | 4 | 5 | 6 | 7 | 8 | 9 | 10 |
|---|---|---|---|---|---|---|---|---|---|---|
| **Wheat** | 12 | 10 | 15 | 19 | 21 | 16 | 18 | 9 | 25 | 10 |
| **Rice** | 22 | 29 | 12 | 23 | 18 | 15 | 12 | 34 | 18 | 12 |

Calculate for each crop,

(i) Range

(ii) Q.D.

(iii) Mean Deviation about Mean

(iv) Mean Deviation about Median

(v) Standard Deviation

(vi) Which crop has greater variation?

(vii) Compare the values of different measures for each crop.

[**Hint: Case of Wheat:**

Firstly, arrange the data in ascending order:

| District | Wheat (X) | Deviation from Mean $\lvert d\bar{x}\rvert = \lvert X - \bar{X}\rvert$ $\bar{X}=15.5$ | Deviation from Median $\lvert dm\rvert = \lvert X - M\rvert$ M=15.5 | Deviation $(x = X - \bar{X})$ $\bar{X} = 15.5$ | Square of Deviation $(x^2)$ |
|---|---|---|---|---|---|
| 1 | 9 | 6.5 | 6.5 | –6.5 | 42.25 |
| 2 | 10 | 5.5 | 5.5 | –5.5 | 30.25 |
| 3 | 10 | 5.5 | 5.5 | –5.5 | 30.25 |
| 4 | 12 | 3.5 | 3.5 | –3.5 | 12.25 |
| 5 | 15 | 0.5 | 0.5 | –0.5 | 0.25 |
| 6 | 16 | 0.5 | 0.5 | 0.5 | 0.25 |
| 7 | 18 | 2.5 | 2.5 | 2.5 | 6.25 |
| 8 | 19 | 3.5 | 3.5 | 3.5 | 12.25 |
| 9 | 21 | 5.5 | 5.5 | 5.5 | 30.25 |
| 10 | 25 | 9.5 | 9.5 | 9.5 | 90.25 |
| N = 10 | $\Sigma X = 155$ | $\Sigma\lvert d\bar{x}\rvert = 43$ | $\Sigma\lvert dm\rvert = 43$ | $\Sigma x=0$ | $\Sigma x^2 = 254.5$ |

(i) Range (R) = H – L

Here, H = 25, L = 9

$\therefore$ R = 25 – 9 = 16

(ii) $Q_1 = \text{Size of}\left(\frac{N+1}{4}\right)\text{th item}$

$= \text{Size of}\left(\frac{10+1}{4}\right)\text{th item}$

= Size of 2.75th item

$= \text{Size of 2nd item} + \frac{3}{4}\text{(Size of 3rd item – Size of 2nd item)}$

$$= 10 + \frac{3}{4}(10 - 10)$$

$$= 10 + 0 = 10$$

$$Q_3 = \text{Size of } 3\left(\frac{N+1}{4}\right)\text{th item}$$

$$= \text{Size of } 3\left(\frac{10+1}{4}\right)\text{th item}$$

$$= \text{Size of 8.25th item}$$

$$= \text{Size of 8th item} + \frac{1}{4}(\text{Size of 9th item} - \text{Size of 8th item})$$

$$= 19 + \frac{1}{4}(21 - 19) = 19 + \frac{2}{4} = 19.5$$

$$\text{Quartile Deviation} = \frac{Q_3 - Q_1}{2} = \frac{19.5 - 10}{2} = \frac{9.5}{2} = 4.75$$

(iii) $\text{Mean } (\overline{X}) = \frac{\Sigma X}{N} = \frac{155}{10} = 15.5$

$$\text{Mean Deviation from Mean } (MD_{\overline{X}}) = \frac{\Sigma|d\overline{x}|}{N} = \frac{43}{10} = 4.3$$

(iv) $\text{Median (M)} = \text{Size of}\left(\frac{N+1}{2}\right)\text{th item}$

$$= \text{Size of}\left(\frac{10+1}{2}\right)\text{th item}$$

$$= \text{Size of 5.5th item}$$

$$= \frac{\text{Size of 5th item + Size of 6th item}}{2}$$

$$= \frac{15 + 16}{2} = 15.5$$

$$\text{Mean Deviation from Median } (MD_m) = \frac{\Sigma|dm|}{N} = \frac{43}{10} = 4.3$$

(v) $\text{Standard Deviation } (\sigma) = \sqrt{\frac{\Sigma x^2}{N}} = \sqrt{\frac{254.5}{10}} = \sqrt{25.45} = 5.04$

(vi) $\text{Coefficient of Variation (CV)} = \frac{\sigma}{\overline{X}} \times 100 = \frac{5.04}{15.5} \times 100 = 32.52]$

[**Note:** Students are advised to repeat this exercise using data for the rice crop. To assess the degree of variation, compare CV for the two cases.]

6. A batsman is to be selected for a cricket team. The choice is between X and Y on the basis of their five previous scores which are:

| **X** | 25 | 85 | 40 | 80 | 120 |
|---|---|---|---|---|---|
| **Y** | 50 | 70 | 65 | 45 | 80 |

Which batsman should be selected if we want,

(i) a higher run getter, or

(ii) a more reliable batsman in the team?

[

**Estimation of Mean and CV**

| Batsman-X | | | Batsman-Y | | |
|---|---|---|---|---|---|
| X | Deviation from Mean ($x = X - \bar{X}$) $\bar{X} = 70$ | Square of Deviation ($x^2$) | Y | Deviation from Mean ($y = Y - \bar{Y}$) $\bar{Y} = 62$ | Square of Deviation ($y^2$) |
| 25 | – 45 | 2,025 | 50 | – 12 | 144 |
| 85 | 15 | 225 | 70 | 8 | 64 |
| 40 | – 30 | 900 | 65 | 3 | 9 |
| 80 | 10 | 100 | 45 | – 17 | 289 |
| 120 | 50 | 2,500 | 80 | 18 | 324 |
| $\Sigma X = 350$ | | $\Sigma x^2 = 5{,}750$ | $\Sigma Y = 310$ | | $\Sigma y^2 = 830$ |

**Batsman X:** $\bar{X} = \frac{\Sigma X}{N} = \frac{350}{5} = 70$

$$\sigma_X = \sqrt{\frac{\Sigma x^2}{N}} = \sqrt{\frac{5{,}750}{5}} = \sqrt{1{,}150} = 33.91$$

and $$CV_X = \frac{\sigma}{\bar{X}} \times 100 = \frac{33.91}{70} \times 100 = 48.44$$

**Batsman Y:** $\bar{Y} = \frac{\Sigma Y}{N} = \frac{310}{5} = 62$

$$\sigma_Y = \sqrt{\frac{\Sigma y^2}{N}} = \sqrt{\frac{830}{5}} = \sqrt{166} = 12.88$$

and $$CV_Y = \frac{\sigma}{\bar{Y}} \times 100 = \frac{12.88}{62} \times 100 = 20.77$$

Because average score of X is more than that of Y, we conclude that X is a higher run getter. But batting of X shows greater CV than Y. Hence, Y is a more reliable batsman in the team.]

7. To check the quality of two brands of lightbulbs, their life in burning hours was estimated as under for 100 bulbs of each brand.

| Life (in hours) | Number of bulbs | |
|---|---|---|
| | Brand A | Brand B |
| 0–50 | 15 | 2 |
| 50–100 | 20 | 8 |
| 100–150 | 18 | 60 |
| 150–200 | 25 | 25 |
| 200–250 | 22 | 5 |
| | 100 | 100 |

(i) Which brand gives higher life?

(ii) Which brand is more dependable?

[

**Calculation of Mean and Coefficient of Variation**

| Life (in hours) | Mid-value $\left(m = \frac{l_1 + l_2}{2}\right)$ | Deviation from Assumed Average (dx = m – A) A = 125 | Step-deviation $\left(dx' = \frac{m - A}{C}\right)$ C = 50 | Brand A | | | Brand B | | |
|---|---|---|---|---|---|---|---|---|---|
| | | | | Frequency (f) | fdx′ | fdx′² | Frequency (f) | fdx′ | fdx′² |
| 0–50 | 25 | –100 | –2 | 15 | – 30 | 60 | 2 | –4 | 8 |
| 50–100 | 75 | –50 | –1 | 20 | – 20 | 20 | 8 | –8 | 8 |
| 100–150 | 125 (A) | 0 | 0 | 18 | 0 | 0 | 60 | 0 | 0 |
| 150–200 | 175 | 50 | 1 | 25 | 25 | 25 | 25 | 25 | 25 |
| 200–250 | 225 | 100 | 2 | 22 | 44 | 88 | 5 | 10 | 20 |
| | | | | N = Σf = 100 | Σfdx′ =19 | Σfdx′² =193 | N = 100 | Σfdx′ = 23 | Σfdx′² = 61 |

**Brand A:**

$$\overline{X} = A + \frac{\Sigma fdx'}{\Sigma f} \times C$$

$$= 125 + \frac{19}{100} \times 50$$

$$= 125 + 9.5 = 134.5$$

$$\sigma_x = \sqrt{\frac{\Sigma fdx'^2}{N} - \left(\frac{\Sigma fdx'}{N}\right)^2} \times C$$

$$= \sqrt{\frac{193}{100} - \left(\frac{19}{100}\right)^2} \times 50$$

$$= \sqrt{1.93 - 0.0361} \times 50$$

$$= \sqrt{1.8939} \times 50$$

$$= 1.38 \times 50 = 69$$

$$CV_A = \frac{\sigma}{\overline{X}} \times 100$$

$$= \frac{69}{134.5} \times 100 = 51.3$$

**Brand B:**

$$\overline{X} = A + \frac{\Sigma fdx'}{\Sigma f} \times C = 125 + \frac{23}{100} \times 50$$

$$= 125 + 11.5 = 136.5$$

$$\sigma = \sqrt{\frac{\Sigma fdx'^2}{N} - \left(\frac{\Sigma fdx'}{N}\right)^2} \times C$$

$$= \sqrt{\frac{61}{100} - \left(\frac{23}{100}\right)^2} \times 50$$

$$= \sqrt{0.61 - 0.0529} \times 50$$

$$= \sqrt{0.5571} \times 50$$

$$= 0.75 \times 50 = 37.5$$

$$CV_B = \frac{\sigma}{\overline{X}} \times 100 = \frac{37.5}{136.5} \times 100 = 27.47$$

(i) Brand B gives higher life because average hours of life is more in this case than that of Brand A.

(ii) CV is more in case of Brand A than Brand B, therefore, Brand B is more dependable.]

8. Averge daily wage of 50 workers of a factory was ₹ 200 with a standard deviation of ₹ 40. Each worker is given a raise of ₹ 20. What is the new average daily wage and standard deviation? Have the wages become more or less uniform?

[Given: $\overline{X} = 200, \sigma = 40, N = 50$

This is a case of change of origin since each worker is given a raise of ₹ 20. Change of origin will affect the value of mean but not that of standard deviation. Therefore, in this case, new mean will be:

$$\text{New } \overline{X} = \text{Old } \overline{X} + 20$$
$$= 200 + 20$$
$$= 220$$

while,

$$\text{New } \sigma = \text{Old } \sigma$$
$$= 40$$

Hence, $\text{New } \overline{X} = 220$

$\text{New } \sigma = 40$

Standard deviation being constant, wages show the same amount of uniformity.]

9. If in the previous question, each worker is given a hike of 10% in wages, how are the mean and standard deviation values affected?

[Suppose the wage of *i*th worker is $x_i$.

Now, each worker is given a hike of 10% in wages, new wage of the *i*th worker will be:

$$\text{New wage} = x_i + 10\% \text{ of } x_i$$
$$= x_i + \frac{10}{100} \times x_i$$
$$= \frac{100x_i + 10x_i}{100} = \frac{110x_i}{100}$$
$$= 1.1\ x_i$$

Thus, each observation of *i*th worker is multiplied by 1.1. Since it is case of change of scale, new mean and standard deviation will be:

$$\text{New } \overline{X} = \text{Old } \overline{X} \times 1.1$$
$$= 200 \times 1.1$$
$$= 220$$

while,

$$\text{New } \sigma = \text{Old } \sigma \times 1.1$$
$$= 40 \times 1.1$$
$$= 44$$

∴ New mean = 220.

New standard deviation = 44.]

**10.** Calculate the Mean Deviation about Mean and Standard Deviation for the following distribution:

| Classes | Frequencies |
|---|---|
| 20–40 | 3 |
| 40–80 | 6 |
| 80–100 | 20 |
| 100–120 | 12 |
| 120–140 | 9 |
| | 50 |

[ **Calculation of Mean Deviation from Mean and Standard Deviation**

| Classes | Mid-value $\left(m = \frac{l_1 + l_2}{2}\right)$ | Frequencies (f) | Multiple of Mid-value and Frequency (fm) | Deviation from Mean $\lvert d\bar{x} = m - \bar{X}\rvert$ $\bar{X} = 94.8$ | Multiple of Frequency and the Corresponding Frequency $(f\lvert d\bar{x}\rvert)$ | Deviation from Mean $(x = m - \bar{X})$ $\bar{X} = 94.8$ | Square of Deviation $(x^2)$ | $fx^2$ |
|---|---|---|---|---|---|---|---|---|
| 20–40 | 30 | 3 | 90 | 64.8 | 194.4 | – 64.8 | 4,199.04 | 12,597.12 |
| 40–80 | 60 | 6 | 360 | 34.8 | 208.8 | – 34.8 | 1,211.04 | 7,266.24 |
| 80–100 | 90 | 20 | 1,800 | 4.8 | 96 | – 4.8 | 23.04 | 460.8 |
| 100–120 | 110 | 12 | 1,320 | 15.2 | 182.4 | 15.2 | 231.04 | 2,772.48 |
| 120–140 | 130 | 9 | 1,170 | 35.2 | 316.8 | 35.2 | 1,239.04 | 11,151.36 |
| | | N = 50 | $\Sigma fm$ =4,740 | $\lvert d\bar{x}\rvert$ =154.8 | $\Sigma f\lvert d\bar{x}\rvert$ =998.4 | | | $\Sigma fx^2$ =34,248 |

$$\bar{X} = \frac{\Sigma fm}{\Sigma f} = \frac{4,740}{50} = 94.8$$

$$\text{Mean Deviation from Mean} = \frac{\Sigma f\lvert d\bar{x}\rvert}{\Sigma f} = \frac{998.4}{50} = 19.968$$

$$\text{Standard Deviation} = \sqrt{\frac{\Sigma fx^2}{\Sigma f}}$$

$$= \sqrt{\frac{34,248}{50}}$$

$$= \sqrt{684.96} = 26.17$$

∴ Mean deviation from mean = 19.968.

Standard deviation = 26.17.]

**11.** The sum of 10 values is 100 and the sum of their squares is 1,090. Find the Coefficient of Variation.

[Given: $\Sigma X = 100$, $\Sigma X^2 = 1,090$, $N = 10$

$$\bar{X} = \frac{\Sigma X}{N} = \frac{100}{10} = 10$$

$$\sigma = \sqrt{\frac{\Sigma X^2}{N} - \left(\frac{\Sigma X}{N}\right)^2}$$

$$= \sqrt{\frac{1,090}{10} - \left(\frac{100}{10}\right)^2}$$

$$= \sqrt{109 - 100} = \sqrt{9} = 3$$

$$CV = \frac{\sigma}{\overline{X}} \times 100$$

$$= \frac{3}{10} \times 100 = 30$$

Coefficient of variation = 30.]

# Correlation

12

## 1. What is Correlation?

The statistical methods so far studied in this book focus on the analysis of one variable or one statistical series only. In real life however, two or more than two statistical series may be found to be mutually related. For instance, change in price leads to change in quantity demanded. Increase in supply of money causes increase in price level. Increase in level of employment results in increase in output. Such situations necessitate simultaneous study of two or more statistical series. The focus of study in such situations is on the degree of relationship between different statistical series. The statistical technique that studies the degree of such relationships is called the **technique of correlation.**

**What is Correlation?**

It is a statistical method or a statistical technique that measures quantitative relationship between different variables, like between price and demand.

### Definition

According to **Croxton and Cowden**, "*When the relationship is of a quantitative nature, the appropriate statistical tool for discovering and measuring the relationship and expressing it in a brief formula is known as correlation.*"

In the words of **Boddington**, "*Whenever some definite connection exists between the two or more groups, classes or series or data there is said to be correlation.*"

**Relationship between Two Variables may just be a Coincidence**

One may find a relationship between two variables which is just a coincidence. Example: When there is a departure of migratory birds from a sanctuary, you may find a fall in wedding ceremonies in the country. Such relationships are meaningless. These are in other words, spurious relationships which are devoid of any meaningful conclusion. Such relationships are not to be treated as correlations. Only those relationships are to be treated as correlations which offer some meaningful conclusions. Example: Increase in rainfall and increase in rice production is a relationship that makes sense; increase in per capita income and decrease in death rate is a meaningful relationship; Good percentage of marks in physics may be related to good percentage of marks in mathematics; and so on.

### Positive and Negative Correlation

Correlation between different variables may either be positive or negative. Here is a brief description of the two:

### (1) Positive Correlation

When two variables move in the same direction, that is, when one increases the other also increases and when one decreases the other also decreases, such a relation is called positive correlation.

Relationship between price and supply may be cited as an example. Check the following table as an illustration:

**Table 1. Positive Correlation between the Variables**

| (A) Simultaneous Increase in the Values of both Variables | | (B) Simultaneous Decrease in the Values of both Variables | |
|---|---|---|---|
| **X** | **Y** | **X** | **Y** |
| 10 | 100 | 50 | 200 |
| 20 | 150 | 40 | 150 |
| 30 | 200 | 30 | 100 |
| 40 | 250 | 20 | 50 |

### (2) Negative Correlation

When two variables change in different directions, it is called negative correlation. Relationship between price and demand, may be cited as an example. The following table demonstrates this relation.

**Table 2. Negative Correlation between the Variables**

| Rise in the Value of One Variable is accompanied with a fall in the other | |
|---|---|
| **X** | **Y** |
| 1 | 5 |
| 2 | 4 |
| 4 | 2 |
| 5 | 1 |

**What does Correlation Measure?**

Often the students tend to believe that correlation suggests a relationship between two variables where one is the cause of the other. Example: This is correlation between price and quantity demanded of a commodity. Clearly, an increase in price causes a decrease in quantity demanded, and vice versa. Change in price causes changes in quantity demanded. But to be emphatically noted is the point that cause and effect relationship between the variables is not at all any pre-condition in the theory of correlation. Correlation just measures the degree and intensity of relationship between the two variables, with or without any cause and effect relationship. Of course the established relationship between the variables should be capable of offering us some meaningful conclusion. Example: Students who are good in academics may be good in sports also. Certainly, it is a meaningful relationship (or correlation) if one finds it. But surely there is no cause and effect relationship between the two variables.

### Linear and Non-Linear Correlation

Correlation may be linear or non-linear.

#### (1) Linear Correlation

When two variables change in a constant proportion, it is called linear correlation. If the two sets of data bearing fixed proportion to each other are shown on a graph paper, their relationship will be indicated by a straight line. Thus, linear correlation implies a straight line relationship.

#### (2) Non-linear Correlation

When the two variables do not change in any constant proportion, the relationship is said to be non-linear. Such a relationship does not form a straight line relationship.

**The Basic Difference between Linear and Non-linear Correlation**

In case of linear correlation, the two sets of data show some fixed proportion to each other and therefore, form a straight line on a graph paper. In case of non-linear correlation, the two sets of data do not show any fixed proportion to each other, and therefore, do not make a straight line on a graph paper.

**Illustration.**

**Linear Correlation**

| | | | | | | | |
|---|---|---|---|---|---|---|---|
| **(a)** | 2 | 4 | 6 | 8 | 10 | 12 | 14 |
| **(b)** | 5 | 10 | 15 | 20 | 25 | 30 | 35 |

Thus, for every change in variable (a) by 2 units there is a change in variable (b) by 5 units.

**Non-linear Correlation**

| | | | | | | | |
|---|---|---|---|---|---|---|---|
| **(a)** | 2 | 4 | 6 | 8 | 10 | 12 | 14 |
| **(b)** | 3 | 7 | 12 | 18 | 25 | 35 | 45 |

Here there is no specific relationship between the two variables, though both tend to change in the same direction. That is, both are increasing, but not in any constant proportion.

### Simple and Multiple Correlation

#### (1) Simple Correlation

Simple correlation implies the study of relationship between two variables only. Like the relationship between price and demand or the relationship between money supply and price level.

**Partial Correlation**

When more than two variables are involved and out of these the relationship between only two variables is studied treating other variables as constant, then the correlation is partial.

#### (2) Multiple Correlation

When the relationship among three or more than three variables is studied simultaneously, it is called multiple correlation. In case of such correlation, the entire set of independent and dependent variables is simultaneously studied. For instance, effects of rainfall, manure, water, etc., on per hectare productivity of wheat are simultaneously studied.

## 2. Degree of Correlation

Degree of correlation refers to the Coefficient of Correlation. There can be the following degrees of positive and negative correlation.

(1) **Perfect Correlation:** When two variables change in the same proportion it is called perfect correlation. It may be of two kinds:

**Correlation and Causation**

Correlation is a numerical measure of direction and magnitude of the mutual relationship between the values of two or more variables. But the presence of correlation should not be taken as the belief that the two correlated variables necessarily have causal relationship as well. Correlation does not always arise from causal relationship but with the presence of causal relationship, correlation is certain to exist.

(i) **Perfect Positive:** Correlation is perfectly positive when proportional change in two variables is in the same direction. In this case, coefficient of correlation is positive (+1).

(ii) **Perfect Negative:** Correlation is perfectly negative when proportional change in two variables is in the opposite direction. In this case, coefficient of correlation is negative (–1).

(2) **Absence of Correlation:** If there is no relation between two series or variables, that is, change in one has no effect on the change in other, then those series or variables lack any correlation between them.

(3) **Limited Degree of Correlation:** Between perfect correlation and absence of correlation there is a situation of limited degree of correlation. In real life, one mostly finds limited degree of correlation. Its coefficient (r) is more than zero and less than one ($r > 0$ but $< 1$). The degree of correlation between 0 and 1 may be rated as:

(i) **High:** When correlation of two series is close to one, it is called high degree of correlation. Its coefficient lies between 0.75 and 1.

(ii) **Moderate:** When correlation of two series is neither large nor small, it is called moderate degree of correlation. Its coefficient lies between 0.25 and 0.75.

(iii) **Low:** When the degree of correlation of two series is very small, it is called low degree of correlation. Its coefficient lies between 0 and 0.25.

All these degrees of correlations may be positive or negative.

**Degree of Correlation**

| Degree | Positive | Negative |
|---|---|---|
| Perfect | +1 | –1 |
| High | Between + 0.75 and +1 | Between – 0.75 and –1 |
| Moderate | Between + 0.25 and + 0.75 | Between – 0.25 and – 0.75 |
| Low | Between 0 and + 0.25 | Between 0 and – 0.25 |
| Zero | 0 | 0 |

## 3. Methods of Estimating Correlation

Various methods are available for estimating correlation between different sets of statistical series. Some of the important ones are as under:

(1) **Scattered Diagram Method,**

(2) **Karl Pearson's Coefficient of Correlation, and**

(3) **Spearman's Rank Correlation Coefficient.**

**Line of Best Fit**

Line of Best Fit is the one that passes through the scattered points such that it represents most of these points. Roughly, half of the scattered points should be on either side of the line.

### Scattered Diagram

*Scattered diagram offers a graphic expression of the direction and degree of correlation*. To make a Scattered Diagram, data are plotted on a graph paper. A dot is marked for each value. The course of these dots would indicate direction and closeness of the variables. Following pictures show some of the possible directions and the degrees of closeness of the variables.

As should be clear from the scattered diagrams, closeness of the dots towards each other in a particular direction indicates higher degree of correlation. If the dots are scattered (showing neither the closeness nor any direction), it is an indication of low degree of correlation.

> **A Note**
>
> Scattered diagram only shows an approximation of the relationship or closeness of two sets of data. Precise measurement of the relationship is not possible.

**Graph: Scattered Diagram**

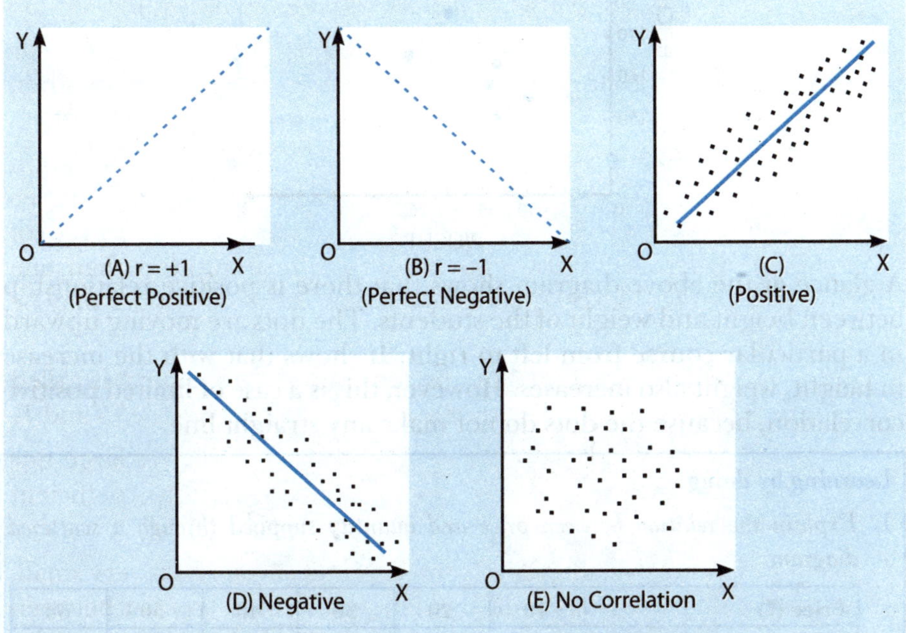


## Merits and Demerits of Scattered Diagram

### Merits

(1) Scattered diagram is a very simple method of studying correlation between two variables.

(2) Just a glance at the diagram is enough to know if the values of the variables have any relation or not.

(3) Scattered diagram also indicates whether the relation is positive or negative.

### Demerits

(1) A scattered diagram does not measure the precise extent of correlation.

(2) It gives only an approximate idea of the relationship.

(3) It is not a quantitative measure of the relationship between the variables. It is only a qualitative expression of the quantitative change.

**Illustration.**

The following table gives height and weight of the students of a class. Make a scattered diagram to show if the relationship is positive or negative and if the relationship is strong or weak.

| **Height (cm)** | 180 | 150 | 158 | 165 | 175 | 163 | 195 | 155 |
|---|---|---|---|---|---|---|---|---|
| **Weight (kg)** | 65 | 54 | 55 | 65 | 60 | 54 | 63 | 50 |

**SOLUTION:**

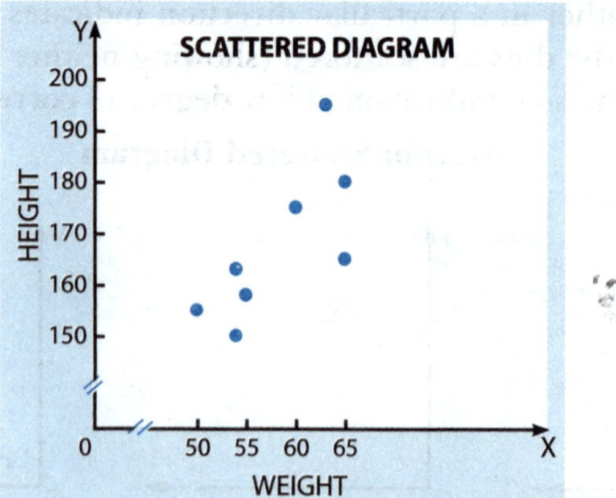


A glance at the above diagram shows that there is positive relationship between height and weight of the students. The dots are moving upward in a particular course from left to right. It shows that with the increase in height, weight also increases. However, this is a case of limited positive correlation, because the dots do not make any straight line.

*Learning by doing*

1. *Explain the relation between price and quantity supplied through a scattered diagram.*

| **Price (₹)** | 10 | 20 | 30 | 40 | 50 | 60 |
|---|---|---|---|---|---|---|
| **Quantity Supplied** | 25 | 50 | 75 | 100 | 125 | 150 |

2. *Show the relationship between X and Y through a scattered diagram.*

| **X** | 8 | 16 | 24 | 31 | 42 | 50 |
|---|---|---|---|---|---|---|
| **Y** | 70 | 58 | 50 | 32 | 26 | 12 |

3. *Visit your nearest mother dairy store. Get information on the daily price and quantity sold of bananas for the last 30 days. Draw a scattered diagram of the statistical information. Write your observation on the relationship (closeness) between price and quantity sold of bananas.*

## KARL PEARSON'S COEFFICIENT OF CORRELATION

Scattered diagram method of correlation merely indicates the direction of correlation but not its precise magnitude. *Karl Pearson has given a quantitative method of calculating correlation. It is an important and widely used method of studying correlation. Karl Pearsons' coefficient of correlation is generally written as 'r'.*

### FORMULA

According to Karl Pearson's method, the coefficient of correlation is measured as

$$r = \frac{\Sigma xy}{N\sigma_x\sigma_y}$$

Where,

r = Coefficient of correlation

x = $X - \overline{X}$

$y \quad = Y - \overline{Y}$

$\sigma_x \quad$ = Standard deviation of X series

$\sigma_y \quad$ = Standard deviation of Y series

N = Number of observations.

**Note**

Karl Pearson's coefficient of correlation does not apply to those series where deviations are calculated on the basis of assumed mean.

This formula is applied only to those series where deviations are worked out from actual average of the series, it does not apply to those series where deviations are calculated on the basis of assumed mean. Value of the coefficient of correlation calculated on the basis of this formula may vary between +1 and –1.

However, the situations, when r = +1, r =–1, or r = 0, are rather rare. Generally, value of 'r' varies between +1 and – 1.

### A Modified Version of Karl Pearson's Formula

In it there is no need to calculate standard deviation of 'X' and 'Y'. Coefficient of correlation may be worked out directly using the following formula:

$$r = \frac{\sum xy}{\sqrt{\sum x^2 \times \sum y^2}}$$

Here, $x = (X - \overline{X})$; $y = (Y - \overline{Y})$.

**ILLUSTRATION.**

Calculate coefficient of correlation, given the following data:

| X | 2 | 3 | 4 | 5 | 6 | 7 | 8 |
|---|---|---|---|---|---|---|---|
| Y | 4 | 7 | 8 | 9 | 10 | 14 | 18 |

**SOLUTION:**

**Calculation of Coefficient of Correlation**

| X | Deviation ($x = X - \overline{X}$) $\overline{X} = 5$ | Square of Deviation ($x^2$) | Y | Deviation ($y = Y - \overline{Y}$) $\overline{Y} = 5$ | Square of Deviation ($y^2$) | Multiple of Deviations (xy) |
|---|---|---|---|---|---|---|
| 2 | – 3 | 9 | 4 | – 6 | 36 | +18 |
| 3 | – 2 | 4 | 7 | – 3 | 9 | + 6 |
| 4 | – 1 | 1 | 8 | – 2 | 4 | + 2 |
| 5 | 0 | 0 | 9 | – 1 | 1 | 0 |
| 6 | 1 | 1 | 10 | 0 | 0 | 0 |
| 7 | 2 | 4 | 14 | 4 | 16 | + 8 |
| 8 | 3 | 9 | 18 | 8 | 64 | +24 |
| $\Sigma X = 35$ N = 7 $\overline{X} = 5$ | $\Sigma x = 0$ | $\Sigma x^2 = 28$ | $\Sigma Y = 70$ N = 7 $\overline{Y} = 10$ | $\Sigma y = 0$ | $\Sigma y^2 = 130$ | $\Sigma xy = 58$ |

$$r = \frac{\Sigma xy}{\sqrt{\Sigma x^2 \times \Sigma y^2}}; \; x = (X - \overline{X}); \; y = (Y - \overline{Y})$$

The table shows that, $\Sigma xy = 58$, $\Sigma x^2 = 28$, $\Sigma y^2 = 130$.

Substituting the values,

$$r = \frac{58}{\sqrt{28 \times 130}} = \frac{58}{\sqrt{3,640}} = \frac{58}{60.33} = +0.96$$

Coefficient of Correlation (r) = +0.96.

It is a situation of high positive correlation.

**Here is another illustration.**

**ILLUSTRATION.**

Calculate the coefficient of correlation between the age of husbands and wives:

| Age of Husband (Years) | 21 | 22 | 28 | 32 | 35 | 36 |
|---|---|---|---|---|---|---|
| Age of Wife (Years) | 18 | 20 | 25 | 30 | 31 | 32 |

**SOLUTION:**

| Age of Husband (X) | Deviation $(x = X - \overline{X})$ $\overline{X} = 29$ | Square of Deviation $(x^2)$ | Age of Wife (Y) | Deviation $(y = Y - \overline{Y})$ $\overline{Y} = 26$ | Square of Deviation $(y^2)$ | Multiple of Deviations (xy) |
|---|---|---|---|---|---|---|
| 21 | − 8 | 64 | 18 | − 8 | 64 | 64 |
| 22 | − 7 | 49 | 20 | − 6 | 36 | 42 |
| 28 | − 1 | 1 | 25 | − 1 | 1 | 1 |
| 32 | + 3 | 9 | 30 | + 4 | 16 | 12 |
| 35 | + 6 | 36 | 31 | + 5 | 25 | 30 |
| 36 | + 7 | 49 | 32 | + 6 | 36 | 42 |
| $\Sigma X = 174$ | $\Sigma x = 0$ | $\Sigma x^2 = 208$ | $\Sigma Y = 156$ | $\Sigma y = 0$ | $\Sigma y^2 = 178$ | $\Sigma xy = 191$ |

$$x = (X - \overline{X});\ y = (Y - \overline{Y})$$

$$\overline{X} = \frac{\Sigma X}{N} = \frac{174}{6} = 29; \overline{Y} = \frac{\Sigma Y}{N} = \frac{156}{6} = 26$$

$$\Sigma xy = 191,\ \Sigma x^2 = 208,\ \Sigma y^2 = 178$$

$$r = \frac{\Sigma xy}{\sqrt{\Sigma x^2 \times \Sigma y^2}}$$

$$r = \frac{191}{\sqrt{208 \times 178}}$$

$$= \frac{191}{\sqrt{37,024}} = \frac{191}{192.42} = 0.993$$

Coefficient of Correlation (r) = 0.993.

Thus, there is a high degree of positive correlation between the age of husband and wife.

## Short-cut Method

This method is used when mean value is not in whole number but in fractions. In this method, deviation is calculated by taking the assumed mean of both the series. It involves the following steps:

(1) Any convenient value in X and Y series is taken as assumed mean $A_X$ and $A_Y$.

(2) With the help of assumed mean of both the series, deviation of the values of individual variable, *i.e.*, dx $(X - A_X)$ and dy $(Y - A_Y)$ are calculated.

(3) Σdx and Σdy are found by adding the deviations.

(4) Deviations of the two series are multiplied, as dx.dy, and the multiples added up to obtain Σdxdy.

(5) Squares of the deviations $dx^2$ and $dy^2$ are added up to find out $\Sigma dx^2$ and $\Sigma dy^2$.

(6) Finally, coefficient of correlation is calculated using the following formula:

**FORMULA**

$$r = \frac{\Sigma dxdy - \frac{(\Sigma dx) \times (\Sigma dy)}{N}}{\sqrt{\Sigma dx^2 - \frac{(\Sigma dx)^2}{N}} \times \sqrt{\Sigma dy^2 - \frac{(\Sigma dy)^2}{N}}}$$

Here,

dx = Deviation of X series from the assumed mean = (X – A)

dy = Deviation of Y series from the assumed mean = (Y – A)

Σdxdy = Sum of the multiple of dx and dy

$\Sigma dx^2$ = Sum of square of dx

$\Sigma dy^2$ = Sum of square of dy

Σdx = Sum of deviation of X series

Σdy = Sum of deviation of Y series

N = Total number of items.

**ILLUSTRATION.**

Calculate coefficient of correlation between the price and quantity supplied:

| **Price (₹)** | 4 | 6 | 8 | 15 | 20 |
|---|---|---|---|---|---|
| **Supply (kg)** | 10 | 15 | 20 | 25 | 30 |

**SOLUTION:**

| **Price (X)** | **Deviation (dx = X – A) A = 8** | **Square of Deviation ($dx^2$)** | **Supply (Y)** | **Deviation (dy = Y – A) A = 20** | **Square of Deviation ($dy^2$)** | **Multiple of Deviations (dxdy)** |
|---|---|---|---|---|---|---|
| 4 | – 4 | 16 | 10 | – 10 | 100 | 40 |
| 6 | – 2 | 4 | 15 | – 5 | 25 | 10 |
| 8 (A) | 0 | 0 | 20 (A) | 0 | 0 | 0 |
| 15 | 7 | 49 | 25 | 5 | 25 | 35 |
| 20 | 12 | 144 | 30 | 10 | 100 | 120 |
| N = 5 | Σdx = 13 | $\Sigma dx^2 = 213$ | N = 5 | Σdy = 0 | $\Sigma dy^2 = 250$ | Σdxdy = 205 |

$$r = \frac{\Sigma dxdy - \frac{(\Sigma dx) \times (\Sigma dy)}{N}}{\sqrt{\Sigma dx^2 - \frac{(\Sigma dx)^2}{N}} \times \sqrt{\Sigma dy^2 - \frac{(\Sigma dy)^2}{N}}}$$

$$r = \frac{205 - \frac{(13)\times(0)}{5}}{\sqrt{213 - \frac{(13)^2}{5}} \times \sqrt{250 - \frac{(0)^2}{5}}}$$

$$r = \frac{205 - 0}{\sqrt{213 - 33.80} \times \sqrt{250 - 0}}$$

$$r = \frac{205}{\sqrt{179.20} \times \sqrt{250}}$$

$$= \frac{205}{13.39 \times 15.81}$$

$$r = \frac{205}{211.70}$$

$$= +\ 0.97$$

Coefficient of Correlation (r) = + 0.97.

This is a situation of a high degree of positive correlation.

### Step-deviation Method

The method involves the following steps:

(1) Repeat Step-1 and Step-2 of the short-cut method.

(2) Now divide 'dx' and 'dy' by some common factor as $dx' = \frac{dx}{C_1}$, $dy' = \frac{dy}{C_2}$; here $C_1$ is common factor for series X and $C_2$ is common factor for series Y. And dx′ and dy′ are step-deviations.

(3) $\Sigma dx'$ and $\Sigma dy'$ are found by adding the deviations.

(4) Deviations of the two series are multiplied, as $dx' \times dy'$, and the multiples added up to obtain $\Sigma dx'dy'$.

(5) Squares of the deviations $dx'^2$ and $dy'^2$ are added up to find out $\Sigma dx'^2$ and $\Sigma dy'^2$.

(6) Finally, coefficient of correlation is calculated using the following formula.

**FORMULA**

$$r = \frac{\Sigma dx'dy' - \frac{(\Sigma dx') \times (\Sigma dy')}{N}}{\sqrt{\Sigma dx'^2 - \frac{(\Sigma dx')^2}{N}} \times \sqrt{\Sigma dy'^2 - \frac{(\Sigma dy')^2}{N}}}$$

### Illustration

Calculate coefficient of correlation between the price and quantity demanded:

| Price (₹) | 5 | 10 | 15 | 20 | 25 |
|---|---|---|---|---|---|
| Demand (kg) | 40 | 35 | 30 | 25 | 20 |

### Solution:

| Price (X) | dx = X – $A_x$ $A_x$ =15 | $dx' = \frac{dx}{C_1}$ $C_1 = 5$ | $dx'^2$ | Demand (Y) | dy = Y – $A_y$ $A_y$ = 30 | $dy' = \frac{dy}{C_2}$ $C_2 = 5$ | $dy'^2$ | dx'dy' |
|---|---|---|---|---|---|---|---|---|
| 5 | – 10 | – 2 | 4 | 40 | 10 | 2 | 4 | – 4 |
| 10 | – 5 | – 1 | 1 | 35 | 5 | 1 | 1 | – 1 |
| 15 | 0 | 0 | 0 | 30 | 0 | 0 | 0 | 0 |
| 20 | 5 | 1 | 1 | 25 | –5 | –1 | 1 | – 1 |
| 25 | 10 | 2 | 4 | 20 | –10 | –2 | 4 | – 4 |
| N = 5 | | Σdx' = 0 | $\Sigma dx'^2 = 10$ | N = 5 | | Σdy' = 0 | $\Sigma dy'^2 = 10$ | Σdx'dy' =–10 |

$$r = \frac{\Sigma dx'dy' - \frac{(\Sigma dx') \times (\Sigma dy')}{N}}{\sqrt{\Sigma dx'^2 - \frac{(\Sigma dx')^2}{N}} \times \sqrt{\Sigma dy'^2 - \frac{(\Sigma dy')^2}{N}}}$$

$$= \frac{-10 - \frac{0}{5}}{\sqrt{10 - \frac{0}{5}}\sqrt{10 - \frac{0}{5}}}$$

$$= \frac{-10}{\sqrt{10} \times \sqrt{10}} = \frac{-10}{10} = -1$$

Coefficient of Correlation (r) = – 1.

This is a situation of a perfectly negative correlation between price and quantity demanded.

### Properties of Correlation Coefficient

(1) r has no unit. It is a pure number. It means units of measurement are not parts of r.

(2) A negative value of r indicates an inverse relation, and if r is positive, the two variables move in the same direction.

(3) If r = 0, the two variables are uncorrelated. There is no linear relation between them. However, other types of relation may be there.

(4) If r = 1 or r = – 1, the correlation is perfect or proportionate. A high value of r indicates strong linear relationship, *i.e.*, + 1 or –1.

(5) The value of the correlation coefficient lies between minus one and plus one, *i.e.*, $-1 \leq r \leq +1$. If the value of r lies outside this range, it indicates error in calculation.

**Learning by doing**

1. *Find out coefficient of correlation between the age of Husband and Wife, using Karl Pearson's method based on actual mean value of the following series.*

| Age of Husband | 20 | 23 | 27 | 31 | 35 | 38 | 40 | 42 |
|---|---|---|---|---|---|---|---|---|
| Age of Wife | 18 | 20 | 24 | 30 | 32 | 34 | 36 | 38 |

(**Ans.** *r* = + 0.994)

2. *Calculate Karl Pearson's coefficient of correlation, between the age and weight of children.*

| Age (Years) | 1 | 2 | 3 | 4 | 5 |
|---|---|---|---|---|---|
| Weight (kg) | 3 | 4 | 6 | 7 | 10 |

(**Ans.** *r* = + 0.98)

3. *Calculate coefficient of correlation, using Karl Pearson's formula based on actual mean value of the series given below.*

| Year | Index of Industrial Production | Number of Unemployed People in thousand |
|---|---|---|
| 2006 | 100 | 11.3 |
| 2007 | 102 | 12.4 |
| 2008 | 104 | 14.0 |
| 2009 | 107 | 11.1 |
| 2010 | 105 | 12.3 |
| 2011 | 112 | 12.2 |
| 2012 | 103 | 19.1 |
| 2013 | 94 | 26.4 |

(**Ans.** *r* = – 0.673)

## Spearman's Rank Correlation Coefficient

In 1904, **Charles Edward Spearman** developed a formula to calculate coefficient of correlation of qualitative variables. It is popularly known as *Spearman's Rank Difference Formula or Method*. There are some variables whose quantitative measurement is not possible. These variables are known as qualitative variables (or more precisely 'attributes') such as beauty, bravery, wisdom, ability, virtue, etc.

The attributes cannot be expressed in numbers or quantitative terms. Their relative merit can be determined on the basis of their order of preference or ranking. For instance, in a fancy dress competition two judges may rank the participants in order of preference. Similarly, the selection committee may prepare a list of successful candidates in order of preference. We experience many such examples in our day-to-day life.

It is in such situations that we use Spearman's Rank Difference Method.

**FORMULA**

$$r_k = 1 - \frac{6\Sigma D^2}{N^3 - N}$$

Here,

$r_k$ = Coefficient of rank correlation;

D = Rank differences; and

N = Number of pairs.

We shall study the calculation of rank correlation in three different situations:

(i) When Ranks are given;

(ii) When Ranks are not given;

(iii) When the values of the series are the same.

Following illustration explains the calculation of Rank Correlation.

### Coefficient of Rank Correlation when Ranks are given

**ILLUSTRATION.**

In a fancy-dress competition, two judges accorded following ranks to the 10 participants:

| Judge X | 1 | 2 | 3 | 4 | 5 | 6 | 7 | 8 | 9 | 10 |
|---|---|---|---|---|---|---|---|---|---|---|
| Judge Y | 10 | 6 | 5 | 4 | 7 | 9 | 8 | 2 | 1 | 3 |

Calculate coefficient of rank correlation.

**SOLUTION:**

$$r_k = 1 - \frac{6\Sigma D^2}{N^3 - N}$$

| Judge I, X = $R_1$ | Judge II, Y= $R_2$ | D = $R_1 - R_2$ | $D^2$ |
|---|---|---|---|
| 1 | 10 | – 9 | 81 |
| 2 | 6 | – 4 | 16 |
| 3 | 5 | – 2 | 4 |
| 4 | 4 | 0 | 0 |
| 5 | 7 | – 2 | 4 |
| 6 | 9 | – 3 | 9 |
| 7 | 8 | – 1 | 1 |
| 8 | 2 | 6 | 36 |
| 9 | 1 | 8 | 64 |
| 10 | 3 | 7 | 49 |
| N = 10 | | | $\Sigma D^2 = 264$ |

$$r_k = 1 - \frac{6\Sigma D^2}{N^3 - N}$$

Here, N = 10; $\Sigma D^2 = 264$

$$r_k = 1 - \frac{6 \times 264}{(10)^3 - 10} = 1 - \frac{1,584}{990}$$

$$= 1 - 1.6 = -0.6$$

Coefficient of Rank Correlation ($r_k$) = – 0.6.

There is a negative coefficient of rank correlation to the tune of – 0.6 which is fairly high. **High negative correlation suggests that two sets of judgements are fairly opposite to each other.**

### Coefficient of Rank Correlation when Ranks are not given

Sometimes, only data are given and not the ranks. In such situations, ranks are to be accorded by the student himself. While according the ranks, uniform procedure should be adopted for both the series. For example, if the highest rank is accorded to the lowest value in one series, the same must be done for the second series as well.

**ILLUSTRATION.**

In a Poetry Recitation Competition, 10 participants were accorded following marks by two different judges, X and Y:

| X | 15 | 17 | 14 | 13 | 11 | 12 | 16 | 18 | 10 | 9 |
|---|---|---|---|---|---|---|---|---|---|---|
| Y | 15 | 12 | 4 | 6 | 7 | 9 | 3 | 10 | 2 | 5 |

Calculate the coefficient of rank correlation.

**SOLUTION:**

There are 10 items each in the two series in this question. We may accord, the highest rank, *i.e.*, 10 to highest value/item in each series, *i.e.*, 18 in series X and 15 in series Y, and accord the lowest rank, *i.e.*, 1 to the lowest value/item in each series, *i.e.*, 9 in series X and 2 in series Y.

| X | Rank $R_1$ | Y | Rank $R_2$ | $D = R_1 - R_2$ | $D^2$ |
|---|---|---|---|---|---|
| 15 | 7 | 15 | 10 | – 3 | 9 |
| 17 | 9 | 12 | 9 | 0 | 0 |
| 14 | 6 | 4 | 3 | 3 | 9 |
| 13 | 5 | 6 | 5 | 0 | 0 |
| 11 | 3 | 7 | 6 | – 3 | 9 |
| 12 | 4 | 9 | 7 | – 3 | 9 |
| 16 | 8 | 3 | 2 | 6 | 36 |
| 18 | 10 | 10 | 8 | 2 | 4 |
| 10 | 2 | 2 | 1 | 1 | 1 |
| 9 | 1 | 5 | 4 | – 3 | 9 |
| N = 10 | | | | | $\Sigma D^2 = 86$ |

$$r_k = 1 - \frac{6\Sigma D^2}{N^3 - N}$$

Here, $N = 10; \Sigma D^2 = 86$

$$r_k = \frac{6 \times 86}{(10)^3 - 10} = 1 - \frac{516}{1,000 - 10}$$

$$= 1 - 0.52 = 0.48$$

Coefficient of Rank Correlation ($r_k$) = 0.48.

Thus, there is a positive rank correlation of a moderate degree of 0.48.

### Coefficient of Rank Correlation when Ranks are Equal

Sometimes, two or more items in the series have equal ranks. In such situations, average of the two ranks (say 7.5 of the ranks 7 and 8) is accorded to each value. But one is likely to commit mistake in this procedure. In order to avoid the possibility of error, the following formula is used for the calculation of coefficient of rank correlation in such situations:

**FORMULA**

$$r_k = 1 - \frac{6[\Sigma D^2 + \frac{1}{12}(m_1^3 - m_1) + \frac{1}{12}(m_2^3 - m_2) + ...]}{N^3 - N}$$

Here, m = Number of items of equal ranks.

**ILLUSTRATION.**

Calculate coefficient of rank correlation between the marks in Economics and Statistics, as indicated by 8 answer books of each of the two examiners.

| Marks in Statistics | 15 | 10 | 20 | 28 | 12 | 10 | 16 | 18 |
|---|---|---|---|---|---|---|---|---|
| Marks in Economics | 16 | 14 | 10 | 12 | 11 | 15 | 18 | 12 |

**SOLUTION:**

There are 8 answer books each in Economics and Statistics indicating different marks. Rank 1 is accorded to the highest score. In Statistics, two answer books indicate 10 marks each. Hence, the first answer book has been given Rank 8 and the second 7. Thus, the average rank = $\frac{8+7}{2}$ = 7.5 has been accorded to both. Likewise, in Economics two answer books indicate 12 marks each. The average rank = $\frac{6+5}{2}$ = 5.5 has, therefore, been accorded to both.

**Calculation of Coefficient of Rank Correlation**

| Marks in Statistics (X) | Rank $R_1$ | Marks in Economics (Y) | Rank $R_2$ | $D = R_1 - R_2$ | $D^2$ |
|---|---|---|---|---|---|
| 15 | 5 | 16 | 2 | 3.0 | 9.00 |
| 10 | 7.5 | 14 | 4 | 3.5 | 12.25 |
| 20 | 2 | 10 | 8 | – 6 | 36.00 |
| 28 | 1 | 12 | 5.5 | – 4.5 | 20.25 |
| 12 | 6 | 11 | 7 | – 1 | 1.00 |
| 10 | 7.5 | 15 | 3 | 4.5 | 20.25 |
| 16 | 4 | 18 | 1 | 3.0 | 9.00 |
| 18 | 3 | 12 | 5.5 | – 2.5 | 6.25 |
| N = 8 | | | | | $\Sigma D^2 = 114$ |

Here, number 10 is repeated twice in series X and number 12 is repeated twice in series Y. Therefore, in X, m = 2 and in Y, m = 2.

$$r_k = 1 - \frac{6[\Sigma D^2 + \frac{1}{12}(m_1^3 - m_1) + \frac{1}{12}(m_2^3 - m_2)]}{N^3 - N}$$

$$= 1 - \frac{6[114 + \frac{1}{12}(2^3 - 2) + \frac{1}{12}(2^3 - 2)]}{8^3 - 8}$$

$$= 1 - \frac{6\left[114 + \frac{1}{12}(6) + \frac{1}{12}(6)\right]}{512 - 8}$$

$$= 1 - \frac{6\left[114 + \frac{1}{2} + \frac{1}{2}\right]}{504} = 1 - \frac{6[115]}{504} = 1 - \frac{690}{504}$$

$$= 1 - 1.36 = -0.36$$

Coefficient of Rank Correlation ($r_k$) = – 0.36.

### Merits and Demerits of Rank Correlation

#### Merits

(1) Spearman's rank correlation method is easier than Pearson's method of correlation.

(2) Rank correlation method is very convenient method when the series give only order of preference and not the actual values of the variables.

(3) Rank correlation is a superior method of analysis in case of qualitative distributions such as those relating to virtue, wisdom or ignorance.

#### Demerits

(1) Rank correlation method cannot be used in case of group frequency distributions.

(2) It can handle only a limited number of observations. It is generally not used when the number of observations exceeds 20.

*Learning by doing*

1. *10 students obtained following ranks in their mathematics and statistics examinations. Find out the extent to which the knowledge of students is correlated in the two subjects.*

| Ranks in Statistics | 1 | 2 | 3 | 4 | 5 | 6 | 7 | 8 | 9 | 10 |
|---|---|---|---|---|---|---|---|---|---|---|
| Ranks in Mathematics | 2 | 4 | 1 | 5 | 3 | 9 | 7 | 10 | 6 | 8 |

*(Ans. $r_k$ = + 0.76)*

2. *Calculate coefficient of rank correlation, given the following data set.*

| X | 20 | 11 | 72 | 65 | 43 | 29 | 50 |
|---|---|---|---|---|---|---|---|
| Y | 60 | 63 | 26 | 35 | 43 | 51 | 37 |

*(Ans. $r_k$ = – 1)*

## 4. Importance or Significance of Correlation

Following observations highlight the importance or significance of correlation as a statistical method:

(1) **Formation of Laws and Concepts:** The study of correlation shows the direction and degree of relationship between the variables. This has helped the formation of various laws and concepts in economic theory, such as, the law of demand and the concept of elasticity of demand.

(2) **Cause and Effect Relationship:** Correlation coefficient sometimes suggests cause and effect relationship between different variables. This helps in understanding why certain variables behave the way they behave.

(3) **Business Decisions:** Correlation analysis facilitates business decisions because the trend path of one variable may suggest the expected changes in the other. Accordingly, the businessman may plan his business decisions for the future.

(4) **Policy Formulation:** Correlation analysis also helps policy formulation. If the Government finds a negative correlation between tax rate and tax collection, it should pursue the policy of low tax rate. Because, low tax rate would lead to high tax collection.

## MISCELLANEOUS ILLUSTRATIONS

### ILLUSTRATION 1.

From the following data, compute the coefficient of correlation between X and Y series.

| | X-Series | Y-Series |
|---|---|---|
| Number of Items | 6 | 6 |
| Arithmetic Mean | 350 | 138 |
| Squares of Deviations from Mean | 19 | 94 |

Summation of product of deviations of X and Y series from their respective arithmetic mean = 41.

**SOLUTION:**

We are given:

$N = 6, \overline{X} = 350, \overline{Y} = 138, \Sigma x^2 = 19, \Sigma y^2 = 94, \Sigma xy = 41$

$$r = \frac{\Sigma xy}{\sqrt{\Sigma x^2 \times \Sigma y^2}}$$

Substituting the values, we get

$$r = \frac{41}{\sqrt{19 \times 94}} = \frac{41}{\sqrt{1{,}786}} = \frac{41}{42.26} = 0.97$$

Coefficient of Correlation (r) = + 0.97.

### ILLUSTRATION 2.

From the following table, calculate the coefficient of correlation by Karl Pearson's method:

| X | 6 | 2 | 10 | 4 | 8 |
|---|---|---|---|---|---|
| Y | 9 | 11 | – | 8 | 7 |

Arithmetic means of X and Y series are 6 and 8 respectively.

**SOLUTION:**

Let us first find the missing value of Y and let us denote it by *a*.

$$\overline{Y} = \frac{\Sigma Y}{N} = \frac{9 + 11 + a + 8 + 7}{5} = \frac{35 + a}{5}$$

$$\Rightarrow \quad 8 = \frac{35 + a}{5}$$

$\therefore \quad 35 + a = 40$

$\Rightarrow \quad a = 5$

Thus, the complete series is:

| X | 6 | 2 | 10 | 4 | 8 |
|---|---|---|---|---|---|
| Y | 9 | 11 | 5 | 8 | 7 |

Now we find the coefficient of correlation.

**Calculation of Coefficient of Correlation**

| X | Deviation $(x=X-\overline{X})$ $\overline{X}=6$ | Square of Deviation $(x^2)$ | Y | Deviation $(y=Y-\overline{Y})$ $\overline{Y}=8$ | Square of Deviation $(y^2)$ | Multiple of Deviations (xy) |
|---|---|---|---|---|---|---|
| 6 | 0 | 0 | 9 | 1 | 1 | 0 |
| 2 | – 4 | 16 | 11 | 3 | 9 | –12 |
| 10 | 4 | 16 | 5 | – 3 | 9 | –12 |
| 4 | – 2 | 4 | 8 | 0 | 0 | 0 |
| 8 | 2 | 4 | 7 | – 1 | 1 | –2 |
| $\Sigma X=30$ | $\Sigma x=0$ | $\Sigma x^2=40$ | $\Sigma Y=40$ | $\Sigma y=0$ | $\Sigma y^2=20$ | $\Sigma xy=-26$ |

$$r = \frac{\Sigma xy}{\sqrt{\Sigma x^2 \times \Sigma y^2}}$$

The table shows that $\Sigma xy = -26$, $\Sigma x^2 = 40$, $\Sigma y^2 = 20$

Substituting the values, we get

$$r = \frac{-26}{\sqrt{40 \times 20}}$$

$$= \frac{-26}{\sqrt{800}} = \frac{-26}{28.28}$$

$$= -0.92$$

Coefficient of Correlation (r) = – 0.92.

**ILLUSTRATION 3.**

From the data given below, find the number of items (N):

$r = 0.5$, $\Sigma xy = 120$, Standard Deviation of $Y(\sigma_y) = 8$, $\Sigma x^2 = 90$

where, x and y are deviations from arithmetic mean.

**SOLUTION:**

Given: $r = 0.5$, $\Sigma xy = 120$, $\Sigma x^2 = 90$, $\sigma_y = 8$

Now, $\quad \sigma_y = \sqrt{\frac{\Sigma y^2}{N}}$

when $y = Y - \overline{Y}$ [Formula of standard deviation]

$$8 = \sqrt{\frac{\Sigma y^2}{N}}$$

Squaring both sides, we get

$$64 = \frac{\Sigma y^2}{N} \quad \Rightarrow \quad \Sigma y^2 = 64N$$

Now, $$r = \frac{\Sigma xy}{\sqrt{\Sigma x^2 \times \Sigma y^2}} \quad \Rightarrow \quad 0.5 = \frac{120}{\sqrt{90 \times 64N}}$$

Squaring both sides

$$0.25 = \frac{(120)^2}{90 \times 64N}$$

$$\Rightarrow \quad 0.25 = \frac{14,400}{5,760N}$$

$$\Rightarrow \quad (0.25)(5,760)N = 14,400$$

$$\Rightarrow \quad (1,440)\ N = 14,400$$

$$\therefore \quad N = \frac{14,400}{1,440} = 10$$

Number of Items = 10.

**ILLUSTRATION 4.**

Find the coefficient of correlation from the following data:

| X | 10 | 12 | 18 | 16 | 15 | 19 | 18 | 17 |
|---|---|---|---|---|---|---|---|---|
| Y | 30 | 35 | 45 | 44 | 42 | 48 | 47 | 46 |

**SOLUTION:**

**Calculation of Coefficient of Correlation**

| X | Deviation (dx = X – A) A=16 | Square of Deviation ($dx^2$) | Y | Deviation (dy = Y – A) A=42 | Square of Deviation ($dy^2$) | Multiple of Deviations (dxdy) |
|---|---|---|---|---|---|---|
| 10 | – 6 | 36 | 30 | – 12 | 144 | 72 |
| 12 | – 4 | 16 | 35 | – 7 | 49 | 28 |
| 18 | + 2 | 4 | 45 | + 3 | 9 | 6 |
| 16 (A) | 0 | 0 | 44 | + 2 | 4 | 0 |
| 15 | – 1 | 1 | 42 (A) | 0 | 0 | 0 |
| 19 | + 3 | 9 | 48 | + 6 | 36 | 18 |
| 18 | + 2 | 4 | 47 | + 5 | 25 | 10 |
| 17 | + 1 | 1 | 46 | + 4 | 16 | 4 |
| ΣX = 125 N = 8 | Σdx = – 3 | $\Sigma dx^2 = 71$ | ΣY = 337 N = 8 | Σdy = 1 | $\Sigma dy^2 = 283$ | Σdxdy = 138 |

$$\overline{X} = \frac{\Sigma X}{N} = \frac{125}{8} = 15.625;$$

$$\overline{Y} = \frac{\Sigma Y}{N} = \frac{337}{8} = 42.125$$

Since the actual means are not whole numbers, we take 16 as assumed mean for X and 42 as assumed mean for Y.

Applying the formula,

$$r = \frac{\Sigma dxdy - \frac{(\Sigma dx) \times (\Sigma dy)}{N}}{\sqrt{\Sigma dx^2 - \frac{(\Sigma dx)^2}{N}} \times \sqrt{\Sigma dy^2 - \frac{(\Sigma dy)^2}{N}}}$$

$$= \frac{138 - \frac{(-3) \times (1)}{8}}{\sqrt{71 - \frac{(-3)^2}{8}} \times \sqrt{283 - \frac{(1)^2}{8}}}$$

$$= \frac{138 - (-0.375)}{\sqrt{71 - 1.125} \times \sqrt{283 - 0.125}}$$

$$= \frac{138 + 0.375}{\sqrt{69.875} \times \sqrt{282.875}}$$

$$= \frac{138.375}{8.36 \times 16.82}$$

$$= \frac{138.375}{140.6152}$$

$$= +0.98$$

Coefficient of Correlation (r) = + 0.98.

**ILLUSTRATION 5.**

If r = 0.997, $\Sigma xy = 46$, $\overline{X} = 4$, $\overline{Y} = 8$, $\Sigma x^2 = 28$, what will be the value of $\Sigma y^2$?

**SOLUTION:**

$$r = \frac{\Sigma xy}{\sqrt{\Sigma x^2 \times \Sigma y^2}}$$

Given: r = 0.997, $\Sigma xy = 46$, $\overline{X} = 4$, $\overline{Y} = 8$, $\Sigma x^2 = 28$

Substituting the values, we get

$$0.997 = \frac{46}{\sqrt{28 \times \Sigma y^2}}$$

Squaring both sides, we get

$$0.994 = \frac{2,116}{28 \times \Sigma y^2}$$

$$\Rightarrow 27.832 \times \Sigma y^2 = 2,116$$

$$\Sigma y^2 = 76.03$$

Value of $\Sigma y^2 = 76.03$.

**ILLUSTRATION 6.**

Two ladies were asked to rank 10 different types of cell phone. The ranks given by them are given below:

| Cell Phone | A | B | C | D | E | F | G | H | I | J |
|---|---|---|---|---|---|---|---|---|---|---|
| Neelu | 1 | 6 | 3 | 9 | 5 | 2 | 7 | 10 | 8 | 4 |
| Neena | 6 | 8 | 3 | 7 | 2 | 1 | 5 | 9 | 4 | 10 |

Calculate Spearman's rank correlation coefficient.

**SOLUTION:**

**Calculation of Rank Correlation Coefficient**

| Rank $R_1$ | Rank $R_2$ | $D = R_1 - R_2$ | $D^2$ |
|---|---|---|---|
| 1 | 6 | – 5 | 25 |
| 6 | 8 | – 2 | 4 |
| 3 | 3 | 0 | 0 |
| 9 | 7 | + 2 | 4 |
| 5 | 2 | + 3 | 9 |
| 2 | 1 | + 1 | 1 |
| 7 | 5 | + 2 | 4 |
| 10 | 9 | + 1 | 1 |
| 8 | 4 | + 4 | 16 |
| 4 | 10 | – 6 | 36 |
| N=10 | | $\Sigma D = 0$ | $\Sigma D^2 = 100$ |

$$r_k = 1 - \frac{6\Sigma D^2}{N^3 - N}$$

Here, $N = 10$; $\Sigma D^2 = 100$

Substituting the values, we get

$$r_k = 1 - \frac{6 \times 100}{10^3 - 10}$$

$$= 1 - \frac{600}{1{,}000 - 10}$$

$$= 1 - \frac{600}{990}$$

$$= 1 - 0.606 = 0.394$$

Coefficient of Rank Correlation ($r_k$) = 0.394.

**ILLUSTRATION 7.**

Calculate coefficient of correlation by means of ranking method from the following data:

| X | 40 | 50 | 60 | 60 | 80 | 50 | 70 | 60 |
|---|---|---|---|---|---|---|---|---|
| Y | 80 | 120 | 160 | 170 | 130 | 200 | 210 | 130 |

**SOLUTION:**

**Calculation of Rank Correlation Coefficient**

| X | Rank $R_1$ | Y | Rank $R_2$ | $D = R_1 - R_2$ | $D^2$ |
|---|---|---|---|---|---|
| 40 | 8 | 80 | 8 | 0 | 0 |
| 50 | 6.5 | 120 | 7 | – 0.5 | 0.25 |
| 60 | 4 | 160 | 4 | 0 | 0 |
| 60 | 4 | 170 | 3 | 1 | 1 |
| 80 | 1 | 130 | 5.5 | – 4.5 | 20.25 |
| 50 | 6.5 | 200 | 2 | 4.5 | 20.25 |
| 70 | 2 | 210 | 1 | 1 | 1 |
| 60 | 4 | 130 | 5.5 | – 1.5 | 2.25 |
| N = 8 | | | | $\Sigma D = 0$ | $\Sigma D^2 = 45$ |

In this question in X series, the values 60 and 50 are repeated thrice and twice. The average rank for the value 60 is 4 (3 + 4 + 5 ÷ 3) while for the value 50 it is 6.5 (6 + 7 ÷ 2). In both the cases, the correlation factor will be $\frac{1}{12}(3^3 - 3)$ and $\frac{1}{12}(2^3 - 2)$ respectively. In series Y, the 130 is repeated twice. The average rank for the value 130 is 5.5 (5 + 6 ÷ 2). In this case, correlation factor will be $\frac{1}{12}(2^3 - 2)$.

$$r_k = 1 - \frac{6\left[\Sigma D^2 + \frac{1}{12}(m_1^3 - m_1) + \frac{1}{12}(m_2^3 - m_2) + \frac{1}{12}(m_3^3 - m_3)\right]}{N^3 - N}$$

Here, $\Sigma D^2 = 45$; $m_1 = 3$; $m_2 = 2$; $m_3 = 2$; $N = 8$

By substituting values in the above formula, we get

$$r_k = 1 - \frac{6\left[45 + \frac{1}{12}(3^3 - 3) + \frac{1}{12}(2^3 - 2) + \frac{1}{12}(2^3 - 2)\right]}{(8)^3 - 8}$$

$$= 1 - \frac{6\left[45 + \frac{1}{12}(24) + \frac{1}{12}(6) + \frac{1}{12}(6)\right]}{512 - 8}$$

$$= 1 - \frac{6\left(45 + 2 + \frac{1}{2} + \frac{1}{2}\right)}{504} = 1 - \frac{6(48)}{504} = 1 - \frac{288}{504}$$

$$= 1 - 0.571 = 0.429$$

Coefficient of Rank Correlation ($r_k$) = 0.429.

## EXERCISE

### 1. Very Short Answer Type Questions [1 mark]

**A. Multiple Choice Questions: Choose the Correct Answer**

1. When two variables change in the same direction, then such a correlation is called:
   (a) negative (b) positive
   (c) no correlation (d) all of these
2. When the relation of three or more variables is studied simultaneously, it is called:
   (a) simple correlation (b) partial correlation
   (c) multiple correlation (d) none of these
3. Relation between price and demand is:
   (a) positive (b) negative
   (c) one to one (d) no relationship
4. When coefficient of correlation lies between +0.25 and + 0.75, it is called:
   (a) perfect degree of correlation (b) high degree of correlation
   (c) moderate degree of correlation (d) low degree of correlation
5. Coefficient of correlation lies always between:
   (a) 0 and +1 (b) –1 and 0
   (c) –1 and +1 (d) none of these
6. Rank correlation is a superior method of analysis in case of ________ distribution.
   (a) qualitative (b) quantitative
   (c) frequency (d) none of these
7. Which of the following equations is correct?
   (a) $r_k = 1 - \frac{6\Sigma D^2}{N}$ (b) $r_k = 1 - \frac{6\Sigma D^2}{N^2 - N}$
   (c) $r_k = 1 - \frac{6\Sigma D^2}{N^3 - N}$ (d) $r_k = 1 - \frac{6\Sigma D^2}{N^4 - N}$
8. Formula of Karl Pearson's coefficient of correlation is:
   (a) $\frac{N\sigma_X\sigma_Y}{\Sigma xy}$ (b) $\frac{\Sigma xy}{N\sigma_X\sigma_Y}$
   (c) $\frac{\sigma_X\sigma_Y}{\Sigma xy}$ (d) $\frac{\Sigma xy}{\sigma_X\sigma_Y}$
9. When two variables change in a constant proportion, it is called:
   (a) linear correlation (b) non-linear correlation
   (c) partial correlation (d) none of these

Ans. 1. (b), 2. (c), 3. (b), 4. (c), 5. (c), 6. (a), 7. (c), 8. (b), 9. (a).

## B. True or False

State whether the following statements are True or False:

1. Definite relation between two or more than two groups or series is called correlation. (True/False)
2. Coefficient of correlation, is always positive. (True/False)
3. In scattered diagram, more the different points are close to each other, less will be the value of correlation. (True/False)
4. If the value of coefficient of correlation is +1, it implies that correlation between the two variables is perfectly positive. (True/False)
5. Karl Pearson's method of correlation apply to those series where deviations are calculated on the basis of assumed mean. (True/False)
6. There is always a cause and effect relationship between the two series showing high coefficient of correlation. (True/False)

Ans.1. True, 2. False, 3. False, 4. True, 5. False, 6. False.

## C. Concepts/Definitions & Knowledge-based Questions

1. Define correlation.

Ans. Correlation is a statistical method or a statistical technique that measures quantitative relationship between different variables, like between price and demand.

2. Define partial correlation.

Ans. When more than two variables are involved and out of these the relationship between only two variables is studied treating other variables as constant, then the correlation is partial.

3. What is the line of best fit?

Ans. Line of Best Fit is the one that passes through the scattered points such that it represents most of these points. Roughly, half of the scattered points should be on either side of the line.

4. Name the principal methods of calculating coefficient of correlation.

Ans. There are three principal methods of calculating coefficient of correlation:

(1) Scattered Diagram Method,

(2) Karl Pearson's Coefficient of Correlation, and

(3) Spearman's Rank Correlation Coefficient.

5. What is the difference between positive and negative correlation?

Ans. The difference between positive and negative correlation is that in positive correlation, variables move in the same direction whereas in the negative correlation, they move in different directions.

6. What is the nature of correlation of two variables, when they move in the same direction?

Ans. When two variables move in the same direction, such correlation is positive in nature.

7. Coefficient of correlation is between – 1 and + 1. How would you express it arithmetically?

Ans. When coefficient of correlation is – 1, correlation is perfect negative and
when coefficient of correlation is + 1, correlation is perfect positive.

8. When is rank correlation method used?

Ans. Rank correlation method is used when variables are qualitative in nature, such as beauty, bravery, wisdom, virtue, etc.

## 2. Short Answer Type Questions [3-4 marks]

1. Define correlation. Give its importance.
2. Describe the various degrees of correlation.
3. What are the different methods of finding correlation?
4. Explain the various kinds of correlation.
5. Explain the scattered diagram method of correlation.
6. Explain the merits and demerits of scattered diagram method.
7. Describe Karl Pearson's method of calculating coefficient of correlation.
8. State the properties of correlation coefficient.
9. Discuss Spearman's rank difference method.
10. State the merits of rank correlation coefficient.
11. What kind of relationship between X and Y is indicated, if the points of the scattered diagram tend to cluster about
    (i) a straight line parallel to the X-axis
    (ii) a straight line parallel to the Y-axis
    (iii) a straight line sloping upward, and
    (iv) straight line sloping downward?
12. If the points in a scattered diagram tend to cluster about a straight line which makes an angle of 30° with the X-axis, what would you say about the strength of association between X and Y?

## 3. Long Answer Type Questions [6 marks]

1. Define correlation. Give its importance in Statistics.
2. What is meant by correlation? Explain its various kinds.
3. Discuss Karl Pearson's method of calculating coefficient of correlation. Give its merits and limitations.
4. Discuss Spearman's method of calculating coefficient of correlation. Give its merits and limitations.
5. Explain the concept of correlation. What is the basic difference between: (i) linear and non-linear correlation, and (ii) positive and negative correlation.
6. (i) How is Karl Pearson's coefficient of correlation defined?
   (ii) What are the limits of the correlation coefficient r?
   (iii) If r = +1 in one situation and r = –1 in the other, what kind of relationship exists between the variables X and Y?
7. (i) Define Spearman's rank correlation ($r_k$).
   (ii) What are the limits of $r_k$?
   (iii) If the values of X and Y have been ranked and we compute correlation between ranks of X and Y, will this correlation be equal to the value of $r_k$?

## 4. Essential Practicals

1. Make a scattered diagram of the data given below. Does any relationship exist between the two?

| X | 4 | 5 | 6 | 7 | 8 | 9 | 10 | 11 | 12 | 13 | 14 | 15 |
|---|---|---|---|---|---|---|---|---|---|---|---|---|
| Y | 78 | 72 | 66 | 60 | 54 | 48 | 42 | 36 | 30 | 24 | 18 | 12 |

2. Calculate coefficient of correlation of the age of husband and wife using Karl Pearson's method.

| Husband (Age) | 23 | 27 | 28 | 29 | 30 | 31 | 33 | 35 | 36 |
|---|---|---|---|---|---|---|---|---|---|
| Wife (Age) | 18 | 20 | 22 | 27 | 29 | 27 | 29 | 28 | 29 |

(Ans. r = + 0.86)

3. Calculate correlation of the following data using Karl Person's method:

| Series A | 112 | 114 | 108 | 124 | 145 | 150 | 119 | 125 | 147 | 150 |
|---|---|---|---|---|---|---|---|---|---|---|
| Series B | 200 | 190 | 214 | 187 | 170 | 170 | 210 | 190 | 180 | 181 |

(Ans. r = – 0.85)

4. Using assumed average in Karl Pearson's formula, calculate coefficient of correlation, given the following data:

| X | 78 | 89 | 97 | 69 | 59 | 79 | 68 | 61 |
|---|---|---|---|---|---|---|---|---|
| Y | 125 | 137 | 156 | 112 | 107 | 106 | 123 | 138 |

(Ans. r = + 0.597)

5. Find out Karl Pearson's coefficient of correlation:

| Capital Units (in '000) | 10 | 20 | 30 | 40 | 50 | 60 | 70 | 80 | 90 | 100 |
|---|---|---|---|---|---|---|---|---|---|---|
| Profit Receipt | 2 | 4 | 8 | 5 | 10 | 15 | 14 | 20 | 22 | 30 |

(Ans. r = + 0.96)

6. Seven students of a class secured following marks in Economics and History. Calculate coefficient of correlation with the help of these data.

| Economics | 66 | 90 | 89 | 55 | 58 | 44 | 42 |
|---|---|---|---|---|---|---|---|
| History | 58 | 76 | 65 | 58 | 53 | 49 | 56 |

(Ans. $r_k$ = + 0.79)

7. Find out rank difference correlation of X and Y:

| X | 80 | 78 | 75 | 75 | 58 | 67 | 60 | 59 |
|---|---|---|---|---|---|---|---|---|
| Y | 12 | 13 | 14 | 14 | 14 | 16 | 15 | 17 |

(Ans. $r_k$ = – 0.714)

8. Calculate coefficient of correlation of the following data with rank difference and Karl Pearson's methods:

| Economics (Marks) | 77 | 54 | 27 | 52 | 14 | 35 | 90 | 25 | 56 | 60 |
|---|---|---|---|---|---|---|---|---|---|---|
| Hindi (Marks) | 35 | 58 | 60 | 46 | 50 | 40 | 35 | 56 | 44 | 42 |

(Ans. $r_k$ = – 0.703, r = – 0.69)

9. Seven methods of teaching Economics in two universities are shown below. Calculate rank difference correlation.

| Teaching Methods | I | II | III | IV | V | VI | VII |
|---|---|---|---|---|---|---|---|
| Rank of 'A's Students | 2 | 1 | 5 | 3 | 4 | 7 | 6 |
| Rank of 'B's Students | 1 | 3 | 2 | 4 | 7 | 5 | 6 |

(Ans. $r_k = + 0.5$)

10. Give three examples of perfect correlation. Find out rank difference coefficient of correlation with the help of the following data:

| X | 48 | 33 | 40 | 9 | 16 | 65 | 26 | 15 | 57 |
|---|---|---|---|---|---|---|---|---|---|
| Y | 13 | 13 | 22 | 6 | 14 | 20 | 9 | 6 | 15 |

(Ans. $r_k = + 0.758$)

11. Calculate coefficient of correlation of the following data:

| X | 10 | 6 | 9 | 10 | 12 | 13 | 11 | 9 |
|---|---|---|---|---|---|---|---|---|
| Y | 9 | 4 | 6 | 9 | 11 | 13 | 8 | 4 |

(Ans. $r = + 0.90$)

12. Deviation of two series X and Y are shown. Calculate coefficient of correlation.

| X | +5 | – 4 | –2 | +20 | –10 | 0 | +3 | 0 | – 15 | –5 |
|---|---|---|---|---|---|---|---|---|---|---|
| Y | +5 | –12 | – 7 | +25 | –10 | – 3 | 0 | +2 | –9 | – 15 |

(Ans. $r = + 0.89$)

13. In a baby competition, two judges accorded following ranks to 12 competitors. Find the coefficient of rank correlation.

| Entry | A | B | C | D | E | F | G | H | I | J | K | L |
|---|---|---|---|---|---|---|---|---|---|---|---|---|
| Judge X | 1 | 2 | 3 | 4 | 5 | 6 | 7 | 8 | 9 | 10 | 11 | 12 |
| Judge Y | 12 | 9 | 6 | 10 | 3 | 5 | 4 | 7 | 8 | 2 | 11 | 1 |

(Ans. $r_k = – 0.455$)

14. In a Fancy-dress competition, two judges accorded the following ranks to eight participants:

| Judge X | 8 | 7 | 6 | 3 | 2 | 1 | 5 | 4 |
|---|---|---|---|---|---|---|---|---|
| Judge Y | 7 | 5 | 4 | 1 | 3 | 2 | 6 | 8 |

Calculate coefficient of rank correlation. (Ans. $r_k = 0.619$)

15. In a beauty contest, three judges accorded following ranks to 10 participants:

| Judge I | 1 | 6 | 5 | 10 | 3 | 2 | 4 | 9 | 7 | 8 |
|---|---|---|---|---|---|---|---|---|---|---|
| Judge II | 3 | 5 | 8 | 4 | 7 | 10 | 2 | 1 | 6 | 9 |
| Judge III | 6 | 4 | 9 | 8 | 1 | 2 | 3 | 10 | 5 | 7 |

Find out by Spearman's Rank Difference Method which pair of judges has a common taste in respect of beauty. (Ans. $r_k$ (I & II) = – 0.212, $r_k$ (II & III) = – 0.297, $r_k$ (I & III) = + 0.636)
(It means there is a good deal of concurrence in the judgement of I and III.)

16. Following data relates to age group and percentage of regular players. Calculate Karl Pearson's coefficient of correlation.

| **Age Group** | 20–25 | 25–30 | 30–35 | 35–40 | 40–45 | 45–50 |
|---|---|---|---|---|---|---|
| **% of Regular Players** | 40 | 35 | 28 | 20 | 15 | 5 |

(Ans. r = – 0.996)

17. From the following data, relating to playing habits in various age group of 900 students. Calculate coefficient of correlation between age group and playing habits.

| **Age Group** | 15–16 | 16–17 | 17–18 | 18–19 | 19–20 | 20–21 |
|---|---|---|---|---|---|---|
| **Number of Students** | 250 | 200 | 150 | 120 | 100 | 80 |
| **Regular Players** | 200 | 150 | 90 | 48 | 30 | 12 |

(Ans. r = – 0.992)

18. Following data relates to density of population, number of deaths and population of various cities. Calculate death rate and Karl Pearson coefficient between density of population and death rate.

| **Cities** | P | Q | R | S | T | U |
|---|---|---|---|---|---|---|
| **Density of Population** | 200 | 500 | 700 | 500 | 600 | 900 |
| **Number of Deaths** | 840 | 300 | 312 | 560 | 1,440 | 1,224 |
| **Population** | 42,000 | 30,000 | 24,000 | 40,000 | 90,000 | 72,000 |

(Ans. r = – 0.247)

19. From the following data, determine Karl Pearson's coefficient of correlation between X and Y series for 15 pairs:

| | **X-Series** | **Y-Series** |
|---|---|---|
| **Mean** | 80 | 120 |
| **Sum of Squares of deviation from Arithmetic Mean** | 56 | 156 |
| **Sum of product of deviations of X and Y from their respective Means** | 92 | |

(Ans. r = 0.98)

20. From the following information, determine coefficient of correlation between X and Y series:

| | **X-Series** | **Y-Series** |
|---|---|---|
| **Number of Items** | 15 | 15 |
| **Mean** | 25 | 18 |
| **SD** | 3.01 | 3.03 |
| **Sum of Squares of deviation from Mean** | 136 | 138 |
| **Sum of product of deviations of X and Y from their respective Means** | 122 | |

(Ans. r = 0.89)

## 5. NCERT Textbook Questions [With Hints to Answers]

1. The unit of correlation coefficient between height in feet and weight in kg is:
   (i) kg/feet
   (ii) percentage
   (iii) non-existent
   [(iii)]
2. The range of simple correlation coefficient is:
   (i) 0 to infinity
   (ii) minus one to plus one
   (iii) minus infinity to infinity
   [(ii)]
3. If $r_{xy}$ is positive the relation between X and Y is of the type:
   (i) when Y increases X increases
   (ii) when Y decreases X increases
   (iii) when Y increases X does not change
   [(i)]
4. If $r_{xy} = 0$, the variable X and Y are:
   (i) linearly related
   (ii) not linearly related
   (iii) independent
   [(ii)]
5. Of the following three measures which can measure any type of relationship?
   (i) Karl Pearson's coefficient of correlation
   (ii) Spearman's rank correlation
   (iii) Scatter diagram
   [(iii), as it can measure both linear and non-linear relationships.]
6. If precisely measured data are available the simple correlation coefficient is:
   (i) more accurate than rank correlation coefficient
   (ii) less accurate than rank correlation coefficient
   (iii) as accurate as the rank correlation coefficient
   [(i)]
7. Can r lies outside the –1 and 1 range depending on the type of data?
   [No. When r lies outside the range –1 and 1, it only indicates error in calculation.]
8. Does correlation imply causation?
   [No. Correlation only implies covariation.]
9. When is rank correlation more precise than simple correlation coefficient?
   [When a precise measurement of the variables is not possible.]

**10.** Does zero correlation mean independence?

[Zero correlation only means that there is no linear relationship between the two variables. It does not mean that the two variables are independent of each other.]

**11.** Can simple correlation coefficient measure any type of relationship?

[No. Simple correlation measures only linear relationship between the variables.]

**12.** Interpret the values of r as 1, –1 and 0.

[When r = 1, the correlation is perfect positive. In this case, proportional change in two variables is linear and is in the same direction.

When r = –1, the correlation is perfect negative. In this case, proportional change in two variables is linear and is in the opposite direction.

When r = 0, the two variables are uncorrelated. There is no linear relationship between them. However, it does not imply that the two variables are independent.]

**13.** Why does rank correlation coefficient differ from Pearsonian correlation coefficient?

[Rank correlation coefficient is more often used to measure the linear relationship between the qualitative variables whereas Karl Pearson's method of correlation coefficient measures the linear relationship between the quantitative variables.]

**14.** Calculate the correlation coefficient between the heights of fathers in inches (X) and their sons (Y):

| **X** | 65 | 66 | 57 | 67 | 68 | 69 | 70 | 72 |
|---|---|---|---|---|---|---|---|---|
| **Y** | 67 | 56 | 65 | 68 | 72 | 72 | 69 | 71 |

[

| **X** | **Deviation (dx = X – A) A = 68** | **Square of Deviation ($dx^2$)** | **Y** | **Deviation (dy = Y – A) A = 72** | **Square of Deviation ($dy^2$)** | **Multiple of Deviations (dxdy)** |
|---|---|---|---|---|---|---|
| 65 | – 3 | 9 | 67 | – 5 | 25 | 15 |
| 66 | – 2 | 4 | 56 | – 16 | 256 | 32 |
| 57 | – 11 | 121 | 65 | – 7 | 49 | 77 |
| 67 | – 1 | 1 | 68 | – 4 | 16 | 4 |
| 68 | 0 | 0 | 72 | 0 | 0 | 0 |
| 69 | 1 | 1 | 72 | 0 | 0 | 0 |
| 70 | 2 | 4 | 69 | – 3 | 9 | – 6 |
| 72 | 4 | 16 | 71 | – 1 | 1 | – 4 |
| N = 8 | $\Sigma dx = -10$ | $\Sigma dx^2 = 156$ | N = 8 | $\Sigma dy = -36$ | $\Sigma dy^2 = 356$ | $\Sigma dxdy = 118$ |

$$r = \frac{\Sigma dxdy - \frac{(\Sigma dx) \times (\Sigma dy)}{N}}{\sqrt{\Sigma dx^2 - \frac{(\Sigma dx)^2}{N}} \times \sqrt{\Sigma dy^2 - \frac{(\Sigma dy)^2}{N}}}$$

$$= \frac{118 - \frac{(-10) \times (-36)}{8}}{\sqrt{156 - \frac{(-10)^2}{8}} \times \sqrt{356 - \frac{(36)^2}{8}}}$$

$$= \frac{118 - 45}{\sqrt{156 - 12.5} \times \sqrt{356 - 162}}$$

$$= \frac{73}{\sqrt{143.5} \times \sqrt{194}}$$

$$= \frac{73}{11.98 \times 13.93}$$

$$= \frac{73}{166.88} = 0.44$$

Correlation coefficient (r) = 0.44.]

**15.** Calculate the correlation coefficient between X and Y and comment on their relationship:

| **X** | – 3 | –2 | –1 | 1 | 2 | 3 |
|---|---|---|---|---|---|---|
| **Y** | 9 | 4 | 1 | 1 | 4 | 9 |

[

| **X** | **Deviation ($x = X - \overline{X}$) $\overline{X} = 0$** | **Square of Deviation ($x^2$)** | **Y** | **Deviation ($y = Y - \overline{Y}$) $\overline{Y} = 4.67$** | **Square of Deviation ($y^2$)** | **Multiple of Deviations (xy)** |
|---|---|---|---|---|---|---|
| – 3 | – 3 | 9 | 9 | 4.33 | 18.75 | – 12.99 |
| – 2 | – 2 | 4 | 4 | – 0.67 | 0.45 | 1.34 |
| – 1 | – 1 | 1 | 1 | – 3.67 | 13.47 | 3.67 |
| 1 | 1 | 1 | 1 | – 3.67 | 13.47 | – 3.67 |
| 2 | 2 | 4 | 4 | – 0.67 | 0.45 | – 1.34 |
| 3 | 3 | 9 | 9 | 4.33 | 18.75 | 12.99 |
| $\Sigma X = 0$ N = 6 | 0 | $\Sigma x^2 = 28$ | $\Sigma Y = 28$ N = 6 | | $\Sigma y^2 = 65.34$ | $\Sigma xy = -18 + 18 = 0$ |

$$\overline{X} = \frac{\Sigma X}{N} = \frac{0}{6} = 0; \quad \overline{Y} = \frac{\Sigma Y}{N} = \frac{28}{6} = 4.67$$

Here, $\Sigma xy = 0, \Sigma x^2 = 28, \Sigma y^2 = 65.34$

$$r = \frac{\Sigma xy}{\sqrt{\Sigma x^2 \times \Sigma y^2}}$$

$$= \frac{0}{\sqrt{28 \times 65.34}} = 0$$

Correlation coefficient (r) = 0

Since r = 0, the two variables X and Y are uncorrelated. That is, there is no linear relationship between X and Y.]

**16.** Calculate the correlation coefficient between X and Y and comment on their relationship.

| **X** | 1 | 3 | 4 | 5 | 7 | 8 |
|---|---|---|---|---|---|---|
| **Y** | 2 | 6 | 8 | 10 | 14 | 16 |

[

| X | Deviation (dx = X – A) A = 5 | Square of Deviation ($dx^2$) | Y | Deviation (dy = Y – A) A = 10 | Square of Deviation ($dy^2$) | Multiple of Deviations (dxdy) |
|---|---|---|---|---|---|---|
| 1 | – 4 | 16 | 2 | – 8 | 64 | 32 |
| 3 | – 2 | 4 | 6 | – 4 | 16 | 8 |
| 4 | – 1 | 1 | 8 | – 2 | 4 | 2 |
| 5 | 0 | 0 | 10 | 0 | 0 | 0 |
| 7 | 2 | 4 | 14 | 4 | 16 | 8 |
| 8 | 3 | 9 | 16 | 6 | 36 | 18 |
| N = 6 | $\Sigma dx = -2$ | $\Sigma dx^2 = 34$ | N = 6 | $\Sigma dy = -4$ | $\Sigma dy^2 = 136$ | $\Sigma dxdy = 68$ |

$$r = \frac{\Sigma dxdy - \frac{(\Sigma dx) \times (\Sigma dy)}{N}}{\sqrt{\Sigma dx^2 - \frac{(\Sigma dx)^2}{N}} \times \sqrt{\Sigma dy^2 - \frac{(\Sigma dy)^2}{N}}}$$

$$= \frac{68 - \frac{(-2) \times (-4)}{6}}{\sqrt{34 - \frac{(-2)^2}{6}} \times \sqrt{136 - \frac{(-4)^2}{6}}}$$

$$= \frac{68 - \frac{8}{6}}{\sqrt{34 - \frac{4}{6}} \times \sqrt{136 - \frac{16}{6}}}$$

$$= \frac{\frac{408 - 8}{6}}{\sqrt{\frac{204 - 4}{6}} \times \sqrt{\frac{816 - 16}{6}}}$$

$$= \frac{\frac{400}{6}}{\sqrt{\frac{200}{6} \times \frac{800}{6}}}$$

$$= \frac{\frac{400}{6}}{\frac{1}{6}\sqrt{200 \times 800}}$$

$$= \frac{400}{6} \times \frac{6}{1} \times \frac{1}{\sqrt{1,60,000}}$$

$$= \frac{400}{400} = 1$$

Correlation coefficient (r) = 1

This is a situation of a perfectly positive correlation between X and Y.]

# Index Numbers 13

The concept of index number can be best understood through an illustration. Let us consider a situation of rising prices during the year 2014. In this context, we are faced with three basic questions. *First,* compared to which year have the prices risen during 2014? *Second,* how do we handle the situation when the prices of some goods rise more than the others? *Thirdly,* can prices of different goods be expressed in terms of any standard unit or different units are to be used to express prices of different goods and services, such that the price of milk is to be expressed in terms of rupees per litre, of cloth in terms of rupees per metre and of sweets in terms of rupees per kilogram. The study of Index Numbers answers all these questions: *First,* rise in prices during 2014 would be studied only with reference to some previous years like 2001 or 2004. Otherwise, the mere statement that prices during 2014 have tended to rise would make no sense. 2014 will be treated as the current year and 2001 or 2004 as the base year. Prices during the base year are taken as 100. Prices during the current year are related to the base year price. So that, we find out percentage change in price level over the years. Level of price is called the index of price. Since price of the base year is assumed to be 100, we can say that index of price of the base year is always 100. If base year is 2004 and the price index is 100, and if in the year 2014 prices are doubled, we shall conclude that the index of price in the year 2014 has shot up to 200 compared to 100 in the base year. As regards the *second* question (how do we handle the situation when prices of some goods change more than the others) the study of index numbers suggests to take average change. Thus, if the price of Potatoes has risen from 100 to 200 and the price of Onions has risen from 100 to 300, we shall consider average change only, *viz.* $\frac{200 + 300}{2} = 250$.

Thus, it is the average index of prices for the various goods and services which is constructed for different years, and compared with the base year.

*Third,* as regards the problem of expressing the prices of various goods and services in some homogeneous units, the theory of Index Numbers suggests to consider only percentage change in prices of various goods and services. Once a change in price is expressed as a percentage change, the unit of the commodity (like litre of a milk, or metre of a cloth) loses its relevance.

**Thus, what does the study of Index Numbers do? It helps us to find out percentage change in the values of different variables (may be prices of different goods or production of different commodities) over time with reference to some base year which happens to be the year of comparison. When various goods are studied simultaneously, the percentage change is taken as the average for all the goods.**

### Definition

In the words of **Spiegel**, *"An Index Number is a statistical measure designed to show changes in a variable or group of related variables with respect to time, geographic location or other characteristics"*.

According to **Croxton** and **Cowden**, *"Index Numbers are devices for measuring difference in the magnitude of a group of related variables"*.

## 1. Features or Characteristics of Index Numbers

Following are the three specific features or characteristics of index numbers:

(1) **Measures of Relative Changes:** Index numbers measure relative or percentage changes in the variable(s) over time. Index number of prices, for example, is not simply a statement of prices at different dates, it presents estimates of percentage changes in the prices over years with reference to some selected base year. If index of prices stands at 200 in 2014 compared to 100 in 2004-05 (the base year) it suggests that compared to the base year, prices have risen by 100 per cent.

(2) **Quantitative Expression:** Index numbers offer a precise measurement of the quantitative change in the concerned variable(s) over time. The index of prices, for example, will tell us that between the years 2013 and 2014, prices have risen by 7 per cent, or that industrial production has declined by 3 per cent or that national income has risen just by 3.5 per cent during this period. The index numbers are not the qualitative statements like prices are rising or falling.

(3) **Averages:** Index numbers show changes in terms of averages. For example, when it is said that between the years 2013 and 2014, prices have risen by 7 per cent but it does not mean that prices of all goods and services have uniformly risen by 7 per cent; it only means that on an average there has been a 7 per cent rise in the prices of various goods and services, even when prices of certain goods might have risen by more than 7 per cent and of certain others by less than 7 per cent.

## 2. Difficulties or Problems in the Construction of Index Numbers

(1) **Purpose of Index Number:** There are various types of index numbers, constructed with different objectives. Before constructing an index number, one must define the objective. The construction of index number is significantly influenced by the objective or purpose of the study. Thus, for example, if the objective is to study the impact of

change in the value of money on the consumers one should construct consumers' price index number. If we are to study the impact of change in the purchasing power of money on the producers, we shall construct index number on the basis of wholesale prices. **Haberler** has rightly pointed out that, "*Different index numbers are constructed to fulfil different objective and before setting to construct a particular index number, one must clearly define one's object of study because, it is on the objective of the study, that the nature and format of the index number depends.*"

(2) **Selection of Base Year:** Selection of Base Year is another problem in the construction of index number. Base year is the reference year. It is the year with which prices of the current year are compared. As far as possible, Base Year should be a normal year.

That is, it should be the one without much ups and downs. Otherwise, the index values would fail to capture the real change in the variable. The year 2004-05 is treated as base year in India, at present.

(3) **Selection of Goods and Services:** Having defined the objective, the problem is of the selection of goods or services to be included in the index number. To construct the Consumers' Price Index, for example, all commodities are not included. **It is neither possible nor desirable to include all the goods and services produced in the country. We have to choose those goods and services which represent most of others in the market.** In other words, commodities selected should be such as are widely consumed, for example, rice, milk, ghee, cloth, etc. Larger the number of goods and services more representative is the index number.

(4) **Selection of the Prices of the Goods and Services:** Having selected the goods and services, the problem arises of prices to be selected. Broadly, in the construction of Price Index, the problem is whether to adopt retail prices or wholesale prices, controlled or open market prices. The choice would depend upon the objective or purpose of the study.

(5) **To Find Out the Average Prices:** In the construction of index number, base year value is assumed to be 100 and other values of different years are related to 100. Thus, if cloth price is ₹ 5 per metre in the base year and is found to be ₹ 10 per metre in the current year, the index of prices of cloth would be $\frac{10}{5} \times 100 = 200$ for the current year. Likewise, price relatives for other commodities are worked out and average for these price relatives is determined and compared with the base year value of 100. It may be noted here that average of base year remains 100, but the average of the year under investigation may be more or less than 100. In case the average of the year under investigation is more than the average of the base year, it means that general price level has gone up. If it is less than the base year, it means that general price level has gone down. Generally, base year is indicated as '0' and current year as '1'. Price index is written as $P_{01}$ and it is read as price index of year 1 in relation year 0.

**Purpose of Constructing Index Number of (i) Prices, and (ii) Quantities**

(i) Purpose of constructing index number of prices is to know the relative change or percentage change in the price level (made up of simple or weighted average of the prices of different goods and services) over time. A rising general price level over time is a pointer towards inflation, while a falling general price level is a pointer towards deflation. Both inflation as well as deflation have notable consequences for an overall economic activity in the economy.

(ii) Purpose of constructing index number of quantity is to know relative change or percentage change in the quantum or volume of output of different goods and services over time. This reflects the level of economic activity in the economy and its different sectors. A rising index of quantity suggest a rising level of economic activity and *vice versa*.

(6) **Selection of Method of Weighting:** In working out the average price, every care should be taken of the relative significance of different commodities. While constructing index number, weights are accorded to different commodities according to their relative significance. There are several methods of according weight, *e.g.*, Fisher's method, Paasche's method, Laspeyre's method. While constructing weighted index number, one must justify his choice of weighting technique in accordance with the nature and objective of his study.

(7) **Problem of Finding Average:** In finding out average values, different kinds of average may be used, geometric average, arithmetic average, etc. The choice of average significantly influences the results. Different kinds of averages may give different index number of a given change in price.

(8) **Selection of Formula:** Index numbers can be constructed with the help of many formulae, such as, Laspeyre's method, Paasche's method, Dorbish and Bowley's method, Fisher's method. One has to decide about the method to be used while constructing the index number.

## 3. Advantages or Uses of Index Numbers

Some of the main advantages or uses of index numbers are as under.

(1) **Measurement of Change in the Price Level or the Value of Money:** Most important use of index numbers is that index numbers measure the value of money during different periods of time. We can use index numbers to know the impact of the change in the value of money on different sections of the society. Accordingly, devices or means can be worked out to correct inflationary or deflationary gaps in the system.

(2) **Knowledge of the Change in Standard of Living:** Index numbers help to ascertain the living standards of people. Money incomes may increase but if index numbers show a decrease in the value of money, living standards may even decline. Thus, index numbers indicate change in real income.

(3) **Adjustments in Salaries and Allowances:** Cost of living index is a useful guide to the Government and Private Enterprises to make necessary adjustments in salaries and allowances of the workers. Increase in the cost of living index suggests increase in salaries and allowances.

(4) **Useful to Business Community:** Price index numbers serve as a useful guide to the business community in their planning and decisions. Trend of the prices significantly influence their production decisions.

(5) **Information Regarding Production:** Index numbers of production shows whether the level of agricultural and industrial production in the economy is increasing or decreasing. Accordingly, agricultural and industrial development policies are formulated.

(6) **Information Regarding Foreign Trade:** Index of exports and imports provides useful information regarding foreign trade. Accordingly, export-import policies are formulated.

(7) **Useful to Politicians:** Politicians come to know of the real economic condition in the country on the basis of index numbers. They offer constructive criticism of government's economic policies and give suggestions for economic reforms in the country.

(8) **Useful to Government:** It is with the help of index numbers that the government determines its monetary and fiscal policies and takes concrete steps for the economic development of the country. In other words, with the help of index numbers government formulates appropriate policies to increase investment, output, income, employment, trade, price level, consumption, etc.

## 4. Limitations of Index Numbers

In the construction of index numbers, there are some practical difficulties and theoretical limitations. The same are as under:

(1) **Not Completely True:** Index numbers are not fully true. For example, one can only make an estimate of change in the value of money with the help of index numbers. The index numbers simply indicate arithmetical tendency of the temporal changes in the variable.

(2) **International Comparison is not Possible:** Different countries have different basis of index numbers. These do not help international comparisons.

(3) **Difference of Time:** With the passage of time, it is difficult to make comparisons of index numbers. With the changing times, man's habits, tastes, etc., also undergo a change. Consequently, index numbers constructed on the basis of old consumption pattern cannot be compared with the index numbers constructed on the basis of new consumption pattern.

(4) **Limited Use:** Index numbers are prepared with certain specific objective. If they are used for another purpose they may lead to wrong conclusions. For example, index numbers prepared to know about the economic condition of the teachers cannot be used to know about the economic condition of the labourers.

(5) **Lack of Retail Price Index Numbers:** Most of the index numbers are prepared on the basis of wholesale prices. But in real life, retail prices are most relevant, but it is difficult to collect retail prices. Index numbers based on wholesale prices may be misleading.

With regard to the limitations of index numbers, **Coulbourn** has rightly said, "*In this changing world it is difficult to escape from the theoretical defects and in future, as far as we can see, it will not be possible, from theoretical point of view, to make use of the best method of constructing the index number*."

**The Principal Limitations of Index Numbers**

These are:

(i) there are no scientific techniques of according weightage to different items included in the index numbers.

(ii) weightage to different items often has a blend of personal bias.

(iii) owing to difference in the unit of currency as well as difference in the composition of production (and consumption) across different countries of the world, it is often very difficult to construct Index Numbers that facilitate international comparisons.

## 5. Simple and Weighted Index Numbers

'Simple' and 'weighted' are the two broad categories of index numbers. Here is a brief description of these concepts.

### Simple Index Numbers

These are the index numbers in which all items of the series are accorded equal weightage or importance. In case of a simple index of prices, for example, all goods and services are to be accorded equal weightage, no matter whether sale/purchase of certain goods is more than that of the others. It will be a simple average of the prices of different goods and services.

**The Basic Difference between Simple Index and Weighted Index**

In the simple index, all items of the series are treated as of equal importance. In the weighted index, weights are accorded to different items depending on their relative importance.

### Weighted Index Numbers

These are the index numbers in which different items of the series are accorded different weightage, depending upon their relative importance. It is not a simple average of prices of different goods and services, as in case of a simple price index. Instead, it is to be a weighted average of the prices of different goods. Thus, if the expenditure on rice is twice the expenditure on cloth, then in the construction of price index, price of rice may be accorded '2' as the weight compared to the weightage of '1' to the price of cloth.

Though difficult to construct, weighted index numbers certainly offer a much more realistic view of the change over time compared to the simple index numbers.

## 6. Methods of Constructing Index Numbers

The following chart shows the various methods of constructing index numbers (Simple as well as weighted):

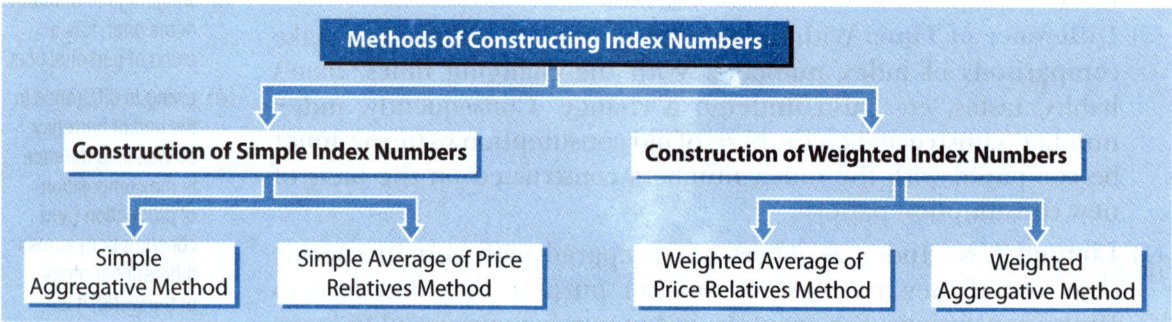


Let us attempt a brief description of the various methods.

## Construction of Simple Index Numbers

There are two methods of constructing simple index numbers:

### (i) Simple Aggregative Method

In this method, aggregate of the prices of commodities in the current year are divided by the aggregate of their prices in the base year and multiplied by 100 to get index value for the current year. It is expressed by the following formula:

**FORMULA**

$$P_{01} = \frac{\sum P_1}{\sum P_0} \times 100$$

Here, $P_{01}$ = Price index of the current year.

$\Sigma P_1$ = Sum of the prices of the commodities in the current year.

$\Sigma P_0$ = Sum of the prices of the commodities in the base year.

**Current Year:** Current year is the year for which average change is to be measured or index number is to be calculated.

**Base Year:** Base year is the year of reference from which we want to measure extent of change in the current year. The index number of base year is generally assumed to be 100.

**ILLUSTRATION.**

Given the following data and assuming 2004 as the base year, find out index value of the prices of different commodities for the year 2014.

| Commodity | A | B | C | D | E |
|---|---|---|---|---|---|
| Price in 2004 (₹) | 50 | 40 | 10 | 5 | 2 |
| Price in 2014 (₹) | 80 | 60 | 20 | 10 | 6 |

**SOLUTION:**

**Construction of a Simple Index Number—Simple Aggregative Method**

| Commodity | 2004 Price (₹) ($P_0$) | 2014 Price (₹) ($P_1$) |
|---|---|---|
| A | 50 | 80 |
| B | 40 | 60 |
| C | 10 | 20 |
| D | 5 | 10 |
| E | 2 | 6 |
| Total | $\Sigma P_0 = 107$ | $\Sigma P_1 = 176$ |

$$P_{01} = \frac{\Sigma P_1}{\Sigma P_0} \times 100 = \frac{176}{107} \times 100 = 164.49$$

Price Index = 164.49.

## (II) SIMPLE AVERAGE OF PRICE RELATIVES METHOD

According to this method, we first find out price relatives for each commodity and then take simple average of all the price relatives.

### What is Price Relative?

A price relative is the percentage ratio of the value of a variable in the current year to its value in the base year. In other words, a price relative is a percentage ratio between price of a commodity in the current year and that in the base year.

$$\text{Price Relatives, } P_{01} = \frac{\text{Current Year Price } (P_1)}{\text{Base Year Price } (P_0)} \times 100$$

We can find out price index number of the current year by using the following formula.

**FORMULA**

$$P_{01} = \frac{\Sigma\left(\frac{P_1}{P_0} \times 100\right)}{N}$$

(Here, $\frac{P_1}{P_0} \times 100$ = Price relatives; N = Number of goods; $P_1$ = Current year's value; $P_0$ = Base year's value.)

**Base Year and its Characteristics**

Base year is the year of comparison, also called reference year. It should bear the following characteristics:

(i) It should be a normal year, not showing wide fluctuations in the parameters related to the index number.

(ii) It should be a year for which reliable statistical data are available, so that comparison of the performance of the other years with the base year becomes meaningful.

(iii) It should not be a year too far from the period of study. Otherwise, relative change over time would not make much sense.

(iv) It should be neither very long nor very short period. Generally, it is not more than a year and not less than a month.

**An Important Caution**

Prices for different commodities are expressed with reference to different units of measurement. Price of steel, for example, is expressed as rupee per kg, while the price of milk is expressed as rupee per litre, and the price of cloth is expressed as rupee per metre. Simple aggregate method of index numbers cannot be used for commodities with different units of measurement. It can be used only for those commodities which have a common unit of measurement.

**Notation of 0 and 1**

Often the notation of 0 stands for the base year, and 1 stands for the current year.

**ILLUSTRATION.**

Given the following data and using the Price Relatives Method, construct an index number for the year 2014 in relation to 2004 prices.

| Commodity | Wheat | Ghee | Milk | Rice | Sugar |
|---|---|---|---|---|---|
| **2004 Price (₹)** | 100 (per qt.) | 8 (per kg) | 2 (per *l*) | 200 (per qt.) | 1 (per kg) |
| **2014 Price (₹)** | 200 | 40 | 16 | 800 | 6 |

**SOLUTION:**

**Construction of a Simple Index Number—
Simple Average of Price Relative Method**

| Commodity | Base Year 2004 Price ($P_0$) | 2014 Price ($P_1$) | Price Relatives of 2014 in relation to 2004 $\left(\frac{P_1}{P_0} \times 100\right)$ |
|---|---|---|---|
| Wheat | 100(per qt) | 200 (per qt) | $\frac{200}{100} \times 100 = 200$ |
| Ghee | 8 (per kg) | 40 (per kg) | $\frac{40}{8} \times 100 = 500$ |
| Milk | 2 (per *l*) | 16 (per *l*) | $\frac{16}{2} \times 100 = 800$ |
| Rice | 200 (per qt) | 800 (per qt) | $\frac{800}{200} \times 100 = 400$ |
| Sugar | 1 (per kg) | 6 (per kg) | $\frac{6}{1} \times 100 = 600$ |
| N = 5 | | | $\Sigma\left(\frac{P_1}{P_0} \times 100\right) = 2,500$ |

$$P_{01} = \frac{\Sigma\left(\frac{P_1}{P_0} \times 100\right)}{N}$$

$$= \frac{2,500}{5} = 500$$

Price Index = 500.

## Construction of Weighted Index Numbers

There are two methods of constructing weighted index numbers, as discussed below:

### (I) WEIGHTED AVERAGE OF PRICE RELATIVES METHOD

According to this method, weighted sum of the price relatives is divided by the sum total of the weights. In this method, goods are given weight according to their quantity. Thus,

**FORMULA**

$$P_{01} = \frac{\sum RW}{\sum W}$$

(Here, $P_{01}$ = Index number for the current year in relation to the base year; W = Weight; R = Price relative.)

**Not all Commodities are Ever Included**

Not all commodities are ever included in the construction of an Index Number. Only a sample of commodities is taken which represents characteristics of the entire group of commodities under study.

**ILLUSTRATION.**

Given the following data and using Weighted Average Price Relative Method, construct index number for 2014 based on 2004 prices.

| Goods | Weight | 2004 Price (₹) | 2014 Price (₹) |
|---|---|---|---|
| Wheat | 40 | 100 (per qt) | 200 (per qt) |
| Rice | 30 | 200 (per qt) | 800 (per qt) |
| Milk | 15 | 2 (per *l*) | 16 (per *l*) |
| Ghee | 10 | 8 (per kg) | 40 (per kg) |
| Sugar | 5 | 1 (per kg) | 6 (per kg) |

**SOLUTION:**

| Goods | Weight (W) | 2004 Price ($P_0$) | 2014 Price ($P_1$) | $R = \frac{P_1}{P_0} \times 100$ | RW |
|---|---|---|---|---|---|
| Wheat | 40 | ₹ 100 per qt | ₹ 200 per qt | $\frac{200}{100} \times 100 = 200$ | $200 \times 40 = 8{,}000$ |
| Rice | 30 | ₹ 200 per qt | ₹ 800 per qt | $\frac{800}{200} \times 100 = 400$ | $400 \times 30 = 12{,}000$ |
| Milk | 15 | ₹ 2 per *l* | ₹ 16 per *l* | $\frac{16}{2} \times 100 = 800$ | $800 \times 15 = 12{,}000$ |
| Ghee | 10 | ₹ 8 per kg | ₹ 40 per kg | $\frac{40}{8} \times 100 = 500$ | $500 \times 10 = 5{,}000$ |
| Sugar | 5 | ₹ 1 per kg | ₹ 6 per kg | $\frac{6}{1} \times 100 = 600$ | $600 \times 5 = 3{,}000$ |
| Total | $\Sigma W = 100$ | | | | $\Sigma RW = 40{,}000$ |

$$P_{01} = \frac{\Sigma RW}{\Sigma W} = \frac{40{,}000}{100} = 400$$

Price Index = 400.

### (II) WEIGHTED AGGREGATIVE METHOD

Under this method different goods are accorded weight according to the quantity bought. Economists have different views in this respect. Should the weight be given (i) on the basis of the quantity bought in the current year or (ii) on the basis of the quantity bought in the base year or (iii) on the basis of the quantities bought in both the years? Different economists have, therefore, suggested different techniques of weighting. Some of the well known methods are as under:

**What is the basic difference between Laspeyre's and Paasche's methods of construction of Weighted index Numbers?**

Laspeyre uses base year quantities as the weights of different items. Paasche on the other hand, uses current year quantities as weights.

**(1) Laspeyre's Method:** Laspeyre's uses *base year quantities* ($q_0$) as weights of different items. His formula for estimating Index values is:

**FORMULA**

$$P_{01} = \frac{\sum p_1 q_0}{\sum p_0 q_0} \times 100$$

**(2) Paasche's Method:** Paasche's on the other hand uses *current year's quantities* ($q_1$) as weight. His formula to construct the Index value is:

**FORMULA**

$$P_{01} = \frac{\sum p_1 q_1}{\sum p_0 q_1} \times 100$$

(3) **Fisher's Method:** Fisher has combined the techniques of Laspeyre's and Paasche's method. He used *both base year as well as current year quantities* ($q_0$, $q_1$) as weight. His formula to construct Index Number is:

**FORMULA**

$$P_{01} = \sqrt{\frac{\sum p_1 q_0}{\sum p_0 q_0} \times \frac{\sum p_1 q_1}{\sum p_0 q_1}} \times 100$$

Fisher's method is treated as Ideal Formula.

## Fisher's Index Number as an Ideal Method

The choice of method for the construction of an index number will depend upon the object with which a particular index number is constructed. Many formulae may be used for the construction of index numbers but all may not be suitable for the specific purpose in hand. Some of the important formulae do not conform to certain appropriate test of consistent behaviour; it implies that these formulae give us biased results.

However, Fisher's Method is considered as an ideal method for constructing index numbers:

$$P_{01} = \sqrt{\frac{\Sigma p_1 q_0}{\Sigma p_0 q_0} \times \frac{\Sigma p_1 q_1}{\Sigma p_0 q_1}} \times 100$$

Fisher's method is considered as 'ideal' because

(1) It is based on variable weights.

(2) It takes into consideration the price and quantities of both the base year and current year.

(3) It is based on geometric mean (GM) which is regarded as the best mean for calculating index number.

(4) Fisher's index number satisfies both the **Time Reversal Test and Factor Reversal Test**. The time reversal test implies that the formula for calculating an Index Number should be such that will give the same ratio between one point of comparison and the other, no matter which of the two is taken as base. Time Reversal means that if we change base year to current year and vice versa then the product of two indexes should be equal to unity. Thus, an index number should work both ways, *i.e.*, forward as well as backward. On the other hand, Factor Reversal Test implies, just as our formula should permit the interchange of two items without giving inconsistent results, so it ought to permit interchange of prices and quantities without giving inconsistent results, *i.e.*, the two results multiplied together should be equal to value ratio.

**ILLUSTRATION.**

Construct index numbers of prices of the items in the year 2014 from the following data by:

(i) Laspeyre's Method,

(ii) Paasche's Method, and

(iii) Fisher's Method.

| Items | 2004 (Base Year) | | 2014 (Current Year) | |
|---|---|---|---|---|
| | Price | Quantity | Price | Quantity |
| A | 10 | 10 | 20 | 25 |
| B | 35 | 3 | 40 | 10 |
| C | 30 | 5 | 20 | 15 |
| D | 10 | 20 | 8 | 20 |
| E | 40 | 2 | 40 | 5 |

**SOLUTION:**

**Construction of Price Index Numbers**

| Items | Base Year (2004) | | Current Year (2014) | | $p_0q_0$ | $p_0q_1$ | $p_1q_0$ | $p_1q_1$ |
|---|---|---|---|---|---|---|---|---|
| | Price ($p_0$) | Quantity ($q_0$) | Price ($p_1$) | Quantity ($q_1$) | | | | |
| A | 10 | 10 | 20 | 25 | 100 | 250 | 200 | 500 |
| B | 35 | 3 | 40 | 10 | 105 | 350 | 120 | 400 |
| C | 30 | 5 | 20 | 15 | 150 | 450 | 100 | 300 |
| D | 10 | 20 | 8 | 20 | 200 | 200 | 160 | 160 |
| E | 40 | 2 | 40 | 5 | 80 | 200 | 80 | 200 |
| | | | | | $\Sigma p_0q_0 = 635$ | $\Sigma p_0q_1 = 1{,}450$ | $\Sigma p_1q_0 = 660$ | $\Sigma p_1q_1 = 1{,}560$ |

**(i) Laspeyre's Method:** $P_{01} = \dfrac{\Sigma p_1q_0}{\Sigma p_0q_0} \times 100$

$$= \frac{660}{635} \times 100 = 103.94$$

**(ii) Paasche's Method:** $P_{01} = \dfrac{\Sigma p_1q_1}{\Sigma p_0q_1} \times 100$

$$= \frac{1,560}{1,450} \times 100 = 107.59$$

**(iii) Fisher's Method:** $P_{01} = \sqrt{\dfrac{\Sigma p_1q_0}{\Sigma p_0q_0} \times \dfrac{\Sigma p_1q_1}{\Sigma p_0q_1}} \times 100$

$$= \sqrt{\frac{660}{635} \times \frac{1,560}{1,450}} \times 100$$

$$= \sqrt{1.03 \times 1.07} \times 100$$

$$= \sqrt{1.1021} \times 100$$

$$= 1.05 \times 100 = 105$$

**ILLUSTRATION**

Find out index value from the following data using (i) Laspeyre's method, (ii) Paasche's method, and (iii) Fisher's method.

| Items | Base Year Quantity | Base Year Price (₹) | Current Year Quantity | Current Year Price (₹) |
|---|---|---|---|---|
| A | 6 | 10 | 8 | 12 |
| B | 4 | 15 | 5 | 20 |
| C | 5 | 8 | 3 | 16 |
| D | 3 | 9 | 6 | 1 |

**SOLUTION:**

| Items | $q_0$ | $p_0$ | $q_1$ | $p_1$ | $p_1q_0$ | $p_0q_0$ | $p_1q_1$ | $p_0q_1$ |
|---|---|---|---|---|---|---|---|---|
| A | 6 | 10 | 8 | 12 | 72 | 60 | 96 | 80 |
| B | 4 | 15 | 5 | 20 | 80 | 60 | 100 | 75 |
| C | 5 | 8 | 3 | 16 | 80 | 40 | 48 | 24 |
| D | 3 | 9 | 6 | 1 | 3 | 27 | 6 | 54 |
| | | | | | $\Sigma p_1q_0 = 235$ | $\Sigma p_0q_0 = 187$ | $\Sigma p_1q_1 = 250$ | $\Sigma p_0q_1 = 233$ |

**(i) Laspeyre's Method:** $P_{01} = \frac{\Sigma p_1q_0}{\Sigma p_0q_0} \times 100$

$= \frac{235}{187} \times 100 = 125.67$

**(ii) Paasche's Method:** $P_{01} = \frac{\Sigma p_1q_1}{\Sigma p_0q_1} \times 100$

$= \frac{250}{233} \times 100 = 107.29$

**(iii) Fisher's Method:** $P_{01} = \sqrt{\frac{\Sigma p_1q_0}{\Sigma p_0q_0} \times \frac{\Sigma p_1q_1}{\Sigma p_0q_1}} \times 100$

$= \sqrt{\frac{235}{187} \times \frac{250}{233}} \times 100$

$= \sqrt{1.2567 \times 1.0729} \times 100$

$= \sqrt{1.3483} \times 100$

$= 1.1612 \times 100 = 116.12$

**ILLUSTRATION.**

From the following data construct Fisher's Ideal Index:

| Commodity | Base Year Price | Base Year Quantity | Current Year Price | Current Year Quantity |
|---|---|---|---|---|
| A | 5 | 50 | 7 | 60 |
| B | 6 | 15 | 8 | 10 |
| C | 8 | 8 | 11 | 12 |
| D | 7 | 20 | 10 | 15 |

**SOLUTION:**

| Commodity | $p_0$ | $q_0$ | $p_1$ | $q_1$ | $p_1q_0$ | $p_0q_0$ | $p_1q_1$ | $p_0q_1$ |
|---|---|---|---|---|---|---|---|---|
| A | 5 | 50 | 7 | 60 | 350 | 250 | 420 | 300 |
| B | 6 | 15 | 8 | 10 | 120 | 90 | 80 | 60 |
| C | 8 | 8 | 11 | 12 | 88 | 64 | 132 | 96 |
| D | 7 | 20 | 10 | 15 | 200 | 140 | 150 | 105 |
| | | | | | $\Sigma p_1q_0 = 758$ | $\Sigma p_0q_0 = 544$ | $\Sigma p_1q_1 = 782$ | $\Sigma p_0q_1 = 561$ |

$P_{01} = \sqrt{\frac{\Sigma p_1q_0}{\Sigma p_0q_0} \times \frac{\Sigma p_1q_1}{\Sigma p_0q_1}} \times 100$

$= \sqrt{\frac{758}{544} \times \frac{782}{561}} \times 100$

$= \sqrt{1.9423} \times 100 = 1.3937 \times 100 = 139.37$

*Learning by doing*

1. *Using Simple Aggregate Method and Price Relatives Method, find out index values for the year 2014 from the following data:*

| **Items** | A | B | C | D | E |
|---|---|---|---|---|---|
| **2004 Price (₹)** | 15 | 33 | 38 | 25 | 50 |
| **2014 Price (₹)** | 30 | 35 | 57 | 35 | 63 |

*(**Ans.** 136.64, 144.412)*

2. *Find out index value by the Price Relative Method for the year 2014 from the following data:*

| **Items** | A | B | C | D | E | F | G |
|---|---|---|---|---|---|---|---|
| **2004 Price (₹)** | 100 | 10 | 5 | 4 | 1 | 2 | 3 |
| **2014 Price (₹)** | 100 | 9 | 4 | 2 | 1 | 2.50 | 2.25 |

*(**Ans.** 88.57)*

3. *Construct an index number by Price Relatives Method using 2004 as base year:*

| **Goods** | A | B | C | D |
|---|---|---|---|---|
| **2004 Price (₹)** | 8 | 10 | 15 | 20 |
| **2013 Price (₹)** | 10 | 12 | 18 | 22 |
| **2014 Price (₹)** | 12 | 14 | 20 | 25 |

*(**Ans.** 118.75, 137.08)*

4. *Construct an index of prices using 2004 as the base year and Price Relatives Method:*

| **Goods** | **Weight** | **2004** | **2013** | **2014** |
|---|---|---|---|---|
| A | 5 | 10 | 12 | 14 |
| B | 3 | 5 | 6 | 8 |
| C | 2 | 4 | 5 | 7 |

*(**Ans.** 121, 153)*

## 7. Consumer Price Index or Cost of Living Index Number

So far we have been focusing on general price indices. But these indices do not precisely explain how the change in general price level affects the cost of living of the various classes of society. This is because different classes of people consume different goods and services. Accordingly, the change in prices affect them differently. To know the effects of changing prices on the living of different classes of society, we need a special type of price index, called **Consumer Price Index or Cost of Living Index Number**.

*The consumer price index is the index number which measures the average change in prices paid by the specific class of consumers for goods and services consumed by them in the current year in comparison with base year.* Change in the price level affects the cost of living of the concerned class of consumers. Accordingly, consumer price indices are also called **cost of living indices**.

In India, the consumer price indices are mainly constructed for the following consumer groups:

(i) Industrial Workers (IW),

(ii) Urban-Non Manual Employees (UNME), and

(iii) Agricultural Labourers (AL).

## Construction of Consumer Price Index

Construction of the consumer price index number involves the following steps:

**(1) Selection of the Consumer Class:** Consumers are classified into various classes like industrial labour, government employees, agricultural labour, teachers, etc. We should select the class of consumer according to the requirement of our study.

**(2) Information about the Family Budget:** After the decision about the group, a sample of persons should be selected from the group and following information about their family budgets should be obtained:

(i) Commodities which they consume.

(ii) Quantity of consumption.

(iii) Prices of the concerned goods and services.

(iv) Money spent on these goods and services.

The items which are generally consumed may be classified in groups like (i) Food, (ii) Clothing, (iii) Fuel and light, (iv) House rent, (v) Education, health and sanitation, (vi) Miscellaneous.

**(3) Choice of Base Year:** The base year should be the year of economic stability. It should not be too distant from the current year.

**(4) Information about Prices:** The retail prices of selected items/ commodities should be collected from the region where the group of selected person lives and makes the purchases.

**(5) Weightage:** The importance of various items for different classes of people is different. Therefore, the selected items should be given weights according to their relative importance. As discussed earlier, there are two ways of according weights:

**(i) Quantity Weights:** These weights are given in proportion to the quantities consumed in the base period.

**(ii) Expenditure Weights:** These weights are given in proportion to the total expenditure on the items consumed in the base period.

## Methods of Constructing Consumer Price Index (CPI)

Corresponding to the two methods of assigning weights to different commodities, there are two methods of the construction of Consumer's Price Index.

**(i) Aggregative Expenditure Method**, and

**(ii) Family Budget Method.**

**(i) Aggregative Expenditure Method:** This method is similar to the *Laspeyre's method* (already discussed).

The following formula is used in this method.

**FORMULA**

$$\text{Consumer Price Index (CPI)} = \frac{\Sigma p_1 q_0}{\Sigma p_0 q_0} \times 100$$

Where, $p_1$ = Price of the commodities in the current year.

$p_0$ = Price of the commodities in the base year.

Thus,

$q_0$ = Quantity consumed in base year.

$\Sigma p_1 q_0$ shows aggregate expenditure in the current year.

$\Sigma p_0 q_0$ shows aggregate expenditure in the base year.

$$P_{01} = \frac{\Sigma p_1 q_0}{\Sigma p_0 q_0} \times 100$$

**(ii) Family Budget Method:** The following formula is used in this method to find Consumer's Price Index.

**FORMULA**

$$\text{Consumer's Price Index} = \frac{\Sigma RW}{\Sigma W}$$

Where, R = Current year's price relative of various items.

W = Weights of various items.

CPI is calculated by this method in following steps:

(i) The current year's price ($p_1$) of each commodity is divided by the base year's price ($p_0$) of the respective commodities. Then the resultant is multiplied by 100. These are called price relatives of the current year.

Therefore,

$$\text{Price Relatives of the Current year} = \frac{\text{Price of the Current Year}}{\text{Price of the Base Year}} \times 100$$

$$i.e., \quad R = \frac{p_1}{p_0} \times 100$$

(ii) Aggregate expenditure on each item is considered as the weight of the item. Hence, the weight (W) of a commodity is calculated by multiplying the price ($p_1$) of a commodity in the base year with the quantity ($q_0$) of the commodity consumed in the base year.

(iii) The price relative (R) of each item is multiplied with their respective weights ($W = p_0 q_0$). These products are added to find $\Sigma RW$.

(iv) The sum of weights $\Sigma W$ or $\Sigma p_0 q_0$ is calculated.

(v) These values are substituted in the following formula to find the consumer's price index.

Consumer Price Index

$$= \frac{\text{Sum of Products of the Price relative with weights}}{\text{Sum of Weights}}$$

Thus:

$$P_{01} = \frac{\Sigma RW}{\Sigma W}$$

**ILLUSTRATION.**

Find the Consumer Price Index or the Cost of Living Index Number for the current year from the following data by (i) Aggregate Expenditure method, and (ii) Family Budget Method.

| Articles | Quantity Consumed in Base Year | Price in Base Year | Price in Current Year |
|---|---|---|---|
| Rice | 5 qt | 24 per qt | 30 per qt |
| Wheat | 1 qt | 16 per qt | 20 per qt |
| Pulses | 2 qt | 12 per qt | 18 per qt |
| Ghee | 4 kg | 5 per kg | 6.25 per kg |
| Oil | 5 *l* | 4 per *l* | 5 per *l* |
| Clothing | 40 metres | 1 per metre | 1.50 per metre |
| Firewood | 10 qt | 2 per qt | 2.50 per qt |
| House Rent | 1 house | 20 per house | 25 per house |

**SOLUTION:**

**(I) AGGREGATIVE EXPENDITURE METHOD**

From the given data we derive the following table:

| Articles | Quantity Consumed in Base Year ($q_0$) | Price in Base Year ($p_0$) | Price in Current Year ($p_1$) | Aggregate Expenditure in Base Year ($p_0q_0$) | Aggregate Expenditure in Current Year ($p_1q_0$) |
|---|---|---|---|---|---|
| Rice | 5 qt | 24 | 30 | 120 | 150 |
| Wheat | 1 qt | 16 | 20 | 16 | 20 |
| Pulses | 2 qt | 12 | 18 | 24 | 36 |
| Ghee | 4 kg | 5 | 6.25 | 20 | 25 |
| Oil | 5 *l* | 4 | 5 | 20 | 25 |
| Clothing | 40 m | 1 | 1.50 | 40 | 60 |
| Firewood | 10 qt | 2 | 2.50 | 20 | 25 |
| House Rent | 1 house | 20 | 25 | 20 | 25 |
| | | | | $\Sigma p_0q_0 = 280$ | $\Sigma p_1q_0 = 366$ |

$$\text{Index Number for Current Year} = \frac{\Sigma p_1q_0}{\Sigma p_0q_0} \times 100$$

$$= \frac{366}{280} \times 100 = 130.71$$

## (II) Family Budget Method

| Articles | Quantity Consumed in Base Year ($q_0$) | Price in Base Year ($p_0$) | Price in Current Year ($p_1$) | Price Relative for Current Year ($R = \frac{p_1}{p_0} \times 100$) | Weights (Value consumed in Base Year) ($W = p_0q_0$) | Product of Price Relative and Weight (RW) |
|---|---|---|---|---|---|---|
| Rice | 5 qt | 24 | 30 | 125 | 120 | 15,000 |
| Wheat | 1 qt | 16 | 20 | 125 | 16 | 2,000 |
| Pulses | 2 qt | 12 | 18 | 150 | 24 | 3,600 |
| Ghee | 4 kg | 5 | 6.25 | 125 | 20 | 2,500 |
| Oil | 5 *l* | 4 | 5 | 125 | 20 | 2,500 |
| Clothing | 40 metres | 1 | 1.50 | 150 | 40 | 6,000 |
| Firewood | 10 qt | 2 | 2.50 | 125 | 20 | 2,500 |
| House Rent | 1 house | 20 | 25 | 125 | 20 | 2,500 |
| | | | | | $\sum W = 280$ | $\sum RW = 36,600$ |

Now CPI for Current Year $= \frac{\Sigma RW}{\Sigma W} = \frac{36,600}{280} = 130.71$

**Illustration.**

Calculate the Cost of Living Index from the following data.

| Items | Quantity Consumed in the given Year | Price per unit in ₹ | |
|---|---|---|---|
| | | Base Year | Given Year |
| Rice | $2\frac{1}{2}$ qt ×12 | 12 | 25 |
| Pulses | 3 kg ×12 | 0.4 | 0.6 |
| Oil | 2 *l* ×12 | 1.5 | 2.2 |
| Clothing | 6 metres ×12 | 0.75 | 10 |
| Housing | 12 months | 20 per month | 30 per month |
| Miscellaneous | Expenditure of 12 months | 10 per month | 15 per month |

**Solution:**

| Items | Quantity Consumed in the given Year ($q_1$) | Price | | Aggregate Expenditure in the Base Year ($p_0q_1$) | Aggregate Expenditure in the Current Year ($p_1q_1$) |
|---|---|---|---|---|---|
| | | Base Year ($p_0$) | Current Year ($p_1$) | | |
| Rice | 30 qt | 12 | 25 | 360 | 750 |
| Pulses | 36 kg | 0.4 | 0.6 | 14.4 | 21.6 |
| Oil | 24 *l* | 1.5 | 2.2 | 36 | 52.8 |
| Clothing | 72 metres | 0.75 | 10 | 54 | 720 |
| Housing | 12 months | 20 per month | 30 per month | 240 | 360 |
| Miscellaneous | 12 months expenditure | 10 per month | 15 per month | 120 | 180 |
| | | | | $\sum p_0q_1 = 824.4$ | $\sum p_1q_1 = 2,084.4$ |

$$\text{Cost of Living Index} = \frac{\Sigma p_1 q_1}{\Sigma p_0 q_1} \times 100$$

$$= \frac{2,084.4}{824.4} \times 100 = 252.84$$

**ILLUSTRATION.**

Construct Cost of Living Index for 2004 based on 2014 from the following data:

| Group | Food | Housing | Clothing | Fuel and Light | Miscellaneous |
|---|---|---|---|---|---|
| **Group Index Number for 2014 (Based on 2004)** | 122 | 140 | 112 | 116 | 106 |
| **Weights** | 32 | 10 | 10 | 6 | 42 |

**SOLUTION:**

| Group | Group Index Number (R) | Weights (W) | Weighted Relative (RW) |
|---|---|---|---|
| Food | 122 | 32 | 3,904 |
| Housing | 140 | 10 | 1,400 |
| Clothing | 112 | 10 | 1,120 |
| Fuel and light | 116 | 6 | 696 |
| Miscellaneous | 106 | 42 | 4,452 |
| | | $\Sigma W = 100$ | $\Sigma RW = 11,572$ |

$$\text{Thus, Cost of Living Index} = \frac{\Sigma RW}{\Sigma W} = \frac{11,572}{100} = 115.72$$

### IMPORTANCE OF THE CONSUMER PRICE INDEX OR COST OF LIVING INDEX

**Uses**

(i) Formulation of Price Policy.

(ii) Wage Adjustment.

(iii) Measurement of Real Value.

(iv) Analysis of Markets.

(v) National Income Deflator.

(1) **Formulation of Price Policy:** The consumer price indices are used by government to frame policies on prices. On the basis of these indices government decides whether the prices are to be controlled, dual price policy should be adopted or public distribution system is to be introduced, etc. Also, government policies like rent control and taxation, general economic and fiscal policies etc. are framed on the basis of the consumer price index numbers to a large extent.

(2) **Wage Adjustment:** Cost of living index numbers are used as basis for the wage adjustments. The rates of dearness allowances are decided by the government on the basis of these indices. These indices are also used for wage contracts and wage agreements of the workers.

(3) **Measurement of Real Value:** These index numbers are used to measure the real value of the rupee or its purchasing power and real income (or revenue), etc.

(4) **Analysis of Markets:** The consumer price indices are also used for the analysis of the market of specific commodities for their demand and supply.

(5) **National Income Deflator:** These indices are also used as deflators of national income. Accordingly, real change in national income is estimated.

### Difficulties in the Construction of Consumer Price Index

There are many difficulties in the construction of consumer price index. These are as follows:

**(1) Difference in the Standards of Living:** Consumption pattern of different classes of consumers are different and therefore, have different living standards. Thus, there cannot be one consumer price index number for different classes of society.

**(2) Difference in Prices:** The price indices are constructed on the basis of retail prices. But the retail prices vary from place to place and even at the same place from shop to shop. As such it is very difficult to find a representative price for the calculation of consumer price index.

**(3) Difference in the Proportion of Expenditure:** All the members of any particular group do not spend on various items of consumption in same ratio and even one person does not spend on various commodities in the same ratio at two different periods of time. A consumer's purchase ratio depends upon his/her taste, habits, etc. Accordingly, it is difficult to construct a cost of living index that truly reflects a change in the cost of living over time.

## 8. Wholesale Price Index (WPI)

The Wholesale Price Index (WPI) measures the relative changes in the prices of commodities traded in the wholesale markets. In India, the wholesale price index numbers are constructed on weekly basis.

In India, the new Wholesale Price Index (WPI) series with base 2004-05 = 100 became effective from 2010 shifting from the earlier base of 1999-2000. Presently, 2004-05 is being used as the base year. The Government plans to further shift the base year to 2011-12. However, detailed modalities of this change are yet to be worked out.

### Commodity Group and Weightage of Wholesale Price Index

In India, all the commodities have been classified in the following three groups:

| Commodity Group | Name of Commodities | Weightage |
|---|---|---|
| (1) Primary Articles | These include 98 commodities like Rice, Fruits, Pulses, Vegetables and non-food articles like Cotton, Jute, metals. | 22.02 |
| (2) Fuel, Power, Light and Lubricants | These include 19 items like Coal, Petroleum Products, Electricity, LPG. | 14.23 |
| (3) Manufacturing | It includes 318 items like Textiles, Sugar, Paper, Machinery, Chemicals, Fertilizers, Leather, etc. | 63.75 |

### Uses of Wholesale Price Index

**(1) Forecasting Demand and Supply:** The wholesale price indices are often used to forecast demand and supply situation in the economy. An increase in wholesale price index is an indication of excess demand. It is a situation in which demand is greater than supply. On the other hand, a decrease in wholesale price index implies deficient demand. It is a situation in which demand is less than supply.

**Note: The Basic Difference of purpose behind the Consumer Price Index Number and the Wholesale Price Index Number**

In case of consumer price index number, the basic purpose is to know cost of living of a specified group of consumers in the society. In case of wholesale index number, the basic purpose is to assess the situations of overall demand and supply in the economy. Rising prices indicate a situation of excess demand, while falling prices suggest a situation of deficient demand. Wholesale price index focuses on the rate of inflation in the economy.

**Producer Price Index**

As in many countries, in India also, efforts are afoot to shift from WPI (Wholesale Price Index) to Producer Price Index. Producer - Price refers to the basic price including taxes, trade margins and transport cost. Producer Price Index is expected to offer better insights into the analysis of price trends in the country.

(2) **Estimation of Monetary Value and Real Value:** The wholesale price index can be used to estimate the monetary value and real value of aggregates like national income and expenditure. Monetary value is the value estimated at current year prices. Real value is the value estimated at base year prices or at constant prices. The monetary aggregate can be converted into real aggregate by applying the following formula:

$$\text{Real Aggregate of the Current Year} = \text{Monetary Aggregate of the Current Year} \times \frac{\text{Price Index of Base Year}}{\text{Price Index of Current Year}}$$

(3) **Indicator of Rate of Inflation:** The wholesale price index is also applied to calculate the rate of inflation in a country. It refers to the rate at which prices tend to increase over time.

**What is Rate of Inflation?**

Wholesale price index is prepared for every week. If for week 1, wholesale price index is $A_1$ and for week 2, the wholesale price index is $A_2$, then the rate of inflation between week 1 and week 2 would be estimated as under:

$$\frac{A_2 - A_1}{A_1} \times 100$$

**Illustration.**

If wholesale price index for week 1 = 200 and for week 2 = 250, then

$$\text{Rate of inflation} = \frac{250-200}{200} \times 100$$

$$= \frac{50}{200} \times 100 = 25\%$$

**Annual rate of inflation is estimated by considering average of the wholesale price index for all weeks of the year.**

## 9. Index Number of Industrial Production

Index number of industrial production is that index which measures the relative increase or decrease in the level of industrial output in a country in comparison to the level of production in the base year. In India, the base year for the current series is 2004-05. These index numbers tell us about the changes in the quantum of production. These index numbers are useful in estimating the growth of industrial production in the economy.

### Construction of Index Number of Industrial Production

Construction of the index number of industrial production involves the following steps:

(1) **Classification of Industries:** To construct index number of industrial production the industries are classified into following groups:

(i) Mining, (ii) Manufacturing, and (iii) Electricity.

(2) **Statistics or Data Related to Industrial Production:** The data relating to the production of the above mentioned industries are collected either monthly, quarterly or yearly.

**(3) Weightage:** Weights are given on the basis of the relative importance of different industries. The weights are based on the values of net output of different industries, and their contribution to national income.

In India, the following weightage is given to different groups at present:

| Group | Weightage |
|---|---|
| (1) Mining | 10.47 |
| (2) Manufacturing | 79.36 |
| (3) Electricity | 10.17 |
| Total | 100.00 |

Index Number of Industrial Production is calculated by using the following formula:

**FORMULA**

$$\text{Index Number of Industrial Production} = \frac{\sum\left(\frac{q_1}{q_0}\right)W}{\sum W} \times 100$$

Where, $q_1$ = Level of production in the current year.

$q_0$ = Level of production in the base year.

W = Weight or relative importance of industrial output.

**ILLUSTRATION.**

Construct index number of industrial production from the following data:

| Industry | Output | | | Units |
|---|---|---|---|---|
| | Base Year | Current Year | Weights | |
| Manufacturing Production | 122 | 300 | 85 | Mill. Tonnes |
| Electrical Products | 203 | 400 | 5 | Th. Nos. |
| Mining | 65 | 87 | 10 | Mill. Tonnes |

**SOLUTION:**

From the given data we have

| Industry | Output | | Relative Value $\left(R = \frac{q_1}{q_0} \times 100\right)$ | Weights (W) | Weighted Relative (RW) |
|---|---|---|---|---|---|
| | Base Year ($q_0$) | Current Year ($q_1$) | | | |
| Manufacturing Production | 122 | 300 | $\frac{300}{122} \times 100 = 245.90$ | 85 | 20,901.50 |
| Electrical Products | 203 | 400 | $\frac{400}{203} \times 100 = 197$ | 5 | 985.00 |
| Mining | 65 | 87 | $\frac{87}{65} \times 100 = 134$ | 10 | 1,340.00 |
| | | | | $\Sigma W = 100$ | $\Sigma RW = 23,226.50$ |

Index Number of Industrial Production

$$= \frac{\Sigma RW}{\Sigma W} = \frac{23,226.50}{100} = 232.27 \text{ (approx.)}$$

## 10. Inflation and Index Numbers

Inflation refers to a situation of rise in the general price level in a country over a fairly long period of time. Often, inflation is measured in terms of wholesale price index. A consistent rise in the wholesale price index over time implies a situation of inflation. **Example:** If wholesale price index rises from 100 in 2004-05 (base year) to 150 in 2014, and if the increase in price has almost been consistent over time (like, every year the general price level has been rising by 5-10%), it would be deemed as a situation of inflation. Implying a continuous erosion in the value of money or purchasing power of money. Value of money (or purchasing power of money) reduces to half if wholesale price index rises by 100%. Obviously, double the price level, half the purchasing power of a rupee. If money income of the people remains constant, 10% increase in the price level implies a 10% decrease in purchasing power of the people.

Inflation causes erosion of purchasing power of the people, if their money income remains constant. Accordingly, often we find workers pestering the government for dearness allowance (DA) to compensate for the loss of purchasing power during periods of inflation.

### Fall in the Rate of Inflation does not Imply Fall in the Price Level

Students here must appreciate the distinction between inflation and the rate of inflation. Inflation is measured as a percentage increase in the general price level, like from 100 in 2011 to 115 in 2012, implying a 15% increase in the price level during the period of one year. While prices have tended to increase during the year, these may not be rising at the same pace (or the same rate) every week within the year. Relative change in the price index from week to week measures the rate of inflation.

$$\text{Rate of Inflation} = \frac{A_2 - A_1}{A_1} \times 100$$

Where $A_1$ = Wholesale price index for week 1, and $A_2$ = Wholesale price index for week 2. Thus, within the year, rate of inflation may increase or decrease. It only implies the increase or decrease in the pace of inflation or increase/decrease in the speed of inflation not a fall in the price level. To illustrate, in week 1 the rate of inflation may be 5% while in week 2, the rate of inflation may be 4%. Fall from 5% to 4% should not be interpreted as a fall in the price level. It only implies a fall in the speed at which prices tend to rise.

> Inflation is measured in terms of changes in the wholesale price index, based on weekly quotations of wholesale prices.
>
> Increase in the wholesale price index over a long period of time implies a situation of inflation. It causes erosion of purchasing power of money.
>
> In a situation of inflation, trade unions often pester for higher money wages to compensate for the fall in the purchasing power of a rupee.

> **Sensex**
>
> Sensex is the index showing changes in the Indian stock market. It is a short form of Bombay Stock Exchange Sensitive Index. It is constructed with 1978-79 as the reference year or the base year. It consists of 30 stocks of the leading companies in the country. Changes in these stocks are expected to represent changes in the entire stock market. Rise in sensex implies an overall increase in share prices. This shows increase in expected earnings from investments in the stock market. This also implies robust performance of the principal industries in the economy.

## MISCELLANEOUS ILLUSTRATIONS

### ILLUSTRATION 1.

The following are the prices of commodities in 2004 and 2014. Construct a price index based on price relatives taking 2004 as base year.

| Commodity | A | B | C | D | E |
|---|---|---|---|---|---|
| Price in 2004 | 50 | 40 | 80 | 110 | 20 |
| Price in 2014 | 70 | 60 | 90 | 120 | 20 |

**SOLUTION:**

**Construction of a Price Index—Simple Average of Price Relatives**

| Commodity | Price in 2004 ($P_0$) | Price in 2014 ($P_1$) | Price Relatives $\left(\frac{P_1}{P_0} \times 100\right)$ |
|---|---|---|---|
| A | 50 | 70 | $\frac{70}{50} \times 100 = 140$ |
| B | 40 | 60 | $\frac{60}{40} \times 100 = 150$ |
| C | 80 | 90 | $\frac{90}{80} \times 100 = 112.5$ |
| D | 110 | 120 | $\frac{120}{110} \times 100 = 109.1$ |
| E | 20 | 20 | $\frac{20}{20} \times 100 = 100$ |
| N = 5 | | | $\Sigma\left(\frac{P_1}{P_0} \times 100\right) = 611.6$ |

$$P_{01} = \frac{\Sigma\left(\frac{P_1}{P_0} \times 100\right)}{N} = \frac{611.6}{5} = 122.32$$

### ILLUSTRATION 2.

Construct index numbers of prices in the year 2014 from the following data by using: (i) Laspeyre's Method, (ii) Paasche's Method, and (iii) Fisher's Method.

| Commodity | 2004 (Base Year) | | 2014 (Current Year) | |
|---|---|---|---|---|
| | Price | Quantity | Price | Quantity |
| A | 2 | 8 | 4 | 6 |
| B | 5 | 10 | 6 | 5 |
| C | 4 | 14 | 5 | 10 |
| D | 2 | 19 | 2 | 15 |

**SOLUTION:**

**Construction of Various Index Numbers**

| Commodity | Base Year (2004) | | Current Year (2014) | | $p_1q_0$ | $p_0q_0$ | $p_1q_1$ | $p_0q_1$ |
|---|---|---|---|---|---|---|---|---|
| | $p_0$ | $q_0$ | $p_1$ | $q_1$ | | | | |
| A | 2 | 8 | 4 | 6 | 32 | 16 | 24 | 12 |
| B | 5 | 10 | 6 | 5 | 60 | 50 | 30 | 25 |
| C | 4 | 14 | 5 | 10 | 70 | 56 | 50 | 40 |
| D | 2 | 19 | 2 | 15 | 38 | 38 | 30 | 30 |
| | | | | | $\Sigma p_1q_0 = 200$ | $\Sigma p_0q_0 = 160$ | $\Sigma p_1q_1 = 134$ | $\Sigma p_0q_1 = 107$ |

**(i) Laspeyre's Method:**

$$P_{01} = \frac{\Sigma p_1 q_0}{\Sigma p_0 q_0} \times 100$$

$$= \frac{200}{160} \times 100 = 125$$

**(ii) Paasche's Method:**

$$P_{01} = \frac{\Sigma p_1 q_1}{\Sigma p_0 q_1} \times 100$$

$$= \frac{134}{107} \times 100 = 125.23$$

**(iii) Fisher's Method:**

$$P_{01} = \sqrt{\frac{\Sigma p_1 q_0}{\Sigma p_0 q_0} \times \frac{\Sigma p_1 q_1}{\Sigma p_0 q_1}} \times 100$$

$$= \sqrt{\frac{200}{160} \times \frac{134}{107}} \times 100$$

$$= \sqrt{1.5654} \times 100$$

$$= 1.2512 \times 100 = 125.12$$

**ILLUSTRATION 3.**

From the following data, construct a price index number by using Fisher's Ideal Formula:

| Commodity | Base Year | | Current Year | |
|---|---|---|---|---|
| | Price per unit | Expenditure (₹) | Price per unit | Expenditure (₹) |
| A | 2 | 40 | 5 | 75 |
| B | 4 | 16 | 8 | 40 |
| C | 1 | 10 | 2 | 24 |
| D | 5 | 25 | 10 | 60 |

**SOLUTION:**

Since we are given the expenditure and the price, we can obtain the quantity by dividing total expenditure by the price for each commodity. We can then apply Fisher's Formula.

| Commodity | Base Year | | Current Year | | $p_1q_0$ | $p_0q_0$ | $p_1q_1$ | $p_0q_1$ |
|---|---|---|---|---|---|---|---|---|
| | $p_0$ | $q_0$ | $p_1$ | $q_1$ | | | | |
| A | 2 | 20 | 5 | 15 | 100 | 40 | 75 | 30 |
| B | 4 | 4 | 8 | 5 | 32 | 16 | 40 | 20 |
| C | 1 | 10 | 2 | 12 | 20 | 10 | 24 | 12 |
| D | 5 | 5 | 10 | 6 | 50 | 25 | 60 | 30 |
| | | | | | $\Sigma p_1q_0 = 202$ | $\Sigma p_0q_0 = 91$ | $\Sigma p_1q_1 = 199$ | $\Sigma p_0q_1 = 92$ |

By Fisher's Formula:

$$P_{01} = \sqrt{\frac{\Sigma p_1q_0}{\Sigma p_0q_0} \times \frac{\Sigma p_1q_1}{\Sigma p_0q_1}} \times 100$$

$$= \sqrt{\frac{202}{91} \times \frac{199}{92}} \times 100$$

$$= \sqrt{4.8015} \times 100$$

$$= 2.1912 \times 100$$

$$= 219.12$$

**ILLUSTRATION 4.**

Based on the following data, construct Laspeyre's and Paasche's Price Indices for 2013 and 2014 with 2004 as base:

| Items | 2004 | | 2013 | | 2014 | |
|---|---|---|---|---|---|---|
| | Price (in ₹) | Quantity (in kg) | Price (in ₹) | Quantity (in kg) | Price (in ₹) | Quantity (in kg) |
| A | 2 | 6 | 4 | 6 | 4 | 8 |
| B | 0.4 | 40 | 0.7 | 40 | 1 | 36 |
| C | 0.5 | 24 | 0.2 | 40 | 0.25 | 32 |

**SOLUTION:**

**Construction of Laspeyre's Price Indices**

| Items | 2004 | | 2013 | 2014 | $p_0q_0$ | $p_1q_0$ | $p_2q_0$ |
|---|---|---|---|---|---|---|---|
| | $q_0$ | $p_0$ | $p_1$ | $p_2$ | | | |
| A | 6 | 2 | 4 | 4 | 12 | 24 | 24 |
| B | 40 | 0.4 | 0.7 | 1 | 16 | 28 | 40 |
| C | 24 | 0.5 | 0.2 | 0.25 | 12 | 4.8 | 6 |
| | | | | | $\Sigma p_0q_0 = 40$ | $\Sigma p_1q_0 = 56.8$ | $\Sigma p_2q_0 = 70$ |

Laspeyre's Price Index:

$$P_{01}(2013) = \frac{\Sigma p_1q_0}{\Sigma p_0q_0} \times 100$$

$$= \frac{56.8}{40} \times 100$$

$$= 142$$

$$P_{02}(2014) = \frac{\Sigma p_2q_0}{\Sigma p_0q_0} \times 100$$

$$= \frac{70}{40} \times 100$$

$$= 175$$

### Construction of Paasche's Price Indices

| Items | 2004 | | 2013 | | 2014 | | $p_0q_1$ | $p_1q_1$ | $p_0q_2$ | $p_2q_2$ |
|---|---|---|---|---|---|---|---|---|---|---|
| | $q_0$ | $p_0$ | $q_1$ | $p_1$ | $q_2$ | $p_2$ | | | | |
| A | 6 | 2 | 6 | 4 | 8 | 4 | 12 | 24 | 16 | 32 |
| B | 40 | 0.4 | 40 | 0.7 | 36 | 1 | 16 | 28 | 14.4 | 36 |
| C | 24 | 0.5 | 40 | 0.2 | 32 | 0.25 | 20 | 8 | 16 | 8 |
| | | | | | | | $\Sigma p_0q_1 = 48$ | $\Sigma p_1q_1 = 60$ | $\Sigma p_0q_2 = 46.4$ | $\Sigma p_2q_2 = 76$ |

Paasche's Price Index:

$$P_{01}(2013) = \frac{\Sigma p_1q_1}{\Sigma p_0q_1} \times 100$$

$$= \frac{60}{48} \times 100 = 125$$

$$P_{02}(2014) = \frac{\Sigma p_2q_2}{\Sigma p_0q_2} \times 100$$

$$= \frac{76}{46.4} \times 100 = 163.79$$

**ILLUSTRATION 5.**

From the following data, find the Cost of Living Index Number of 2014 on the basis of 2004 by (i) Aggregate Expenditure Method, and (ii) Family Budget Method:

| Items | Quantity Consumed in 2004 | Prices | |
|---|---|---|---|
| | | 2004 | 2014 |
| Wheat | 2 qt | 75 | 125 |
| Rice | 20 kg | 12 | 16 |
| Sugar | 10 kg | 12 | 16 |
| Ghee | 5 kg | 10 | 15 |
| Clothing | 25 m | 4.5 | 5 |
| Fuel | 40 kg | 10 | 12 |
| Rent | 1 house | 25 | 40 |

**SOLUTION:**

(i) **Construction of Cost of Living Index Number —Aggregative Expenditure Method**

| Items | Quantity Consumed in 2004 ($q_0$) | Prices in 2004 ($p_0$) | Prices in 2014 ($p_1$) | Aggregate Expenditure in 2004 ($p_0q_0$) | Aggregate Expenditure in 2014 ($p_1q_0$) |
|---|---|---|---|---|---|
| Wheat | 2 qt | 75 | 125 | 150 | 250 |
| Rice | 20 kg | 12 | 16 | 240 | 320 |
| Sugar | 10 kg | 12 | 16 | 120 | 160 |
| Ghee | 5 kg | 10 | 15 | 50 | 75 |
| Clothing | 25 m | 4.5 | 5 | 112.5 | 125 |
| Fuel | 40 kg | 10 | 12 | 400 | 480 |
| Rent | 1 house | 25 | 40 | 25 | 40 |
| | | | | $\Sigma p_0q_0$=1,097.5 | $\Sigma p_1q_0$=1,450 |

$$\text{Cost of Living Index Number} = \frac{\Sigma p_1 q_0}{\Sigma p_0 q_0} \times 100$$

$$= \frac{1,450}{1,097.5} \times 100$$

$$= 132.12$$

**(ii) Construction of Cost of Living Index Number —Family Budget Method**

| Items | Quantity Consumed in 2004 ($q_0$) | Prices in 2004 ($p_0$) | Prices in 2014 ($p_1$) | Price Relative $(R = \frac{p_1}{p_0} \times 100)$ | Weights (Value Consumed in 2004) ($W = p_0 q_0$) | Weighted Relative (RW) |
|---|---|---|---|---|---|---|
| Wheat | 2 qt | 75 | 125 | 166.7 | 150 | 25,005 |
| Rice | 20 kg | 12 | 16 | 133.3 | 240 | 31,992 |
| Sugar | 10 kg | 12 | 16 | 133.3 | 120 | 15,996 |
| Ghee | 5 kg | 10 | 15 | 150 | 50 | 7,500 |
| Clothing | 25 m | 4.5 | 5 | 111.1 | 112.5 | 12,498.75 |
| Fuel | 40 kg | 10 | 12 | 120 | 400 | 48,000 |
| Rent | 1 house | 25 | 40 | 160 | 25 | 4,000 |
| | | | | | ΣW =1,097.5 | ΣRW=1,44,991.75 |

$$\text{Cost of Living Index} = \frac{\Sigma RW}{\Sigma W} = \frac{1,44,991.75}{1,097.5}$$

$$= 132.11$$

**ILLUSTRATION 6.**

Construct the Cost of Living Index for 2014 on the basis of 2004 from the following data and give your comments:

| Item | Prices in 2004 (₹) | Prices in 2014 (₹) | Weights |
|---|---|---|---|
| Food | 39 | 47 | 4 |
| Fuel | 8 | 12 | 1 |
| Clothing | 14 | 18 | 3 |
| Rent | 12 | 15 | 2 |
| Miscellaneous | 25 | 30 | 1 |

**SOLUTION:**

Since weights are directly given along with the prices in 2004 and 2014, we first determine price relatives (P) and then multiply it with weights (W).

**Calculation of Cost of Living Index**

| Items | $P_0$ | $P_1$ | $R = \frac{P_1}{P_0} \times 100$ | Weights (W) | Weighted Relative (RW) |
|---|---|---|---|---|---|
| Food | 39 | 47 | 120.51 | 4 | 482.04 |
| Fuel | 8 | 12 | 150 | 1 | 150 |
| Clothing | 14 | 18 | 128.57 | 3 | 385.71 |
| Rent | 12 | 15 | 125 | 2 | 250 |
| Miscellaneous | 25 | 30 | 120 | 1 | 120 |
| | | | | ΣW = 11 | ΣRW=1,387.75 |

$$\text{Cost of Living Index} = \frac{\Sigma RW}{\Sigma W}$$

$$= \frac{1,387.75}{11} = 126.16$$

It shows that the cost of living has gone up by 26.16% in 2014 compared to 2004.

**ILLUSTRATION 7.**

In 2004 wheat was selling at an average price ₹ 120 per 20 kg, cloth ₹ 20 per metre, house rent ₹ 300 per house and other items ₹ 100 per unit. By 2014 cost of wheat rose by ₹ 180 per 20 kg, house rent by ₹ 450 and other items doubled in price. Using relative prices, index number for the year 2014 with 2004 as base year was 160. By how much the cloth rose in price during the period?

**SOLUTION:**

Let the rise in price of cloth be X.

| Commodity | Price in 2004 ($P_0$) | Price in 2014 ($P_1$) | Price Relative $\left(\frac{P_1}{P_0} \times 100\right)$ |
|---|---|---|---|
| Wheat | 120 | 180 | $\frac{180}{120} \times 100 = 150$ |
| Cloth | 20 | X | $\frac{X}{20} \times 100 = 5X$ |
| House Rent | 300 | 450 | $\frac{450}{300} \times 100 = 150$ |
| Miscellaneous | 100 | 200 | $\frac{200}{100} \times 100 = 200$ |
| N = 4 | | | $\Sigma\left(\frac{P_1}{P_0} \times 100\right) = 500 + 5X$ |

$$P_{01} = \frac{\Sigma\left(\frac{P_1}{P_0} \times 100\right)}{N}$$

$$\Rightarrow \quad 160 = \frac{500 + 5X}{4}$$

$$\Rightarrow \quad 640 = 500 + 5X$$

$$\Rightarrow \quad 5X = 140$$

$$\Rightarrow \quad X = \frac{140}{5} = 28$$

Hence, the rise in the price of cloth = ₹ 28 – ₹ 20 = ₹ 8 per metre.

# EXERCISE

## 1. Very Short Answer Type Questions [1 mark]

### A. Multiple Choice Questions: Choose the Correct Answer

1. Whose formula is considered ideal for the construction of index number?
   (a) Paasche's formula (b) Laspeyer's formula
   (c) Fisher's formula (d) None of these
2. If the index of prices is estimated to be 112 in 2013, it means that in comparison to the base year, prices in 2013 are higher by:
   (a) 12% (b) 12 × 2 = 24%
   (c) 112% (d) none of these
3. Which of the following formulae is propounded by Fisher?
   (a) $P_{01} = \frac{\Sigma p_1q_1}{\Sigma p_0q_1}$ (b) $P_{01} = \frac{\Sigma p_1q_0}{\Sigma p_0q_0} \times 100$
   (c) $P_{01} = \sqrt{\frac{\Sigma p_1q_0}{\Sigma p_0q_0} \times \frac{\Sigma p_1q_1}{\Sigma p_0q_1}} \times 100$ (d) None of these
4. In notation $P_{01}$, 1 stand for:
   (a) current year (b) reference year
   (c) both (a) and (b) (d) none of these
5. Which of the following equations is correct?
   (a) $P_{01} = \frac{\Sigma RW}{\Sigma W} \times 100$ (b) $P_{01} = \frac{\Sigma RW}{\Sigma W}$
   (c) $P_{01} = \frac{\Sigma W}{\Sigma RW} \times 100$ (d) $P_{01} = \frac{\Sigma W}{\Sigma RW}$
6. Base year is also known as:
   (a) current year (b) reference year
   (c) periodic year (d) both (a) and (c)
7. Price Relatives = $\frac{\text{Current Year Price}}{?} \times 100$.
   (a) Reference year price (b) Periodic year price
   (c) Base year price (d) Both (a) and (c)
8. $P_{01} = \frac{\Sigma p_1q_0}{\Sigma p_0q_0} \times 100$ is the formula of:
   (a) Laspeyre's Method (b) Paasche's Method
   (c) Fisher's Method (d) none of these
9. Fisher's method of calculating index numbers is based on:
   (a) arithmetic mean (b) harmonic mean
   (c) geometric mean (d) none of these

10. Fisher's index number is considered ideal because:
    (a) it is based on variable weights (b) it satisfies Time Reversal Test
    (c) it satisfies Factor Reversal Test (d) all of these
11. Consumer Price Index is also known as:
    (a) Industrial Production Index (b) Cost of Living Index
    (c) Wholesale Price Index (d) none of these
12. Rate of inflation is equal to:
    (a) $\frac{A_1}{A_2 + A_1} \times 100$ (b) $\frac{A_2 + A_1}{A_1} \times 100$ [A = Price index]
    (c) $\frac{A_1}{A_2 - A_1} \times 100$ (d) $\frac{A_2 - A_1}{A_1} \times 100$

Ans. 1. (c), 2. (a ), 3. (c), 4. (a), 5. (b), 6. (b), 7. (d), 8. (a), 9. (c), 10. (d), 11. (b), 12. (d).

### B. True or False

State whether the following statements are True or False:

1. Index numbers measure relative changes in the variables over time. (True/False)
2. A rising index of price suggest a rising level of economic activity. (True/False)
3. In weighted index, weights are accorded to different items depending on their relative importance. (True/False)
4. Consumer price index numbers are constructed to measure the effect of average changes in wholesale prices on consumers living in different places. (True/False)
5. Simple index number can be constructed only by the simple aggregative method. (True/False)
6. Inflation is measured in terms of changes in wholesale price index, based on weekly statements of wholesale prices. (True/False)

Ans. 1. True, 2. False, 3. True, 4. False, 5. False, 6. True.

### C. Concepts/Definitions & Knowledge-based Questions

1. Define index number.

Ans. In the words of Spiegel, "An Index Number is a statistical measure designed to show changes in a variable or group of related variables with respect to time, geographic location or other characteristics".

2. Define simple index numbers.

Ans. Simple index numbers are the index numbers in which all items of the series are accorded equal weightage or importance.

3. Define weighted index numbers.

Ans. Weighted index numbers are the index numbers in which different items of the series are accorded different weightage, depending upon their relative importance.

4. What is price relative?

Ans. A price relative is the percentage ratio of the value of a variable in the current year to its value in the base year.

5. Define consumer price index number.

Ans. The consumer price index is the index number which measures the average change in prices paid by the specific class of consumers for goods and services consumed by them in the current year in comparison with base year.

6. Define wholesale price index.

Ans. The wholesale price index measures the relative changes in the prices of commodities traded in the wholesale markets.

7. State the two types of price index numbers.

Ans. The two types of price index numbers are:

(i) Consumer Price Index, and

(ii) Wholesale Price Index.

8. What should be the base year like?

Ans. Base year should be an year which is without wide fluctuations, not far from the period of study, neither very long nor very short and for which reliable data are available.

9. Name the consumer groups for which consumer price index number is computed.

Ans. The consumer groups for which consumer price index, in India, is computed are:

(i) Industrial Workers (IW),

(ii) Urban-Non Manual Employees (UNME), and

(iii) Agricultural Labourers (AL).

10. State one principal limitation of index numbers.

Ans. One principal limitation of index number is that owing to difference in the unit of currency as well as difference in the composition of production (and consumption) across different countries of the world, it is often very difficult to construct Index Numbers that facilitate international comparisons.

## 2. Short Answer Type Questions [3-4 marks]

1. State the principal types of index numbers.
2. What is the difference between simple index number and weighted index number?
3. Define base year. What is its importance?
4. What is price relative method of constructing index number?
5. Discuss the 'weighted' and 'unweighted' index of prices.
6. What are the four principal features of index numbers?
7. State four difficulties of constructing index numbers.
8. State the four principle importance of index numbers.
9. State the qualities of a good base year.
10. What is meant by wholesale price index number? What do the changes in wholesale price index indicate?
11. What does an index of industrial production measure?

12. What is the purpose of constructing an index number of (i) prices, and (ii) quantities?
13. What are the considerations underlying the choice of base period in the constructions of an index number?

## 3. Long Answer Type Questions [6 marks]

1. What is an index number? Point out its utility and limitations.
2. Describe the uses of index number. What considerations are taken into account while selecting the base year for the preparation of an index number?
3. Explain the needs and problems of 'weighting' in the construction of index number.
4. Describe the main problems which are faced in the construction of index number of prices.
5. What are the uses of wholesale price index number?
6. Discuss the general method of constructing an index number and uses of an index number.
7. What are the considerations underlying the selection of

   (i) weights, and (ii) commodities in the construction of a weighted index of prices?

## 4. Essential Practicals

1. Taking 2004 as base year, construct the index numbers of the years 2005 and 2009.

| Year | 2004 | 2005 | 2006 | 2007 | 2008 | 2009 |
|---|---|---|---|---|---|---|
| Prices (₹) | 10 | 14 | 16 | 20 | 22 | 24 |

(Ans. Index Numbers = 140, 240)

2. Construct index number by Price Relative Method taking 2004 as base year.

**Price per Unit in ₹**

| Year | A | B | C | D |
|---|---|---|---|---|
| 2004 | 25 | 18 | 16 | 21 |
| 2012 | 20 | 22 | 24 | 22 |
| 2013 | 25 | 20 | 25 | 25 |
| 2014 | 28 | 24 | 30 | 26 |

(Ans. Index Number = 114.25, 121.60, 139.16)

3. Compute a Price Index for the following by (i) Simple Aggregative Method, and (ii) Average of Price Relative Method:

| Commodities | A | B | C | D | E | F |
|---|---|---|---|---|---|---|
| Price in 2009 (₹) | 20 | 30 | 10 | 25 | 40 | 50 |
| Price in 2014 (₹) | 25 | 30 | 15 | 35 | 45 | 55 |

(Ans. (i) By Simple Aggregative Index Method = 117.14,
(ii) By Price Relative Index Method = 122.92)

4. Construct price index number of the following data by using:
(i) Laspeyre's Method, (ii) Paasche's Method, and (iii) Fisher's Method.

| Items | Base Year | | Current Year | |
|---|---|---|---|---|
| | Quantity | Price | Quantity | Price |
| A | 3 | 5 | 2 | 8 |
| B | 7 | 4 | 5 | 6 |
| C | 4 | 7 | 3 | 10 |
| D | 6 | 6 | 5 | 7 |

(Ans. (i) By Laspeyre's Method = 138.32,
(ii) By Paasche's Method = 137.04,
(iii) By Fisher's Method = 137.66)

[**Note:** Answers by all the methods are more or less equal. Nevertheless, Fisher's Index number is regarded as an ideal method.]

5. Construct an index number for the year 2014, taking 2004 as base year by any method you deem ideal:

| Year | Good I | | Good II | | Good III | |
|---|---|---|---|---|---|---|
| | Price | Quantity | Price | Quantity | Price | Quantity |
| 2004 | 5 | 10 | 8 | 6 | 6 | 3 |
| 2014 | 4 | 12 | 7 | 7 | 5 | 4 |

(Ans. Fisher's Method = 83.59)

6. Given the following data and taking 2004 as the base year, construct index of prices using:
(i) Laspeyre's Method, (ii) Paasche's Method, and (iii) Fisher's Method.

| Year | Commodities | | | | | | | |
|---|---|---|---|---|---|---|---|---|
| | A | | B | | C | | D | |
| | Price | Quantity | Price | Quantity | Price | Quantity | Price | Quantity |
| 2004 | 24 | 8 | 9 | 3 | 16 | 5 | 10 | 3 |
| 2014 | 30 | 10 | 10 | 4 | 20 | 8 | 9 | 4 |

(Ans. (i) By Laspeyre's Method = 120.67,
(ii) By Paasche's Method = 120.72,
(iii) By Fisher's Method = 120.69)

7. Construct a weighted index number of the following data using price relative method:

| **Item** | A | B | C | D | E |
|---|---|---|---|---|---|
| **Base Year (Quantity)** | 24 | 14 | 8 | 4 | 8 |
| **Base Year (Price)** | 2 | 4 | 6 | 10 | 5 |
| **Current Year (Price)** | 3 | 5 | 9 | 12 | 5 |

(Ans. Weighted Index Number = 130)

8. Find out the index number of the following data with Laspeyre's Method:

| Commodity | 2013 | | 2014 | |
|---|---|---|---|---|
| | Price | Quantity | Price | Quantity |
| A | 70 | 7 | 80 | 6 |
| B | 62 | 3 | 74 | 2 |

(Ans. Laspeyre's Method = 115.68)

9. Construct index numbers of the following data with Laspeyre's and Paasche's Methods:

| Commodity | Base Year | | Current Year | |
|---|---|---|---|---|
| | Quantity | Price | Quantity | Price |
| A | 10 | 0.80 | 11 | 0.70 |
| B | 8 | 0.85 | 9 | 0.90 |
| C | 5 | 1.30 | 5.5 | 0.80 |

(Ans. Laspeyre's Method = 85.45, Paasche's Method = 85.59)

10. Construct index numbers of the following data by Fisher's Method:

| Commodity | Base Year | | Current Year | |
|---|---|---|---|---|
| | Price | Value | Price | Value |
| A | 3 | 18 | 7 | 14 |
| B | 5 | 35 | 10 | 100 |
| C | 6 | 42 | 11 | 55 |
| D | 4 | 32 | 6 | 60 |
| E | 8 | 24 | 9 | 36 |

(Ans. Fisher's Method = 171.21)

[**Hint:** Here value does not stand for quantity. Rather quantity is to be worked out of value. To find quantity of base year ($q_0$) we make use of the following formula:

$$q_0 = \frac{\text{Value}}{\text{Price}} = \frac{18}{3} = 6$$

Similarly, we find quantity of current year ($q_1$) and solve the question using Fisher's Method.]

11. Construct Cost of Living Index on the basis of the following data:

| Items | Price | Weight |
|---|---|---|
| Wheat | 241 | 10 |
| Rice | 150 | 4 |
| Maida | 200 | 2 |
| Pulses | 170 | 2 |
| Oil | 125 | 2 |

(Ans. Cost of Living Index = 200)

12. Construct Consumer Price Index Number with the help of the following data:

| Consumer Items | Price | Weight |
|---|---|---|
| Food | 125 | 40 |
| Fuel | 120 | 10 |
| Cloth | 66.67 | 25 |
| House Rent | 120 | 15 |
| Miscellaneous | 150 | 10 |

(Ans. Consumer Price Index Number = 111.67)

13. From the following data find Consumer Price Index or Cost of Living Index:

| Items | Quantity Consumed in Current Year | Price in Base Year | Price in Current Year |
|---|---|---|---|
| Rice | 30 qt | 12 | 25 |
| Pulses | 36 kg | 0.4 | 0.6 |
| Oil | 24 *l* | 1.5 | 2.2 |
| Clothing | 72 metres | 0.75 | 10 |
| Housing | per month | 20 | 30 |
| Miscellaneous | per month | 20 | 15 |

(Ans. Consumer Price Index = 315.1)

14. Construct Cost of Living Index Number for the year 2014 from the following statistics:

| Commodity | 2004 Price | 2004 Quantity | 2014 Price |
|---|---|---|---|
| A | 25 | 16.0 | 35 |
| B | 36 | 7.0 | 48 |
| C | 12 | 3.5 | 16 |
| D | 6 | 2.5 | 10 |
| E | 28 | 4.0 | 28 |

(Ans. Cost of Living Index Number = 132.64)

15. Find the Consumer Price Index from the following data. Using
(i) Aggregative Expenditure Method, and
(ii) Family Budget Method.
Is there any difference between the two results?

| Commodity | Quantity Consumed in the Year 2004 | Unit | Price in 2004 (₹) | Price in 2014 (₹) |
|---|---|---|---|---|
| Rice | 6 | Quintal | 100 | 120 |
| Wheat | 8 | Quintal | 80 | 90 |
| Bajra | 1 | Quintal | 70 | 70 |
| Arhar | 2 | Quintal | 120 | 115 |
| Desi Ghee | 20 | kg | 12 | 15 |
| Sugar | 1 | Quintal | 160 | 170 |

(Ans. Consumer Price Index = 113.33)

16. Construct index number of industrial production in the year 2014 from the following data on the basis of 2005's production:

| Industry | Unit | 2005 | 2014 | Weight |
|---|---|---|---|---|
| Electrical and Electronics | Mill. Nos. | 12 | 70 | 36 |
| Metallurgical | Th. Tonnes | 22 | 37 | 12 |
| Mechanical | Th. Tonnes | 72 | 105 | 10 |
| Mining | Th. Tonnes | 100 | 123 | 22 |
| Textiles | Mill. Mtrs. | 60 | 130 | 8 |
| Miscellaneous | Th. Tonnes | 123 | 270 | 12 |

(Ans. Index Number of Industrial Production = 315.5)

17. Construct index number of industrial production from the following data:

| Item | Unit | Production or Output | | Weight |
|---|---|---|---|---|
| | | Base Year | Current Year | |
| Mechanical | Mill. Nos. | 237 | 400 | 5 |
| Sugar and Tea | Th. Tonnes | 62 | 150 | 10 |
| Textile | Mill. Mtrs. | 572 | 820 | 35 |
| Mining | Th. Tonnes | 165 | 200 | 15 |
| Transportation | Mill. Nos. | 335 | 727 | 20 |
| Electricity and Electronics | Mill. Nos. | 87 | 323 | 15 |

(Ans. Index Number of Industrial Production = 200.08)

18. Construct index number of industrial production from the following data:

| Industry | Number of Items | | Weight |
|---|---|---|---|
| | Base Year | Current Year | |
| Mining and Quarrying | 35 | 107 | 10 |
| Manufacturing | 413 | 1225 | 85 |
| Electricity and Electronics | 10 | 27 | 5 |

(Ans. Index Number of Industrial Production = 296.19)

## 5. NCERT Textbook Questions [With Hints to Answers]

1. An index number which accounts for the relative importance of the items is known as:
   (i) weighted index (ii) simple aggregative index
   (iii) simple average of relatives
   [(i)]
2. In most of the weighted index numbers the weight pertains to:
   (i) base year (ii) current year
   (iii) both base and current year
   [(i), as changing the weight every year is cumbersome.]
3. The impact of change in the price of a commodity with little weight in the index will be:
   (i) small (ii) large
   (iii) uncertain
   [(i)]
4. A consumer price index measures changes in:
   (i) retail prices (ii) wholesale prices
   (iii) producers prices
   [(i)]
5. The item having the highest weight in consumer price index for industrial workers is:
   (i) food (ii) housing
   (iii) clothing
   [(i)]

6. In general, inflation is calculated by using:

   (i) wholesale price index (ii) consumer price index

   (iii) producers' price index

   [(i)]

7. Why do we need an index number?

   [Page 342, 343]

8. What are the desirable properties of the base period?

   [Page 345]

9. What does a consumer price index for industrial workers measure?

   [The consumer price index for industrial workers measures the average change in prices paid by the specific class of consumers for goods and services consumed by them in the current year in comparison with base year.]

10. What is the difference between a price index and a quantity index?

    [Price index measures the relative or percentage change in the price level of certain goods and services. Whereas, quantity index measures the change in the physical volume of production, construction and employment.]

11. The monthly per capita expenditure incurred by workers for an industrial centre during 1980 and 2005 on the following items are given below. The weights of these items are 75, 10, 5, 6 and 4 respectively. Prepare a weighted index number for cost of living for 2005 with 1980 as the base.

| Items | Price in 1980 | Price in 2005 |
|---|---|---|
| Food | 100 | 200 |
| Clothing | 20 | 25 |
| Fuel & Lighting | 15 | 20 |
| House Rent | 30 | 40 |
| Miscellaneous | 35 | 65 |

[

| Items | Price in 1980 ($p_0$) | Price in 2005 ($p_1$) | Price Relative $\left(R = \frac{p_1}{p_0} \times 100\right)$ | Weights (W) | Product of Price Relative and Weights (RW) |
|---|---|---|---|---|---|
| Food | 100 | 200 | $\frac{200}{100} \times 100 = 200$ | 75 | 15,000 |
| Clothing | 20 | 25 | $\frac{25}{20} \times 100 = 125$ | 10 | 1,250 |
| Fuel & Lighting | 15 | 20 | $\frac{20}{15} \times 100 = 133.33$ | 5 | 666.65 |
| House Rent | 30 | 40 | $\frac{40}{30} \times 100 = 133.33$ | 6 | 799.98 |
| Miscellaneous | 35 | 65 | $\frac{65}{35} \times 100 = 185.71$ | 4 | 742.84 |
| | | | | $\Sigma W = 100$ | $\Sigma RW = 18{,}459.47$ |

$$\text{Weighted Index Number} = \frac{\Sigma RW}{\Sigma W}$$

$$= \frac{18{,}459.47}{100}$$

$$= 184.5947 \sim 184.6$$

∴ Weighted index number = 184.6.]

12. An enquiry into the budgets of the middle class families in a certain city gave the following information:

| **Expenses on Items** | Food 35% | Fuel 10% | Clothing 20% | Rent 15% | Miscellaneous 20% |
|---|---|---|---|---|---|
| **Price (in ₹) in 2004** | 1,500 | 250 | 750 | 300 | 400 |
| **Price (in ₹) in 1995** | 1,400 | 200 | 500 | 200 | 250 |

What is the cost of living index of 2004 as compared with 1995?

[

| **Items** | **Price in 1995 ($p_0$)** | **Price in 2004 ($p_1$)** | **Price Relative $\left(R = \frac{p_1}{p_0} \times 100\right)$** | **Weights (W)** | **Product of Price Relative and Weights (RW)** |
|---|---|---|---|---|---|
| Foodz | 1,400 | 1,500 | $\frac{1{,}500}{1{,}400} \times 100 = 107.14$ | 35 | 3,750 |
| Fuel | 200 | 250 | $\frac{250}{200} \times 100 = 125$ | 10 | 1,250 |
| Clothing | 500 | 750 | $\frac{750}{500} \times 100 = 150$ | 20 | 3,000 |
| Rent | 200 | 300 | $\frac{300}{200} \times 100 = 150$ | 15 | 2,250 |
| Miscellaneous | 250 | 400 | $\frac{400}{250} \times 100 = 160$ | 20 | 3,200 |
| | | | | $\Sigma W = 100$ | $\Sigma RW = 13{,}450$ |

$$\text{Cost of Living Index} = \frac{\Sigma RW}{\Sigma W}$$

$$= \frac{13{,}450}{100} = 134.50$$

∴ Cost of living index = 134.50.]

# Use of Statistical Tools: Developing Projects in Statistics

You have now completed your study on statistical methods relating to:

(1) Collection of Data, (2) Classification of Data,

(3) Presentation of Data, (4) Analysis of Data, and

(5) Interpretation of Data.

**Let us be practical now.** How exactly are you going to use these statistical methods as a student of Economics? We can discuss this by taking up some project work.

Of course, in the context of any project work, the students are expected to use their own thought process based on their understanding of the statistical methods. However, certain guidelines are offered to them just to facilitate their recapitulation of the subject matter and its application in practice. This present chapter focuses on the following projects:

(1) Consumer Awareness among Households.

(2) Demographic Structure of a Neighbourhood.

(3) Changing prices of a few vegetables in a market.

(4) Study of a cooperative institution: Milk Cooperative.

## 1. Project Report on Consumer Awareness among Households using Primary Data

### What is Consumer Awareness?

It is the basic question the students must understand before they take up the project work.

**Here is an outright warning:** Do not confuse consumer awareness with product awareness. Product awareness implies knowledge of the consumers or households regarding availability of a certain product in the market. While product awareness may mean popularity of a certain product among the households. Producers may conduct statistical surveys to ascertain this fact about their products.

Consumer awareness is a much broader and wider concept. It covers the following questions:

(1) Are the consumers aware that the product they are using is a certified product? It should be certified as ISI, AGMARK, ISO-9002, etc.

(2) Are the households, aware of the statutory requirement that the product should show MRP (Maximum Retail Price), date of manufacture and the date showing 'best before use' or the expiry date of the product.

(3) Are the households aware that the product in question (like Kerosene oil or sugar) may be available at the Fair Price Shops regulated by the Government?

(4) Are the households aware of the consumer courts which are meant to protect their interest against fraudulent practices by the shopkeepers?

(5) Are the households aware of the fact that if they buy goods against cash memos, they are ensuring purchase of genuine products as well as tax revenue to the Government?

(6) Do the households update their consumer awareness through electronic media or print media?

**Briefly, consumer awareness among households facilitates and promotes consumer welfare. Greater awareness implies greater welfare through better purchase of the goods and services.**

## Essential Steps on Preparing a Project Report on Consumer Awareness

### (i) Designing a Questionnaire

Students are required to prepare a project report on consumer awareness among households through collection of primary data by designing a questionnaire. Accordingly, designing a questionnaire becomes the first step of the project work.

Students are advised to design a questionnaire covering the various aspects of consumer awareness as detailed in the previous section.

Thus, their questionnaire may assume the following form, or include the following questions:

**A Questionnaire on Consumer Awareness**

| QUESTIONS | RESPONSE | |
|---|---|---|
| 1. Name........................................................ | | |
| 2. Address...................................................... | | |
| 3. Occupation................................................ | | |
| 4. Are you aware that the product you buy should be a certified product like ISI, AGMARK, ISO-9002? | (YES) ...... | (NO) ...... |
| 5. Do you check MRP, Manufacturing Date and Expiry Date while buying a product? | (YES) ...... | (NO) ...... |
| 6. Do you confirm the availability of the product at Fair Price Shops? | (YES) ...... | (NO) ...... |
| 7. Are you aware of consumer courts to protect your rights? | (YES) ...... | (NO) ...... |
| 8. Do you insist on Cash Memo at the time of purchase to ensure genuine purchase and tax revenue to the Government? | (YES) ...... | (NO) ...... |
| 9. Are you updating your awareness through electronic media or print media? | (YES) ...... | (NO) ...... |

[**Note:** You must bear in mind characteristics of a good questionnaire while designing it.]

### (ii) Framing a Sample

Having designed a questionnaire, you must define the sample size of your study. Covering all households in the country or even in a state, a city or a village (you are residing in) may not be possible for a student of Class XI. Best would be to take a sample of 50 households, 25 from the urban area and another 25 from the rural area. Rural-urban comparison should make your study interesting and more meaningful.

In your choice of a sample you can rely upon your knowledge of the various sampling techniques, like random or systematic sampling.

### (iii) Collection of Data

Nature of the statistical inquiry suggests that you should collect data through direct personal oral investigation. You will thus have 50 response sheets, 25 of urban respondents and 25 of the rural respondents. You may personally approach each and every respondent or seek the help of your friends or classmates.

### (iv) Classification of Data

Raw Data need to be classified. Check your knowledge of the classification of data. When classified, the data may assume the following form:

**(A) Data Relating to Rural Households**

Q.4. Certified Product

YES: || = 02

NO: 𝍸 𝍸 𝍸 𝍸 ||| = 23

Q.5. MRP, Expiry and Mfg. Date.

YES: ||| = 03

NO: 𝍸 𝍸 𝍸 𝍸 || = 22

Q.6. Fair Price Shops

YES: 𝍸 𝍸 𝍸 𝍸 = 20

NO: 𝍸 = 05

Q.7. Consumer Courts

YES: NIL = 0

NO: 𝍸 𝍸 𝍸 𝍸 𝍸 = 25

Q.8. Cash Memo

YES: NIL = 0

NO: 𝍸 𝍸 𝍸 𝍸 𝍸 = 25

Q.9. Updating Awareness

YES: NIL = 0

NO: 𝍸 𝍸 𝍸 𝍸 𝍸 = 25

**(B) Data Relating to Urban Households**

Q.4. Certified Product

YES: 𝍸 𝍸 𝍸 𝍸 || = 22

NO: ||| = 03

Q.5. MRP, Expiry and Mfg. Date.

YES: 𝍸 𝍸 𝍸 𝍸 ||| = 23

NO: || = 02

Q.6: Fair Price Shops

YES: NIL = 0

NO: 𝍸 𝍸 𝍸 𝍸 𝍸 = 25

Q.7. Consumer Courts

YES: 𝍸 𝍸 ||| = 13

NO: 𝍸 𝍸 || = 12

Q.8. Cash Memo

YES: NIL = 0

NO: 𝍸 𝍸 𝍸 𝍸 𝍸 = 25

Q.9. Updating Awareness

YES: 𝍸 𝍸 𝍸 𝍸 𝍸 = 25

NO: NIL = 0

### (v) Presentation of Data

Now comes the stage of presentation of data. Check the relevant chapters on the presentation of data. Given the nature of data, you might like to present data in a tabular form as under.

**Table 1. Consumer Awareness Among Households**

| Parameters of Awareness ↓ / Extent of Awareness → | Number of Households showing Awareness | | Number of Household lacking Awareness | |
|---|---|---|---|---|
| | Urban | Rural | Urban | Rural |
| 1. Looking for certified product ISI, AGMARK, ISO-9002 | 22 | 02 | 03 | 23 |
| 2. Checking MRP, date of manufacture and expiry date of the product | 23 | 03 | 02 | 22 |
| 3. Awareness of Fair Price Shops | NIL | 20 | 25 | 05 |
| 4. Awareness of Consumer Courts | 13 | NIL | 12 | 25 |
| 5. Insistence on Cash Memos | NIL | NIL | 25 | 25 |
| 6. Updating Awareness through electronic media and print media | 25 | NIL | NIL | 25 |

**Note:** It is a sample survey of 50 households, 25 each from rural and urban areas.

**Source:** Direct Personal Oral Investigation.

### (vi) Analysis of Data

It means you are to further summarise the data in terms of percentages or averages, so that the interpretation of data becomes easy and meaningful. Here is a summary table for your reference.

**Table 2. Summary Table on Consumer Awareness Among Rural and Urban Households**

| Parameters of Awareness ↓ / Extent of Awareness → | Percentage of Households showing Awareness | | Percentage of Households Lacking Awareness | |
|---|---|---|---|---|
| | Urban | Rural | Urban | Rural |
| 1. Looking for certified product ISI, AGMARK, ISO-9002 | 88 | 8 | 12 | 92 |
| 2. Checking MRP, date of manufacture and expiry date of the product | 92 | 12 | 8 | 88 |
| 3. Awareness of Fair Price Shops | NIL | 80 | 100 | 20 |
| 4. Awareness of Consumer Courts | 52 | NIL | 48 | 100 |
| 5. Insistence on Cash Memos | NIL | NIL | 100 | 100 |
| 6. Updating Awareness through Electronic Media and Print Media | 100 | NIL | NIL | 100 |

### (vii) Interpretation of Data—The Project Report

You are now ready for the interpretation of data, or preparing a statement of conclusions of your study. This will be your project report. Some interesting conclusions that you can draw from the Summary Table and which you can include in your project report are as follows:

(1) There is a general lack of consumer awareness among rural households while urban households show a high degree of consumer awareness. Lack of education among rural households perhaps is the principal cause.

(2) Looking for Fair Price Shops is the only element of consumer awareness where rural households excel over the urban households. Perhaps, it is poverty of the rural masses that compels them to look for cheaper options of purchase.

(3) Both rural as well as urban households are almost completely ignorant of the fact that insistence on cash memos ensures genuine purchases as well as tax revenue to the state.

(4) Electronic Media and Print Media are playing an important role in updating consumer awareness among the urban households.

## PRODUCTIVITY AWARENESS

### EXERCISE

Do a similar exercise on **Productivity Awareness** among the enterprises. You may do this exercise using secondary data. You are to find these data from Newspapers, Economic Surveys, RBI Bulletin, Budget of the Central and the State Governments, Census Reports, NSS reports, etc.

You are to check your library or seek your teacher's help for procuring these reports.

**HINTS:**

(i) Productivity should not be confused with total output.

(ii) $\text{Productivity} = \dfrac{\text{Total Output}}{\text{Units of the factor used}}$

Thus,

$$\text{Labour Production} = \frac{\text{Total Output}}{\text{Total Number of Workers Employed}}$$

$$\text{Land Productivity} = \frac{\text{Total Output}}{\text{Units of Land Used}}$$

(iii) Productivity and cost are reciprocal of each other: Higher productivity implies lower cost, and vice versa.

(iv) Higher productivity ⟶ Lower cost ⟶ Higher profits.

(v) Productivity awareness implies awareness among the producers of the objective of maximising profits.

(vi) In the industrial sector in India, Productivity awareness is fairly high, but in the agricultural sector, it is comparatively low. It is due to the fact that production in industrial sector is governed by the profit motive but in the agricultural sector, production is largely dictated by the subsistence motive, not the profit motive.

## 2. Project Report on Demographic Structure of a Neighbourhood

### INTRODUCTION

**Demography** is the study of the characteristics of human population, such as size, growth, density, distribution, and vital statistics.

**Demographic structure** represents a fundamental approach to the understanding of human society. Its primary tasks are to ascertain the number of people in a given area, to determine what change that number represents from a previous census, to explain the change, and to estimate the future trends of population changes. The demographer also traces the origins of population changes and studies their impact. Demographers compile and analyse data that are useful for understanding various social systems and for establishing public policy in such areas as housing, education, and unemployment.

The primary aim of this project is to practically find out what constitutes the structure of population, and analyse it statistically. For this, the students need to conduct a statistical study in their neighbourhood, analyse the accumulated data and draw inferences about their neighbourhood. If their neighbourhood or locality generally represents the city or the district as a whole, the analysis and interpretation could be assumed to be applicable to the entire city or the district.

### STEPS INVOLVED

#### (i) Designing a Questionnaire

To prepare a project report on the demographic structure of their neighbourhood (say, their colony), the students need to collect certain primary data by designing a questionnaire. A sample questionnaire is drawn up below for reference. The students can supplement this questionnaire with more questions after consulting their teacher. The sample questionnaire has been filled up with hypothetical information.

**A Questionnaire on Demographic Structure**

1. Name of head of the family — Mr ABC
2. Address — 123, Friends Colony, Mathura Road, New Delhi
3. Telephone Number — 23456789
4. Details of family members

**Table 3**

| Member | Sex (M/F) | Age (Years) | Educational Qualification | Occupation (Primary/ Secondary/Tertiary) |
|---|---|---|---|---|
| Husband | M | 42 | | |
| Wife | F | 40 | | |
| Son | M | 13 | | |
| Daughter | F | 17 | | |
| Father | M | 65 | | |
| Mother | F | 58 | | |
| Brother | M | 23 | | |

**Note:** All members of the household should be included in the survey.

**(ii) Collection of Data**

The exercise involves the collection of primary data. Due to enormity of the task, it is recommended that 3-4 students work simultaneously across different parts of the colony to timely complete the survey. The students must ensure that they cover each and every house for collecting the requisite information.

**(iii) Classification of Data**

The raw data now needs to be classified, after which the data may assume the following form (Here again, hypothetical figures have been filled in for ease of understanding):

**Area of the colony:** 0.25 sq km (500m × 500m approx).

**Age Structure in Years:**

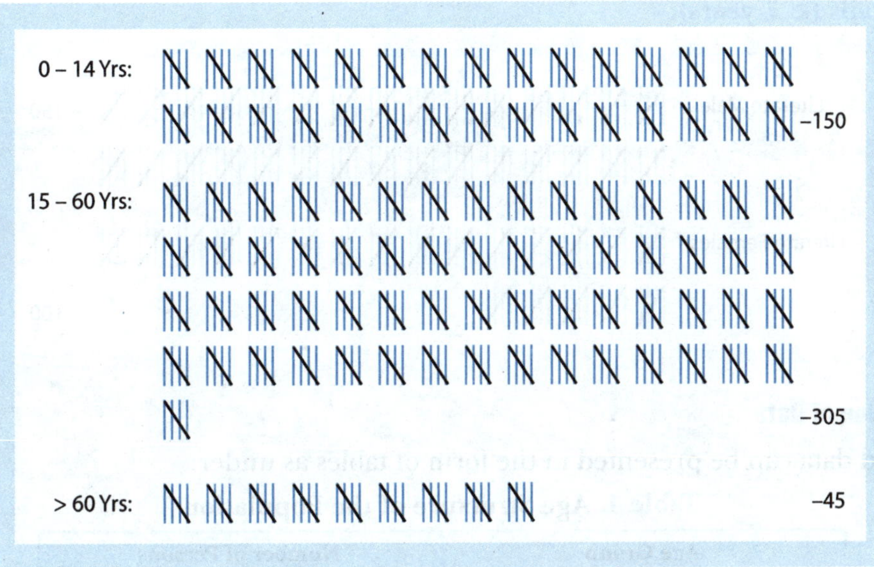


**Sex Distribution:**

**Sector-wise Employment:**

**Literacy Details (≥ 7 years):**

### (iv) Presentation of Data

The classified data can be presented in the form of tables as under:

**Table 4. Age Structure of the Population**

| Age Group | Number of Persons |
|---|---|
| 0-14 Years | 150 |
| 15-60 Years | 305 |
| > 60 Years | 45 |
| | Total Population = 500 |

**Table 5. Occupational Structure of the Population**

| Sector | Number of Persons Employed |
|---|---|
| Primary | 25 |
| Secondary | 90 |
| Tertiary | 135 |
| | Total Employed = 250 |

**Table 6. Literacy Structure of the Population**

| Sex | Number of Persons |
|---|---|
| Males | 150 |
| Females | 100 |
| | Total Literates = 250 |

**Note:** A person who is aged 7 years or above and can both read and write with understanding a short simple statement on his/her everyday life is considered a literate.

### (v) Analysis of Data

**Table 7. Age Structure (in Years)**

| Age Group | Actual Figures | Percentage (of Total Population) |
|---|---|---|
| 0-14 Years | 150 | 30 |
| 15-60 Years | 305 | 61 |
| > 60 Years | 45 | 9 |
| | Total Population = 500 | 100 |

**Table 8. Occupational Structure**

| Sector Type | Actual Figures | Percentage (of Total Employed) |
|---|---|---|
| Primary | 25 | 10 |
| Secondary | 90 | 36 |
| Tertiary | 135 | 54 |

**Table 9. Literacy Structure**

| | Actual Figures | Literacy Rate |
|---|---|---|
| Males | 150 | 75% |
| Females | 100 | 66.67% |
| Difference in Literacy Rate | N/A | 8.33% |

**Male Literacy Rate**

= (Number of Literate Males ÷ Total Number of Males ≥ 7 years) × 100

= (150 ÷ 200) × 100 = 75%

**Female Literacy Rate**

= (Number of Literate Females ÷ Total Number of Females ≥ 7 years) × 100

= (100 ÷ 150) × 100 = 66.67%

**Overall Literacy Rate**

= (Number of Literates × Total Number of Persons ≥ 7 years) × 100

= (250 ÷ 350) × 100 = 71.43%

**Density of Population**

= Total Population ÷ Area of the Colony

= 500 ÷ 0.25 = 2,000 per sq km

**Sex Ratio**

= (Number of Women ÷ Number of Men) × 1,000

= (200 ÷ 300) × 1,000

= 667 women per 1,000 men

**Percentage of Persons Employed**

= (Number of Persons Employed ÷ Total Population) × 100

= (250 ÷ 500) × 100 = 50%

### (vi) Interpretation of Data

Following inferences can now be drawn from the compiled data:

The colony has a **dynamic population** since ratio of young population (0-14 years) is high (30%). This, however, also means that **birth rate is high which can have adverse effect on the quality of life of the people.**

Also, the **percentage of unproductive population is high** (0-14 years = 30% and > 60 years = 9%) which means that there is a high dependency ratio.

**Most persons are employed in secondary and tertiary sectors.**

Together the employment in these sectors, *i.e.*, 36% + 54% = 90%. This is a sign of a high level of economic development.

**Sex ratio is low** (only 667 females per 1000 males) indicating that males outnumber females and that **more importance be given to the girl child.**

**Overall literacy rate is 71.43% which is reasonably high** and indicates a well educated and developed demographic structure. Also male and female literacy rates are 75% and 66.67% respectively, indicating that the society needs to give greater importance to female education.

## 3. Project on Changing Prices of a Few Vegetables in a Market Using Primary Data

### INTRODUCTION

The aim of the project is to study the trend in prices of vegetables over a two-month period and identify reasons causing change in prices.

The study assumes significance in view of the fact that vegetable prices affect every household. If vegetable prices tend to rise, consumption of vegetables will reduce. In fact, in the face of rising vegetable prices, marginal families (or poor families) may not be in a position to buy vegetables at all. Implying a significant adverse impact on their quality of life.

### STEPS INVOLVED

### (i) Designing a Format

A sample format is given below to help the students collect data on changing prices of vegetables in their market. Students should focus on those vegetables which are widely sold in the market. Implying that these are widely consumed by the households. They may approach the vegetable outlets of the cooperative societies or the private vendors in their locality to collect price quotations.

**Vegetable Prices at Mother Dairy Vegetable Outlet during Jan-Feb 2014**

| Vegetables | Price (in ₹/kg) | | | | | | | | |
|---|---|---|---|---|---|---|---|---|---|
| | 1st Week | 2nd Week | 3rd Week | 4th Week | 5th Week | 6th Week | 7th Week | 8th Week | 9th Week |
| Potato | 8 | 9 | 10 | 12 | 14 | 10 | 15 | 11 | 11 |
| Onion | 16 | 16 | 18 | 24 | 28 | 22 | 22 | 21 | 21 |
| Tomato | 7 | 8 | 8 | 12 | 15 | 11 | 13 | 15 | 17 |
| Cauliflower | 12 | 13 | 15 | 21 | 24 | 17 | 18 | 17 | 17 |
| Peas | 13 | 14 | 16 | 24 | 27 | 22 | 22 | 23 | 24 |
| Spinach | 7 | 8 | 8 | 12 | 14 | 8 | 8 | 9 | 10 |
| Carrot | 8 | 8 | 9 | 12 | 14 | 11 | 11 | 12 | 13 |
| Radish | 4 | 4 | 4 | 7 | 9 | 6 | 5 | 6 | 7 |
| Cucumber | 16 | 18 | 18 | 25 | 28 | 24 | 32 | 24 | 25 |
| Ginger | 50 | 52 | 52 | 60 | 62 | 58 | 56 | 56 | 56 |

| Nature of change in prices | | Increase in prices | | Spurt in Prices or a significant increase in prices | | Decrease in Prices | Increase in Prices | Prices are generally stable | |
|---|---|---|---|---|---|---|---|---|---|
| Reasons for change in prices | | Unseasonal Rains-resulting in delay in supplies | | Truckers' strike | | Strike over | Festival week | Marginal increase because of season coming to an end. | |
| Effect on Purchase and Consumption | — | ↓ | ↓ | ↓ | ↓ | ↑ | ↓ | ↔ | ↔ |

**Vegetable Prices at Private Vendor during Jan-Feb 2014**

| Vegetables | Price (in ₹/kg) | | | | | | | | |
|---|---|---|---|---|---|---|---|---|---|
| | 1st Week | 2nd Week | 3rd Week | 4th Week | 5th Week | 6th Week | 7th Week | 8th Week | 9th Week |
| Potato | 10 | 12 | 12 | 15 | 17 | 12 | 20 | 14 | 14 |
| Onion | 20 | 21 | 22 | 30 | 34 | 26 | 26 | 24 | 24 |
| Tomato | 8 | 10 | 10 | 15 | 19 | 15 | 18 | 20 | 21 |
| Cauliflower | 15 | 17 | 19 | 25 | 28 | 20 | 21 | 20 | 20 |
| Peas | 16 | 17 | 20 | 26 | 32 | 27 | 27 | 28 | 30 |
| Spinach | 8 | 10 | 10 | 15 | 18 | 10 | 10 | 12 | 14 |
| Carrot | 10 | 10 | 12 | 15 | 18 | 13 | 13 | 15 | 17 |
| Radish | 5 | 5 | 5 | 8 | 10 | 7 | 6 | 7 | 8 |
| Cucumber | 20 | 22 | 22 | 30 | 34 | 30 | 38 | 30 | 32 |
| Ginger | 60 | 62 | 62 | 75 | 78 | 72 | 70 | 70 | 70 |
| Nature of change in prices | | Increase in prices | | Increase in prices | | Decrease in Prices | Increase in Prices | Prices are generally stable | |
| Reasons for change in prices | | Unseasonal Rains-resulting in delay in supplies | | Truckers' strike | | Strike over | Festival week | Marginal increase because of season coming to an end. | |
| Effect on Purchase and Consumption | — | ↓ | ↓ | ↓ | ↓ | ↑ | ↓ | ↔ | ↔ |

### (ii) Collection of Data

The formats may be written/printed on a computer and the same may be stuck on a cardboard/ filed so that prices can be noted daily. Obviously, data are to be collected through direct personal oral investigation.

### (iii) Classification of Data

The data is already classified since it has been collected in a tabular form.

### (iv) Graphic Presentation of Data

The data in the tables can be represented using vegetable-wise Time series graphs for both mother dairy and the private vendor. An example is given below:

**Time Series Graph Showing Variation in Prices of Potatoes over Jan-Feb 2014**

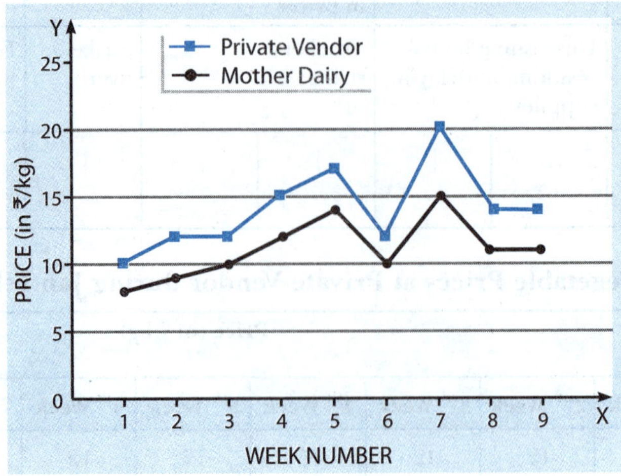


[**Note:** Similar graphs can be drawn for each of the vegetables.]

### (v) Analysis of Data

| | | Price as on 1st Week | Price as on 9th Week | Change % |
|---|---|---|---|---|
| **Potato** | Mother Dairy | 8 | 11 | 37.50 ↑ |
| | Private Vendor | 10 | 14 | 40.00 ↑ |
| **Onion** | Mother Dairy | 16 | 21 | 31.25 ↑ |
| | Private Vendor | 20 | 24 | 20.00 ↑ |
| **Tomato** | Mother Dairy | 7 | 17 | 142.86 ↑ |
| | Private Vendor | 8 | 21 | 162.50 ↑ |
| **Cauliflower** | Mother Dairy | 12 | 17 | 41.67 ↑ |
| | Private Vendor | 15 | 20 | 33.33 ↑ |
| **Peas** | Mother Dairy | 13 | 24 | 84.62 ↑ |
| | Private Vendor | 16 | 30 | 87.50 ↑ |
| **Spinach** | Mother Dairy | 7 | 10 | 42.86 ↑ |
| | Private Vendor | 8 | 14 | 75.00 ↑ |
| **Carrot** | Mother Dairy | 8 | 13 | 62.50 ↑ |
| | Private Vendor | 10 | 17 | 70.00 ↑ |
| **Radish** | Mother Dairy | 4 | 7 | 75.00 ↑ |
| | Private Vendor | 5 | 8 | 60.00 ↑ |
| **Cucumber** | Mother Dairy | 16 | 25 | 56.25 ↑ |
| | Private Vendor | 20 | 32 | 60.00 ↑ |
| **Ginger** | Mother Dairy | 50 | 56 | 12.00 ↑ |
| | Private Vendor | 60 | 70 | 16.67 ↑ |

### (vi) Interpretation of Data

The prices of vegetables have shown the following trends:

(1) The prices marginally increased during 2nd and 3rd week due to unseasonal rains resulting in delay in supplies.

(2) The prices showed sudden spurt during the 4th and 5th week due to truckers' strike resulting in only limited supplies from the fields and farms.

(3) Prices of selected vegetables (potato and cucumber) shot up in the 7th week because of anticipated increase in demand due to festival season (Shivratri).

(4) The prices from the 1st week to the 9th week increased considerably because of the prime season for most vegetables coming to an end.

(5) Prices of private vendor were higher which was justified because of the better quality of vegetables being sold by him.

(6) Change in prices directly affected the purchase and consumption of vegetables. Generally, whenever the prices decreased, the purchase increased and when the prices increased, the purchase decreased.

(7) During festival seasons purchases continued to be high even when prices were high. In fact, prices ruled high simply because purchases were high.

## 4. Study of a Cooperative Institution: Milk Cooperative

Students are introduced to the actual study jointly conducted by the College of Veterinary and Animal Sciences and the College of Agriculture, Pantnagar, Uttaranchal. They can use this study as a source of secondary data. Using the secondary data they can draw their own conclusions and inferences relating to the objective/purpose of their study.

### Introduction

Dairy farming is one of the most important economic activities in the rural mountain areas of Uttaranchal. Rural communities fondly relish dairy products. Apart from ensuring nutrient supplies to the families owning dairy farms, dairying also offers promising employment opportunities and handsome economic returns. In Uttaranchal mountains, dairying is especially a promising economic activity for small holders who constitute the majority of farming communities in the region. However, despite the fact that smallholder dairy farming is increasingly gaining importance as a source of family income in the Uttaranchal mountains, the system is yet not well organised.

The first dairy farms to be tempted for milk sale in the nearby market place would be those located in the periphery of urban areas. The peri-urban farms would be at special advantage because of greater chances of their relationship with the easily accessible market centre.

### Objective of the Study

Here, a note of caution is essential. Since you are using secondary data, your objective of study must be a little different from the objective of study conducted by the College of Veterinary and Animal Sciences. If the objective of the study is exactly the same and you are using the secondary data, your study makes no sense. Let us illustrate this point further. We know that the objective of study of the College of Veterinary and Animal Sciences was to estimate the livestock population (including its composition and size), milk production and marketing of milk (including different channels of marketing). Using data collected by the college, you may be interested in finding how far milk cooperative has been a success story in the rural mountains of Uttaranchal. Thus, you are focusing on one issue: How far people in the rural mountains of Uttaranchal sell milk through the Cooperative Society. If most dairy owners are marketing milk through the cooperative society, you may conclude that Milk Cooperative is a success story. Otherwise not.

## Methods of Study

### Data

In accordance with the objective of your study, you need to have data on the flow of milk through different marketing channels in the area of study. The study conducted by the College of Veterinary and Animal Sciences offers you statistical information as in Table 10.

**Table 10. Milk Flow through Different Marketing Channels in Study Area (All figures are in litres)**

| Village | Milk Production per Village Per Day | Milk Marketing through Different Channels | | | Total Milk Marketed |
|---|---|---|---|---|---|
| | | Producer Consumer Channel | Producer-Trader/ Middleman Consumer Channel | Producer-Cooperative-Consumer Channel | |
| Patan | 430 | 112 | 34 | — | 146 |
| Kaligaon | 430 | 168 | 15 | — | 183 |
| Chauri | 652 | 306 | 27 | 4 | 337 |
| Raikote Kunwar | 648 | 362 | — | — | 362 |
| Motyuraj | 708 | 76 | 147 | 73 | 296 |
| Rautali Mara | 377 | 127 | 14 | — | 141 |
| Overall (Average) | 541 | 192 | 39 | 13 | 244 |

You must also apprise yourself of the method of study, and the area covered. Six villages nestled on the periphery of the township of Lohaghat in the district of Champawat in Uttaranchal were selected for the study. In each village, 20% of the farm households were selected for detailed investigation. Implying, that it was a 'sample study', not a census investigation. Day-to-day visits of the dairy farms in the research villages was undertaken continuously for 45 days (from 15 June to 31 July 2005).

## Analysis and Conclusion

Most of the milk produced at the dairy farms was sold through producer-consumer channel (192 litres or 70% of the total milk marketed). Average milk marketed through producer-trader/middleman-consumer channel per village per day was 39 litres (or only 16% of the total milk marketed). Producer- cooperative- consumer channel of milk marketing was not so active. Merely 5% of the total milk marketed was routed through this channel.

Thus, the pattern of milk flow via different marketing channels reveals that dairy farms in the rural mountains of Uttaranchal tend to establish direct contact with the consumers, as they are easily accessible to them. The consumers also seem to have preference for their own milk suppliers, as they prefer fresh whole milk.

Why is the milk cooperative not an effective channel of the marketing of milk? Perhaps, because cooperatives offer lesser price for full whole milk than the consumers or traders.

# Add-on Numericals

## Organisation of Data

**1. Convert the following inclusive series into exclusive series:**

| Marks | Frequency |
|---|---|
| 19–24 | 2 |
| 25–29 | 7 |
| 30–34 | 6 |
| 35–39 | 2 |
| 40–44 | 3 |

**Sol.** **Conversion of Inclusive Series into Exclusive Series**

| Marks | Frequency |
|---|---|
| 18.5–24.5 | 2 |
| 24.5–29.5 | 7 |
| 29.5–34.5 | 6 |
| 34.5–39.5 | 2 |
| 39.5–44.5 | 3 |

**2. The monthly salary of some families in a society is given below:**

| Monthly Salary (₹ in thousand) | No. of Families |
|---|---|
| 10–20 | 6 |
| 20–30 | 9 |
| 30–40 | 12 |
| 40–50 | 17 |
| 50–60 | 11 |
| 60–70 | 5 |

(i) What is the lower limit of the second class interval?

(ii) What is the upper limit of the last class interval?

(iii) What is the class size of each class interval?

(iv) What is the mid-value of the third class interval?

(v) How many families earn ₹ 50,000 or more in a month?

(vi) How many families earn less than ₹ 20,000 in a month?

**Sol.** (i) Lower limit of the second class interval = 20.

(ii) Upper limit of the last class interval = 70.

(iii) Class Size = Upper limit – Lower limit = 10.

(iv) Mid-value = $\dfrac{\text{Upper limit + Lower limit}}{2} = \dfrac{30+40}{2} = \dfrac{70}{2} = 35.$

(v) Families earning ₹ 50,000 or more in a month = 11 + 5 = 16.

(vi) Families earning less than ₹ 20,000 in a month = 6.

**3. Convert the following cumulative frequency distribution into a simple frequency distribution:**

| Marks | Number of Students |
|---|---|
| More than 0 | 55 |
| More than 5 | 51 |
| More than 10 | 43 |
| More than 15 | 28 |
| More than 20 | 16 |
| More than 25 | 6 |
| More than 30 | 0 |

**Sol.** **Conversion of Cumulative Frequency Distribution into Simple Frequency Distribution**

| Marks | Number of Students (f) |
|---|---|
| 0–5 | 55 – 51 = 4 |
| 5–10 | 51 – 43 = 8 |
| 10–15 | 43 – 28 = 15 |
| 15–20 | 28 – 16 = 12 |
| 20–25 | 16 – 6 = 10 |
| 25–30 | 6 – 0 = 6 |
| 30–35 | 0 |

**4. Following are the marks obtained by 25 students in Statistics. Prepare a frequency distribution by taking a class interval of 4 on exclusive basis.**

| 5 | 6 | 8 | 10 | 11 | 13 | 6 | 8 | 5 | 13 | 8 | 10 | 3 |
|---|---|---|---|---|---|---|---|---|---|---|---|---|
| 18 | 6 | 8 | 5 | 16 | 11 | 8 | 5 | 8 | 5 | 8 | 6 | |

**Sol.** The lowest value is 3 and highest value is 18. We have to take a class interval of 4. The various classes will be 0–4, 4–8 and so on up to 16–20.

**Frequency Distribution**

| Marks | Tally Bars | Frequency (f) |
|---|---|---|
| 0–4 | \| | 1 |
| 4–8 | ~~\|\|\|\|~~ \|\|\|\| | 9 |
| 8–12 | ~~\|\|\|\|~~ ~~\|\|\|\|~~ \| | 11 |
| 12–16 | \|\| | 2 |
| 16–20 | \|\| | 2 |
| | | $\Sigma f = 25$ |

**5. For the following raw data prepare a frequency distribution with a class interval of 5 on inclusive basis:**

| Marks | | | | | | | | | |
|---|---|---|---|---|---|---|---|---|---|
| 12 | 36 | 40 | 16 | 10 | 10 | 19 | 20 | 28 | 30 |
| 19 | 27 | 15 | 21 | 33 | 45 | 7 | 19 | 20 | 26 |
| 26 | 37 | 6 | 5 | 20 | 30 | 37 | 17 | 21 | 20 |

**Sol.** The lowest value is 5 and highest value is 45. We take class interval of 5 on inclusive basis. The various classes will be 5–9, 10–14 and so on up to 45–49.

**Formation of a Frequency Distribution**

| Marks | Tally Bars | Number of Students (f) |
|---|---|---|
| 5–9 | \|\|\| | 3 |
| 10–14 | \|\|\| | 3 |
| 15–19 | ~~\|\|\|\|~~ \| | 6 |
| 20–24 | ~~\|\|\|\|~~ \| | 6 |
| 25–29 | \|\|\|\| | 4 |
| 30–34 | \|\|\| | 3 |
| 35–39 | \|\|\| | 3 |
| 40–44 | \| | 1 |
| 45–49 | \| | 1 |
| | | $\Sigma f = 30$ |

**6. Convert the following series into a simple frequency distribution:**

| Marks | Number of Students |
|---|---|
| More than 0 | 21 |
| More than 10 | 19 |
| More than 20 | 14 |
| More than 30 | 7 |
| More than 40 | 2 |

**Sol.** **Simple Frequency Distribution**

| Marks | Number of Students |
|---|---|
| 0–10 | 21 – 19 = 2 |
| 10–20 | 19 – 14 = 5 |
| 20–30 | 14 – 7 = 7 |
| 30–40 | 7 – 2 = 5 |
| 40–50 | 2 – 0 = 2 |

7. **Convert the following series into a simple frequency distribution:**

| **Mid-value** | 5 | 15 | 25 | 35 | 45 | 55 |
|---|---|---|---|---|---|---|
| **Frequency** | 2 | 8 | 15 | 12 | 7 | 6 |

**Sol.** **Conversion of a Series with Mid-values into a Series with Class Interval**

| **Mid-value** | **Frequency** | **Classes** | **Technique** |
|---|---|---|---|
| 5 | 2 | 0–10 | $l_1 = 5 - \frac{10}{2} = 0, \quad l_2 = 5 + \frac{10}{2} = 10$ |
| 15 | 8 | 10–20 | $l_1 = 15 - \frac{10}{2} = 10, l_2 = 15 + \frac{10}{2} = 20$ |
| 25 | 15 | 20–30 | $l_1 = 25 - \frac{10}{2} = 20, l_2 = 25 + \frac{10}{2} = 30$ |
| 35 | 12 | 30–40 | $l_1 = 35 - \frac{10}{2} = 30, l_2 = 35 + \frac{10}{2} = 40$ |
| 45 | 7 | 40–50 | $l_1 = 45 - \frac{10}{2} = 40, l_2 = 45 + \frac{10}{2} = 50$ |
| 55 | 6 | 50–60 | $l_1 = 55 - \frac{10}{2} = 50, l_2 = 55 + \frac{10}{2} = 60$ |

## Presentation of Data—Textual and Tabular Presentation

1. **Following information relates to the production of Wheat and Rice in India in different years. Present it in the form of a table.**

| **Year** | 2010 | 2011 | 2012 | 2013 | 2014 | 2015 |
|---|---|---|---|---|---|---|
| **Wheat (in million tonnes)** | 28 | 35 | 33 | 62 | 40 | 52 |
| **Rice (in million tonnes)** | 45 | 59 | 36 | 56 | 46 | 58 |

**Sol.** **Table 1. Production of Wheat and Rice in India**

**(in million tonnes)**

| **Years** | **Wheat** | **Rice** | **Total** |
|---|---|---|---|
| 2010 | 28 | 45 | 73 |
| 2011 | 35 | 59 | 94 |
| 2012 | 33 | 36 | 69 |
| 2013 | 62 | 56 | 118 |
| 2014 | 40 | 46 | 86 |
| 2015 | 52 | 58 | 110 |
| Total | 250 | 300 | 550 |

**2. Following are the data about the number of men and women in different age groups in a society. Present the information in the form of a two-way table.**

| Age (in years) | 0–10 | 10–20 | 20–30 | 30–40 | 40–50 | 50–60 |
|---|---|---|---|---|---|---|
| Men | 8 | 15 | 33 | 25 | 30 | 22 |
| Women | 5 | 10 | 24 | 35 | 25 | 18 |

**Sol.** **Table 2. Number of Persons in Different Age Groups**

(according to Age and Sex)

| Age (in years) | Number of Persons | | Total |
|---|---|---|---|
| | Men | Women | |
| 0–10 | 8 | 5 | 13 |
| 10–20 | 15 | 10 | 25 |
| 20–30 | 33 | 24 | 57 |
| 30–40 | 25 | 35 | 60 |
| 40–50 | 30 | 25 | 55 |
| 50–60 | 22 | 18 | 40 |
| Total | 133 | 117 | 250 |

**3. Draw a table to show the sale of LED TV's of different dealers in a year.**

| Dealer | A | B | C | D | E | F |
|---|---|---|---|---|---|---|
| Sale (in thousand) | 18 | 24 | 20 | 25 | 26 | 28 |

**Sol.** **Table 3. Sale of LED TV's**

| Dealer | Sale (in thousand) |
|---|---|
| A | 18 |
| B | 24 |
| C | 20 |
| D | 25 |
| E | 26 |
| F | 28 |
| Total | 141 |

## Diagrammatic Presentation of Data: Bar Diagrams and Pie Diagrams

**1. The following table shows the interest of students of a school in different games:**

| Games | Table Tennis | Volleyball | Hockey | Basketball | Cricket |
|---|---|---|---|---|---|
| Number of Students | 500 | 300 | 350 | 400 | 550 |

**Represent the data by using a simple bar diagram.**

**Sol.**

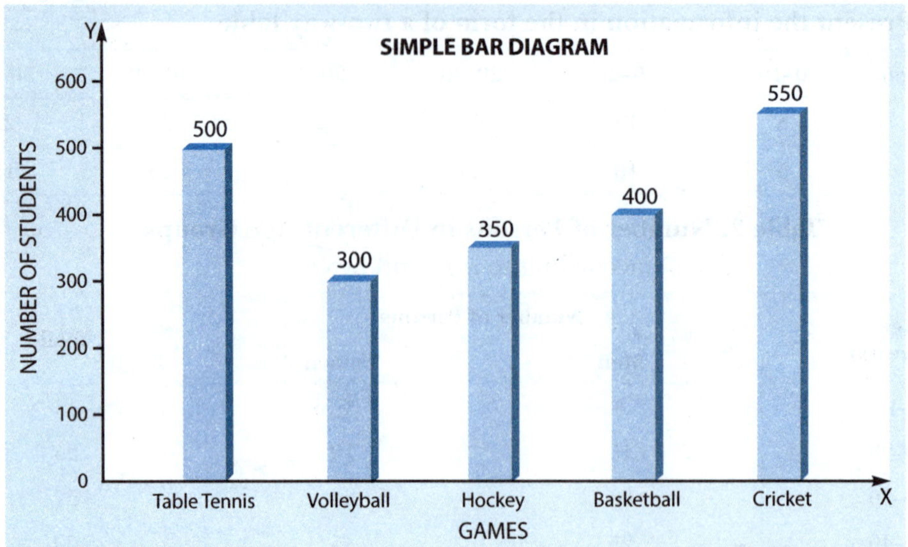


**2. The following table gives the data on the marks obtained by two students 'A and B' in five subjects:**

| **Subject** | Maths | English | Economics | Accountancy | Business Studies |
|---|---|---|---|---|---|
| **Student A** | 75 | 82 | 88 | 90 | 82 |
| **Student B** | 80 | 78 | 85 | 92 | 88 |

**Represent the data by a multiple bar diagram.**

**Sol.**

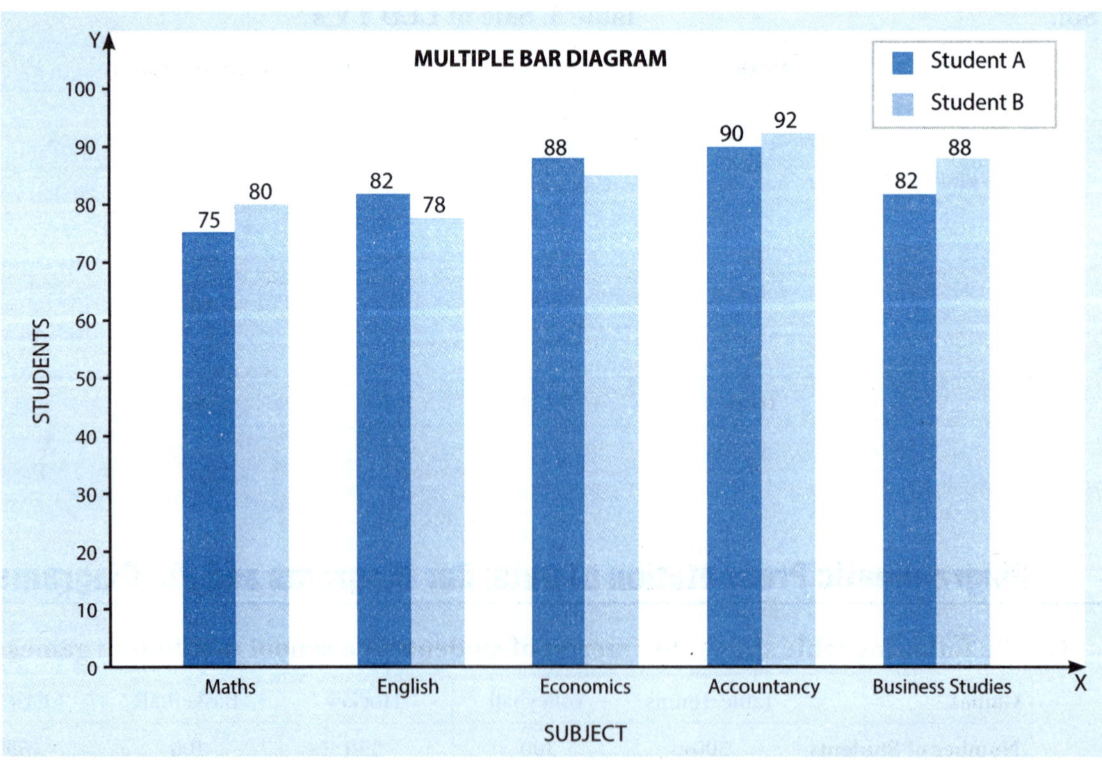

**3. The following table shows the monthly expenditure of different families on different items:**

| Family | Education | Clothing | Food | Rent | Others | Total Expenditure |
|---|---|---|---|---|---|---|
| **A** | 1,500 | 1,000 | 1,250 | 750 | 500 | 5,000 |
| **B** | 1,700 | 850 | 1,200 | 850 | 600 | 5,200 |
| **C** | 1,600 | 700 | 1,500 | 800 | 600 | 5,200 |

**Represent the data in the form of a sub-divided bar diagram.**

**Sol.**

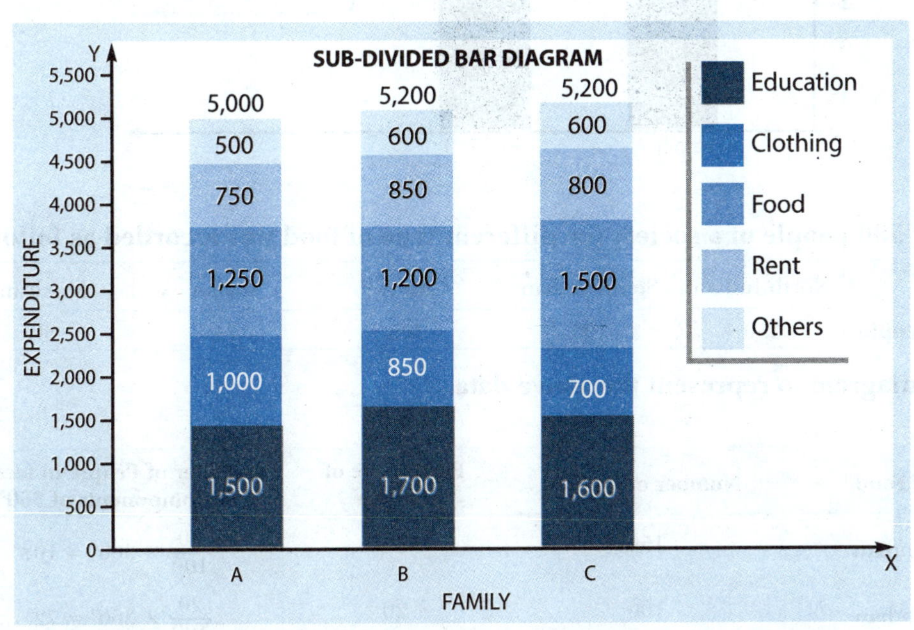


**4. Represent the following data, using a percentage bar diagram:** **(in ₹)**

| Items of Expenditure | Food | Clothing | House Rent | Fuel and Lighting | Miscellaneous |
|---|---|---|---|---|---|
| **Family A** | 200 | 100 | 80 | 40 | 80 |
| **Family B** | 252 | 200 | 100 | 48 | 200 |

**Sol.**

**Percentage Table**

| Item | Family A | | | Family B | | |
|---|---|---|---|---|---|---|
| | **Expenditure (₹)** | **Expenditure (%)** | **Cumulative Percentage** | **Expenditure (₹)** | **Expenditure (%)** | **Cumulative Percentage** |
| Food | 200 | 40 | 40 | 252 | 31.5 | 31.5 |
| Clothing | 100 | 20 | 60 | 200 | 25.0 | 56.5 |
| House Rent | 80 | 16 | 76 | 100 | 12.5 | 69 |
| Fuel and Lighting | 40 | 8 | 84 | 48 | 6 | 75 |
| Miscellaneous | 80 | 16 | 100 | 200 | 25.0 | 100 |
| Total | 500 | 100 | | 800 | 100 | |

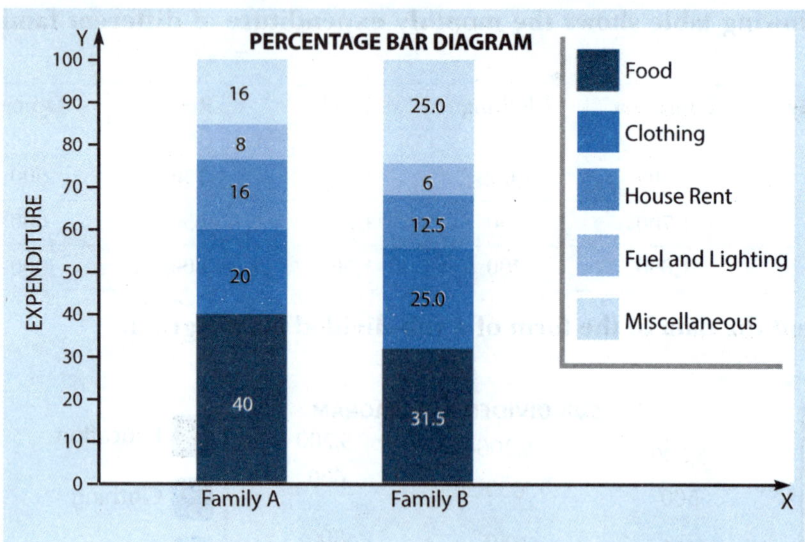


**5. The taste of 500 people of a society for different type of food was recorded as follows:**

| **Type of Food** | North Indian | South Indian | Chinese | Italian | Mexican |
|---|---|---|---|---|---|
| **Number of People** | 150 | 100 | 125 | 75 | 50 |

**Draw a pie diagram to represent the above data.**

**Sol.**

| Type of Food | Number of People | Percentage of People | Number of People in terms of Components of 360° |
|---|---|---|---|
| North Indian | 150 | 30 | $\frac{30}{100} \times 360° = 108°$ |
| South Indian | 100 | 20 | $\frac{20}{100} \times 360° = 72°$ |
| Chinese | 125 | 25 | $\frac{25}{100} \times 360° = 90°$ |
| Italian | 75 | 15 | $\frac{15}{100} \times 360° = 54°$ |
| Mexican | 50 | 10 | $\frac{10}{100} \times 360° = 36°$ |
| Total | 500 | | 360° |

**Pie Diagram**

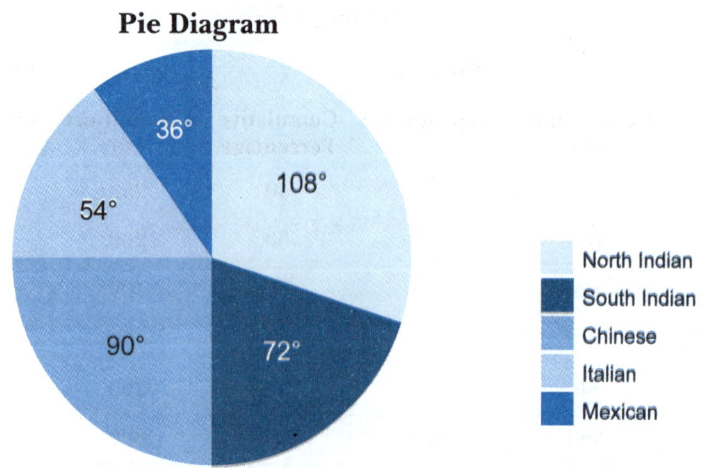

1. **Construct a histogram from the following data:**

| Marks | 0–10 | 10–20 | 20–30 | 30–40 | 40–50 | 50–60 | 60–70 |
|---|---|---|---|---|---|---|---|
| Number of Students | 5 | 12 | 20 | 35 | 24 | 12 | 4 |

**Sol.** **Number of Students Corresponding to Different Range of Marks**

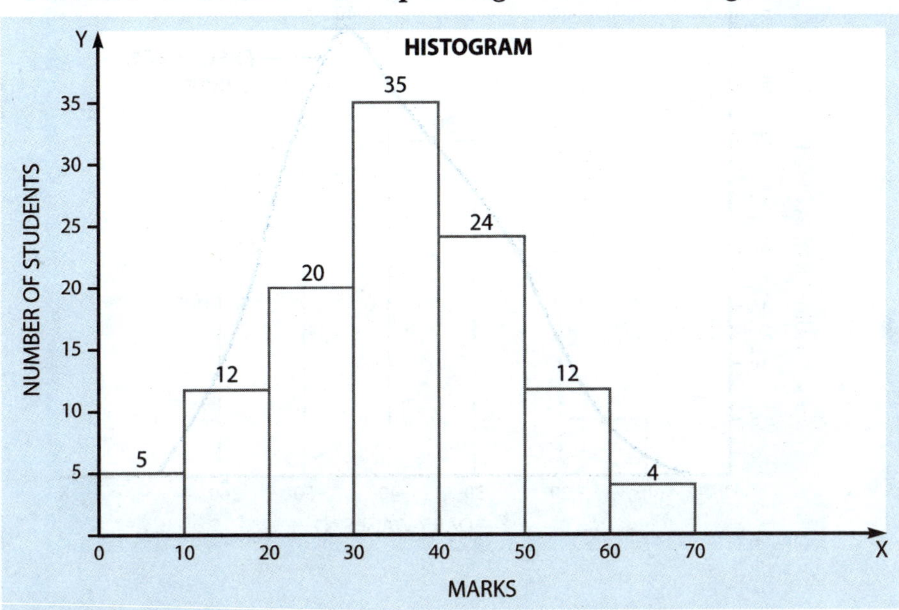


2. **Draw histogram and frequency polygon for the following distribution:**

| Age (Years) | 0–10 | 10–20 | 20–30 | 30–40 | 40–50 | 50–60 | 60–70 | 70–80 |
|---|---|---|---|---|---|---|---|---|
| Number of Residents | 30 | 40 | 60 | 100 | 70 | 40 | 30 | 20 |

**Sol.** **Number of Residents Corresponding to Different Age Groups**

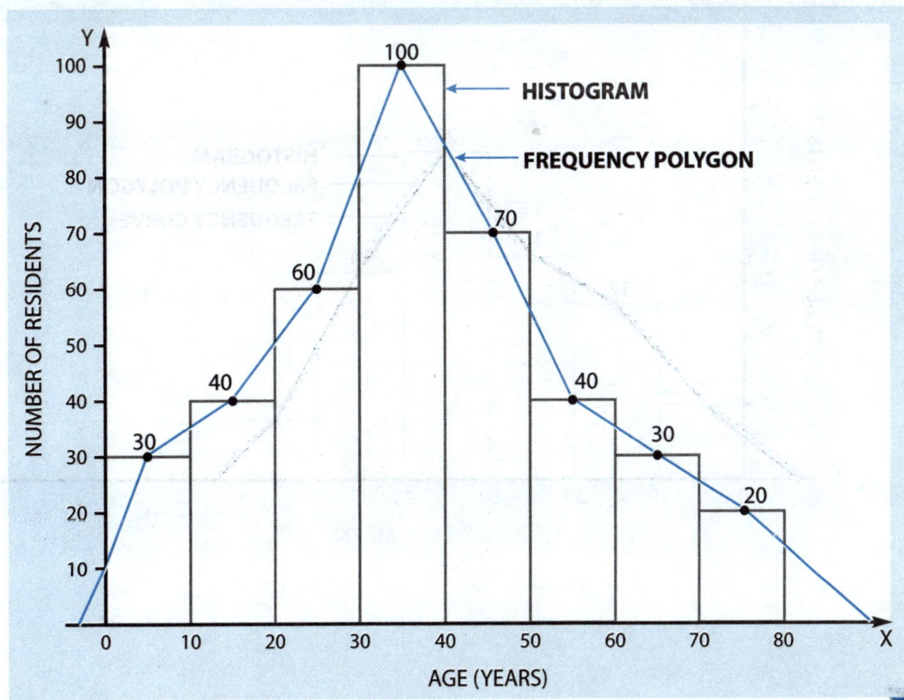

**3. Represent the following data by frequency curve:**

| Daily Wages (₹) | 10–20 | 20–30 | 30–40 | 40–50 | 50–60 |
|---|---|---|---|---|---|
| Number of Workers | 5 | 20 | 30 | 40 | 20 |

**Sol.** **Number of Workers Corresponding to Different Range of Wages**

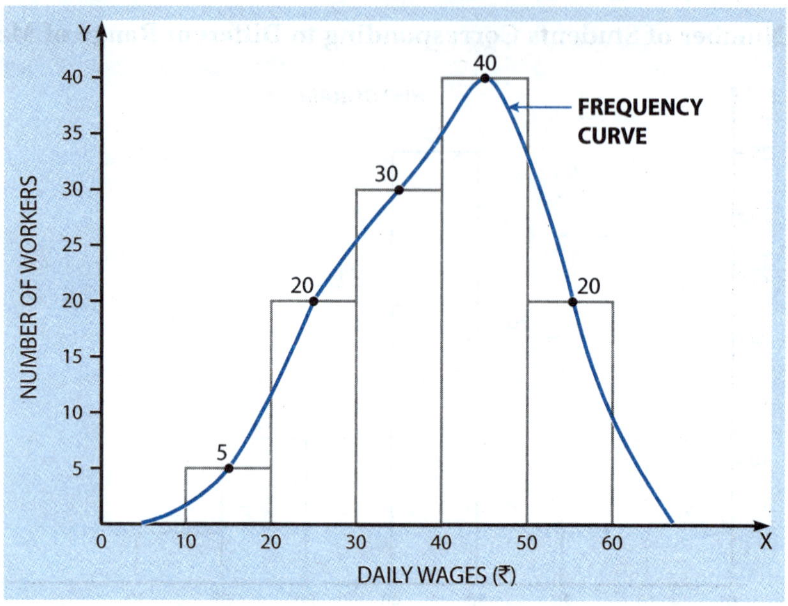


**4. Draw a histogram, a frequency polygon and frequency curve of the following data:**

| Marks | 0–10 | 10–20 | 20–30 | 30–40 | 40–50 | 50–60 |
|---|---|---|---|---|---|---|
| Number of Students | 5 | 12 | 15 | 22 | 14 | 4 |

**Sol.**

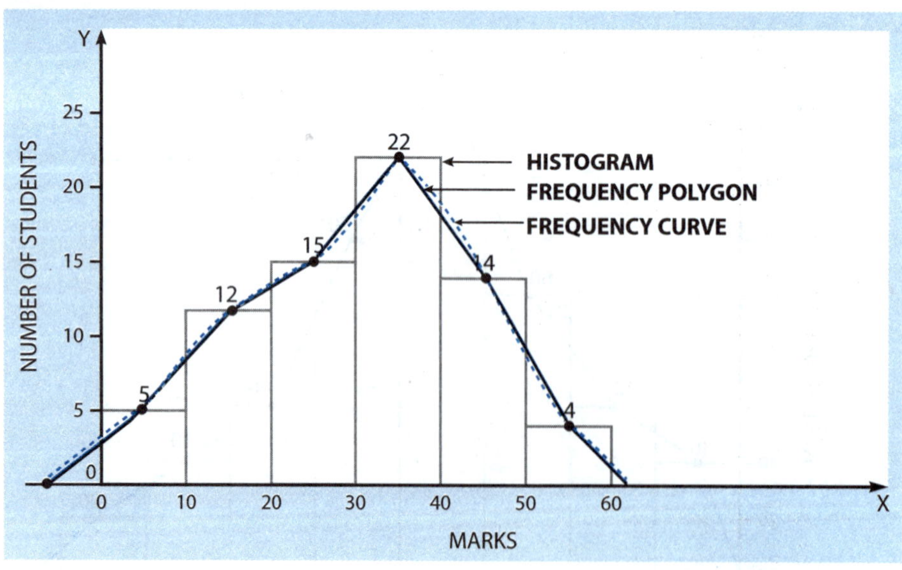

5. **Draw the 'less than' and 'more than' ogive on the same graph paper from the following data:**

| **Marks** | 0–20 | 20–40 | 40–60 | 60–80 | 80–100 |
|---|---|---|---|---|---|
| **Number of Students** | 40 | 51 | 64 | 38 | 7 |

**Sol.** **Cumulative Frequency Table**

| **'Less than' Method** | | **'More than' Method** | |
|---|---|---|---|
| **Marks** | **Cumulative Frequencies** | **Marks** | **Cumulative Frequencies** |
| Less than 20 | 40 | More than 0 | 200 |
| Less than 40 | 40 + 51 = 91 | More than 20 | 200 – 40 = 160 |
| Less than 60 | 91 + 64 = 155 | More than 40 | 160 – 51 = 109 |
| Less than 80 | 155 + 38 = 193 | More than 60 | 109 – 64 = 45 |
| Less than 100 | 193 + 7 = 200 | More than 80 | 45 – 38 = 7 |
| | | More than 100 | 7 – 7 = 0 |

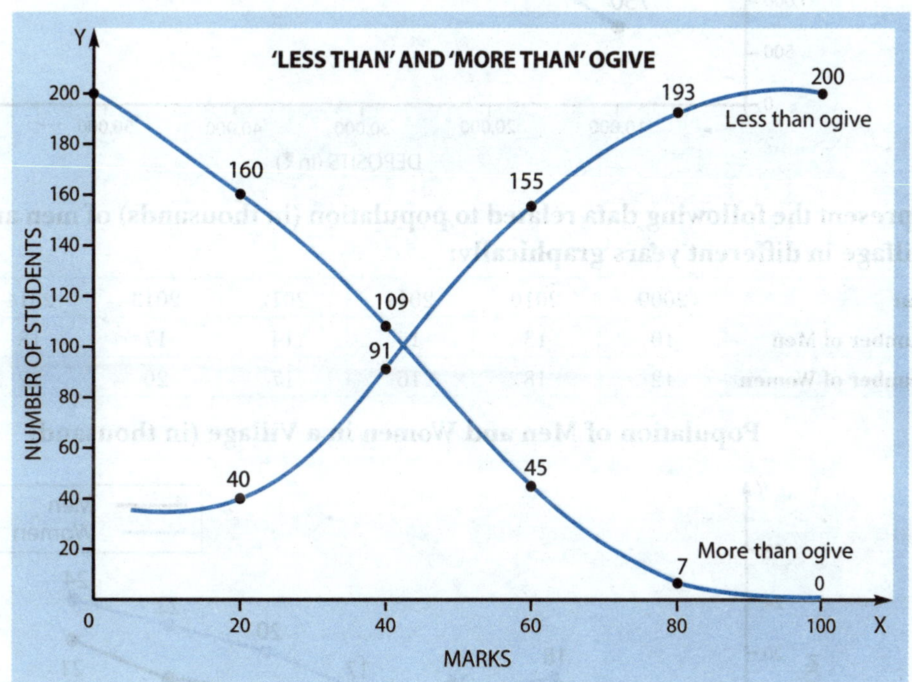

## Arithmetic Line-Graphs or Time Series Graphs

**1. Draw the graph of interest on deposits for a year:**

| Deposits (in ₹) | 10,000 | 20,000 | 30,000 | 40,000 | 50,000 |
|---|---|---|---|---|---|
| Interest (in ₹) | 750 | 1,500 | 2,350 | 3,300 | 4,400 |

**Sol.** **Interest on Deposits for a Year (in ₹)**

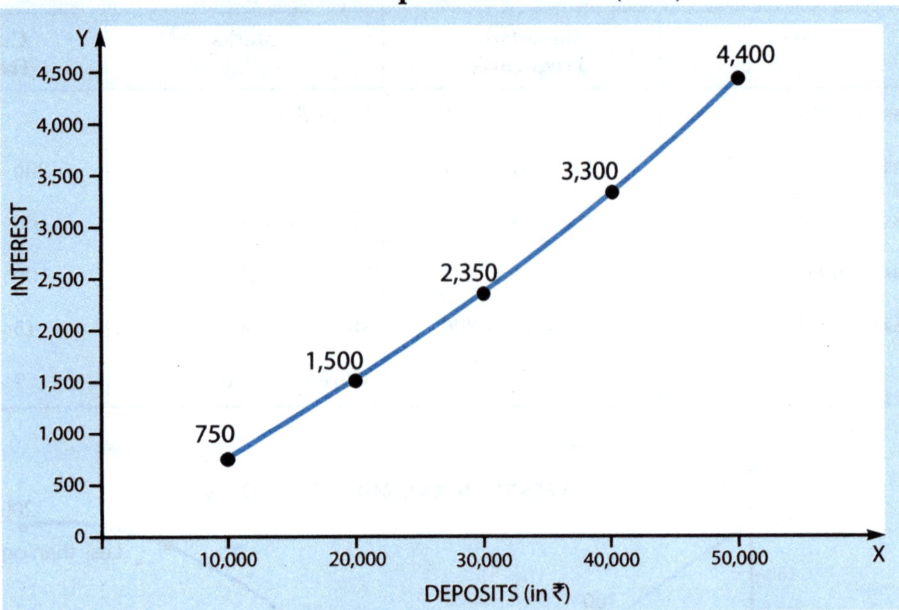


**2. Represent the following data related to population (in thousands) of men and women in a village in different years graphically:**

| Year | 2009 | 2010 | 2011 | 2012 | 2013 | 2014 | 2015 |
|---|---|---|---|---|---|---|---|
| Number of Men | 10 | 13 | 15 | 14 | 17 | 18 | 21 |
| Number of Women | 12 | 18 | 16 | 17 | 20 | 22 | 24 |

**Sol.** **Population of Men and Women in a Village (in thousand)**

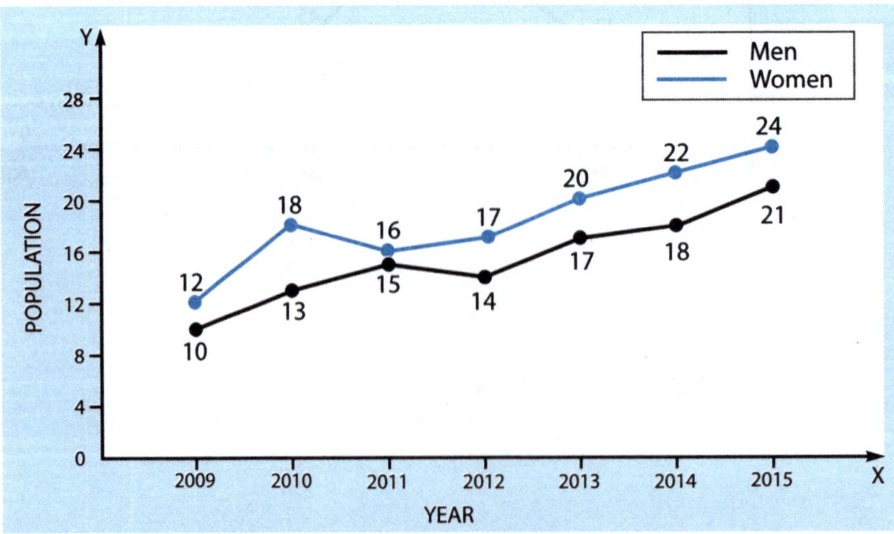

**1. Following are the marks of 37 students:**

| Marks | 4 | 6 | 8 | 10 | 12 | 14 |
|---|---|---|---|---|---|---|
| No. of Students | 5 | 7 | 6 | 8 | 6 | 5 |

**Calculate mean marks, using Short-cut Method.**

**Sol.**

| Marks (X) | Number of Students or Frequency (f) | Deviation (d = X – A) (A = 10) | Multiple of Deviation and Frequency (fd) |
|---|---|---|---|
| 4 | 5 | – 6 | – 30 |
| 6 | 7 | – 4 | – 28 |
| 8 | 6 | – 2 | – 12 |
| 10 | 8 | 0 | 0 |
| 12 | 6 | 2 | 12 |
| 14 | 5 | 4 | 20 |
| | Σf = 37 | | Σfd = – 38 |

$$\overline{X} = A + \frac{\Sigma fd}{\Sigma f}$$

$$= 10 + \frac{-38}{37}$$

$$= 10 - 1.03 = 8.97$$

Mean Marks = 8.97.

**2. Find out the arithmetic mean by the Step-deviation Method of the following:**

| Class Interval | 0–10 | 10–20 | 20–30 | 30–40 | 40–50 | 50–60 | 60–70 | 70–80 |
|---|---|---|---|---|---|---|---|---|
| Frequency | 12 | 16 | 32 | 52 | 42 | 32 | 18 | 12 |

**Sol.**

| Class Interval (X) | Mid-value $\left(m = \frac{l_1 + l_2}{2}\right)$ | Frequency (f) | Deviation (d = m – A) (A = 45) | Step-deviation (d′ = d/C) (C = 10) | Multiple of Step-deviation and Frequency (fd′) |
|---|---|---|---|---|---|
| 0–10 | 5 | 12 | – 40 | – 4 | – 48 |
| 10–20 | 15 | 16 | – 30 | – 3 | – 48 |
| 20–30 | 25 | 32 | – 20 | – 2 | – 64 |
| 30–40 | 35 | 52 | – 10 | – 1 | – 52 |
| 40–50 | 45 | 42 | 0 | 0 | 0 |
| 50–60 | 55 | 32 | 10 | 1 | 32 |
| 60 70 | 65 | 18 | 20 | 2 | 36 |
| 70–80 | 75 | 12 | 30 | 3 | 36 |
| | | Σf = 216 | | | Σfd′ = – 108 |

$$\overline{X} = A + \frac{\Sigma fd'}{\Sigma f} \times C$$

$$= 45 + \frac{-108}{216} \times 10$$

$$= 45 - 5 = 40$$

Arithmetic Mean = 40.

**3. Calculate the mean marks from the following data:**

| Marks | 20–25 | 25–30 | 30–35 | 35–40 | 40–45 | 45–50 | 50–55 |
|---|---|---|---|---|---|---|---|
| No. of Students | 10 | 12 | 8 | 20 | 11 | 4 | 5 |

**Sol.**

| Marks (X) | Mid-value $\left(m = \frac{l_1 + l_2}{2}\right)$ | Number of Students or Frequency ($f$) | Deviation (d = m – A) (A = 37.5) | Multiple of Deviation and Frequency (fd) |
|---|---|---|---|---|
| 20–25 | 22.5 | 10 | – 15 | – 150 |
| 25–30 | 27.5 | 12 | – 10 | – 120 |
| 30–35 | 32.5 | 8 | – 5 | – 40 |
| 35–40 | 37.5 | 20 | 0 | 0 |
| 40–45 | 42.5 | 11 | 5 | 55 |
| 45–50 | 47.5 | 4 | 10 | 40 |
| 50–55 | 52.5 | 5 | 15 | 75 |
| | | Σf = 70 | | Σfd = – 140 |

$$\overline{X} = A + \frac{\Sigma fd}{\Sigma f} = 37.5 + \frac{-140}{70}$$

$$= 37.5 - 2 = 35.5$$

Mean Marks = 35.5.

**4. Find out the arithmetic mean from the following data:**

| Marks (less than) | 5 | 10 | 15 | 20 | 25 | 30 |
|---|---|---|---|---|---|---|
| Number of Students | 10 | 23 | 30 | 54 | 69 | 80 |

**Sol.** Since, we are given cumulative frequency distribution, at first we will convert the series into a simple frequency distribution and then, find out the mean marks.

| Marks (X) | Mid-value $\left(m = \frac{l_1 + l_2}{2}\right)$ | Number of Students or Frequency (f) | Deviation (d = m – A) (A = 12.5) | Step-deviation (d′ = d/C) (C = 5) | Multiple of Step-deviation and Frequency (fd′) |
|---|---|---|---|---|---|
| 0–5 | 2.5 | 10 | – 10 | – 2 | – 20 |
| 5–10 | 7.5 | 13 | – 5 | – 1 | – 13 |
| 10–15 | 12.5 | 7 | 0 | 0 | 0 |
| 15–20 | 17.5 | 24 | 5 | 1 | 24 |
| 20–25 | 22.5 | 15 | 10 | 2 | 30 |
| 25–30 | 27.5 | 11 | 15 | 3 | 33 |
| | | Σf = 80 | | | Σfd′ = 54 |

$$\overline{X} = A + \frac{\Sigma fd'}{\Sigma f} \times C$$

$$= 12.5 + \frac{54}{80} \times 5$$

$$= 12.5 + 3.375 = 15.875$$

Arithmetic Mean = 15.875.

**5. Calculate the weighted mean from the following data:**

| **Marks** | 60 | 75 | 63 | 59 | 55 |
|---|---|---|---|---|---|
| **Weight** | 2 | 1 | 5 | 5 | 3 |

**Sol.**

| **Marks (X)** | **Weight (W)** | **WX** |
|---|---|---|
| 60 | 2 | 120 |
| 75 | 1 | 75 |
| 63 | 5 | 315 |
| 59 | 5 | 295 |
| 55 | 3 | 165 |
| | ΣW = 16 | ΣWX = 970 |

$$\overline{X}_W = \frac{\Sigma WX}{\Sigma W}$$

$$= \frac{970}{16} = 60.625$$

Weighted Mean = 60.625.

**6. Mean of 100 observations is found to be 40. If at the time of computation two items are wrongly taken as 30 and 27 instead of 3 and 72, find the correct mean.**

**Sol.** Given: N = 100, $\overline{X} = 40$

$$\overline{X} = \frac{\Sigma X}{N}$$

Or,
$$40 = \frac{\Sigma X}{100}$$

∴
$$\Sigma X \text{ (Wrong)} = 40 \times 100 = 4{,}000$$

$$\text{Correct values} = 3 + 72 = 75$$

$$\text{Incorrect values} = 30 + 27 = 57$$

$$\text{Correct } \overline{X} = \frac{\Sigma X \text{ (Wrong)} + \text{(Correct Value)} - \text{(Incorrect Value)}}{N}$$

$$= \frac{4{,}000 + 75 - 57}{100}$$

$$= \frac{4{,}018}{100} = 40.18$$

Corrected Mean = 40.18.

7. **The mean monthly salary paid to 77 employees in a company was ₹78. The mean salary of 32 of them was ₹45 and of the other 25 was ₹82. What was the mean salary of the remaining?**

**Sol.** Given: $N = 77, \overline{X}_{123} = 78$

$N_1 = 32, \overline{X}_1 = 45$

$N_2 = 25, \overline{X}_2 = 82$

$N_3 = 77 - 32 - 25 = 20$

Using the formula of combined arithmetic mean, we have

$$\overline{X}_{123} = \frac{\overline{X}_1 N_1 + \overline{X}_2 N_2 + \overline{X}_3 N_3}{N_1 + N_2 + N_3}$$

$$78 = \frac{45 \times 32 + 82 \times 25 + \overline{X}_3 \times 20}{77}$$

$$78 = \frac{1{,}440 + 2{,}050 + 20\overline{X}_3}{77}$$

$$78 = \frac{3{,}490 + 20\overline{X}_3}{77}$$

$$3{,}490 + 20\overline{X}_3 = 6{,}006$$

$$20\overline{X}_3 = 6{,}006 - 3{,}490$$

$$20\overline{X}_3 = 2{,}516$$

$$\overline{X}_3 = \frac{2{,}516}{20} = 125.8$$

Mean salary of the remaining employees= ₹125.8.

8. **The average marks of 39 students of a class is 50. The marks obtained by 40th student are 39 more than the average marks of all the 40 students. Find the mean marks of all the 40 students.**

**Sol.** Let the mean marks of all the 40 students = $\overline{X}$

Given: $\overline{X}_1 = 50, N_1 = 39$

Marks obtained by the 39 students.

$$\Sigma X = 50 \times 39 = 1{,}950$$

Marks obtained by the 40th student

$$= \overline{X} + 39$$

Mean marks of all the 40 students

$$\overline{X} = \frac{\Sigma X}{N}$$

$$\overline{X} = \frac{1{,}950 + \overline{X} + 39}{40}$$

$$40\overline{X} = 1{,}989 + \overline{X}$$

$$40\overline{X} - \overline{X} = 1{,}989$$

$$39\overline{X} = 1{,}989$$

$$\overline{X} = \frac{1{,}989}{39} = 51$$

Thus, Mean marks of all the 40 students = 51.

**1. Calculate the median of the following items:**
**15, 23, 20, 20, 23, 35, 26, 27, 25, 40**

**Sol.** The data is first arranged in ascending order:

| S. No. | X |
|---|---|
| 1 | 15 |
| 2 | 20 |
| 3 | 20 |
| 4 | 23 |
| 5 | 23 |
| 6 | 25 |
| 7 | 26 |
| 8 | 27 |
| 9 | 35 |
| 10 | 40 |
| N = 10 | |

$$M = \text{Size of}\left(\frac{N+1}{2}\right)\text{th item}$$

$$= \text{Size of}\left(\frac{10+1}{2}\right)\text{th item}$$

$$= \text{Size of 5.5th item}$$

$$= \frac{\text{Size of 5th item + Size of 6th item}}{2}$$

$$\therefore \quad = \frac{23+25}{2} = \frac{48}{2} = 24$$

Median = 24.

**2. Find out median marks from the following data:**

| **Marks** | 0–10 | 10–20 | 20–30 | 30–40 | 40–50 |
|---|---|---|---|---|---|
| **Number of Students** | 8 | 30 | 40 | 12 | 10 |

**Sol.**

| Marks (X) | Frequency (f) | Cumulative Frequency (c.f.) |
|---|---|---|
| 0–10 | 8 | 8 |
| 10–20 | 30 | **38 (c.f.)** |
| **($l_1$) 20–30** | **40 (f)** | 78 |
| 30–40 | 12 | 90 |
| 40–50 | 10 | 10 |
| | $\Sigma f = N = 100$ | |

$$M = \text{Size of}\left(\frac{N}{2}\right)\text{th item}$$

$$= \text{Size of}\left(\frac{100}{2}\right)\text{th item} = \text{Size of 50th item}$$

50th item lies in the class interval 20–30.

$$M = l_1 + \frac{\frac{N}{2} - c.f.}{f} \times i$$

$$= 20 + \frac{\frac{100}{2} - 38}{40} \times 10$$

$$= 20 + \frac{50 - 38}{40} \times 10$$

$$= 20 + \frac{12}{40} \times 10$$

$$= 20 + 3 = 23$$

Median Marks = 23.

**3. Following is the distribution of marks in Statistics obtained by 32 students:**

| **Mid-value** | 5 | 15 | 25 | 35 | 45 | 55 |
|---|---|---|---|---|---|---|
| **Frequency** | 4 | 6 | 10 | 7 | 3 | 2 |

**Calculate the median marks.**

**Sol.** Since, we are given the mid-values, we should first find out the upper and lower limits of the various classes. As the mid-values are 5, 15, 25, 35, 45, 55, so, class size is 10 (= 15 – 5). For determining limits of different classes, applying the formula:

$$\text{Lower limit: } l_1 = m - \frac{1}{2} \times i \text{ and}$$

$$\text{Upper limit: } l_2 = m + \frac{1}{2} \times i$$

where, $i$ = difference between two mid-values.

In this case, the upper and the lower limits of the first mid-value are:

$$l_1 = 5 - \frac{1}{2} \times 10 = 0 \text{ and } l_2 = 5 + \frac{1}{2} \times 10 = 10$$

*i.e.*, 0–10 class interval.

Similarly, class intervals for other mid-values are obtained as:

| Class | Frequency (f) | Cumulative Frequency |
|---|---|---|
| 0–10 | 4 | 4 |
| 10–20 | 6 | **10 (c.f.)** |
| **($l_1$) 20–30** | **10 (f)** | 20 |
| 30–40 | 7 | 27 |
| 40–50 | 3 | 30 |
| 50–60 | 2 | 32 |
| | Σf = N = 32 | |

$$M = \text{Size of} \left(\frac{N}{2}\right)\text{th item}$$

$$= \text{Size of} \left(\frac{32}{2}\right)\text{th item} = \text{Size of 16th item}$$

Hence, median lies in the class 20–30.

$$M = l_1 + \frac{\frac{N}{2} - c.f.}{f} \times i$$

$$= 20 + \frac{\frac{32}{2} - 10}{10} \times 10$$

$$= 20 + \frac{16 - 10}{10} \times 10$$

$$= 20 + \frac{6}{10} \times 10$$

$$= 20 + 6 = 26$$

Median Marks = 26.

**4. Find the missing frequency of the group 20–30 when the median is 24.**

| **Size** | 0–10 | 10–20 | 20–30 | 30–40 | 40–50 |
|---|---|---|---|---|---|
| **Frequency** | 5 | 25 | — | 18 | 7 |

**Sol.** Let the missing frequency be denoted by $f_1$.

| Size | Frequency (f) | Cumulative Frequency |
|---|---|---|
| 0–10 | 5 | 5 |
| 10–20 | 25 | **30 (c.f.)** |
| **($l_1$) 20–30** | **$f_1$** | $30 + f_1$ |
| 30–40 | 18 | $48 + f_1$ |
| 40–50 | 7 | $55 + f_1$ |
| | $N = 55 + f_1$ | |

Since, Median = 24, it lies in the class 20–30.

$$M = l_1 + \frac{\frac{N}{2} - c.f.}{f} \times i$$

$$24 = 20 + \frac{\frac{55+f_1}{2} - 30}{f_1} \times 10$$

$$4 = \frac{\frac{55+f_1}{2} - 30}{f_1} \times 10$$

$$\Rightarrow \quad 4f_1 = \left(\frac{55 + f_1}{2} - 30\right) \times 10$$

$$\Rightarrow \quad 4f_1 = \left(\frac{55 + f_1 - 60}{2}\right) \times 10$$

$$\Rightarrow \quad 4f_1 = \left(\frac{f_1 - 5}{2}\right) \times 10$$

$$\Rightarrow \quad 8f_1 = 10f_1 - 50$$

$$\Rightarrow \quad 10f_1 - 8f_1 = 50$$

$$\Rightarrow \quad 2f_1 = 50$$

$$\Rightarrow \quad f_1 = \frac{50}{2} = 25$$

Thus, Missing Frequency = 25.

**5. Locate the median graphically from the following data:**

| **Marks** | 0–10 | 10–20 | 20–30 | 30–40 | 40–50 |
|---|---|---|---|---|---|
| **Number of Students** | 10 | 20 | 30 | 20 | 10 |

**Sol.** Firstly we convert the given distribution into 'less than' and 'more than' cumulative frequencies distribution.

| **Less than method** | |
|---|---|
| **Marks** | **Cumulative Frequency** |
| Less than 10 | 10 |
| Less than 20 | 30 |
| Less than 30 | 60 |
| Less than 40 | 80 |
| Less than 50 | 90 |

| **More than method** | |
|---|---|
| **Marks** | **Cumulative Frequency** |
| More than 0 | 90 |
| More than 10 | 80 |
| More than 20 | 60 |
| More than 30 | 30 |
| More than 40 | 10 |
| More than 50 | 0 |

**Method I:**

Using the 'less than ogive' and 'more than ogive' method, the median is computed graphically as follows:

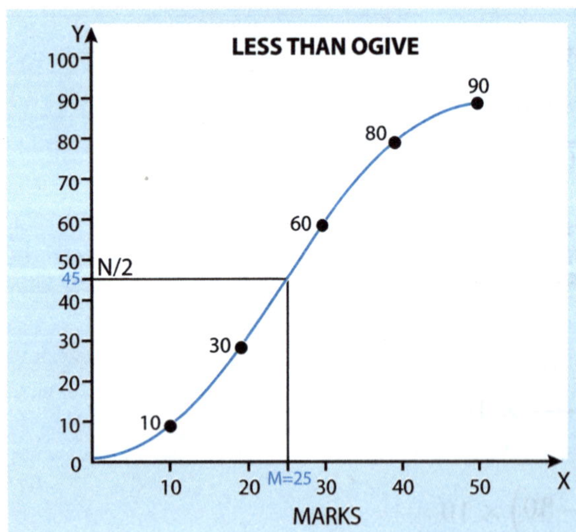


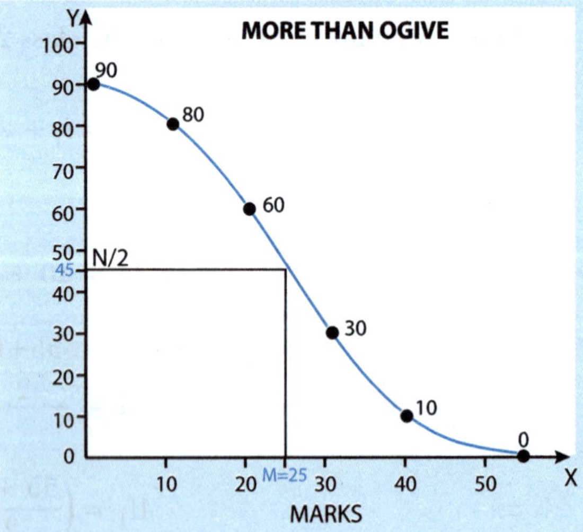


$$M = \text{Size of} \left(\frac{N}{2}\right) \text{th item}$$

$$= \text{Size of} \left(\frac{90}{2}\right) \text{th item} = \text{Size of 45th item}$$

It lies in the class interval 20–30.

**Method II.**

By making use of both the ogive curves together, the median is computed graphically as follows:

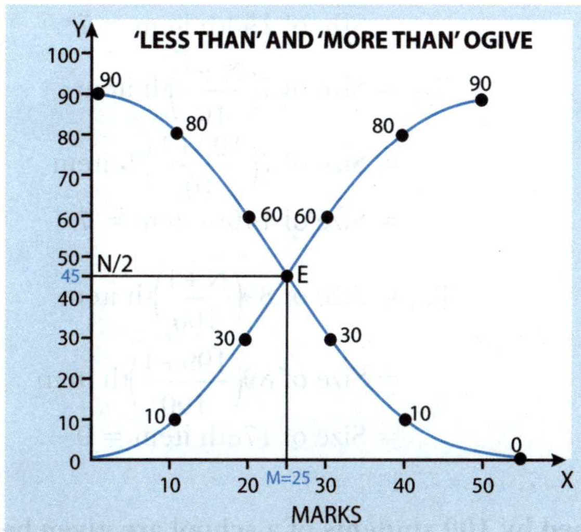


It is clear from the above figure that less than ogive curve and more than ogive curve meet each other at point E. The value of median is 25.

Median = 25.

**6. Calculate $Q_1$, $Q_3$, $D_7$ and $P_{89}$ from the following data:**

| Size | 1 | 2 | 3 | 4 | 5 | 6 | 7 | 8 | 9 | 10 | 11 |
|---|---|---|---|---|---|---|---|---|---|---|---|
| Frequency | 5 | 8 | 15 | 22 | 36 | 44 | 28 | 17 | 12 | 9 | 3 |

**Sol.**

| Size | Frequency (f) | Cumulative Frequency |
|---|---|---|
| 1 | 5 | 5 |
| 2 | 8 | 13 |
| 3 | 15 | 28 |
| 4 | 22 | 50 |
| 5 | 36 | 86 |
| 6 | 44 | 130 |
| 7 | 28 | 158 |
| 8 | 17 | 175 |
| 9 | 12 | 187 |
| 10 | 9 | 196 |
| 11 | 3 | 199 |
| | N = 199 | |

$$Q_1 = \text{Size of}\left(\frac{N+1}{4}\right)\text{th item}$$

$$= \text{Size of}\left(\frac{199+1}{4}\right)\text{th item}$$

$$= \text{Size of 50th item} = 4$$

$$Q_3 = \text{Size of } 3\left(\frac{N+1}{4}\right)\text{th item}$$
$$= \text{Size of } 3\left(\frac{199+1}{4}\right)\text{th item}$$
$$= \text{Size of 150th item} = 7$$
$$D_7 = \text{Size of } 7\left(\frac{N+1}{10}\right)\text{th item}$$
$$= \text{Size of } 7\left(\frac{199+1}{10}\right)\text{th item}$$
$$= \text{Size of 140th item} = 7$$
$$P_{89} = \text{Size of } 89\left(\frac{N+1}{100}\right)\text{th item}$$
$$= \text{Size of } 89\left(\frac{199+1}{100}\right)\text{th item}$$
$$= \text{Size of 178th item} = 9$$

Thus, $Q_1 = 4, Q_3 = 7, D_7 = 7, P_{89} = 9$.

**7. The marks obtained by 100 students of a school are given below.**

| **Marks** | 0–5 | 5–10 | 10–15 | 15–20 | 20–25 | 25–30 | 30–35 | 35–40 |
|---|---|---|---|---|---|---|---|---|
| **No. of Students** | 4 | 6 | 10 | 10 | 25 | 22 | 18 | 5 |

**Find out $Q_1$, $Q_3$, $D_6$ and $P_{95}$.**

**Sol.**

| Marks | Frequency (f) | Cumulative Frequency |
|---|---|---|
| 0–5 | 4 | 4 |
| 5–10 | 6 | 10 |
| 10–15 | 10 | 20 |
| 15–20 | 10 | 30 |
| 20–25 | 25 | 55 |
| 25–30 | 22 | 77 |
| 30–35 | 18 | 95 |
| 35–40 | 5 | 100 |
| | N = 100 | |

$$Q_1 = \text{Size of}\left(\frac{N}{4}\right)\text{th item} = \text{Size of}\left(\frac{100}{4}\right)\text{th item}$$
$$= \text{Size of 25th item}$$

25th item lies in the class interval 15–20.

$$Q_1 = l_1 + \frac{\frac{N}{4} - \text{c.f.}}{f} \times i = 15 + \frac{\frac{100}{4} - 20}{10} \times 5$$
$$= 15 + \frac{25 - 20}{10} \times 5 = 15 + \frac{5}{10} \times 5$$
$$= 15 + 2.5 = 17.5$$
$$Q_3 = \text{Size of } 3\left(\frac{N}{4}\right)\text{th item} = \text{Size of } 3\left(\frac{100}{4}\right)\text{th item}$$
$$= \text{Size of 75th item}$$

75th item lies in the class interval 25–30.

$$Q_3 = l_1 + \frac{3\left(\frac{N}{4}\right) - \text{c.f.}}{f} \times i = 25 + \frac{3\left(\frac{100}{4}\right) - 55}{22} \times 5$$

$$= 25 + \frac{75 - 55}{22} \times 5 = 25 + \frac{20}{22} \times 5 = 25 + 4.55 = 29.55$$

$$D_6 = \text{Size of } 6\left(\frac{N}{10}\right)\text{th item} = \text{Size of } 6\left(\frac{100}{10}\right)\text{th item}$$

$$= \text{Size of 60th item}$$

60th item lies in the class interval 25–30.

$$D_6 = l_1 + \frac{6\left(\frac{N}{10}\right) - \text{c.f.}}{f} \times i = 25 + \frac{6\left(\frac{100}{10}\right) - 55}{22} \times 5$$

$$= 25 + \frac{60 - 55}{22} \times 5 = 25 + \frac{5}{22} \times 5 = 25 + 1.14 = 26.14$$

$$P_{95} = \text{Size of } 95\left(\frac{N}{100}\right)\text{th item} = \text{Size of } 95\left(\frac{100}{100}\right)\text{th item}$$

$$= \text{Size of 95th item}$$

95th item lies in the class interval 30–35.

$$P_{95} = l_1 + \frac{95\left(\frac{N}{100}\right) - \text{c.f.}}{f} \times i = 30 + \frac{95\left(\frac{100}{100}\right) - 77}{18} \times 5$$

$$= 30 + \frac{95 - 77}{18} \times 5 = 30 + \frac{18}{18} \times 5 = 30 + 5 = 35$$

$Q_1 = 17.5$, $Q_3 = 29.55$, $D_6 = 26.14$, $P_{95} = 35$.

**8. Find the mode from the following data:**

**5, 8, 4, 5, 5, 8, 4, 7, 8, 5**

**Sol.** Arrange the series in an ascending order as:

4, 4, 5, 5, 5, 5, 7, 8, 8, 8

An inspection of the series shows that the value 5 occurs most frequently in the series.

Hence, Mode (Z) = 5.

**9. Calculate mode from the following data:**

| **Class Interval** | 30–40 | 40–50 | 50–60 | 60–70 | 70–80 | 80–90 | 90–100 |
|---|---|---|---|---|---|---|---|
| **Frequency** | 3 | 4 | 6 | 10 | 6 | 4 | 3 |

**Sol.**

| **Class Interval** | **Frequency** |
|---|---|
| 30–40 | 3 |
| 40–50 | 4 |
| 50–60 | 6 ($f_0$) |
| **($l_1$) 60–70** | **10 ($f_1$)** |
| 70–80 | 6 ($f_2$) |
| 80–90 | 4 |
| 90–100 | 3 |

A glance at the above table reveals that modal class is 60–70. The actual value of mode is

$$Z = l_1 + \frac{f_1 - f_0}{2f_1 - f_0 - f_2} \times i$$

$$= 60 + \frac{10 - 6}{2(10) - 6 - 6} \times i$$

$$= 60 + \frac{4}{20 - 12} \times 10$$

$$= 60 + \frac{4}{8} \times 10$$

$$= 60 + 5 = 65$$

Mode = 65.

**10. Calculate mean in an asymmetrical distribution if mode is 16 and median is 15.73.**

**Sol.** Given: Mode (Z) = 16, Median (M) = 15.73

$$Z = 3M - 2\overline{X}$$

Substituting the values, we get

$$16 = 3 \times 15.73 - 2\overline{X}$$

$$16 = 47.19 - 2\overline{X}$$

$$2\overline{X} = 47.17 - 16$$

$$2\overline{X} = 31.19$$

$$\overline{X} = \frac{31.19}{2} = 15.6$$

Mean = 15.6.

**11. The arithmetic mean, the mode and the median of a group of 75 observations were calculated to be 27, 34 and 29 respectively. It was later discovered that one observation was wrongly read as 43 instead of the correct value 53. Examine to what extent the calculated values of the three averages will be affected by the error.**

**Sol.** Given: N = 75, $\overline{X}$ = 27

We know, $\overline{X} = \frac{\Sigma X}{N}$ or $\Sigma X = N\overline{X}$

$$\therefore \quad \Sigma X = 75 \times 27 = 2,025$$

$$\text{Corrected } \Sigma X = 2,025 - 43 + 53 = 2,035$$

$$\text{Corrected } \overline{X} = \frac{2,035}{75} = 27.13$$

Thus, the value of mean is affected. But the values of median and mode will not be affected by this error because these are positional averages and the median value is 29 which is far away from the values 43 and 53. Similarly, the value of mode would not be affected by the error since the modal value 34 is far away from the values 43 and 53.

**12. Calculate mean, median and mode from the following data:**

| **Class Interval** | 30–40 | 40–50 | 50–60 | 60–70 | 70–80 | 80–90 |
|---|---|---|---|---|---|---|
| **Frequency** | 18 | 37 | 45 | 27 | 15 | 8 |

**Sol.** **Calculation of Mean, Median and Mode**

| Class Interval | Frequency (f) | c.f. | Mid-Value (m) | Deviation (d = m – A) (A = 55) | Step-deviation $\left(d' = \frac{d}{C}\right)$ (C = 10) | fd' |
|---|---|---|---|---|---|---|
| 30–40 | 18 | 18 | 35 | – 20 | – 2 | – 36 |
| 40–50 | 37 | 55 | 45 | – 10 | – 1 | – 37 |
| 50–60 | 45 | 100 | 55 | 0 | 0 | 0 |
| 60–70 | 27 | 127 | 65 | 10 | + 1 | 27 |
| 70–80 | 15 | 142 | 75 | 20 | + 2 | 30 |
| 80–90 | 8 | 150 | 85 | 30 | + 3 | 24 |
| | Σf = N = 150 | | | | | Σfd' = 8 |

$$\overline{X} = A + \frac{\Sigma fd'}{\Sigma f} \times i = 55 + \frac{8}{150} \times 10$$

$$= 55 + 0.53 = 55.53$$

$$M = \text{Size of}\left(\frac{N}{2}\right)\text{th item}$$

$$= \text{Size of}\left(\frac{150}{2}\right)\text{th item} = \text{Size of 75th item}$$

Median lies in the class interval 50–60.

$$M = l_1 + \frac{\frac{N}{2} - c.f.}{f} \times i$$

$$= 50 + \frac{75 - 55}{45} \times 10$$

$$= 50 + \frac{20}{45} \times 10$$

$$= 50 + 4.44 = 54.44$$

By inspection, mode lies in the class interval 50–60.

$$\therefore \quad Z = l_1 + \frac{f_1 - f_0}{2f_1 - f_0 - f_2} \times i$$

$$= 50 + \frac{45 - 37}{2(45) - 37 - 27} \times 10$$

$$= 50 + \frac{8}{90 - 64} \times 10$$

$$= 50 + \frac{8}{26} \times 10$$

$$= 50 + 3.08 = 53.08$$

Thus, Mean ($\overline{X}$) = 55.53, Median (M) = 54.44, Mode (Z) = 53.08.

**1. Find out the range and coefficient of range from the following data:**
**6, 12, 30, 24, 45, 52, 40**

**Sol.** Here, L = 6, H = 52

$$\text{Range (R)} = H - L = 52 - 6 = 46$$

$$\text{Coefficient of Range (CR)} = \frac{H - L}{H + L} = \frac{52 - 6}{52 + 6} = \frac{46}{58} = 0.79$$

**2. Calculate the range and its coefficient from the following data:**

| Marks | 10–20 | 20–30 | 30–40 | 40–50 | 50–60 |
|---|---|---|---|---|---|
| Number of Students | 8 | 10 | 12 | 8 | 4 |

**Sol.**

| Marks | Number of Students |
|---|---|
| 10–20 | 8 |
| 20–30 | 10 |
| 30–40 | 12 |
| 40–50 | 8 |
| 50–60 | 4 |

Here, L = 10, H = 60

$$\text{Range (R)} = H - L = 60 - 10 = 50$$

$$\text{Coefficient of Range (CR)} = \frac{H - L}{H + L} = \frac{60 - 10}{60 + 10} = \frac{50}{70} = 0.71$$

**3. Calculate interquartile range, quartile deviation and the coefficient of quartile deviation from the following data:**

| Wages (₹) | 10 | 20 | 30 | 40 | 50 | 60 |
|---|---|---|---|---|---|---|
| Number of Workers | 2 | 8 | 20 | 35 | 42 | 20 |

**Sol.**

| Wages (₹) (X) | Number of Workers (f) | Cumulative Frequency (c.f.) |
|---|---|---|
| 10 | 2 | 2 |
| 20 | 8 | 10 |

| 30 | 20 | 30 |
|---|---|---|
| 40 | 35 | 65 |
| 50 | 42 | 107 |
| 60 | 20 | 127 |
| | N = 127 | |

$$Q_1 = \text{Size of} \left(\frac{N+1}{4}\right)\text{th item}$$
$$= \text{Size of} \left(\frac{127+1}{4}\right)\text{th item}$$
$$= \text{Size of 32th item} = 40$$
$$Q_3 = \text{Size of } 3\left(\frac{N+1}{4}\right)\text{th item}$$
$$= \text{Size of } 3\left(\frac{127+1}{4}\right)\text{th item}$$
$$= \text{Size of 96th item} = 50$$
$$\text{Interquartile Range} = Q_3 - Q_1 = 50 - 40 = 10$$
$$\text{Quartile Deviation (QD)} = \frac{Q_3 - Q_1}{2} = \frac{50-40}{2} = \frac{10}{2} = 5$$
$$\text{Coefficient of QD} = \frac{Q_3 - Q_1}{Q_3 + Q_1} = \frac{50-40}{50+40} = \frac{10}{90} = 0.11$$

**4. Calculate quartile deviation and its coefficient from the following data:**

| **Class Interval** | 30–32 | 32–34 | 34–36 | 36–38 | 38–40 | 40–42 | 42–44 |
|---|---|---|---|---|---|---|---|
| **Frequency** | 12 | 18 | 16 | 14 | 12 | 8 | 6 |

**Sol.**

| Class Interval | Frequency (f) | Cumulative Frequency (c.f.) |
|---|---|---|
| 30–32 | 12 | 12 |
| 32–34 | 18 | 30 |
| 34–36 | 16 | 46 |
| 36–38 | 14 | 60 |
| 38–40 | 12 | 72 |
| 40–42 | 8 | 80 |
| 42–44 | 6 | 86 |
| | N = 86 | |

$$Q_1 = \text{Size of} \left(\frac{N}{4}\right)\text{th item}$$
$$= \text{Size of} \left(\frac{86}{4}\right)\text{th item}$$
$$= \text{Size of 21.5th item}$$

21.5th item lies in the class 32–34. Thus,

$$Q_1 = l_1 + \frac{\frac{N}{4} - \text{c.f.}}{f} \times i$$
$$= 32 + \frac{21.5 - 12}{18} \times 2$$

$$= 32 + \frac{9.5}{18} \times 2$$

$$= 32 + 1.05 = 33.05$$

$$Q_3 = \text{Size of } 3\left(\frac{N}{4}\right)\text{th item}$$

$$= \text{Size of } 3\left(\frac{86}{4}\right)\text{th item}$$

$$= \text{Size of 64.5th item}$$

64.5th item lies in 38–40 median class.

Thus,

$$Q_3 = l_1 + \frac{3\left(\frac{N}{4}\right) - \text{c.f.}}{f} \times i$$

$$= 38 + \frac{3\left(\frac{86}{4}\right) - 60}{12} \times 2$$

$$= 38 + \frac{64.5 - 60}{12} \times 2 = 38 + \frac{4.5}{12} \times 2$$

$$= 38 + 0.75 = 38.75$$

$$\text{Quartile Deviation (QD)} = \frac{Q_3 - Q_1}{2}$$

$$= \frac{38.75 - 33.05}{2} = \frac{5.7}{2}$$

$$= 2.85$$

$$\text{Coefficient of QD} = \frac{Q_3 - Q_1}{Q_3 + Q_1}$$

$$= \frac{38.75 - 33.05}{38.75 + 33.05} = \frac{5.7}{71.8}$$

$$= 0.079$$

**5. Estimate mean deviation and its coefficient from the following data:**

**7, 9, 13, 13, 15, 17, 19, 21, 23**

**Sol.**

| **X** | **Deviation from Mean** $\lvert d\bar{x}\rvert = \lvert X - \bar{X}\rvert$ $\bar{X} = 15.22$ |
|---|---|
| 7 | 8.22 |
| 9 | 6.22 |
| 13 | 2.22 |
| 13 | 2.22 |
| 15 | 0.22 |
| 17 | 1.78 |
| 19 | 3.78 |
| 21 | 5.78 |
| 23 | 7.78 |
| $\Sigma X = 137, N = 9$ | $\Sigma\lvert d\bar{x}\rvert = 38.22$ |

$$\bar{X} = \frac{\Sigma X}{N} = \frac{137}{9} = 15.22$$

Mean Deviation from Mean

$$MD_{\bar{x}} = \frac{\Sigma|d\bar{x}|}{N} = \frac{38.22}{9} = 4.25$$

$$\text{Coefficient of Mean Deviation} = \frac{MD_{\bar{x}}}{\bar{X}} = \frac{4.25}{15.22} = 0.279$$

**6. Find out the mean deviation from the median and its coefficient from the following data:**

| **Class** | 0–3 | 3–6 | 6–9 | 9–12 | 12–15 | 15–18 | 18–21 |
|---|---|---|---|---|---|---|---|
| **Frequency** | 2 | 7 | 10 | 12 | 9 | 6 | 4 |

**Sol.**

| **Class** | **Mid-value** $\left(m = \frac{l_1 + l_2}{2}\right)$ | **Frequency (f)** | **Cumulative Frequency (c.f.)** | **Deviation from Median \|dm\| = \|m – M\| M = 10.5** | **Multiple of Deviation and the Corresponding Frequency (f\|dm\|)** |
|---|---|---|---|---|---|
| 0–3 | 1.5 | 2 | 2 | 9 | 18 |
| 3–6 | 4.5 | 7 | 9 | 6 | 42 |
| 6–9 | 7.5 | 10 | 19 | 3 | 30 |
| 9–12 | 10.5 | 12 | 31 | 0 | 0 |
| 12–15 | 13.5 | 9 | 40 | 3 | 27 |
| 15–18 | 16.5 | 6 | 46 | 6 | 36 |
| 18–21 | 19.5 | 4 | 50 | 9 | 36 |
| | | Σf = N = 50 | | | Σf\|dm\| = 189 |

$$M = \text{Size of} \left(\frac{N}{2}\right)\text{th item}$$

$$= \text{Size of} \left(\frac{50}{2}\right)\text{th item} = \text{Size of 25th item}$$

Hence, 9–12 is the Median Class.

$$M = l_1 + \frac{\frac{N}{2} - c.f.}{f} \times i$$

$$= 9 + \frac{\frac{50}{2} - 19}{12} \times 3$$

$$= 9 + \frac{25 - 19}{12} \times 3$$

$$= 9 + \frac{6}{12} \times 3 = 9 + 1.5 = 10.5$$

Mean Deviation from Median

$$MD_m = \frac{\Sigma f|dm|}{N} = \frac{189}{50} = 3.78$$

$$\text{Coefficient of Mean Deviation} = \frac{MD_m}{M} = \frac{3.78}{10.5} = 0.36$$

7. **Calculate the standard deviation and coefficient of standard deviation of the following series:**

| Size | 7 | 10 | 12 | 13 | 15 | 20 | 21 | 28 | 29 | 35 |
|---|---|---|---|---|---|---|---|---|---|---|

**Sol.** **Calculation of Standard Deviation—Direct Method**

| S. No. | Size (X) | Deviation ($x = X - \overline{X}$) $\overline{X} = 19$ | Square of Deviation $x^2 = (X - \overline{X})^2$ |
|---|---|---|---|
| 1 | 7 | – 12 | 144 |
| 2 | 10 | – 9 | 81 |
| 3 | 12 | – 7 | 49 |
| 4 | 13 | – 6 | 36 |
| 5 | 15 | – 4 | 16 |
| 6 | 20 | 1 | 1 |
| 7 | 21 | 2 | 4 |
| 8 | 28 | 9 | 81 |
| 9 | 29 | 10 | 100 |
| 10 | 35 | 16 | 256 |
| N = 10 | ΣX = 190 | Σdx = 0 | $\Sigma dx^2 = 768$ |

$$\overline{X} = \frac{\Sigma X}{N} = \frac{190}{10} = 19$$

$$\sigma = \sqrt{\frac{\Sigma x^2}{N}} = \sqrt{\frac{768}{10}}$$

$$= \sqrt{76.8} = 8.76$$

$$\text{Coefficient of SD} = \frac{\sigma}{\overline{X}} = \frac{8.76}{19} = 0.46$$

Standard Deviation = 8.76, Coefficient of Standard Deviation = 0.46.

8. **Calculate standard deviation from the following data:**

| Size | 10 | 20 | 30 | 40 | 50 | 60 | 70 |
|---|---|---|---|---|---|---|---|
| Frequency | 3 | 5 | 7 | 9 | 8 | 5 | 3 |

**Sol.**

**Calculation of Standard Deviation—Short-cut Method**

| Size (X) | Frequency (f) | Deviation from Assumed Average (dx = X – A) A = 40 | Square of Deviation ($dx^2$) | Multiple of Deviation and the Corresponding Frequency (fdx) | $fdx^2$ |
|---|---|---|---|---|---|
| 10 | 3 | – 30 | 900 | – 90 | 2,700 |
| 20 | 5 | – 20 | 400 | – 100 | 2,000 |
| 30 | 7 | – 10 | 100 | – 70 | 700 |
| 40(A) | 9 | 0 | 0 | 0 | 0 |
| 50 | 8 | + 10 | 100 | + 80 | 800 |
| 60 | 5 | + 20 | 400 | + 100 | 2,000 |
| 70 | 3 | + 30 | 900 | + 90 | 2,700 |
| | N = 40 | | | Σfdx=+10 | $\Sigma fdx^2$=10,900 |

$$\sigma = \sqrt{\frac{\Sigma fdx^2}{N} - \left(\frac{\Sigma fdx}{N}\right)^2}$$

$$= \sqrt{\frac{10,900}{40} - \left(\frac{10}{40}\right)^2} \times 10$$

$$= \sqrt{272.5 - 0.0625}$$

$$= \sqrt{272.4375}$$

$$= 16.51$$

Standard Deviation = 16.51.

**9. Calculate mean and standard deviation from the following data:**

| Daily Wages | 0–10 | 10–20 | 20–30 | 30–40 | 40–50 |
|---|---|---|---|---|---|
| Number of Workers | 2 | 7 | 10 | 5 | 3 |

**Sol.**

| Daily Wages | Mid-value (m) | Number of Workers (f) | Multiple of Mid-value and Frequency (fm) | Deviation from Mean Value ($x = m - \overline{X}$) $\overline{X} = 25$ | Square of Deviation ($x^2$) | $fx^2$ |
|---|---|---|---|---|---|---|
| 0–10 | 5 | 2 | 10 | – 20 | 400 | 800 |
| 10–20 | 15 | 7 | 105 | – 10 | 100 | 700 |
| 20–30 | 25 | 10 | 250 | 0 | 0 | 0 |
| 30–40 | 35 | 5 | 175 | 10 | 100 | 500 |
| 40–50 | 45 | 3 | 135 | 20 | 400 | 1,200 |
| | | $\Sigma f = N = 27$ | $\Sigma fm = 675$ | | | $\Sigma fx^2 = 3,200$ |

$$\overline{X} = \frac{\Sigma fm}{\Sigma f} = \frac{675}{27} = 25$$

$$\sigma = \sqrt{\frac{\Sigma fx^2}{N}}$$

$$= \sqrt{\frac{3,200}{27}}$$

$$= \sqrt{118.52} = 10.89$$

Mean = 25, Standard Deviation = 10.89.

**10. Two samples of size 100 and 150 respectively have means 15 and 16 and standard deviations 3 and 4 respectively. Find the combined mean and standard deviation of size 250.**

**Sol.** Given: $N_1 = 100, \overline{X}_1 = 15, \sigma_1 = 3$

$N_2 = 150, \overline{X}_2 = 16, \sigma_2 = 4$

Now,

$$\overline{X}_{12} = \frac{N_1\overline{X}_1 + N_2\overline{X}_2}{N_1 + N_2}$$

$$= \frac{100 \times 15 + 150 \times 16}{100 + 150}$$

$$= \frac{1,500 + 2,400}{250} = \frac{3,900}{250} = 15.6$$

$d_1 = \overline{X}_1 - \overline{X}_{12} = 15 - 15.6 = -0.6$
$d_2 = \overline{X}_2 - \overline{X}_{12} = 16 - 15.6 = 0.4$

$$\sigma_{12} = \sqrt{\frac{N_1\sigma_1^2 + N_2\sigma_2^2 + N_1 d_1^2 + N_2 d_2^2}{N_1 + N_2}}$$

$$= \sqrt{\frac{100 \times (3)^2 + 150 \times (4)^2 + 100 \times (-0.6)^2 + 150 \times (0.4)^2}{100 + 150}}$$

$$= \sqrt{\frac{100 \times 9 + 150 \times 16 + 100 \times 0.36 + 150 \times 0.16}{250}}$$

$$= \sqrt{\frac{900 + 2{,}400 + 36 + 24}{250}}$$

$$= \sqrt{\frac{3{,}360}{250}} = \sqrt{13.44}$$

$$= 3.67$$

Hence, the combined mean is 15.6 and combined standard deviation is 3.67.

**11. For a group containing 100 observations, the arithmetic mean and standard deviation are 8 and $\sqrt{10.5}$. For 50 observations selected from the 100 observations, the mean and standard deviations are 10 and 2 respectively. Find the arithmetic mean and the standard deviation of the other half.**

**Sol.** Given: $N = 100, \ \overline{X}_{12} = 8, \ \sigma_{12} = \sqrt{10.5}$
$N_1 = 50, \ \overline{X}_1 = 10, \ \sigma_1 = 2$
$N_2 = 100 - N_1 = 100 - 50 = 50$

We know that,

$$\overline{X}_{12} = \frac{N_1\overline{X}_1 + N_2\overline{X}_2}{N_1 + N_2}$$

$$8 = \frac{50\,(10) + 50(\overline{X}_2)}{100}$$

$$800 = 500 + 50\,\overline{X}_2$$

$$50\overline{X}_2 = 800 - 500$$

$$50\overline{X}_2 = 300$$

$$\overline{X}_2 = \frac{300}{50} = 6$$

$d_1 = \overline{X}_1 - \overline{X}_{12} = 10 - 8 = 2$
$d_2 = \overline{X}_2 - \overline{X}_{12} = 6 - 8 = -2$

$$\sigma_{12} = \sqrt{\frac{N_1\sigma_1^2 + N_2\sigma_2^2 + N_1 d_1^2 + N_2 d_2^2}{N_1 + N_2}}$$

Substituting the values, we get

$$\sqrt{10.5} = \sqrt{\frac{50 \times (2)^2 + 50\sigma_2^2 + 50 \times (2)^2 + 50 \times (-2)^2}{100}}$$

$$\sqrt{10.5} = \sqrt{\frac{50 \times 4 + 50\sigma_2^2 + 50 \times 4 + 50 \times 4}{100}}$$

Squaring both sides,

$$10.5 = \frac{200 + 50\sigma_2^2 + 200 + 200}{100}$$

$$10.5 \times 100 = 600 + 50\sigma_2^2$$

$$1{,}050 = 600 + 50\sigma_2^2$$

$$\therefore \quad 50\sigma_2^2 = 450$$

$$\therefore \quad \sigma_2^2 = \frac{450}{50} = 9$$

$$\Rightarrow \quad \sigma_2 = 3$$

Thus, $\overline{X}_2 = 6, \sigma_2 = 3.$

**12. Calculate coefficient of variation from the following data-set:**

| Class Interval | 0–10 | 10–20 | 20–30 | 30–40 | 40–50 | 50–60 | 60–70 |
|---|---|---|---|---|---|---|---|
| Frequency | 10 | 15 | 25 | 25 | 10 | 10 | 5 |

**Sol.**

| Class Interval | Mid-value (m) | Frequency (f) | Deviation from Assumed Average (dx = m – A) A = 35 | $dx' = \frac{dx}{C}$ C = 10 | $dx'^2$ | fdx′ | $fdx'^2$ |
|---|---|---|---|---|---|---|---|
| 0–10 | 5 | 10 | – 30 | – 3 | 9 | – 30 | 90 |
| 10–20 | 15 | 15 | – 20 | – 2 | 4 | – 30 | 60 |
| 20–30 | 25 | 25 | – 10 | – 1 | 1 | – 25 | 25 |
| 30–40 | 35 | 25 | 0 | 0 | 0 | 0 | 0 |
| 40–50 | 45 | 10 | 10 | 1 | 1 | 10 | 10 |
| 50–60 | 55 | 10 | 20 | 2 | 4 | 20 | 40 |
| 60–70 | 65 | 5 | 30 | 3 | 9 | 15 | 45 |
| | | Σf=N=100 | | | | Σfdx′ =–40 | $\Sigma fdx'^2$= 270 |

$$\overline{X} = A + \frac{\Sigma fdx'}{\Sigma f} \times C$$

$$= 35 + \frac{-40}{100} \times 10 = 35 - 4 = 31$$

$$\sigma = \sqrt{\frac{\Sigma fdx'^2}{N} - \left(\frac{\Sigma fdx'}{N}\right)^2} \times C$$

$$= \sqrt{\frac{270}{100} - \left(\frac{-40}{100}\right)^2} \times 10$$

$$= \sqrt{2.7 - (0.4)^2} \times 10$$

$$= \sqrt{2.7 - 0.16} \times 10 = \sqrt{2.54} \times 10$$

$$= 1.594 \times 10 = 15.94$$

$$CV = \frac{\sigma}{\overline{X}} \times 100 = \frac{15.94}{31} \times 100 = 51.42$$

Coefficient of Variation = 51.42.

**1. Calculate the coefficient of correlation using Karl Pearson's formula of the series given below:**

| X | 10 | 12 | 15 | 23 | 20 |
|---|---|---|---|---|---|
| Y | 14 | 17 | 23 | 25 | 21 |

**Sol.** **Calculation of Coefficient of Correlation**

| X | Deviation ($x = X - \bar{X}$) $\bar{X} = 16$ | Square of Deviation ($x^2$) | Y | Deviation ($y = Y - \bar{Y}$) $\bar{Y} = 20$ | Square of Deviation ($y^2$) | Multiple of Deviations ($xy$) |
|---|---|---|---|---|---|---|
| 10 | –6 | 36 | 14 | –6 | 36 | 36 |
| 12 | –4 | 16 | 17 | –3 | 9 | 12 |
| 15 | –1 | 1 | 23 | 3 | 9 | –3 |
| 23 | 7 | 49 | 25 | 5 | 25 | 35 |
| 20 | 4 | 16 | 21 | 1 | 1 | 4 |
| $\Sigma X = 80$ | $\Sigma x = 0$ | $\Sigma x^2 = 118$ | $\Sigma Y = 100$ | $\Sigma y = 0$ | $\Sigma y^2 = 80$ | $\Sigma xy = 84$ |

$$\bar{X} = \frac{\Sigma X}{N} = \frac{80}{5} = 16;\ \bar{Y} = \frac{\Sigma Y}{N} = \frac{100}{5} = 20$$

$$r = \frac{\Sigma xy}{\sqrt{\Sigma x^2 \times \Sigma y^2}}$$

Here, $\Sigma xy = 84$, $\Sigma x^2 = 118$, $\Sigma y^2 = 80$

Substituting the values, we get

$$r = \frac{84}{\sqrt{118 \times 80}} = \frac{84}{\sqrt{9,440}}$$

$$= \frac{84}{97.16} = 0.864$$

Coefficient of Correlation (r) = 0.864.

**2. Calculate coefficient of correlation from the following data:**

| X | 100 | 200 | 300 | 400 | 500 | 600 |
|---|---|---|---|---|---|---|
| Y | 110 | 120 | 135 | 140 | 160 | 165 |

**Sol.**

| X | $dx = X - A_x$ $A_x = 300$ | $dx' = \frac{dx}{C_1}$ $C_1 = 100$ | $dx'^2$ | Y | $dy = Y - A_Y$ $A_Y = 135$ | $dy' = \frac{dy}{C_2}$ $C_2 = 5$ | $dy'^2$ | $dx'dy'$ |
|---|---|---|---|---|---|---|---|---|
| 100 | –200 | –2 | 4 | 110 | –25 | –5 | 25 | 10 |
| 200 | –100 | –1 | 1 | 120 | –15 | –3 | 9 | 3 |
| 300 | 0 | 0 | 0 | 135 | 0 | 0 | 0 | 0 |
| 400 | 100 | 1 | 1 | 140 | 5 | 1 | 1 | 1 |
| 500 | 200 | 2 | 4 | 160 | 25 | 5 | 25 | 10 |
| 600 | 300 | 3 | 9 | 165 | 30 | 6 | 36 | 18 |
| N=6 | | $\Sigma dx' = 3$ | $\Sigma dx'^2 = 19$ | N=6 | | $\Sigma dy' = 4$ | $\Sigma dy'^2 = 96$ | $\Sigma dx'dy' = 42$ |

$$r = \frac{\Sigma dx'dy' - \frac{(\Sigma dx')\times(\Sigma dy')}{N}}{\sqrt{\Sigma dx'^2 - \frac{(\Sigma dx')^2}{N}} \times \sqrt{\Sigma dy'^2 - \frac{(\Sigma dy')^2}{N}}}$$

$$= \frac{42 - \frac{(3)\times(4)}{6}}{\sqrt{19 - \frac{(3)^2}{6}} \times \sqrt{96 - \frac{(4)^2}{6}}}$$

$$= \frac{42 - 2}{\sqrt{19 - 1.5} \times \sqrt{96 - 2.67}}$$

$$= \frac{40}{\sqrt{17.5} \times \sqrt{93.33}}$$

$$= \frac{40}{4.18 \times 9.66}$$

$$= \frac{40}{40.3788} = 0.99$$

Coefficient of Correlation (r) = 0.99.

**3. Calculate Karl Pearson's coefficient of correlation between the values of X and Y for the following data:**

| **X** | 78 | 89 | 96 | 69 | 59 | 79 | 68 | 61 |
|---|---|---|---|---|---|---|---|---|
| **Y** | 125 | 137 | 156 | 112 | 107 | 136 | 123 | 108 |

**Assume 69 and 112 as the mean values for X and Y respectively.**

**Sol.**

| **X** | **Deviation ($dx = X - \overline{X}$) $\overline{X} = 69$** | **Square of Deviation ($dx^2$)** | **Y** | **Deviation ($dy = Y - \overline{Y}$) $\overline{Y} = 112$** | **Square of Deviation ($dy^2$)** | **Multiple of Deviations (dxdy)** |
|---|---|---|---|---|---|---|
| 78 | 9 | 81 | 125 | 13 | 169 | 117 |
| 89 | 20 | 400 | 137 | 25 | 625 | 500 |
| 96 | 27 | 729 | 156 | 44 | 1,936 | 1,188 |
| 69 | 0 | 0 | 112 | 0 | 0 | 0 |
| 59 | –10 | 100 | 107 | –5 | 25 | 50 |
| 79 | 10 | 100 | 136 | 24 | 576 | 240 |
| 68 | –1 | 1 | 123 | 11 | 121 | –11 |
| 61 | –8 | 64 | 108 | –4 | 16 | 32 |
| N=8 | Σdx=47 | $\Sigma dx^2$=1,475 | N = 8 | Σdy=108 | $\Sigma dy^2$=3,468 | Σdxdy=2,116 |

$$r = \frac{\Sigma dxdy - \frac{(\Sigma dx)\times(\Sigma dy)}{N}}{\sqrt{\Sigma dx^2 - \frac{(\Sigma dx)^2}{N}} \times \sqrt{\Sigma dy^2 - \frac{(\Sigma dy)^2}{N}}}$$

$$= \frac{2{,}116 - \frac{(47)\times(108)}{8}}{\sqrt{1{,}475 - \frac{(47)^2}{8}} \times \sqrt{3{,}468 - \frac{(108)^2}{8}}}$$

$$= \frac{2,116 - 634.5}{\sqrt{1,475 - 276.125} \times \sqrt{3,468 - 1,458}}$$

$$= \frac{1,481.5}{\sqrt{1,198.875} \times \sqrt{2,010}}$$

$$= \frac{1,481.5}{34.62 \times 44.83}$$

$$= \frac{1,481.5}{1,552.0146} = 0.955$$

Coefficient of Correlation (r) = 0.955.

**4. From the following data, compute Karl Pearson coefficient of correlation:**

| | X-Series | Y-Series |
|---|---|---|
| **Number of Items** | 7 | 7 |
| **Arithmetic Mean** | 4 | 8 |
| **Sum of squares of Deviations from Arithmetic Mean** | 28 | 76 |

**Summation of product of deviations of X and Y series from their respective means is 46.**

**Sol.** We are given:

$N = 7, \overline{X} = 4, \overline{Y} = 8, \Sigma x^2 = 28, \Sigma y^2 = 76, \Sigma xy = 46$

$$r = \frac{\Sigma xy}{\sqrt{\Sigma x^2 \times \Sigma y^2}}$$

Substituting the values, we get

$$r = \frac{46}{\sqrt{28 \times 76}} = \frac{46}{\sqrt{2,128}}$$

$$= \frac{46}{46.13} = 0.997$$

Coefficient of Correlation (r) = 0.997.

**5. If $r = 0.25$, $\Sigma xy = 45$, $\sigma_y = 3$, $\Sigma x^2 = 50$, where x and y denote deviations from their respective means, find the number of items.**

**Sol.** Given: $r = 0.25, \Sigma xy = 45, \sigma_y = 3, \Sigma x^2 = 50$

Now, $$\sigma_y = \sqrt{\frac{\Sigma y^2}{N}}$$

When $y = Y - \overline{Y}$ [Formula of Standard Deviation]

$$3 = \sqrt{\frac{\Sigma y^2}{N}}$$

Squaring from both sides, we get

$$9 = \frac{\Sigma y^2}{N} \quad \Rightarrow \quad \Sigma y^2 = 9N$$

Now, $$r = \frac{\Sigma xy}{\sqrt{\Sigma x^2 \times \Sigma y^2}} \quad \Rightarrow \quad 0.25 = \frac{45}{\sqrt{50 \times 9N}}$$

Squaring both sides

$$0.0625 = \frac{(45)^2}{50 \times 9N}$$

$$0.0625 = \frac{2,025}{50 \times 9N}$$

$$\Rightarrow \quad 0.0625 = \frac{2,025}{450N}$$

$$\Rightarrow \quad (0.0625)(450)N = 2,025$$

$$\Rightarrow \quad (28.125)N = 2,025$$

$$\therefore \quad N = \frac{2,025}{28.125} = 72$$

Number of Items = 72.

**6. The ranks of 8 same students in tests in Mathematics and Statistics were as follows:**

| **Rank in Mathematics** | 1 | 2 | 3 | 4 | 5 | 6 | 7 | 8 |
|---|---|---|---|---|---|---|---|---|
| **Rank in Statistics** | 4 | 2 | 1 | 6 | 8 | 3 | 5 | 7 |

**Calculate the coefficient of rank correlation.**

**Sol.**

| **Rank in Mathematics ($R_1$)** | **Rank in Statistics ($R_2$)** | **$D = R_1 - R_2$** | **$D^2$** |
|---|---|---|---|
| 1 | 4 | –3 | 9 |
| 2 | 2 | 0 | 0 |
| 3 | 1 | 2 | 4 |
| 4 | 6 | –2 | 4 |
| 5 | 8 | –3 | 9 |
| 6 | 3 | 3 | 9 |
| 7 | 5 | 2 | 4 |
| 8 | 7 | 1 | 1 |
| N = 8 | | | $\Sigma D^2 = 40$ |

$$r_k = 1 - \frac{6\Sigma D^2}{N^3 - N}$$

Here, $N = 8$; $\Sigma D^2 = 40$

Substituting the values, we get

$$r_k = 1 - \frac{6 \times 40}{(8)^3 - 8}$$

$$= 1 - \frac{240}{512 - 8}$$

$$= 1 - \frac{210}{504}$$

$$= 1 - 0.48 = 0.52$$

Coefficient of Rank Correlation ($r_k$) = 0.52.

7. **Find out the coefficient of rank correlation between X and Y:**

| **X** | 46 | 56 | 39 | 45 | 54 | 58 | 36 | 40 |
|---|---|---|---|---|---|---|---|---|
| **Y** | 30 | 60 | 40 | 50 | 70 | 70 | 30 | 50 |

**Sol.**

| **X** | **Rank $R_1$** | **Y** | **Rank $R_2$** | **$D = R_1 - R_2$** | **$D^2$** |
|---|---|---|---|---|---|
| 46 | 5 | 30 | 1.5 | 3.5 | 12.25 |
| 56 | 7 | 60 | 6 | 1 | 1 |
| 39 | 2 | 40 | 3 | –1 | 1 |
| 45 | 4 | 50 | 4.5 | –0.5 | 0.25 |
| 54 | 6 | 70 | 7.5 | –1.5 | 2.25 |
| 58 | 8 | 70 | 7.5 | 0.5 | 0.25 |
| 36 | 1 | 30 | 1.5 | –0.5 | 0.25 |
| 40 | 3 | 50 | 4.5 | – 1.5 | 2.25 |
| N = 8 | | | | | $\Sigma D^2 = 19.5$ |

Here numbers 30, 50 and 70 are repeated twice in series Y. Therefore, m = 2 in Y.

$$r_k = 1 - \frac{6[\Sigma D^2 + \frac{1}{12}(m_1{}^3 - m_1) + \frac{1}{12}(m_2{}^3 - m_2) + \frac{1}{12}(m_3{}^3 - m_3)]}{N^3 - N}$$

$$= 1 - \frac{6[19.5 + \frac{1}{12}(2^3 - 2) + \frac{1}{12}(2^3 - 2) + \frac{1}{12}(2^3 - 2)]}{8^3 - 8}$$

$$= 1 - \frac{6[19.5 + \frac{1}{12}(6) + \frac{1}{12}(6) + \frac{1}{12}(6)]}{512 - 8}$$

$$= 1 - \frac{6[19.5 + 0.5 + 0.5 + 0.5]}{504}$$

$$= 1 - \frac{6[21]}{504} = 1 - \frac{126}{504}$$

$$= 1 - 0.25 = 0.75$$

Coefficient of Rank Correlation ($r_k$) = 0.75.

8. **The rank correlation coefficient between marks obtained by 10 students in English and Statistics was found to be 0.5. Find the sum of squares of difference of ranks.**

**Sol.** Given: r = 0.5, N = 10

Now,
$$r = 1 - \frac{6\Sigma D^2}{N^3 - N}$$

$$\frac{6\Sigma D^2}{N^3 - N} = 1 - r$$

$$\frac{6\Sigma D^2}{10^3 - 10} = 1 - 0.5$$

$$\frac{6\Sigma D^2}{1000 - 10} = 0.5$$

$$\frac{6\Sigma D^2}{990} = 0.5$$

$\Rightarrow$ $6\Sigma D^2 = 0.5 \times 990$

$\Rightarrow$ $6\Sigma D^2 = 495$

$\Rightarrow$ $\Sigma D^2 = \frac{495}{6}$

$\Rightarrow$ $\Sigma D^2 = 82.5$

Sum of Squares of Difference of Ranks = 82.5.

## Index Numbers

**1. Construct the price index from the following data, by taking 2004 as the base year**

| Items | A | B | C | D | E |
|---|---|---|---|---|---|
| **Price in 2004 (₹)** | 6 | 2 | 4 | 10 | 8 |
| **Price in 2015 (₹)** | 15 | 3 | 8 | 14 | 16 |

**Sol.**

| Items | Price in 2004 (₹) ($P_0$) | Price in 2015 (₹) ($P_1$) |
|---|---|---|
| A | 6 | 15 |
| B | 2 | 3 |
| C | 4 | 8 |
| D | 10 | 14 |
| E | 8 | 16 |
| Total | $\Sigma P_0 = 30$ | $\Sigma P_1 = 56$ |

$$P_{01} = \frac{\Sigma P_1}{\Sigma P_0} \times 100 = \frac{56}{30} \times 100$$

$$= 186.67$$

Price Index = 186.67.

**2. Compute a price index from the following by (i) simple aggregative method, and (ii) average of price relative method.**

| Commodity | A | B | C | D | E | F |
|---|---|---|---|---|---|---|
| **Price in 2004 (₹)** | 200 | 300 | 100 | 250 | 400 | 500 |
| **Price in 2015 (₹)** | 250 | 300 | 150 | 350 | 450 | 550 |

**Sol.** (i) **Simple Index Number—Simple Aggregative Method**

| Commodity | Price in 2004 (₹) ($P_0$) | Price in 2015 (₹) ($P_1$) |
|---|---|---|
| A | 200 | 250 |
| B | 300 | 300 |
| C | 100 | 150 |
| D | 250 | 350 |
| E | 400 | 450 |
| F | 500 | 550 |
| | $\Sigma P_0 = 1{,}750$ | $\Sigma P_1 = 2{,}050$ |

$$P_{01} = \frac{\Sigma P_1}{\Sigma P_0} \times 100$$

$$= \frac{2{,}050}{1{,}750} \times 100$$

$$= 117.14$$

(ii) **Simple Index Number—Average of Price Relative Method**

| Commodity | Base Year Price (₹) 2004 ($P_0$) | 2015 Price (₹) ($P_1$) | Price Relatives of 2015 in relation to 2004 $\left(\frac{P_1}{P_0} \times 100\right)$ |
|---|---|---|---|
| A | 200 | 250 | $\frac{250}{200} \times 100 = 125$ |
| B | 300 | 300 | $\frac{300}{300} \times 100 = 100$ |
| C | 100 | 150 | $\frac{150}{100} \times 100 = 150$ |
| D | 250 | 350 | $\frac{350}{250} \times 100 = 140$ |
| E | 400 | 450 | $\frac{450}{400} \times 100 = 112.5$ |
| F | 500 | 550 | $\frac{550}{500} \times 100 = 110$ |
| N = 6 | | | $\Sigma\left(\frac{P_1}{P_0}\right) \times 100 = 737.5$ |

$$P_{01} = \frac{\Sigma\left(\frac{P_1}{P_0} \times 100\right)}{N}$$

$$= \frac{737.5}{6}$$

$$= 122.92$$

**3. Construct Index Number of prices from the following data by (i) Laspeyre's method, (ii) Paasche's method, and (iii) Fisher method.**

| Commodity | 2004 | | 2015 | |
|---|---|---|---|---|
| | Price (₹) | Expenditure (₹) | Price (₹) | Expenditure (₹) |
| A | 8 | 100 | 10 | 90 |
| B | 10 | 60 | 11 | 66 |
| C | 5 | 100 | 5 | 100 |
| D | 3 | 30 | 2 | 24 |
| E | 2 | 8 | 4 | 20 |

**Sol.** Since we are given the total expenditure and the price, we can obtain the quantity figure by dividing the total expenditure by price for each commodity.

**Construction of Various Index Numbers**

| Commodity | 2004 | | 2015 | | $p_0q_0$ | $p_1q_0$ | $p_0q_1$ | $p_1q_1$ |
|---|---|---|---|---|---|---|---|---|
| | $p_0$ | $q_0$ | $p_1$ | $q_1$ | | | | |
| A | 8 | 12.5 | 10 | 9 | 100 | 125 | 72 | 90 |
| B | 10 | 6 | 11 | 6 | 60 | 66 | 60 | 66 |
| C | 5 | 20 | 5 | 20 | 100 | 100 | 100 | 100 |
| D | 3 | 10 | 2 | 12 | 30 | 20 | 36 | 24 |
| E | 2 | 4 | 4 | 5 | 8 | 16 | 10 | 20 |
| | | | | | $\Sigma p_0q_0 = 298$ | $\Sigma p_1q_0 = 327$ | $\Sigma p_0q_1 = 278$ | $\Sigma p_1q_1 = 300$ |

**(i) Laspeyre's Method:** $P_{01} = \dfrac{\Sigma p_1q_0}{\Sigma p_0q_0} \times 100$

$$= \frac{327}{298} \times 100 = 109.73$$

**(ii) Paasche's Method:** $P_{01} = \dfrac{\Sigma p_1q_1}{\Sigma p_0q_1} \times 100$

$$= \frac{300}{278} \times 100 = 107.91$$

**(iii) Fisher's Method:** $P_{01} = \sqrt{\dfrac{\Sigma p_1q_0}{\Sigma p_0q_0} \times \dfrac{\Sigma p_1q_1}{\Sigma p_0q_1}} \times 100$

$$= \sqrt{\frac{327}{298} \times \frac{300}{278}} \times 100$$

$$= \sqrt{\frac{98,100}{82,844}} \times 100$$

$$= \sqrt{1.18415} \times 100$$

$$= 1.0882 \times 100$$

$$= 108.82$$

**4. From the following data, find Fisher's Ideal Index Number:**

| Items | 2015 | | 2004 | |
|---|---|---|---|---|
| | Price | Quantity | Price | Quantity |
| A | 10 | 60 | 6 | 50 |
| B | 2 | 120 | 2 | 100 |
| C | 6 | 60 | 4 | 60 |

**Sol.** **Construction of Fisher's Ideal Index Numbers**

| Items | 2004 | | 2015 | | $p_1q_0$ | $p_0q_0$ | $p_1q_1$ | $p_0q_1$ |
|---|---|---|---|---|---|---|---|---|
| | $p_0$ | $q_0$ | $p_1$ | $q_1$ | | | | |
| A | 6 | 50 | 10 | 60 | 500 | 300 | 600 | 360 |
| B | 2 | 100 | 2 | 120 | 200 | 200 | 240 | 240 |
| C | 4 | 60 | 6 | 60 | 360 | 240 | 360 | 240 |
| | | | | | $\Sigma p_1q_0 = 1{,}060$ | $\Sigma p_0q_0 = 740$ | $\Sigma p_1q_1 = 1{,}200$ | $\Sigma p_0q_1 = 840$ |

Fisher's Ideal Index Number, $P_{01} = \sqrt{\dfrac{\Sigma p_1q_0}{\Sigma p_0q_0} \times \dfrac{\Sigma p_1q_1}{\Sigma p_0q_1}} \times 100$

$$= \sqrt{\frac{1{,}060}{740} \times \frac{1{,}200}{840}} \times 100$$

$$= \sqrt{2.0463} \times 100$$

$$= 1.4305 \times 100$$

$$= 143.05$$

**5. Calculate price index from the following data by using weighted average price relative method:**

| Commodity | Base Year Price | Current Year Price | Weights |
|---|---|---|---|
| A | 6 | 8 | 240 |
| B | 3 | 3.2 | 240 |
| C | 2 | 3 | 40 |

**Sol.** **Weighted Average Price Relative Method**

| Commodity | Base Year Price ($p_0$) | Current Year Price ($p_1$) | $R = \frac{p_1}{p_0} \times 100$ | Weights (W) | Weighted Relative (RW) |
|---|---|---|---|---|---|
| A | 6 | 8 | 133.33 | 240 | 31,999.2 |
| B | 3 | 3.2 | 106.67 | 240 | 25,600.8 |
| C | 2 | 3 | 150 | 40 | 6,000 |
| | | | | $\Sigma W = 520$ | $\Sigma RW = 63{,}600$ |

$$P_{01} = \frac{\Sigma RW}{\Sigma W}$$

$$= \frac{63{,}600}{520} = 122.31$$

Price Index = 122.31.

# Stats & Indian Mix: Statistical Knowledge and Evaluation of the Indian Economy

**1. The following table shows Gross National Income at constant prices in India (Economic Survey, 2015-16):**

| Year | Gross National Income (GNP) (₹ in crore) |
|---|---|
| 2011-12 | 86,59,215 |
| 2012-13 | 91,18,709 |
| 2013-14 | 97,17,062 |
| 2014-15 | 1,04,27,701 |
| 2015-16 | 1,12,14,077 |

**(i) Represent the data in the form of a bar diagram.**

**(ii) How do you explain the fact that despite a rise in GNP, the farmers are committing suicide across all parts of the country?**

**Sol.** (i) **Gross National Income (at constant prices) in India**

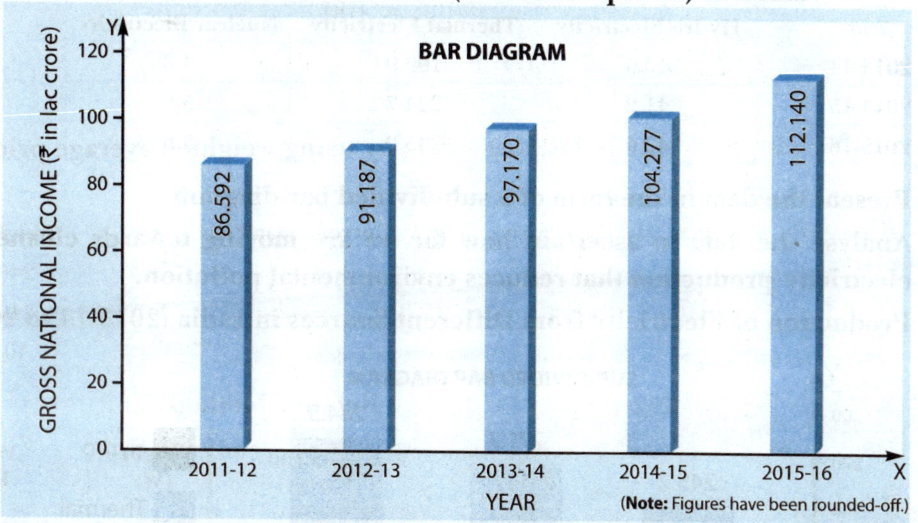


(ii) Low share of agriculture in GNP is owing to slow (or even negative) growth of agricultural sector. Implying low level of income of the farmers. Low income combined with the staggering burden of debt (particularly on the small and marginal farmers) compels the farmers for desperate acts like suicide.

**2. The following table shows Gross National Product/Income at constant prices and exports of India (Economic Survey, 2015-16):**

| Year | 2011-12 | 2012-13 | 2013-14 | 2014-15 |
|---|---|---|---|---|
| GNP (₹ in crore) | 86,59,215 | 91,18,709 | 97,17,062 | 1,04,27,701 |
| Exports (₹ in crore) | 14,65,959 | 16,34,318 | 19,05,011 | 18,96,348 |

**(i) Prepare a multiple bar diagram.**

**(ii) Comment on the growth of exports in India in relation GNP.**

**Sol.** (i) **Gross National Product (at constant prices) and Exports of India**

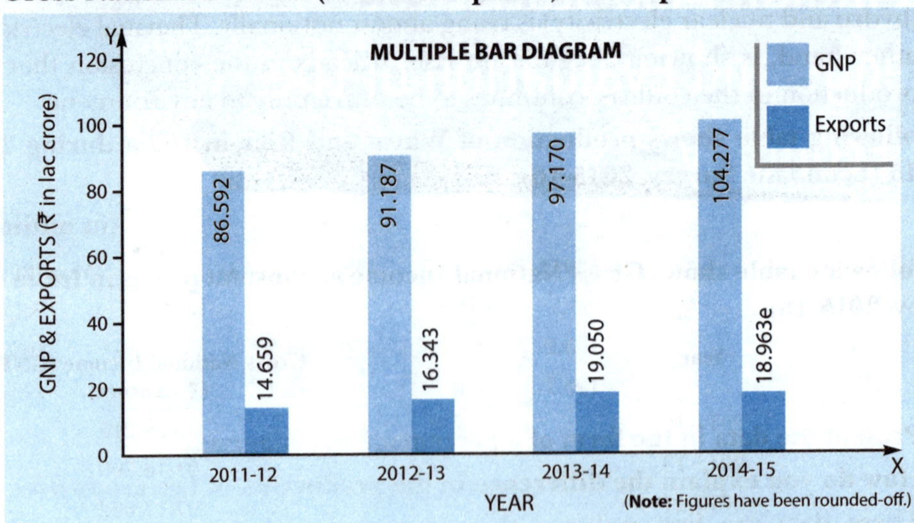


(ii) It is clear from the above diagram that GNP has been rising in India. But there has been very dismal growth of exports as compared to GNP in India. Implying that our GNP growth is driven by and large by the domestic demand, not the global demand.

**3. The following table shows production of electricity from different sources in India during 2013-14 to 2015-16 (Economic Survey, 2015-16):**

**(in thousand MW)**

| Year | Hydro Electricity | Thermal Electricity | Nuclear Electricity | Total |
|---|---|---|---|---|
| 2013-14 | 40.5 | 199.9 | 4.8 | 245.2 |
| 2014-15 | 41.2 | 224.7 | 5.8 | 271.7 |
| 2015-16 | 42.6 | 235.9 | 5.8 | 284.3 |

**(i) Present the data in the form of a sub-divided bar diagram.**

**(ii) Analyse the data to ascertain how far we are moving towards cleaner form of electricity production that reduces environmental pollution.**

**Sol.** (i) **Production of Electricity from Different Sources in India (2013-14 to 2015-16)**

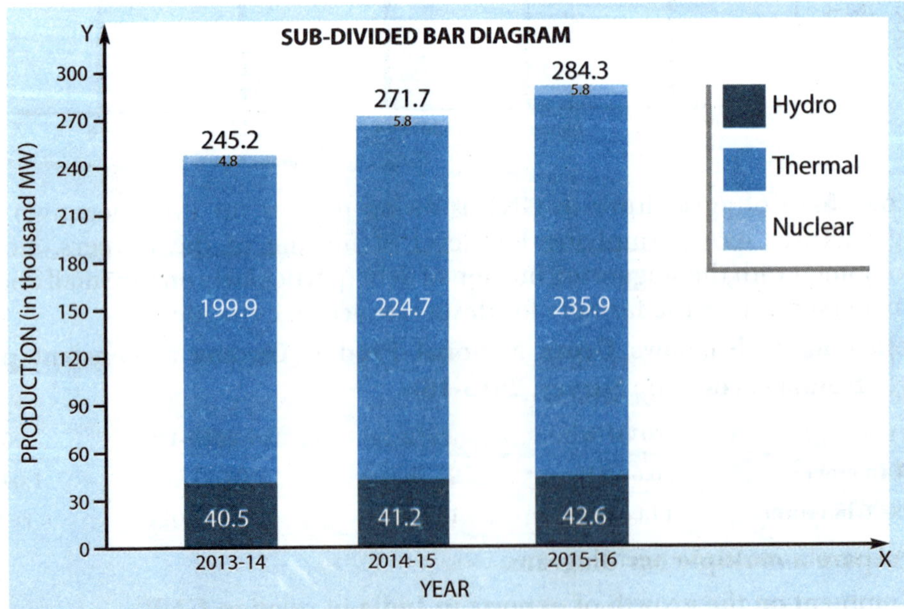

(ii) It is clear from the above data that over time, production of cleaner forms of electricity (hydro and nuclear electricity) is rising almost notionally. Thermal electricity, on the other hand, is showing a significant rise. It leads to the conclusion that electricity production in the country continues to be unfriendly to environment.

**4. The following table shows production of Wheat and Rice in India during 2012-13 to 2014-15 (Economic Survey, 2015-16):**

**(in million tonnes)**

| Crop | Year (2012-13) | Year (2013-14) | Year (2014-15) |
|---|---|---|---|
| Wheat | 93.5 | 95.8 | 88.9 |
| Rice | 105.2 | 106.6 | 104.8 |
| Total | 198.7 | 202.4 | 193.7 |

**(i) Present the data in the form of a percentage bar diagram.**

**(ii) How do you explain the difference in the production of two crops over time?**

**Sol.** (i) These data are first reduced to percentages and then presented in terms of percentage bar diagram, as under:

**Percentage Contribution of Wheat and Rice**

**(in million tonnes)**

| Crop | Year (2012-13) | Cumulative Percentage | Year (2013-14) | Cumulative Percentage | Year (2014-15) | Cumulative Percentage |
|---|---|---|---|---|---|---|
| Wheat | 47.05 | 47.05 | 47.33 | 47.33 | 45.9 | 45.9 |
| Rice | 52.95 | 100 | 52.67 | 100 | 54.1 | 100 |
| Total | 100 | | 100 | | 100 | 100 |

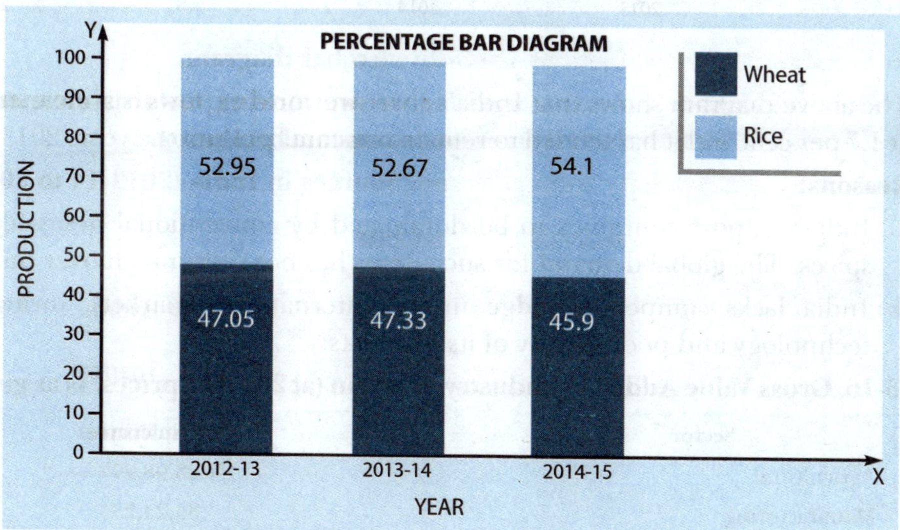


(ii) It is clear from the above diagram that the production of rice (as a percentage of the total production of wheat and rice) has risen over time. On the other hand, percentage production of wheat has declined. It could be because of:

(a) Good monsoon in the Kharif season when rice is grown compared to the monsoon during the Rabi season when wheat is grown, and

(b) Use of innovative technology in the production of rice.

**5. The following table gives India's share in world exports (Economic Survey, 2015-16):**

**(in US dollar million)**

| Year | India's Export | World Exports |
|---|---|---|
| 2013 | 3,14,809 | 1,84,57,704 |
| 2014 | 3,19,757 | 1,86,63,720 |

**(i) Present the data in the form of a percentage bar diagram.**

**(ii) Comment on the share of India's export in the world exports, stating the two possible reasons.**

**Sol.** (i) **India's Share in World Exports**

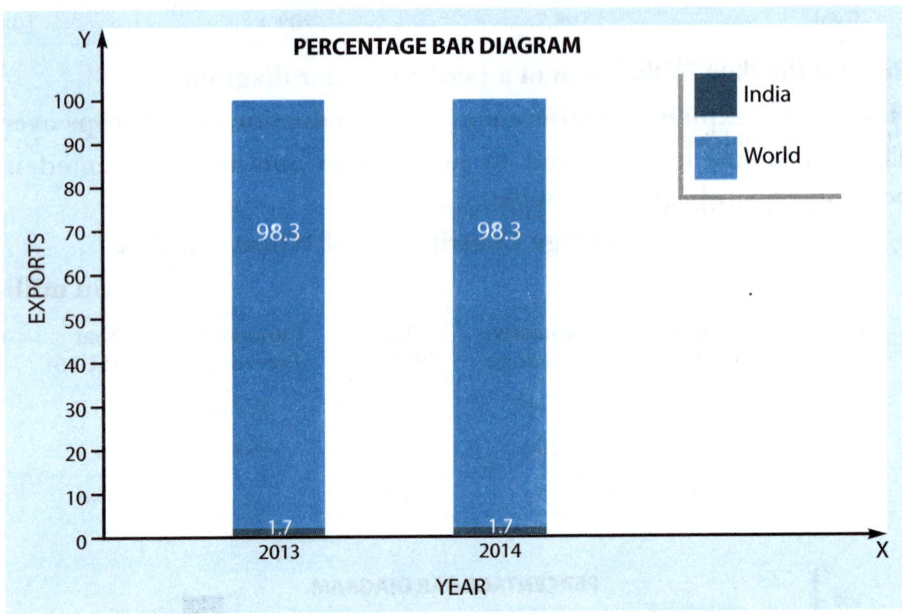


(ii) The above diagram shows that India's share in world exports is almost insignificant at 1.7 per cent and it has tended to remain constant between the years 2013 and 2014.

**Reasons:**

(a) India's export continues to be dominated by conventional items like tea and spices. The global demand for such items has not risen much over time.

(b) India lacks competitive edge in the international markets, owing to poor technology and poor quality of its products.

**6. In 2015-16, Gross Value Added by industry of origin (at 2011-12 prices) is as given below:**

| Sector | ₹ in crore |
|---|---|
| Agricultural | 23,98,277 |
| Manufacturing | 33,24,233 |
| Services | 22,77,734 |
| Finance and Insurance | 25,25,532 |
| Community and Social Services | 17,26,530 |
| Total | 1,22,52,306 |

**(i) Present this information in the form of a pie diagram.**

**(ii) Comment on the relative performance of agriculture and manufacturing, stating the possible reason.**

**Sol.** (i) These data are first reduced to percentages, then percentage values are converted into component parts of 360° of a circle. Finally these are shown as different components of the circle.

| Sector | % Share | Share in terms of Components of 360° |
|---|---|---|
| Agricultural | 19.6 | $\frac{19.6}{100} \times 360° = 70.56°$ |
| Manufacturing | 27.1 | $\frac{27.1}{100} \times 360° = 97.56°$ |
| Services | 18.6 | $\frac{18.6}{100} \times 360° = 66.96°$ |
| Finance and Insurance | 20.6 | $\frac{20.6}{100} \times 360° = 74.16°$ |
| Community and Social Services | 14.1 | $\frac{14.1}{100} \times 360° = 50.76°$ |

**Gross Value Added by Industry of Origin (at 2011-12 prices)**

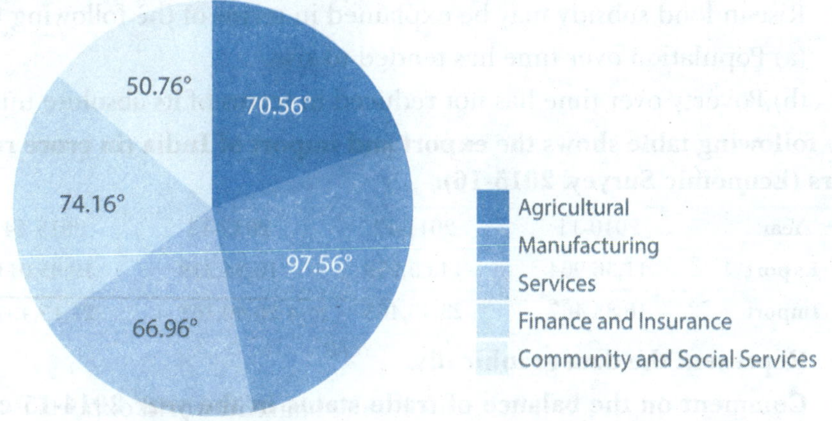


**Pie Diagram**

(ii) The share of agricultural sector in gross value added is less as compared to manufacturing sector.

**Reason:**

Manufacturing sector is growing faster than the agricultural sector. It is a sign of the growing Indian economy.

**7. The following table shows food subsidy in India during 2011-12 to 2015-16 (Economic Survey, 2015-16):**

**(₹ in crore)**

| Year | Food Subsidy |
|---|---|
| 2011-12 | 72,370.90 |
| 2012-13 | 84,554.00 |
| 2013-14 | 89,740.02 |
| 2014-15 | 1,13,171.16 |
| 2015-16 | 1,05,509.41 |

**(i) Represent the information in the form of a one variable time series graph.**

**(ii) How do you explain a consistent rise in food subsidy over time?**

**Sol.** (i) **Food Subsidy in India during 2011-12 to 2015-16**

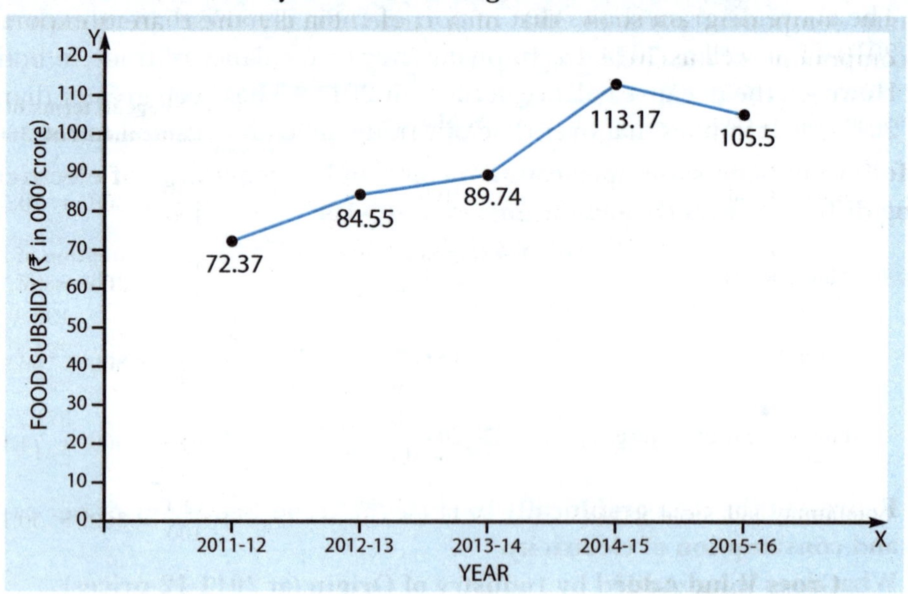


(ii) Rise in food subsidy may be explained in terms of the following factors:

(a) Population over time has tended to rise.

(b) Poverty over time has not reduced in terms of its absolute number.

**8. The following table shows the export and import of India (in crore rupees) in different years (Economic Survey, 2015-16):**

| **Year** | 2010-11 | 2011-12 | 2012-13 | 2013-14 | 2014-15 |
|---|---|---|---|---|---|
| **Export** | 11,36,964 | 14,65,959 | 16,34,318 | 19,05,011 | 18,96,348 |
| **Import** | 16,83,467 | 23,45,463 | 26,69,162 | 27,15,434 | 27,37,087 |

**(i) Represent the data graphically.**

**(ii) Comment on the balance of trade status in the year 2014-15 compared with the year 2010-11.**

**Sol.** (i) **Export and Import of India**

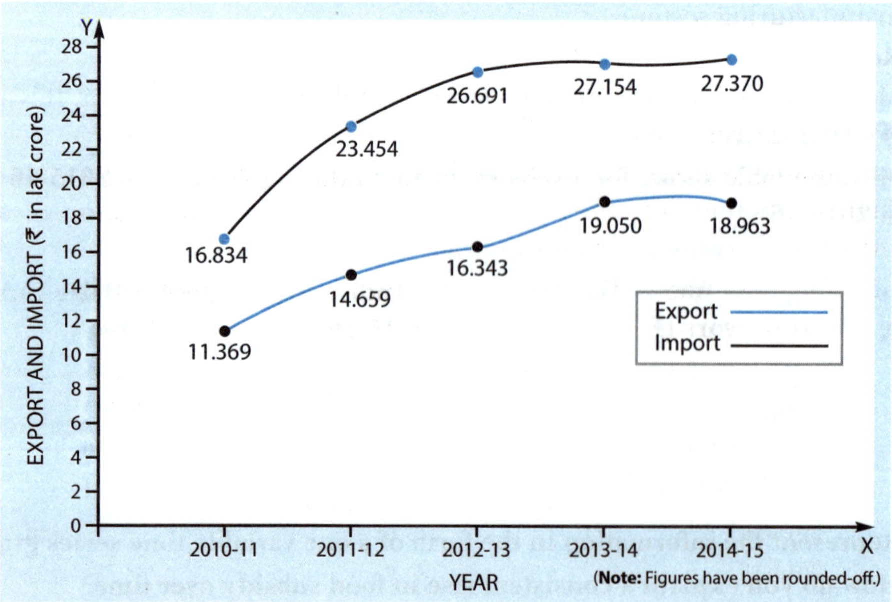

(ii) Balance of trade is the excess of export over import of a country.
The above diagram shows that import of India is more than its export in the year 2010-11 as well as 2014-15. Implying, negative balance of trade in both the years. However, the negative balance in the year 2014-15 has been greater than in the year 2010-11. It implies that over time our trade deficit has tended to rise.

**9. The following table shows per capita income and consumption of electricity in India during different years (Economic Survey, 2015-16):**

| Year | Per Capita Income (₹) | Consumption of Electricity (Thousand MW) |
|---|---|---|
| 2011-12 | 63,460 | 199.9 |
| 2012-13 | 65,664 | 223.4 |
| 2013-14 | 68,867 | 245.2 |
| 2014-15 | 72,889 | 271.7 |
| 2015-16 | 77,431 | 284.3 |

**(i) Represent the data graphically to show the trend behaviour of per capita income and consumption of electricity.**
**(ii) What does it indicate?**

**Sol.** (i)

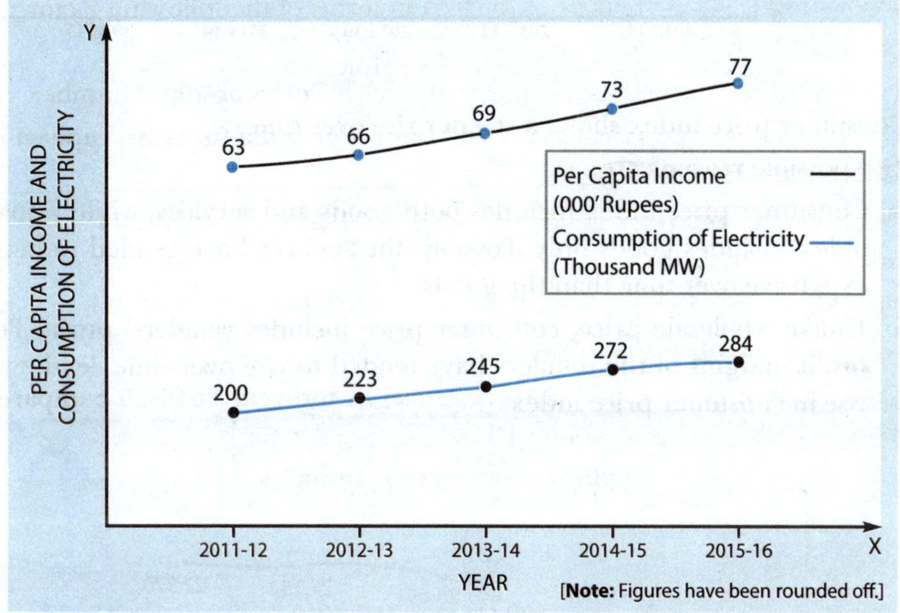


(ii) The two graphs show a similar picture in terms of their movement over time. Both are showing an upward trend. It indicates that higher per capita income leads to higher consumption of electricity. Or that, higher consumption of electricity is indicative of rising per capita income.

**10. The following table shows Wholesale Price Index and Consumer Price Index in India during different years (Economic Survey, 2015-16):**

| Year | Wholesale Price Index | Consumer Price Index |
|---|---|---|
| 2010-11 | 143.3 | 180 |
| 2011-12 | 156.1 | 195 |
| 2012-13 | 167.6 | 215 |
| 2013-14 | 177.6 | 236 |
| 2014-15 | 181.2 | 251 |

**(i) Represent the data in the form of two variable graphs.**

**(ii) Which of the two shows steeper rise over time? State two possible reasons to explain the difference.**

**Sol.** (i) **Wholesale Price Index and Consumer Price Index in India (2010-11 to 2014-15)**

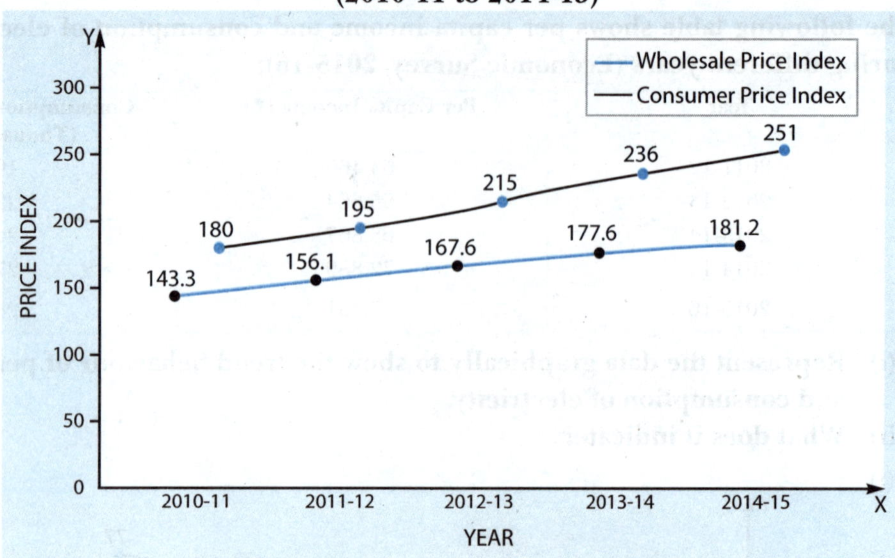


(ii) Consumer price index shows a steeper rise over time.

Two possible **reasons** are:

(a) Consumer price index includes both goods and services, while wholesale price index includes goods only. Possibly, the services have tended to become more expensive over time than the goods.

(b) Unlike wholesale price, consumer price includes retailers' profit. Possibly, the profit margins of the retailers have tended to rise over time, leading to steeper rise in consumer price index.